Marketing Principles

Marketing

William G. Nickels
University of Maryland

Principles

A Broadened Concept
of Marketing

Prentice-Hall, Inc., Englewood Cliffs, New Jersey 07632

Library of Congress Cataloging in Publication Data

Nickels, William G
  Marketing principles.
  Includes bibliographical references.
  1. Marketing. I. Title.
HF5415.N47   658.8   77-24308
ISBN 0-13-558205-9

*To my best friends, Marsha and Joel, to family friends
(yes, and in-laws, too), and to all my other friends.*

Marketing Principles
William G. Nickels

This book has been composed on film in Aster and Helvetica,
with display type in Comstock and Gill Sans Ultra Bold and Light.
Editing and production are by Raymond Mullaney, with the
assistance of Mary Helen Fitzgerald; cover and interior
design are by A Good Thing, Inc.; drawings are by Vantage Art, Inc.

10   9   8   7   6   5   4   3   2   1
Printed in the United States of America

Prentice-Hall International, Inc., *London*
Prentice-Hall of Australia Pty. Limited, *Sydney*
Prentice-Hall of Canada, Ltd., *Toronto*
Prentice-Hall of India Private Limited, *New Delhi*
Prentice-Hall of Japan, Inc., *Tokyo*
Prentice-Hall of Southeast Asia Pte. Ltd., *Singapore*
Whitehall Books Limited, *Wellington, New Zealand*

Contents

Preface to the Instructor

As the market for college graduates grows tighter, students are looking for interesting and relevant courses that will help them prepare for a career. Marketing certainly is one course that meets those criteria. But many introductory texts fail to convey the excitement of marketing. In contrast, this book is designed to portray not only the excitement of marketing, but also its importance in modern society. It answers the kinds of questions students are asking today: Are there interesting careers in marketing? What do marketers do? How can marketers become more socially responsive and responsible? How can marketing help me—an accounting major? Because the text is responsive to student needs, schools that use this text for the first course in marketing are likely to experience more demand for the first course and for other marketing courses as well. This is true even in schools where enrollment in general is declining. Marketing is a subject for tomorrow, and students quickly become aware of those courses that best meet their needs.

But students in the future will need a different kind of marketing education. For instance, seven out of every ten jobs in 1980 will be in the service sector. Yet many introductory marketing texts devote little, if any, material to the special problems of service marketing. Furthermore, the government and other nonprofit organizations play dominant roles in the U.S. economy. Yet, marketing texts usually devote little space to the marketing problems of nonbusiness organizations. This book is for tomorrow's marketers. It has separate chapters on the marketing of services, the marketing of nonbusinesses, and the future of marketing. It is, I believe, the first introductory marketing text that fully recognizes the **broadened concept** of marketing.

A broadened concept of marketing, in addition to covering nonbusiness and service marketing, also portrays marketing as an exchange process, not just a managerial process. Students need to understand that buying is marketing, too; that marketing is not something done *to* buyers by sellers, but something buyers and sellers do *with* each other. This text explains the basic concepts of marketing management, including product, distribution, promotion, and price decisions. But unlike many texts, it doesn't stop there. It goes on to explain the role of buyers in marketing and the social issues involved in the marketing process. Every effort is made to stress concepts and principles to minimize overlap with a second course in marketing management—a real problem in some schools.

Because this text is so comprehensive, it is appropriate for the introductory marketing course at all colleges and universities. It also makes an excellent reading assignment for executive-development programs. In fact, this book—together with the study guide—is appropriate for anyone who wants to learn marketing principles. But the text is aimed primarily at undergraduate students taking their first marketing course.

Most undergraduate students today are very concerned about environmental problems. They face a future in which ecology, conservation, productivity, population control, and other quality-of-life questions will dominate much governmental and business decision making. This text addresses all these issues and presents a philosophy of marketing management (a societal marketing concept) that all readers will find interesting and challenging.

A variety of teaching aids, which are discussed fully in the Preface to the Student, help to make this course attractive for the instructor as well as the student. For example, each chapter begins with learning goals so that students and instructors can agree on what is to be learned. Furthermore, each chapter ends with thought-provoking questions and cases that help to generate lively class discussion. The teacher's manual has sample lesson guides, lecture suggestions, lecture sources, examination questions, and other helpful materials.

But what makes a course worthwhile to instructors and students is material that is up-to-date and forward looking. Students, for example, desperately need help in marketing themselves for a job, and yet most texts don't even discuss this relevant marketing problem. Students appreciate material that is designed to meet their needs, and the material in this book is obviously student-oriented.

An instructor is not confined to one teaching approach when using this text, as is usually the case with principles texts. This text uses a conceptual approach to marketing and encompasses all the traditional approaches: functional, institutional, managerial, and environmental. This allows the instructor to make the first course in marketing an introduction to all the other courses. Majors and nonmajors alike will appreciate the comprehensive coverage of basic concepts. I hope you find that your course evaluations rise and your classroom experiences become more gratifying as you use this text. I know that you share my goal of making marketing the best course on your campus.

Preface to the Student

Marketing is one of the most interesting and useful subjects you can study. Students usually get most enthusiastic about subjects that give them the ability to apply their new knowledge to everyday problems. You will be able to apply the concepts in this text to become a more informed and effective consumer, to promote your ideas and your skills, and to help improve the quality of life for all people. Most students today are also interested in challenging and rewarding careers. For this reason, this text has an entire chapter on careers in marketing and techniques for landing the right job. You may want to read this chapter first if you are uncertain about a career.

Before you begin reading the text, glance through the table of contents and read the introductions to each of the seven parts. This will give you a better feel for what the text is all about and what approach is used. Although any introductory course is designed to teach you the terminology and basic concepts of the field, you will also want to apply what you have learned. To get you involved in marketing decision making, each chapter is followed by several thought-provoking questions and two short cases that require some analysis. Discussion of these materials helps the text to come alive and makes the first course in marketing only an introduction to other, more specialized marketing courses.

This book was designed to capture the excitement and challenge of marketing. I have tried to make it the most interesting and most readable marketing principles text. Every effort has been made to make the book visually attractive and easy to learn from. For example, each chapter begins with learning goals to guide you as you study. Key concepts and key terms are highlighted in color and are printed in bold type. It is easier, therefore, to learn and remember important concepts and to review such concepts when needed. To further aid such review, each chapter concludes with a summary of key concepts and key terms. Each chapter has boxed quotations that emphasize fundamental issues and introduce you to current writings in marketing. Cartoons and advertisements are also used to illustrate important concepts and to show examples of marketing in action.

A study guide has been prepared for use with the text. This guide is intended to make studying more structured and to prepare you for examinations and class discussion. Helpful hints are given for reading the book, for taking class notes, and for studying for exams. In addition, each chapter is summarized in a few pages. The guide reinforces your reading through programmed learning exercises and helps you prepare for exams by giving sample exam questions. In short, you should use the study guide whether or not it is formally assigned.

It is my pleasure to share with you my enthusiasm for marketing. I hope you are as enthusiastic after reading this book.

Acknowledgments

The road to writing a principles book is crowded with people who are willing and eager to help. Most important, perhaps, are those who offer encouragement to begin in the first place. I am grateful, therefore, to my family and friends for helping me through the first few difficult steps down the road.

Someone also has to help keep you on the path along which lie the principles to be learned. Noel Zabriskie at the University of North Florida inspired me to develop basic principles. My students helped me to refine them. And my teachers and colleagues at The Ohio State University and the University of Maryland helped me to put them in the proper framework. Special thanks go to the faculty and instructors at the University of Maryland who have critically reviewed the material and tested it in the classroom. Notable contributors include Tom Greer, Marvin Jolson, Paul Bloom, Gary Ford, Cecil Hynes, and Ron Hill.

It is tempting when writing a text to follow the well-worn path of previous writers. But some people are so influential that they can lead you off to newer and better routes. One such person is Philip Kotler at Northwestern University. His writings have taught all marketers to broaden their perspectives and to look to the future. It was Philip Kotler who introduced the broadened concept of marketing that provides the framework for this text. He also drove home the important point that buying is marketing, too. And his articles on consumerism, social responsibility, and marketing management have revolutionized traditional thinking. I join my marketing colleagues in thanking him for his insight. Only the late Wroe Alderson has done as much to inspire my thinking.

Translating new material into an attractive, readable text involves many more participants. The office staff at the University of Maryland was extremely helpful throughout the process. My graduate assistants helped prepare the materials for the teacher's manual and study guide. Special thanks go to Robin Sloan, Joy Luna, Anne Rowland, and Brenda Toan for their help.

The people who are the most help toward the end of the road are those in publishing. Judy Rothman and David Culverwell are two of the most competent and hard-working individuals I have ever worked with. They showed me the benefits of following the Prentice-Hall path. John Covell helped launch the manuscript, and I thank him. But Ray Mullaney was the editor who cut and smoothed and shaped the raw material into an attractive total package. Ray has earned not just my thanks, but my respect and my admiration.

Finally, the road ends with faculty members and students who make the whole trip worthwhile. Some faculty members gave their time and expertise to reviewing the text and making helpful suggestions. For this help I am thankful to:

James H. Donnelly, University of Kentucky
John W. Ernest, Los Angeles City College
Ronald E. Frank, University of Pennsylvania
Roy R. Grundy, College of DuPage
Mark Jones, Chabot College
James McCormack, Monroe Community College
Vincent F. Orza, Jr., Central State University
George A. Smith, Norwalk Community College
Richard E. Stanley, University of South Carolina
John H. Sullivan, Jr., North Shore Community College
Sumner M. White, Massachusetts Bay Community College

At the end of the road, one can be grateful to all who helped, but the responsibility for the trip is on the author. I accept responsibility for any flaws remaining in the manuscript. It is hoped that you, the reader, will be one of the last contributors. If you see any mistakes or want to make any suggestions for improving the book, please write. There are other roads to travel, and help is always appreciated.

1

Introduction

One of the best ways to learn about an activity is to watch several people engaged in it. Chapter 1 will introduce you to Jeff Charles, Marsha Norman, Maria Rodriguez, Ira Bernstein, and other people whose experiences will give you a feel for the marketing process. These experiences will reveal some basic concepts and principles that apply in all marketing situations. (All of the examples in this book are based on actual cases, but the names and situations may be changed somewhat to make a point or to protect the privacy of those involved.) Chapter 1 will also introduce a definition of marketing that stresses mutually satisfying exchange relationships.

In Chapter 2, we shall explore some basic functions of marketing. If you now feel that marketing is something sellers do *to* buyers, you will be surprised to find that both buyers and sellers perform all the marketing functions. Marketing is discussed as a way of creating exchanges by overcoming the obstacles between buyers and sellers.

Marketing has changed its focus over the years, and the philosophy behind marketing has changed as well. Chapter 3 traces the evolution of marketing and the marketing concept (the managerial philosophy that helps guide marketing management). A new marketing philosophy that puts more emphasis on marketing's role in society is now emerging. We shall look at this new philosophy and what it could mean for all social organizations. We shall begin Part 1 by reviewing the ways in which marketing exchanges are part of our everyday lives.

Introduction to Marketing

exchange concepts

1

LEARNING GOALS After you have read and studied this chapter, you should be able to:

1. Define the term marketing as used in the book.
2. List three mutually satisfactory exchange relationships that you have experienced.
3. Discuss the ways in which both buying and selling are part of marketing.
4. Explain why marketing is described as a process.
5. Name four constraints on the marketing process.
6. Describe at least four different exchange relationships other than that of business and consumers.
7. Differentiate between wants and needs.
8. Explain why marketing concepts may be applied in both profit-making and nonprofit organizations.
9. Define the following terms: micro-marketing; macro-marketing; positive marketing; normative marketing; the profit sector; situational management; mutually satisfying exchange.
10. Develop your own definition of marketing that shows your understanding of exchange concepts.

> *Exchange is the central concept underlying marketing. It calls for the offering of value to someone in exchange for value. Through exchanges, various social units—individuals, small groups, organizations, whole nations—attain [what] they need.*
>
> Philip Kotler*

INTRODUCTION You have been participating in marketing exchanges all your life. If you're like most people, your first marketing experience was probably exchanging toys with a friend—after both of you negotiated a deal. Of course, exchange situations gradually become more complex and expensive, but the same basic concepts and principles still apply. For example, your exchanges in retail stores probably started with bubble gum and led up to automobiles and stereo sets.

You probably also take part in exchanges involving ideas, political and religious concepts, charitable causes, and other nonbusiness ventures. No matter where you go or what you do, your life will be a whole series of exchange situations in which you will be asked to give up something such as time or money to get something in return. Marketing will teach you how to better manage such exchange relationships. You will learn how to make marketing exchanges that lead to greater satisfaction for you *and* for other persons.

From this book you will learn how marketing techniques can be used to begin satisfying many of society's basic needs. You will also see how marketing can be used to satisfy many of your *personal* needs. Let's begin our discussion of marketing by introducing a few people who have effectively applied marketing concepts to satisfy their needs.

Jeff Charles was a college student in the eastern United States when he noticed that many of his friends had difficulty meeting and dating the kind of people they preferred. Suddenly Jeff had an idea. He had been working with computers as part of his class projects, and he decided to begin a computerized dating service. He asked young men and women to fill out computer-coded questionnaires and used their responses to select suitable dating partners. Jeff saw a need and filled it, and now he has a good income from this service.

Edwin H. Land saw that people had to go through a lot of fuss and bother to get their films processed. In fact, film often sat in the camera for months until people used up the roll. Land invented a camera that would turn out instant pictures that were developed inside the camera. He took his idea to Kodak but was turned down. He then turned to a company named Polaroid that made sunglasses (Land had founded the company in 1937). Of course, you know the rest. Land made a fortune with the Polaroid Land camera.[1]

* *Marketing for Nonprofit Organizations* (Englewood Cliffs, N.J.: Prentice-Hall, Inc., 1975), p. 5.

[1] You can read about the success of this camera and the introduction of Kodak's competitive version in "The Camera Boom," *Newsweek*, May 3, 1976, pp. 69–72.

Marsha Norman got her good idea while serving on a church committee. The congregation wanted to become more socially involved in the community and to make better use of its facilities. Marsha discovered that many women in the community wanted to work full time but had difficulty finding good places to leave their children. Marsha then checked the building codes and other requirements and eventually opened a day-care center in the basement of the church. Teachers were hired, and children could be cared for in a happy, enriching environment while their parents were at work. Marsha found a need and filled it, and in return she got satisfaction from serving others.

These examples show how several people learned a basic concept of marketing. They learned that successful marketing begins with the study of people's wants and needs. These successful marketers also found that satisfying the wants and needs of others brought a satisfactory return to them as well. The guiding concept behind all successful marketing exchanges, therefore, is:

› **Find a need and fill it.**

The natural result of such efforts is that the business, person, or private organization that satisfies others probably will be satisfied also. In fact, *marketing may be defined as an attempt to form mutually satisfying exchange relationships.* Let's look at some other marketing cases to see how these relationships are sometimes begun.

Maria Rodriguez had three young children and wanted to attend classes at the local community college. But Maria needed someone to watch her children while she was away. She found eight other women in her community with similar needs and started a baby-sitting club in which the women shared baby-sitting chores. Maria had a need and satisfied it herself. In doing so, she satisfied the needs of others as well.

Ira Bernstein was an elderly gentleman who needed someone to help around the house, go shopping, and generally manage the household. So Ira put an ad in the paper telling people of his need. A coed from a local college answered Ira's ad and has proved to be truly helpful.

Marketing helps to improve exchange relationships.

Maria and Ira discovered that people have many wants and needs that no one has satisfied. To fill *their own* needs, Maria and Ira searched out others and established their own mutually satisfying exchange relationships. They learned that marketing may be initiated by the buyer as well as by the seller. The guiding concept for buyers is:

> ❯ **Find your own needs and get others to satisfy them.**

Buying Is Marketing Too

Buyer marketing is a valid procedure to improve the buyer's position. Just as sellers use various marketing techniques to attract buyers, buyers can resort to various marketing measures to gain a response from sellers. Just as sellers study buyer behavior, buyers may study seller behavior. . . .

In general, *both parties* to the market transaction have the most to gain when they view their relation as one of mutual benefit rather than conflicting interest.

From Philip Kotler and Sidney J. Levy, "Buying Is Marketing Too!" *Journal of Marketing*, January 1973, p. 59. Reprinted with permission of the American Marketing Association.

Have you noticed how many people advertise in the newspapers to find solutions to their wants and needs? Businesses seek employees through the want ads. Couples expecting children place ads seeking used baby furniture. Take a brief look at the classified ads in your newspaper. You will find ads from people trying to buy or sell new and used furniture, cars, and a host of other goods and services (see Figure 1.1). The classified ad section of any newspaper can give you a good feeling for what marketing is all about. A basic concept that might help you understand the marketing process better is:

> ❯ **Marketing is an attempt to satisfy the needs of both the buyer and the seller.**

This book is based on the premise that marketing is a process that creates solutions to people's wants and needs. Marketing is thus one of the most interesting and useful subjects one can study. It has been estimated that from one-fourth to one-third of all people employed in the United States (excluding the military) are in jobs directly or closely related to marketing.[2]

Everyone in the United States has wants and needs, almost everyone uses marketing to satisfy those wants and needs, and everyone could benefit from a more thorough knowledge of the principles and concepts behind market behavior. This book should help you be a better marketer, so that you may more fully satisfy your own wants and needs.

---

[2] William J. Stanton, *Fundamentals of Marketing*, 4th ed. (New York: McGraw-Hill, Inc., 1975), p. 9.

Figure 1.1 PART OF A TYPICAL CLASSIFIED AD SECTION

EVOLUTION OF THE DEFINITION OF MARKETING

Marketing has not always been thought of as an exchange relationship. A brief review of the history of marketing education will give you a better idea of how marketing has evolved through the years.

Marketing was first taught as a business subject in 1902. At that time, the courses had names like "The Distribution of Products," and marketing was thought of as a distribution process.[3] In fact, the American Marketing Association still officially defines marketing as "the performance of business activities that direct the flow of goods and services from producer to consumer or user."[4]

One popular definition in the 1950s viewed marketing as "the delivery of a standard of living to society."[5] Throughout the period from 1900 to 1960, marketing was generally thought of as a *business* activity. The emphasis in texts was on the description of marketing functions and

---

[3] See Robert Bartels, *The Development of Marketing Thought* (Homewood, Ill.: Richard D. Irwin, Inc., 1962).

[4] "Report of the Definitions Committee," *Journal of Marketing*, October 1948, pp. 202–217. The American Marketing Association is now working on a new, better definition.

[5] Paul Mazur, *The Standards We Raise* (New York: Harper & Row, Publishers, 1953), pp. 18–28.

7

institutions. During this period, there were many different concepts about the meaning of marketing:

It has been described by one person as a business activity; as a group of related business activities; as a trade phenomenon; as a frame of mind; as a coordinative, integrative function in policy making; as a sense of business purpose; as an economic process; as a structure of institutions; as the process of exchanging or transferring ownership of products; as a process of concentration, equalization, and dispersion; as the creation of time, place, and possession utilities; as a process of demand and supply adjustment; and as many other things.[6]

During the 1960s, the emphasis in marketing (and in marketing texts) shifted to marketing management. The definitions thus emphasized *management* of the flows of goods and services from producer to consumer.

But the 1970s saw the emergence of a new direction in marketing thought. Marketing concepts were broadened to include the activities of nonprofit organizations, and the definitions changed as well.[7]

The newer, more progressive texts recognize marketing as an exchange activity applicable in all exchange situations. Thus, marketing is now referred to as "those activities performed by individuals or organizations, either profit or nonprofit, that enable, facilitate, and encourage exchange to the satisfaction of both parties";[8] or as "human activity directed at satisfying wants and needs through exchange processes";[9] or as "exchange activities conducted by individuals and organizations for the purpose of satisfying human wants."[10]

You should develop your own definition of marketing that you can remember and discuss with others. As you develop a definition, keep these concepts in mind:

> Marketing is performed by both individuals and organizations.
> The goal of marketing is to enable, facilitate, and encourage exchange.
> The purpose of exchanges is to satisfy human wants and needs.
> Marketing is performed by both the seller and the buyer.

[6] *Statement of the Philosophy of Marketing of the Marketing Faculty* (Columbus: Ohio State University, Bureau of Business Research, 1964).

[7] See Philip Kotler and Sidney J. Levy, "Broadening the Concepts of Marketing," *Journal of Marketing*, January 1969, pp. 10–15.

[8] Burton Marcus et al., *Modern Marketing* (New York: Random House, Inc., 1975), p. 4.

[9] Philip Kotler, *Marketing Management*, 3rd ed. (Englewood Cliffs, N.J.: Prentice-Hall, Inc., 1976), p. 5.

[10] Ben M. Enis, *Marketing Principles: The Management Process*, 2nd ed. (Santa Monica, Calif.: Goodyear Publishing Co., Inc., 1977), p. 17.

Marketing is performed by individuals and by all types of organizations, including cities.

St. Louis
Less dollars coming. A lot more going.

Be a hero! Land your people right smack in the middle of things. St. Louis will make you a hero because of the money everyone can save and earn.

At the population center of the U.S., St. Louis is closer to more Americans than any other city. And, one-third of all Americans (nearly 80 million people) live within 500 miles of St. Louis. So, if you have people coming from all over the map, travel costs will probably average less to St. Louis.

Convenient transportation that's our forte . . . non-stop service from all major air hubs in the nation via ten airlines, AMTRAK, two international bus lines and four Interstate Highways converging on St. Louis. And, we are the nation's largest inland port, and second largest trucking and railroad center. Yes, if you're moving people or exhibiting products, you can probably bring them to St. Louis from all parts of the country for less money and more conveniently than to any other location.

Top hotel facilities are here to accommodate groups of every size and type. You'll be amazed at the variety and quality of our meeting facilities and to top it all off, the new St. Louis Gateway Convention and Exhibition Center is opening next year.

Great attractions! We are the historic city that keeps old man river young with stern-wheelers and ragtime, Six Flags, world-famous zoo, fabulous restaurants, sports, theatre, and symphony in the shadow of the soaring Gateway Arch.

Economic diversity that includes you . . . St. Louis has the most diversified economy of any U.S. city. So, whatever you're buying, selling, making, or communicating, you'll probably be right at home, and a success, in St. Louis.

A mid-America welcome awaits you. So, be a hero and bring your group to St. Louis. We're a great meeting town, coming and going.

All right, show me how my group can come to St. Louis for less and have a lot more going.

Name

Organization

Address

City

State   Zip

Preferred Dates   No. of People

CONVENTION AND VISITORS BUREAU OF GREATER ST. LOUIS
500 N. Broadway/St. Louis, Missouri 63102/314-421-1023
WARREN L. TRAFTON, Executive Director

Courtesy of Convention and Visitors Bureau of St. Louis.

A DEFINITION FOR THE FUTURE Marketing is a constantly changing function that adapts to the changing needs of society and of individuals within society. The following definition recognizes marketing's social role: **Marketing** is a process in a society that, subject to constraints, attempts to establish mutually satisfying product-exchange relationships between people with diverse wants and needs and people or machines that can partially satisfy those wants and needs.[11]

This definition introduces several key concepts that provide a foundation for studying all marketing relationships. Let's review the eight key elements of this definition as a basis for further discussion.

1. Marketing is a whole series of activities. The term used to describe such a series is "process." Marketing is a process of satisfying wants and needs.
2. Marketing activities are different in various situations ("in a society"). The *environment* (surroundings) affect what is done and how.
3. Marketing activities are limited by various outside influences; therefore, marketing is subject to *constraints*.
4. Marketing's goal is to create exchange relationships, but marketing can only *attempt* to create such relationships.
5. Marketing attempts to create mutual satisfaction.
6. Marketing involves *products*.
7. Marketing relationships may be between two or more people or between people and mechanical devices or machines.
8. Marketing satisfies both *wants* and *needs*.

The following sections will explain more fully what each of these eight elements mean. The idea is to give you a complete background in basic concepts and principles.

Marketing Is a Process To say that marketing is a process means simply that marketing is a continuing development, or a series of activities, involving many changes. The marketing process continually changes over time in response to new social needs and wants. The basic concept behind the discussion is:

> **Marketing is a process, not a single exchange, and that process involves a series of activities.**

Marketing Operates within a Society Marketing as a process changes depending upon the society (environment) in which it operates. The political, social, technological, and physical characteristics of a society determine what form marketing will take.

The nature of marketing is therefore different in various societies and even within particular geographic areas or particular social groups.

[11] This definition was first used in William G. Nickels, *Marketing Communications and Promotion* (Columbus, Ohio: Grid, Inc., 1976), p. 10.

Thus, in a socialistic country (for example, Russia), the government has a much larger say in what gets produced, where, when, and how. In a capitalistic country (for example, the United States), more of the production and marketing decisions are left to free enterprise systems and consumer choice.

The nature of marketing exchanges also varies greatly between developed and developing nations. In the United States, for example, services are a major element in personal consumption expenditures. In developing nations, services are a minor item, and basic products such as food and housing dominate consumer expenditures. The concept that applies here is:

> **Marketing is based on society's wants and needs; therefore, marketing varies among societies, and its tasks change as a society's wants and needs change.**

Marketing Is Subject to Constraints Marketing's *attempts* to form mutually satisfactory exchange relationships are not always successful. Often, various constraints prevent or hinder the marketing process. For example, some people have wants and needs that are not socially acceptable in their societies; these wants and needs can be satisfied only by breaking some legal or moral guidelines. The marketing process is thus subject to social, political, and ethical constraints.

Often marketers do not have the resources or the technology to satisfy selected wants and needs. Marketing is thus subject to financial and technological constraints.

Many of our needs can be met only through personal effort or group cooperation; often, marketing can merely assist in this effort. For example, the needs for peace, self-satisfaction, leisure time, friendship, and international cooperation have not been fully met.

Marketing is also constrained by its reliance on persuasion and information rather than on force. It cannot *make* people happy or content.

Many of the criticisms of marketing today grow from the fact that there is still imperfect communication between and among marketing participants. Also, products, distribution, credit, and service systems are often faulty. One of the constraints on marketing is that the process involves people, and people may cheat and make mistakes. One concept of marketing that emerges from this discussion is:

> **The marketing process cannot and will not satisfy all of society's wants and needs because various constraints prevent or hinder this objective.**

When people satisfy their wants in one area, they seek satisfaction of other wants; however, no society ever seems to find complete serenity and bliss. In search for such satisfactions, people will seek religious, social, or psychological answers to their wants and needs. Marketing will always be needed in a society because people always seem to have unsatisfied wants—including peace, a clean environment, and understanding.

Marketing Forms Exchanges Marketing is concerned mainly with establishing and maintaining exchange relationships. Exchange relationships, such as goods for money, may be broadly interpreted to include also the exchanging of goods for goods (barter), services for votes (elections), knowledge for knowledge (pooled scientific information), people for money (entertainers and athletes), ideas for money (education), time for personal fulfillment (charitable work), and all other exchange relationships, including civic (government) transactions[12] (see Figure 1.2).

The two-way nature of the marketing exchange process is perhaps most vividly illustrated in barter arrangements (that is, the trading of goods). If Jones makes shoes and Smith makes hats, Smith and Jones may trade their merchandise in a mutually satisfactory exchange. Either one may initiate the contact, and either one may try to persuade the other to alter the offer. In other words, either may assume the role of "buyer" or "seller." The same is true of the exchange of money for goods, services, persons, places, or ideas. Either party may make the initial contact, and either may request some adjustment from the other.

Thus, *marketing is an interaction that attempts to establish exchange relationships.* It is not simply a one-way attempt to generate sales. Exchange is only one step in the marketing process. Marketing takes

[12] Enis, *Marketing Principles,* p. 22.

Figure 1.2 EXAMPLES OF MARKETING EXCHANGE RELATIONSHIPS

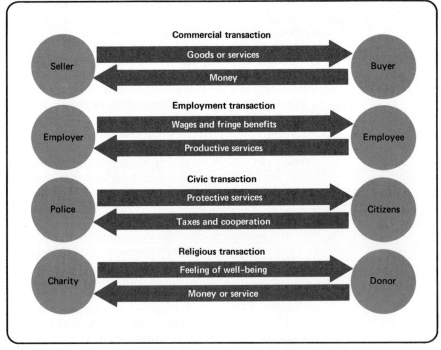

Redrawn from Philip Kotler, *Marketing for Nonprofit Organizations* (Englewood Cliffs, N.J.: Prentice-Hall, Inc., 1975), p. 24.

place before and after the exchange. Because marketing is an exchange process, we shall not concentrate on marketing *management* (that is, management of the firm). Instead, we shall look at marketing from the perspective of both buyers and sellers.

Emphasis in most of the popular introductory marketing texts has been on marketing management. Specifically, there has been much discussion of the four *p*'s of marketing management: product, place, promotion, and price.[13] These four factors collectively have become known as the **marketing mix.**

It is important to know and understand the importance of product, place, promotion, and price, and so this book will have chapters on each. But the emphasis will not be on the management of the factors in the marketing mix by a business manager. Instead, the emphasis will be on these four factors as elements in the exchange process. They are as important to the buyer as they are to the seller, and it is the *concepts behind* the managerial decisions that are most important. Here is what one text says about the traditional managerial approach:

There are two basic reasons as to why traditional discussions of marketing are inadequate. First, technological, managerial, and social changes cause rapid innovation in marketing institutions and practices; thus, descriptive materials soon become obsolete. Second, management methods which accomplish the marketing task vary greatly with different firms; therefore, a description of the management methods used by some firms is incomplete and inadequate. Academicians and managers have come to agree that marketing needs to be viewed as an integrated body of conceptual knowledge. When so viewed, marketing institutions, functions, and practices are described as concepts. These concepts are all interconnected with a root or basic concept . . . that all marketing activity begins and ends with the consumer.[14]

A popular myth is that marketing is something sellers do *to* buyers. Marketing is thus considered to be synonymous with selling and/or advertising. But marketing is not what sellers do *to* buyers; it is what buyers and sellers do together or what sellers do *with* buyers. Buying is part of marketing too.[15] Thus, two basic concepts of marketing are:

➤ **Marketing is an exchange process that involves a two-way interaction: buying and selling are both important to exchanges.**

➤ **Marketing relationships may be initiated by anyone.**

---

[13] The most popular example is E. Jerome McCarthy, *Basic Marketing: A Managerial Approach*, 5th ed. (Homewood, Ill.: Richard D. Irwin, Inc., 1975), pp. 75–80.

[14] Weldon J. Taylor and Roy T. Shaw, Jr., *Marketing: An Integrated Analytical Approach* (Cincinnati, Ohio: South-Western Publishing Co., 1975), pp. 29–30.

[15] Philip Kotler and Sidney J. Levy, "Buying Is Marketing Too!" *Journal of Marketing*, January 1973, pp. 54–59.

Why Study Concepts?

Concepts have been identified as the fundamental units marketers use in their everyday marketing activities; concepts are the building blocks of the propositions and theories that marketers use in explaining, predicting, and controlling marketplace phenomena. It is essential that a basic understanding of concepts be achieved.

From Gerald Zaltman, Christian R. A. Pinson, and Reinhard Angelmar, *Metatheory and Consumer Research* (New York: Holt, Rinehart and Winston, Inc., 1973), p. 47.

Marketing Attempts to Create Mutual Satisfaction Early in this chapter, we discussed Edwin H. Land's invention of a camera that automatically produces developed photographs. The story of Land's invention clearly points out the following basic concept of marketing:

> People who recognize a need and fill it usually can satisfy some of their own needs as well.

The goal of marketing is *mutually satisfactory exchanges.* This does not mean that *all* marketers have the best interests of the public in mind when they attempt a transaction. It does mean, however, that such marketers will tend to fail in the long run, because, without mutual satisfaction, the marketing process is likely to end. (This generally happens unless there is no alternative marketing strategy, in which case, a half a loaf may be better than none.) This is true for both the seller and the buyer. For example, if sellers are not satisfied with the prices they receive or the profits they make, they will likely stop the marketing relationship by going out of business or seeking other markets. Buyers also have the right to buy or not buy, and they will exercise that right depending on their view of the gain or loss of an exchange.

It is obvious from the number of consumer complaints today that not all marketing transactions are mutually satisfying. Often the buyer or seller feels cheated when he or she analyzes his or her gain or loss over time. One function of marketing is to open up channels of communication, so that such dissatisfactions can be resolved. The marketing process is an *attempt* to provide mutual satisfaction, but this is not always possible.

Some marketing exchanges may turn out to be unsatisfactory. Such dissatisfaction should be resolved so that in the long run the marketing process comes close to providing mutual satisfaction. But you know that all of your needs and wants (for example, peace in the world) may never be filled. And so a basic concept of marketing is:

> People's needs and wants are endless, and so there always will be a need for marketing.

Another concept that emerges from a discussion of mutually satisfactory relationships is:

> **If any party in a marketing exchange relationship is dissatisfied, the relationship will likely end unless that dissatisfaction is resolved.**

Marketing Involves Products It may be difficult for you at this point to think of persons, places, ideas, and services as "products," but, as far as marketing is concerned, they are. Anything that can satisfy a person's wants and needs may be viewed as a product or a part of a product.

When the term "marketing" was first used, products were thought of as food, steel, cotton, and other *physical goods*. Later, the marketing of *services*, such as those offered by banks, insurance companies, and airlines, become a major concern of marketing, and goods *and* services were thought of as products. Today people want education, culture, art, health, safety, and other products that are not provided by manufacturers or economic service institutions. Table 1.1 relates some of today's needs to various kinds of products.

Table 1.1 is meant to be only a sample of the many needs we have and of the kinds of things that may be viewed as products. One product of the Lung Association is the prevention and treatment of respiratory ailments; a product of a football team may be entertainment or winning; products of a restaurant include food, atmosphere, and service; and so on.

Product concepts and principles are highly complex and will be given full treatment in Chapter 8. However, at this point it is important that you understand this concept:

> **A product in marketing may be a person, place, idea, physical good, service, social cause, or some combination of these.**

Deception and Fraud in Marketing

Some educators* and most of the general public feel that marketing is *not* an attempt to establish mutually satisfying exchange. Many consumers feel it is an attempt by sellers to deceive, manipulate, and exploit naïve buyers. In fact, such practices do occur, but it is obvious that they hurt marketing and marketers as much as they do the public. No one can market effectively in an atmosphere of mistrust, doubt, and misinformation. One key principle of marketing needs to be emphasized throughout this book and throughout the marketing world:

Deception, fraud, and all other questionable marketing practices hinder the creation of mutually satisfying marketing exchanges and are thus antimarketing; therefore, one objective of marketing is to minimize such practices.

---

* For example, see Robert M. Fulmer, *The New Marketing* (New York: Macmillan Publishing Co., Inc., 1976), pp. 5–6.

Table 1.1 SOME NEEDS AND THE PRODUCTS THAT SATISFY THEM

Need	Products that satisfy need
Education	Ideas, concepts, principles
Health	Nutritional information, medical care, illness prevention
Culture	Books, music, dance, art
Aid for the disadvantaged	Charities, social causes, foundations
Spiritual guidance	Churches, religions, occult practices
Cooperative living	Unions, food co-ops, communes, government
Protection	Insurance, police, military

It might be helpful to recognize that the product is what the consumer *perceives* it to be, not what it actually *is*. If a little girl believes in Santa Claus, then Santa Claus is just as real and important to her as friends or relatives. From a marketing perspective, if a person *feels* a product is superior to other products, it *is* superior for him or her, regardless of whether it is objectively inferior to other goods or not. Another concept, then, which will be explained in detail later is:

> **The product is what a person perceives it to be.**

Marketing Involves People or Machines Most people think of buying, selling, and other marketing activities as interpersonal exchanges, but in this age of automation and technological growth, machines have taken over many of the marketing activities. For example, people can obtain insurance, food, money, trinkets, and dozens of other items from vending machines. People can also buy goods through the mail or by phones connecting them to a computer. The concept is:

> **Marketing relationships may be interpersonal, or they may involve man/machine exchanges or even machine/machine exchanges.**

Many stores have automatic reordering systems that send computer cards to the manufacturer, whose computer system analyzes the order and begins the distribution process. Of course, people are behind all marketing exchanges, but many of the functions people perform may be performed better and more efficiently by machines.

Marketing Attempts to Satisfy Wants and Needs You may have wondered why the discussion thus far has referred to both wants and needs. What is the difference? People *need* very few things in life: a little food, some water, enough warmth to stay alive, and so forth. But people *want* all kinds of things: electric knives, tennis rackets, ice cream, phonograph records, and much, much more.

Machine Marketing

Women shoppers know how they like to be served, and nowhere is this more true than in Japan, where women have just struck a blow against automated shopping.

Susuma Iida is a fully automated supermarket in the Tokyo suburb of Kokubunji. Customers chose from 3,000 products, stored in a battery of 67 vending machines, by inserting a plastic card and pushing a button specifying the name and quantity of the desired article.

The goods were then taken to a human cashier for wrapping. The customer's plastic card was placed into another machine that computed payment in 0.7 seconds. The store's computerized section handled items ranging from tinned and bottled products to frozen foods. In the rest of the supermarket, meat, fish, clothing and other goods are sold in the conventional manner.

The government had taken great interest in the system, for the computerized store was developed under Trade Ministry supervision at a cost of around $1 million.

It attracted customers at first—because of its novelty—and daily sales amounted to around $3,400. But by the time the project was dropped recently sales had dropped to a fifth of that figure.

In the end, the computerized section of the store was attracting less than 300 customers a day, while more than 2,000 on average were using the conventional section.

Behind this decline was a basic unhappiness at being unable to touch or check the quality and freshness of goods, especially perishables, before purchase.

Once the goods were removed from the display cases they could not be replaced. A shopper had to go to the trouble of requesting a refund from the cashier.

Other shoppers apparently felt uncomfortable at "being controlled by a machine."

Japanese shoppers are used to a high level of personal service. In big department stores, polite women dressed in custom-designed uniforms and white gloves bow customers on to escalators. Purchases are also beautifully wrapped at no extra charge. All this, of course, was missing at Kokubunji.

The Trade Ministry does not rule out further experiments in the future. But officials admit it was a mistake to set up a store with both automated and manned sections, especially when the public was not accustomed to computerized shopping.

There were also teething troubles. The Kokubunji machines did not always deliver the goods and the computer did not always get its arithmetic right. Automation clearly has some advantages, though. A non-automated supermarket is thought to need at least a staff of 25, while the automated operation can get by with a fifth of that number.

From Mark Murray, "Machine Marketing," *The Washington Post,* October 3, 1976. © *New York Times/Observer.*

Marketing tries to satisfy people's wants and needs. Much of what people want is determined by cultural influences (for example, elaborate weddings, fancy clothes, special foods, and beds). People also want what others have. (Children are especially prone to this, but adults are almost the same.) We shall analyze consumer wants and behavior later on in Chapter 7. The concept to remember is:

> ▸ People *need* very little in life but *want* much, and so marketing is usually more concerned with wants than needs.

Changing Needs to Wants

The individual is not always conscious of his needs. To want a product is to recognize it explicitly as a means of meeting a situation which is regarded as both probable and important. Marketing creates wants by making consumers aware of needs and by identifying specific products as means of meeting these needs.

From Wroe Alderson, *Marketing Behavior and Executive Action* (Homewood, Ill.: Richard D. Irwin, Inc., 1957), p. 280.

Many people are concerned about the frivolous desires of the U.S. public and wish they could change the public's values. Those persons who wish to install a different set of values in society (for example, churchgoers, environmentalists, consumerists, moralists, and parents) can apply marketing principles to the task to improve their effectiveness. Marketing is a tool that is available to anyone—anyone who has a need or anyone who is responsive to the needs of others.

MARKETING'S LIMITS Some people may not be comfortable with the definitions and principles of marketing that have been outlined in this chapter. They may wonder where marketing ends and just what functions and activities are included in marketing. The answers to such questions have led to much debate among marketing scholars. Let's take a look at the key issues in this debate.

Marketing has traditionally been limited to exchanges involving the transfer of money for goods and services. The problems of such a narrow definition of marketing are threefold. First, the differences between the marketing activities of certain profit-making institutions and certain nonprofit institutions are minimal, if there are differences at all. For example, there is little difference between the marketing of the pairs of institutions listed in Table 1.2.

Second, by concentrating on economic (money) exchange relationships, marketing scholars and practitioners may not make sufficient effort toward solving the marketing problems of the government, politicians, unions, charities, social causes, and other noneconomic institutions.

Third, emphasis on the economic aspect of marketing may put too

Table 1.2 PROFIT-MAKING INSTITUTIONS AND PARALLEL NONPROFIT INSTITUTIONS

Profit-making institution	Nonprofit institution
Private universities	Public universities
Private, profit-making hospitals	Public hospitals
Professional theater	Amateur theater (free)
Professional football	College football
Supermarkets	Food co-ops
Employment agencies	State employment agencies
Private day-care center	Public day-care center

much emphasis on profits and marketing management. Scant attention may then be given to the needs of society and to the buying side of exchange relationships.

This does not mean that marketing as an economic process is less important or that less attention should be given marketing management. The point here is that more attention should be given to marketing as a tool that is available to all people and organizations. The principles of marketing are universal principles; they can be applied in any interpersonal situation involving an exchange. As Erich Fromm says in *The Art of Loving:*

Our whole culture is based on . . . the idea of a mutually favorable exchange. . . . Two persons thus fall in love when they feel they have found the best object available . . . considering the limitations of their own exchange values.[16]

The point is that marketing principles can be used and are used in social relationships as well as in economic exchanges. So what are the limits of marketing? For all practical purposes, you can assume that marketing concepts are applicable in any and all exchange relationships involving people. The concept is:

> **Any person or organization that becomes involved in the process of need satisfaction may apply marketing principles to that task.**

Some of the many types of organizations involved in marketing today are listed in Table 1.3.

Some organizations and groups that were once very important have become obsolete. For example, we need fewer carriage makers today than we did in the 1800s. On the other hand, some organizations have emerged for which there was less recognized need in the past. For example, the Environmental Protection Agency was not created until people recognized the environmental harm that resulted from poor planning or from single-minded concern for more basic needs (for

[16] Erich Fromm, *The Art of Loving* (New York: Basic Books, Inc., 1970).

Table 1.3 SOME EXAMPLES OF MARKETING ORGANIZATIONS

Nonprofit organizations	Consumer organizations	Business organizations	Government organizations	Private organizations
Charities Unions Police departments Social causes Boys clubs Girl Scouts Churches Foundations	Better business bureaus Public-interest research groups Nader's groups Common Cause Consumer's Union	Manufacturers Wholesalers Retailers Bankers Insurance companies Transportation firms Consultants	Environmental Protection Agency Department of Transportation Department of the Interior Department of Defense Department of Agriculture Office of Consumer Affairs Local government	SPCA Sierra Club Fraternities Entertainers American Automobile Association Sororities

example, for food, housing, raw materials, electricity, transportation and so forth). It is also clear that some organizations have always been needed and probably always will be. For example, we will probably always have farms of some type, clothing producers, and builders.

This discussion reveals two basic concepts of marketing:

> People and organizations will prosper or falter based on the growth or decline of the want or need for them.

> Those people and organizations that succeed in spite of falling demand do so by adapting their activities to satisfy new or different social needs.[17]

For example, consider the March of Dimes organization. Originally it was formed to solve society's need to cure polio. Once that need was satisfied, the organization survived by responding to another need—the need to prevent and treat birth defects. Thus, it survived through adaptation, as called for in the second concept just cited.

THE NATURE AND SCOPE OF MARKETING Because there has been some debate about the definition and scope of marketing, it is important to show what will be included in a principles of marketing text. We shall be looking at marketing concepts as they apply in both profit-making and nonprofit organizations. We shall look at present marketing practices (sometimes this is called the "positive"

---

[17] This and other survival strategies are expanded upon in Wroe Alderson, *Marketing Behavior and Executive Action* (Homewood, Ill.: Richard D. Irwin, Inc., 1957), pp. 55–57.

approach) and at ways to improve present practices (sometimes known as the "normative" approach). We shall discuss the marketing practices of individuals and firms (micro-marketing), but we shall also look at the total marketing system to see if it is as effective and efficient as it might be (macro-marketing). The entire marketing process is summarized in Figure 1.3. The following definitions will help in your analysis of the table and will provide the foundation for the discussion that follows:

1. **Macro-marketing** refers to the entire marketing system that emerges to satisfy society's wants and needs.
2. **Micro-marketing** refers to the exchange relationship between one organization and the people it serves.
3. **Positive marketing** describes how marketing is practiced in different organizations.
4. **Normative marketing** suggests ways to improve the marketing process to better serve people's wants and needs.
5. The **profit sector** includes all organizations whose objectives include the desire for monetary profit.
6. The **nonprofit sector** includes all organizations whose objectives do not include the desire for monetary profit.

Macro-marketing Figure 1.3 shows some of the issues that are involved in the study of macro-marketing. Basically, macro-marketing is the study of the total exchange system in a society and how it operates. It includes the study of the following:[18]

1. Whether marketing helps or hinders economic development
2. Whether existing distribution systems (for both private and public goods) are efficient
3. How marketing differs among various nations
4. What kind of laws regulating marketing are optimal
5. Whether marketing should have special social responsibilities
6. Whether the demand for public goods should be stimulated

These issues and others will be discussed fully throughout the text. Marketing is an evolving discipline, and the study of macro-marketing helps clarify the issues and improve marketing practices.

Micro-marketing Micro-marketing is the study of problems and issues related to particular organizations or individuals. It looks at decisions regarding products, prices, promotions, distribution systems, international exchanges, and marketing management in general.

Much of this book will be concerned with describing present efforts to market businesses, government agencies, social causes, and other orga-

---

[18] Much of this section is based on Shelby D. Hunt, "The Nature and Scope of Marketing," *Journal of Marketing*, July 1976, pp. 17–27.

Figure 1.3 THE SCOPE OF MARKETING

		Positive	Normative
Profit Sector	Micro	(1) Problems, issues, theories, and research concerning: a. Individual consumer buyer behavior b. How firms determine prices c. How firms determine products d. How firms determine promotion e. How firms determine channels of distribution f. Case studies of marketing practices	(2) Problems, issues, normative models, and research concerning how firms *should*: a. Determine the marketing mix b. Make pricing decisions c. Make product decisions d. Make promotion decisions e. Make packaging decisions f. Make purchasing decisions g. Make international marketing decisions h. Organize their marketing departments i. Control their marketing efforts j. Plan their marketing strategy k. Apply systems theory to marketing problems l. Manage retail establishments m. Manage wholesale establishments n. Implement the marketing concept
Profit Sector	Macro	(3) Problems, issues, theories, and research concerning: a. Aggregate consumption patterns b. Institutional approach to marketing c. Commodity approach to marketing d. Legal aspects of marketing e. Comparative marketing f. The efficiency of marketing systems g. Whether the poor pay more h. Whether marketing spurs or retards economic development i. Power and conflict relationships in channels of distribution j. Whether marketing functions are universal k. Whether the marketing concept is consistent with consumers' interests	(4) Problems, issues, normative models, and research concerning: a. How marketing can be made more efficient b. Whether distribution costs too much c. Whether advertising is socially desirable d. Whether consumer sovereignty is desirable e. Whether stimulating demand is desirable f. Whether the poor should pay more g. What kinds of laws regulating marketing are optimal h. Whether vertical marketing systems are socially desirable i. Whether marketing should have special social responsibilities
Nonprofit Sector	Micro	(5) Problems, issues, theories, and research concerning: a. Consumers' purchasing of public goods b. How nonprofit organizations determine prices c. How nonprofit organizations determine products d. How nonprofit organizations determine promotion e. How nonprofit organizations determine channels of distribution f. Case studies of public goods marketing	(6) Problems, issues, normative models, and research concerning how nonprofit organizations *should*: a. Determine the marketing mix (social marketing) b. Make pricing decisions c. Make product decisions d. Make promotion decisions e. Make packaging decisions f. Make purchasing decisions g. Make international marketing decisions (e.g., CARE) h. Organize their marketing efforts i. Control their marketing efforts j. Plan their marketing strategy k. Apply systems theory to marketing problems
Nonprofit Sector	Macro	(7) Problems, issues, theories, and research concerning: a. The institutional framework for public goods b. Whether television advertising influences elections c. Whether public service advertising influences behavior (e.g., "Smokey the Bear") d. Whether existing distribution systems for public goods are efficient e. How public goods are recycled	(8) Problems, issues, normative models, and research concerning: a. Whether society should allow politicians to be "sold" like toothpaste b. Whether the demand for public goods should be stimulated c. Whether "low informational content" political advertising is socially desirable (e.g., ten-second "spot" commercials) d. Whether the U.S. Army should be allowed to advertise for recruits

From Shelby D. Hunt, "The Nature and Scope of Marketing," *Journal of Marketing*, July 1976, pp. 17–27. Reprinted with permission of the American Marketing Association.

New Frontiers in Macro-marketing

Marketing is being challenged to adjust to . . . an age of public interest. Academicians are becoming more concerned with ethics, morals, values, and marketing-government relationships. The result will be reformulations of the domain, concepts, and models of marketing.

In this perspective, marketing . . . is a formative force in our culture, an institution of social control, a social process for delivering a standard of living and satisfying society's wants and needs. . . .

Marketing frontiers are being extended to encompass intrinsic as well as exchange values. Included are markets based on social concern, markets of the mind, and markets related to the development of people to the fullest extent of their capabilities. Hence, marketing is becoming more involved in the solution of current, functional problems: the elimination of poverty, urban renewal, ecological shifts and balances, enhancement of the quality of life, and improved human relationships.

From William Lazer, "Marketing Education: Commitment for the 1970s," *Journal of Marketing*, July 1970, pp. 7–11. Reprinted with permission of the American Marketing Association.

nizations. Some suggestions will be made about ways to improve present practices as well.

Although this book stresses certain basic concepts that one may apply in marketing situations, it is important to recognize that marketing cannot be described by a few such concepts or procedures. Marketing experts, more than most other people, must be open to change. The marketing environment today may be described as one involving: (1) rapid social change; (2) fierce competition (both at home and from foreign nations); (3) unpredictable government rules, regulations, and actions; (4) declines in natural resources; (5) more involvement of consumerists, environmentalists, and other interest groups; (6) unprecedented technological potential; and (7) shifts in the basic values, attitudes, and behavior of many consumers.[19]

Situational Management

Marketing management in such an environment calls for sensitivity, flexibility, creativity, and a commitment to ethical behavior and social as well as managerial responsibility. The process of adapting organizations to a continually changing environment is called **situational management.** Situational management often demands a rather decentralized organizational structure that emphasizes a continuous monitoring of, and adapting to, market situations. It also may require a comprehensive marketing communication system that enables the organization to respond quickly to new opportunities, competitive changes, and other environmental situations. Finally, situational management demands people who are open to change, who are cooperative, responsible, and

[19] These concepts are from Ross A. Webber, *Management* (Homewood, Ill.: Richard D. Irwin, Inc., 1975), pp. 209–218, 435–439.

dedicated. Such people would make good marketing managers in all organizations.

You will find that flexibility and responsiveness are also needed in your personal marketing relationships. Most of the marketing concepts that are applicable in an organizational setting are also applicable in face-to-face exchanges.

MARKETING CAREERS The reason marketing is such an interesting subject to study is that it is so widely applicable. As a result, it also provides many career opportunities. Everyone would benefit by knowing something about marketing, because everyone is a consumer. Marketing helps make us better consumers as well as better sellers of our ideas, goods, and services.

You are probably familiar with many of the careers available to a person trained in marketing, but perhaps there are some with which you are not so familiar. Later on, after we have discussed marketing more fully, we shall take a detailed look at marketing careers (Chapter 21). At this point, it may be sufficient to say that almost all organizations could use people trained in marketing. These organizations include the government, churches, unions, athletic teams, schools, social causes, charities, hospitals, and businesses. Job categories include marketing researcher, consumer representative, sales representative, advertising manager, display coordinator, credit manager, retailer, wholesaler, distribution specialist, consumer-affairs specialist, public relations director, purchasing agent, buyer, product manager, and many others.

Traditionally, marketing has provided as many job opportunities as any other career field. The lifetime incomes of marketing professionals are generally above average, and often such professionals have many desirable fringe benefits. For example, salespersons not only earn good incomes but are relatively free from desk work. This is true to a lesser extent of buyers, marketing researchers, consumer-affairs specialists, and others in marketing. We hope that you will find marketing an interesting subject to study and perhaps an interesting career as well.

FOR REVIEW

Key Terms

Among the more important terms and expressions discussed in this chapter are the following:

Marketing is a process in a society that, subject to constraints, attempts to establish mutually satisfying product-exchange relationships between people with diverse wants and needs and people or machines that can partially satisfy those wants and needs.

Macro-marketing refers to the entire marketing system that emerges to satisfy society's wants and needs.

Micro-marketing refers to the exchange relationship between one organization and the people it serves.

Nonprofit (noneconomic) institutions carry out exchanges that do not have monetary profit as a prime objective.

The **nonprofit sector** includes all nonprofit institutions.

Normative marketing suggests ways to improve the marketing process to better serve people's wants and needs.

Positive marketing describes how marketing is practiced in different organizations.

Profit-making (economic) institutions carry out exchanges that involve the transfer of money for goods or services.

The **profit sector** includes all profit-making institutions.

Situational management is the process of adapting organizations to a continually changing environment.

Key Concepts

Among the more important marketing concepts introduced in this chapter are the following:

> **Marketing is a process, not a single exchange, and that process involves a series of functions.**

> **Marketing is based on society's wants and needs, and its tasks change as society's wants and needs change.**

> **The marketing process cannot and will not satisfy all of society's wants and needs because various constraints prevent or hinder this objective.**

> **If any party in a marketing exchange relationship is dissatisfied, the relationship will likely end, unless that dissatisfaction is resolved.**

> **Marketing is an exchange process that involves a two-way interaction; buying and selling are both important to exchanges.**

> **Marketing relationships may be initiated by anyone.**

> **A product in marketing may be a person, place, idea, physical good, service, social cause, or some combination of these.**

> **People *need* very little in life, but *want* much, and so marketing is usually more concerned with wants than with needs.**

> **People's wants and needs are endless, and so there will always be a need for marketing.**

> **Deception, fraud, and all other questionable marketing practices hinder the creation of mutually satisfying exchanges and are thus antimarketing; therefore, one objective of marketing is to minimize such practices.**

Discussion Questions

1. The United States needs more oil. What constraints keep marketers from filling that need?

2. Sandy Myer needs to take medicine for an illness she has. The medicine is very expensive, and Sandy does not like to pay the price. Is Sandy's purchase of medicine a mutually satisfying exchange? Why or why not?

3. How could you as a buyer help to make the following marketing exchanges more mutually satisfying: (a) getting a checkup from a doctor; (b) having a home built; and (c) taking courses in college?

4. Write your own definition of marketing and explain the terminology you use.

5. Give two examples of marketing exchanges that you have had with mechanical devices. Who was replaced by those devices? Are exchanges with machines sometimes more effective and efficient than those with persons? Discuss.

6. "Deception, fraud, and all other questionable marketing practices hinder the creation of mutually satisfying marketing exchanges and are thus antimarketing." Do you agree? Give examples to support your position.

7. "People's needs and wants are endless, and so there will always be a need for marketing." Do you agree? Give examples to support your position.

8. Do manufacturers and consumers have equal right to sell or not sell, buy or not buy? Do oil companies have an obligation to look for and sell more oil? Do you have an obligation to buy it? Explain your position.

9. Do you think marketing "*creates* wants and needs"? Give examples to prove your point.

10. American car manufacturers had too many large cars in inventory at the beginning of the 1970s and too many small cars in inventory by the mid-1970s. What environmental factors are affecting the automobile industry? How can auto manufacturers better adapt to these external factors?

CASES

Army Recruiting
Meeting the Needs of the Market

Barry Schwartz went to college during the 1960s. He learned that marketing was "a business activity that directs the flow of goods and services from producer to consumer or user." Barry is now a recruiter for the U.S. Army. He is not working for a "business," nor is he dealing with what he calls a "consumer." He is working for the government and has had some success in getting young persons to join the Army. However, the Army is concerned because many new recruits tend to be poorly educated and do not fill its need for highly skilled technicians and experts of all kinds. Barry needs some marketing assistance to get the kind of recruits he wants, including college graduates and people with special training in electronics and other skilled areas.

1. What is the "product" of the Army recruiter?

2. Do you prefer the definition of marketing Barry learned in school or the one that says that marketing is "those activities performed by individuals or organizations, either profit or nonprofit, that enable, facilitate, and encourage exchange to the satisfaction of both parties"? Why?
3. What need in society is being met by the Army?
4. What needs must the Army meet in order to get more highly educated recruits?
5. What changes in society have made Army recruiting more difficult?
6. Can you think of anything that Barry could do to help him recruit more college graduates?

Bank Marketing
What Is the Product?

Sylvester Rockwell is the president of a large bank with several branches in the city and surrounding suburbs. The bank is one of the older banks in the region and has a reputation for reliability, integrity, and conservative management of funds. Lately the bank has experienced increased competition and the number of depositors (and dollars deposited) has fallen.

Frank DiFlorio, a representative of a nationally known bank-supply firm, has proposed that the bank install automatic tellers at several suburban shopping centers. These automatic tellers would enable the bank to transact deposits and withdrawals 24 hours a day. Installation of automatic tellers would call for a large capital investment, and the bank president needs some marketing advice.

1. Are bank deposits and withdrawals marketing exchanges?
2. Would the convenience of automatic tellers that are open 24 hours a day appeal to enough people to make the investment worthwhile?
3. Does the bank or its customer usually initiate the first marketing exchange? Why?
4. What is the "product" of a bank?
5. Could machines ever replace tellers entirely?

What Marketers Do
a functional approach

2

LEARNING GOALS

After you have read and studied this chapter, you should be able to:

1. Explain who is included in the term "marketing participants."
2. Define what a universal marketing function is.
3. Explain the concept of exchange potential.
4. Name the five separations that divide marketers.
5. List the six universal marketing functions and briefly explain each.
6. Apply the six functions to any marketing situation.
7. List at least fifteen marketing activities other than the six universal functions.
8. Define the following terms: market separations; concentrated marketing; differentiated marketing; market targeting.

> *Functionalism is the most promising approach for theoretical development in marketing because it deals with concepts which can be applied to all types of [products] and all types of [organizations] which participate in marketing. The first step is to identify the marketing functions and then show how they apply in one situation after another.*
>
> Wroe Alderson*

INTRODUCTION In Chapter 1 we discussed *what* marketing is trying to accomplish—mutually satisfactory product-exchange relationships—but we said little about *how* this is to be done. Therefore, this chapter will answer the question, "What do marketers do to resolve the separations between marketing participants and to create market transactions?"

The first thing we should establish is just who the people are that are performing the marketing functions. That brings us back to you, because you, as a consumer, are one of the marketing participants. Other marketing participants include producers, wholesalers, retailers, credit agencies, advertising agencies, and a host of other people and organizations. What is of most concern to us at this point are the marketing activities performed by these people.

You should keep in mind as you read this chapter that the functions discussed here are performed by everyone in the marketing process. This means that the burden for creating exchanges *does not* fall on the seller in all marketing situations. For example, if you need a doctor who is a specialist in plastic surgery, chances are you will contact the doctor and try to establish a marketing relationship. You probably won't sit around waiting for the doctor to contact you. The basic concept is:

> **The person who initiates marketing contacts and tries the hardest to establish an exchange usually is the person who has the greater need.**

The example of doctors is only one such situation. In periods of scarcity, individuals and organizations actively search out and buy from suppliers, and suppliers often try to *control* rather than *increase* sales.[1]

The marketing literature has always stressed the marketing efforts of the seller, but, in today's market, the buyer is often the more active participant in the marketing process. But buyers and sellers should work together to accomplish the marketing functions, so that the needs of both are examined, recognized, and satisfied.

---

* *Marketing Behavior and Executive Action* (Homewood, Ill.: Richard D. Irwin, Inc., 1957), p. 23.

[1] Philip Kotler and Sidney Levy, "Demarketing, Yes, Demarketing," *Harvard Business Review*, November–December 1971, pp. 74–80.

> **Role of Buyer and Seller**
>
> A transaction transfers ownership from seller to buyer. Initiative may come from either the buyer or seller. The buyer searches the market to satisfy his wants, and the seller seeks to stimulate demand through activities preceding negotiations.

From George Fisk, *Marketing Systems: An Introductory Analysis* (New York: Harper & Row, Publishers, 1967), p. 315.

MARKETING FUNCTIONS

People involved in the marketing process perform many different functions or activities. A few of these activities seem to be common to all marketing situations and thus form the basis for all the other activities. In a market economy, those activities or functions that are inherent in the marketing process and pervade it throughout, including the activities of nonprofit organizations, are called **universal marketing functions.**[2] All the other activities that marketers perform may be called **facilitating functions,** or activities that assist persons in the performance of the basic, universal marketing functions.

A universal marketing function, then, is one that is necessary in both profit-making and nonprofit marketing organizations. It is performed by all marketing components including utility-consuming (buyers) and utility-producing (producers and middlemen) organizations and individuals. ("Utility" here simply means something useful or something of value.)

Dozens of lists of marketing functions have been compiled over the past 50 years. This indicates that no one is absolutely sure whether there is a set number of marketing functions or what they are. The functions of marketing change as society's needs change, and so no list of functions is necessarily permanent or "right."

The functions discussed in this chapter have been derived from observation and from careful analysis of other writings on marketing. They should give you a better idea of what marketers do and how they do it.

Marketing Functions and Exchange Potential

Before we explore the universal marketing functions, let us review the basic concepts behind the marketing process. Such a review will set the stage for the material that follows. We have learned that marketing starts with people with diverse wants and needs. The presence of those wants and needs is called **exchange potential.**

Whenever a producer or a utility-producing entity of any kind develops some good, service, idea, or other want-satisfying product, that producer has a need to find someone with whom to trade his products.[3]

[2] See Theodore N. Beckman, William R. Davidson, and W. Wayne Talarzyk, *Marketing*, 9th ed. (New York: The Ronald Press Company, 1973), p. 422.

[3] The concepts in this section are based on William McInnes, "A Conceptual Approach to Marketing," in *Theory in Marketing*, ed. Reavis Cox, Wroe Alderson, and Stanley J. Shapiro (Homewood, Ill.: Richard D. Irwin, Inc., 1964), pp. 51–67.

Figure 2.1 EXCHANGE POTENTIAL

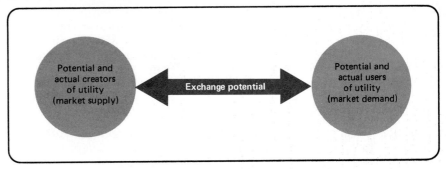

The presence of such products or the potential for creating such products also may be called exchange potential. We can picture exchange (marketing) potential as shown in Figure 2.1.

Notice in the figure that utility producers and utility consumers or users are separated by a gap. That gap may be geographical (spatial), in that the producer may be in Detroit and the consumer or user may be in Atlanta. Some marketing function or functions are needed to close this geographical gap. Either the producer or the consumer may initiate such activities, but no exchange can take place without them. If you try to picture the two marketing entities being discussed, you might envision something like Figure 2.2.

The division of labor in most advanced countries has created many situations such as the one in Figure 2.2, where producers and consumers are hundreds or even thousands of miles apart. Sometimes the producer

Figure 2.2 GEOGRAPHICAL SEPARATION

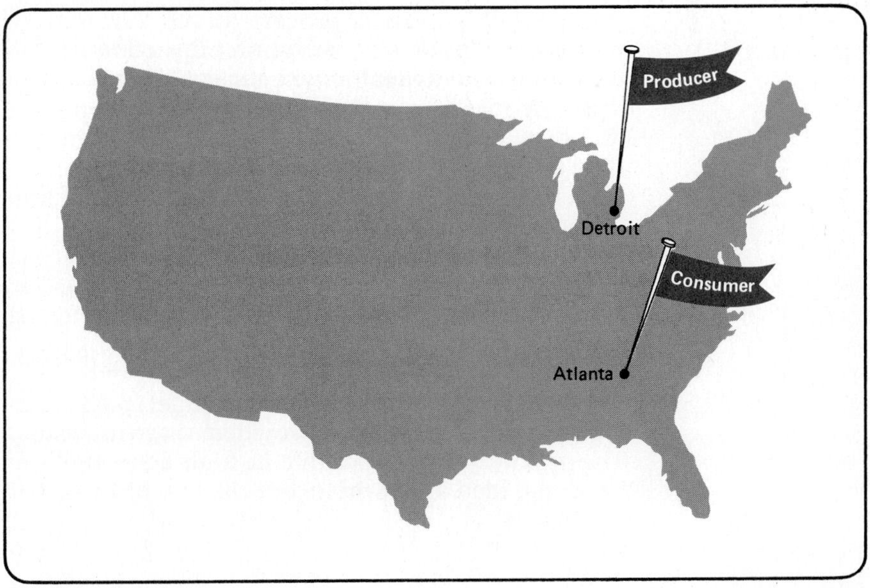

will be in one country and the consumer in some other country halfway around the world. The greater the distance between producer and consumer, the greater is the need for marketing functions to close the gap. The key concepts behind this discussion are:

› **Whenever there is an individual with unsatisfied wants or needs, exchange potential exists.**

› **Whenever there are individuals or organizations that have the ability to satisfy wants or needs, exchange potential exists.**

› **The greater the separations between those who seek satisfaction and those who can provide it, the greater is the need for marketing functions.**

Market Separations Are the Basis for Marketing Functions The concept of market separations has been developed very well by McInnes in "A Conceptual Approach to Marketing."[4] In this article, he points out that the most visible dimension of a market is *spatial separation*, as shown in Figure 2.2. One important concept behind McInnes's theory is:

› **People are separated geographically from those who can satisfy their needs; therefore some function(s) must be performed to establish contact and to begin the marketing process.**

McInnes goes on to say that spatial separation is also accompanied by *time separation*. One concept that explains this problem is:

› **People want products at a certain time, but they are not always available at those times; therefore some function(s) must be performed to have what people want available *when* they want it.**

An example of this is grocery stores that stay open 24 hours a day. Another example is the frozen-food section of a store where fruits and vegetables are available whenever people want them.

But people do not always know about supply sources, and producers do not always know where markets are. Therefore, McInnes suggests that there is a *perceptional separation* between producers and consumers. Part of this problem is due to a lack of knowledge and part to a lack of interest. The concept is:

› **People do not know about available products, and producers do not know about available markets unless some function(s) are performed to provide that information.**

Even though marketing (exchange) participants may be brought together and information provided, there may still be a *value separation*. The producer has a price that he finds acceptable, and the consumer also has some idea about price, but the two prices may not be the same. The concept is:

[4] Ibid.

> Markets are not perfect, and the value placed on products varies among people; therefore, some function(s) must be performed to adjust the product to the market and/or the market to the product.

Those exchanges involving money may be resolved by adjusting the price. But not all exchanges involve money, and so other adjustments must be made. McInnes goes on to discuss *ownership separation.* The concept is:

> Even when fully informed and motivated marketing participants are brought together, no exchange is completed until the people actually transfer something of value; therefore, some marketing function(s) must be performed to complete the exchange.

Market Separations That Must Be Closed by Marketing Functions

1. Space
2. Time
3. Perception
4. Values
5. Ownership

This discussion shows that the participants in a marketing exchange are often separated by space, time, perception, values, and ownership. In each case, there is a need for marketing functions to close the separations. McInnes was talking about the market for goods and services, but his concepts may be applied to the markets of nonprofit organizations, government markets, and all other marketing exchanges. In the following section, we shall discuss six marketing functions that close market separations and that are present in all marketing situations.

SIX UNIVERSAL MARKETING FUNCTIONS In a market economy, at least six functions meet the criteria for being called "universal marketing functions." The criteria are: (1) the function must be inherent in both economic (profit-making) and social (nonprofit) marketing situations; and (2) the function must be performed by both buyers and sellers. The six universal marketing functions are:

1. Market analysis
2. Marketing communication
3. Product differentiation
4. Market segmentation
5. Valuation
6. Exchange

The following sections will demonstrate how marketers use these six functions to satisfy needs in both business and nonbusiness marketing situations.

The Market-Analysis Function How do businesses and other organizations learn what you and other consumers want and need? On the other hand, how do you and all the other consumers and satisfaction seekers find people and organizations that can satisfy your needs? The answer is that all marketing participants must perform some function designed to inform them about the market (that is, about supply and demand) and about market characteristics. This function is called **market analysis.**

For sellers, market analysis takes the form of an activity called *marketing research.*[5] This may or may not be the work of a formal department in the organization, but the activity takes place nonetheless. For buyers, market analysis is simply the process called *shopping.* Shopping does not necessarily involve physically going from place to place, but may be as simple as reading newspaper ads, reviewing catalogs, talking to friends, or any other technique for gathering marketing facts. The

[5] *Market* research, which we shall discuss in detail later, is just one aspect of *marketing* research.

Figure 2.3 MARKET ANALYSIS BY BUYER AND SELLER

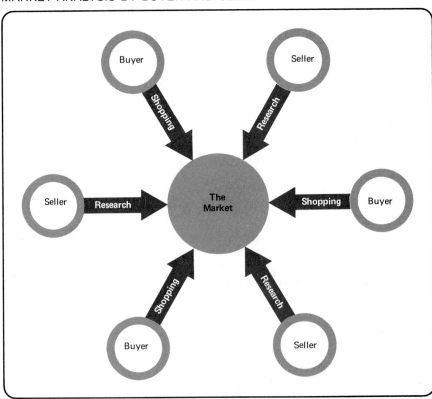

market-analysis function may be pictured as shown in Figure 2.3. Note that research and shopping are both elements of the market-analysis function.

Through the market-analysis function, sellers are able to estimate how many potential buyers there are, where they are, and other such helpful information. Buyers use market analysis to find out how many potential sellers there are, where they are, how much they charge, and other information relevant to them. The sum of all potential exchanges at any one time is called *the market*. Any market, therefore, is made up of many potential exchange relationships. Two concepts emerge from this discussion:

> **Market analysis is a universal marketing function that enables marketing participants to learn about the supply of, and demand for, given product offers or potential offers.**

> **The sum of all potential exchanges at any one time for a particular good, service, or anything else is called the market.**

Market analysis is a continual process that occurs before, during, and after marketing exchanges. Market analysis measures the demand for the ideas, goods, or services (satisfactions) that organizations or individuals are capable of creating. It also includes the activities of buyers or users in their search for satisfaction of their wants and needs.

It is important to emphasize that market analysis continues *after* exchange relationships are established. It measures the satisfactions of such exchanges, the potential for further exchanges, and the adjustments necessary to optimize all such relationships.

All marketers engage in some form of market analysis. The degree of sophistication varies greatly, but the process occurs universally. Market analysis helps resolve the market separations of space (by searching out others), perception (by the gathering of information), and values (by comparing alternatives).

The Communication Function

most imp. of the 6

Once buyers and sellers have analyzed the market, how do they contact one another to begin the exchange process? The answer is through marketing communication, a second universal function performed by all participants. Although communication is mentioned second, there is no particular order in which these functions are performed. Communication, for example, takes place throughout the marketing process. Communication in fact helps resolve all of the marketing separations and is probably the most important function of all. As one expert has put it: "Communication is without doubt the adhesive which binds the market forces together and forms a network of information flows that provide the basis for knowledgeable behavior of all members of our market system."[6]

Communication enables the management of society's diverse organizations to make intelligent decisions about the wants and needs of the public. Communication also enables the public to select those products,

[6] Rom J. Markin, *The Psychology of Consumer Behavior* (Englewood Cliffs, N.J.: Prentice-Hall, Inc., 1969), p. 188.

programs, services, ideas, and causes that best serve its interests. Imperfect communication results in imperfect markets. At the macro (societal) level, marketing communications include all the information flows among individuals and organizations in their mutal search to establish satisfactory marketing relationships.

The Marketing-Communication Function

In the beginning, there is the *seller* and there is the *buyer*. And if they are to interact . . . as the marketing concept requires . . . they must *communicate* with one another. And in fact they do . . . in a variety of ways.

Typically, the buyer communicates with the seller through the answers he gives to the seller's *market research*. And the seller, in turn, communicates with the buyer through his *advertising*.

In greater detail . . . their communications go like this:

1. The buyer expresses his wants and needs, his desires and satisfactions.
2. The seller, sensing the opportunity for profit, makes the product or service that is called for.
3. Then, through his advertising, the seller tells the buyer that he has just the thing the buyer was asking for.
4. And if the seller has correctly understood what the buyer was saying . . . and if he has actually made what was asked of him . . . the buyer will probably buy.

Of course, the transaction is not quite that brief, or that simple. In the course of the dialogue the seller has had to ask a *lot of questions* . . . and he has had to ask them *quite skillfully* . . . to benefit from what the buyer was saying.

From a speech by John G. Marder, executive vice-president of Grey Advertising, published in *Grey Matter*, a publication of Grey Advertising, Inc., January–February 1975.

The communication function involves flows of information *and* persuasion. These flows are multidirectional, pervasive (they occur throughout the marketing process), and dynamic (they are constantly changing). The communication flows in marketing are multidirectional because information travels from sellers to buyers, from buyers to sellers, and through various communications middlemen. Producers sponsor marketing research and advertise to determine what the market desires and to inform potential markets about their products. The public provides information to firms through their participation in marketing research, through their preferences in the marketplace, and through organizations such as Consumer's Union and Common Cause.

Communication flows are pervasive because they occur at micro and macro levels in the marketing process. At the macro level, trade associations, government public relations personnel, consumer organizations, and others communicate about relevant market issues. At the micro level, firms provide specific product information, the government provides detailed information about various programs, and individuals communicate with firms and other organizations regarding their preferences.

Because information is the key to informed decision making, communication is an extremely important marketing function. Furthermore, because consumers' needs and wants are continually evolving, as are the product and service capabilities of organizations, communication flows are constantly changing.

Negotiation activities are part of the communication function in that they involve all efforts to reach an agreement between marketing participants. Activities that facilitate the communication function may include advertising, personal selling, sales promotion, public relations, publicity, and marketing research. Because the product offering itself may also communicate need-satisfying information, product design, packaging, branding, and pricing may also be viewed as potential facilitating activities.

Some concepts that evolve from the discussion of marketing communication are:

> **Marketing communication is a universal marketing function that enables marketing participants to better understand one another and to negotiate an exchange.**

> **Communication flows in marketing are multidirectional, pervasive, and dynamic.**

The second concept is important. Too many people view marketing as a one-way attempt of a seller to influence a buyer. But buyers also attempt, often successfully, to influence sellers, and the goal of marketing is to establish and maintain an open "multilogue" (a multidirectional dialogue) between and among all marketing participants.

The Product-Differentiation Function   Through the functions of market analysis and marketing communication, marketers learn where potential exchanges are and other pertinent market facts, but how do they adjust their products so that there can be mutually satisfying exchanges? The marketing function that adjusts the offer of the seller to meet buyer needs and/or adjusts the offer of the buyer to satisfy seller needs is called **product differentiation.** It involves all the minor adjustments that must be made before the people involved are willing to make an exchange. Many of the adjustments may be psychological rather than physical, as the participants adjust their demands to acceptable levels.

Some of the changes sellers might make are:

1. Actual changes in the physical good, service, or idea
2. Changes in the packaging, branding, pricing, or location
3. Changes in the information made available to buyers

4. Changes in the attitudes or practices of those involved in the negotiating process

Some of the changes buyers might make are:

1. Increasing the amount they are willing to pay
2. Offering to perform some of the exchange tasks such as pick up and storage
3. Changes in the information they supply to sellers to clarify problems
4. Changes in their attitudes or practices.

Product Differentiation—From Chickens to Airplanes

Millions of chickens are raised and sold in the area known as Maryland's Eastern Shore. One of the most famous producers is Frank Perdue. Perdue chickens are sold at a premium to restaurants and in supermarkets in New York City and all through the eastern United States. Perdue chickens stand out from competitive chickens because they are fed "secret ingredients" that make them yellow. Furthermore, Frank Perdue promises "your money back if you don't like the chickens." Frank Perdue is proof that a homogeneous product like chickens can be differentiated from competition *and sold at a premium.* Whereas most producers found it difficult to create product differentiation for chickens, Frank Perdue did not.

A similar story concerns tennis shoes. For years, no product lacked a special identity more than did tennis shoes (sneakers). But through careful promotion and product differentiation, tennis shoes with names like Adidas, Puma, and Bata have captured a large share of the market—again at premium prices. Whereas plain sneakers might cost $5.95, these new tennis shoes may cost $20.00 and more. Adidas products are so popular that the name Adidas on a T-shirt is a status symbol in some areas. Product differentiation and promotion made Adidas stand out from "ordinary" tennis shoes.

Mary Wells, the head of a well-known advertising agency, was able to create a similar preference for Braniff Airlines. At the time she took the account, Braniff was a little-known, local airline. By painting the planes wild colors, dressing the hostesses in attractive outfits, and changing the name of the airline to Braniff International, Wells was able to create product differentiation for an airline.

Similar stories could be told about sunglasses (Foster Grant), bananas (Chiquita), and oranges (Sunkist). Product differentiation and promotion generated special interest in these products that is hard to beat. Could similar preferences be generated for other homogeneous products like milk, eggs, butter, and gasoline?

Product Differentiation for Buyers

Through self-maneuvers which are the counter-part of featuring, styling, branding, and packaging, the buyer can use the *product variable* to become an attractive "product" to the seller. The buyer must analyze the seller's perception in order to create a favorable impression. The buyer might even offer to improve the product; e.g., a prospective tenant offers to remodel the apartment.

From Philip Kotler and Sidney J. Levy, "Buying Is Marketing Too!" *Journal of Marketing*, January 1973, p. 59.

In addition to adjusting products to better meet the needs of others, the product-differentiation function also enables marketers to differentiate their products from other competing products. That is, a product can be designed so as to stand out from all the similar competing products. Some of the ways in which this is done are explored in the insert "Product Differentiation—From Chickens to Airplanes."

In spite of all the efforts of buyers to make their needs known and of sellers to design products that meet the needs of others, most market contacts do not result in a transaction. Think of the thousands of items you have shopped for and how many you rejected before you bought the few you own. Clearly, product differentiation by itself is not sufficient to satisfy market demands. Some guiding concepts in such decisions are:

> **Product differentiation is a universal marketing function that adjusts the product offers of both buyers and sellers so that a mutually beneficial exchange can take place.**

> **Product differentiation enables a marketer to create a product offer that stands out from that of competitors and that will be preferred by the market.**

> **Product changes may involve physical changes, changes in information, psychological changes, or any other changes in the need-satisfying nature of the product.**

> **Product differentiation narrows the gap between buyers' perceptions of what a product should be and sellers' perceptions of what they should offer.**

Later, in Chapter 8, we shall discuss in greater detail the problems of product design and adaptation of the market offering. Let's look now at a related function—market segmentation.

The Market-Segmentation Function Because no one seller can satisfy all buyers, and no one buyer can satisfy all sellers, there is need for a marketing function to narrow the market. That function is one part of the market-segmentation process.

As a consumer, you select a few stores where you shop and choose a few doctors and other service organizations and people to meet your

Figure 2.4 MARKET SEGMENTATION

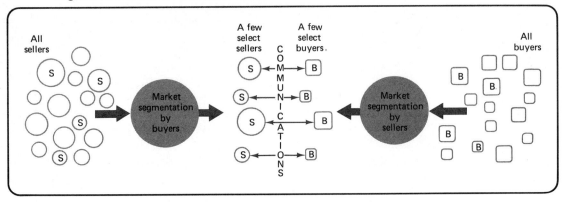

needs. The seller goes through a similar process. Rather than have all sellers communicating with all buyers, market segmentation works as shown in Figure 2.4. Thus, through the market-segmentation function, buyers and sellers can concentrate their marketing efforts. Together with product differentiation, market segmentation is an effective way to target in on a market.[7]

Some guiding concepts for market segmentation are:

› **Market segmentation is a universal marketing function that narrows the potential participants in a given market to those most likely to act or to find mutual satisfaction by an exchange.**

› **Both buyers and sellers use market-segmentation strategies to make their marketing task easier.**

For the seller, market segmentation helps to resolve market separations by targeting marketing efforts toward those people who are in the right place at the right time and who have the kinds of perceptions and price orientation that are compatible with the product in question. In a heterogeneous market, the seller has three targeting options: (1) Introduce only one product, hoping to get as many people to buy as possible. This is called **undifferentiated marketing.** (2) Go after one particular market segment and develop the ideal product for them. This is called **concentrated marketing.** (3) Introduce several product versions, each appealing to a different group. This is called **differentiated marketing.** [8] Note that the determination of market segments and the selection of market targets are separate problems. **Market segmentation** is the process of dividing the total population (market) into several submarkets or segments that tend to have similar characteristics. **Market targeting** is

[7] See Wendell R. Smith, "Product Differentiation and Market Segmentation as Alternative Marketing Strategies," *Journal of Marketing,* July 1956, pp. 3–8.

[8] Philip Kotler, *Marketing Management: Analysis, Planning, and Control,* 3rd ed. (Englewood Cliffs, N.J.: Prentice-Hall, Inc., 1976), p. 142.

the process by which an organization decides which market segments to serve.[9] Note also that product decisions and segmentation decisions are closely related.

The Valuation Function

Cost-benefit function

After participants in a marketing relationship have established contact and have communicated their wants and needs to one another, everyone involved must determine whether the benefits of a marketing exchange would exceed the costs. This cost-benefit analysis is called the **valuation function.** Like the market-analysis function, valuation is a continual process that occurs before a relationship is established, during negotiations, and after any exchange.

* One of the primary facilitating activities of the valuation function is pricing. Of course, not all marketing relationships involve a price. However, they all involve some cost-benefit trade-off by all the participants. A major emphasis in marketing is to ensure that the benefits of an exchange relationship exceed the costs. Cost here means more than money—it also means time, effort, thought, and other factors. Benefits may be physical, psychological, or spiritual.

At the macro (societal) level, for example, marketing valuation helps determine whether the values of providing consumer satisfaction exceed the possible social costs of pollution and health impairment. There is a social cost associated with all marketing systems, and the valuation function measures net social contribution. If social costs exceed social values, the system should adjust and adapt. The communication function facilitates such adaptation.

At the micro (individual transaction) level, facilitating activities for the valuation function include cost-benefit analyses, price comparisons, distribution-cost analyses, return-on-investment measures, and other such studies.

Some concepts that help clarify the valuation function are:

➤ **Valuation is a universal marketing function whereby each of the participants tries to determine whether the benefits of a transaction would exceed the costs.**

➤ **Cost-benefit analyses in marketing involve monetary costs and all other costs such as time and effort; benefits can be physical, psychological, or spiritual.**

➤ **If the benefits of a potential exchange do not appear to exceed the cost, no exchange is likely to occur.**

➤ **Values (satisfactions) may be increased for either party by increasing the benefits or lowering the costs.**

➤ **In any free-market exchange, all participants would experience an increase in satisfaction because benefits would exceed costs.**

As you review some of your past transactions, you may decide that the benefits you received did not exceed your costs. This knowledge will guide you in future purchases, but in a free market such as exists in the

[9] Ibid.

United States, where there is the potential for the greatest amount of satisfaction, you should recognize that there are also potentials for deception and dissatisfaction.

The Exchange Function   After the parties to a marketing relationship have negotiated an agreement and have decided that the cost-benefit trade-offs are satisfactory, there often is a problem of actually carrying out the exchange. Often, one of the major problems is financing. Without some sort of credit arrangements, the marketing of homes, cars, furniture, medical care, travel, appliances, and other major purchases would be greatly impaired. The exchange function involves the arrangement of necessary financing. It also may involve delivery, installation, servicing, guarantees, storage, barter arrangements, or other such adjustments to facilitate the exchange. These activities help resolve the ownership gap in marketing.

Nonprofit organizations are also concerned about implementing the exchange process. The establishment of trusts, will agreements, and other financial arrangements facilitate donor giving. To facilitate giving, charities often include self-addressed stamped envelopes in their mailings. They also place containers in retail outlets and other convenient places and solicit funds door to door. All such activities are part of the exchange function and resolve market separations.

It should be noted that although exchange is a universal marketing function in that the goal of all marketing efforts is a transaction, an exchange does not always result from marketing efforts. If no exchange occurs, however, the marketing *process* would end; therefore, in the long run, all marketing processes involve an exchange.

Do not feel that marketing ends with the exchange simply because it is the last function listed. Quite the contrary, an exchange is just one step in the ongoing process. After the exchange, the valuation function continues, communication about the exchange continues, and the knowledge gained from the exchange becomes input for further market analysis. Some concepts to keep in mind, therefore, are:

Figure 2.5 ROLE OF MARKETING FUNCTIONS

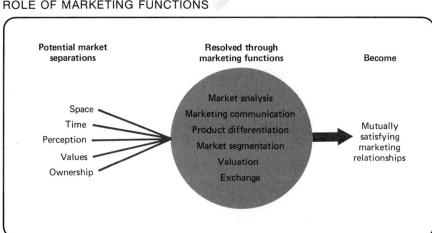

> Exchange is a universal marketing function that facilitates a transfer of benefits (need satisfactions).

> Not all marketing *efforts* result in an exchange, but the total marketing *process* always involves exchanges.

> Exchange is not the end of the marketing process, but merely one more step.

The role of marketing functions is summarized in Figure 2.5.

APPLYING FUNCTIONS TO EVERYDAY LIFE

Let us review the marketing functions once more and try to apply them to a rather basic exchange relationship. The functions are:

1. Market analysis
2. Marketing communication
3. Product differentiation
4. Market segmentation
5. Valuation
6. Exchange

Although most people do not think of dating as a marketing activity, it is an exchange process, it involves people, and marketing concepts can be applied. For example, through *market analysis,* a person can find where potential dates are, how many there are, and other such market information. Through *market segmentation,* a person eliminates all of the people whom he or she has learned to avoid because the potential for friendly relations with them has proved in the past to be minimal. *Communication* enables one person to establish contact with another, and the possibility of a date can be discussed. Because no one is perfect, both people may have to adjust their wants and their offer to meet the needs of the other ("Busy on Friday? How about Saturday?"). This adjustment is technically known as *product differentiation.* Despite all of one's attempts to make dates with others, more often than not the answer may be "no" (unless you are a great marketer). The *valuation function* explains why you may change your mind given the demands ("I'll go out only if we can go to dinner at The Four Seasons.") or why the other person may not want to go ("Sky diving is not my thing, thank you!"). But, as a person becomes more experienced at dating, the effectiveness of his or her approach may improve.

It may seem frivolous to cite dating as a marketing problem. The point to be made is that all interpersonal relationships may be approached from a *marketing (exchange) perspective.* Thus, marketing functions are important to politicians, teachers, and all other individuals and organizations that want to establish long-term relationships with others. The concepts are:

> Any interpersonal relationship may be viewed from a marketing perspective.

> The six universal marketing functions may be used to facilitate any interpersonal relationship.

OTHER KEY Some marketing activities are not universally applicable, but they are
MARKETING nevertheless of sufficient importance to bear special study. Most of these
ACTIVITIES activities (for example, transportation and storage) concern the distribution of *goods* from the raw materials state to the final consumer as a finished product. Other activities are so important that they, too, demand emphasis. They include packaging, branding, credit, and product design (all parts of the product-differentiation function); advertising, selling, sales promotion, public relations, publicity, and display (all parts of the communication function); and pricing (part of the valuation function).

Each of these key supporting activities will receive detailed attention as our analysis of the marketing process develops. Actually, there are so many marketing activities that one could get confused by discussing them all at once. For this reason, we have emphasized the six universal marketing functions.

Marketing Activities

No chapter could give a detailed analysis of all the activities performed by marketers. Below are listed some of the activities that facilitate the performance of the six universal marketing functions.

Buying	Packaging	Standardization
Selling	Branding	Grading
Transportation	Trademarking	Channel selection
Storage	Pricing	Establishing guarantee policy
Finance (credit)	Risk taking	Determining terms of sale
Advertising	Negotiation	Delivery
Sales promotion	Marketing research	Installation
Public relations	Location	Handling complaints
Publicity	Shopping	Customer service
Product design	Product service	Maintaining business standards
Inventory taking	Labeling	Cooperating with government
Planning	Display	

FOR REVIEW

Key Terms

Among the more important terms and expressions used in this chapter are the following:

Concentrated marketing refers to the development of a product to suit one particular market segment.

Differentiated marketing refers to the marketing of several versions of a product, each of which is designed to suit a particular segment of a market.

Exchange is a universal marketing function that facilitates the transfer of benefits (need satisfactions).

Exchange potential exists when individuals or organizations have unsatisfied wants and needs and other individuals or organizations have the ability to satisfy these wants and needs.

Facilitating marketing functions are activities that assist persons in the performance of the universal marketing functions.

The **market** is the sum of all potential exchanges at any one time for a particular good, service, or anything else.

Market analysis is a universal marketing function that enables marketing participants to learn about the supply of, and demand for, given product offers and potential offers.

Marketing communication is a universal marketing function involving flows of information and persuasion that enable marketing participants better to understand one another and to negotiate an exchange.

Market segmentation, a universal marketing function, is the process of dividing the total population (market) into several submarkets or segments that tend to have similar characteristics.

Market separations are gaps in space, time, perception, values, or ownership that tend to separate buyer and seller and thus hinder the exchange process.

Market targeting is the process by which an organization decides which market segments to serve.

Product differentiation is a universal marketing function that adjusts the product offers of both buyers and sellers so that a mutually beneficial exchange can take place.

Undifferentiated marketing refers to the marketing of a single product to the mass market rather than to segmented markets.

A **universal marketing function** is one that is necessary in both profit-making and nonprofit marketing organizations and is performed by both buyers and sellers.

Valuation is a universal marketing function whereby each of the participants in a marketing exchange determines whether the benefits of a transaction would exceed the costs.

Key Concepts

Among the more important marketing concepts introduced in this chapter are the following:

▸ **The person who initiates marketing contacts and tries the hardest to establish an exchange is usually the person who has the greater need.**

▸ **Whenever there is an individual with unsatisfied wants or needs, market potential exists.**

▸ **Market separations may be of space, time, perception, values, and ownership.**

» The existence of potential exchange relationships is called a market.
» Both buyers and sellers use market segmentation to make their marketing easier.
» Valuation may be increased by either party by increasing the benefits or lowering the costs.
» In a free-market exchange, all participants would experience an increase in satisfaction because benefits would exceed costs.

Discussion Questions

1. "The person who initiates marketing contacts and tries the hardest to establish an exchange usually is the person who has the greater need." Do you agree? Give several examples to illustrate your point.

2. The six universal marketing functions as outlined in this chapter are (1) market analysis, (2) marketing communication, (3) product differentiation, (4) market segmentation, (5) valuation, and (6) exchange. Explain how you would use each of these functions, as a buyer, when you go to the supermarket. What is your product offer?

3. "The greater the separations between those who seek satisfaction and those who can provide it, the greater is the need for marketing." Illustrate this concept by comparing a primitive village with the total U.S. market.

4. "Communication helps resolve all the marketing separations and is probably the most important function of all." Do you agree? Explain the relative importance of communication for the following purchases: (1) a movie ticket, (2) a new color TV, (3) an airline ticket.

5. Think back to your last major purchase. What were the costs and benefits you consciously or subconsciously considered in evaluating the exchange?

6. The text uses dating as an example of a situation in which marketing concepts can be applied. Do you agree? Is this a proper application of marketing? Why or why not?

7. Some traditional texts consider transportation, storage, finance, and grading to be universal marketing functions. Do you agree? Why or why not?

8. Are buying and selling universal marketing functions? Give examples to prove your point.

9. "Whenever there is an individual with unsatisfied wants or needs, market potential exists." Do you agree? What if the individual has no money?

10. "In a free-market exchange, all participants would experience an increase in satisfaction because benefits would exceed costs." Do you agree? Give evidence to support your position.

CASES

Wycomiat Lumber Company
Buyer Marketing

The Wycomiat Lumber Company in Maine is enjoying one of its better years. It produces lumber and other building materials, much of which is in very short supply. Wycomiat has more orders than it can fill and is beginning to discourage more orders. Sigmund Vonderheidt, the owner, wants to serve preferred customers first.

The Lanore Construction Company in Rhode Island is falling behind on its contracts. The company cannot get some of the lumber materials it needs, and these delays are holding up the electricians and plumbers, as well as the carpenters. Michael Lanore has searched all over for materials and eventually contacted Wycomiat Lumber. Mr. Lanore intends to go to Maine to talk with Mr. Vonderheidt.

1. What "separations" must Mr. Lanore overcome in order to get his materials?
2. Show how Mr. Lanore can use the six universal marketing functions outlined in this chapter to improve his chances of getting Mr. Vonderheidt to sell to him.
3. What, other than more money, could Mr. Lanore offer Mr. Vonderheidt to make the sale more appealing?
4. What would you suggest that Mr. Lanore do if he fails to get the materials he wants from Wycomiat?

Birth Control in India
Marketing a Cause

Government officials in India have been concerned about population growth in their country. Various birth-control measures have been employed, including the offering of incentives (for example, a transitor radio) for having a vasectomy, the free distribution of birth-control devices, and state-imposed sanctions on families that have more than two children. Nevertheless, population growth continues, and starvation and death often result.

1. Is state control of population a marketing problem? Explain.
2. What are the market separations between the people of India and the population-control experts?
3. How could the government of India use the six universal marketing functions to increase the use of birth-control methods? Should the government be involved in such decisions?
4. Who has the greater perceived need for birth control—the government or the people? Given your answer, who would you expect to initiate a marketing relationship?

The Marketing Concept
a philosophy
for tomorrow's marketers

> *The marketing concept has been widely accepted as an adequate state-ment of the function and role of marketing in today's society as well as in the business firm. In recent years, however, there has been a growing indication that the concept has faltered to the point where it is no longer an adequate statement. Evidence exists to support the questioning of the marketing concept.*
>
> Martin L. Bell and C. William Emory*

INTRODUCTION Now that we have explored what marketers are trying to accomplish and some of the functions marketers perform, we can begin to analyze more fully the philosophy behind the management of marketing in an organi-zation. The concepts in this chapter were first developed as a guide for business firms, but we shall show how basic managerial concepts in marketing can apply also to nonbusiness organizations and to individ-uals (buyers and sellers).

Marketing is more than a process that attempts to establish mutually satisfactory product-exchange relationships. It is also a philosophy of management, a philosophy that has been called the "marketing man-agement concept" or, more recently, the "marketing concept." It took many years for business to evolve such a philosophy. A look at how the marketing concept developed will help to clarify where we are today and how we got there; for this reason, we shall briefly trace its history in American business. Then we shall present a new, broadened marketing philosophy to guide marketing decision making in the future.

HISTORY OF THE MARKETING CONCEPT From the time the first settlers began their struggle to survive in America until after the Civil War, the general philosophy of business was, "Pro-duce as much as you can because there is a limitless market." Given the limited production capability and the vast demand for products in those days, such a philosophy was both logical and profitable. Businesspeople were mostly farmers, carpenters, and trade workers who were catering to the public's basic needs for housing, food, and clothing. There was a need for greater and greater productive capacity, and businesses natu-rally had a **production orientation**. This means that the goals of business centered on production and that little attention was given to marketing. This was satisfactory at that time because most goods were bought as soon as they became available.

The Era of Mass Production After the Civil War, U.S. businesses began to grow much larger. By 1890, some had become so large and complex that a law called the Sherman Antitrust Act was passed to forbid such things as contracts, combina-tions, or conspiracies in restraint of trade and monopolies or attempts to monopolize any part of trade or commerce. In part, this act, which had little immediate effect, was passed to prevent larger corporations from driving smaller firms out of business.

* "The Faltering Marketing Concept," *Journal of Marketing*, October 1971, p. 37.

Pillsbury's Sales Orientation in the 1930s

We are a flour-milling company, manufacturing a number of products for the consumer market. We must have a first-rate sales organization which can dispose of all the products we can make at a favorable price. We must back up this sales force with consumer advertising and market intelligence. We want our salesmen and our dealers to have all the tools they need for moving the output of our plants to the consumer.

Changed in the 1960s to:

At Pillsbury . . . marketing will become the basic motivating force for the entire corporation. Soon it will be true that activity of the corporation—from finance to sales to production—is aimed at satisfying the needs and desires of the consumer.

Statements of Pillsbury management, as quoted in Robert J. Keith, "The Marketing Revolution," *Journal of Marketing*, January 1960, pp. 38–39. Reprinted with permission of the American Marketing Association.

During the period from 1890 to 1920, businesses turned to mass production; automobile assembly lines are a prime example of this development. This was also a time when large corporations had control over much of the sugar industry, the oil industry (remember this was before cars were widely available), and other major industries. Production capacity often exceeded the immediate market demand, and the marketing philosophy turned from a production orientation to a **sales orientation**. Businesses turned their attention to *promoting* their products and mobilized much of the firm's resources into the sales effort.

In the 1920s, books on selling were written by psychologists and other trained professionals. They usually emphasized techniques for "getting your foot in the door," "overcoming objections," "winning the order"; they generally tried to show how psychological concepts could be used to persuade others to buy. The customer was usually viewed as a pawn to be moved and manipulated in the quest for increased profits.

During the 1920s, most salespeople found little resistance to their appeals, for these were the "roaring twenties," a period of rapid economic growth. But the decade ended in a sudden collapse in 1929. The Great Depression that followed lasted through much of the 1930s. These were hard times, with unemployment reaching 24 percent, and selling and marketing in general were in a depressed state.

World War II moved the United States away from depression and unemployment to mobilization for war. Mass-production techniques were employed to produce military products rather than consumer products. Because of the war effort, few consumer goods were available, and many were rationed. It was not a time for salespeople to be pushing consumer goods.

After the war, there was a tremendous demand for goods and services among the returning soldiers who were starting a new life with new families. It was during these postwar years that the "baby boom" (the sudden large increase in the birthrate after the war) started, and a "boom" in consumer spending was also launched.

The Philosophy of the 1950s The United States entered a period of relative prosperity after the war (1945 to 1950), and businesses began to recognize the need to *work with* their customers rather than continue the philosophy of *selling to* customers. The sales orientation that had dominated businesses for so many years (from about 1870 until the early 1950s) was being slowly replaced by what is now known as the "marketing concept."

The traditional **marketing concept** was interpreted differently by various authors, but it basically called for three managerial strategies:

1. A consumer orientation
2. The coordination and integration of corporate efforts
3. A profit orientation

Consumer Orientation Henry Ford is reported to have said, "You can have any color car as long as it's black." He seemed more interested in production than in adapting to consumer wants and needs. He felt that the best car was a good, reliable, inexpensive one. In fact, Ford sold half the new cars made in this country up to 1926.[1] But the people at General Motors talked with

[1] For an analysis of this case and several others, see Robert F. Hartley, *Marketing Mistakes* (Columbus, Ohio: Grid, Inc., 1976).

The marketing Concept in practice:

Pioneer Acceptance of Marketing Concept by General Electric

In 1952 your Company's operating managers were presented with an advanced concept of marketing, formulated by the Marketing Services Division. This, in simple terms, would introduce the marketing man at the beginning rather than the end of the production cycle and would integrate marketing into each phase of the business. Thus marketing, through its studies and research, would establish for the engineer, the designer and the manufacturing man what the consumer wants in a given product, what price he is willing to pay, and where and when it will be wanted. Marketing would have authority in product planning, production scheduling and inventory control, as well as the sales distribution and servicing of the product. This concept, it is believed, will tighten control over business operations and will fix responsibility, while making possible greater flexibility and closer teamwork in the marketing of the company's products.

From an address by Ralph J. Cordiver, president of General Electric, in *GE Annual Report*, 1952.

Is giving consumers what they want always a good idea?

BROOM HILDA   By Russell Myers

FRUIT   VEGETABLES   JUNK FOOD

consumers and found a basic desire for individuality and status. They began making cars in *all* colors and shapes and eventually took away much of Ford's market. Today, General Motors has over 50 percent of the new car market. This is an example of **consumer orientation** at work. The marketing concept behind it is:

> **Give consumers what research and past experience show they want.**

Consumers often say they want products and product features that they do not really want or buy. Marketers must therefore probe deeply to find what really motivates consumers and what they *will* buy rather than what they *say* they will buy.

Coordination and Integration of the Firm In order to provide optimum consumer satisfaction, all elements of marketing must be coordinated and integrated in that cause. For example, salespersons often promise delivery on a certain date, and then the delivery people fail to show up. Such lack of coordination annoys the consumer and prevents consumer satisfaction. Similarly, a salesperson may write up a sale and promise credit terms, only to find that the credit department turns down the customer's application. Again, this may cause resentment and bad feelings among all parties concerned. Other examples would show that all marketing functions should be coordinated and integrated. The concept is:

> **To provide optimum consumer satisfaction and to minimize conflicts, all marketing activities should be coordinated and integrated.**

One solution to the problem of coordination and integration is to have one person responsible for all marketing activities—a marketing manager. Since the early 1950s, there has been a slow but consistent trend toward having such a position in the larger firms.[2]

[2] For a description of today's chief marketing executive, see "Profile of a Chief Marketing Executive," *The Marketing News,* May 15, 1972, p. 1.

As firms began the process of restructuring in order to develop better consumer relations, it became obvious that functions other than marketing would have to become involved. The research and development department would have to design products that were safe and reliable; and the finance, accounting, legal, and personnel departments would all have to participate in a unified effort to help consumers satisfy their needs. The marketing principles of consumer orientation and coordinated marketing activities became a managerial philosophy. The concept to remember is:

> **Every person and every department in the organization is involved in a coordinated effort to provide consumer satisfaction so that the goals of the organization (for example, profit) can be realized.**

This new philosophy was embodied in a strategy called "management by objectives."[3] First, the objectives of the firm are established (to achieve consumer satisfaction at a profit). Then, the objectives of each department are determined. No one department is to stress its objective to the detriment of either the objective of another department or the overall corporate objectives. *Or suboptimization would result.*

✓ Profit Orientation The purpose of adopting a new philosophy of business was to improve consumer relations because better relationships would also benefit the firm and increase profits. One goal of all business firms is to optimize profits. This is called **profit orientation**. Profit enables a firm to grow and hire more people, to provide even more satisfaction to consumers, and to strengthen the economy as a whole.

Many firms do not have profit goals but instead set goals of increased sales or a greater share of the market. But if they come at huge expense, increased sales may lead to less profit rather than more profit. The concept to be followed is:

> **One goal of business firms is to make a profit, for without profits the business will eventually fail.**

[3]See, for example, George S. Odiorne, *Management by Objectives* (New York: Pitman Publishing Corporation, 1965), or Steven J. Carroll, Jr., and Henry L. Tosi, Jr., *Management by Objectives: Applications and Research* (New York: Macmillan, Inc., 1973).

Marketing Means Customer Orientation

To me—and to put it quite simply—the sales concept alone concerns itself primarily with volume. Marketing means customer orientation—a true alliance with the fellow at the other end of the pipeline, but it insists upon a course of action of mutual benefit.

From a speech of Fred J. Borch to the American Management Association, 1957.

Some people believe that profits are the only or the major goal that businesses should work toward.[4] But most firms have many goals, including providing a pleasant atmosphere for employees, contributing to society, and providing safe and satisfying goods and services to selected market segments. It must be kept in mind, however, that all social goals of an organization are dependent upon the firm's survival and long-term growth, and these are not possible without profits.

Is a Profit Orientation Anticonsumer? Some people feel that an organization cannot be profit oriented and socially oriented at the same time. They feel that if there is a conflict between the goal of profit and the goal of consumer satisfaction, the emphasis will be on profits. Other people feel that a profit orientation prevents a firm from being socially responsible. (See the insert "Social Responsibility versus Social Responsiveness," in which Robert Hartley explains the relationship between profits and social responsibility.)

There is not necessarily a conflict between the goals of social responsibility for business firms and the goal of profit. Without profits, a firm cannot afford to hire more people, and demographics being what they are today, we will need over two million new jobs each year just to stay even with population growth. When profits fell during the recession in

[4] See Theodore Levitt, "Dangers of Social Responsibility," *Harvard Business Review*, September–October 1958, p. 44.

Social Responsibility versus Social Responsiveness

There is a subtle difference between *social responsibility* and *social responsiveness*. As generally used, social responsibility suggests that a firm recognize a responsibility to more than its stockholders, perhaps a responsibility to its employees, its customers, its suppliers, the community in which it does business and, projected to its furthest, a responsibility to society at large. Since the needs and demands of these groups differ and are not always compatible, some priorities of corporate responsibility must be established. A complete acceptance of social responsibility would be a willingness to sacrifice profits for other priorities, especially those of a social and environmental nature.

Social responsiveness . . . suggests a more active response to the environment. It is oriented to action that attempts to correct or improve certain conditions. This could mean a commitment to social needs at the expense of profit, but it can also indicate a willingness to forego short-run profit in favor of long-range profitability. . . . It implies not shying away from running efficient passenger trains or opening supermarkets in the ghetto; rather it would be concerned with finding innovative approaches to bring such "do-good" endeavors to profitability.

From Robert F. Hartley, *Marketing Fundamentals for Responsive Management* (New York: Dun-Donnelley Publishing Corporation, 1976), p. 84.

Profits Are Reward for Meeting Needs

Today's professional marketers are not primarily motivated by the pure axiomatic concept of profit. In fact the marketers' primary goal is in meeting the needs of a designated market. Thus, resulting profits would then be a reward for successfully meeting a given market's needs. This relatively new concept is now universally followed by astute marketing practitioners. Let's remember, however, that this new marketing concept did not gain overnight acceptance, nor would any innovation that demanded change in historical attitudes, philosophies, or conventional routine. That fact is, however, that those corporations and marketers who readily accepted this new concept of marketing and adjusted to the change have already left their more reluctant competitors far behind.

From an editorial by Michael D. Wallach in *Impact,* newsletter of the Washington, D.C., chapter of the American Marketing Association, February 1971, p. 2.

the early 1970s, unemployment reached levels unmatched since the Great Depression of the 1930s. The goals of full employment and profit are thus congruent; when profits rise, employment usually rises.

Furthermore, society wants to provide for its retired and disabled members. If businesses are to contribute their share to this social goal, they will need enough money (capital) to cover the cost of pensions. With people living longer and longer, the burden of supporting the aged will grow tremendously, and economic growth (real business growth) is needed to support them. The social security system was designed to provide an income *supplement,* and, for many workers, private pension plans have to supply the basic income. There is no real conflict, then, between the social goal of support for the aged and the goal of profit, because earnings are needed to fund pension plans.

A strong, healthy economy is one in which businesses are competitive in international markets so that there can be a balance of trade. To remain competitive, businesses need capital to buy modern equipment and machinery. This capital comes mostly from earnings reinvested in the firm. Thus, profit goals do not conflict with goals of economic growth and national survival.

The capital made available through profits may also be used to provide pollution control, to train the disadvantaged, to support social causes, and to accomplish other socially responsible goals. Certainly, without profits, few of these things are possible.

There is much misunderstanding in society about profits and their role in providing for social betterment. Part of the problem has been that businesspeople have fought for profits, worked for profits, and defended the need for profits, but they have done little to educate the public about profits. As a consequence, the public seems to favor minimum profits, taxing of "excess profits," and social control of businesses to prevent them from earning "unreasonable" profit. Profit to many people has become a dirty word, a socially irresponsible goal, and an evil to be cut out from society. The concepts are:

» **There is no inherent conflict between a profit orientation in business and social responsibility.**

» **Profit orientation is not the same as sales orientation; one can greatly increase sales without increasing profits.**

Educating the Public on Profits

Many businesses are trying to educate the public about the role of, and necessity for, profits. For example, in 1976, Allied Chemical planned to spend $350,000 in a campaign with the theme, "Where profits are for people."

Phillips Petroleum prepared a TV commercial with the theme, "Free enterprise. Sometimes we forget how well it works." The ad explains that newsboys in the United States earn more money than 50 percent of the people on earth.

The nonprofit Advertising Council introduced a series on free enterprise in 1976.

These are only a few of the recent efforts by organizations to explain profits and the free-enterprise system in general. Opinion Research Corp. found that the public's estimate of the average manufacturer's after-tax profit is 33 percent, more than six times the true amount. The public felt that oil companies' profits were 61 percent, more than eight times the true amount. Obviously, the public needs more information and education in this area.

A NEW MARKETING CONCEPT The marketing concept evolved as a philosophy of management for business firms. But marketing applications have been broadened to include nonbusiness organizations as well. Furthermore, the marketing concept has been a guiding philosophy for sellers, but not for buyers. The following sections outline a new marketing concept for the future. Progressive organizations seem to be moving toward a new marketing concept that has four main elements:

1. A new *societal orientation* is replacing the more narrow consumer orientation.
2. A *systems orientation* is replacing the traditional emphasis on coordination and integration of individual organizations.
3. A *human orientation* is replacing the traditional profit orientation.
4. The marketing concept is being applied to *buyers* as well as sellers.

Each of these changes is discussed in more detail in the following sections. The philosophy of marketing is still evolving, and so this material can only give you a feel for the direction marketing may be taking.

A Societal Several authors have suggested that the traditional marketing concept
Orientation has not been an effective philosophy for marketing managers.[5] Special
attention has been given the idea of consumer orientation. It has been
argued that "a consumer orientation is not a logical normative proposition or a workable descriptive proposition."[6] Furthermore it has been
said that:

> A consumer orientation directs the attention of [an organization] only
> to some fraction of the population which supports it. Moreover, inso-
> far as present or potential consumers are concerned, the consumer
> orientation generates concern only with the individual's role as a
> buyer or consumer of a particular product or service. Thus, the con-
> sumer orientation is limited in scope and one-dimensional in nature.[7]

A consumer orientation directs the attention of an organization to its
customers and neglects to mention the other "publics" of an organization such as the government, the community, and stockholders. There is
no doubt that an organization should focus attention on satisfying the
wants and needs of consumers, but this focus should not blind the
organization to the broader needs of society. Often, products that meet
the short-run needs of individual consumers have a negative effect on
society and on individuals as well:) IMP.

1. Alcohol, cigarettes, and marijuana are examples of products that may
   provide short-run consumer satisfaction but could prove harmful in
   the long run.
2. Large, gas-consuming automobiles may satisfy the needs of individual
   consumers but tend to pollute the air, use scarce resources too
   rapidly, and cause traffic congestion; eventually, such automobiles
   may result in long-run dissatisfaction to owners and society.
3. Some popular foods such as soda (pop), potato chips, and candies
   may provide short-run satisfaction to users but may lead to tooth
   decay, weight problems, and other such problems.

The point is this: The objective of marketing is not simply to provide
consumer satisfaction; it also attempts to create a better quality of life. A
better quality of life includes satisfaction of basic wants and needs (such
as food, protection, health). But it also includes a clean and healthy
environment, an intelligent use of resources, and a recognition of the

[5] For example, see Leslie M. Dawson, "The Human Concept: New Philosophy
for Business," *Business Horizons*, December 1969, pp. 29–38; Andrew G. Kaldor,
"Imbricative Marketing," *Journal of Marketing*, April 1971, p. 21; Martin Bell
and C. William Emory, "The Faltering Marketing Concept," *Journal of Marketing*, October 1971, pp. 37–42; and C. Glenn Walters, D. Wayne Norvell, and
Sam J. Bruno, "Is There a Better Way Than Consumer Orientation?" in *Proceedings: Southern Marketing Association, 1975 Conference*, ed. Henry W. Nash
and Donald P. Robin (Mississippi State University, 1976), pp. 79–81.
[6] Walters et al., "Is There a Better Way Than Consumer Orientation?" p. 79.
[7] Dawson, "The Human Concept," p. 33.

How much for social responsibility?

Some people say we must reach "zero" pollution.
But at what cost? And how fast?

At Bethlehem Steel, we work hard—every day—to control pollution. But the cost is high. We've already spent approximately $400 million to clean up a major portion of the pollutants from the air and water we use. We consider this money well spent.

$600 million more

In an effort to meet existing pollution control laws and regulations, we have many more projects under way or anticipated in the near future. These projects are expected to cost us some $600 million over the next five years.

Where does that leave us?

Depending upon how far regulatory agencies go in stringent interpretation of the present laws and regulations, we may be faced with spending hundreds of millions more to try to remove the last traces of pollution. We do not think that this would be money well spent.

Attempting to remove the last increment of pollution involves new and uncertain technology. The attempt will consume a considerable amount of scarce energy and natural resources. And, in many cases, it will merely transfer pollution problems to the power companies or chemical manufacturers.

Is it time for a rearrangement of priorities?

We are faced as a nation with troublesome alternatives. Do we continue our headlong rush to implement some of the air and water clean-up standards that have yet to be proved necessary—or even sound—or shall we give equal consideration to jobs, our energy requirements, capital needs, and other demands for social priorities?

We believe the national interest now requires that we face up to the dual necessity of preserving our environment while at the same time assuring our economic progress.

Our booklet, "Steelmaking and the Environment," tells more about the problems of pollution and what we're doing to help solve them. For a free copy, write: Public Affairs Dept., Room 476-WSJ, Bethlehem Steel Corp., Bethlehem, PA 18016.

Bethlehem

Courtesy of Bethlehem Steel Corporation.

needs of society as well as of individuals. In addition to giving consumers what they want and need, marketers have some obligation to help consumers buy more intelligently.[8] (See the insert "The Societal Marketing Concept for Business.")

The Societal Marketing Concept for Business

The dilemma for the marketer, forced into the open by consumerism, is that he cannot go on giving the consumer only what pleases him without considering the effect on the consumer's and society's well-being. On the other hand, he cannot produce products which the consumer will not buy. The problem is to somehow reconcile company profit, consumer desires, and consumer long-run interests. The original marketing concept has to be broadened to the societal marketing concept.

The societal marketing concept calls for a *customer orientation* backed by *integrated marketing* aimed at generating *customer satisfaction* and *long-run consumer welfare* as the key to attaining long-run profitable volume.) IMP.

Philip Kotler, "What Consumerism Means for Marketers," *Harvard Business Review*, May–June 1972, p. 54. Copyright 1972 by the President and Fellows of Harvard College. All rights reserved.

There is some evidence today that organizations are adopting a broader **societal orientation** that includes a consumer orientation. For example, many large business firms and nonprofit organizations have become involved in programs designed to train the disadvantaged, improve the community, reduce the use of energy, cut back pollution, provide consumer information and consumer education, involve employees in community projects, and generally respond to the broader needs of society. Consumer orientation thus has become only one of the many social goals of today's progressive organizations. There is also growing cooperation between government and business organizations in developing programs to reduce unemployment and solve many of the other problems facing society. The concepts are:

> **A societal orientation directs an organization's marketing activities toward creating a better quality of life, including providing consumer satisfaction and creating a healthy environment, using resources carefully, and responding to the broader needs of society.**

> **A societal orientation is designed to help buyers to buy more intelligently, sellers to be more responsive and responsible, and government agencies to be more effective in promoting social welfare.**

[8] To learn how the new societal concept affects marketing management, see Adel I. El-Ansary, "Societal Marketing: A Strategic View of the Marketing Mix in the 1970s," *Journal of the Academy of Marketing Science*, Fall 1974, pp. 553–566.

Principles Behind a Societal Marketing Orientation

"Social Responsibility" is not an obligation imposed on marketing, but an inherent aspect of the nature of marketing. . . .

If marketing is recognized as an effective instrument of society, then there could be no perceived difference between the goals and values of the marketing system and those of society in general.

The marketing process is judged effective only to the extent that it produces results desired by *society, throughout society.*

Marketing is not something that is done to another party, but a process which is participated in by all members of a society.

Marketing is . . . a fundamental societal process which necessarily and inherently evolves within a society to facilitate the effective and efficient resolution of the society's needs for exchange of . . . values.

From Daniel J. Sweeney, "Marketing: Management Technology or Social Process?" *Journal of Marketing,* October 1972, pp. 7–8. Reprinted with permission of the American Marketing Association.

A Systems Orientation The traditional marketing concept calls for the coordination and integration of organizational efforts to provide consumer satisfaction at a profit. One problem with this concept is that it is too narrow. Successful marketers of the future will broaden their focus away from the firm as an entity unto itself to a **systems orientation** that includes the entire channel of distribution (that is, manufacturers, wholesalers, and retailers) and outside influences (for example, the government).[9]

Prior to the 1970s, almost all the management literature concentrated on managerial cooperation *within the firm.* Management by objectives, for example, was a concept that explained how to coordinate functions within one organization. But most businesses today depend on the coordination and integration of interfirm relationships (systems relationships). Concepts such as management by objectives should therefore be broadened to include the entire marketing system.

Much competition today is between entire channel systems. The systems that survive are those that are most efficient and most effective in solving society's as well as individual's wants and needs. Our discussion of a societal orientation in marketing shows the interrelationships between business organizations, the government, and the public. A true systems orientation would view the firm as part of a channel, the channel as part of the national economy, and the national economy as part of a world economy. Such a broad perspective would reveal the relationship between economic and social survival and growth.

[9] See, for example, Lee Alder, "Systems Approach to Marketing," *Harvard Business Review,* May–June 1967, pp. 105–118; and Samuel V. Smith, Richard H. Brien, and James E. Stafford, eds., *Readings in Marketing Information Systems* (Boston: Houghton Mifflin Company, 1969).

To implement the coordination and integration of interfirm systems, marketers will have to control information flows throughout the channel and between channel systems and their markets. To control such large information flows, marketers will have to adopt marketing information systems. Part of a systems orientation, therefore, is the use of marketing information systems and other such managerial tools. We shall discuss these systems in detail in Chapter 6.

In the future, there may be much more interfirm cooperation and integration. Even now, the whole world is becoming more economically interdependent, and international, interfirm relationships are becoming more common. For example, a Japanese firm may develop a high-quality, medium-priced tape recorder or automobile. Rather than sell such merchandise through their own distributorships in the United States, they might contract with U.S. firms to do the marketing tasks. That was the situation with Chrysler, which sold the Dodge Colt, a Japanese-made car.

Firms in the United States may develop similar relationships with other nations of the world. One country may make products; another country may ship them; and a third country may handle all the other marketing tasks. The concepts behind coordinated and integrated systems are:

> **Survival of a world economy calls for marketing cooperation between and among nations, because all economies are interdependent.**

> **Marketing management is expanding to mean management of the total marketing system, not just of one department or organization.**

> **A systems orientation in marketing calls for the use of marketing information systems to control information flows.**

> **Those organizations that are part of a coordinated and integrated marketing system will continue to dominate the market and force other organizations to be more competitive by adopting systems concepts.**

The Perils of Noncooperation You only have to look at the health-care industry in much of the United States to see how the lack of coordination and integration between and among organizations causes social havoc. In any large city, there are likely to be several hospitals with duplicate facilities, empty beds, and wasted resources. Meanwhile, millions of Americans are receiving poor health care, if any. Rather than work together in a spirit of cooperation, hospitals tend to plan independently of one another and to resist overall health-care planning. Wouldn't the coordination and integration of health-care facilities throughout a given area be beneficial to both the community *and* the various health-care agencies? The health-care industry needs to adopt a systems orientation as part of its new marketing philosophy.

Similar reorientation is needed by universities, businesses, unions, and other groups. They are all part of a social system that needs a balanced set of priorities. Each organization in society naturally concentrates on solving some group's wants or needs, but it should not be to the exclusion of other, more general social needs.

> **How Coordination and Integration Cuts Costs**
>
> Eight hospitals in the Hartford, Connecticut, area have formed a regional consortium and are pooling their resources, sharing staffs and purchasing jointly in bulk. One advantage of the consortium is that it stops unnecessary duplication and the competitive scramble by every hospital to have the best cobalt radiation machine, its own coronary unit, its own special clinics. The practicing physician, through the consortium medical staff bylaws, is able to admit patients to any of the eight hospitals, so that full utilization of facilities meets the needs of the public.
>
> Medical costs have risen too high for hospitals to go on competing like grocery stores. As the industry faces up to getting its costs under control, the regional consortium looks more and more like the pattern for the future.

From *Business Week*, May 26, 1975.

A Human Orientation   Perhaps no other concept has done more to harm the public's impression of marketing than the traditional focus on a profit orientation. Emphasis on a profit orientation makes marketers look greedy and unfeeling—as if they would do anything for a dollar. Part of this image may be overcome with the new emphasis on societal marketing. But marketing experts must also look at the other side of the relationship—the seller side. Traditionally the seller has been portrayed as some large, impersonal *organization* that has forced its products or ideas upon individual, comparatively defenseless consumers. But sellers are people too. They also have wants and needs that must be satisfied by marketing exchanges. Profits are certainly one important element in providing seller satisfaction, but just *one* element.

The broadened marketing concept calls for a **human orientation** that directs management's attention toward the needs of stockholders, managers, and employees and balances these human needs with the need for meeting overall organizational goals such as profit.[10] A human orientation emphasizes the fact that organizations have objectives other than profit. Table 3.1 gives some indication of how business leaders view profit and social responsibility. Note that the vast majority feel that profit is the *primary* concern, but that social responsibility is another major goal. Of those business leaders surveyed, 94 percent said that their companies were involved in programs such as employing and training the hard-core unemployed.

Note that a human orientation is applicable in all organizations (profit and nonprofit). The traditional profit orientation was a philosophy for *businesses* only. Note also that the needs of individuals are given attention along with the needs of the organization as a whole. The long-run

[10] This concept was introduced by Dawson in "The Human Concept."

Table 3.1 HOW 300 BUSINESS LEADERS VIEW THE ROLE OF PROFITS AND SOCIAL RESPONSIBILITY

Response categories	Percent who agree
"Business should assume responsibilities even at the cost of reduced profits."	17
"The sole business of business is profits."	10
"Business must first make an *adequate* profit, then must assume public responsibilities that may not be profitable."	42
"Business should concentrate on profits, but pay more in 'taxes and human resources' to solve social problems."	20
"Business should develop know-how in solving social problems and make its skills available to the government at a profit."	8
No reply	3

Constructed from material in Arthur M. Louis, "What Business Thinks," *Fortune*, September 1969, p. 94.

Look over

success of any organization depends upon a cooperative and effective structure of people as well as buildings, machinery, and the like. Dawson summarizes the need for a human concept in business rather than a profit orientation like this:

The point is, simply, that the firm concerned only with profit performance may find its lack of other internal or external social purpose to be a growing threat to its survival in an increasingly humanistic world. To borrow from the lexicon of economics, profit may become the necessary, but not sufficient, condition for the survival of the firm.[11]

Some stockholders (owners) are becoming more concerned with a human orientation in business. Much stock today is being purchased by large organizations such as pension funds, university development funds, and so forth. Often these organizations have established criteria for investment that include concern for the environment and other humanistic issues. A human orientation in organizations, therefore, is good for employees, good for owners, and good for society as a whole.

There is not necessarily a conflict between a profit orientation, as practiced by many organizations, and a human orientation. Profits are necessary for a firm to provide employee programs, stockholder dividends, and managerial training. A profit orientation that explicitly recognizes these humanistic goals is the same as a human orientation. But the term "human orientation" is better because it does not have all the potentially unfavorable connotations of a "profit" orientation.

[11] Ibid., p. 38.

Societal Orientation Combines with Human Orientation
Although there were often conflicts between the traditional consumer orientation and profit orientation in the past, there is no conflict between a societal orientation and a human orientation. The goals of all organizations are broadening as the needs of society become more pressing. Organizations are beginning to realize that narrow goals, such as profit, are simply not satisfactory bases for planning.[12] Every organization must also have other goals that may be secondary but are still an integral part of a total marketing strategy.

One goal, as we have noted, is to meet better the needs of managers and employees. Thus, organizations have developed recreational programs, vacation resorts, continuing education opportunities, training programs, and other personal-development programs. Such programs are part of an internal marketing program designed to earn the loyalty and support of employees. The concepts are:

> **A human orientation directs management's attention toward the needs of stockholders, managers, and employees and balances these human needs with the need for meeting overall organizational goals such as profit.**

> **A human orientation provides a foundation for meeting the needs of all people—consumers, stockholders, employees, and members of the community.**

> **A human orientation recognizes that profits are a necessary, but not a sufficient, objective of corporate policy.**

> **A human orientation and a societal orientation combine to give marketing a philosophy that stresses need satisfaction of all people, including people not directly involved in the exchange process.**

The goal of marketing is to establish mutually satisfying exchange relationships between people. The new broadened marketing concept, with its human orientation, recognizes the fact that the needs of society and of workers must also be met if such exchanges are to be satisfying in the long run. The concept is:

> **The broadened marketing concept provides a new philosophy for marketers who recognize that marketing exchanges have an effect on the overall quality of life; therefore, every effort is made to balance the needs of buyers, sellers, and society. This calls for a societal orientation, a systems orientation, and a human orientation.**

Some authors feel that the broadened marketing concept demands radical changes in the attitudes and direction of marketing:

The marketer will, in essence, have to become vitally concerned with human welfare rather than economic gain, and with the broader

---

[12] See Charles F. Phillips, Jr., "What Is Wrong With Profit Maximization?" *Business Horizons*, Winter 1963, pp. 73–80.

needs, aspirations, and potentialities of society rather than merely the problems of competition, sales volume, and profit. All of this implies and requires an expansion of marketing's point of view, frame of reference, purpose, methods, and skills. To accomplish the necessary adjustments entailed by this expansion might prove the greatest challenge to the marketing profession that it has yet experienced.[13]

Problems with Implementation Several studies have shown that the greatest problems with the marketing concept come in the implementation stage. Businesses seem to accept the concept but are not always able to make it work.[14] Executives in nonprofit organizations and government agencies often do not know what the marketing concept is; therefore, if they do implement it, it is often by accident rather than by design.

The greatest pressure to adopt some kind of broadened marketing concept probably will not come from educators or business leaders. It is most likely to come from consumerists and other public-interest groups. There is much evidence that the time has come for such changes:

In short, the major challenge is the development of operational definitions of the marketing concept which will allow the idea to be implemented on a day-to-day basis. As business enters an era that is becoming more complex and hostile, a time when consumers are likely to be more vocal and more demanding, this challenge will become more urgent.[15]

In the long run, though, educators and others interested in marketing will have to demonstrate the advantages of a new marketing philosophy for all organizations and individuals. The public today tends to think of the marketing philosophy as one of "get what you can" and "use any device you can to get it." To change that image will be a major challenge. We hope you will recognize the potential of a worldwide marketing philosophy based on open, mutually satisfying exchanges. We hope further that you will help implement that philosophy in your own life, with your employer, and in all other social organizations. (For a good summary of the ways in which businesses must relate to other aspects of society, see the insert "A Situation Orientation." Note that a situation orientation is one way to determine what to emphasize in the broader societal organization.)

[13] F. Kelly Shuptrine and Frank A. Osmanski, "Marketing's Changing Role: Expanding or Contracting?" *Journal of Marketing,* April 1975, p. 65.

[14] See Hiram C. Barksdale and Bill Darden, "Marketers' Attitudes toward the Marketing Concept," and Martin L. Bell and C. William Emory, "The Faltering Marketing Concept," in the *Journal of Marketing,* October 1971, pp. 29–42; and Carlton P. McNamara, "The Present Status of the Marketing Concept," *Journal of Marketing,* January 1972, pp. 50–57.

[15] Barksdale and Darden, "Marketers' Attitudes toward the Marketing Concept," p. 36.

A Situation Orientation

The philosophy that best describes actual business practice is a situation orientation. Under this philosophy it is recognized that the firm functions within a total environment. . . . A grouping of components that comprise the total business environment are listed [below] along with their purpose or function. . . .

COMPONENTS OF THE TOTAL BUSINESS ENVIRONMENT

Types of variables	Components	Functions in the system
Internal	Business firm	Economic satisfaction
External	Competition Natural resources Economic (business cycle) Government Social and cultural Buyers	Business efficiency Environmental balance System productivity Group's protection Social order Satisfaction from use

The important point of a situation orientation is that any of these objectives can singly or in some combination be the object of business policy. . . . The firm is pulled in several directions simultaneously by the various factors. . . . In the final analysis, the success or failure of the business may be directly related to management's ability to effect meaningful compromises among the situational factors.

From C. Glenn Walters, D. Wayne Norvell, and Sam J. Bruno, "Is There a Better Way Than Consumer Orientation?" in *Proceedings: Southern Marketing Association, 1975 Conference,* ed. Henry W. Nash and Donald P. Robin (Mississippi State University, 1976), p. 81.

The Marketing Concept for Buyers

The marketing concept has traditionally been presented as a managerial function, thus implying that the responsibility for establishing mutually satisfying exchanges is on the seller. It also implies that sellers should be socially responsible and act in the best interest of their customers and society as a whole. But little mention is made of the responsibilities and functions of the buyer.[16]

Buyers should also learn to temper their individual demands to fit the broader needs of society. For example, a person may prefer to buy throwaway bottles and cans, to keep his or her home at 78 degrees, and to eat many steaks and chops, but concerns for the environment, the energy shortage, and world hunger should also be important considerations. *Buyers* should use a societal orientation too.

[16] See George Fisk, "Criteria for a Theory of Responsible Consumption," *Journal of Marketing,* April 1973, pp. 24–31.

Furthermore, buyers should learn to coordinate and integrate their efforts to present their case more effectively and efficiently. Such joint effort may take the form of local consumer cooperatives, consumerist organizations designed to organize consumer research and education (for example, the Consumers' Union), and local consumer organizations that meet to discuss ways to influence political and business decisions.

Finally, buyers should adopt a broadly based human orientation that recognizes the needs of all factors of society, including business, government organizations, and consumers. Environmentalists, for example, should balance their concerns for the land, sea, and air with concerns for the needs of people and economic growth. All members of society should learn to make rational cost-benefit analyses of social programs. That is, care should be taken to measure the costs of any socially beneficial program as well as its benefits. The concepts behind a broadened marketing concept for buyers as well as sellers are:

> **The broadened marketing concept provides an exchange philosophy for both sellers and buyers that stresses a societal orientation, coordination and integration of efforts, and a broadly based human orientation that recognizes the needs of individuals and of society as a whole.**

> **Everyone is partially responsible for creating a better society: No one institution or organization can create a better standard of living without the cooperation and assistance of other members of society.**

FOR REVIEW

Key Terms

Among the more important terms and expressions discussed in this chapter are the following:

A **consumer orientation** is a managerial philosophy that emphasizes research on, and satisfaction of, the expressed or unexpressed wants and needs of consumers.

A **human orientation** is a managerial philosophy that expands the profit orientation to include the satisfaction of the wants and needs of workers and owners within an organization.

The **new marketing concept** is a managerial philosophy that, in general, calls for (1) a societal orientation, (2) a systems orientation, (3) a human orientation, and (4) application of the marketing concept to buyers as well as sellers.

A **production orientation** is a managerial philosophy that emphasizes production rather than marketing.

A **profit orientation** is a managerial philosophy that emphasizes increased profits rather than merely increased sales.

A **sales orientation** is a managerial philosophy that emphasizes the promotion and sales of products rather than merely their production.

A **situation orientation** embodies elements of the societal, systems, and human orientations and emphasizes flexibility of marketing objectives.

A societal orientation is a managerial philosophy that expands the consumer orientation to include the wants and needs of all aspects of society.

A systems orientation is a managerial philosophy that emphasizes coordination and integration, not of individual organizations, but of the entire marketing system, including information flows.

The traditional marketing concept is a managerial philosophy that, in general, calls for (1) a consumer orientation, (2) the coordination and integration of corporate efforts, and (3) a profit orientation.

Key Concepts

Among the more important marketing concepts introduced in this chapter are the following:

> One goal of business firms is to make a profit, for without profits the business will eventually fail.

> There is no inherent conflict between a profit orientation in business and social responsibility.

> A societal orientation directs an organization's marketing activities toward creating a better quality of life, including providing consumer satisfaction and creating a healthy environment, using resources carefully, and responding to the broader needs of society.

> A societal orientation is designed to help buyers to buy more intelligently, sellers to be more responsive and responsible, and government agencies to be more effective in promoting social welfare.

> Marketing management is expanding to mean management of the total marketing system, not just of one department or organization.

> A human orientation directs management's attention toward the needs of managers and employees and balances these human needs with the need for meeting overall organizational goals such as profit.

> A human orientation and a societal orientation combine to give marketing a philosophy that stresses need satisfaction of all people, including people not directly involved in the exchange process.

> The broadened marketing concept provides an exchange philosophy for both sellers and buyers that stresses a societal orientation, coordination and integration of efforts, and a broadly based human orientation that recognizes the needs of individuals and of society as a whole.

Discussion Questions

1. A production orientation to marketing means that an organization will produce a product first and *then* try to sell it. Give several examples of organizations that have such an orientation today. How would such organizations change if they were to adopt a consumer orientation or a human orientation?

2. "One goal of business firms is to make a profit, for without profits the business will eventually fail." Do you agree? Why or why not? How

much profit do you feel the average business now makes? In your opinion, how much *should* they make? Why?

3. Give examples of businesses that still seem to have a sales orientation. What would they do differently if they adopted a societal orientation? A human orientation?

4. "The societal marketing concept calls for a *customer orientation* backed by *integrated marketing* aimed at generating *customer satisfaction* and long-run *consumer welfare* as the key to attaining long-run profitable volume." Do you like the societal orientation? Why or why not? Is it an improvement over a consumer orientation? How?

5. A human orientation recognizes the needs of managers and employees as well as organizational needs for profit. How would such a philosophy be implemented on a college campus?

6. "Pressure to adopt a broadened marketing concept is likely to come from consumerists and other public-interest groups." Do you agree? Is there a better way? How?

7. "If marketing is recognized as an effective instrument of society, then there could be no perceived difference between the goals and values of the marketing system and those of society in general." Do you agree? Is this possible?

8. "Survival of a world economy calls for marketing cooperation between and among nations, for all economies are interdependent." Do you agree? Why or why not? Are we moving closer or further away from this concept?

9. There is no conflict between the goal of profit and the goal of social responsibility. Do you agree? Why or why not?

10. Give several examples of how buyers could implement the new marketing philosophy of human orientation through coordinated and integrated programs.

CASES

Parade of Values Supermarket
Applying the Marketing Concept

The Parade of Values Supermarket (PVS) has been operating in the same neighborhood for 10 years. There has always been a friendly atmosphere at the PVS, and the managers know many of the customers by name. A few years ago, the PVS stopped giving stamps to its customers and promoted its policy of "lower prices" instead. But ever since that time, prices at the supermarket have risen higher and higher. Recently there was a significant hike in milk and beef prices, and the PVS passed the price increase on to customers. This caused quite a fuss in the community, and some neighborhood people began to picket the store demanding lower prices and accusing the store of insensitivity to customer needs, excess profits, and betrayal of the neighborhood's trust. The store managers agreed to lower the milk and beef prices, but the neighbor-hood people did not seem as friendly anymore, and the old atmosphere of trust was gone.

1. Would the new broadened marketing concept be of any help in this case? How?
2. How could the PVS implement such a program? What would be the major problems?
3. Do you think it was a good idea to lower the milk and beef prices? Why or why not?

Bosworth Steel Company
Societal Marketing

The Bosworth Steel Company has produced specialty steel products in the same location for over 50 years. The plant is located on the shores of a large lake because the steelmaking process used by Bosworth calls for lots of water. Furthermore, the lake is a convenient dumping ground for the steel shavings and other debris created in the manufacturing process.

Recently, city officials have found potentially dangerous traces of chemicals in the lake water that were traced directly to Bosworth's dumping site. The city has demanded that Bosworth find another site for dumping. Bosworth management is not able to find an alternate dumping site that is economically feasible. They have decided to close the plant if the city forces them to comply to new pollution standards. This would mean firing over 1,300 employees in a town of 30,000 people. Most of the people in the town are either employees of Bosworth or are family or relatives who depend upon Bosworth employee's for their support.

1. Would Bosworth have avoided this conflict if it had adopted the traditional marketing concept that called for a coordinated and integrated effort to provide consumer satisfaction at a profit?
2. If you were a city official, what kind of mutually satisfying exchange could you make with the management of the steel company that would save the jobs of your people and minimize pollution problems as well?
3. Show how other manufacturing firms could use the new marketing concept to avoid such potential problems as the need to close the plant because of pollution problems.
4. Using this case as an example, explain why it is necessary to coordinate the efforts of business and government to solve tomorrow's needs for goods, services, and a better standard of living.

2

Learning
about Markets

In a very simplified form, marketing management can be summarized as: "Find a need and fill it." Part 2 goes into more detail about market analysis—the "find a need" part of the job. A person or firm cannot satisfy the needs of everyone, and so some procedure must be followed to narrow the market to manageable size. That procedure is part of the market-segmentation process. Chapter 4 introduces procedures for defining the market (who, when, where, why, and how often), segmenting the market, and positioning products to capture selected markets. Positioning basically means creating an image (or market position) for your product offer that clearly separates it from the offer of competitors.

You will get some feel for the size and other details about markets in Chapter 5. You will be introduced to the consumer market, the industrial market (business-to-business sales), the government market, the farm market, and international markets.

An individual or organization "finds a need" by means of marketing research. Marketing research involves a *periodic* review of marketing situations. It is one part of a total marketing information system. A marketing information system enables a marketing organization to monitor the market *continually* and to use that information to make marketing management more efficient and effective in "satisfying needs." All of this is discussed in Chapter 6.

The market of concern to most marketers is the consumer market. As you will see in Chapter 7, by studying consumers' behavior marketers can better understand their needs and what influences their purchasing decisions. This information can lead to more satisfying exchanges for everyone involved.

Defining and Segmenting Markets

whom should we serve?

LEARNING GOALS After you have read and studied this chapter, you should be able to:

1. Define the term market as used in this book.

2. Explain the differences among the following segmentation strategies: demographics; psychographics; geographic segmentation; benefit segmentation; usage segmentation; situation segmentation.

3. List the criteria to be used for determining the proper segmentation technique (or techniques) to be used for a particular organization.

4. Show how product positioning is related to market segmentation.

5. List the various techniques for segmenting the market using demographics.

6. Explain why an organization should use several segmentation techniques rather than just one.

7. Give an example that illustrates why situation segmentation is important for reaching seemingly complex markets.

8. Explain why the largest market segment is not always the best segment for a particular organization.

9. Show how buyers can use segmentation tools to be more effective and efficient.

10. Outline a segmentation strategy for a nonbusiness organization such as a political party.

INTRODUCTION

The new marketing concept requires a careful analysis of people's wants and needs. Any such analysis will reveal that people's needs differ greatly, as does their exchange behavior. This means that organizations must develop different marketing programs for various groups within the total population. **Market segmentation** is the process of dividing the total population (market) into several submarkets or segments that tend to have similar characteristics. For example, a total market may be divided by separating men from women or young people from older people. A couple of examples may help clarify what segmentation is like.

General Motors (GM) wants to meet the automotive needs of as many market segments as are profitable. There is one large segment, for example, that wants a small, economical car. For them, GM provides the Chevette. Another key segment prefers a large, comfortable luxury sedan. For them, GM provides Cadillacs, Buicks, and Oldsmobiles. There seems to be a trend toward smaller luxury cars that get better gas mileage. Therefore, GM came out with a smaller Cadillac and other smaller versions of luxury cars. In addition GM makes station wagons, trucks, buses, and other motor vehicles to satisfy the needs of special groups.

General Motors competes with the other U.S. car manufacturers to better meet the needs of particular market segments. For example, American Motors (AMC) tries to compete in the market for small and intermediate-sized cars. Many foreign car manufacturers (for example, Datsun, Toyota, Volkswagen, Fiat) also compete for the small-car market segment. There is also much competition from overseas producers for the luxury-car market segment (for example, Mercedes Benz, Volvo, Rolls Royce).

One can see from this example that the automobile market is not one, large, homogeneous group. Rather it is made up of many smaller market segments that want different things from a car. The new marketing concept requires the identification of these market segments and the design of marketing programs to satisfy selected segments.

As another example of segmentation, consider Cherise Brown. She is a tall (5′ 10″) professional woman who likes to dress in the latest styles. Cherise has learned, to her dismay, that many of the local clothing stores do not stock outfits that fit. The pants are usually too short, and the coat sleeves come halfway up her arm. Cherise has found several stores that cater to tall women, and some large department stores that have special sections devoted to tall sizes.

Market Analysis (New York: McGraw-Hill Book Co., 1925), p. 1.

74

Various market segments respond differently to the same product offer.

"How come you don't look that happy when I prepare a tv dinner for you?"

Cherise has a friend, Donna, who is pregnant. Donna needed a bathing suit to wear to their beach house and other clothes for special occasions. Donna found a couple of maternity shops that carried a wide selection of clothes for pregnant women. Donna also found that department stores carry assorted maternity clothes but that the selection tends to be limited.

Both Cherise and Donna have learned to concentrate their shopping trips on those stores where they are most likely to find what they want. They use market segmentation to improve the marketing process. It is interesting to note that several retailers have specialized in market segments such as tall women, maternity clothes, short women, and so forth.

This chapter explains how marketers (1) define markets, (2) segment markets, and (3) position products to reach particular market segments. All of these activities may be viewed as facilitating activities to the market-segmentation function. The concepts upon which this chapter elaborates are:

> **Market segmentation is a universal marketing function that enables buyers and sellers to concentrate their efforts on people who are most likely to participate in a mutually satisfying exchange.**

> **Market-segmentation strategies are just one aspect of total marketing programs that are designed to meet the wants and needs of people.**

MARKET DEFINITION Before we get involved in the details of market-segmentation strategies, perhaps we should look for a moment at the total market. The term market has so many meanings that one could get quite confused. People speak of the stock market, the used-car market, the real-estate market, the government market, the youth market, the job market, and so forth. All of these markets have several things in common: (1) They consist of groups of people with different wants and needs, and (2) these people have the potential for participating in marketing exchanges. In Chapter 2, we defined a market as the sum of all potential exchanges at any one time for a particular good or service. For our purposes here, we can sharpen our definition as follows: A **market** is a particular group of people and/or organizations that have wants and needs that may be partially satisfied through a marketing exchange.

This definition stresses the idea that markets represent a *potential*. As was discussed in Chapter 2, market potential exists on both the buying and selling side. When people produce an economic good, develop a new service, or think of a new solution to society's problems, they begin to look for people who could use their creations. They have the potential for satisfying others with what they have. Conversely, whenever a person feels a need or desire for new satisfactions, he or she looks for others to satisfy his or her wants. He or she has the potential for using the results of another person's efforts. Based on these concepts, a *market* may be further defined as the *potential* that exists for a mutually satisfying exchange between the producers of want-satisfying products and the buyers or users of such products.

One of the primary tasks of any organization is to measure the total marketing potential for the category of product it intends to produce (**primary demand**) and whether or not the market for the product of that particular organization is large enough to be worth the effort (this is called **selective demand**).

Suppose, for example, that you're thinking of opening a tennis shop in your home town. You've noticed that the demand for tennis equipment (the primary demand) has increased tremendously over the last few years and that tennis shops seem to be doing well (there are now over 35 million tennis players in the United States—up 350 percent in just 5 years). But before you invest your money, you'd like to know more details about how large the market will be in the *next* few years, how well other tennis shops are actually doing, and how big a market share (selective demand) you might hope to get.

You might begin your analysis by talking with the owners of other tennis shops and with the companies that supply them with rackets, balls, clothes, and other materials. Your investigation might reveal that the most successful shops handle more than one sport—for example, tennis and skiing. If so, you could then contact suppliers of ski equipment to get their ideas. You could also contact the trade associations involved with sports equipment and study the data published in tennis and ski magazines.

The potential growth of the tennis and ski markets may also be determined by studying the trends in leisure-time activities in general. The age distribution of the local area may also give some clues. You might find, for example, that there will be a tremendous increase in the number of people between the ages of 25 and 40 who would have the money for equipment and the potential interest in sports activities such as tennis and skiing. You might also be concerned about the future state of the economy, because when the economy is bad (for example, high unemployment), the demand for expensive recreation activities such as skiing often falls off. Related to the economic situation is the amount of money people have to spend on recreation and the trends in family size.

If the market for a tennis shop or a ski and tennis shop seemed worthwhile, you'd then like to know more about the local area—the media that are most popular, the life-style of the people, and so forth. All of these things are part of a comprehensive study of the market and market characteristics (**market definition**). The following sections describe in more detail the process of defining overall markets and target markets. Basically, the problem is to decide whom to serve, where, when, how, and with what return to the seller.

Selecting Target Markets

As we discussed in Chapter 2, some organizations have a strategy of **undifferentiated marketing**.[1] This means that the organization will try to develop a single product that will meet the needs of *all* or *most* of the people. It is the marketing of a single product to the mass market rather than to segmented markets. Examples might include a soft drink manufacturer that tries to make a drink that appeals to everyone. Such a firm would use mass marketing techniques (for example, mass advertising) to reach mass markets. It is unusual to find an organization that defines its market as "everyone."

Most organizations practice **differentiated marketing**, which means that the organization tries to identify particular subgroups of buyers (market segments) in order to divide the market into two or more groups.[2] It is the marketing of several versions of a product, each of which is designed to suit a particular segment of a market. The objective is (1) to select those subgroups that the organization will serve and (2) to design products that will satisfy those subgroups. Marketing managers use a three-step approach to reach selected subgroups (called **target markets**):

1. They develop a market description that defines the total market for their products.
2. They divide the total target market into logical, identifiable, reasonably homogeneous submarkets, or segments.
3. They design the most effective marketing strategy possible to reach the various segments of the total target market. In practice, management may assign priorities to certain market segments. Or, it may decide that the potential of one segment does not justify any promotional effort at all.[3]

[1] See Philip Kotler, *Marketing Management: Analysis, Planning, and Control*, 3rd ed. (Englewood Cliffs, N.J.: Prentice-Hall, Inc., 1976), p. 151.

[2] Ibid., p. 152.

[3] David Schwartz, *Marketing Today* (San Francisco: Harcourt Brace Jovanovich, Inc., 1973), p. 72.

In defining the market, an organization must take care that it recognizes the potential influence of people not in the target group. No organization can afford to concentrate its marketing efforts on a target market exclusively, because other organizational publics may interfere with the exchange relationship. Such interference is illustrated in the following example.

The Bondick brothers have operated a stock car racetrack for several years. The racing season is relatively short, lasting from late spring until the end of September. Races are run every Friday night, and the crowds are generally quite large. The Bondick brothers decided to expand the races to Friday *and* Saturday nights. They made arrangements with the various racing authorities and had the season all planned. But a local citizen's association blocked the expanded schedule because the racetrack was too noisy, and the spectators disrupted the neighborhood. The Bondick brothers learned the hard way that they had more than one "public" to serve. The concepts are:

➤ **All organizations must develop marketing relationships with several "publics," including customers, suppliers, stockholders, members of the surrounding community, and government leaders. The concept of "find a need and fill it" applies to all those publics and begins with a definition of just who the various publics are (market definition).**

➤ **Market-segmentation strategies and the marketing programs that are developed as a result should be aimed at target markets *and* all other groups that might have an effect on the marketing program.**

MARKET SEGMENTATION

Question: What problem do top market executives feel is the most important? Answer: Recognizing, defining, understanding, and segmenting markets. That was the conclusion of a survey of chief marketing officers of 200 member companies of the American Marketing Association (see Table 4.1).

One reason market segmentation was chosen as the most important problem is that market-segmentation decisions affect all the other marketing activities. For example, if a retail store decided to serve middle-class women on the east side of Cleveland with stylish clothes priced at a moderate level, such a decision would affect where the store should be located, what suppliers to use, what advertising media to use, price levels, and many other marketing decisions. A marketing vice-president of a $4 billion conglomerate said about market segmentation, "It is the basis upon which all marketing and advertising strategies are established."[4] Thus, you can see that market segmentation is a major problem for small retail stores and for billion-dollar conglomerates.

Segmentation decisions often commit an organization to a long-term policy that can be changed only by spending considerable time and money. However, market-segmentation strategies and tactics may be

[4] Charles N. Waldo, "What's Bothering Marketing Chiefs Most? Segmentation," *Advertising Age*, June 4, 1976, p. 77.

Table 4.1 HOW MARKETING EXECUTIVES RATE THEIR PROBLEMS

Choice	Times mentioned	Ranking points (total)	Times mentioned		
			1st	2nd	3rd
Problems in effectively communicating with general, staff, and functional managers	49	196	14	7	10
Problems and practices in long-range marketing planning	74	283	22	14	8
Discovering and establishing effective channels of distribution	41	152	1	14	11
Problems in recognizing, defining, understanding, and segmenting markets	**71**	**308**	**27**	**14**	**10**
Understanding and coping with governmental laws and regulations as applied to marketing, that is, the legal issues in marketing	29	63	—	2	4
The issue of social responsibility and the marketer	18	47	1	2	1
Developing effective advertising and sales-promotion strategies	66	229	7	13	11
Problems in establishing and maintaining an effective field force	61	209	9	8	11
Current and future practices in new product planning	66	211	7	9	8
Practices and problems in measuring effectiveness and controlling marketing costs	74	246	5	13	16
Special problems in selling to international markets	5	9	—	—	—
Current and future practices in physical distribution and warehousing	10	27	—	1	2

Reprinted with permission from Charles N. Waldo, "What's Bothering Marketing Chiefs Most? Segmentation," *Advertising Age*, June 4, 1973, p. 77. Copyright 1973 by Crain Communications, Inc.

used on a short-term basis to make decisions such as: To which area of town should we send a catalog? Should we buy winter coats for all sizes or should we concentrate on the more popular sizes? Should we use local radio, newspapers, or direct mail to reach our college-age market? Obviously, segmentation decisions are important to all phases of a marketing program.

Segmentation Strategies Although it may seem obvious to you that marketing efforts would be more successful if they were directed at a specific, well-defined market, segmentation strategies are a relatively new concept in marketing. Even today most organizations use only a very basic segmentation strategy. For example, the retail tennis shop mentioned earlier might choose as a target market men and women aged 17 to 45 in the upper middle class. All of the segmentation variables used (age, sex, and social class) are called **demographic variables.** Research suggests that such variables are not very effective when used by themselves.[5]

More progressive organizations are combining demographic variables with **psychographic variables** in a multidimensional approach to segmentation. That is, they take an overall look at variables such as activities, interests, values, and life-style, in addition to age, sex, income, and other demographic variables.

Even a casual observer could see that other segmentation strategies may be helpful. For example, a tennis shop would likely serve only a selected geographic area and could use **geographic segmentation.** One could also concentrate on heavy versus light users (tennis fanatics versus occasional players). This is called **usage segmentation.** Or one could concentrate on the benefits sought by users as illustrated by the GM case discussed at the beginning of this chapter. This is called **benefit segmentation.** Finally, one might discover that the best segmentation strategy would be determined by the situation—the economic, social, and political environment in which the marketing will take place. Such flexibility calls for **situational segmentation.**

In the following sections, we shall discuss each of these strategies in more detail. Note that the emphasis is on the seller in this discussion. Buyers may also use segmentation strategies, but there is little written on the subject. This is to be expected, because segmentation is usually most important for the seller. We shall be looking at the following segmentation strategies:

1. Geographic segmentation
2. Demographic segmentation
3. Psychographic segmentation
4. Benefit segmentation
5. Situation segmentation
6. Usage segmentation

Later we shall discuss how these strategies may be applied by industrial sellers, by buyers, and by nonbusiness organizations.

Geographic Segmentation One of the more basic techniques for segmenting markets is to use geographic boundaries (see Figure 4.1). People who live near a local store, for example, are more likely to respond to that store's offers. Also, an organization or individual may find areas that are not being served by competitors. For example, many cities in the United States have no doctor at all. Other cities have an abundance; therefore, a doctor could find a ready market by locating in a geographic area in which there is little or no competition. Some typical geographic segmentation variables are listed in Table 4.2.

One helpful source of information about various geographic markets

[5] See, for example, Daniel Yankelovich, "New Criteria for Market Segmentation," *Harvard Business Review,* March–April 1964, pp. 83–90.

Figure 4.1 REGIONAL DIVISIONS OF THE UNITED STATES

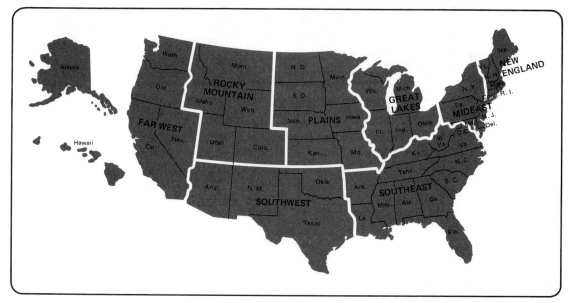

is *Sales and Marketing Management's Annual Survey of Buying Power* (see Figure 4.2). This magazine supplement lists income figures and other relevant data for every region in the country. Note that Figure 4.2 includes data for retail sales by store group, age distribution of population, buying power, and household income. Such figures help a marketer find the geographic areas with the best potential for future exchanges. The concept to keep in mind when analyzing geographic segments is:

‣ **People who live in different geographic areas (for example, city versus country) have different wants and needs; therefore, an effective segmentation strategy is to select those geographic areas where the people are most likely to want what you have to offer.**

Demographic Segmentation Another of the more basic segmentation strategies is demographics. Demographic variables (see Table 4.3) are widely used because the breakdowns often are based on common sense and the procedures are relatively easy.

Table 4.2 GEOGRAPHIC SEGMENTATION VARIABLES

Variable	Typical segments
Region	New England, Mideast, Great Lakes, Plains, Southeast, Southwest, Rocky Mountain, Far West
City or county size	Under 5,000; 5,000–19,999; 20,000–49,999; 50,000–99,999; and so on
Population density	Urban, suburban, rural

Figure 4.2 A SAMPLE OF AVAILABLE REGIONAL DATA

NEW HAMPSHIRE

POPULATION—12/31/75 / RETAIL SALES BY STORE GROUP 1975

N.H. METRO AREAS / COUNTIES / CITIES	Total Pop. (Thousands)	% Of U.S.	Median Age Of Pop.	18-24 Years	25-34 Years	35-49 Years	50 & Over	Households (Thousands)	Total Retail Sales ($000)	Food ($000)	Eating & Drinking Places ($000)	General Mdse. ($000)	Furnit.-Furnish.-Appl. ($000)	Automotive ($000)	Drug ($000)
MANCHESTER - NASHUA	247.0	.1151	28.4	12.3	13.3	16.5	24.7	81.7	783,569	183,474	51,917	133,630	26,929	156,559	20,134
Hillsborough	247.0	.1151	28.4	12.3	13.3	16.5	24.7	81.7	783,569	183,474	51,917	133,630	26,929	156,559	20,134
• Manchester	82.5	.0385	31.4	12.3	11.0	16.6	29.4	29.6	332,324	75,258	27,034	42,702	11,187	81,519	9,922
• Nashua	65.6	.0306	27.3	12.3	14.5	16.8	22.1	21.7	261,688	58,921	14,721	53,904	10,991	53,705	4,794
SUBURBAN TOTAL	98.9	.0460	27.2	12.3	14.7	16.1	22.3	30.4	189,557	49,295	10,162	37,024	4,751	21,335	5,418
OTHER DESIGNATED COUNTIES															
Belknap	36.8	.0171	30.5	12.8	12.0	16.1	28.5	12.7	137,092	29,287	11,129	7,946	3,031	32,403	4,160
Cheshire	57.9	.0270	29.2	13.5	13.3	16.2	26.1	19.3	171,430	47,866	13,073	16,584	5,139	28,931	5,169
Coos	33.4	.0155	30.5	14.0	10.5	15.5	29.8	11.4	83,967	25,758	4,948	5,157	2,720	17,620	1,799
Grafton	59.7	.0279	28.4	18.1	13.2	14.9	26.3	19.6	219,997	61,062	13,362	27,915	8,668	30,057	4,416
Merrimack	90.8	.0423	30.4	12.7	13.3	16.1	27.8	30.1	230,507	49,109	13,817	20,854	8,159	52,234	6,017
Rockingham	162.6	.0758	27.6	11.9	13.7	17.5	22.4	52.6	547,247	134,553	29,501	89,056	20,724	92,607	8,123
Strafford	81.7	.0381	26.9	16.9	12.7	15.9	23.8	25.5	225,013	52,161	12,968	41,597	12,564	36,543	4,825
Sullivan	33.0	.0154	29.9	12.9	11.7	15.9	28.1	11.6	107,744	27,357	2,897	12,981	2,740	27,769	2,496
TOTAL METRO COUNTIES	409.6	.1909	28.1	12.1	13.6	16.9	23.7	134.3	1,330,816	318,027	81,418	222,686	47,653	249,166	28,257
TOTAL DESIGNATED COUNTIES	802.9	.3742	28.6	13.4	13.2	16.3	25.2	264.5	2,506,566	610,627	153,612	355,720	90,674	474,723	57,139
TOTAL STATE	826.0	.3850	28.7	13.3	13.1	16.3	25.4	273.1	2,601,115	632,372	161,056	361,603	92,901	488,744	58,326

EFFECTIVE BUYING INCOME 1975

% Of Hslds. By EBI Group: (A) $8,000-$9,999 (B) $10,000-$14,999 (C) $15,000-$24,999 (D) $25,000 & Over

N.H. METRO AREAS / COUNTIES / CITIES	Total EBI ($000)	Median Hsld. EBI	A	B	C	D	Buying Power Index
MANCHESTER - NASHUA	1,165,618	13,166	7.9	24.6	31.9	8.8	.1167
Hillsborough	1,165,618	13,166	7.9	24.6	31.9	8.8	.1167
• Manchester	386,129	11,778	8.7	24.1	27.2	7.2	.0424
• Nashua	329,680	14,109	7.1	24.8	35.3	10.0	.0346
SUBURBAN TOTAL	449,809	13,793	7.8	24.8	33.9	9.7	.0397
OTHER DESIGNATED COUNTIES							
Belknap	192,043	12,981	8.5	22.0	31.4	10.2	.0192
Cheshire	260,990	12,073	10.0	27.8	27.6	6.5	.0262
Coos	130,921	10,422	10.8	27.9	20.1	4.4	.0134
Grafton	282,258	11,651	10.0	24.5	25.5	8.4	.0298
Merrimack	433,378	12,532	9.0	24.8	29.5	8.4	.0401
Rockingham	785,661	13,724	8.3	24.4	33.8	10.0	.0794
Strafford	321,896	11,246	10.8	28.3	23.7	5.2	.0339
Sullivan	149,909	11,188	10.9	26.8	24.0	5.9	.0155
TOTAL METRO COUNTIES	1,951,279	13,383	8.1	24.5	32.6	9.3	.1961
TOTAL DESIGNATED COUNTIES	3,722,674	12,555	9.0	25.3	29.5	8.2	.3742
TOTAL STATE	3,819,403	12,463	9.1	25.3	29.2	8.0	.3857

From *Sales & Marketing Management's 1976 Survey of Buying Power,* July 26, 1976, p. C-125. Reprinted by permission from *Sales & Marketing Management* magazine. Copyright 1976.

For example, let's say that you were asked to develop a segmentation strategy for your local library. You could use a basic demographic breakdown to help reach separate markets.

One way you could segment the library market is by different age groups. You could develop a program for young children that might include periodic puppet shows, movies, book discussion groups, special displays of particularly interesting children's books, and a whole display of toys and games for children to use and take home. Such activities would encourage children to visit the library on a regular basis.

Teenagers might be approached by offering a wide selection of records to listen to at the library or take home. Special displays of books on sports, cards, and other interesting subjects might also be developed. Sports personalities might be asked to give periodic talks at the library, and there could be films, book discussion groups, and other interesting events.

A different type of program could be developed for middle-aged women and men, the elderly, and college students. The point is that age is often an important segmentation tool.

For other products, stage in the family life cycle may be an important demographic variable. Table 4.4 gives a good overview of the family life cycle and how it affects purchase decisions. Note, for example, that an older married couple with all their children away from home tends to keep their house, whereas when one of the partners dies, the house is likely to be sold. Table 4.4 points out the importance of tracing life-cycle trends, because such trends reveal much about what is likely to be sold and to whom. Almost all organizations use demographic segmentation to better define their markets. Let's look at two other demographic variables, race and religion, to see how they are used: A restaurant may establish as its target market upper-class Orientals who wish to bring their families for special meals. A nightclub may want to reach a mostly black target market, or a newspaper may be directed at a Catholic or Jewish audience. You can see how helpful demographic segmentation can be. The basic concept is:

> **There are readily apparent differences between people of different ages, sexes, incomes, social classes, and other demographic characteristics that allow for rather basic segmentation decisions.**

Demographic variables are only the foundation for more detailed segmentation strategies, however, and are rarely effective by themselves.

Table 4.3 DEMOGRAPHIC SEGMENTATION VARIABLES

Variable	Typical segments
Age	Under 5; 5–10; 11–18; 19–34; 35–49; 50–64; 65 and over
Education	Grade school or less; some high school; high school graduate; some college; college graduate; advanced college degree
Family size	1; 2–3; 4–5; over 6
Family life cycle	Young, single; young, married, no children; young, married, oldest child less than 6 years old; young, married, youngest child 6 or over; older, married, with children; older, married, no children; older, single; other
Income	Under $5,000; $5,000–$9,999; $10,000–$14,999; $15,000–$19,000; over $20,000
Nationality	American, Asian, British, Eastern European, French, German, Italian, Japanese, Latin American, Middle Eastern, Scandinavian, and so forth
Occupation	Professional, managerial; technical, officials, and proprietors; clerical, sales; supervisors; operatives; farmers; students; home managers; retired; unemployed
Race	White, black, Indian, Oriental, and so forth
Religion	Catholic, Protestant, Jewish, and so forth
Sex	Male, female
Social class	Lower lower, upper lower, lower middle, upper middle, lower upper, upper upper

Note, though, that even such broad segments as children versus adults could help tremendously in product, promotion, and other marketing decisions. Note also how the needs of the target audience (segments) determine the product rather than the other way around. A library, for example, would not concentrate on books alone as its product but would also offer films, records, magazines, demonstrations, and other educational aids *according to the wants and needs of the community it serves.* The concept is:

> **Demographic market segmentation helps a seller select rather broad classes of people that can be better served because their wants and needs can be more clearly defined and products can be developed to meet them.**

Table 4.4 STAGES IN THE FAMILY LIFE CYCLE

Stage in life cycle	General characteristics	Likely purchases
Bachelor stage; young, single people not living at home	Few financial burdens. Fashion opinion leaders. Recreation-oriented.	Basic kitchen equipment, basic furniture, cars, equipment for the mating game, vacations.
Newly married couples; young, no children.	Better off financially than they will be in the near future. Highest purchase rate and highest average purchase of durables.	Cars, refrigerators, stoves, sensible and durable furniture, vacations.
Full nest I; youngest child under age 6	Home purchasing at peak. Liquid assets low. Dissatisfied with financial position and amount of money saved. Interested in new products. Like advertised products.	Washers, dryers, TV, baby food, chest rubs and cough medicine, vitamins, dolls, wagons, sleds, skates.
Full nest II; youngest child 6 or over	Financial position better. Some wives work. Less influenced by advertising. Buy larger-sized packages, multiple-unit deals.	Many foods, cleaning materials, bicycles, music lessons, pianos.
Full nest III; older married couples with dependent children	Financial position still better. More wives work. Some children get jobs. Hard to influence with advertising. High average purchase of durables.	New, more tasteful furniture, auto travel, nonnecessary appliances, boats, dental services, magazines.

Table 4.4 *Continued*

Stage in life cycle	General characteristics	Likely purchases
Empty nest I; older married couples, no children living with them, head in labor force	Home ownership at peak. Most satisfied with financial position and money saved. Interested in travel, recreation, self-education. Make gifts and contributions. Not interested in new products.	Vacations, luxuries, home improvements.
Empty nest II; older married couples, no children living at home, head retired.	Drastic cut in income. Keep home.	Medical appliances, medical care, products which aid health, sleep, and digestion.
Solitary survivor, in labor force	Income still good but likely to sell home.	Same as other retired group.
Solitary survivor, retired	Drastic cut in income. Special need for attention, affection, and security.	Same as other retired group.

Adapted from William D. Wells and George Gubar, ''Life Cycle Concept in Marketing Research,'' *Journal of Marketing Research*, August 1968, p. 267. Reprinted with permission of the American Marketing Association.

4 P's

Product, place, promotion, and price decisions are all clearly aided by segmenting the market into broad, general classes such as male versus female, young versus old, rich versus poor, and other demographic segments.

Psychographic Segmentation Some marketers have found that the more traditional segmentation variables (for example, geographic and demographic) do not define their target audience accurately enough.[6] For this reason, they have begun using more personal data such as the activities, values, interests, lifestyles, and opinions of their target markets (psychographic variables). People with the same demographic characteristics often vary greatly on these other factors, some of which are listed in Table 4.5. Researchers have found that psychographic variables are useful in segmenting both industrial and consumer markets.[7] The following discussion will focus on consumer markets, but keep in mind that the concepts are applicable in industrial markets as well.

[6] There is some evidence that demographic segmentation may be more effective than supposed; see Donald E. Morrison, ''Evaluating Market Segmentation Studies: The Properties of R^2,'' *Management Science*, July 1973, pp. 1213–1220.

[7] See, for example, David T. Wilson, H. Lee Matthews, and Timothy W. Sweeney, ''Industrial Buyer Segmentation: A Psychographic Approach,'' in Fred C. Allvine, *Combined Proceedings, Spring and Fall Conferences* (Chicago: American Marketing Association, 1971), pp. 327–331.

"The sudden inexplicable glee you've been feeling is common among women reaching your time of life. It's called the empty nest syndrome."

Courtesy of *New Woman* magazine. Copyright © 1976 by New Woman, Inc.

Psychographic segmentation often involves the use of several variables such as personality, interests, activities, life-styles, and values to discover styles of living and ways of making decisions that explain buyer behavior.[8] A complete psychographic study may include: (1) product-related variables such as perceived benefits and usage rates, (2) promotion variables such as brand imagery and media habits, and (3) consumer variables such as personality and self-image.

The use of psychographics is relatively new among marketers, and the procedures are still being perfected. There is no doubt, though, that a combination of demographic and psychographic data is very helpful for pinpointing and understanding the behavior of target audiences. The concept behind using psychographics is:

➤ **Data that show the interests, values, and other personal information about potential buyers add tremendously to the more general information obtained from demographic research; such facts are gathered through psychographic research.**

[8] See, for example, Edgar A. Pessemier and Douglas J. Tigert, "Personality, Activity, and Attitude Predictors of Consumer Behavior," in *New Ideas for Successful Marketing*, ed. John S. Wright and Jac L. Goldstucker (Chicago: Proceedings of the American Marketing Association, 1966); Joseph T. Plummer, "Life Style Patterns and Commercial Bank Credit Card Usage," *Journal of Marketing*, April 1971, and Ruth Ziff, "Psychographics for Market Segmentation," *Journal of Advertising Research*, April 1971.

Table 4.5 PSYCHOGRAPHIC SEGMENTATION VARIABLES

Variable	Typical segments
Attitudes Behavior patterns Interests Life-styles Opinions Personality Self-image Values	There are no typical breakdowns in psychographic analysis because the technique is new and still being developed.

For example, a firm that sold customized vans (trucks) that contained refrigerators, carpeting throughout, and other such accessories might target in on young males (under 35) who are single, who have a self-image of being "swingers," and who place a great value on sociability. Research might show that such men read *Playboy* magazine and frequently attend sports events. One marketing strategy, therefore, might be to advertise in *Playboy* and have a display of customized vans at various sports events, ski shows, and resort areas.

Even after a market has been defined more clearly using psychographics, there may still be some question about what features or benefits various groups might prefer. In the case of vans, for example, should refrigerators be made standard? What about air conditioning? Should there be a window in the roof or not? Such questions are answered best by another marketing tool called benefit segmentation. Some authors view benefit segmentation as one aspect of psychographics, but it really deserves special emphasis.

Benefit Segmentation The idea of benefit segmentation is to divide the market based on the perceived benefits of the good, service, or idea desired (see Table 4.6). For example, a car manufacturer may find one large segment primarily concerned with good gas mileage, another primarily interested in space (for a large family), and a third primarily wanting comfort and luxury. Each segment would call for a different kind of product, price, advertising strategy, and sales effort.

Table 4.6 BENEFIT SEGMENTATION VARIABLES

Variable	Typical segments
Comfort Convenience Durability Economy Health Luxury Safety Status	Benefit segmentation divides an already established market into smaller, more homogeneous segments. Those people who desire economy in a car would be an example. The benefit desired varies by product.

Table 4.7 TOOTHPASTE MARKET SEGMENT DESCRIPTION

Variable	Segment name			
	The sensory segment	The sociables	The worriers	The independents
Principal benefit sought	Flavor, product appearance	Brightness of teeth	Decay prevention	Price
Demographic strengths	Children	Teens, young people	Large families	Men
Special behavioral characteristics	Users of spearmint flavored toothpaste	Smokers	Heavy users	Heavy users
Brands dispropor-tionately favored	Colgate, Stripe	Macleans, Plus White, Ultra Brite	Crest	Brands on sale
Personality characteristics	High self-involve-ment	High sociability	High hypo-chondriasis	High autonomy
Life-style char-acteristics	Hedonistic	Active	Conservative	Value-oriented

From Russell I. Haley, "Benefit Segmentation: A Decision-Oriented Research Tool," *Journal of Marketing*, July 1968, p. 33. Reprinted with permission of the American Marketing Association.

Benefit segmentation helps the seller to get a better picture of why the consumer buys: What is the consumer's principal buying motive? What needs are dominant? The answers to these questions help the seller to better predict actual behavior than do broader segmentation variables such as age, sex, social class, or income.

It has been found, for example, that the toothpaste market is made up of various segments: those who are most concerned with decay preven-tion (for example, large families); others who are interested in bright teeth (for example, smokers and teenagers); and still others who are most concerned with flavor or price. It has also been found that each segment could be further identified as to demographics (especially men versus women and age), brands favored, heavy versus light users, and psychographics (for example, high self-involvement versus high socia-bility).[9] As a result of all this information (summarized in Table 4.7), a toothpaste manufacturer might develop several brands with different characteristics. He would also know something about the market for each brand and how to promote it (for example, what to say, in what media, and so forth).

The whole idea of benefit segmentation is to take a relatively large market segment made up of different kinds of people and break it down into smaller, more similar segments. Furthermore, each of these smaller market segments can be studied more intensively to learn more about the wants and needs of the buyers, their personalities and values, and

[9] Russell I. Haley, "Benefit Segmentation: A Decision-Oriented Research Tool," *Journal of Marketing*, July 1968, pp. 30–35.

their media habits. The concept behind benefit segmentation can be summarized as follows:

› **Within each broad market segment (such as women), there are many smaller segments (groups) that look for different things in a product; therefore, the market may be divided into smaller segments that put more emphasis on particular benefits such as economy, social appeal, convenience, and durability.**

Situation Segmentation One interesting finding that has resulted from research on benefit segmentation is that people change their desires for particular benefits in different situations. It helps to understand why this occurs, and so this section discusses how to adapt segmentation strategies to the situation.[10]

One of the assumptions behind traditional segmentation strategies is that people can be placed into some recognizable categories that are relatively fixed and measurable. But persons actually assume many different personalities (roles) as they adjust themselves to the various groups to which they belong.

For example, let's examine the behavior of a college professor as she assumes different roles. One night the professor and her husband may have the dean of the college to their home for dinner. For such an occasion, the family might use their finest china and linen napkins, serve expensive wine, and prepare a gourmet meal. Her role this night is one of a professional and a gourmet. The next night the professor and her family might have pot pies for dinner, no napkins, and milk to drink. Dessert may be instant Jello. The professor's role this night is that of mother and busy family member.

This example shows that the same person may use different products for the same purposes based on the demands of the situation. Traditional segmentation strategies do not recognize these variances in behavior that are caused by the diverse roles people assume at a given time.

It has been suggested, therefore, that marketers use *situation segmentation.* The idea is to "identify the psychological variables that operate in different usage situations, and offer a product . . . that satisfies the wants and needs implicit in them."[11] The following are some of the situations that call for different marketing strategies: (1) when people are on vacation, (2) when people are moving into a new neighborhood, (3) when people are celebrating an important occasion with close friends, and (4) when families are trying to economize on living costs.

Notice how each situation would result in different purchasing behavior. People on vacation tend to spend more on housing and meals than they would normally. They are also more prone to buy products such as souvenirs, sunglasses, and other accessories and symbols of leisure living. These same people might have special low-cost meals at home and would ordinarily never even think of buying the kinds of junk

[10] Material in this section is based on Norman Goluskin, "Every Man a Walter Mitty," *Sales Management,* July 7, 1975, pp. 45–46.

[11] Ibid.

they purchase while on vacation. When a special occasion such as a twenty-fifth wedding anniversary arrives, this same family might serve an elaborate meal by candlelight, with an expensive wine. After all, a special occasion calls for special preparations. And that is the point of situation segmentation; it recognizes the fact that people buy different products for different reasons based on the social situation of the time.

A person who normally buys margarine shops for butter for certain special events. A family that carefully counts calories periodically shops for elaborate cakes and ice cream (for example, for a child's first birthday). Situation segmentation accounts for such behavior by analyzing the motives and desires that people have in different buying circumstances. The concept behind a discussion of situational segmentation is:

Combining Psychographics with Demographics

Life-style is based on the proposition that the more you know about with whom you are attempting to communicate, the more effectively you can communicate with them. The "whom" in life-style is usually the heavy user of the product under consideration, that relatively small segment of consumers who often account for the bulk of a product's sales volume. What we want to know about this heavy user segment is: In what ways are they different from the light or nonuser of the product? Traditionally we have looked at this heavy user segment in terms of demographic characteristics. With life-style we are attempting to provide a more three-dimensional view of these consumers that may be helpful in creating the advertising for them. The life-style characteristics combined with the demographic characteristics help construct a portrait of the heavy user so that the creator of the advertising can get a better, more real-life picture of whom he is trying to communicate to about a product.

In the life-style questionnaire that is mailed to the panel of respondents, there are three basic areas of inquiry. First, there are 300 activity interests and opinion (AIO) statements that the respondent rates on a six-point agreement scale. Second, there are a number of media usage questions and, third, a large section on average product usage of over 100 different products. The new dimension of this approach is of course the AIO items which measure the "life-style" of the respondents. The items that make up the questionnaires come from many sources, and are still being refined. Basically we view a person's life-style as composed of his activities—how he spends his time at work and leisure; his interests—what he places importance on in his immediate surroundings; his opinions—where he stands on issues, society, and himself; and some basic facts—his social class, stage in life cycle, and his purchasing patterns.

From Joseph T. Plummer, "Life-Style and Advertising Case Studies," in *Combined Proceedings, Spring and Fall Conferences*, ed. Fred C. Allvine (Chicago: American Marketing Association, 1972), p. 291. Reprinted with permission of the American Marketing Association.

> A person who falls into a particular market segment one day may not fit into that same segment on a different day or under different circumstances; therefore, marketers should not feel a particular segment is permanent—rather, a policy of studying buyer behavior under different conditions should be followed.

The "normal" market for a given product may be quite large and predictable, but the chance for expansion of that market is greater if the occasional shopper is also given some recognition and marketing effort. This brings up the subject of whether or not a marketer should go after heavy users, light users, nonusers, or some combination. These categories may also be included in the broad strategy called psychographics.

Usage Segmentation An effective segmentation tool, but one that can be overdone, is segmentation by heavy and light users (see Table 4.8). The questions asked are: Who uses the product the most and the least? Who does not use the product at all? And why?

Studies of heavy and light users often are quite revealing. For example, Table 4.9 shows the difference in market potential between light and heavy buyers of a group of selected products. Note in the table that heavy buyers of catsup bought almost eight times as much catsup as did light buyers. Note also that for some products (for example, candy bars, beer, and hair spray), there is a tremendous difference in market potential between the two segments. Table 4.9 combines demographic segmentation (age, income, education, and so forth) with usage segmentation.

Some beer companies, for example, have effectively implemented a usage-segmentation strategy. Schaefer beer decided to go after the heavy user with the slogan, "The one beer to have when you're having more than one." There are many people who are not heavy beer drinkers, however, and they are more likely to respond to such slogans as, "The champagne of bottled beer."

For many nonprofit groups, usage segmentation is often the most effective of the segmentation strategies. Those people who have attended art shows, dance performances, concerts, and other such events (and those people who have given to a charity or supported a cause) are the ones most likely to go or give again. It is important to keep a list of such patrons and to update the names constantly.

The nonattenders or nondonors who have fixed attitudes about the

Table 4.8 USAGE MARKET SEGMENTATION

Variable	Typical segments
Heavy users	
Light users	Segmentation by usage is self-explanatory.
Nonusers	
Loyalty status	None; medium; strong; absolute (repeat purchases)

Table 4.9 LIGHT AND HEAVY BUYERS BY MEAN PURCHASE RATES FOR DIFFERENT SOCIOECONOMIC GROUPS—SELECTED PRODUCTS

Product	Description		Mean consumption rate ranges		Ratio of highest to lowest rate
	Light buyers	Heavy buyers	Light buyers	Heavy buyers	
Catsup	Unmarried or married over age 50 without children	Under 50, three or more children	0.74–1.82	2.73–5.79	7.8
Frozen orange juice	Under 35 or over 65, income less than $10,000, not college graduates, two or fewer children	College graduates, income over $10,000, between 35 and 65	1.12–2.24	3.53–9.00	8.0
Pancake mix	Some college, two or fewer children	Three or more children, high school or less education	0.48–0.52	1.10–1.51	3.3
Candy bars	Under 35, no children	35 or over, three or more children	1.01–4.31	6.56–22.29	21.9
Cake mix	Not married or under 35, no children, income under $10,000, TV less than 3½ hours.	35 or over, three or more children, income over $10,000	0.55–1.10	2.22–3.80	6.9
Beer	Under 25 or over 50, college educated, nonprofessional, TV less than 2 hours	Between 25 and 50, not college graduate, TV more than 3½ hours	0–12.33	17.26–40.30	∞[a]
Cream shampoo	Income less than $8,000, at least some college, fewer than five children	Income $10,000 or over with high school or less education	0.16–0.35	0.44–0.87	5.5
Hair spray	Over 65, under $8,000 income	Under 65, over $10,000 income, not college graduate	0–0.41	0.52–1.68	∞[a]
Toothpaste	Over 50, fewer than three children, income less than $8,000	Under 50, three or more children over $10,000 income	1.41–2.01	2.22–4.39	3.1
Mouthwash	Under 35 or over 65, less than $8,000 income, some college	Between 35 and 65, income over $8,000, high school or less education	0.46–0.85	0.98–1.17	2.5

[a] Infinity symbol.

From Frank M. Bass, Douglas J. Tigert, and Ronald T. Lonsdale, "Market Segmentation: Group versus Individual Behavior," *Journal of Marketing Research*, August 1968, p. 267. Reprinted with permission of the American Marketing Association.

subject are usually not worth pursuing. Such people would give reluctant support, if they were to give at all, and might divert much useful effort from other, more responsive segments. However, if the organization sponsoring such programs or causes wishes to broaden its support, it could do so by giving free performances or free demonstrations, in order to expose more people to the organization and its benefits. The concept behind usage segmentation is:

> **Almost all goods, services, and ideas are subject to an 80/20 rule; that is, 20 percent of the people will buy 80 percent of the output. Therefore, it is often an effective strategy to identify the 20 percent of the people who are heavy users or use some procedure to more effectively reach the remaining 80 percent of the market. It is also important to identify nonusers to see what causes their dissatisfaction because they often represent a large, untapped market.**

How to Select Segmentation Variables In every marketing situation, several segmentation variables might be used. The problem is to decide which strategy is best. Suppose you were a consultant to the United Way cause as a service to your community. How would you know whether to use income or occupation as a key segmentation variable? Which one is best?

1. The prime reason for selecting a particular segment should be whether or not the factor separates an identifiable market that can be effectively reached at a minimum cost. For example, income may be a very good determinant of people who are likely to give the most to a charity, but how do you reach these people? Perhaps it would be better to select certain geographic regions, or even certain businesses, for intensive soliciting. Again, the idea is to select a segment or segments that are likely to respond to a workable marketing program at a reasonable cost.

    Some segmentation variables, such as sex, age, and income, are relatively easy to determine and measure but give little guidance as to marketing strategy. Another criterion for selecting a segmentation strategy, therefore, is whether or not it makes the marketing strategy for reaching that market more apparent. At times, psychographic variables such as self-image and values are harder to determine but more revealing for promotional decisions. For example, a person who is concerned about the causes supported by the United Way might be reached effectively if one knew his or her self-image and media habits.

3. Finally, pursuing a market segment should be worth the trouble. This means that it should be a large enough segment to make a whole marketing program pay off without costing too much in time or money. Some charities have found that some segments, such as the very wealthy or the largest firms, are small in number but large in potential. Naturally, such segments deserve special emphasis and should return a satisfactory payoff. Salespeople (volunteers), rather than advertising, are usually used to solicit such accounts.

    The selection of a particular market segment or segments is such a critical decision that each variable should be carefully analyzed and tested for its ability to generate an effective marketing program, to reach the market without too much cost, and to add to an overall marketing program for reaching multiple segments. Some guiding concepts to use in selecting segmentation variables are:

> It is more effective to use several segmentation variables rather than just one; that is, some combination of demographics and psychographics is the most effective.

> There is a cost associated with any segmentation research, so there must be some trade-off between the desire to know more about the market and the need to minimize costs.

> Market segmentation and product differentiation are joint decisions: If you change the product, you change the segments it would appeal to and vice versa.

> The largest market segment is not necessarily the most desirable, because competition for that segment will no doubt be high. For this reason, there must be some decision as to which segments have the most real potential (as opposed to total potential).

> There are three criteria for evaluating a segmentation tool: (1) Does the factor separate an identifiable market that can be reached effectively at a minimum cost? (2) Does it help clarify other marketing decisions (for example, promotion)? (3) Will serving the market segment result in a mutually satisfying exchange?

Segmenting Industrial Markets   Many of the same techniques used to segment consumer markets may also be used in industrial markets. For example, *geographic segmentation* may be used to target in on organizations in a certain part of the country. Often, transportation costs will dictate a geographic segmentation strategy.

Some manufacturers use *industry segmentation*. That is, they concentrate their sales effort on particular industries. The sales force is specially trained to know the problems of selected industries, and the entire marketing effort is targeted on those few industries.

The 80/20 rule applies to industrial organizations also. Often a firm will concentrate on key accounts (that is, the accounts that bring in 80 percent of the business). This strategy is sometimes known as *customer-size segmentation*.

One very useful segmentation tool is provided by the federal government. It is called the Standard Industrial Classification System (SIC). Using SIC data, a firm can identify relatively small segments of its industrial market. All types of businesses in the United States are divided into ten groups, and a range of two-digit classification code numbers is assigned to each group. Using these codes, a firm can find many potential users of its goods and services. The concepts are:

> Industrial markets can be segmented much like consumer markets so that marketing efforts can be placed where the best chances are found for establishing mutually satisfying exchanges.

Industrial market segmentation is often easier than consumer market segmentation because there are fewer potential customers and much data is available from the government to help firms find markets.

Segmentation by the Buyer

It may be just as important for buyers to analyze and segment the market as it is for sellers. Consumers and purchasing agents should learn how to select those firms that are most likely to satisfy their wants and needs. Such a selection process involves market segmentation.

Consumers, for example, learn that retail stores can be classified as either low in price (discount stores), very high in price and in quality (Neiman Marcus, Saks Fifth Avenue, specialty shops), and moderate in price and quality (most traditional department stores such as Sears). Through a segmentation strategy, a consumer can minimize shopping time by going to the store most appropriate for the product in question. For example, if price is the prime consideration, discount stores are usually a good place to shop. If better quality is desired at a slightly higher price, department stores are usually better places to shop, and so on.

It is very helpful to both the buyer and the seller if the buyer makes his or her wants and needs known and works closely with selected suppliers to get desired goods and services. If some businesses fail to meet consumer expectations, consumers must learn to avoid such businesses and to inform other consumers about their experience. Such communication helps consumers to segment the market for more satisfying exchanges.

Buyers for retail stores and manufacturing organizations have learned how to evaluate and select suppliers carefully. They use segmentation strategies also, including geographic segmentation (for example, they buy from suppliers in New York and California) and benefit segmentation (they choose sellers that offer the best "package" of benefits). Buyers for retail stores must keep in mind the people they wish to sell to when making purchases, for "goods well bought are half sold." Middlemen such as wholesalers and retailers thus use market segmentation strategies for both buying and selling.

Segmentation in the Public Sector

One can become so involved with different segmentation strategies that basic principles can be forgotten. For example, let's review the marketing decision making of the educational sector over the last 30 years. Immediately after World War II, there was a sharp increase in the number of children born each year. Demographic analysis would show this immediately. Did school districts immediately begin planning to handle additional demands? Most did not. In fact, some districts were so surprised by increased enrollments that they had to teach school in hastily designed shifts that disrupted entire school systems for several years. Children often would attend either morning sessions or afternoon sessions, and one family might have several children going to school at different times of the day.

Did the experience of the grade schools generate immediate changes in the junior and senior high schools? Not to any great extent. Instead, when the enrollment increased, there was often a frantic scramble to find new teachers, more classrooms, and so forth. Temporary buildings were erected, and everything operated on a semicrisis basis. Remember, though, that these students were born at least 12 years before, and so there was plenty of time to plan and implement changes. But common sense and basic segmentation research often lost out to tradition, indifference, and poor marketing planning.

Did colleges recognize this trend and begin plans to adapt? Not to the extent needed. Schools were overcrowded, "getting into college" was a major issue, and there was another minicrisis in education.

The school system recovered from its shock in the 1960s and began building more schools and colleges across the country. These schools are now built and ready, but there are fewer students. So schools are being closed, teachers laid off, and a new crisis is developing. There are too many teachers being trained, and primary education in general is being criticized on several fronts. Reading and math scores are lower than in the past, and plans are being made to revise curricula (again).

The basic principles of market analysis and market segmentation were not practiced very well by the educational sector over the last 30 years. Will this change in the future? There are still too many colleges turning out teachers with the wrong skills for today's markets. Now that birthrates have fallen, there may be even less demand for school facilities. Are plans being made now for such changes? The answer is "yes" in some areas, but "no" in many others. The basic concepts that have been violated by some school districts are:

> Market analysis and segmentation begins by a simple counting of the market to determine its size and its characteristics.
> Counting must be done continuously, for market changes are often sudden and dramatic.
> Changes in the market should lead to immediate changes in marketing plans to adapt to the new situation.
> Before plans are implemented, there should be a new check of the market to be sure the situation has not changed.

These basic principles are violated daily by government, business, and private causes. Ford Motor Company counted the market for the Edsel, researched market wants and needs, but forgot to review the market before implementation. By the time the Edsel was introduced, the market had changed, and the car lost millions of dollars for the firm.

General Motors had similar problems throughout the 1970s. First, the energy crisis caused a tremendous demand for small cars. GM made very expensive and extensive product-line changes to produce more small cars. As the energy crisis subsided somewhat in the mid-1970s, people started buying larger cars, and GM was forced to change again. It has cut the size and weight of their luxury and full-size cars in response to new market needs. These examples show that businesses (even the largest, most sophisticated ones) can make mistakes in market analysis and market segmentation. How large will the small-car segment be in the 1980s? That is the question car manufacturers must answer. The concepts are:

> Consumer behavior is subject to change as the economy changes (for example, shortages in fuel).

> Market-segmentation strategies should be based on studies of the social, economic, technological, and political environment as well as on consumer studies.

> All organizations (business, government, and nonprofit) must develop better market-analysis and market-segmentation strategies in the future if the United States is to avoid disruptions such as the energy crisis, the wheat crisis, the meat crisis, and the educational crisis of the past.

Social Market Segmentation   The new marketing concept calls for the application of marketing techniques to solve the needs of society as well as those of particular subsegments. For example, a key social problem today is air pollution. One study of consumers found that the usual segmentation tools were not effective in finding consumers interested in ecology. The most important segmentation variable was "concern about the issue at hand," whether the issue be nonreturnable bottles, high-phosphate detergent, excessive use of paper products, or air pollution.[12] A more recent study looked at the energy-conscious consumer as a market segment.[13] The use of segmentation tools to solve social problems is a relatively new concept in marketing, but one that is receiving increased attention. In the future, we should see a much greater use of segmentation strategies by non-business organizations and by business firms that try to satisfy society's needs.

Too Much Segmentation?   In their attempt to capture a small share of a larger market, some organizations have developed new products that differ only slightly from other competing products. During a period of rapid growth in a society, such a strategy has proved quite successful. But in a period of stability or recession, people become more concerned with basic values, and, more importantly, organizations shift their attention away from a growth in sales to a growth in profit. That is, organizations become more selective about the markets they try to serve and cut back greatly on new-product introductions and eliminate many old, unprofitable products from their offerings.

There can be too much market segmentation. There can also be too many organizations competing for a particular market. For example,

Do away w/slightly differing product, to prevent loss of profit in the promotion of it.

[12] See Harold H. Kassarjian, "Incorporating Ecology into Marketing Strategy: The Case of Air Pollution," *Journal of Marketing,* July 1971, pp. 61–65.

[13] See Richard C. Reizenstein and David J. Barnaby, "An Analysis of Selected Consumer Energy-Environment Trade-Off Segments," in *Marketing: 1776–1976 and Beyond,* ed. Kenneth Bernhardt (Chicago: American Marketing Association, 1976), pp. 522–526.

dressmakers may try to serve the wants of women to the point where there are too many styles to select from and too many competitors. Eventually some of the organizations may fail. But more important to society is the fact that too many products designed for too narrow segments often use up resources better spent elsewhere. Marketers must be careful not to concentrate all their efforts on serving *individual* markets to the point where it hurts the firm and/or society as a whole. Usually the laws of supply and demand will eliminate most products that differ only slightly from others. But the cost of producing them, promoting them, and distributing them has already been incurred. This is wasteful and cuts into profits. Careful market segmentation thus benefits society as well as the organizations using it.

PRODUCT POSITIONING Market-segmentation studies help an organization determine some of the characteristics of its target markets. The process of using that data to design products and promotions that will capture an acceptable market share is called **product positioning.** Positioning in basic terms means making a product stand out from competing products and making it more attractive to the buyer. It may involve basic changes in the good or service or changes in the package, price, brand name, promotion, or any other aspects of marketing that affect consumer perceptions.

Positioning means many different things to marketers, but most would agree that market-segmentation and positioning strategies are closely related. Often the best way to sell a product is to concentrate on one segment of the market, preferably a segment that has been largely

---

Confusion over Positioning

What is meant by *positioning?* Ask a dozen practitioners and you will likely come up with a dozen . . . answers. Academicians tend to ascribe an even broader range of denotations to the word. . . . Behavioral theory suggests that consumer purchase decisions are influenced by the individual's perception of the physical object, its accompanying marketing effort, and the individual's beliefs about the item or what is more commonly referred to as the image of the product. . . . A definition of a product's position [according to the author] would be the perceived image consumers have of one product in relation to their perceived image of (1) similar products marketed by competing firms, and (2) kindred brands which might be offered by the innovating firm. And profitable positioning is a strategy for creating a unique product image which increases *total* profits.

From John H. Holmes, ''Profitable Product Positioning,'' *MSU Business Topics,* Spring 1973, pp. 27–28. Reprinted by permission of the publisher, Division of Research, Graduate School of Business Administration, Michigan State University.

ignored by the leading sellers. For example, when the market leader captured the *all-day* cold-relief market (Contac), positioning strategy led competition to go after the night time cold-relief market (Ny Quil).

Positioning advocates also recommend that an organization *not* try to compete head to head with established leaders. The idea is to analyze behavioral life-styles or other segmentation figures and "position" your product where others have not.[14] If one company has the market for deodorant soaps, competition might seek the market for soaps with beauty cream. If one firm has the market for the heavy beer drinker, another could go after the occasional drinker or the diet-conscious drinker, and so forth.

Positioning Strategy   Market segmentation is linked with product positioning when the seller tries to design a product that best fits the needs of a selected market segment. Here are steps to follow in developing a positioning strategy:

1. Determine the wants and needs of selected market segments.
2. Analyze the benefits of your product offer compared to those offered by other organizations serving those market segments.
3. Determine which benefits are most important to the markets desired and which are least important.
4. Study what benefits are being offered by competing organizations and how the market views the total offer.
5. Adjust your product offer so that the groups of benefits you offer better meet the needs of a particular market segment.
6. Promote your product to create the image that you want the market to see and understand.   *Product Positioning*

Anheuser-Busch, for example, has three distinctive beer brands positioned to fit three different market segments. Michelob is positioned as a super-premium beer, Budweiser as a premium beer, and Busch as a popular brand.[15] The company differentiates the three beers by price and taste so that sales do not cut into one another, and there are three distinct market positions. Positioning strategies involve the advertising too. Budweiser stresses fun, fellowship, and quality and is advertised during football and hockey games. Busch emphasizes quality and price during baseball games. Michelob, on the other hand, is for the "snooty" set and stresses quality and social suitability during "country club" sports.[16]

---

[14] See, for example, Lewis Alpert and Ronald Gatly, "Product Positioning by Behavioral Life-Styles," *Journal of Marketing*, April 1969, pp. 65–69.
[15] "Three Marketing Elements Combine to Make and Sell Three Distinctive Beers," *Marketing News*, September 26, 1975, p. 9.
[16] Ibid.

Positioning and Social Accountability

We hear a good deal currently about positioning products. I suggest that products will also be positioned for social accountability. Johnson and Johnson, in its new marketing strategy, plans a program designed to locate areas of greatest consumer dissatisfaction with all of the company's consumer products. That's a splendid example of using a social audit to achieve improved service to the public—and improved profit performance.

From E. B. Weiss, "Advertising Meets Its Era of Social Accountability," *Advertising Age*, October 23, 1972, p. 78.

Profitable Positioning The Anheuser-Busch example shows how one company can position three very similar products so that an increase in sales of one brand does not harm the sales of the company's other brands. Such a strategy is called **profitable positioning** and means that the program is designed to increase profits, not just sales. That is, the sales of one company brand will not cut into the sales of other company brands.

Companies must establish a positioning strategy whenever they introduce a new brand. Coca Cola, for example, wanted a product to meet the needs of a diet-conscious market. Rather than introduce "Diet Coke," which might have hurt the sales of Coke, the company introduced Tab as

Questions to Ask before Positioning a Product

Positioning starts with the product. What does it do? How is it perceived? Does it attack competitive market shares by doing the same thing, only better, or does it open up a totally new field and thereby additional buyers? What are, and who are, its potential customers?

How will the product be used? When? Where? By whom? What are the consumers' acknowledged feelings about the product and its use? What are their hidden, or subconscious, attitudes in that field of use?

Are these same feelings universally present and fairly uniform for your product's entire consumer population? Or do they shift and vary by region? By income? By educational level? By ethnic origin?

Here's what we do with the answers to all these questions: We develop a concise, detailed product profile, . . . a product character that will serve to guide us in positioning it. Thus, positioning is a precise description of the product's actual and perceived attributes, of the way it responds to consumer needs, . . . and most important, of the strategy that will differentiate it from competition and position it within the competitive market environment.

From Robert Lee Dickens, "How Creative Packaging Can Help You Position Your Product," *Advertising Age*, September 1, 1975, p. 28.

a new brand.[17] Later the company added Fresca to capture the part of the diet segment that was more interested in fruity tastes. The sales of Coke, Tab, and Fresca all add to profits without seriously affecting the sales of one another.

Companies also *reposition* their products to gain higher profits. One pet-food company had a brand that was priced about the same as three other brands. Several lower-priced and several higher-priced brands also were on the market. The company found that the consumer was very concerned about convenience.[18] All it took to make the product more convenient was a packaging change, and sales rose dramatically as promotion stressed the convenience of the new package. The company was able to increase its profits without any drastic change in the product through an effective repositioning strategy. This example shows that positioning may involve any of a number of product changes, including packaging, branding, and pricing.

Positioning and Product Differentiation To fully understand positioning strategies within an organization, you will have to learn more about how to analyze and design promotable products. We shall discuss this topic in detail in Chapter 8. It is important at this point that you recognize the interrelationships among market analysis, market segmentation, product differentiation, and product positioning. Therefore let's briefly review some concepts that will tie together these terms:

› **Market analysis is the function that enables buyers and sellers to learn about the supply of, and demand for, products. The seller uses *marketing research* and the buyer uses *shopping* in the process of market analysis.**

› **Market segmentation narrows the market to those persons most likely to be satisfied through an exchange; segmentation is carried out by both the buyer and seller.**

› **Product differentiation is the function that adjusts the product offers of the buyer and seller so that an exchange can take place. It usually takes place after market segmentation.**

› **Product positioning is a managerial strategy that uses the information gathered through research and segmentation studies to create an image for the product that makes it desirable to the target market or markets. It is one strategy within the product-differentiation function.**

Later we shall discuss how marketing research is conducted and how to design promotable products effectively. The center of all this attention is the *market*. In the following chapter, you will learn more about the size and nature of world and national markets.

[17] John H. Holmes, "Profitable Product Positioning," *MSU Business Topics,* Spring 1973, pp. 27–32.

[18] Jack Springer, "1975: Bad Year for New Products, Good Year for Segmentation," *Advertising Age,* February 10, 1975, pp. 38–40.

FOR REVIEW

Key Terms

Among the more important terms and expressions discussed in this chapter are the following:

Benefit segmentation involves dividing a market into subgroups based on the benefits users seek from a product.

Demographic segmentation involves dividing a market into subgroups based on objective factors such as age, sex, education, and so forth.

Differentiated marketing refers to the marketing of several versions of a product; each of which is designed to suit a particular market.

Geographic segmentation involves dividing a market into subgroups based on geographic boundaries.

A **market** is a particular group of people and/or organizations that have wants and needs that may be partially satisfied through a marketing exchange.

Market definition is the comprehensive study of the market and market characteristics.

Market segmentation is the process of dividing the total population (market) into several submarkets or segments that tend to have similar characteristics.

Primary demand indicates the total marketing potential for a particular category of product.

Product positioning is the process of using data on characteristics of a target market to design products and promotional strategies that will capture an acceptable market share.

Profitable positioning is a strategy designed to increase profits, not just sales.

Psychographic segmentation involves dividing a market into subgroups based on subjective factors, such as the interests, values, attitudes, and other personal characteristics of the potential market.

Selective demand indicates the total marketing potential for a specific organization's brand within a wider category of product.

Situational segmentation involves dividing a market into subgroups based on the economic, social, and political environment (situation) in which the marketing will take place.

A **target market** is a particular market segment chosen to be served by a particular organization.

Undifferentiated marketing is the marketing of a single product to the mass market rather than to segmented markets.

Usage segmentation involves dividing a market into subgroups based on the use (heavy or light) or nonuse of a product.

Key Concepts

Among the more important marketing concepts introduced in this chapter are the following:

› Market segmentation is a universal marketing function that enables buyers and sellers to concentrate their efforts on people who are most likely to participate in a mutually satisfying exchange.

› Market-segmentation strategies and the marketing programs that are developed as a result should be aimed at target markets *and* all other groups that might have an effect on the marketing program.

› People who live in different geographic areas (for example, city versus country) have different wants and needs; therefore, an effective segmentation strategy is to select those geographic areas where the people are most likely to want what you have to offer.

› Demographic market segmentation helps a seller select rather broad classes of people that can be better served because their wants and needs can be more clearly defined and products can be developed to meet them.

› Data that show the interests, values, and other personal information about potential buyers add tremendously to the more general information obtained from demographic research; such facts are gathered through psychographic research.

› Within each broad market segment (such as women), there are many smaller segments (groups) that look for different things in a product; therefore, the market may be divided into smaller segments that put more emphasis on particular benefits such as economy, social appeal, convenience, and durability.

› It is more effective to use several segmentation variables rather than just one; that is, some combination of demographics and psychographics is the most effective.

› There are three criteria for evaluating a segmentation tool: (1) Does the factor separate an identifiable market that can be reached effectively at a minimum cost? (2) Does it help clarify other marketing decisions (for example, promotion)? (3) Will serving the market segment result in a mutually satisfying exchange?

› Product positioning is a managerial strategy that uses the information gathered through research and segmentation studies to create an image for the product that makes it desirable to the target market or markets. It is one strategy within the product-differentiation function.

Discussion Questions

1. It has been said that a new cereal company could never compete against the present companies because a new company could never compete with the advertising of the larger firms. Do you agree? How could a new cereal avoid national competition with established

brands? Clue: How could the company define and segment the market?

2. Discuss the importance of geographic segmentation for the sales of the following products: women's dresses, food, and sports equipment.

3. Explain the difference between an organization's "public" and its "target market" using your local university as an example.

4. Explain how buyers segment the market before shopping for automobiles.

5. There was a discussion of public schools in the chapter and their efforts at market segmentation. Do you feel that schools are now adapting to the future demands for education? What are the trends in birthrates and how will they affect elementary education?

6. How would you segment the market for a new candy bar that was high in nutrition and low in calories? Would you go after one segment or many segments? Why?

7. How has your life-style changed over the last 5 years? How do you think it will change during the next 5 years? How will that affect your purchasing decisions? Discuss.

8. Why would a family want a big car other than for comfort and prestige? Using your answer to this question as a start, show how benefit segmentation can be used in the automobile industry.

9. Give several examples of how your purchase behavior varies from situation to situation; for example, when you are on a vacation versus when you are at home.

10. Discuss how the 80/20 rule applies to class discussion. Can you identify the 20 percent who do 80 percent of the talking? Are you part of the 20 percent or the 80 percent?

CASES

Opening a Children's Bookstore
Segmentation and Positioning Strategies

Sheila Gold worked in the children's section of the library. Parents often complained to her that it was hard to find good children's books at the local stores. Sheila enjoyed helping the parents find the right kind of books for their children and thought that she might enjoy running a children's book store.

Sheila found a place to open a store in a shopping center away from the center of town. She bought children's books for all age groups (young people from age 1 to 10).

After paying the initial costs of opening the store and buying the materials, Sheila had little money left for promotion. She decided to concentrate her promotional efforts on the most receptive market segments.

1. What segmentation strategies would you recommend?
2. How could Sheila position the store to make it more attractive than other book stores?
3. Notice that Sheila did no market research before selecting a site and ordering books. Was this a mistake? Remember she was an experienced librarian.
4. What other "publics" besides parents should Sheila be concerned about?

Conducting an Election Campaign
Reaching All the Publics

Virginia Langley, a 38-year-old mother of three, had been active in political matters most of her adult life. Virginia had helped at the office of her state senator for several election campaigns and had been involved in promoting several bond issues and in defeating others. Virginia has spent her entire life in a growing city of approximately 29,000 people. Her parents were one of the first families to settle in her town, and her brothers and sisters were all well-known citizens.

One day some out-of-town developers proposed to the city council a large high-rise motel complex that could "revitalize the dying downtown area." Virginia realized that such a complex would also ruin the friendly atmosphere of the downtown area, overtax the sewer system, create severe traffic congestion, and violate the city's development plan. Nevertheless, the city council and the mayor were in favor of the proposal. Virginia and her friends mobilized to put the matter to a vote. She succeeded in her efforts, and the motel-complex issue was defeated.

Virginia decided that she had had enough headaches from city council and the mayor. She decided to run for mayor herself and support a full slate of new council members. But Virginia was forced to run against Mayor Peterson, a man who had been in office for 12 years and who was rather popular among voters.

Virginia had very little money to support her election campaign. Nevertheless, she hoped to appeal to a broad segment of the population, especially those people who had opposed the new motel complex.

Her opponent had good financial backing and was running on his record. He had instituted many popular programs in the city, but he did have a reputation for being in favor of rather questionable zoning changes.

1. What kind of segmentation strategy or strategies would you recommend for Virginia?
2. Virginia was positioning herself as an anti-motel-complex candidate and a hard-liner on zoning. Would you recommend this strategy?
3. What "publics" will Virginia have to appeal to if she is elected?

National and International Markets

exploring different markets

LEARNING GOALS After you have read and studied this chapter, you should be able to:

1. Explain what population shifts are occurring in the United States and how such shifts will affect governmental and business organizations.

2. Identify changes in the labor market and their effect on the career choices of today's college students.

3. Describe some of the changes occuring in the role of women in society and the implications for marketing.

4. Show your understanding of the changing age distribution of the population by identifying those products or services that might be expected to have increased markets and those that might have decreased markets.

5. Give a good explanation of why marketers feel that the standard of living in the United States today is much higher than it was 20 years ago.

6. Contrast the industrial market with the consumer market in the United States.

7. Explain how the farm market is expanding even though the number of farms is declining.

8. Explain why a wealthy nation like the United States should trade with the less developed nations of the world.

9. Define the following terms: the Sunbelt; the industrial belt; input-output analysis; personal income; disposable income; the industrial market; international marketing; theory of competitive advantage; multinational corporation; the service sector.

10. Discuss future career possibilities in organizations serving the following markets: consumers; industry; the government; farmers; and foreign countries.

> *A market is an exchange relationship among buyers and sellers. Whether we think of the traditional marketplace for local fresh produce and handicrafts, or the market for consumer goods in a metropolitan area, or the national and international market for steel, chemicals, or industrial equipment, the essential nature of a market remains the same.*
>
> Lee E. Preston*

INTRODUCTION Because all of us are consumers, we have a special interest in the consumer market and the changes that are taking place in it. This chapter will look at the consumer market and some of its characteristics including size, geographic mobility, occupational shifts, age distribution, income distribution, and the changing role of women.

We shall also look at nonconsumer markets because these markets as a whole are larger than the consumer market, and they offer good career possibilities. We shall briefly explore the industrial market, the farm market, and the government market to give you an idea of the differences among these markets and consumer markets. This discussion will show that the concept of "find a need and feel it" does not apply only to consumers. Farmers, businesses, government agencies, and other organizations also have needs that must be met by the marketing system. (Remember that in Chapter 4 we defined a market as a particular group of people *and/or organizations* that have wants and needs that may be partially satisfied through marketing exchanges.)

The nations of the world have become so interdependent that one should not discuss national markets without looking at international markets as well, for national markets are greatly affected by world conditions. We shall end this chapter, therefore, by looking at international marketing exchanges, including the role of multinational corporations. We shall begin our analysis of markets by looking at the one you are most familiar with: the consumer market.

THE CONSUMER MARKET The population of the United States is approaching 220 million people, more than double the population in 1910. The *rate* of growth in the United States has slowed in recent years, but there is still a large overall increase in the total number of people every year. Many young people are just now reaching the family-starting age, and there may be a new spurt in population growth if these people decide to have average-sized families (see Figure 5.1). But even if population growth in the United States were to level off, the increase in world population would still have a tremendous effect. For example, marketers might shift much of their sales effort to the expanding nations of the world. Or many of the world's resources may be shifted to less developed countries, leaving the United States short of the materials it needs for continued growth.

* *Markets and Marketing: An Orientation* (Glenview, Ill.: Scott, Foresman and Company, 1970), p. 1.

Figure 5.1 PROJECTIONS OF U.S. POPULATION GROWTH BASED ON 2-CHILD OR 3-CHILD FAMILY

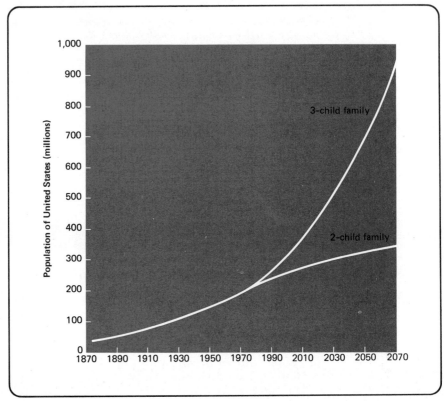

Redrawn from Carl P. Swanson, *The Natural History of Man* (Englewood Cliffs, N.J.: Prentice-Hall, Inc., 1973), p. 346.

In the following sections, we shall explore some of the trends in U.S. consumer markets. First, we shall explore *where* the people are and where they are going. Then we shall discuss *what* they are doing and the changing role of women in the job market. Then we shall look at other characteristics of the market such as age and income.

Population Shifts in the United States It is interesting and instructive to study geographic differences in markets within the United States. The number of people living in different areas of the country varies greatly, and there is a constant movement of people from one area to another. One very useful source of population data is *Sales & Marketing Management's* (SMM) 5-year projection of 300 metropolitan markets. This magazine supplement has data on population, households, effective buying income (EBI),[1] effective buying income per household, retail sales, and buying power indexes for all 300

[1] Effective buying income equals personal income less personal taxes and nontax payments (fines, fees, penalties), as well as personal contributions for social insurance.

areas. These data give marketing managers much of the information they need to plan personnel needs (for example, number of salespersons per geographic area) and allocation of resources (for example, which territories should be given special attention).

A brief glance at SMM's 5-year projections reveals that the Rocky Mountain states will experience the fastest growth in the 1975–1980 period with a 9.6 percent increase in population (see Table 5.1; for a map of the regions, see Figure 4.1). But the Rocky Mountain states have relatively small populations, and so an increase is less significant here than are similar increases elsewhere. For example, the real growth in numbers will be in the Southeast (9.4 percent gain), the Southwest (9.1 percent gain), and the Far West (7.2 percent gain). It should be noted that the gains in these areas (sometimes known as the Sunbelt) follow similar gains in the previous 5-year period. It is significant that Jimmy Carter won the presidency of the United States in 1976 as a result of carrying the South. This indicates that the South is becoming stronger politically and economically as its population increases dramatically:

In sharp contrast to those growth rates [in the Sunbelt], the other parts of the country will lag behind. The farm states of the Plains region are expected to increase their population 2.3% and the Great

Table 5.1 REGIONAL GROWTH'S CONTINUING IMBALANCE

Region[a]	Projected 1980 total population (1,000)	Percent change 1975–1980	Projected 1980 metro population (1,000)	Percent change 1975–1980	Projected 1980 EBI per household	Percent change 1975–1980
New England	12,316.8	+0.8	10,340.7	+0.2	$20,092	+26.4
Middle Atlantic	42,802.5	−0.1	37,467.6	−1.0	20,488	+26.9
Great Lakes	41,540.1	+1.1	32,882.0	+0.3	20,945	+32.1
Plains	17,267.6	+2.3	8,962.9	+0.7	19,913	+40.7
Southeast	51,652.5	+9.4	31,523.9	+8.1	17,919	+37.9
Southwest	20,274.5	+9.1	14,850.1	+9.8	18,027	+33.9
Rocky Mountain	6,303.3	+9.6	3,878.0	+8.5	19,826	+42.4
Far West	31,081.4	+7.2	26,984.2	+6.6	19,100	+25.6
United States	**223,238.7**	**+4.1**	**166,889.4**	**+3.4**	**$19,437**	**+31.4**

[a]**New England**—Conn., Me., Mass., N.H., R.I., Vt. **Middle Atlantic**—Del., D.C., Md., N.J., N.Y., Pa. **Great Lakes**—Ill., Ind., Mich., Ohio, Wis. **Plains**—Iowa, Kan., Minn., Mo., Neb., N.D., S.D. **Southeast**—Ala., Ark., Fla., Ga., Ky., La., Miss., N.C., S.C., Tenn., Va., W.Va. **Southwest**—Ariz., N.M., Okla., Texas. **Rocky Mountain**—Colo., Idaho, Mont., Utah, Wyo. **Far West**—Alaska, Cal., Hawaii, Nev., Ore., Wash.

Reprinted by permission from *Sales & Marketing Management's 1976 Survey of Buying Power—Part II, Sales & Marketing Management*, October 25, 1976, p. 8. Copyright 1976.

Lakes region, 1.1%. The northeast section will remain a stagnant pocket, the New England area scratching out a minuscule 0.8% gain, the Middle Atlantic Area suffering a 0.1% decline.[2]

The Southeast is expected to have a 4.4 million increase in population and the Southwest, 1.7 million. What all these figures mean is that there is a strong shift in population away from the industrial belt (Massachusetts, New York, Pennsylvania, Ohio, Michigan, Illinois, and Indiana) toward the Sunbelt (Florida, Alabama, Mississippi, Louisiana, Texas, New Mexico, Arizona, and California) (see Figure 5.2). If the projections are accurate, the industrial belt's population by 1980 will be only 714,500 more than it was in 1970, whereas the Sunbelt's population will have increased by 10.2 million.[3] Such dramatic differences will change *where* the largest markets are in the United States and *what* they may be buying. It will mean that corporations, government agencies, and most other organizations will have to shift some of their attention and efforts to the Sunbelt. This does not mean that the other regions of the country will receive less attention, but only that the growing regions will need more. Figure 5.2 gives you some idea of where the growth will be. Note that areas like New Jersey, Pennsylvania, and Massachusetts may experience *declining* populations.

It is important to recognize that population shifts affect the marketing programs of cities, states, and other governmental units as well as businesses. Population shifts, for example, affect school building programs, welfare loads, unemployment problems, city planning, and other governmental decisions. Businesses also need to plan where to locate warehouses, where to assign sales territories, how to measure sales potential in a given area, and other such marketing decisions. The concepts are:

› All marketers are affected by population shifts within and among various states and countries.

› Population projections that are available from governmental and private sources should be carefully studied when marketing plans are being made.

Occupational Shifts You can get some idea of how rapidly markets change by looking at the trends in farming over a 50-year period. In 1920, about one out of every three people were living on a farm. By 1945, less than one out of five were on farms, and, by 1970, the number had lowered to less than one out of twenty. This means that fewer and fewer people are supplying the food needs of more and more people. The amount of food produced per farmer (productivity) has greatly increased over these years, but there is some question whether farm production can keep up with population growth in the future.

[2] *Sales & Marketing Management—1976 Survey of Buying Power*, October 25, 1976, p. 8.
[3] Ibid., p. 16.

Figure 5.2 GROWTH RATES OF THE STATES

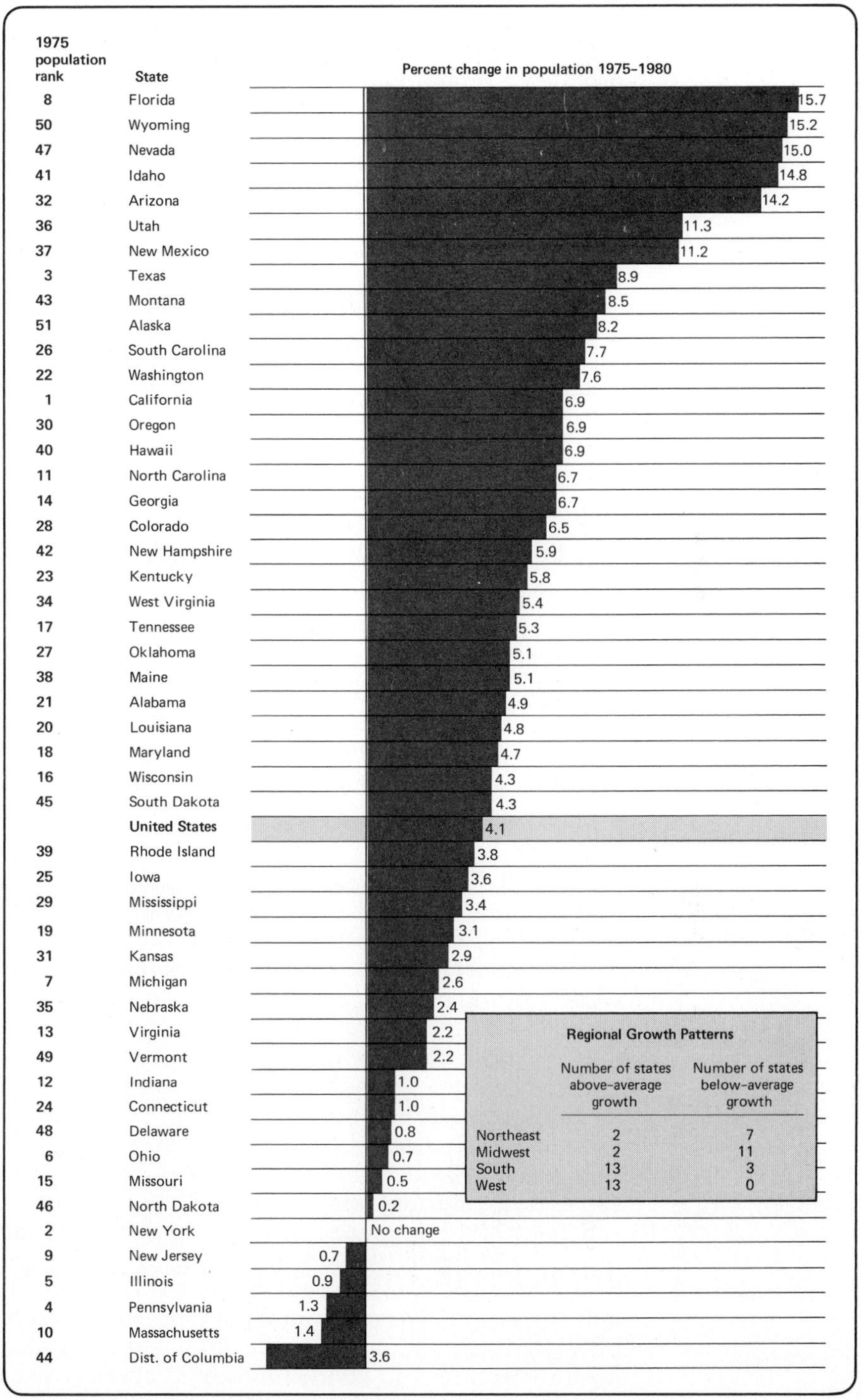

1975 population rank	State	Percent change in population 1975-1980
8	Florida	15.7
50	Wyoming	15.2
47	Nevada	15.0
41	Idaho	14.8
32	Arizona	14.2
36	Utah	11.3
37	New Mexico	11.2
3	Texas	8.9
43	Montana	8.5
51	Alaska	8.2
26	South Carolina	7.7
22	Washington	7.6
1	California	6.9
30	Oregon	6.9
40	Hawaii	6.9
11	North Carolina	6.7
14	Georgia	6.7
28	Colorado	6.5
42	New Hampshire	5.9
23	Kentucky	5.8
34	West Virginia	5.4
17	Tennessee	5.3
27	Oklahoma	5.1
38	Maine	5.1
21	Alabama	4.9
20	Louisiana	4.8
18	Maryland	4.7
16	Wisconsin	4.3
45	South Dakota	4.3
	United States	4.1
39	Rhode Island	3.8
25	Iowa	3.6
29	Mississippi	3.4
19	Minnesota	3.1
31	Kansas	2.9
7	Michigan	2.6
35	Nebraska	2.4
13	Virginia	2.2
49	Vermont	2.2
12	Indiana	1.0
24	Connecticut	1.0
48	Delaware	0.8
6	Ohio	0.7
15	Missouri	0.5
46	North Dakota	0.2
2	New York	No change
9	New Jersey	0.7
5	Illinois	0.9
4	Pennsylvania	1.3
10	Massachusetts	1.4
44	Dist. of Columbia	3.6

Regional Growth Patterns

	Number of states above-average growth	Number of states below-average growth
Northeast	2	7
Midwest	2	11
South	13	3
West	13	0

Reprinted by permission from *Sales & Marketing Management's 1976 Survey of Buying Power—Part II, Sales & Marketing Management.* October 25, 1976, p. 9. Copyright 1976.

There is a similar but not so drastic movement away from goods-producing (manufacturing) industries to service industries such as the arts, finance, government, insurance, real estate, transportation, and utilities. Around 1900, seven out of ten persons in the United States were producing goods. By 1980, it is estimated that only three out of ten will be producing goods; the rest will be in the service industries. Chances are good, therefore, that your future career will be in a service industry rather than in manufacturing. Today about one-third of those in the service sector work for nonprofit organizations. One of the largest service sectors, and a growing one still, is the government.

The shift away from goods-producing industries toward service industries means that the markets for health care, education, recreation, travel, entertainment, and other services will experience continued growth. Marketers must learn how to better analyze and satisfy these markets. This may mean less emphasis on traditional marketing areas such as transportation (physical distribution) and storage and more emphasis on such marketing functions as communication, market segmentation, and product differentiation. The concepts are:

> Some marketing emphasis in the future will shift from the promotion of manufactured goods to the promotion of services, including government services.

> The shift in consumer demand from the goods sector to the service sector will affect employment possibilities for all people and has special impact on students of marketing; more jobs will be available in the government and in service industries than in the manufacturing industries.

The Changing Role of Women   In the United States today, more and more women are opting for careers outside the home (see Figure 5.3). About half the labor force (those 16 years of age and older) are women. Married women as well as single women have chosen to follow careers (44.4 percent of married women were working in 1975), and this leads to all kinds of marketing implications.[4]

First of all, there is an increased demand for labor-saving devices around the home as men and women find less time for housework. This expands the market for products such as microwave ovens, dishwashers, and automatic washers and dryers. It also opens up new service markets such as child care, baby-sitting, carpet cleaning and general household assistance, catering, and other work-saving services.

Second, the presence of a second family income adds greatly to overall income and leads to such marketing opportunities as (1) more meals away from home, (2) more recreational demand, (3) more money available for all goods, services, and government programs, and (4) a different life-style from the past. Families today are less likely to eat their meals together at home, to divide household chores by sex (for example, men

[4] See "Working Wives Becoming Major Marketing Force," *Advertising Age* (April 5, 1976), p. 34.

Figure 5.3 WOMEN IN THE U.S. LABOR FORCE, 1940–1975

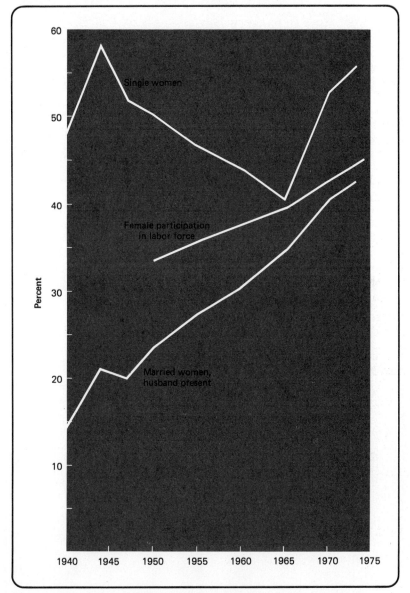

Based on figures in *Statistical Abstract of the United States, 1974*, pp. 336, 341.

are more likely to do some cooking, cleaning, baby-sitting, and other household chores), or to concentrate on the career of the man (families often move, for example, because of new career opportunities for the woman).

But the changing role of women goes way beyond careers and household chores. Women are also becoming more active in consumerism, environmental causes, politics, religion (for example, women ministers), and all other aspects of society. One marketing task for groups such as the National Organization for Women (NOW) is to alter the traditional attitudes and practices of all segments of society toward women. As the roles of women and the attitudes toward women change, the market for goods, services, and ideas also changes.

More women, for example, are enrolling in graduate schools, professional schools, and other adult-education programs. Women are also becoming more involved in sports—both as spectators and participants. Women's tennis, for example, has experienced explosive growth. The marketers of educational and sports programs must take account of these changes if they wish to satisfy these new markets. The concept is:

> ◗ The changing role of women in society is affecting all areas of marketing by opening up entire new markets in the service sector, by increasing overall family incomes, and by involving more women in all phases of society, including religion, government, politics, and sports.

Figure 5.4 HOW THE AGE MIX WILL CHANGE, 1975–1990

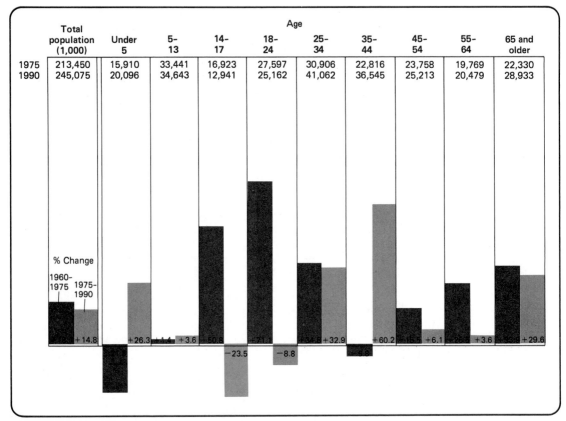

	Total population (1,000)	Under 5	5–13	14–17	18–24	25–34	35–44	45–54	55–64	65 and older
1975	213,450	15,910	33,441	16,923	27,597	30,906	22,816	23,758	19,769	22,330
1990	245,075	20,096	34,643	12,941	25,162	41,062	36,545	25,213	20,479	28,933

Age Marketers in the United States have concentrated on the youth market
Distribution for many years—and with good reason. The market was huge because of
of the Market the baby boom after World War II, and young people set the trends in
such areas as fashions, movies, music, and attitudes toward sex. But
yesterday's teenagers are tomorrow's young adults, and this growing-up
process has serious consequences for marketers (see Figure 5.4 and the
insert "Dramatic Shifts Coming in Age Groups").

Dramatic Shifts Coming in Age Groups

Exit the Pepsi generation. It's becoming the Budweiser gang.

That's the demographic shape of tomorrow's markets, as indicated by
the Census Bureau's newest set of population projections. Although total
population growth is expected to continue at a slower pace, averaging
0.9% in the 1975–90 period vs. 1.1% in the 1960–75 period, the actual
increase in numbers of people will be considerable. The projected 1990
population, at 245.1 million, is 31.6 million more than the current level, a
numerical gain equivalent to the aggregate populace of the five biggest
metropolitan markets—New York, Chicago, Los Angeles-Long Beach,
Philadelphia, and Detroit.

What's important to marketers, however, is the striking change in the age
profile that will take place as a result of the plummeting birth rates of the
past several years. The youthquake of 1960–75, when the 14–17 and 18–24
year olds increased at phenomenal rates, will be replaced by a middle-
aged tempo in 1975–90 as the 35–44 and 25–34 year olds, in that order, set
the pace. And the "Don't trust anyone over 30" rebel cry of the 1960s will
be muted as the median age of the population rises from today's 28.8 to
32.3 by 1990.

Marketers who focus on particular age groups will have to reset their
sights. For example, those who cater to the high school crowd will see
their prospects dwindle by more than 20%, whereas those who sell to the
more sedate (but prosperous) 35–44 year olds will see their prospects
increase by 60%.

One especially encouraging factor is that household heads who fall into
tomorrow's two fastest-growing age groups account for over 40% of U.S.
household money income. Thus despite all the talk about the new
Spartan lifestyles, this trend may keep personal consumption expenditures rising at a brisk clip in the next 15 years.

Reprinted by permission from *Sales & Marketing Management* magazine,
December 8, 1975. Copyright 1975.

Soon those in the 25–34 age groups will head 26 percent *of all families*.
This means a growing market for family items such as clothing, food,
and housing (apartments too). It also means a demand for related items
such as carpeting, drapes, furniture, bedding, appliances, and other
household items. There may be a renewed interest in child rearing, and
that would set off a new explosion in population. There is no doubt that
young families will be a huge market in the near future.

The danger of concentrating on this highly visible, growing market segment is that marketers may ignore the even larger older market. Grey Advertising recently reminded the readers of *Grey Matter* that: "Consumers under 35 years of age are at the head of 20 million units—families plus unrelated individuals. In contrast, persons 55 years or older are heads of 25 million units." They go on to say that "earnings of families and individuals aged over 55 years added up to 200 billion dollars . . . about 15% more than the under 35 group."[5] The concept to keep in mind is:

> **The market may be divided into various age groups and analyzed accordingly. One should be careful to study shifts in age patterns so as not to miss significant trends.**

In the United States, for example, the market of those people over 55 years of age is big and getting bigger. People are living longer than ever before, and many have high incomes. In 1972, people under 35 accounted for 16 percent of those earning $15,000 or more, but people over 55 accounted for 25 percent of that income bracket.[6]

Older people are interested in travel, recreation, and other services to improve their quality of life. Health care is important to them, and so there is much interest in special foods, drugs, and related health-care items. But older people are also interested in much the same things as younger groups. They like to shop, to wear good clothes, to go to movies, and so forth. The problem has been that society is so youth-oriented that there have been limited opportunities for older people to buy the kind of clothes they prefer (trend-setting, youth-oriented fashions are not their style), to attend "good" movies (too much sex and violence), or to find a comfortable place in society (they were often ignored, retired too early, and forgotten even by their families).

A marketer would be wise to keep a close watch on population and age patterns. Of course not everyone is simply either young or old, for there is a whole range of age groups. Each group has its own characteristics and special wants and needs. Because some of these segments are being ignored by the majority of sellers, they represent a vast, untapped market for aware new marketers. The concepts are:

> **Shifts in the age distribution of the population will have a tremendous impact on marketing in the near future: a decline in the youth segment will affect school systems, clothing manufacturers, and the whole entertainment industry; an increase in the segment of people starting new families will expand markets for housing, travel, and recreation; and an increase in older people will strain the social security system, create a demand for senior-citizen housing, and create vast new markets for leisure industries.**

> **Shifts in age distribution will cause shifts in income distribution and create new opportunities for some marketers and new problems for others.**

[5] *Grey Matter*, May 1973.
[6] Ibid.

Income All social organizations must recognize age groups *and* the distribution
Distribution of wealth and income among them. The government has some control
over the distribution of wealth and income through its system of taxation
and social programs. In structuring our system of taxation, the government may have at least two goals: (1) the creation of incentives to invest
and to produce what is needed and (2) the establishment of a society in
which everyone has an equal chance for happiness, success, and self-
fulfillment.

Businesses are especially concerned with the distribution of wealth
and income because it helps determine which markets have the most
potential. Of some concern is **personal income**, which is the money
received from wages, interest, dividends, and the like. But of more
concern is **disposable income**, which is the amount of money left after
taxes and other such payments, or the amount of money individuals can
spend on their own wants and needs.

Over the last 25 years, both personal income and disposable income
have risen (see Table 5.2). For most people, this means that they are able
to enjoy a better standard of living. For example, people today have
many products, including cars, television sets, dishwashers, refrigerators,
and automatic washers and dryers, that were considered luxuries only a
generation ago. In fact, in the United States most people have such ready

Table 5.2 PERSONAL AND DISPOSABLE INCOME, 1950–1974

Year	Personal income ($ billions)		Disposable income ($ billions)	
	Current dollars	1974 dollars	Current dollars	1974 dollars
1950	227.6	446.3	206.9	405.6
1955	310.9	544.5	275.3	482.1
1956	333.0	571.2	293.2	502.6
1957	351.1	584.2	308.5	513.2
1958	361.2	587.3	318.8	518.0
1959	383.5	615.6	337.3	541.1
1960	401.0	633.5	350.0	552.8
1961	416.8	652.3	364.4	569.9
1962	442.6	685.1	385.3	596.9
1963	465.5	712.9	404.6	619.6
1964	497.5	752.6	438.1	662.8
1965	538.9	804.3	473.2	706.9
1966	587.2	856.0	511.9	745.7
1967	629.3	893.9	546.3	775.9
1968	688.9	945.0	591.0	810.9
1969	750.9	988.0	634.4	834.6
1970	808.3	1,015.5	691.7	869.0
1971	864.0	1,044.7	746.4	902.5
1972	944.9	1,111.7	802.5	943.3
1973	1,055.0	1,174.8	903.7	1,006.8
1974	1,150.5	1,150.5	979.7	979.7

From Helen Axel, ed., *A Guide to Consumer Markets 1975/1976* (New York: The Conference
Board, 1975), p. 116.

access to what they need in the way of *goods* that they are shifting their spending to the **service sector,** where they seek satisfaction from travel, recreation, better health care, education, and more time for the arts and culture.

In spite of the generally satisfactory life-style of most of the people in the United States, there is still much poverty and hunger. And many of the nations of the world are far behind our standard of living. Marketing can do much to raise the standard of living of all people by promoting better health, nutritional knowledge, and education, and by setting up better systems for producing and distributing the products people want and need. It will take even more marketing expertise in the future to sell the need for planned population growth and more productivity to raise everyone's standard of living.

 Monitoring income and wealth changes throughout the United States and the world is an important marketing function. Figure 5.5 shows the revolution in the distribution of income in the United States since 1930 and projects the redistribution to 1980. This type of broad social change obviously has an enormous effect on all aspects of the marketing of goods and services. Presently, some nations are experiencing unexpected wealth because they own huge reserves of oil. Other nations are discovering similar natural resources (including labor) and are improving their citizens' lives. In the United States, our life-styles may become more rertricted as our money is used to purchase more expensive raw materials such as oil and precious metals. All of these changes will have tremendous impact on markets and marketing in the future.

Figure 5.5 REDISTRIBUTION OF INCOME—A REVOLUTION

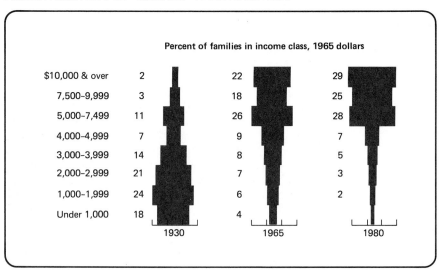

THE
INDUSTRIAL
MARKET
Most people tend to think of marketing as an exchange between consumers and manufacturers or retailers. But there is a vast nonconsumer market that is even more important to some marketers. Attempts to establish exchange relationships in the nonconsumer area are known as **industrial marketing.** Industrial marketing does not include those sales made to middlemen (wholesalers and retailers) who intend to sell products *in the same form* in which they were purchased. The concept is:

> **All products bought for industrial or business use are industrial products, and the marketing of them constitutes industrial marketing.**[7]

"The task of industrial marketing involves about one-half of the output of manufacturing industries, practically all of the production of the nonfarm extractive industries, about four-fifths of agricultural production, some one-half of the goods imported from other countries, and all industrial and business service."[8] As you can see, industrial marketing is a tremendously important aspect of the total marketing system. You can get a better feel for this market by looking at this sample list of business buyers or "industries":

1. Agriculture, forestry, and fisheries
2. Banking, finance, and insurance
3. Communications
4. Construction
5. Government
6. Manufacturing
7. Mining
8. Public utility
9. Service
10. Transportation

Note that industrial buyers include the government, farmers, public utilities, insurance agencies, and other organizations that are not always thought of as part of industry. Some of the major purchases such organizations make include: raw materials such as iron ore and agricultural products; semimanufactured goods such as sheet metal; parts, such as the frame for an automobile; machinery (for example, an automatic screw machine); equipment (for example, fixtures); supplies (for example, stationery); and business services of all kinds.

[7] This definition is from Theodore N. Beckman, William R. Davidson, and W. Wayne Talarzyk, *Marketing,* 9th ed. (New York: The Ronald Press Company, 1973), p. 152.
[8] Ibid.

Characteristics of the Industrial Market Establishing mutually satisfying exchanges in the industrial market is similar to what occurs in consumer marketing, but there are important differences. Some characteristics of industrial markets are:

1. The market for industrial goods is a *derived* demand; that is, the demand for consumer products such as automobiles creates the demand for industrial goods and services including tires, batteries, glass, metal, plastics, and engines.
2. The demand for industrial goods is relatively inelastic; that is, the demand does not always change significantly with minor changes in price. The reason for this is that industrial products are made up of so many parts that a price increase for one part is not usually a significant problem.
3. The number of customers in the industrial market is relatively few; that is, there are just a few construction firms or mining operations compared to the consumer market of 70 million or so households.
4. The size of industrial customers is relatively large; that is, a few large organizations account for most of the employment and production of various goods and services.
5. Industrial markets tend to be concentrated; for example, oil fields tend to be concentrated in the Southwest and Alaska. Consequently marketing efforts often may be concentrated on a particular geographic area, and distribution problems are often minimized by locating warehouses near industrial "centers."
6. Industrial buyers generally are more rational in their selection of goods and services; they use specifications and carefully weigh the "total product offer" including quality, price, and service.
7. Industrial sales tend to be direct. Manufacturers will sell products such as tires directly to automobile manufacturers, but would tend to use wholesalers and retailers to sell to consumers.

Sources of Information on Industrial Marketing You can find helpful data about industrial markets in the government-produced *Census of Manufacturers*. There you will find the number of establishments in various industrial classifications broken down by geographic location. You will also find listed the major types of materials used in these industries. But such data are very general and can only give you a feel for the more detailed aspects of these huge markets.

Another helpful information source is the government's Standard Industrial Classification system (SIC), which enables an industrial marketer to identify relatively small elements of the total industrial market.[9] All types of businesses are divided into ten groups, and a two-digit code number is assigned to each. These ten groups are further

[9] For a thorough presentation of the SIC system and a list of all SIC classifications, see *Standard Industrial Classification Manual* (Washington, D.C.: Government Printing Office, 1972). See also John Revett, "SIC Offers Helpful Answers to Marketer's Big Questions," *Advertising Age*, July 14, 1975, p. 81.

divided into smaller segments, so that marketers can get a good idea of the total industrial market and its key components.

You can learn something about the interrelationships between various industrial organizations and their suppliers by looking at the input-output tables that are prepared by the Office of Business Economics of the U.S. Department of Commerce. These tables are much more detailed than those mentioned previously (for example, they employ 367 industrial classifications). Using these figures, a marketer can determine where various goods and services are sold (that is, where the output goes) and where the sellers got their input of raw materials, semifinished products, and services. Using these tables you can trace, for example, the effect that a 1-million-unit increase in new-car sales over last year will have on almost all of the industries involved. You would see the effect on frame manufacturers and their suppliers of raw materials. You could also trace the effect on tire manufacturers and their suppliers. The concepts are:

> **Input-output data enable marketers to trace the interindustry exchanges of goods and services that result from a change in the national or international market for consumer goods and services.**

> **The Census of Manufacturers, Standard Industrial Classification data, and other such published information give marketers a rather complete picture of the industrial market, including information such as total number of businesses, their location, employment, and value of their output.**

Of course, you can also find much helpful data about industrial marketing in the textbooks designed for industrial marketing courses. Reading such texts will give you a quick introduction to industrial marketing and an overview of the marketing process within industrial markets.[10]

Careers in Industrial Marketing Some of the most challenging and best-paying marketing careers are in the industrial area. This is especially true of industrial sales. Industrial salespeople have become marketing consultants to their clients and are quite sophisticated marketing experts (see Chapter 14 for details).

Often an industrial sales representative must have an advanced degree such as an MBA (Master of Business Administration). You can learn more about this exciting field by registering for a course in industrial marketing or reading some of the many books in this area. An engineering degree or a similar background plus an MBA is an effective way to get a good job in industrial sales. A course in industrial marketing should reveal whether or not such a career would be what you are looking for.

[10] See, for example, Richard M. Hill, Ralph S. Alexander, and James S. Cross, *Industrial Marketing*, 4th ed. (Homewood, Ill.: Richard D. Irwin, Inc., 1975), or Robert Haas, *Industrial Marketing Management* (New York: Petrocelli/Charter, 1976).

THE GOVERNMENT MARKET

The largest buyer of goods and services in the United States is the government. About (one-third) of the **gross national product** (the total value of the goods and services produced in a given year) is spent by various government units (federal, state, and local).

The government usually buys by establishing specifications for what it wants and requesting bids from various sellers. Often the agency must accept the lowest bid; therefore, the specifications must be very complete and clear or else the merchandise may be inferior, or the services (for example, delivery, installation, or repair) accompanying the sale may be unsatisfactory. Often contract terms have to be changed because the government failed to specify certain needed elements in its request for bids.

Many government needs cannot be met effectively through the bid system, either because there may be few suppliers or because the exact nature of the product may not be clear (for example, a new weapons system or fighter plane must be designed and built). In such cases, the government may negotiate a contract with a major manufacturer. Some contracts are on a "cost-plus" basis (the cost of producing the product *plus* a fair profit). In the past this practice has led to alleged abuses by the contractors. Newspapers are continually reporting cost overruns, questionable contracts, and inferior products that have resulted from government contracts.

The government has set up many checks and balances designed to minimize unsatisfactory or overly expensive purchases, but mistakes happen nonetheless. We cannot begin to describe the elaborate process involved in government buying at federal and state levels. But we would like to point out that this is a very large market that marketers should not ignore. Smaller businesses can get helpful advice on how to bid on government contracts from the Small Business Administration. Larger businesses can also find many books and articles describing procedures for capturing the government market.[11]

THE FARM MARKET

The farm market in the United States is huge and still growing. Fewer and fewer farms are producing more and more food. Today less than a million farms produce nearly 90 percent of the nation's farm output, and it has been predicted that someday a mere 10,000 farm units will control 80 percent of farm output.[12] Total farm assets in 1976 were over $530 billion. That is equal to about three-fifths of all the capital assets of all U.S. manufacturers.

American farms are extremely efficient, partly because of the huge investment farmers make in equipment. On the average, each farm worker in 1976 supplied enough food for fifty-six people. As recently as 1957, each farmer had fed only twenty-three people, and in 1945, only fifteen—an increase of 273 percent in 30 years. It is widely believed that

[11] For example, see Cecil Hynes and Noel Zabriskie, *Marketing to Governments* (Columbus, Ohio: Grid, Inc., 1976).

[12] E. B. Weiss, "When 10,000 Farm Units Control 80% of Farm Output," *Advertising Age*, January 20, 1969, p. 56.

continued increases in farm efficiencies can occur only through increased size of farms. It has been predicted that by 1985, 53 percent fewer dairy producers with 10 percent fewer animals will produce 14 to 20 percent more than is produced today.[13]

What all this means to marketers in general is this: The farm market will continue to be one of the largest single markets in the United States. There are about 4.5 million farm workers who buy much the same household supplies as their urban counterparts.[14] The farmer should no longer be viewed as a small, independent worker who tends to can preserves and generally act like the small farmer in the movies. Rather, most of the farms of the future will be part of huge corporate systems that are made up of highly professional, sophisticated farm managers who are quite willing to spend money for equipment, supplies, and other farm materials, including items for personal use.

Farmers Adopt a Systems Orientation

Like all progressive organizations, farmers have adopted a systems orientation to make them better buyers and sellers (marketers). In the future, more and more farms will be organized as corporations, rather than proprietorships (independent, owner-operated farms), mainly because that will be the only way to obtain the tax benefits and the capital needed for an industrialized facility.[15] The vast majority of farmers already belong to cooperatives. Cooperatives enable farmers to buy needed materials more efficiently, help them to determine what crops to plant and when, and provide them with a more assured market for what they produce. For example, for an annual membership fee, the Central Iowa Farm Management Association provides a computer analysis of a farmer's total operation plus a weekly "grain alert" newsletter.[16] The computer analysis lets farmers know which operations are profitable. For example, one farmer gave up raising chickens when the analysis showed they were a losing investment.

International Harvester dealers are providing a similar service through a farm management program called Pro Ag.[17] Using a computer, the service analyzes variables such as crop choice, acreage utilization, capital investment, and equipment choice. As a result of the computer analysis, one farmer in Indiana put up a grain drying and handling center. Then he bought an additional combine. Later he tested the benefits of a 12-row corn planter over a 6-row planter.

One can see that farmers are not only systematized, but they have also become quite sophisticated in their farm-management programs. (They are also profit-oriented.)

[13] "Agrimarketers Told Farm Market Steady, More Industrialization Seen," *Advertising Age*, May 17, 1976, p. 2.

[14] See "U.S. Farm/Ranch Market: Fewer . . . Larger . . . Richer," *Sponsor*, March 6, 1967, pp. 31–34.

[15] "Agrimarketers Told Farm Market Steady, More Industrialization Seen," p. 2.

[16] See "The New Up Life Down on the Farm," *Newsweek*, May 31, 1976, p. 61.

[17] See "The Corn Is Green, and Farm Equipment Manufacturers Reap a Harvest," *Barron's*, June 7, 1976, p. 5.

Eventually, a systems orientation among farm industries will lead to more huge corporate structures that will manage food production, processing, and distribution (agribusiness). Such corporations will have tremendous buying power and will tend to deal directly with suppliers of farm equipment and other farm needs. Suppliers will adapt to the new, huge agribusinesses by becoming larger and more sophisticated also. Suppliers will establish operations that will provide for the total needs of a farmer including seed, fertilizer, equipment, fuel, computerized management advice, on-site consulting, and credit assistance. One key to the success of future farming is capital. As feed, fertilizer, fuel, equipment, and other necessities become more and more expensive, farmers will have tremendous capital requirements. The farm marketing system, therefore, will include insurance companies, banks, and other investment corporations as part of the total system.

Marketing relationships with farmers will be quite different in the future. The farm market, like the industrial market, will be easily identifiable and will consist largely of a few, huge producers. These producers will be reached mainly through personal selling, but more use will also be made of the various media. More farm magazines are available today than ever before.[18] Furthermore, there are radio stations that concentrate on the farm market.[19] The concepts that relate to the farm market are:

> **The farm industry is the largest cohesive market in the United States.**

[18] See "Farm Advertisers Widen Media; Survey Shows Radio, TV Impact," *Advertising Age*, August 25, 1975, p. 20.
[19] See "Reach-the-Farmer Pays Off," *Sponsor*, March 6, 1967, pp. 44–47.

Marketing Concept Reaches the Farmer

The first requirement of successful agriculture in the future will be to determine the market opportunity before making the crucial production decisions. Traditionally, the situation was reversed; farmers grew what they felt they could grow successfully, then when it was harvested they began to think about marketing it. We still have too many farmers ignoring the important marketing phase of management. More importantly, we have too many farm marketing organizations (both cooperative and proprietary) also ignoring this vital phase of management. . . .

Once the market opportunity has been determined, the successful farm managers of the future will apply the latest technology to produce to the specifications of that market with maximum efficiency. (In other words, farming has been *production*-oriented; it is now becoming *marketing*-oriented.)

From E. B. Weiss, "When 10,000 Farm Units Control 80% of Farm Output," *Advertising Age*, January 20, 1969, p. 56. Copyright 1969 by Crain Communications, Inc.

> Farm markets in the future will be dominated by a relatively small number of large organizations (corporations and cooperatives) that will be highly sophisticated buyers and sellers.

> A systems orientation will make farm marketing more effective and efficient in meeting the needs for food in an expanding world.

Farming and Foreign Trade It is estimated that within 10 years agricultural exports could lead to an $8 billion annual gain in the U.S. balance of payments. After feeding his fellow citizens, the U.S. farmer has left over nearly 60 percent of his wheat and rice, 50 percent of his soybeans, 25 percent of his grain sorghum, and 20 percent of his corn.[20] Much of the world depends upon the U.S. farmer for basic food needs. The United States will continue to supply food to other countries as long as such surplus production is available. One of the major political problems in the future will be establishing policy for the trading of farm commodities in international markets. The next section discusses international markets in more detail.

THE INTERNATIONAL MARKET The U.S. market is affected greatly by the world market, and this means that you are affected as well. When the United States sells wheat, corn, and other food products to other countries, the price you pay for food products may rise because of the reduced domestic supply. The same may be true when the United States *gives* food products free to other countries. On the other hand, when other countries raise the price of oil and other natural resources, the price you pay for gas and other products is greatly affected.

Oil is used to make fertilizer, fertilizer is needed to raise grain, and grain is used to feed cattle. Therefore, when oil prices rise, fertilizer prices rise, grain prices rise, and cattle prices rise. This is just one example of how international exchanges affect the prices we pay. Furthermore, because people need gas in their cars, drivers in the United States may be forced to drive smaller, better-mileage cars when gas prices soar. The concept is this:

> Everyone in the United States is affected by marketing exchanges with other countries in terms of the prices they pay for everyday goods and services.

In the 1970s, the United States went through a period of unexpected inflation and relatively high unemployment. One report attributes 40 percent of U.S. inflation to international events: "About 15 percent of consumer price rises were caused by exchange rate changes" said the report, and "about 25 percent was caused by increases in prices of oil, grains, and other foods, and commodities used as industrial inputs."[21]

[20] Data from an ad by Sperry Rand Corporation, *The Washington Post*, June 3, 1976, p. C 20.

[21] "International Events Caused 40% of U.S. Inflation Woes, Says Reports," *Marketing News*, September 12, 1975, p. 5.

This discussion is not meant to imply that international trade always raises prices. On the contrary, free and open world trade often opens vast new markets for U.S. products, lowers the cost of production, and in the long run has the potential for increasing the welfare of everyone.

All consumers benefit from what the United States is able to import from other countries. Would life be as nice without the coffee, tea, bananas, chocolate, and vanilla that businesses import? Producers could not operate as effectively without imported minerals such as manganese and bauxite. Similarly, other countries would not enjoy as high a standard of living without the food, computers, machinery, and other items they buy from the United States. As Figure 5.6 shows, there has been a dramatic increase in the volume of imports and exports over the past few years. The United States tries to maintain a balance between imports and exports, with emphasis being given to a favorable balance of trade (that is, exports exceed imports). The concept is:

› **International exchanges of goods, services, and cultural events can increase the welfare of all countries that participate.**

Size of the World Market   One of the most significant aspects of world markets is the growing number of people whose wants and needs marketers attempt to fill. A look at population growth figures projected over time will give you an idea of the problem (or the opportunity). From the time humans first appeared on earth until the year 1850, the human race had grown to only a billion people. It took only 75 more years to double that figure. In the next 35 years, another billion were added; and it took about 15 years to add the fourth billion. It has been projected that by 1985 the world population will reach 5 billion people.

Notice how rapidly the world population is increasing. In 1970, for example, over 72 million people were added to the population. That means that as many people as live in all of England and Wales, Scotland, Ireland, Sweden, and Norway are added to the world population every year.[22] It also means that there are that many more people to house, feed, clothe, educate, and assure some satisfactory style of life. The question is, "Do we have the resources and the marketing skills needed to satisfy all of the people of the world?" The answer from some areas

[22] Shirley Foster Hartley, *Population Quantity Vs. Quality* (Englewood Cliffs, N.J.: Prentice-Hall, Inc., 1972), p. 5.

Why International Marketing?

Basically, the reason for marketing internationally is the same as for marketing domestically. Someone has a want or need and someone else has a product or service to satisfy it. The buyer and seller both have opportunities to gain through the exchange.

From Robert J. Holloway and Robert S. Hancock, *Marketing In a Changing Environment* (New York: John Wiley & Sons, Inc., 1968), pp. 422–424.

Figure 5.6 U.S. IMPORTS AND EXPORTS, 1960–1974

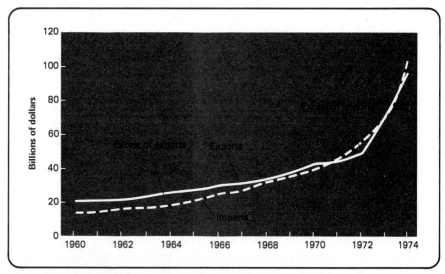

Based on data from U.S. Bureau of the Census.

seems to be "no." There may not be enough food, energy, and other necessary goods and services for all. One of the roles of marketing is to study such problems and develop the means to solve them. Population control may be one way; new food-growing techniques may be another; and a better distribution of wealth may be a third alternative.

By the time today's college students are in their 40s, the world population may be over 6.5 billion people. Because about 37 percent of the world's population is under 15 years of age, the potential for increased births in the future remains high.

People in the United States cannot ignore the explosive growth of world population. All peoples of the world will be competing for the same raw materials, and, if there is not enough to go around, one nation may war with another to correct any imbalances. World hunger is just one among many worldwide problems that no country can ignore without opening itself to possible military threat. Thus, international marketing exchanges will take on new importance in the future. Also, marketing in the United States will change as more and more people compete for fewer available goods and services.

Why Trade with Other Nations? There are several reasons why one country would trade with other countries. First, no country, even a technologically advanced one, can produce all of the products that its people want and need. Second, even if a country could become self-sufficient, other countries would demand trade with that country in order to meet the needs of their people. Third, some countries have an overabundance of natural resources and a lack of technological know-how. Other countries (for example, Japan) have vast technological skills, but few natural resources. Trade relations enable each country to produce what it is most capable of producing and buy what else it needs in a mutually beneficial exchange relationship. By modifying slightly the definition of marketing presented in

"Better let me have another gross of the #101 thunderbird ashtrays, two gross of the #473 beaded souvenir moccasins, and two dozen #87 turquoise and silver runner pins."

Reprinted by permission from *Sales & Marketing Management* magazine, July 7, 1975. Copyright 1975.

Chapter 1, we can come up with a definition of international marketing that explains its rationale. *International marketing is the process in worldwide markets that, subject to constraints, attempts to establish mutually satisfying exchange relationships between countries with diverse wants and needs and other countries that can satisfy those wants and needs.*

Marketing exchanges between and among countries involve more than goods and services. Countries also exchange art, athletes (for international competition and friendly relations), cultural events (plays, dance performances, and so forth), medical advances, space exploration (for example, the USSR–U.S.A. space program), and labor. The guiding principle behind international economic exchanges is the economic theory of competitive advantage. In concept form, this theory is:

> > A country should produce and sell to other countries those products that it produces most effectively and efficiently and should buy from other countries those goods and services it cannot produce as effectively and/or efficiently.

Alternatives to International Marketing Exchanges

There are alternatives to establishing free and open marketing exchanges between and among countries, but none seem too favorable. One alternative is *isolationism.* Under such a plan, a country would try to become self-sufficient and not rely on other countries for what it needs. It is always a good idea to rely on oneself for as much as possible, but such a policy has its dangers. Other countries may demand trade relations or threaten to take what they need by force.

A second kind of trade relationship, therefore, is one determined by force. One country could steal what it wanted or take what it needs through war or corrupt political deals. It would appear that a better solution would be free and open exchange. One executive feels that international marketing exchanges may be a strong force toward world peace:

The wishes of consumers for goods and services, and the desires of businessmen to provide them, must lead to an insistence that governments provide situations encouraging free trade . . . the commitment of international business, of world traders headquartered on all the continents, calls for an open interchange of goods, services, communications, and ideas. Increasingly this will mean a dynamic force toward world peace.[23]

Constraints on International Trade

All marketing exchanges are subject to constraints, but none is as complex as the constraints on international trade. Some of the major constraints are political, economic, technological, and legal. Let's look at how each of these constraints hinders world trade.

First, there is the real problem of different political beliefs. One country might be socialistic and another capitalistic. In order to prove their system is "better," each country may try to keep its products from benefiting the other. In fact, political considerations have caused many countries to establish embargoes (legal constraints) that prevent their companies from trading with other countries.

Second, economic constraints often hinder international trade. For example, some nations are so poor that they have little or nothing with which to trade. Other countries have found that international trade drains them of money they cannot afford to lose from their economy.

Third, technological constraints may make it difficult or impossible to carry on effective trade. For example, some less developed countries

---

[23] J. Paul Austin, "World Marketing as a New Force for Peace," *Journal of Marketing,* January 1966, p. 3.

have such primitive transportation and storage systems that international food exchanges are ineffective because the food is spoiled by the time it reaches those in need.

Each country tries to optimize its own gain through marketing exchanges. To do this, a country might establish import quotas on certain products (that is, specify how much can be bought from other countries) to protect its own producers. Most countries have established various kinds of restrictions, regulations, and restraints on international trade. These constraints are further complicated by the tremendous geographic distances separating some countries. The guiding concepts are:

- There are serious constraints on world trade, including political, economic, technological, and legal constraints. Different monetary systems are also a problem.
- There are tremendous geographic constraints on world trade that make it difficult to exchange some commodities.
- Different religious beliefs have a great effect on what people want in the way of goods and services; these religious beliefs can constrain exchange relations.
- One of the major barriers to open exchange is the wide variety of languages spoken in different countries; communication between and among international marketers is often difficult at best.
- Each country has its own social norms of behavior and life-styles; these differences often cause difficulties in developing and promoting products that would be acceptable in world markets.

International Trade Cooperatives

To strengthen their trading position with other parts of the world, some countries have become partners in a mutually beneficial trade agreement. Several European countries for example have joined together in the European Economic Community (better known as the European "Common Market") to strengthen trade relations among member countries. This alliance also gives these countries more power when dealing with outside nations. Other such trade cooperatives include the European Free Trade Association, the Central American Common Market, and the Latin American Free Trade Association.

Such trade cooperatives are evidence that these countries recognize the benefits of free and open marketing exchanges. The United States also recognizes the benefits of a marketing approach to world relations. For example, the United States has adopted a policy of exchanging goods, services, art, and other products with Russia and China to keep a dialogue going and to minimize world tensions. In fact the word *détente*, which has been used to describe our present relations with Russia and China, comes from the French word *détendre*, which means "to relax."

Multinational Corporations

There has been much discussion recently about the power of multinational corporations. It is helpful to understand just what they are and what they mean for international trade. A **multinational corporation** is a business that, while headquartered in one country, does much of its marketing with other countries, either by itself or in cooperation with businesses in the other countries.

Multinational corporations of the past and of today have been formed to expand world markets, to take advantage of lower wage rates in other countries, and generally to improve profits for the company. Today's multinationals also have become a symbol of world trade, in that they demonstrate that there can be international cooperation and trade on a coordinated, integrated basis. "The social and economic benefits of multinationals are equally important aspects of their operations," according to F. Perry Wilson of Union Carbide. "The companies' foreign investments have a 'push effect' on the economics of host nations. The infusion of capital and technology, the introduction of training programs, the addition of jobs, payroll dollars and the creation of management opportunities for local nationals have an energizing effect. . . ."[24]

An example of a large multinational is Du Pont, which has forty-four principal foreign subsidiaries or affiliated companies employing nearly 32,000 people. Total sales in 1974 outside the United States amounted to $2.17 billion, of which over $800 million were U.S. exports.[25] "At last count, some 3,500 U.S. corporations had more than $125 billion worth of direct investments abroad. Foreign internationals had $70 billion—some $20 billion of it in the United States."[26] The concepts are:

> Multinational corporations may facilitate mutually beneficial exchange relationships between and among nations.

> Multinational corporations are evidence of the application of the systems approach to international markets.

Sources of Information on International Trade
This book can only touch upon the wealth of information available about international marketing. If you want to learn more about the subject, here is where you might look:

1. The main source of information is the U.S. government. For example, the Department of Commerce and the Bureau of International Commerce can give you a bibliography of government publications on international trade. Other government agencies will also provide helpful assistance to those interested in overseas sales.

2. Government agencies of foreign nations also publish helpful information that is usually readily available at one of their consulates.

3. The U.S. Chamber of Commerce publishes information on foreign markets, as do the Chambers of Commerce in other countries.

[24] F. Perry Wilson, "The Highest Self-Interest," *Newsweek*, November 24, 1975, p. 23.
[25] Figures are from "Why Companies Do Business Abroad," *Reader's Digest*, November 1975, pp. 26–28
[26] Ibid., p. 28.

It's helped more businessmen make more money than any "how to" book in history.

First, because the world of exporting is worth billions of dollars. And second, because in just 52 pages, this little book provides the in-depth introduction you need to cash in. Step by step, it covers such subjects as locating foreign reps, payment, financing, shipping, documentation, overseas promotions—to name a few. Clear, concise, easy-to-understand, it will help show you that marketing internationally is no more difficult than marketing domestically. So send us the coupon now. And we'll show you why it could be the most profitable you've ever clipped.

U. S. Department of Commerce

Rogers C. B. Morton, Secretary of Commerce
U.S. Department of Commerce, BIC 5A
Washington, D.C. 20230
Please send me a copy of "A Basic Guide to Exporting."

Name_____
Title_____
Company_____
Address_____
City_____State_____Zip_____

A Public Service of This Magazine & The Advertising Council.

Reprinted with permission of The Advertising Council.

4. Many good international marketing texts are available that summarize much of what a student would like to know about this area.[27]

Future Trends in International Trade Many U.S. business firms have concentrated so intently on competing for domestic (U.S.) markets that they have tended to avoid international markets. In addition, the recent growth of foreign competition in automobiles, bicycles, cameras, and motorcycles has caused American firms to work harder on regaining the U.S. market rather than expanding to other countries. But this may not be the case for long. Many firms now recognize the fact that much of the marketing opportunity of the future will come from foreign markets. Presently the United States is *last* among the advanced trading nations in percentage of gross national product exported.

Careers in International Marketing Many U.S. firms hire native workers (including marketing personnel) in their overseas operations. Nevertheless, there are many interesting and challenging career opportunities in international marketing. Much of the growth in this area will come from a large increase in exports from the United States. But there will always be opportunities in the import business as well. Furthermore, there are many government positions available for an expert in international marketing. Some universities specialize in international marketing, and others have advanced degree programs. If you are interested in international marketing, you are encouraged to take an undergraduate course at your local university or read some of the many texts in this area. This exposure will help you decide whether a career in international marketing is for you.

[27] See, for example, Philip R. Cateora and John M. Hess, *International Marketing*, rev. ed. (Homewood, Ill.: Richard D. Irwin, Inc., 1971), or Warren J. Keegan, *Multinational Marketing Management* (Englewood Cliffs, N.J.: Prentice-Hall, Inc., 1974).

FOR REVIEW

Key Terms

Among the more important terms and expressions discussed in this chapter are the following:

Disposable income is the amount of personal income that is left after taxes and other such payments and that can therefore be used by a person to satisfy his or her wants and needs.

The **gross national product** of any country is the total value of goods and services produced in a given year.

Industrial marketing consists of exchange relationships in the nonconsumer area that involve the transfer of products designed for industrial or business *use* rather than for *resale*.

International marketing is the process in worldwide markets that, subject to constraints, attempts to establish mutually satisfying exchange relationships between countries with diverse wants and needs and other countries that can satisfy those wants and needs.

A **multinational corporation** is a business that, while headquartered in one country, does much of its marketing with other countries, either by itself or in cooperation with businesses in other countries.

Personal income consists of all monies received from wages, interest, dividends, and the like.

The **service sector** is that segment of a market in which exchanges involve intangible products such as travel, entertainment, health care, education, and the like.

According to the **theory of competitive advantage,** a country should produce and sell to other countries those products that it produces most effectively and efficiently and should buy from other countries those goods and services it cannot produce as effectively and/or efficiently.

Key Concepts

Among the more important marketing concepts introduced in this chapter are the following:

> **Some marketing emphasis in the future will shift from the promotion of manufactured goods to the promotion of services, including government services.**

> **The changing role of women in society is affecting all areas of marketing by opening up entire new markets in the service sector, by increasing overall family incomes, and by involving more women in all phases of society, including religion, government, politics, and sports.**

> **Shifts in age distribution will cause shifts in income distribution and create new opportunities for some marketers and new problems for others.**

> **The farm industry is the largest cohesive market in the United States.**

> **Farm markets in the future will be dominated by a relatively small number of large organizations (corporations and cooperatives) that will be highly sophisticated buyers and sellers.**

> **There are serious constraints on world trade, including political, economic, technological, and legal constraints. Different monetary systems are also a problem.**

> **Multinational corporations may facilitate mutually beneficial exchange relationships between and among nations.**

Discussion Questions

1. "The projected 1990 population, at 245.1 million, is 31.6 million more than the current level, a numerical gain equivalent to the aggregate populace of the five biggest metropolitan markets—New York, Chicago, Los Angeles–Long Beach, Philadelphia, and Detroit." What

effect will this increase in population have on the standard of living in the United States? Why? What effect will it have on marketing? Why?

2. There is a major population shift toward the Sunbelt, an area that encompasses the U.S. Southeast and the Southwest. Is this a "plus" or a "minus" for the southern states? How will it affect northern industrial states?

3. More and more women are entering the labor force, and this includes half of those women with children. What effect does this have on marketing?

4. Most people do not prepare for their retirement until late in life, but today's young college student may have reason to do otherwise. Why? What effect will the baby boom have on the old-age market when today's college students retire about 40 years from now? Will social security be a major relief? Why or why not? Discuss how population shifts affect the standard of living of retired people.

5. "The largest buyer of goods and services in the United States is the government." Is this market likely to grow faster or slower than the consumer market over the next decade? How will this affect today's college students in marketing?

6. "A country should produce and sell to other countries those products that it produces most effectively and efficiently and buy from other countries those goods and services it cannot produce as effectively and/or efficiently." Do you agree? Why or why not?

7. One author quoted in this chapter indicated that more free trade between nations could lead to world peace. Do you agree? Why or why not?

8. Could a nation like the United States apply the societal marketing concepts outlined in Chapter 3 to world trade? Explain your answer.

9. Are multinational corporations a benefit to world relations or a drawback? Give examples to explain your answer.

10. Most graduate students seem to shy away from the industrial market as a career goal. Is this a good idea? Why or why not?

CASES

Littlefield College
Changing Markets

Littlefield was one of the colleges that suffered a surprising drop in enrollment in the early 1970s. Littlefield is a relatively small, liberal arts college with an enrollment of about 2,200 students. Although not well known nationally, Littlefield has an outstanding music department and is very strong in history and political science.

Littlefield never had an enrollment problem until the 1970s. In fact, its problem had been one of screening out students rather than seeking them. But for the last several years enrollment has been declining, and many of the students who do apply have scores on the admission test that are too low.

The administrators and faculty at Littlefield are divided over what should be done. Some administrators, faced with a lower budget (donations are down also), have proposed larger classes, higher tuition, and minimum salary increases. Faculty members have called for lower admission standards and an all-out promotional campaign. The Littlefield campus promises to be quite tense until this problem is resolved.

1. Do the demographic trends of the future (for example, age distribution of the population) show that Littlefield College will have less or more trouble finding students to enroll?
2. Littlefield College is located in a small midwestern city. Do population shifts among states indicate more or less people will be moving to the Midwest?
3. How could Littlefield College change its marketing program to attract students who are older and are taking courses part-time, especially at night?
4. Will family-income changes in the future increase or decrease the enrollments in private colleges? Why?

Careers in Consumer and Industrial Markets
A Difficult Choice

Marion Elsapp graduated from college with a degree in journalism and a minor in business. His first job was in the advertising department of a chain of hardware stores where he handled all phases of advertising (copywriting, layout, some art, and so on). Marion later got a job with a medium-sized advertising agency in the city. He worked on accounts as diverse as banks, auto dealers, department stores, boutiques, and dry cleaners. Marion was happy at his job, but felt underpaid and overworked.

Marion heard about a job at an industrial advertising agency in town. The salary was higher than he was making, and the agency was much smaller. Marion felt this might be his chance to be a "big fish in a small pond."

1. What differences between the consumer market and the industrial market would have an effect on Marion's choice?
2. Would Marion be working in different media for industrial markets? Why or why not?
3. Would you recommend that he take the job at the industrial ad agency? Why or why not?

Marketing Information Systems and Marketing Research

analyzing the market

LEARNING GOALS After you have read and studied this chapter, you should be able to:

1. Explain the relationships between the market-analysis function and marketing information systems.

2. List the three parts of a total marketing information system and briefly explain each.

3. Explain the difference between marketing intelligence and marketing research.

4. Describe how you could benefit personally from establishing a marketing information system in your home.

5. Define the following terms: marketing information system; marketing research; primary research; sales forecasting; secondary data.

6. Show how buyers and sellers benefit from using marketing research.

7. List the five major types of marketing research.

8. Discuss each of the fourteen steps in conducting a marketing research study.

9. Describe how an interfirm marketing information system would be implemented.

10. Give examples of situations in which nonbusiness organizations could use the concepts and principles of marketing research and marketing information systems.

> *Marketing effectiveness depends significantly on communication effectiveness. The market, in reality, is energized (or activated) through information flows.*
>
> Thomas A. Staudt and Donald A. Taylor[*]

INTRODUCTION The basis for all marketing exchanges is marketing information. Politicians need to know who their potential supporters are, where they are, and how they might be mobilized to help in their campaigns. A school principal needs to know how much money to expect from the government and other sources, how many students will be enrolling, where teachers are needed, and other such information. A minister needs to know something about what the congregation does and does not want in a service, what resources are available for church programs, and what services he or she is expected to perform for the membership. Businesses need information about consumers and consumer behavior, suppliers, government actions, and other such data.

Consumers and buyers for all organizations must also learn something about market conditions, price changes, and sources of supply. In short, information is one key to increased marketing success for everyone. But how does one get such information? How is such information best used? And what is the cost of getting such information? These are some of the questions that need to be answered in a discussion of marketing research and marketing information systems. First, let's put marketing research into some perspective relative to the marketing functions we discussed back in Chapter 2.

Marketing Research: A Part of the Market-Analysis Function The starting point for most marketing situations is **market analysis.** Market analysis is the first of the six universal marketing functions, and it is often the foundation for all the other activities. It is through market analysis that sellers discover the wants and needs of individuals and society. And it is market analysis that enables individual buyers and organizations to find solutions to their wants and needs. The term normally used to describe the process whereby organizations analyze markets and market potential is **marketing research.** It is the process of locating needs, finding ways to satisfy needs, choosing alternative solutions to one's own needs, and generally learning more about the supply of, and demand for, various products. Marketing research is just one element of a total marketing information system that individuals and businesses may use to be more effective and efficient marketers. This chapter will discuss marketing research and its role in a total marketing information system. A marketing information system is usually the best way to implement the market-analysis function for both the buyer and the seller.

[*] *A Managerial Introduction to Marketing,* 2nd ed. (Englewood Cliffs, N.J.: Prentice-Hall, Inc., 1970), p. 379.

THE MARKETING INFORMATION SYSTEM A marketing information system (MIS) may be defined as a process of gathering, processing, storing, and using information to make better marketing decisions and to improve marketing exchanges. There are three parts of a total system: (1) marketing intelligence gathering, (2) information processing, analysis, storage, and distribution, and (3) promotional communications.

Marketing Intelligence Gathering The flow of information known as marketing intelligence consists of facts, figures, and ideas about institutions and developments in the environment that affect the marketer's opportunities and performance. Buyers and sellers both need to monitor the actions of the government as well as political, social, technological, and economic developments. The concept is:

> **Effective and efficient marketing decision making depends upon continuous, reliable, and factual information; that information is called marketing intelligence.**

There are numerous sources of marketing intelligence; in fact, the problem today tends to be too much information rather than not enough. Consumers are often overwhelmed by the number of new products they must evaluate and the amount of information they must process in order to select products effectively. The problem is usually too much of the wrong kind of information and too little factual, helpful information. The same is true of businesses and other organizations. They have access to literally millions of pieces of information and are often buried in a sea of facts and figures that tends to obscure rather than illuminate a proper course of action. The concept is:

> **Individuals and organizations must carefully select from all available information (intelligence) those facts and figures most relevant to improving their exchange relationships.**

Need for Quality Information

Information is needed on which to base sound judgments . . . yet there are few things that are more difficult to obtain than needed information. Notice the word *needed*. We are inundated with information, but most of it is useless; we have no need for it. . . . All too frequently the manager seeks information haphazardly, only when he needs it. He fails to set up a system that feeds information to him continually. Yet that is precisely what is needed—a system.

From Richard H. Buskirk, *Principles of Marketing*, 4th ed. (Hinsdale, Ill.: Dryden Press, 1975), p. 663.

Talking with Consumers Organizations could begin their intelligence-gathering process by talking directly with consumers. Those people who already are participating in exchanges with the organization can discuss what they like and dislike about the organization and its product offers. People who once were "customers," but have left, are good sources of information about what makes people leave. Those people who have never had any relationships with the organization could explain *why* they have not and what it would take to get them to consider future exchanges. Employees of the organization could also provide information about complaints, compliments, and other data they have learned from their contacts with the public. The concept is:

> **Organizations should monitor consumers to get their opinions and reactions to the organization and its products, policies, and personnel; such information should be gathered from present customers, previous customers, noncustomers, and employees.**

If the organization's "customers" are called clients, patients, or by some other name, and its employees are all volunteers, the same concept applies. *Marketing intelligence is an active, listening function, not just a sorting out of published facts and figures.* The same process should go on for buyers. They should actively seek information about suppliers by talking to customers, noncustomers, previous customers, and employees. The concept is:

> **Marketing intelligence is helpful to all participants in exchange relationships, including buyers and sellers, middlemen, and participants in noneconomic exchanges.**

Intelligence about the Environment Individuals, businesses, and other organizations may seek information from many sources. Some sources are those people and organizations directly involved in the exchange process. They include suppliers, distributors (for example, wholesalers and retailers), credit agencies, and advertising agencies.

Other sources of information include competitors, consultants, trade associations, government publications, nonprofit research foundations, and commercial research organizations. Data should be gathered about legal conditions, political changes, labor markets, cultural trends, lifestyle changes, economic developments, international trade circumstances, market trends, and technological advances. The concepts are:

> **There are numerous sources of intelligence that should be monitored in a comprehensive marketing intelligence program; they include governmental and private sources.**
> **Intelligence about the political, social, economic, and technological environment are part of any complete information-gathering program.**

Internal Data In addition to the information obtained from external sources, every organization should carefully monitor its internal data. Marketers should have ready access to information from their own employees. For example, salespeople, delivery people, marketing research personnel, and service representatives should all be active searchers for, and providers of, information about consumers, competitors, and the general marketing environment.

Marketing decision makers also need data from financial reports, legal rulings, personnel files, accounting sheets, production records, and other internal operations. Stockholders might also be asked for their opinions, reactions, and suggestions. The concept is:

> Marketing intelligence data from external sources should be combined with internally generated data to provide a continuous information flow to marketing decision makers and other personnel.

2.

Information Processing, Analysis, Storage, and Distribution The second part of a total marketing information system, after the gathering of intelligence, is information processing, analysis, storage, and distribution. Information processing and analysis conjure up images of advanced computer systems and other data-processing equipment. In fact, in most larger organizations, computers are very helpful in managing large amounts of information. But for individuals and smaller organizations (such as an independent retailer), data analysis may be nothing more than looking through available material, gathering missing facts and figures, and evaluating the information on some rational basis. The concept is:

> Information gathered through marketing intelligence should be analyzed for its accuracy and reliability and used as a guide to decision making.

Information (marketing intelligence) should also be distributed to decision makers. Of course not *all* the data should be distributed. That is the purpose behind data processing and analysis—to weed out irrelevant material to prevent the overburdening of decision makers with too much detail. Distribution of the material should be to those who want and need the information. Three types of internal information flows are shown in Figure 6.1.

One problem with early attempts to establish marketing information systems was that the managers did not use the information provided. Often the material was provided as computer printouts that managers did not bother to wade through. Also, the material often was not requested by the managers but was sent to them "for their information." Two concepts that emerge from this discussion are:

> Marketing information should be distributed to everyone in an organization who can use it, but only after those people have had a chance to discuss what information is needed and in what form.

> A marketing information system works only if everyone in the organization participates in its design and implementation; if it is managed exclusively by marketing researchers, management scientists, and computer specialists, the material may be largely ignored by marketing decision makers.

Figure 6.1 INTERNAL INFORMATION FLOWS

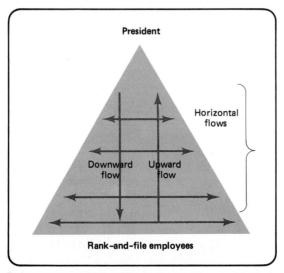

Redrawn and adapted from Philip Kotler, "A Design for the Firm's Marketing Nerve Center," *Business Horizons*, Fall 1966, p. 67.

Interfirm Distribution of Data Marketing information systems have traditionally been managed within the confines of one organization. Today there is so much interdependence among organizations in the marketing system that there should be open exchanges of information between and among organizations (subject to legal and competitive restrictions). For example, many of the smaller manufacturers that supply parts to the automobile companies would go out of business if they were dropped as suppliers. For all practical purposes, one could say that those suppliers are a part of the car companies' manufacturing process. Therefore, the automobile companies should share much of their marketing intelligence data with suppliers to make sure that the suppliers have heard about the latest in materials, technology, and consumer feedback. Such exchange of information benefits both the supplier and the auto manufacturer.

Furthermore, automobile manufacturers should share some intelligence data with their dealers. Comparatively speaking, automobile dealers are very small and cannot afford sophisticated data-gathering and data-processing systems. They rely heavily on the manufacturer for information about such things as sales trends, relevant political developments, consumer attitudes and behavior, and economic trends. The concepts are:

> Marketing intelligence data should be distributed to all members of the channel of distribution (that is, suppliers, manufacturers, distributors, and dealers) on a selected basis to improve the marketing capability of the total system.

> In most instances today competition is between channel systems, not between individual firms; therefore, there should be interfirm cooperation and coordination, which is best managed through interfirm marketing information systems.

> **Industry Use of Marketing Information Systems**
>
> A study by Boone and Kurtz in 1971 showed that 39 percent of the companies responding to their survey of *Fortune's* top 500 companies had an operational marketing information system. Another 38 percent of the firms were developing one. The chief reason expressed for establishing an MIS was to provide management with timely, accurate information. Most firms (63%) had installed their information system in the previous five years (1966–1971).

Based on statistics in Louis E. Boone and David L. Kurtz, "Marketing Information Systems: Current Status in American Industry," in *Combined Proceedings, 1971 Spring and Fall Conferences,* ed. Fred C. Allvine (Chicago: American Marketing Association, 1972), pp. 163–167.

Many conflicts can develop between manufacturers and dealers if there is not an effective *two-way* exchange of information. For example, many managers of service (gas) stations do not agree with the policies and practices of the oil companies. Information tends to come to station managers in the form of orders, directives, and rules. The managers often feel they have little input *to* the oil companies; as a result, these managers may refuse to cooperate in the promotions and programs of their suppliers. Often the relationship between oil companies and their dealers can be described as distant at best and often hostile. The concepts are:

> ‣ If major organizations do not provide open two-way channels of communication with their dealers (or distributors or suppliers), conflict, hostility, and noncooperation may result.

> ‣ An operating marketing information system that opens two-way flows of information among organizations gives all of the organizations a better chance to improve their marketing programs and leads to more cooperation, harmony, and understanding within the entire system.

Promotional Communications   The third part of a total MIS involves sending informative and persuasive messages to the public: it is called **promotional communications.** An organization has many "publics"; potential customers are only one category. Other "publics" may include the local community, government regulators, consumerists, legislators, stockholders, employees, distributors, dealers, and suppliers. A **public** can be defined broadly as a distinct group of people and/or organizations that have an actual or a potential interest and/or impact on an organization.[1]

Not all publics are of equal importance, but a marketer cannot afford to ignore one group just because it does not seem important at the time. For example, the owners of a fast-food restaurant could do research and find that there was a great demand for their product in a certain part of

[1] Philip Kotler, *Marketing for Nonprofit Organizations* (Englewood Cliffs, N.J.: Prentice-Hall, Inc., 1975), p. 17.

town. After acquiring the necessary land and permits, they would in theory be ready to build. But the people in the local community might protest the building of such a restaurant in their neighborhood; they could take the restaurant to court and cause many delays and problems for the owners. The owners might even be forced to give up the location. Such troubles can often be resolved before they happen through a careful analysis of all publics and the establishment of programs to communicate with them throughout the planning process.

Promotional communications are the flows of information and persuasion *from* an organization. They should be based on good marketing intelligence (flows of information *to* the organization) and careful marketing planning. Promotional channels include personal selling, advertising, publicity, public relations, and sales promotion. The product itself often offers much in the way of information to the various publics. Therefore, packaging, branding, labeling, pricing, and product design may all be considered elements of a total promotional program.[2] There will be a thorough discussion of each of these promotional elements as we progress through the book. The concept behind the development is:

> ▸ The third part of a marketing information system is promotional communications between an organization and its publics, including stockholders, the local community, government agencies, customers, and potential customers.

The three flows of a total marketing information system are summarized in Figure 6.2.

Your Personal MIS By following the concepts presented thus far, you could greatly improve your ability as a marketer. The first thing you should do is gather *marketing intelligence* that would help you in your shopping trips and other exchange situations. A good source of information is the newspaper. There you will find articles about nutrition, fabrics, and various consumer issues. You will also be able to get information from the ads and clip coupons for big savings on your food purchases. For larger purchases, you might consult *Consumer Reports, Consumer Bulletin, Changing Times, Money* magazine, *Moneysworth,* and other such materials at the library. Of course, you could talk to your friends, neighbors, and relatives to get their experiences and opinions about various goods, services, people, places, and things.

But it is not enough just to gather intelligence. Usually you hear a lot about various goods and services, but are not in the market at the time. When the time does come to buy, you tend to forget details and where to get helpful information. The second part of a personal MIS, therefore, is some kind of *personal information storage system.* My wife and I keep a file right in the family room. As we read newspapers, magazines, and books, we cut out interesting recipes, coupons, articles, ads, and infor-

---

[2] For a comprehensive look at promotion that incorporates these concepts, see William G. Nickels, *Marketing Communications and Promotion* (Columbus, Ohio: Grid, Inc., 1976).

Figure 6.2 THE THREE FLOWS OF A TOTAL MARKETING
INFORMATION SYSTEM

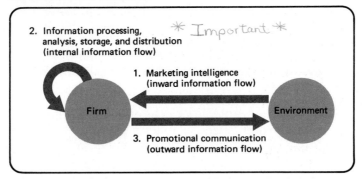

Redrawn and adapted from Philip Kotler, "A Design for the Firm's Marketing Nerve
Center," *Business Horizons*, Fall 1966, p. 67.

 mation. We then file this material under appropriate headings such as:
vacation ideas, food ideas and recipes, savings tips, and current events.
Maybe you would benefit from such a system. The idea is to establish
some location where information is easily stored and found.

The third part of a personal MIS is *promotional communications*. The
idea is to share the information you have gathered with members of your
family, neighbors, and friends. It is also helpful to use your influence to
get local retailers and other marketers to better satisfy your needs and
those of the community. Usually, this is most effectively done when the
entire community cooperates in consumer and political matters.

A personal MIS goes beyond shopping and consumer matters, however. Once you get in the habit of clipping and storing information, you
can begin gathering information about religious, social, political, charitable, environmental, and other relevant issues. You are thus prepared to
discuss such matters more intelligently and with a more factual basis. An
informed businessperson, an informed shopper, and an informed conversationalist all need information to be effective. There is so much
information available that all people could use a personalized MIS to
help organize information for their personal as well as business use.
Such information will help make you a better prepared shopper, a more
aware voter, a more informed conversationalist, and a more knowledgeable member of the community.

MARKETING Marketing research is the formalized process for gathering marketing
RESEARCH intelligence. One corporate executive explains the difference between
marketing research and marketing intelligence in this way:

*The difference between marketing research and marketing intelligence
is like the difference between a flashbulb and a candle. Let's say you
are dancing in the dark. Every 90 seconds you are allowed to set off a
flashbulb. You can use these brief intervals of intense light to chart a
course, but remember everyone else is moving too . . . you may get
bumped and you may stumble . . . but you can dance along.*

On the other hand, you can light a candle. It doesn't yield as much light, but it's a steady light. You are continually aware of the movements of other bodies. You can adjust your course to the courses of others. The intelligence system is a kind of candle. It's no great flash on the immediate state of things, but it provides continuous light as situations shift and change.[3]

The difference between marketing research and marketing intelligence may be summarized as follows. **Marketing research** is a *periodic, structured* process of gathering information[relative to a *particular* marketing problem.] **Marketing intelligence** is the *continuous, flexible* process of actively monitoring relevant external and internal data to provide input into *all* marketing decisions.

[Note]
done because you have a problem. Some co's do however carry on continuous marketing research.

Value of Research Depends on Product   Often consumers will do little or no research to aid their decision making about minor purchases. For example, you might buy a new kind of gum or beverage just to try it out. Research by purchase and use is a relatively inexpensive but sure-fire way to test such low-cost items. But the same techniques are not as applicable in the case of high-cost items. Few people can afford to buy and try a new color TV, car, or stereo system without backing their purchase with some helpful information gathered through research. That research may involve a careful reading of ads; discussions with friends, neighbors, and retailers; analysis of data in *Consumer Reports* and other similar magazines; and personal physical comparisons, price comparisons, and in-store trials. The concept is:

> **The value of information (marketing research) to an individual or organization depends upon the relative importance (for example, cost) of the decision to be made, the complexity of the decision, and the amount of information already available.**

Organizations act much like consumers in their evaluation of the worth of marketing research. If the decision is not very important (the equivalent of buying a pack of gum), an organization will tend to make a decision based on the available information. But when the decision involves the purchase of expensive equipment (for example, a computer), the selection of key markets, or other important areas, an organization will value highly information gathered through research. In fact one should view research information as a marketing cost to be evaluated like all other costs. "Information is a scarce good with its own cost of production," says economist Paul Heyne. "It simply does not pay to go on acquiring information forever before acting. A rational seller will continue acquiring information, therefore, only so long as the anticipated marginal gain from doing so is greater than the anticipated

---

[3] Robert J. Williams, of Mead Johnson, as cited in "Marketing Intelligence Systems: A DEW Line for Marketing Men," *Business Management*, January 1966, p. 32. © 1966 by Macmillan Professional Magazines, Inc. All rights reserved.

marginal cost of acquiring information. A rational buyer will behave in the same way."[4] The concept to follow is this:

imp.

> **Marketing research data has a cost and should be controlled like other costs; gather information only so long as the benefits of acquiring it exceed the cost.**

There are several techniques for determining how much information one should gather relative to the cost. Sophisticated statistical methods and other tools may be used to quantify such decisions. The techniques for doing these calculations are beyond the scope of this book but may be learned in a comprehensive marketing research or marketing statistics course.

Research Techniques Marketing researchers are becoming more and more sophisticated in their ability to manipulate and analyze data. One problem is that some researchers become too involved with technique and not involved enough in preparing clear, understandable, and usable information for managers:

It is common, for example, for some researchers to see research as being the application of certain techniques—those techniques which they know how to apply. Great emphasis has been given to the technicalities, and this has affected the thinking of business executives as well as researchers. As a result, management tends to equate surveys and research and to ask about such things as sample size and cost before clarifying what it really wants to learn. . . . There is a widespread failure to visualize a continuing process of inquiry in which executives are helped to think more effectively.[5]

Marketing research is a relatively new function in many organizations, but its sophistication has increased dramatically. At first, researchers used basic techniques such as personal observation in the marketplace and small consumer surveys. This led to more advanced questionnaire designs, survey techniques, and sampling procedures. Today, one could get overwhelmed by the terminology of marketing research, and, in fact, many people question whether research reports need be so difficult to read. They tend to be full of terms like multiple regression analysis, multidimensional scaling, heuristic programming, preposterior analysis, stochastic models, maximin, minimax, matrix multiplications, canonical correlations, Bayesian statistics, and factor analysis. None of these concepts is particularly difficult to understand, but statistics can be presented in a way that obscures rather than clarifies the useful facts. Anyone interested in marketing management in any organization

[4] Paul T. Heyne, *The Economic Way of Thinking* (Chicago, Ill.: Science Research Associates, Inc., 1973), p. 86.

[5] Joseph W. Newman, "Put Research Into Marketing Decisions," *Harvard Business Review*, March–April 1962, p. 106.

"Aw, be a sport, Miss Demkin. Listen to the multivariate statistical analysis psychographic segmentation presentation one more time.

From *Marketing News,* March 12, 1976, p. 11. Reprinted with permission of the American Marketing Association.

should become familiar with the strategies and techniques of marketing research. You should do this not necessarily so that you could actually do these analyses, but so that you could prepare yourself to read and understand research reports and not be misled by the data.

Much marketing research is being done at universities in order to help all organizations improve their marketing practices. Such research is high level in most cases and may be offered free to certain causes and nonprofit organizations. The marketing faculty of some schools may also be available on a consulting basis to help in research design and implementation. Students should talk with faculty members about such projects and should become involved. There is no better way to learn research techniques than actually to try them.

RESEARCH A great variety of topics are investigated by marketing researchers in a
TOPICS typical organization.[6] The major categories include:

1. Sales and market potential research
2. Product research

[6] Much of the data in this section is based on Dik W. Twedt, ed., *1973 Survey of Marketing Research: Organization, Functions, Budget, Compensation* (Chicago: American Marketing Association, 1973).

3. Advertising research
4. Economic and organizational research
5. Social responsibility research

Each of these areas is discussed briefly in the following sections to give you some idea of the scope of the research area.

Different Research Questions

One of the pillars of the modern marketing concept is decision making based on accurate facts and information. The formal method of obtaining information is marketing research. Let us examine the five fundamental questions that marketing research asks. *5 Fundamental Questions*

a. What is the potential market for a product and what will our company's share of this be in each period? Known as quantitative market research, this question involves a study of total industry volume and a forecast of the company's sales.
b. Who are the present and potential customers? Known as qualitative market research, this question involves the study of the market's characteristics, e.g., age, location, size, etc.
c. How can the company best appeal to this market? This area deals with motivation research, packaging research, pricing, and product research. It suggests appeals for promotion, selling, and advertising.
d. How can the company most effectively reach this market? Having answered the first three questions, it remains to find out the most efficient way of reaching the market. This involves transportation, channel, and media research.
e. How successful is the firm's marketing program and what are its weak areas? It is this question that needs the accountant's specialized skills through his use of distribution cost accounting.

From Bruce E. Mallen and Stephen D. Silver, "Modern Marketing and the Accountant," *Cost and Management*, February 1964, pp. 75–85.

Sales and Market Potential Research Twedt's 1973 survey of marketing research revealed that more companies measured market potentials (68 percent) than any other research area. In that category were analyses of market share (67 percent) and determinations of market characteristics.[7] This book's Chapters 4 and 5 gave you some idea of what these organizations were trying to accomplish and how. As we have noted, one of the better sources of information on market potential is *Sales & Marketing Management's Survey of Buying Power*. It gives facts and figures for city, county, and metropolitan areas regarding population, geographic size, income, and retail sales by categories. Such data reveal market potential for a given geographic area and provide the foundation for more intensive study. Local Chambers of Commerce can often supplement such data.

[7] Ibid.

Using these data, organizations can better determine where to concentrate their marketing efforts. They can also estimate what the results might be. Estimating sales results is called **sales forecasting.** Twedt found that 65 percent of his sample of 1,322 companies did some sales analysis, 57 percent used research to establish sales quotas and territories, and 45 percent did sales compensation studies.[8]

You can learn the details of how to conduct sales forecasts by reading one of the many good sales management texts now available.[9] Courses in sales management and marketing research will often include discussion of such topics as test market studies, distribution channel studies, and other research topics. All of these are research studies that attempt to get more information about consumer wants and needs, consumer income, total market potential for a given product, market potential for a particular brand, and sales potential for a given territory and salesperson. Such studies are not accurate to the dollar, but they do give management a better feel for decisions regarding the introduction of new products, sales quotas, and profit potential.

Product Research The costs of developing and marketing a new product are often difficult to comprehend. Included may be the costs of developing the product and the package, distribution costs, and promotion costs. In total, a nationally introduced product may cost $15 million or more to launch. For example, Brown-Forman Distillers spent about $6.5 million to introduce Frost 8/80 Dry White whiskey and lost about $2 million of that amount. Scott Paper Company is reported to have lost $12.8 million trying to capture the disposable diaper market with Baby Scott in 1971. About $6 million was reported to have been spent on advertising in 1971 alone. The list of product failures is extremely long and the costs are very high: Fact toothpaste failed after more than $5 million was spent in promotion; Vote toothpaste failed after another $5 million was spent in promotion; Resolve couldn't get the market from Alka Seltzer, even after over $11 million was spent in promotion; and so on. The market is strewn with the Edsels, Corfam shoes, and other product failures of the past. And the life cycle of new products is becoming shorter:

Once a new product could look forward to 10, perhaps 20, years of profitable existence. Now its life expectancy is 28 months. That's if the new product survives. Most don't. An estimated 80% of new products fail, and, of those that make it, only one in four becomes a significant source of profit, according to a Booze, Allen & Hamilton study.[10]

---

[8] Ibid.

[9] See, for example, Steven C. Wheelwright and Spyros Makridakis, *Forecasting Methods for Management* (New York: John Wiley & Sons, Inc., 1973), or Marvin A. Jolson, *Sales Management: A Tactical Approach* (New York: Petrocelli/Charter, 1977), Chap. 4.

[10] See Theodore J. Van DeKamp, "How We Can Cope With Future Shock: The Marketing Brokerage Company," *Advertising Age,* June 3, 1974, p. 40.

Table 6.1 TYPES OF PRODUCT RESEARCH

Type of research	Percent of firms doing this research
Potential of new product	77
Product versus competition	74
Product characteristics	63
Product testing	58
Competitive products	54
Length of product line	47
Packaging	44

From Richard D. Crisp, *Company Practices in Marketing Research* (New York: American Management Association, 1953).

The losses companies suffer in introducing new products are borne by the consumer, stockholders, and society in general. Similar losses may occur when the government launches new programs, new weapons systems, or new rules and regulations. All organizations must analyze their "products" to avoid the severe losses that now occur daily in the market. As shown in Table 6.1, this analysis may take many forms. No organization can afford to develop a "product" to meet the public's needs without careful, thorough marketing research of the type listed in Table 6.1. Even though a research study may cost from $20,000 to $150,000, such amounts are very small in relation to the millions lost because of poor research or no research. We cannot give you here the details of how to conduct product research. But we hope you will be interested enough to look through a good book on marketing research or take a course in this critical marketing area.

Advertising Research Marketers spend over $30 billion on advertising each year and need information to make such expenditures more effective and more efficient. Thus far, though, advertising effectiveness is one area in which marketing research has been of limited help. This is not to say that there are not many studies; the problem is that the behavior of consumers is so difficult to predict with any accuracy.

About one-half the organizations studied by Twedt in 1973 did studies of ad effectiveness. Of course, that means *half did not*. Only 37 percent did copy research, and only 30 percent did any motivation research.[11]

Marketing research is very helpful to advertisers in that it explores *what* people want in a product and *why*. It also shows what benefits are most and least desirable, what media (for example, TV and magazines) people are exposed to most, past purchasing behavior, and other important information. Researchers test ads *before* they are run (pretesting) by showing them to panels of consumers and conducting other such tests. Researchers also help select which media to use (for example, TV versus radio) and which particular vehicles are best (for example, *Readers Digest* versus *TV Guide*). Finally, researchers attempt to measure ad effectiveness *after* the ad is run.

[11] Twedt, *1973 Survey of Marketing Research*.

151

The area of advertising effectiveness is where researchers often have the most difficulty. How does one measure effectiveness? Firms cannot simply measure sales, because so many things influence sales besides advertising, including the weather, personal selling, word of mouth, and publicity. If a firm measures how many people *saw* the ad or *read* part of the ad, the firm is really measuring the attractiveness of the ad, *not* the attractiveness of the product.

This is one area of marketing research that has much promise for the future. Many people are working on models and techniques for measuring advertising effectiveness, media selection, and copy effectiveness. Until better procedures are developed, marketing managers will continue to complain, as John Wanamaker once did: "Half the money I spend on advertising is wasted, and trouble is I don't know which half." There are entire books on the measurement of advertising effectiveness.[12] You might glance through one to get some feel for this interesting, challenging area.

Economic and Organizational Research

Marketing has often been referred to as "applied economics." It is no surprise, therefore, to find that economic research is a major aspect of marketing research. This involves short- and long-range forecasting, studies of business trends, pricing studies, location studies, and international economic-exchange studies.

Marketers also must study internal organizational problems such as personnel requirements, product-mix studies, duties and responsibilities of various members of the marketing organization, purchasing procedures, and distribution procedures. There is no internal marketing function that is not studied by researchers.

If you are beginning to get the idea that marketing research and marketing information from that research are the heart of marketing management, you are right. Marketing research is a key to all effective marketing decision making and a key subject that all marketing students should take. As you can see, marketing researchers become involved in all aspects of the economy from international trade problems to analyses of consumer behavior. Could there be a career in marketing research for you? One very interesting area is social responsibility research. Many companies are just starting to conduct such studies.

Social Responsibility Research

As we showed in Chapter 3, marketing is just beginning to adopt a new philosophy of a "societal orientation," a consideration of both needs of society and the needs of individuals. Social responsibility is a major concern of many organizations, and marketing research is needed to measure the organization's success in meeting its broader social objectives. For example: What effect does our organization and its products have on the environment? Are our products being used safely and effectively? If not, how can we educate consumers in product use? What do people value today and how does this differ from what they valued in

[12] See, for example, Darrell B. Lucas and Steuart H. Britt, *Measuring Advertising Effectiveness* (New York: McGraw-Hill Book Company, 1963).

Value of Research to Society

The value of marketing research spreads farther than among business-men. The consumer gains from proper use of quality information on his part as well as on the firm's part. Products are more properly geared to the consumer as a result of the use of information, and they are more efficiently distributed. Indeed, the improvement in the directing of marketing resources aids the consumer just as it aids the business firm.

Manifestly the economy benefits from intelligence. Market information permits governments to anticipate needs in various areas, thereby improving allocation of resources. . . .

Although ours is an affluent society, there remains the need for elimination of waste and for improvement in the allocation of national and private resources . . . the imperfections of our economic system can be eliminated in part, certainly minimized, through the proper use of quality information.

From Robert J. Holloway and Robert S. Hancock, *Marketing in a Changing Environment* (New York: John Wiley & Sons, Inc., 1968), pp. 224–225.

former years? All of these questions and more are the bases for marketing research.

Organizations also are concerned about legal and ethical constraints on their operations and promotions: What laws are now being considered by federal and state legislators? How will they affect us? What input could we or should we make in their deliberations? This too is a matter for marketing research.

Later in this book (Chapter 19) we shall discuss marketing's social responsibility and legal constraints in more detail. It is important to note here, though, that studies on social responsibility have become a major focus of marketing research.

THE RESEARCH PROCESS There is no "best" way to conduct marketing research, nor is there any step-by-step procedure that must be followed to be successful. Nevertheless, some guidelines and basic concepts have proved useful. For example, a researcher might follow these steps in designing a research study:

1. Study the situation as it now exists.
2. Define the strengths of present programs.
3. Define the problem or problems to be resolved.
4. State research objectives in writing.
5. Determine the scope of the project and the estimated costs.
6. Set up controls where necessary.
7. Exhaust secondary sources before doing original research.
8. Gather any data not available in other studies.
9. Analyze and process the data into readable form.

10. Prepare a report.
11. Suggest alternative solutions and reasons for each.
12. Recommend a course of action.
13. Follow up on the implementation.
14. Redefine the situation (that is, strengths and weaknesses).

The remainder of this chapter will discuss some of these steps in more detail.

Study the Situation Most texts on marketing research state that the first step in research design is to "define the problem." But there may be no problem, or the need may be to determine more carefully just what the market situation is. Marketing research is not just a problem-solving function! It is an *analysis function* that feeds information to decision makers. Research does not begin or end with a problem. It begins with the need for good, reliable information. What does the public think about our organization and its products? What do our employees think? How are our sales compared to last year? How is our stock doing? These are the kind of questions that provide bases for further marketing research. The concept is:

› **Marketing research is part of the market-analysis function; its role is to analyze the organization's market situation periodically and to conduct further studies if necessary; it is not merely a problem-solving function.**

Marketing research is part of a total marketing information system. It should be structured so that research data can be combined with less structured or less formal information to give decision makers a comprehensive view of the market.

Define Strengths and Identify Problems Marketing researchers too often are put in the position of "finding answers" to problems and are given little freedom to analyze both *strengths and weaknesses* of present practices. It is as important to know what an organization does well as what it does not do well, and marketing research should report *both sides*.

In many, if not most, organizations, marketing researchers are asked to conduct specific studies. Top management often decides that there is a problem (for example, falling sales or profits, poor corporate image, or ineffective advertising) and specifies what kind of research project they want. Many marketers feel that this is the wrong approach to research. They feel that marketing researchers should be given the freedom to help discover what the problem is, what the alternatives are, what data are needed, and how to go about gathering and analyzing the data. Problem definition is one of the most important steps because it sets the stage for all the other procedures. If marketing research is not included in the problem-analysis stage, it often becomes an ineffective data-gathering and analysis function with little real influence on corporate decision making. This is considered by many to be a misuse of the department.

> **Research is the Basis for Marketing Decisions**
>
> To be market oriented a firm must base *all* its activities on the needs of the market. This requires knowing as much as possible about the market and the strategies and tactics of competitors in their attempts to exploit the market. Marketing research is the process by which firms attempt to obtain such information, and, as such, marketing research is an integral part of the decision-making process.

From Harper W. Boyd and Ralph Westfall, *Marketing Research: Text and Cases* (Homewood, Ill.: Richard D. Irwin, Inc., 1964), pp. 3–4.

State the Objectives and Scope of the Project in Writing Research projects have a momentum of their own once they get started, and every effort should be made at the beginning to clearly state in writing what the research is *and* is not supposed to accomplish. The costs of a research project can easily exceed benefits if the scope of the project is not clearly stated.

Often the best way to establish clear objectives is to state them in the form of hypotheses. For example, a university may want to research why fewer students are taking foreign languages. The hypotheses to be tested might be:

1. Students are not taking foreign languages because the courses are perceived to be too hard.
2. Students are not taking foreign languages because the teachers are poor.
3. Students are not taking foreign languages because they see no practical use for them.

These are only examples and are not presented in ideal research language. Nevertheless, you can see that research objectives are made more precise if put in the form of hypotheses. It may be possible to develop many more hypotheses by doing some preliminary research. The idea is to be quite precise as to what the research question is.

Set Up Controls There should be some mechanism for evaluating the progress of a research project, so that it can be kept on a reasonable time schedule and within set costs. This might mean the development of a simple flow chart that describes what should be done by when. Such a chart lists the various events in a project, the goal of each event, the order in which the events are to occur, and the time schedule that the events are to follow. Periodic checks will reveal whether the program is on target or not. As you go along, it is often important to ask questions such as the following: What information do we now have? Do we need more, and, if so, how much will it cost? Is the information available in published form or do we have to get it ourselves? Often circumstances change and research projects should be altered as well. Periodic review and questioning sessions will keep the research in line with current problems.

Gather
Secondary Data Information already available in published form is called **secondary data.** The cost of information is so high that researchers often should put primary emphasis on these published data. Perhaps the key source is the U.S. government. We shall not go into detail about these government reports because you should go to the library and browse through them yourself. However, here are some that you should look up: *Census of Agriculture; Census of Business; Census of Manufacturers; Census of Housing;* and for more up-to-date information, the *Survey of Current Business,* the *Annual Survey of Manufacturers,* the Current Population Reports, and other government data that your librarian will help you find. One way to find quickly what you are looking for is to look through the annual *Statistical Abstract of the United States* because it summarizes the other data in chart form.

Government
Reports

You should also become familiar with the information that is available from the following sources.

1. *Journals.* Be sure to examine journals such as the *Journal of Marketing Research, Journal of Marketing, Sales & Marketing Management, Advertising Age,* and the *Harvard Business Review.* Also review more popular publications such as *Business Week,* the *Wall Street Journal, Consumer Reports, Changing Times, Newsweek, Moneysworth,* and *Money.*

2. *Trade associations and trade journals.* There is a wealth of data available for manufacturers, middlemen, and retailers in the form of special reports, surveys, and trade magazines that have much current information.

3. *Nonprofit organizations representing both business and the consumer.* Notable examples include Better Business Bureaus, Chambers of Commerce, the National Industrial Conference Board, extension agencies at state universities, and various foundations.

4. *Information services.* Many new organizations and established firms gather secondary and primary data for subscribers. You should become familiar with some of them. For example, all the information from government hearings is available from Congressional Information Service, Inc. (CIS). One of the world's largest sources of secondary data is called The Information Source (TIS). Retailers might contact organizations like Management Horizons, which has its own Retail Intelligence System (RIS). These are only a few of the many resources available to researchers gathering secondary data (see Table 6.2).

5. *Libraries.* The best library for finding published data is the Library of Congress, but information is often difficult to get because the library is so crowded with books and other materials. Often your local representative or senator will help you get information that is particularly hard to find in the Library of Congress. Most libraries in major cities will provide you with more information than you could possibly use. Do not be afraid to ask for help; librarians will help you dig out information, even over the phone!

New Government Information Service

The first comprehensive source book for computer-generated Federal data files, data bases, and related software is now available. It is produced by the U.S. Department of Commerce, National Technical Information Service (NTIS). More than 300,000 government research reports were available in 1975, and 200 reports *per day* were being added. A *custom* search for information might cost $50, but previously prepared packages are available for about $20. The NTIS Directory of Computerized Federal Data Files & Software costs $60. Any researcher should thoroughly search such sources for information before conducting in-house research.

Of course, a key source of secondary data is internally published information. Accounting and auditing reports, production reports, personnel data, legal findings, and other such internal information is often vital to good research. If the research capability of the organization (individual) is limited, consultants are available to provide assistance in gathering secondary data and to conduct new studies. A recent directory lists over 350 such research organizations.[13]

Carry Out Primary Research At times you may have to conduct your own research to determine customer attitudes or to find some other facts that are not available in published form. The process of gathering your own information is called **primary research.** There are many good books available on techniques for gathering marketing research, so we will not go into such details here.[14] Although research studies have become highly sophisticated, there is still much merit in simple personal observation of the market to get a "feel" for the situation. Short, direct questionnaires and surveys are also good for finding answers at a minimum cost in time and money.

A popular technique in the past few years has been focus-group interviewing, group-depth interviewing, or focus-group discussions; these are just different names for a similar procedure. The idea is to bring together a group of about fifteen people with similar interests (a focus group) and discuss with them ideas about an organization and its products, policies, or whatever. Focus-group interviewing is a more structured approach to getting the opinions of the group. Focus-group discussions tend to be unstructured, open sessions in which the participants are free to say whatever they want. Such sessions are very helpful in developing hypotheses that can be tested by further research. Often people talking in an open atmosphere will reveal much more about their true attitudes and beliefs than they will when answering

[13] Ernest S. Bradford, *Bradford's Directory of Marketing Research Agencies and Management Consultants,* 15th ed. (Middleburg, Vt.: Bradford Co., 1973–1974).

[14] For example, see Paul E. Green and Donald S. Tull, *Research for Marketing Decisions,* 4th ed. (Englewood Cliffs, N.J.: Prentice-Hall, Inc., 1978) or Gilbert A. Churchhill, Jr., *Marketing Research* (Hinsdale, Ill.: The Dryden Press, 1976).

Table 6.2 HELPFUL SOURCES OF SECONDARY DATA

Data base	Originator	Scope	Input
ABI/INFORM Abstracted Business Information	ABI, Inc. 620 S. 5th St. Louisville, Ky. 40202	Finance, economics, statistics, marketing, business law	Abstracts from over 300 business management journals
AcCIS American Statistics Index and Congressional Information Service/Index	Congressional Information Service 7101 Wisconsin Ave. Washington, D.C. 20014	CIS/Index and American Statistics Index	All congressional records and statistical data issued by federal government
EIS Economic Information Systems, Inc.	EIS 9 East 41st St. New York, N.Y. 10017	Who buys what, where, and how much	Census material, corporate reports, financial studies, industrial, trade, and telephone directories
IDDD International Demographic Data Directory	U.S. Bureau Census International Statistical Program Center Washington, D.C. 20233	Worldwide demographic and family-planning data, emphasis on developing countries	Surveys, official statistical publications, data from international organizations, census reports
A.C. Nielson Company	A.C. Nielson Co. Nielson Plaza Northbrook, Ill. 60062	Marketing research, TV audience and magazine readership measurement	Field surveys, sample data
NTIS National Technical Information Service	NTIS U.S. Department of Commerce 5825 Port Royal Rd. Springfield, Va. 22151	Government research and development reports and analyses	From *Weekly Government Abstracts*

SOCIAL SCISEARCH (citation searching)[a]	Institute for Scientific Information 325 Chestnut St. Philadelphia, Pa. 19106	Multidisciplinary social sciences	Covers significant items from 1,400 of world's leading social science journals
PREDICASTS, Inc.	PREDICASTS 200 University Circle Research Center 11001 Cedar Ave. Cleveland, Ohio 44106	Maintains six files: (1) domestic statistics (time series, forecasts on U.S. economics, demographics, finance, and production); (2) international statistics; (3) EIS plants (data and classification of industrial plants in United States); (4) F & S indexes (citations to articles relevant to business); (5) market abstracts (chemical and equipment); (6) weekly (current chemical and equipment market information)	

[a] Citation searching means you can ask the system to locate all items that have referenced a specified earlier document, whether it be a journal, article, book, thesis, or any other type of document. System is based on the proved concept that there is a significant subject relationship between an article and the earlier material which it cites.

From Patsy K. Smith, "How to Do a Computerized Literature Search" (unpublished research paper, The University of Maryland, 1976); see also Robert F. Dyer and Joseph P. Weintraub, "How to Plan and Conduct Searches of Computer-Retrievable, Bibliographic Data Bases for Marketing and Consumer Research," *Marketing News*, January 16, 1976, p. 20.

formal questionnaires or survey questions. The goals of focus-group techniques and more quantitative research efforts are complementary:

The goal of focus-group research is to learn and understand what people have to say and why. The emphasis is on getting people talking at length and in detail about the subject at hand—how they feel about it, how it fits into their lives, their emotional involvement with it, and so forth.

At some point, however, when the questions of what and why have been explored, quantitative research needs to be employed to add the dimensions of how much, how many, and to what extent.[15]

Imp.

There are many techniques for gathering and processing marketing data. The proper technique is the one that answers the research problem best and fastest at a minimum cost. At times, nothing more than a brief period of personal observation will be needed. At other times, you might become involved in large nationwide surveys that last an hour or more per respondent and involve several variables. It is important for any marketer (buyers and sellers) to have a good understanding of marketing research principles and techniques. A course on this topic usually provides the best foundation, but research is learned best by doing it. One of the more difficult tasks of marketing researchers is writing a readable, helpful report.

Analyze Data and Prepare a Report A research project should not be considered finished until the information is made available to decision makers and they have resolved the problem. Research is really an ongoing process with no real beginning or end. The data analysis and report presentation should recognize this fact. The report should adapt to the needs of the *user*, not of the researcher. The data analysis may be as complex as needed, but the report on that analysis should be in a language that is readable, understandable, and directly usable. Not all data need go into the report, but they should be available if needed later.

Suggest Alternative Actions and Recommendations Research reports tend to be rather impersonal and full of facts and figures. Too often the researcher is asked to merely gather the facts, not to make recommendations. It is sometimes better, though, if the researcher becomes more personally involved in the problem-definition stage *and* the problem-solution stage. Several alternative courses of action may be recommended, and some indication of the consequences of each may be pointed out. As McInnes has noted: "It is not research information but action based on correct information that can yield results."[16]

---

[15]"Shafer Answers 3 Most Frequently Asked Focus-Group Questions," *Marketing News*, November 21, 1975, p. 8. See also the entire edition of *Marketing News*, January 16, 1976.

[16]William McInnes, "A Conceptual Approach to Marketing," in *Theory in Marketing*, ed. Reavis Cox, Wroe Alderson, and Stanley J. Shapiro (Homewood, Ill.: Richard D. Irwin, Inc., 1964).

Follow Up What was done as a result of the research? Is the problem resolved? Do we need more information? Where are we now? Where do we go next? These are the kinds of questions that should be asked, but often are not asked, after a research project is completed. Research is just one part of a total information system, and so it should be involved continuously in analyzing potential problem situations, gathering data, and working with the information-systems personnel to keep the organization running smoothly. Research projects, together with the results of any action taken, should be stored for future reference. In many firms, research projects are one-shot deals, and any reports are destroyed after use. Each new project must then begin anew, with no past research results to use as a guide. How often have you thrown away information after making a purchase and regretted it later on when a friend needed it? We must learn to gather, process, *and* store data more efficiently so as to make marketing decision making more effective for everyone concerned.

FOR REVIEW

Key Terms

Among the more important terms and expressions discussed in this chapter are the following:

 A **marketing information system (MIS)** is the process of gathering, processing, storing, and using information to make better marketing decisions and to improve marketing exchanges.

Marketing intelligence is the continuous, flexible process of actively monitoring relevant external and internal data to provide input into all marketing decisions.

Marketing research is a periodic, structured process of gathering information relative to a particular marketing problem.

Primary research is the process by which a researcher gathers information on his or her own without relying on secondary data.

Promotional communications involve sending informative and persuasive messages to the public.

A **public** is a distinct group of people and/or organizations that have an actual or a potential interest and/or impact on an organization.

Sales forecasting is the process of estimating future sales results.

Secondary data consist of any information that is readily available in published form. *Be careful of who did it.*

Key Concepts

Among the more important marketing concepts introduced in this chapter are the following:

➤ **Organizations should monitor consumers to get their opinions and reactions to the organization and its products, policies, and personnel;**

such information should be gathered from present customers, previous customers, noncustomers, and employees.

> Marketing intelligence data from external sources should be combined with internally generated data to provide a continuous information flow to marketing decision makers and other personnel.

> An operating marketing information system that opens two-way flows of information among organizations gives all of the organizations a better chance to improve their marketing programs and leads to more cooperation, harmony, and understanding for the whole system.

> Marketing research data has a cost and should be controlled like other costs; gather information only so long as the benefits of acquiring it exceed the cost.

> So much information is available that all people could use a person-alized marketing information system to help organize information: such information helps make better-prepared shoppers, more aware voters, more informed conversationalists, and more knowledgeable members of the community.

> The imperfections of our economic system can be eliminated in part, or at least minimized, through the proper use of quality information.

Discussion Questions

1. Can buyers use marketing research as well as sellers? Explain and give examples to prove your point.

2. Explain the difference between marketing research and marketing intelligence by giving several examples of each.

3. "What organizations need today is more information." Do you agree? If yes, what kind of information? If no, what do organizations need?

4. Most people view marketing intelligence as gathering data about the environment. Explain why internal marketing intelligence is equally important. What are examples of facts and figures that are key internal data?

5. "In most instances, competition today is between channel systems, not between individual firms; therefore, there should be interfirm cooperation and coordination, which is best managed through a marketing information system." Do you agree? Why or why not? Give examples.

6. List the various "publics" of your local bank. Which are the most important? Why?

7. Discuss how you could use MIS concepts to help in your personal life (for example, for vacations, food purchases, voting). Is this unrealistic?

8. "An organization could always use more marketing research; there is never too much information." Do you agree? Why or why not?

9. What are the major categories of marketing research? Do present-day research efforts reflect the marketing concept in action? Discuss.

10. Is marketing research a useful function in nonprofit organizations? Why or why not?

CASES

A North American Oil Company
Controlling the Research Process

A major North American oil company experienced a slow but steady fall-off in profits. Top management decided to call in an expert on consumer behavior to conduct an attitude survey. Management was sure that consumers were not buying for some reason, but they were not sure what the reason was.

The consultant asked the managers which of their products were most profitable. The managers said they did not have profit figures for individual products, only for major groupings. The consultant then asked to see marketing research studies from the past to see what they might reveal. There had been several major studies, but the head of marketing research had left recently, and no one knew where the old reports were. The consultant then asked to meet the marketing manager so that an agreement could be reached on what kind of research was needed and what would be done with the results. The company did not have a marketing manager—only a sales manager, an advertising manager, a distribution manager, and a new marketing research director.

The consultant asked if he could meet with each of these managers to get some feel for corporate marketing practices. He found that there was little coordination between the sales managers and the advertising manager. Neither of these managers knew the distribution manager very well—he was located in another city in a major distribution center. The new marketing research director had never conducted any studies except those specifically requested by top management and had rarely worked closely with the sales or advertising manager.

1. Should the consultant go ahead with his attitude survey? Why or why not?

2. If you were a marketing consultant, what changes would you make at the oil company?

3. What kind of research study (or studies) do you think the company needs?

4. Would a marketing information system benefit this company? How?

Becoming a Better Buyer
Setting up a Personal MIS

Ellen Jean Simpson just could not find the time to be the good consumer she wanted to be. Ellen Jean was taking night courses at the local community college and was rearing three children (ages $1\frac{1}{2}$, 3, and 5) during the day. Although she tried to keep up on current events, Ellen Jean was often embarassed at parties when she did not understand jokes about current political events and could not debate current issues with much background knowledge. In short, Ellen Jean felt trapped by her family obligations and course work.

To keep herself informed about consumer issues, Ellen Jean read *Consumer Reports* and the food section of her daily paper. But whenever she was ready to buy something, Ellen Jean couldn't remember which products were recommended and which weren't. Ellen Jean also read parts of *Time* magazine and other magazines when she had a chance. But she could never remember many details about controversial subjects such as tax reform, social security financing, campaign promises, and the like.

1. How could a marketing information system help Ellen Jean become a better student, conversationalist, and consumer?

2. A marketing information system consists of three elements: marketing intelligence; data analysis, storage, and retrieval; and promotion. How could Ellen Jean use each of these to lower her grocery bill?

3. Ellen Jean must write a paper on private versus national brands. How could she use a marketing information system to make her paper more effective?

4. Ellen Jean found that many of her neighbors and friends have similar problems in finding and remembering facts, figures, and other information. How could Ellen Jean set up a multihousehold MIS for her neighborhood?

Consumer Behavior 7
understanding market influences

LEARNING GOALS After you have read and studied this chapter, you should be able to:

1. Give several examples of external influences on consumer behavior from your own experiences.

2. Explain why consumer behavior varies in different circumstances (for example, a dinner party versus an ordinary family meal.)

3. Define the following terms: attitude; culture; opinion leader; primary group; reference group; and selective perception.

4. Explain the relative importance of promotional communication versus the other external influences on consumer behavior. Are we most influenced by TV?

5. Show how leaders in all organizations can benefit from a knowledge of consumer behavior concepts.

6. Discuss how buyer behavior affects the seller.

7. Draw a diagram of external and internal influences on consumer behavior.

8. Use the concepts of selective exposure, selective perception, and selective retention to explain why many students do poorly in statistics courses.

9. Compare cultural influences in your neighborhood to those of a student in another country.

10. Understand your own consumption behavior better by learning what factors influence you decisions.

> *In every field or discipline there always appear to be a few simple questions that are highly embarrassing because the debate that forever swirls around them seemingly leads only to perpetual failure and ultimately makes ardent fools of the most expert. "Why do customers buy goods?" is an example of just such a question in marketing.*
>
> Rom J. Markin, Jr.*

INTRODUCTION When Horace Lambertson was 16 years old, he wanted an old car to drive around in. He was not particular about how it looked or how much mileage it got. He just wanted to drive! At the time, Horace felt comfortable wearing Levis and different T-shirts, and he had long, curly hair that fell down to his shoulders. Horace did not ride his bicycle much; in fact, Horace did not do much other than hang around with the guys, play music, go to school, and generally fuss around.

A couple of years later, when Horace went to State College, he bought a Volkswagen bus to carry his things to school. He carpeted the whole back end, put in extra speakers for the radio, and painted the exterior with wild colors. Horace still wore Levis most of the time, but he would occasionally wear slacks and a sport shirt. Horace usually wore wire-rim glasses, a wide leather watch band, and Earth shoes; he also kept his hair a little shorter and neater. He rode his bike to school often and carried his books in a sack on his back.

Horace graduated in the middle of his class (he was an economics major) and began looking for a job. He got his hair cut, bought a rather conservative blue suit, and found a job as an adjuster for an insurance company. Horace carried his insurance papers in a brief case and drove a Dodge Dart. He got his own apartment and immediately bought a new stereo, some furniture, a water bed, a clock radio, and an entire new wardrobe of suits, slacks, ties, and dress shoes.

Horace is 38 now, has a house in the suburbs, drives a station wagon, and works for a government agency. He has three children and spends much of his free time taking them hiking and bike riding. Horace is studying for an MBA degree at night, dresses rather conservatively, and works hard at the job and at school.

Horace is also quite active in his church. He had attended church with his parents when he was young, but he did not go to church for several years before, during, and after college. Horace gives money to church and to several charities. He also gives time to the local Boy Scout troop to which his son belongs.

Horace is a typical college graduate who has lived a relatively normal life. From Horace, we can learn something about how people behave, why they behave that way, and what influences their behavior. We are especially interested in Horace's consumption behavior and his attitudes toward today's organizations, because this chapter is about consumer behavior and consumer attitudes toward marketing and its institutions.

* *Consumer Behavior—A Cognitive Approach* (New York: Macmillan Publishing Co., Inc., 1974), p. 3.

We shall highlight the material by returning to our summary of Horace's behavior over the years and by analyzing the forces that may have influenced his actions.

EXTERNAL INFLUENCES ON CONSUMER BEHAVIOR

We shall begin the analysis of consumer behavior by looking at the *external forces* that influence market behavior. For example, we shall look at culture and its influence on attitudes and behavior. We shall also explore various subcultures and social classes and their effect on individuals. We shall then explore the interaction between self-image and the influence of outside individuals and groups. All of these influences are summarized in Figure 7.1.

Consumer behavior is also determined by individuals and their personalities and attitudes. We shall look at consumer perceptions, learning concepts, and other internal variables (see Figure 7.1 for a summary).

We shall conclude the chapter by discussing the influence of consumers on marketers and the importance of consumer behavior concepts in all social organizations. It is important to recognize the fact that consumers are half of the exchange relationship and need as much study and analysis as do businesses and government agencies (the other half of the exchange).

Culture and Consumer Behavior

Much of what Horace and other Americans do is determined by the culture in which they live. **Culture,** essentially, consists of a set of fairly standardized prescriptions concerning what must be done, should be done, may be done, and must not be done.[1] These prescriptions are passed down from generation to generation and remain more or less stable over time. Much of our behavior is socially determined, and we usually give little thought to why we do such socially acceptable things.

For example, Horace went to college right after high school. Why? One important reason is that Americans value higher education. It is socially acceptable, or even socially necessary in some communities, to go to college. The value Americans place on education is just one of many cultural norms (standards of behavior) that have an important influence on behavior.

Cultural norms vary greatly in content, influence, and enforcement, but they affect every action we take. From the time we get up in the morning, we are a product of our culture. Even the fact that we get up at a certain time is culturally determined. Men in the United States often shower every day (unusual cultural behavior by worldwide standards), use deodorant, shave, and use various kinds of sweet smelling lotions (some of this behavior would be considered rather peculiar in most other countries). For breakfast, a man might have orange juice, bacon and eggs, toast, and coffee. Such a breakfast is unheard of in most nations. After breakfast, men like Horace get into their cars, drive to work, eat lunch around noon, quit at 5:00 P.M. or so, and go home for dinner. Some

---

[1] W. Thomas Anderson, Jr., Catherine C. Bentley, and Louis K. Sharpe, *IV, Multidimensional Marketing* (Austin, Tex.: Lone Star Publishers, Inc., 1976), p. 215.

Figure 7.1 FACTORS AND FORCES INFLUENCING CONSUMER BEHAVIOR

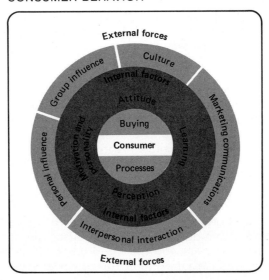

From Robert J. Holloway, Robert Mittelstaedt, and M. M. Vankatesen, *Consumer Behavior: Contemporary Research in Action* (Boston: Houghton Mifflin Company, 1971). Copyright © 1971 by Houghton Mifflin Company. Reprinted by permission of the publisher.

time is spent with the children, and then it's into the family room for TV and on to bed. All of this behavior is patterned after similar behavior of our fathers, our fathers' fathers, and so on. They and their families have taught us what is "right" to do and what is not "right" to do.

The majority of the people who live in the United States have been taught to value activity and work; success has been traditionally determined by wealth; freedom has been something worth dying for, and equality is equally important. Americans are largely materialistic, achievement-oriented, and nationalistic, and they demand ethical and moral behavior if it does not interfere with the other goals. These too are cultural in origin and are part of our very makeup and personality.

Cultural norms are reflected in religious beliefs, customs, laws, government regulations, business codes and standards, union rules, and other such guides to acceptable behavior. These norms affect how marketers sell and how consumers buy. They affect everything people do.

Horace's cultural surroundings have taught him to value religion and religious freedom and to love and respect his family and friends. He has learned that he should donate some of his time and money to others, work hard, and serve his country whenever he is needed. Horace has also learned to fear Communism, to look unfavorably upon homosexual behavior, and to scorn those who are lazy and show little interest in work. His goal is to dress nicely, to own his own home, and to strive for material success in general. What are your own personal values, attitudes, and behavior patterns? Compare them sometime with someone from Japan, India, the USSR, or some other foreign culture (even England); you will see how much your life has been formed by cultural prescriptions and norms of behavior. The concepts one may derive from this discussion are:

> Much of any person's personal behavior and consumption behavior is determined by his or her culture.

> Cultural norms become institutionalized through the church, government, codes of ethics, schools, and other organizations.

> Cultural norms vary considerably from nation to nation and even from neighborhood to neighborhood.

Subcultures in the United States Horace bought much of what he owns and behaves as he does partially because he was reared in a Western subculture. That is, he was influenced by the cultural patterns of Europeans, Americans, and other Western peoples. Because he was reared in the United States, Horace is more influenced by the subcultural influence of the United States. There are various subcultures *within* the United States that also influence personal behavior and consumption behavior. These subcultures are based on ethnic background, religion, social class, language, age, education, occupation, and other factors.

One subculture that you might be familiar with is the youth subculture. You may have noticed that young people seem to prefer certain movies, music, food, and clothing that are different from those chosen by the middle-aged subculture. Similarly, black consumers often choose foods, clothing, and music that differ from those preferred by Oriental consumers. Similarly, the life-style of people who live in California differs from that of people in North Dakota.

Subcultural behavior affects every area of marketing management, including product design, pricing, promotion, and distribution. Some subcultures value innovation and leisure living. Other subcultures stress the "Protestant ethic" and frown on many modern life-styles. The concepts are:

> The U.S. market is made up of many subcultures that influence the success of marketing efforts to establish mutually satisfying exchanges.

> It is better (easier) to appeal to existing cultural patterns of behavior than to create new purchasing patterns or new wants.

> Sellers should establish different market strategies for each major subculture; such strategies should include product, pricing, distribution, and promotional considerations.

Social Class and Consumer Behavior The members of a particular social class tend to have similar attitudes, values, and behavior that vary somewhat from members of other social classes. The following traditional hierarchy of social class was developed several years ago by Warner and Lunt:[2]

1. *Upper-upper*—individuals with old wealth and family status
2. *Lower-upper*—individuals with newer wealth and no family status

---

[2] W. Lloyd Warner and Paul Lunt, *The Social Life of a Modern Community* (New Haven, Conn.: Yale University Press, 1950), pp. 81–91.

3. *Upper-middle*—professionals and managers
4. *Lower-middle*—white-collar workers
5. *Upper-lower*—blue-collar workers
6. *Lower-lower*—unskilled workers

These classes are often based on variables such as occupational status, income (or source of income), level of education, and location of home. Income is no longer a very good indicator of social class because college professors and blue-collar workers may make similar incomes but belong to different social classes. But occupational status and level of education together with income is a pretty good indicator of class position. The concepts are:

› Consumers in the United States can be classified into social-class rankings based on several variables such as income and level of education.

› Members of various social classes tend to have similar values, attitudes, and consumption behavior; marketers can thus use social class as a segmentation variable.

Self-Image and Consumer Behavior Imagine yourself growing up as Horace did, going to college, becoming a parent, assuming more and more responsibilities, and having different images of yourself as you grow older. One very important influence on consumer behavior is self-image (self-concept). Self-image is a view of self that is a combination of how people think about themselves and how they feel others think of them. It is influenced by various psychological, physiological, social, and economic needs.

Horace found that a 16-year-old is often in a hurry to "grow up." He or she may want a car (a symbol of maturity), to "do his or her own thing" (that is, not do what their parents want them to), to smoke and to drink (both symbols of maturity), and to stay out late. A 16-year-old boy often does not have a very positive self-image. As Horace did, he may struggle to prove his worth through externals like a car, clothing, and "being cool." His shopping behavior often reflects that image in that much of what he buys may be influenced by the need to be liked, to look mature, and to be his idea of what a 16-year-old should be.

How quickly a person's image changes depends a lot on how much responsibility he or she has. For example, Horace did not change much during his college years because he was still receiving much of the money he needed from his parents. He still wore the kind of clothes he wore in high school, drove a Volkswagen because it was "cool," and generally acted just as he thought a college student should act.

But during the last couple of months before Horace was graduated from college, a different person emerged. That person was Horace the college graduate, the guy who needed a job, the man with new challenges and opportunities. Horace started thinking more like a businessman than a student. He wore businessman clothes, carried a businessman's brief case, and eventually bought a businessman's car. Actually, what Horace did was buy what he thought a businessman *should* buy.

Horace's self-image was changing from that of a dependent student to a self-reliant, self-confident professional person. Horace found himself drinking liquor instead of beer. He often ate at restaurants rather than fast-food outlets. And he surrounded himself with what he thought a successful person should have (a stereo, a color TV, and so on).

You can imagine how Horace feels now that he is a husband, father, Boy Scout leader, churchgoer, and voting Republican. His self-image still dictates much of what he buys, where he buys it, how much he is willing to pay, and other such decisions. Of course, Horace is now influenced greatly by his wife and children, his straining budget, and other external factors. Let us stop here for a minute and see what concepts we can learn from Horace. The concepts are:

> **Self-image, which is how people think of themselves and how they feel others think of them, is a major determinant of consumer behavior.**

> **A seller who wishes to satisfy consumers should study their self-image and try to emphathize with them; the products offered, the promotional program, the pricing strategy, and the location of the products should all enhance those self-images.**

> **People change their self-image over time, and various demographic segments can be further segmented by self-image characteristics;**

Self-concept and Consumption Behavior

1. An individual does have a self-concept of himself.
2. The self-concept is of value to him.
3. Because this self-concept is of value to him, an individual's behavior will be directed toward the furtherance and enhancement of his self-concept.
4. An individual's self-concept is formed through the interaction process with parents, peers, teachers, and significant others.
5. Goods serve as social symbols and, therefore, are communication devices for the individual.
6. The use of these good-symbols communicates meaning to the individual himself and to others, causing an impact on the intra-action and/or the interaction processes and, therefore, an effect on the individual's self-concept.

Prediction of the model:

7. Therefore, the consuming behavior of an individual will be directed toward the furthering and enhancing of his self-concept through the consumption of goods as symbols.

From Edward L. Grubb and Harrison L. Grathwohl, "Consumer Self-Concept, Symbolism and Market Behavior: A Theoretical Approach," *Journal of Marketing,* October 1967, pp. 22–27. Reprinted with permission of the American Marketing Association.

psychographic segmentation helps a seller to discover a target market's self-concept.

> If a seller can determine what a buyer's self-image is, then the seller can predict what the buyer's goals are and what his or her purchasing behavior is likely to be.

The insert "Self-Concept and Consumption Behavior" is a descriptive model that is helpful in relating consumption behavior to the self-concept (self-image) of individuals. Although the authors of the insert stress the exchange of "goods," the concepts, with only slight changes, apply equally well to services, ideas, and causes. Can you think of how giving a donation to charity would enhance a person's self-concept?

Group Influence on Consumer Behavior
Part of a person's self-image is determined by how he or she feels others think. Another major influence on consumer behavior, therefore, is group influence. The greatest influence comes from those people with whom we have regular, intimate, face-to-face relationships—the family, friends, work groups, and some close social groups. (These are called **primary groups**.) Horace was very surprised to see how his purchasing behavior was influenced by his children ("I want a hamburger"), by his wife, and by his close friends. No longer could Horace go grocery shopping without considering the needs of the family as well as his own needs. And often Horace joined the same clubs, went to the same vacation spots, and ate at the same restaurants as his friends. The concepts are:

> Consumers are greatly influenced in their purchasing behavior by primary groups such as family and friends.

> Marketers often must direct their promotions to groups of people (for example a whole family) rather than to particular individuals.

An individual is also influenced by a whole series of **secondary groups** such as church members, the local community, and casual social groups such as a bowling league. A person tends to go along with the opinions, behavior, and beliefs of such groups (but to a lesser extent than in the case of primary groups). For example, if the church group decides to boycott a certain movie theater because it shows X-rated films, chances are most of the members will agree. The concepts are:

> A person's purchasing behavior is influenced by a whole series of secondary groups who might have a significant influence on particular behavior.

> A seller often would benefit by developing programs that appeal to various social groups, because the group will influence many individuals; for example, a special offer may be made to everyone who belongs to a certain club or bowls in a certain league.

Reference Groups Much of what a person says and does is based on his or her interpretation of what others would expect. A **reference group** is that group (or groups) that an individual uses as a frame of reference in forming ideas about the "right" way of thinking and behaving. For example, Horace's reference group when he was in high school and college was his fellow students. Horace dressed, thought, and behaved according to the norms of his schoolmates.

A reference group is not necessarily a group to which a person actually belongs or will ever join. For example, Horace's reference group when he was a senior in college was business executives. He did not belong to that group, but he began to dress and act *as if* he were a businessman. Other reference groups also influenced his behavior at that time. For instance, he was very impressed by some active members of his church and other adults who volunteered to help others. Eventually Horace became an active church member himself and was a very committed volunteer in the Boy Scouts.

Reference groups can influence what one wears, what clubs one joins, where one lives, how one spends his or her leisure time, and, more importantly for this discussion, where one shops, what one buys, and how one reacts to various market offers. People tend to imitate the opinions and behavior of their reference groups. The concepts are:

> A reference group is a group (or groups) that a person uses as a guide for deciding what is the "right" way of thinking and behaving—including shopping and consumption behavior.

> A person need not belong to a reference group to be influenced by it.

Influence of Opinion Leaders on Consumer Behavior Discussions with Horace revealed that much of his purchasing behavior was influenced by individuals rather than by groups. Such individuals are called **opinion leaders.** Horace called such influence "word-of-mouth advertising" although, strictly speaking, it is neither advertising (because it is not paid for) nor is it restricted to words (that is, others may influence you by what they do as well as what they *say*).

Some marketing experts feel that personal influence occurs in a two-step flow. That is, a seller will promote a new product in the media, some opinion leader will read about it, and the opinion leader will tell others. The two steps are: (1) from medium to opinion leader and (2) from opinion leader to others. Much evidence supports such a model, but other evidence suggests that the model is too one-sided. That is, discussions about products may be initiated by an opinion leader *or* by someone *seeking information* from another person (an opinion seeker). Opinion leaders, therefore, both influence, and are influenced by, others (see Figure 7.2).

Horace says that marketers should try to reach opinion leaders because they are so effective in influencing others. Horace is right, of course—the problem is how to find opinion leaders and how to get them to say nice things about a product.

Horace feels that is easy; just reach people such as congresspersons and movie stars, and they will influence others. This approach is called the "trickle down" theory and assumes that upper-class people will influence middle-class people who will in turn influence lower class people. But research has shown that this is not so. After all, a woman does not consult her local congressperson or TV personality to ask advice about the purchase of a new refrigerator or carpet. Instead, she is likely to ask friends, neighbors, and salespeople.

Research has shown that opinion leaders vary depending on the product. For example, as you might expect, the opinion leader for food tends to be a married woman with several children who is rather outgoing.[3] The opinion leader for fashion tends to be young and outgoing (friendly). Opinion leaders appear in all social classes and are of varying ages, but *rarely are they opinion leaders for more than a couple of products*. There do not seem to be generalized opinion leaders—only people whose opinion is sought on certain specific products. Furthermore, opinion leaders tend to be of the same social class as those they influence; they are generally outgoing, friendly, innovative, and knowledgeable; they tend to follow group norms more closely; but they do not seem to have any distinguishable personality features.[4]

The problem one finds after reviewing all the literature is that opinion leaders are *not* easily identified. In fact, everyone is a potential opinion leader for some product category. Some recommended strategies for sellers include:

[3] See the classic study by Elihu Katz and Paul F. Lazarsfeld, *Personal Influence* (Glencoe, Ill.: The Free Press, 1955).

[4] These conclusions are based on a whole series of studies. You can find up-to-date material on this subject in most consumer behavior texts or communications texts. See, for example, James F. Engel, David T. Kollat, and Roger D. Blackwell, *Consumer Behavior*, 2nd ed. (New York: Holt, Rinehart and Winston, Inc., 1973) or Lee Richardson, ed., *Dimensions of Communication* (New York: Appleton-Century-Crofts, 1969), pp. 193–263.

Figure 7.2 ONE-STEP VERSUS TWO-STEP MODEL OF PROMOTIONAL COMMUNICATION

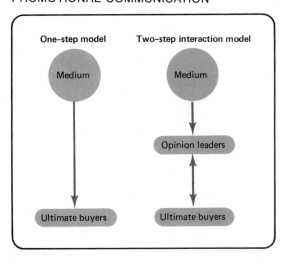

Is Morris an opinion leader?

"How come Morris loves it?"

Reprinted with permission from the April 12, 1976, issue of *Advertising Age.* Copyright 1976 by Crain Communications, Inc.

1. Make opinion leaders by giving people the product and encouraging them to discuss it with others; for example, sell one prominent community leader a new pool at cost to influence others to "keep up with the Joneses."

2. Create artificial opinion leaders in TV commercials; for example, have someone who appears knowledgeable and outgoing explain product benefits to a neighbor in a natural environment. These are sometimes called "slice-of-life" commercials.

3. Use professionals such as doctors, lawyers, dentists, and architects as opinion leaders for products they would be expected to recommend; that is, give them free samples or educate them on the advantages of your product.

4. Use socially prominent people in ads as opinion leaders; for example, a racing car driver could recommend a certain kind of motor oil.

5. Study the characteristics of opinion leaders for a particular product (including what TV shows they prefer) and promote the product where these people will see it.

Promotional Communications and Consumer Behavior

One should not overlook the role promotional communications (marketing communications) play in influencing consumer behavior. One myth in marketing is that producers use promotion to deceive and manipulate consumers. Consumers are not easily deceived or manipulated, but they can be influenced by marketing information and persuasion. Consumers often review newspaper advertisements before setting out to buy groceries, appliances, and even major purchases such as cars and homes. Such advertisements provide basic information about price, location, availability, and a few product benefits.

Studies have shown that advertising may be a factor in influencing where people shop for groceries.[5] Other studies have shown that consumers often turn to the media for information about upcoming purchases.[6] Of course salespeople, displays, sales promotions, and other marketing efforts also influence when and if consumers buy. The concepts are:

> **One major influence on consumer behavior is the information (and persuasion) people receive from marketing organizations.**

> **Marketing information interacts with other external factors such as culture, group influence, and personal influences to create an environment that motivates exchange behavior.**

Economic Influences on Consumer Behavior Two of the more significant influences on consumer behavior are the economic condition of the nation *and* the economic condition of particular consumers. When the economy is booming and the general mood is one of optimism, consumer spending on housing, appliances, and other products opens up. But when economic conditions are bad and the national mood is pessimistic, consumer spending slows considerably (even for those people who are not directly affected by the economy). The concept is:

> **Many industries are affected by perceived national economic conditions in that sales increase when the economy is perceived as doing well and fall when the economy is perceived as doing poorly.**

A more obvious influence on consumer behavior is the personal economic situation of individual consumers. Horace, for example, feels constrained in his desire to satisfy his own needs by the fact that he has a family to help support. Inflation and taxes have lowered Horace's purchasing power recently and he has learned to economize, make do, and generally cut back on spending.

INTERNAL INFLUENCES ON CONSUMER BEHAVIOR In addition to the external factors we have discussed thus far, consumer behavior is influenced by the buyer and his or her internal makeup. Figure 7.1 shows that attitudes, perception, learning, motivation, and personality are all internal factors that a marketer should consider when analyzing consumer behavior. The following sections will give you a brief introduction to the wealth of information available on these sub-

[5] Kenward L. Atkin, "Advertising and Store Patronage," *Journal of Advertising Research*, December 1966, pp. 18–23.

[6] See, for example, William Lazer and William E. Bell, "The Communications Process and Innovation," *Journal of Advertising Research*, September 1966, pp. 2–7.

jects. Let us begin with perception because how we perceive things greatly affects our exchange behavior. Remember the principle we discussed earlier: "The product is what the consumer thinks it is."

Perception Throughout this book, you will be reminded that consumer perception is a critical variable in establishing exchange relationships. How consumers perceive the product offer and the organization making that offer are perhaps *the* most important criteria for choosing between similar products. It is important, therefore, for a marketing student to know something about consumer perception.

One of the more important concepts to understand is *selectivity of perception.* People see largely what they want to see, hear what they want to hear, and believe what they want to believe. Marketers must learn to deal with those realities. People will tend to avoid those messages that conflict with their predispositions. Thus, smokers will tend to avoid articles and commercials about the dangers of smoking, and Democrats will tend to avoid commercials for Republicans. This tendency is called **selective exposure.** It means, for one thing, that people will avoid most promotional messages. To break through this perceptual barrier, marketers must make their messages relevant and interesting to the target market.

Even when messages do reach consumers (which is the exception), there is a tendency to disparage the source or twist the meaning of the communication. This tendency is called **selective perception.** This phenomenon is very obvious during a basketball game, when the referees always seem to favor the other team. The reason is that the home crowd selectively perceives the plays. Similarly, consumers selectively perceive product offers (including promotions) based on their past experiences and prejudices. Marketers must learn to overcome these tendencies by designing messages that are likely to be accepted.

But consumers also tend to forget what is said by marketers. This tendency is called **selective retention.** A 15-year-old girl may remember all the batting averages of her favorite players but forget entirely her piano lesson at 3:00 P.M. Similarly, a consumer will remember dozens of myths ("Toads will give you warts"), but forget which laundry detergent is "bluer than blue."

Part of a person's perception of product offers is based on his or her self-image, as we discussed earlier. But perceptions are also the result of experiences, learning, attitudes, and personality. The concepts are:

> **Perceptions of product offers and the organizations making them are critical to the establishment of exchange relationships.**

> **Perception is largely selective—consumers will avoid most messages (selective exposure), distort those they do see (selective perception), and forget much of what they have seen and heard (selective retention).**

Sometimes marketers use repetition to penetrate the consumer's selective processes. In addition, marketers usually try to design messages that are not offensive to consumers and fit their predispositions of reality and truth. Nonetheless, it is difficult to change consumer attitudes.

Attitudes   No doubt you have formed either positive or negative attitudes about certain products such as American cars, electric razors, and freeze-dried coffee. These attitudes are based partially on your perceptions of these products and what you have learned from experience and from others. In fact, an **attitude** may be defined as a learned tendency to react to a product offer in a consistently favorable or unfavorable manner.

It is a natural tendency to feel that attitudes are a fairly accurate predictor of future behavior. In fact, many marketing studies center on attitudes in the hope of determining what consumers will do. But research has shown that there is not necessarily any correlation between attitudes and behavior:

> *After more than 70–75 years of attitude research, there is still little, if any, consistent evidence supporting the hypothesis that knowledge of an individual's attitude toward some object will allow one to predict the way he will behave with respect to that object. Indeed, what little evidence there is to support any relationship between attitude and behavior comes from studies demonstrating that a person tends to bring his attitude into line with his behavior rather than from studies demonstrating that behavior is a function of attitude.*[7]

One study, for example, probed people's attitudes toward a new rapid-transit system. Almost everyone was in favor of the system and said they would use it. But in fact few of those who said they would use the system actually did use it. Most people seemed to be in favor of the system only because they hoped their neighbor would use it so that they could drive their car on less congested roads.

Nonetheless, several studies have shown that attitudes may be a fairly accurate measure of future behavior. Why the apparent conflict in

[7] Martin Fishbein, "Attitude and the Prediction of Behavior," in *Attitude Theory and Measurement*, ed. Martin Fishbein (New York: John Wiley & Sons, Inc., 1967), p. 477.

Attitudes Important to All Marketers

Almost everyone, regardless of the nature of their occupation or industry, is concerned with the concept of attitudes. The politician and the political scientists are interested in attitudes regarding taxation, housing, urban renewal, and voter appeal. Managers are interested in employees' attitudes as they might affect morale and productivity. Managers are also interested from the marketers point of view in consumers' attitudes regarding the company's products and in competitors' attitudes as they reflect market and product intentions . . . attitudes are, therefore, deemed an important variable in as well as an indicator of behavior in nearly every walk of life: religious, governmental, judiciary, administrative, and commercial.

From Rom J. Markin, Jr., *Consumer Behavior—A Cognitive Approach* (New York: Macmillan Publishing Co., Inc., 1974), p. 260.

results? It may be that some attitude measures are faulty or that the attitude concepts used were sometimes inaccurate. Other behavioral influences may also intervene to confuse the research findings.[8]

There has been some progress recently in designing more effective attitude measures.[9] You may have noted that your attitudes toward one product are much stronger, firmer, or certain than your attitudes toward other products. Strength of attitude is thus an important variable in determining future behavior. If you take a course in consumer behavior or marketing research, you will find that attitude research is becoming quite sophisticated. For our purposes, we hope you remember these basic concepts:

> **An attitude is a learned tendency to react to a product offer in a consistently favorable or unfavorable manner.**

> **Attitudes are not always a good predictor of consumer behavior.**

> **Attitudes can be changed by marketers, especially if the attitude is based on limited knowledge or if the person does not feel strongly about his or her present attitude.**

Personality When people talk about subjects such as attitudes and personality, there is an assumption that everyone is talking about the same thing. But there are dozens of definitions of attitudes and personality, each of which is slightly different. The reason for this is that each person's adjustment to the environment makes him or her different from anyone else. These differences include the way the person perceives the surroundings and the way he or she processes information and reacts to certain product offers or other stimuli. Differences between persons may be called their *personality.*

Marketers are interested in learning more about personality in order to improve market-segmentation techniques and to better understand consumer behavior. There is some question whether a person's personality is relatively fixed or varies over time and from situation to situation. One text has concluded that "future research that attempts to predict buyer behavior or identify market segments based on personality dimensions is destined to a low practical payout."[10]

Marketing researchers are continuing to study personality dimensions and hope to find more valuable information than is now available. We have already discussed how marketers are using activities, interests, and opinions as one technique for segmenting markets (psychographics). The concepts that provide the basis for further research are:

> **Personality differences among consumers affect their perceptions of product offers and their exchange behavior.**

[8] Engel et al., *Consumer Behavior,* p. 272

[9] See, for example, Martin Fishbein, "The Relationships Between Beliefs, Attitudes and Behavior," in *Cognitive Consistency,* ed. S. Feldman (New York: Academic Press, 1966), pp. 199–223.

[10] Engel et al., *Consumer Behavior,* pp. 296–297.

Models of Buyer Behavior

Marshallian man is concerned chiefly with economic cues—prices and income—and makes a fresh calculation before each purchase.

Pavlovian man behaves in a largely habitual way rather than thoughtful way; certain configurations of cues will set off the same behavior because of rewarded learning in the past.

Freudian man's choices are influenced strongly by motives and fantasies which take place deep in his private world.

Veblenian man acts in a way which is shaped largely by past and present social groups.

Hobbesian man seeks to reconcile individual gain with organizational gain.

From Philip Kotler, "Behavioral Models for Analyzing Buyers," *Journal of Marketing,* October 1965, pp. 37–45.

› **Marketers have limited success thus far in using personality as a segmentation variable or as a predictor of consumer behavior.**

The insert "Models of Buyer Behavior" summarizes much of what we have said about consumer behavior. Each of the models describes one element of consumer behavior. Consumers are actually a composite of all these people.

HOW LEARNING INFLUENCES BEHAVIOR Much of a person's consumption behavior is learned from his or her environment. Marketers have borrowed many concepts and principles from psychology and the other behavioral sciences to explain how learning affects behavior. In this section, we shall review some of the basic findings from that literature. We shall explore how people learn from experience, from practice, from association, and from others.

Learning from Experience Have you ever noticed that people tend to buy the same brand-name products each time they go to the store? They might change brands periodically, but they seem to stick with the same brand of cigarettes, coffee, and many other products. One explanation for such behavior is that people learn from experience what they like and do not like. They tend to repeat purchases that are satisfying and to cease purchases that are not satisfying. In psychology, this is called the "law of effect."

Experience has also taught many people that brand names tend to be more expensive, but better; that some stores sell quality and others emphasize price; and that some marketers will try to deceive the public. The concepts are:

› **Consumer behavior is affected by experience; people will tend to repeat purchases that satisfy and to cease purchases that do not satisfy.**

> Over time, consumers tend to repeat purchases that satisfy until the purchase becomes a habit; marketers of new, competing products often have a difficult time changing such habits.

> An experienced consumer is more aware of price/quality trade-offs and is more likely to optimize his or her exchange relationships.

Learning from Practice We learn to ride a bike, swim, and improve our exchange behavior by practicing. Usually children learn very quickly that the offers they see on television and read on packages are often not what they seem to be. Wise parents will let their children practice making marketing decisions. Children will learn from their mistakes and grow up to be more informed, more experienced buyers and sellers.

Shoppers will experiment with different products (practice different shopping behavior) and become more and more skilled at picking the most satisfying assortment. Practice, therefore, leads to experience and "experience is the best teacher," or so the saying goes. But consumers often cannot afford to learn from experience because items such as homes, cars, and color TV sets are too expensive to experiment with in the marketplace. Consumers are much wiser to learn from others' experiences or from education. These concepts are discussed further in the next section.

Learning from Others We have already discussed how people learn behavior (including shopping behavior) from their family, reference groups, and opinion leaders. But we did not emphasize the fact that people often talk to one another about products and purchases and learn much about how to improve their market exchanges. Some marketers call such communication *word-of-mouth* publicity. Certainly word-of-mouth is one of the bigger influences on consumer behavior.

Consumers may also learn from self-education. They may read magazines such as *Consumer Reports*, take courses in real estate, insurance, and other important consumer areas, and read books on personal finance.

Consumers may also learn much by shopping. Salespeople, brochures, and point-of-purchase materials may provide needed information for complex purchases. The consumer should work closely with retail employees and manufacturer's representatives to learn how to optimize the exchange relationship. The concepts are:

> One way to minimize the cost of market research for consumers is to share market information with others through word-of-mouth communication.

> Consumers can greatly improve their purchase behavior through a program of self-education that includes formal courses and informal reading of readily available literature.

> Consumers could make optimum use of their shopping time by consulting with salespeople and using the available brochures and point-of-purchase materials.

Learning from Association

We have learned to associate big cars and homes with wealth and status. We also have learned to associate certain products with feelings of fun and excitement. Promoters tend to reinforce such feelings by showing their products in a setting that creates a favorable image. Thus, one cigarette is associated with "springtime freshness," another with Marlboro country, and still another with women's newly found freedom ("You've come a long way, baby"). Consumers learn from such associations which products will fit their self-chosen image of themselves. Thus, one person may drive a Cadillac because it projects (and fits) a self-image of material success and luxury; another person may choose to drive a small economy car because it projects (and fits) a self-image of wise frugality and environmental awareness. The concept is:

› **Consumers learn to associate certain products with a particular self-image or life-style and will buy those products to fit their own self-image; promoters tend to reinforce such behavior by associating their products with a particular social group or life-style.**

WHY CONSUMER BEHAVIOR VARIES

David Kutz is a salesman for a major manufacturing firm. When Dave is traveling for his firm, he usually goes by plane, stays at moderately priced hotels, eats at the better restaurants, and has his shoes shined by the person in the hotel barber shop. However, when Dave travels with his family, he usually drives the family car, stays at discount motels, eats at fast-food restaurants or cafeterias, and wears old, beat-up shoes. Dave assumes two entirely different personalities in his roles as salesman and father. He is usually a free-spending, well-dressed professional on the job. But he becomes a rather conservative spender and dresses very casually while at home.

There are several other behavior patterns that make Dave a very complex consumer. Sometimes, he drinks Bud, but other times he may drink Michelob or Miller or Heineken beer. Why does he switch? If you ask Dave, he cannot explain. Sometimes Dave shops for clothes at the local discount store. Other times he goes to the most expensive specialty shops. Sometimes Dave and his wife drink wine with dinner and eat gourmet meals. At other times they eat hot dogs and beans and drink Pepsi. Periodically Dave is very concerned about nutrition and cuts down on sugars, fats, and "junk" foods. But, more often than not, Dave grabs a handful of potato chips at a party, eats two donuts for breakfast, and orders pie a la mode for dessert. Does Dave sound different from most other young men and women? Not really; he changes his behavior almost daily and buys a whole range of products that do not seem to fit any set pattern. He buys expensive brand names and cheap, little-known brands. He buys $25 shirts and $6 shirts. He sometimes is very generous to requests for charity, but at other times he is quite resistant. Why does Dave vary his behavior so much? Why do we all follow similar patterns? The concepts are:

› **People have many different roles in life that demand different behaviors; for example, the behavior of a woman changes as she assumes the** role of wife, mother, daughter, home manager, businesswoman, churchgoer, vacationer, and neighbor.

➤ As people assume different roles, their purchasing behavior changes—a person might shop at a discount store in the morning (assuming the role of economical home manager and parent) and at an exclusive shop in the afternoon (assuming the role of partygoer and person on the way up the social ladder).

➤ People cannot be placed into permanent, fixed categories to describe their consumption behavior; their behavior varies considerably depending on the role they are playing, the nearness of payday, and other external factors.

➤ Marketers (sellers) should recognize the diversity of roles people play and adjust their marketing programs accordingly; for example, the appeal to a businessman would differ from the appeal to *that same man* as a father and husband (and the appeal to a businesswoman would differ from the appeal to her as a wife and mother); in one role, they may buy nothing but the best and in the other role buy nothing but discount items.

Pause for a moment and think of your own purchasing behavior. Do you act the same and go to the same places on a date as you do with your parents? Do you sometimes eat at "nice" restaurants and at other times eat at the local "greasy spoon"? Does who is paying make a difference? If you watch a person's buying behavior over a period of time, certain patterns will usually develop, but usually the most obvious pattern is that people will change how, where, and when they buy based on the circumstances in which they find themselves. They will sometimes buy the best and sometimes the cheapest. Consumer behavior is very complex and very changeable. There is no one reason why people do as they do. There are *many* reasons, including the fact the people assume many different roles, and each role calls for different consumption (purchasing) behavior.

Behavior Varies to Fit the Situation

An assumption basic to most personality theories is that people behave consistently. . . . But the empirical evidence for personality consistency is slim. Research over the years has failed to demonstrate much consistency in human behavior either over time or across situations. . . . Because the actions of another person are such a salient feature of any scene, we tend to overestimate the extent to which behavior is caused by personality characteristics or attitudes and underestimate the importance of situational forces that may cause the person to act.

From Ernest R. Hilgard, Richard C. Atkinson, and Rita L. Atkinson, *Introduction to Psychology*, 6th ed. (New York: Harcourt Brace Jovanovich, Inc., 1975), p. 386.

Role of the Family Life Cycle Horace found that his purchasing behavior changed dramatically as he went from bachelorhood to married life. He also found that having children changed his behavior again. He wondered whether other people experienced the same changes and whether there would be other changes in his life equally as important. The answer is yes on both counts. People do follow a certain pattern of living called the family life cycle, and it does change purchasing behavior throughout a person's life. One model of the family life cycle looks like this:[11]

1. Bachelor—young single people
2. Newly married couples—young, no children
3. Full nest, stage one—young married couples with youngest child under age 6
4. Full nest, stage two—young married couples with youngest child 6 or over
5. Full nest, stage three—older married couple with dependent children
6. Empty nest, stage one—older married couple with no children living at home, head of household in labor force
7. Empty nest, stage two—older married couples with no children living at home, head of household retired
8. Solitary survivor, stage one—older single person in labor force
9. Solitary survivor, stage two—older person, retired

This model does not include all the possible family stages, but you should get the general idea. A bachelor would be expected to spend money on basic furniture, a car, and vacations. Newly married couples might spend more on refrigerators and other household items. Children bring on the need for washers and dryers, cribs, baby food, and many toys, games, and other playthings. Empty nesters can spend more money on vacations and meals away from home. Notice, though, that each stage in the family life cycle may be fairly well anticipated, and consumer needs and wants can be determined accordingly. Thus, when the number of marriages increases, as it did in the mid-1970s, marketers can anticipate an increased demand for household goods, soon to be followed by baby needs, and so forth. The recent trend toward having fewer children, and those later in life, changes the cycle but not the basic concepts, which are:

➤ Consumption behavior changes during a person's lifetime based on his or her family situation.

➤ Marketers can learn much about future market demands by studying the trends in family formations and changes in the family life cycle.

[11] William D. Wells and George Gubar, "Life Cycle Concept in Marketing Research," *Journal of Marketing Research*, November 1966, pp. 355–363.

HOW CONSUMERS AFFECT SELLERS   One gets the impression from reading most marketing texts that the sole purpose of studying consumer behavior is to learn how to change consumer attitudes or to get consumers to do what the seller wants. This is really a backward concept of marketing. Marketers should be more concerned about how to get sellers to do what consumers want and how to change seller attitudes. At least there should be some balance.

The most successful sellers are not those who study consumers to determine how to write better ads to better meet their own objectives. The successful seller studies the consumer to find out how to adjust the product to consumer needs to better serve his or her customers. Consumers should be a bigger influence on sellers than the other way around. After all, consumers did not go into business to satisfy the needs of sellers; sellers went into business to satisfy the needs of buyers.

Anyway, it is extremely difficult to change consumer attitudes or consumer behavior. Ask anyone who has tried to get his or her children to eat vegetables, to get a spouse to stop smoking, to get a high school student to wear galoshes, to get a Republican to vote Democratic, or to get a bigot to love all his neighbors. The concepts are:

> **One purpose of studying consumer behavior is to learn more about consumer wants and needs to better serve them.**

> **It is easier, and more profitable, to give consumers what they want than to try to change them through promotion.**

> **It is very difficult to change a person's attitudes or behavior through marketing or any other method.**

The marketers most concerned with *changing* consumer attitudes and behavior are those groups trying to change socially unacceptable behavior. There is need for those who want to stop people from smoking or drinking too much, from polluting the air, water, and land, from eating "junk" foods, and from hating and killing others. But the history of mankind shows that such efforts have been largely futile and fall in the area of *social* marketing rather than *business* marketing because the results are often disappointing to a profit-oriented organization.

EXCHANGE BEHAVIOR AND THE SOCIAL SCIENCES   When it comes to studying human behavior, marketing is a relative newcomer. Other social sciences have led the way for marketers and have given marketers most of the tools and background information for their research.

Students with backgrounds in psychology, sociology, anthropology, and social psychology will find marketing organizations an exciting place to apply their knowledge. Psychology is the study of individual behavior and learning processes. Marketers have adapted many psychological research processes to the study of consumer behavior. Sociology is the study of group behavior, and social psychology is the study of individuals and their interaction with groups. Anthropology, on the other hand, is the study of races, cultures, and social relationships of different regions and historical periods.

You can see that a student of consumer behavior must be well grounded in all behavioral sciences *first*. Techniques of studying consumer behavior have become quite quantitative in order to pinpoint the many variables and their interrelationships. A student of consumer behavior would therefore benefit from having a firm knowledge of statistics, mathematics, and computer use as well.[12] Finally, a marketing student should have some basic understanding of economics, because much consumer behavior is influenced by and is the subject of economics.

Exchange Behavior Is Important to All Organizations

Every organization needs to know how to measure four attributes of the target markets it chooses to serve: their needs, perceptions, preferences, and satisfactions.[13] Consumer analysis, then, is more than a search to understand *why* people do what they do. It is also an attempt to measure *their reactions* to various organizations and to determine whether their wants and needs are being met.

First, an organization must determine what the needs and wants of the target market are. One can learn about such techniques in a course on marketing research or in an advanced course on consumer behavior. It is not easy to determine what consumers want because often they themselves do not know, and, even when they do know, they will often not be open and candid in their discussions with researchers. Often researchers must use advanced psychological-testing procedures to get at true motivations behind purchases (that is, wants and needs).

Organizations also are concerned about measuring consumer perceptions and preferences. What do they like and dislike and why? What is the image of the organization as a whole, its products, its personnel, and its marketing efforts? There are several procedures for determining such answers, but all involve consumer research and analysis.

Finally, an organization should evaluate its effectiveness by measuring consumer satisfaction. Most organizations measure marketing success by looking at profits or sales or goal attainment of other kinds (for example, increased membership). But marketing is an attempt to provide *mutually satisfying relationships*, and so consumer satisfaction should be given equal attention. In the long run, an organization will not be successful unless the people it serves are satisfied. This is true for businesses, churches, schools, charities, and all other organizations.

Analysis of consumer behavior is important to all organizations because all organizations need to know consumer needs, perceptions, preferences, and satisfactions. You will find that many colleges offer entire courses on consumer behavior. There are several good texts available for student use (consult your local college for the one they

---

[12] See Frank M. Bass, Charles W. King, and Edgar A. Pessemier, *Applications of the Sciences in Marketing Management* (New York: John Wiley & Sons, Inc., 1968).

[13] Philip Kotler, *Marketing for Nonprofit Organizations* (Englewood Cliffs, N.J.: Prentice-Hall, Inc., 1975), p. 157.

recommend). We could only touch on some of the basic concepts in this chapter. Consumer behavior is a rapidly growing area in marketing. Within the last few years, there has been a new journal in the area (the *Journal of Consumer Research*) and a new association (the Association for Consumer Research). If you are interested in learning the latest concepts in this field, you might enjoy reading the *Journal* or attending one of the association's national meetings.

FOR REVIEW

Key Terms

Among the more important terms and expressions discussed in this chapter are the following:

An **attitude** is a learned tendency to react to a product offer in a consistently favorable or unfavorable manner.

Culture consists of a set of fairly standardized prescriptions concerning what must be done, should be done, may be done, and must not be done.

Opinion leaders are persons whose views on topics, products, and so forth are especially valued and have a strong influence on the behavior of others.

Primary groups consist of people with whom we have regular, intimate, face-to-face relationships.

Reference groups consist of people whom an individual uses as a frame of reference in forming ideas about the "right" way of thinking and behaving.

Secondary groups consist of people with whom we have casual, nonintimate, and occasional interaction.

Selective exposure refers to the tendency of consumers to avoid most messages.

Selective perception refers to the tendency of consumers to disparage the source or twist the meaning of a communication.

Selective retention refers to the tendency of consumers to forget most of the messages to which they are exposed.

Key Concepts

Among the more important marketing concepts introduced in this chapter are the following:

› **Much of any person's personal behavior and consumption behavior is determined by his or her culture.**

› **Self-image, which is how people think of themselves and how they feel others think of them, is a major determinant of consumer behavior.**

› **Consumers are greatly influenced in their purchasing behavior by primary groups such as family and friends.**

> One major influence on consumer behavior is the information (and persuasion) people receive from marketing organizations.

> Perceptions of product offers and the organizations making those offers are critical to the establishment of exchange relationships.

> Personality differences among consumers affect their perceptions of product offers and their exchange behavior.

> Consumer behavior is affected by experience; people will tend to repeat purchases that satisfy and to cease purchases that do not satisfy.

> As people assume different roles, their purchasing behavior changes.

> Consumption behavior changes during a person's lifetime, based on his or her family situation.

Discussion Questions

1. Talk with one of your classmates who was reared in another country. Discuss what he or she ate for breakfast, lunch, and dinner and how and where these foods were purchased. Compare these events to your own behavior. What are some of the influences that account for the differences in behavior?

2. Look around your neighborhood and notice how different people care for their lawns, what clothes they wear, and what kind of car they drive. Does this give you any clue as to their self-image? Does your dress and behavior reflect your self-image? How?

3. Think of the last three major purchases you have made (for example, a stereo, eyeglasses, and so on). What are some of the factors that influenced *where* you bought them and what kind you bought. Compare your analysis with those of other students. Is your analysis similar to or different from theirs? Why?

4. Who are the opinion leaders that most influence you in the case of the following items: (1) clothes, (2) vacation ideas, (3) cleaning supplies (for example, window cleaner), and (4) what career to follow. Do the same people influence all these decisions? Discuss.

5. How does your personal financial situation affect *what* you buy and *where*. Will you buy different things at different places when you have a better income? Discuss how U.S. economic and personal economic situations affect consumer behavior.

6. What image do you get when you see a person wearing expensive tennis clothes, driving a sports car, and smoking a cigarette? What influences would prompt someone to create such an image? Is it a good image or not? Why?

7. Discuss what influence you and other students have had on sellers. What influence will you have 10 years from now and how will this change seller behavior? For example, what products will you buy then that you do not buy now?

8. What is your reaction as a consumer to appeals from nonprofit organizations at your home (dorm)? What factors influence your reaction?

9. List all the roles that you play (for example, student, sports spectator, churchgoer, and so on). Discuss how your consumption behavior might differ in each of these roles.

10. Explain why students do or do not ride bikes to class, why some dress very neatly and others very sloppily, and why some study hard and others just goof off. Does such behavior reflect social class or personality or peer-group influence or some other influence?

CASES

Children and Family Purchasing Habits
External and Internal Influences on Behavior

Connie Weibard is a 30-year-old mother of twins (age 5) who lives in a small home in a new development. Connie is a college graduate who had a rather successful career as an accountant until she had her twins. Now Connie enjoys taking care of "her boys" and working part-time on income tax returns and other such jobs. Connie still wears some of the outfits she bought for her accounting job, but mostly she prefers to wear jeans and a sweater. Her hair is cut very short for minimum care, and she wears little makeup.

Connie belongs to a baby-sitting club, is active at church (she manages the yearly bazaar), and belongs to an association of women college graduates. She has her own car and feels fairly free to go where she wants (the baby-sitting club is a great help). Connie's husband Mike is a high school teacher and part-time coach. Here are some of the goods and services Connie and her husband have bought in the last few years: a Ford Pinto station wagon, several hanging plants and other household plants, a large turkey to cook for Thanksgiving, a Christmas tree, an attaché case for Mike, and a scarf that says Gucci on it.

1. Discuss what external and internal forces may have influenced these purchases.
2. How many of these purchases, if any, do you feel were influenced primarily by marketing?
3. How different do you suppose the Wiebard's purchasing behavior is now versus before the twins were born?

Pastor Johnson
Consumer Behavior in a Counseling Situation

Pastor Wilfred Johnson has many duties in addition to conducting services and serving his church members. One of his duties is to counsel people about marriage problems, financial problems, emotional problems, and related matters. The pastor would like to learn more about people and their behavior, so that he could improve his counseling skills. He is particularly concerned about the number of people who are deeply in debt and yet continue to charge items at department stores and other retail outlets. He feels that marketers are to blame for much of the problem. He is interested in taking courses in marketing and consumer behavior to learn more about this subject.

1. Discuss some of the reasons why people go deeply into debt. How much of the cause can be traced to marketers (retailers)?
2. What are some of the consumer-behavior factors that could lead to emotional problems and marriage problems?
3. Using the same concepts (for example, role behavior) that explain why people vary the kind of products they buy, explain why church members may be quite generous when asked to give at church but quite reluctant to give when solicited at home.
4. Discuss several benefits a pastor might obtain from a course in consumer behavior.

3

Satisfying Various Markets

All the material in Part 2 was designed to give you some idea of the many markets (unsatisfied needs) in the world today. Part 3 will focus on techniques for satisfying those markets.

Anything that provides satisfaction of a person's wants or needs may be called a product. All organizations produce some product whether the product is tangible (a good) or intangible (a service or idea). Chapter 8 will explore product concepts and techniques for making one product offer more appealing (that is, more satisfying) than someone else's offer. We shall also explore product management; that is, getting control over product decisions.

An important part of the product offer is the package; another important part is the brand. Chapter 9 will discuss packaging and branding concepts and the use of these concepts to design more attractive product offers. One way to make a product more attractive is to offer additional services such as delivery and credit. Such customer services are discussed in Chapter 9.

We all know how important price is in most exchange situations. Chapter 10 discusses various pricing concepts and strategies.

Part 3 ends with an analysis of distribution concepts and systems (Chapter 11). A product is more valuable if it is *where* the customer wants it *when* he or she wants it. Distribution strategy, therefore, may be part of product strategy in that it is one more way to increase the buyer's satisfaction. The systems approach to product management calls for the coordination and integration of packaging, branding, service, pricing, and distribution strategies.

Product Concepts

meeting wants and needs

INTRODUCTION Thus far, most of the material in this book has focused on knowing and understanding what people want and why. All of that material may be classed under the heading: "Find a need." But there comes a time when the research and analysis ends, and the marketer begins the process of "filling needs" or satisfying wants. The marketer must make something, do something, or say something in order to give people what they want. In other words, the marketer must develop a "product."

Earlier we said that anything that satisfies a person's wants or needs may be viewed as a product or part of a product. Thus, a product may be a person, a place, an idea, a physical good, a service, a government program, a charity, a cause, or anything else that somehow provides satisfaction to others. This chapter will concentrate on the concepts and principles involved in creating and managing products that meet the needs of the market.

WHAT IS A PRODUCT? A product may be defined as an intangible sense of value that a consumer perceives when he or she weighs the benefits and drawbacks of making an exchange. Most people tend to think of products as tangible goods that can be seen and felt. They also tend to view products as what producers make in a factory. The following examples will help illustrate

---

* "Systems Approach to Marketing," *Harvard Business Review*, May–June 1967, pp. 105–118.

Products Satisfy Needs

What the product is physically is actually beside the point. To understand what it really is, one must forget its physical aspects and consider its *function in use.* Put another way, a product is nothing more or less than the utility it provides in use. That is, a product is something that satisfies a need, or fills a want, or solves a problem.

But in whose eyes? *In the eyes of the user. . . .* If he perceives that it will satisfy his needs better than they can otherwise be satisfied, he may decide to buy. If he does not perceive the *use* of the product in this positive way, he will likely decide not to buy.

From George D. Downing, *Sales Management* (New York: John Wiley & Sons, Inc., 1969), pp. 21–22.

why traditional thinking about products needs to be changed. The examples will also reveal why a product should be viewed as an *intangible*, at least as perceived by consumers.

What is the product of a professional baseball team? To answer this question, one must decide what perspective to use. From the owner's perspective, the product may be a good team that wins games and attracts crowds. But often winning teams fail to attract a satisfactory crowd. And sometimes a losing team will attract huge crowds. Why? It is not effective to evaluate a product from the perspective of the seller, because more often than not sellers fail to produce products (including baseball teams) that sell.

From the perspective of the buyer, the product of a baseball team is entertainment. Win or lose, the team should be fun to watch and should get the fans involved in action on the field. Baseball fans evaluate many things before paying to see a professional baseball team. Is the parking adequate? Is the stadium area safe? How long does it take to drive to the stadium and back? How much does it cost for parking, tickets, and snacks? How easy is it to get tickets? Is the game on TV? How good are the seats? *And,* is the team fun to watch?

This example should give you the idea that the only way to evaluate a product effectively is to *talk with consumers.* What do they like about it? What don't they like? Because most people will not answer such questions directly, marketers must use research techniques such as focus-group interviews to get honest open answers (see Chapter 6). This example also shows that consumers evaluate a product by looking at many dimensions, not just quality and/or price. In this example, they evaluated parking, safety, convenience, and enjoyment in use. Let us look at one more example before we discuss some key concepts.

What is the product of a library? For years librarians seemed to concentrate on books and reading groups as their main product. But these products failed to attract enough people. So some librarians decided to look at the product from the perspective of the public and then made a drastic change in the product as a result.

In the Salinas, Calif., library, teen-agers have brightly painted a young-adult room where they hold guitar "jams." In the current events room of Pittsburgh's Carnegie Library, a United Press International newsprinter clatters away 12 hours a day. In Erie, Pa., a child can borrow a guinea pig from the library for a week; its juvenile department also boards mice, rats, gerbils and a 42-inch boa constrictor for children to play with. . . .

The Whitmore Library in Salt Lake County, Utah, has opened piano and organ rooms. . . .

In Chicago, as part of an experiment for children aged two to five years, three branch libraries are lending out tools and playthings like toy workbenches, hand puppets, an abacus, a magnet, drums and tambourines.[1]

[1] John J. Ryan, "With a Little Luck, You May Even Find Books in the Library," *The Wall Street Journal*, May 7, 1975, p. 1.

Clearly the "product" of a library today may be *anything that will satisfy the needs of selected market segments* including movies, rental paintings, workshops, and concerts. (See the ad on the facing page put out by the American Library Association). Libraries are much more successful today because they have designed their product to fit the needs of people. Previously they had designed a product (a wide selection of books) and then tried to find people to use it. Recognizing that people evaluate many aspects of a total product offer, libraries have made their product more *convenient* by means of mobile lending units, more *fun* by adding record collections and listening rooms, and more *helpful* by increasing over-the-phone services. In short, libraries have been designing consumer-oriented products.

These examples have demonstrated several basic concepts:

› **There often is a difference between the product as viewed from the perspective of the seller and as viewed by the buyer.**
› **Successful sellers design their products based on the needs of the buyer—those needs are determined through marketing research.**
› **A buyer evaluates a product by looking at many dimensions, including price, quality, convenience, safety, and satisfaction in use.**
› **A product is what a person perceives it to be.**

Some of these concepts are difficult to understand without going into more detail. The following sections expand upon the concepts we have developed in the examples above.

The Product Offer It should be clear at this point that the product is what the buyer buys, not what the seller hopes to sell. What the seller hopes to sell may be called a product offer.

A **product offer** may be defined as anything a marketer does in an attempt to satisfy another's wants and needs. The whole idea of conducting marketing research, consumer analysis, and other such studies is to assure that the product offer is close to what people want. But quite often sellers develop product offers that are not acceptable to buyers. How does this happen, given that sellers spend so much money and effort on marketing research? Let us look at a few cases of product failures to see what we can learn from them.

Believe it or not, there was a company that tried and succeeded in building a "better mousetrap." Supposedly, the world should have beaten a path to the company's door. But, in fact, the product failed. It was a good trap, it was attractive, and it was not messy like the spring-type trap. But the price was 25 cents (versus 10 cents for the spring-set version), and the trap could be used only once. After the product failed in the marketplace, the owner decided that the price was too high.[2]

Another example: A charitable organization made up mostly of businessmen wanted to raise funds for their cause. They went through rather elaborate preparations to bring a circus to town. They thought that they

---

[2] See Chester M. Woolworth, "So We Made a Better Mousetrap," *President's Forum*, Fall 1962, pp. 26–27.

The product offer of a library is much more than books.

You could plan a trip,   borrow a classic film,   get help finding a job,

learn to belly dance,   attend a concert,   get fast answers,

trace your family tree,   stay in shape,   or get your books by mail.

©Walt Disney Productions

AT THE LIBRARY? At the library.
Come see what's new besides books.
American Library Association

Reprinted by permission of the American Library Association.

could sell enough circus tickets to earn a good profit, which they then could donate to the cause. Each member of the organization was given a number of tickets to sell, and signs were placed in several stores promoting the circus. The circus gave several performances (days and evenings), but the ticket sales were so low that, after expenses, the organization had no money left for the charity.

Still another example: A major chemical company invented a new product that was a substitute for leather in shoes. In fact, the material was superior to leather in many ways: It was water resistant, shined without need of polishing, and held its shape. The product was consumer tested and placed on the market. But competition from other, less expensive materials increased; consumer *perceptions* of the benefits of the new substitute were often negative, and production costs were high. Eventually the company sold the patent rights and absorbed a huge loss.[3]

[3] For details on this case and twelve others like it, see Robert F. Hartley, *Marketing Mistakes* (Columbus, Ohio: Grid, Inc., 1976).

The Real Product Is the Benefits Consumers Receive

The "purpose" of the product is not what the engineer explicitly says it is, but what the consumer implicitly demands that it shall be. Thus, the consumer consumes not things, but expected benefits—not cosmetics, but the satisfaction of the allurements they promise; not quarter-inch drills, but quarter-inch holes; not stock in companies, but capital gains; not numerically controlled milling machines, but trouble free and accurately smooth metal parts; not low-cal whipped cream, but self-rewarding indulgence combined with sophisticated convenience.

From Theodore Levitt, "The Morality(?) of Advertising," *Harvard Business Review,* July–August 1970, pp. 84–92. Copyright © 1970 by the President and Fellows of Harvard College. All rights reserved.

In each of these examples, an organization designed what it *thought* was a good product offer. But the success of a marketer depends *not only* on designing a good product offer, *but also* in creating market exchanges. This means that the product offer must be made acceptable to some target market. It must also have the right price, must be available in the right place at the right time, and must have an image that meets the wants and needs of potential buyers.

The mousetrap manufacturer had an excellent offer except for one element—the price was too high. The circus was a good idea, but a product will not sell unless the public knows that it exists, and the circus was not promoted widely enough. The chemical company had a good substitute for leather, but the price was too high, and consumers were not sufficiently educated as to the product's benefits. The concept of *product offer* may be summarized as follows: A product offer is what the seller perceives as the solution to a market need. But the product offer is not what determines whether an exchange will take place or not. It is the buyer's *perception* of the product offer that is important (the product). And often what the seller sees as his product offer and what the buyer sees as the product are quite different. (See the insert "The Real Product Is the Benefits Consumers Receive.")

Consumer Reactions to Product Offers A product may be defined further as what buyers perceive as they analyze the product offer of sellers. As such, a product is not necessarily a tangible object that can be seen or felt. Rather, it is *what the buyer thinks it is.* The concepts that explain this are:

> **A product is what the buyer thinks it is, not what the seller thinks it is.**
> **The way buyers perceive a product depends on their past experiences, cultural influences, the product offer itself, and all the other cues they receive from the market surroundings.**

We have already discussed concepts and principles of consumer behavior. Now you can see how important consumer attitudes are in determining the success or failure of a product offer. A person's past experiences will bias his or her reaction to a product. For example, if you have tried a similar product offer before and did not like it, you may not be very receptive to a new, similar offer. Also, your cultural background will influence your evaluation of a product offer. If your family, friends, or community disapproves of a product offer, those attitudes may also influence your perceptions. In summary, therefore, marketers may follow these concepts:

> **Buyers evaluate products based on their own values and experiences.**
> **The product offer and all the information related to a product offer are screened by buyers and evaluated according to their personal values.**

These concepts explain why it is so important to study and understand consumer behavior. You should also recognize the importance of communication in the marketing exchange process. Communication is the function that enables buyers and sellers to better define what the product is and make adjustments if or where needed.

The insert "Private versus Public Goods" indicates that product concepts apply to both private goods and public goods. Note that private goods and public goods are both designed to meet the needs of the people. Both are *products* of society's efforts to fill wants and needs.

Classifying Goods and Services   Several attempts have been made to classify consumer goods and services. One of the more traditional classifications divides goods and services into three general categories: convenience goods and services, shopping goods and services, and specialty goods and services.

Private versus Public Goods

In our society we usually leave the choice of goods to be consumed to the individual and his own tastes. And the economic goods usually lend themselves to exclusive individual use—that is, they are *private goods.* . . .

But some of our economic needs clearly can only be satisfied by social rather than by individual action. If some economic goods are to be provided in the best way, or at all, they have to be shared by all. These are called *public goods* and differ from private goods in two important respects. The services of public goods are *nondivisible;* it is impossible to keep those who do not pay for them from receiving their benefits. For example, . . . mosquito control keeps everyone in the area from being bitten, and pollution control purifies the water we all use. Also unlike private goods, the services (benefits) of public goods are *nonexhaustible.* . . . A lighthouse protects additional ships with no decline in the services rendered to those already using it. In contrast, a physician tends to see one more patient only at the sacrifice of some other one.

From Kalman Goldberg, *Our Changing Economy* (Boston: Little, Brown and Company, 1976), pp. 248–249.

Convenience goods and services are those products that the consumer wants to purchase frequently and with a minimum of effort (for example, gum, candy, banking). Location is very important for marketers of convenience goods and services. Brand awareness and imagery are also important.

Shopping goods and services are those products that the consumer buys only after comparing quality and price from a variety of sellers. Shopping goods and services are sold largely through shopping centers where consumers can "shop around." Because consumers carefully compare such products, marketers can emphasize price differences, quality differences, or some combination of the two.

Specialty goods and services are those products that have a special attraction to consumers, who are willing to go out of their way to obtain them. Examples include goods like expensive fur coats and organs and services provided by medical specialists or business consultants. These products are often marketed through the classified section of the telephone book or by word of mouth.[4]

Other classification systems have been developed to further differentiate consumer goods, but they are too complex to be discussed in detail here.[5] The basic concepts are:

> **Consumer goods and services may be classified according to the shopping habits of consumers; one such classification is convenience, shopping, and specialty goods and services.**

> **The marketing task varies depending on the kind of product; that is, convenience goods are marketed differently from specialty goods, and so forth.**

EVALUATING THE PRODUCT OFFER   The example of a baseball team showed us that there is often a difference between what sellers perceive as their product and what the buyer perceives. To find out what the product really is, sellers must establish open two-way communication with consumers. Such discussions will bring out the strengths and weaknesses of the product offer and lead to changes that will result in more favorable market exchanges. The concept is:

> **To measure what the product is and should be, sellers must talk with consumers; consumers include present customers, past customers, and potential customers.**

---

[4] For a thorough treatment of the promotion of convenience shopping, and specialty goods and services, see William G. Nickels, *Marketing Communications and Promotion* (Columbus, Ohio: Grid, Inc., 1976.)

[5] For example, see Gordon Miracle, "Product Characteristics and Marketing Strategy," *Journal of Marketing*, January 1965, pp. 18–24, and Leo V. Aspinwall, "The Characteristics of Goods Theory," in *Managerial Marketing: Perspectives and Viewpoints*, ed. William Lazer and Eugene J. Kelley (Homewood, Ill.: Richard D. Irwin, Inc., 1962), pp. 633–643.

In order to analyze both the favorable and unfavorable aspects of a "product," the seller should analyze all three consumer groups. *Present customers* can show what aspects of the product attracted them and which could be improved; *past customers* could explain what aspects of the product attracted them in the first place and what drove them away; and *potential customers* could reveal their impressions of the product (if they have any) and what might be done to attract them. Let us explore an actual case to see how these concepts and principles work.

A marketing consultant was hired by a famous old restaurant to help in its promotional program because sales and profits were falling. The restaurant owner had analyzed his product by himself (a mistake, because the customer determines the product) and had put much money into a new chef and excellent waiters. The owner was particularly concerned about his luncheon business because it was down from previous years.

The consultant did an analysis of the product by talking with consumers, using the concepts outlined above. He went to nearby office buildings and asked present customers, past customers, and potential customers about the favorable and unfavorable aspects of the product.

It was clear from the beginning that the restaurant had the best *physical good* in the area. That is, the local people felt the food was delicious, the atmosphere was comfortable, and the service was outstanding. So why was business so poor?

Lunch took too long! It was just that simple; the local businessmen did not have the *time* to eat at such a "fine" restaurant. To them, the physical good was excellent, but the total product was faulty.

The consultant recommended that the owner set up one large area of the restaurant where the service would be especially prompt but the same excellent food would be served. Sales and profits rose immediately and there was no need for a promotional program at all. Word of mouth from one businessman to another was all that was needed to turn the restaurant's business around. What was needed was a good product based on consumer needs, not more promotion. Customer needs were determined by *listening*.

Product Value When talking with different consumer groups, as the consultant in the example did, it is important to recognize that a product might have positive and negative aspects. That is, the person evaluating a product offer might see things about the product that he or she likes *and* dislikes. The buyer establishes **product value** by adding up all the positive want-satisfying aspects and subtracting the negative aspects. An example may help you visualize this process.

Let us analyze a hypothetical case of a college student who is shopping for an economical car. She goes to a foreign car dealer because she has seen pictures of the car and really likes the sporty look it has. The car has much want-satisfying appeal as a good-looking symbol of youth and "sportiness." The car has several other want-satisfying features such as automatic shift (she has never driven a stick shift), an economical 4-cylinder engine, room for four, and a nice interior design. In short, the car is just what she dreamed of all her life.

But there are some negative aspects to be considered also. The car is sold at a dealership 25 miles from her home, and so bringing the car in for service would be difficult—and she has heard that this car needs frequent tune-ups and adjustments. The price is $2,000 more than competitive models. And there is a 3-month waiting period for the particular features she wants.

Some questions for your analysis are: First, what is the product of the car dealer? Pause here for a moment and mentally list all of the aspects of the product you can think of. Remember, the product is what the *buyer* thinks it is. Did you consider credit (the car was $2,000 more than others), service, friendly salespeople, location, appearance of the dealership, and the car itself? The product, then, is many things, including the buyer's perception that the car would need frequent servicing (a perception that may or may not be true).

A second question for your consideration is: What is the value of the *product* to the college student? Remember that this was the car of her dreams, and so the car per se had all the want-satisfying characteristics she could want. But the car per se is not the product. The product includes the car *plus* its price, the necessity for services, the inconvenience of service, and the fact that other cars were available for significantly less money. These latter factors significantly lowered the value of the car to the college student. Some concepts that emerge from this discussion are:

> Perception of a product may or may not be based on reality.
> Product value to a buyer is the sum of all the perceived want-satisfying aspects of the product minus the perceived negative aspects.

The whole idea behind any marketing exchange is to satisfy some want or need by exchanging a product with lesser value for one of greater value. This is true for all the participants. If one wishes to be an initiator of an exchange, therefore, it is important to design a product offer that others will perceive as a good value, so that they are willing to make a satisfying offer in return.

Keep in mind as you read these concepts and principles that both the buyer and the seller have a product to exchange. The buyer's product offer may be money, but the seller's view of the buyer's product may include many other things. For example, if the buyer looks poor, the seller may lower the price. The product of the buyer is what the *seller* thinks it is and is based on the seller's experiences and values.

The Consumer Ultimately Determines Product Value   Most people analyze products from the perspective of the seller. Often some determination is attempted relative to whether the seller's product is good, better, or best. But the concept that partially demonstrates the problem with such thinking is:

> From a marketing perspective, if buyers perceive the product offer as "good" (that is, it meets their needs well), it *is* a good product; in contrast, if consumers perceive a product as "bad" (that is, it does not

meet their needs), then the product *is* bad regardless of how well it is made or how others feel consumers *should* react.

This point is so important to the understanding of marketing that we shall use another example to explain what this means. Other principles that help clarify the concept of "product" will then emerge.

A leading firm in the tape-recorder industry spent millions of dollars on laboratory research and development trying to make the "best" recorder on the market. The company succeeded in making a *high-quality* recorder but eventually had to get out of the recorder business because of falling sales and profits. Why? The company put its research and development efforts into making what *it* considered to be a "good" product, but what they were making was a good "physical good." The difference between these principles is explained as follows: **A physical good** is something tangible that can be measured, weighed, and evaluated according to some established criteria. In contrast, a "product," as defined earlier, is an intangible sense of value that consumers perceive when they weigh the benefits and drawbacks of making an exchange.

Most people do not want the "best" recorder any more than most people want a Cadillac. Most people want a tape recorder or a car that is of reasonably good quality and has a fair price, attractive appearance, reliable service, and a recognized name (the importance of product names—brands—will be discussed later).

It is a mistake to make the best physical good (meaning best quality) unless people want such high quality. The idea is to give people what they want; not what you think they *should* want or what you are capable of making. As Charles Revson of Revlon once said: "In the factory we make cosmetics; in the store we sell hope." One can learn what consumers want only through a continuous process of market analysis.

Perhaps one more example will help. Louise Jones is an artist who hopes to make enough money selling her paintings to support her family. Louise prefers a certain style of art that some people have described as "modern." But Louise has so much talent that she can create many different styles and moods. Thus far Louise has been rather unsuccessful in selling the paintings *she* likes, but she has earned a fair income selling what she calls "commercial stuff." That is, she knows what art the public likes and will buy, but she does not want to produce such art. Louise is thus faced with a classic marketing problem: Should you give the consumer what the consumer wants (even if you think it is junk?) or should you try to sell what *you think* the consumer *should* want? Often the best strategy is to do both and try to educate consumers to buy the "better" products. But remember that terms like "good," "better," and "best" are all relative. What is a "good" painting to me may be "junk" to you. In marketing, it is the buyer, not the seller who determines what is "good."

**How Not to
Evaluate
a Product** People who are good-looking and who are in tremendous physical shape seem to have a big advantage over the plain-looking, out-of-shape average person. But the fact is that most people end up choosing friends and lovers (at least long-term friends and lovers) who are not necessarily

the best looking or the most physically fit. The reason people do this is that they establish relationships with other people based on a whole range of criteria and not just on the obvious physical factors of the tangible physical good. In other words, the product of a friend or lover is a combination of personality, friendliness, helpfulness, enthusiasm, understanding, warmth, and good looks. How a person looks is just one aspect of the total person. But how many people do you know who spend hours each day working on their appearance but spend little or no time developing their personality, helpfulness, warmth, or other characteristics?

Businesspersons, job seekers, manufacturers, and almost everyone else may make the same basic errors when approaching a marketing problem. They might start by analyzing themselves or their physical good (research and development) *before* they have analyzed the consumer and his or her wants and needs. They have reversed the most basic of marketing concepts. Instead of: "Find a need and fill it," they stress, "Design a product and find someone who needs it."

As a result, students major in areas for which there is no demand, businesses make product improvements for which there is no need, and people in general complain because their work is not appreciated because their efforts are *not filling a need.*

Putting Product Concepts to Use
It should be clear by now that it is important for marketers to be able to view a product from the perspective of the consumer. Consumers are most interested in benefits—what the product will do for them. Sellers cannot make benefits; they can only make product features that will result in benefits. The concept guiding sellers' actions is this:[6]

> **Buyers are interested in the benefits of products rather than features.**

Buyers want clean clothes, not green crystals; healthy, clean teeth, not fluoride; and so forth. Green crystals and fluoride are both product *features.* Clean clothes and healthy, clean teeth are *benefits* that the consumer would obtain *because* of the features.

Sellers should begin the process of product design by determining what benefits consumers want and then designing features that will result in those benefits. Promotional messages from the seller should stress benefits, not features.

The Product as an Intangible
How the consumer *feels* as the result of a marketing transaction may be more important than any *physical* benefit he or she may receive from the item purchased. An item that may seem absolutely worthless to you may

[6] For a sophisticated review of recent theories that show that consumer demand is for certain underlying characteristics rather than for products or brands themselves, see Brian T. Ratchford, "The New Economic Theory of Consumer Behavior: An Interpretive Essay," *Journal of Consumer Research*, September 1975, pp. 65–75.

be a treasured possession of a young child. A painting by a modern artist that looks silly to one person may give someone else an unbelievable feeling of elation. The same is true of some music, poetry, literature, and other "products."

If one understands this concept, it is easy to see why there is little difference in the selling of goods, services, people, places, causes, government programs, charities, or ideas. In every case the goal is to satisfy a need. In every case, the seller should emphasize the benefits of the product. And in every case, the product is the perceived benefits the consumer sees when he or she evaluates the product offer. Whether the product is a physical good, a service, or idea, it is the consumer's *perception* of these things that counts. The product is always an *intangible*—something that the consumer has in his or her mind.

Helping the Consumer Visualize Because the product is what the consumer perceives it to be and because the consumer is more interested in benefits than in features, one role of the seller is to help the buyer visualize the benefits of the product.

Have you noticed how exciting it is to plan a vacation when you are able to visualize where you are going and what you will be doing? Half the fun of a vacation for some people is the anticipation of it and the memories of it. The same is true of other products, for a vacation is a product.

If a salesperson can help you visualize the excitement of owning a boat, or a color TV, or a new stereo, or a fancy fishing rod, he or she is well on the way to making a sale. Remember, the product is what you think it is, and the salesperson's role is to make the pleasures of ownership vivid and real through the process of visualization.

Why Some Consumers Are Dissatisfied If consumers buy only products that they perceive as adding to their satisfaction, why are so many consumers dissatisfied with what they buy? The answer partially is that the product consumers buy is what they *think it is*. But what they *think* and what is *reality* are often quite different. Furthermore, the use of a product adds information to the consumer that *changes his or her perception.*

Many business and consumerist leaders have attempted to give consumers as much information as possible *before* they buy. In the future, such attempts should lessen the number of people who buy inferior products because they do not know any better.

PRODUCT- DIFFERENTIATION STRATEGIES The market is made up of many different buyers and sellers who compete with one another to optimize their personal exchange relationships. Sellers are able to adjust to individual market demands through the product-differentiation function. As discussed in Chapter 2, **product differentiation** is the universal marketing function that adjusts the product offer to meet the needs of particular market segments.

"Product differentiation broadly interpreted, represents a control over supply," Alderson says, "in the sense that only one seller offers a product

Classic Statement of Product Differentiation

A general class of product is differentiated if any significant basis exists for distinguishing the goods (or services) of one seller from those of another. Such a basis may be real or fancied, so long as it is of any importance whatever to buyers and leads to a preference for one variety of the product over another. Where such differentiation exists, even though it be slight, buyers will be paired with sellers, not by chance and at random . . . but according to their preferences.

From E. H. Chamberlin, *The Theory of Monopolistic Competition*, 7th ed. (Cambridge, Mass.: Harvard University Press, 1958), p. 56.

of that exact name and identity."[7] Alderson further states that, "The seller offering a product different from others actually does occupy a monopoly position in that limited sense."[8]

In this section, we shall discuss strategies whereby the seller may adjust his product offer in such a way as to minimize competition and optimize the benefits for both the buyer and the seller. Adjustments to the product offer may involve the following: (1) changes in the physical good itself (if there is one involved); (2) changes in the package, brand, or label; (3) changes in the price; (4) changes in the conditions surrounding the sale (for example, credit, service, guarantees, warranties); or (5) changes in the convenience of making the exchange (for example, through a better location, delivery, installation, and so on). The concepts behind the discussion in this section are:

> The product offer of the seller is a combination of factors that together have the potential of optimizing the satisfactions of the buyer.

> The process of creating product offers to meet the needs of individual buyers is known as the product-differentiation function.

> To create a more satisfying product offer, the seller can vary any of a number of elements such that no two sellers will have the same product offer.

> The seller who has the potential for creating the most acceptable product offer is the one who has the most open communication with buyers.

Differentiation through Communication   One of the more effective ways for a marketer to differentiate his product offering is by giving the consumer information. If one marketer gives the consumer information about a product and competitors do not, the one who gives information is likely to get the buyer's business. One reason for this is that information adds value to the product.

[7] Wroe Alderson, *Marketing Behavior and Executive Action* (Homewood, Ill.: Richard D. Irwin, Inc., 1957), p. 105.
[8] Ibid.

There is no better way to explain how information adds value to products than through an example. Let us say that a new play called *The Game* is coming to town. How much would people be willing to spend to go to the play? The answer is, "It all depends." Depends on what? How good the play is? Nobody knows that for sure until they go! In fact, people can increase or decrease the value they assign to the play before they see it only on the basis of information they obtain.

One bit of information might be that the play has won many awards for excellence. That might add value. Or the play may have been running in New York for 3 years to full houses. That might add value. Or the play might star four of the most famous celebrities in the United States. The point is that the more information people receive the better they are able to *perceive* value and the more likely they are to enter an exchange (if the perceived values are positive). A guiding concept for marketers, therefore, is:

> **To add value to a product, give the potential buyer as much information as possible about the product's want-satisfying characteristics.**

A corollary to this concept is:

> **Information may add or detract from a product's value in the mind of the consumer.**

If the consumer learns unfavorable things about a product (such as a play), the chances of an exchange may be lessened. Control over information, therefore, is part of control over the product, for the product is what it is perceived to be. Positive publicity may benefit a product, but negative publicity may harm it. Good, informative advertising may enhance a product's image, but uninformative, deceptive advertising can do great harm.

Differentiation through Location Placing a product in a convenient location is another way in which a seller can improve (differentiate) a product offer. A bottle of water has much more value to people in the hot, dry desert than in an air-conditioned office. A mobile X-ray unit is more apt to reach the public than is a stationary health clinic.

Product Is Basis for Honesty

I do believe that the product, more often than the marketer himself, sets the pace of deceptive selling.

If the marketer has a good product, he has no need to conceal its faults.

If he has a bad one and is determined to sell it, he has no choice.

From Betty Furness, "Responsibility in Marketing," in *1967 Winter Conference Proceedings*, ed. Reed Moyer (Chicago: American Marketing Association, 1968), p. 25.

Economist Paul Heyne gives an excellent example of how location changes the product:

. . . neither is a gallon of milk at the little store next door the same thing as a gallon of milk three blocks away at the supermarket. If you have no car, are rocking a screaming baby who won't stop until he gets his bottle, and have no one to leave the baby with, the milk three blocks away is a vividly different commodity from the milk at the store next door. Ask any mother.[9]

The concepts are:

› **Sellers can differentiate their products from competitors by making the products easy to obtain.**

› **Products can be made more accessible by locating them in convenient stores, by selling them door to door, by selling through the mail, and by generally having them when and where people want them.**

In Chapter 11, we shall discuss more thoroughly the principles behind product distribution. Distribution is one of the most expensive marketing functions and calls for special emphasis.

Differentiation through Product Quality

One obvious strategy for capturing a share of the market for a product is to give the consumer a better "quality" product.[10] The major problem with such a strategy is defining what "quality" means. Basically it means using pure ingredients, strict standards of production, or superior designs. But quality is not always apparent to consumers. Consumers are usually more impressed with the *appearance* of quality. Quality may be symbolized by price or the package, by the store where the product is sold, or by brand name. The concepts are:

› **Quality may be an effective element in product differentiation, but the product must *appear* to have good quality as well.**

› **Quality images may be created through good engineering and through packaging, branding, pricing, and other marketing efforts.**

Differentiation through Service

One of the most important differentiating strategies any organization can use is customer service. This includes before-exchange services such as analyzing needs and providing advice. It also includes delivery, installation, repair, and credit services. Of nearly 500,000 consumer complaints processed by Better Business Bureaus in 1975, 70 percent involved service or repair problems.[11] This shows how important service is to the

[9] Paul T. Heyne, *The Economic Way of Thinking* (Chicago: Science Research Associates, Inc., 1973), p. 97.

[10] See Alfred A. Kuehn And Ralph L. Day, "Strategy of Product Quality," *Harvard Business Review*, November–December 1962, pp. 100–110.

[11] *Marketing News*, March 26, 1976, p. 2.

Table 8.1 RELATIVE IMPORTANCE OF THE ELEMENTS OF PRODUCT STRATEGY[a]

Product effort activity	Percent of producers rating activity as most important		
	Industrial goods	Consumer durables	Consumer nondurables
Presale service	23.7	12.8	12.1
Postsale service	17.7	14.2	9.2
Technical research and development	34.5	34.6	38.6
Market research	15.7	17.8	27.5
Style research and development	6.1	18.8	9.6
Other	2.3	1.9	3.0
Total	100.0	100.0	100.0

[a] Data are the average responses of 334 industrial, 52 consumer durable, and 87 consumer nondurable goods manufacturers. Eleven responses are excluded because of point allocations not equaling 100.

From Jon G. Udell, "The Perceived Importance of the Elements of Strategy," *Journal of Marketing.* January 1968, p. 38.

consumer because most people do not complain to the Better Business Bureau unless they are particularly upset. A further indication of the importance of service is shown in Table 8.1. Note that for industrial goods, service (both presale and postsale) is the most important element in product strategy. The company that provides better service (and makes sure the public knows about it) often has a clear advantage over competitors. Customer service, packaging, and branding are so important to product management that we shall devote the entire next chapter to these topics.

Differentiation through Exchange Environment
The general environment or atmosphere within which a product exchange takes place often has a great effect on the buyer's perception of value. These external factors are sometimes called **atmospherics**[12] and refer to things like carpeting, lighting, noise (or no noise), and a general mood of honesty, friendliness, and openness.

Motel operators, for example, should think of their signs, bushes, parking lot, lobby, and pool as part of their "product" and design them with as much care as the rooms, beds, and fixtures.

Supermarket operators should be as aware of lighting, cleanliness, and store attractiveness as they are of prices and assortment. All of these combine to make a product offer "better than" or "different from" those of competitors. The concepts are:

> **The product as perceived by the consumer includes the atmosphere of the exchange location including parking, landscaping, signs, lighting, carpeting, and friendly participants.**

[12] See Philip Kotler, "Atmospherics as a Marketing Tool," *Journal of Retailing,* Winter 1973–1974, pp. 48–64.

Products from a Consumer Viewpoint

Because he realizes that unintended outputs are always present in the creation of a product, the consumer tends to reject the traditional definition of product and to accept a new one. . . . The latter takes into account the effect of the existence and marketing of a product on the user, on other individuals, on groups, and on organizations, all of which are inseparable components of society. The crucial difference between the user and the consumer lies in the consumer's awareness of the fact that products have intended as well as unintended outputs. The consumer also differentiates himself from the user in that he recognizes that although the intended utilities built into the product are generally positive and are intended for his personal use and enjoyment, the unintended utilities can be negative as well as positive and can affect a far greater number of people.

From Etienne Cracco and Jacques Rostenne, "The Socio-Ecological Product," *MSU Business Topics*, Summer 1971, pp. 27–34.

> ꞏ **Sellers can differentiate their products from those of competitors (even when the physical good or service is exactly the same) by changing the atmosphere of the exchange situation.**

Ecology and Product Differentiation The basic premise behind this chapter is that a product is something that satisfies the consumer's wants and needs. But today's marketers must also be concerned with the wants and needs of society. A product that meets the needs of individuals (for example, hand guns or aluminum cans) may not meet the broader needs of society for safety or environmental protection.

In the short run, a producer may succeed in selling products that threaten the safety, environment, or moral well-being of society. But in the long run, such products may fail as society brings pressure on the producer and the government to ban them.

One way to differentiate a product, therefore, is to design it to be safer or less harmful to the environment than competitive products. Such a product may be termed a socio-ecological product and is defined as the sum of all positive and negative attitudes that must be accepted by society as a whole in order to allow the satisfaction by users of a certain bundle of needs, wants, or desires in a certain way.[13] As the insert "Products from a Consumer Viewpoint" notes, products may have intended and unintended outputs. In supplying a new product, a manufacturer has as its intended output the product itself and the satisfaction of consumer wants. One unintended positive output might be an increase in the number of available jobs, whereas an unintended negative output might be increased water pollution or air pollution.

[13] See Etienne Cracco and Jacques Rostenne, "The Socio-Ecological Product," *MSU Business Topics*, Summer 1971, pp. 27–34.

PRODUCT MANAGEMENT Product management may be defined as a staff function designed to coordinate all the marketing efforts for a particular product (product line) or brand. When manufacturers of consumer goods analyze all of the variables that can make or break a product in the marketplace, they usually realize that product management is a very complex task. The concept of product management originated over 50 years ago with Procter & Gamble, and over the last 25 years, product managers have come to occupy important positions in many firms. An Association of National Advertisers survey of members found that 85 percent of the companies producing packaged goods, 34 percent of the companies producing other consumer goods, and 55 percent of manufacturers of industrial goods had a product-management system.[14]

Product managers have direct responsibility for one brand or one product line, including all the elements of the marketing mix: product, place, promotion, and price. The problem has been that product managers (brand managers) have not in the past been given the authority that should accompany their responsibility. They had a staff position and as such had to use their powers of persuasion to get company employees to support their efforts. (See the insert "The Role of Product Manager.")

There was a major readjustment in the product-manager concept in the mid 1970s. PepsiCo, Purex, Eastman Kodak, Levi Strauss, and others abandoned the product-management system for some other marketing

[14] *Current Advertising Practices: Opinions as to Future Trends* (New York: Association of National Advertisers, 1974).

The Role of Product Manager

Industrial companies have adapted from consumer companies the product manager concept. Consumer companies, specifically Procter & Gamble, were the initiators of the product manager concept. Typically, a product manager has 100 percent responsibility and 1 percent authority. He's responsible for getting the job done, but the only person that reports to him is his secretary. And, his purpose is to make a profit in his particular product line.

Most companies will divide their products into several categories. The product manager is responsible for maximizing the profits of that particular product line. He does it in a number of ways. He does it through advertising campaigns and promotional programs—but he has to depend on the salesmen to sell his particular product line. Therefore, most product managers are competing with other product managers for the salesman's time. This is an interesting aspect. I often state that I'm really selling to our salesmen rather than to our customers and competing against other product managers who are also responsible for the quality of the product and packaging of the product, and all the way down the line to consumer appeal.

Loren Broadhead of Avery Label, as quoted in Robert W. Frye, *Introduction to the Marketing System* (San Francisco: Canfield Press, 1973), p. 314.

"How do we know it's the recession?
Maybe we've got a lousy product."

Reprinted with permission from the May 24, 1976, issue of *Advertising Age.* Copyright 1976
by Crain Communications, Inc.

structure. But after this shakeout, the product-manager concept still remained, but in slightly altered form.

Product managers were once considered "little presidents" for the brands they managed. But the market became too complex for one person to manage it all, especially the advertising function. Companies such as Procter & Gamble have been using the product-manager system for years—and still do—but the procedures are continually being refined. We cannot go into great detail here about the product manager's duties and responsibilities, so let us simply give you some basic concepts. The concepts are:

> **Those organizations that have many products (brands) to sell often find a product-management system helpful in coordinating and integrating the marketing effort for each brand.**

> **Product managers must learn to take a broad perspective on their brands that recognizes the needs of consumers and society in general—a single-minded sales or profit orientation is no longer acceptable.**

> **Brand managers should be given authority commensurate with their responsibility, subject to the approval or supervision of a marketing manager.**

You can expand your understanding of these concepts by reading some of the current literature on product managers.[15] Also, study

[15] For example, see "The Brand Manager No Longer King," *Business Week,* June 9, 1973, pp. 58–66, and Victor P. Buell, "The Changing Role of the Product Manager in Consumer Goods Companies," *Journal of Marketing,* July 1975, pp. 3–11.

Tasks of the Product Manager

These task areas represent an ascending order of degree of responsibility. The eighth embodies the full realization of the product management vision which has been expressed thus: "It's like setting up each product manager in his own business." The implication is a true planning, decision-making, and profit-producing center which would attain what may be the dream of corporate executives, namely, the downward placement of specialized responsibility to relieve them of the myriad problems of individual products and free them for overall corporate coordination and comprehensive strategy. . . .

. . . Few corporate positions—perhaps no other position short of the top—can offer a comprehensive experience that compares favorably with product management. And it has the plus of intimate marketing orientation that is becoming increasingly required in managing the modern corporation.

1. Furnish an intelligence center on all aspects of a product line or brand (except manufacturing details), including technical information, market situations, and so forth.
2. Create ideas for product improvements, new-product development, and promotion; or gather such ideas from internal and external sources.
3. Advise top management on marketing aspects of a new product line or brand during its implementation through research and development phases.
4. Prepare advertising and marketing concepts for functional management, and provide liaison with advertising and merchandising agencies in the actual development programs.
5. Stimulate interest in and support for a product line or brand among salesmen and distributors (in industrial goods, also among key buyers).
6. Prepare sales forecasts; also provide logistic guidance for production and distribution.
7. Devise product strategy and plans, and propose product goals and budgets for submission to the determining executives.
8. Assume responsibility for product strategy, campaigns, and profitability.

From David J. Luck and Theodore Nowak, "Product Management—Vision Unfulfilled," *Harvard Business Review* May–June 1965, pp. 143–153. Copyright © 1965 by the President and Fellows of Harvard College. All rights reserved.

carefully the insert "Tasks of the Product Manager"; it should give you a good idea of the scope and complexity of the duties of product managers.

PRODUCT MANAGEMENT AND THE PRODUCT LIFE CYCLE

In recent years, many books have been written on the subject of product managers and their tasks. One interesting book deals especially with the product manager's involvement in what has been called the **product life cycle**—the birth, growth and development, and, sometimes, death of a product.[16] Like Peter Pan, some products seem to stay young forever; others seem to hobble along in an eternal old age; some are born, flourish, and die in a matter of months.

It is important that you have a basic understanding of the product life cycle and of the ways in which consumers influence this life cycle. Some consumers accept new products immediately, whereas others adopt a wait-and-see attitude. We shall end this chapter with a review of some of the basic concepts in these areas. You should also take some time to do some reading on your own, because product management is a truly exciting area of marketing.

The Product Life Cycle

You surely have noticed that some products seem to take a while to catch on with the public, but then they become very popular, level off in sales, and gradually decline in popularity and sales. As mentioned earlier, this phenomenon is known as the product life cycle (see Figure 8.1).

[16] Chester R. Wasson, *Dynamic Competitive Strategy and Product Life Cycles* (St. Charles, Ill.: Challenge Books, 1974).

Figure 8.1 THE PRODUCT LIFE CYCLE

Ref pg. 198 in Reader.

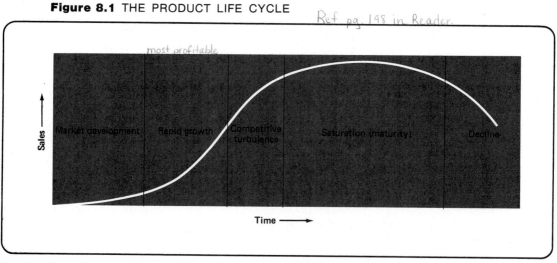

Based on Chester R. Wasson, *Dynamic Competitive Strategy and Product Life Cycles* (St. Charles, Ill.: Challenge Books, 1974). Copyright © 1974 by Chester R. Wasson.

We can perhaps see how this life cycle works by looking at the introduction of instant coffee. When instant coffee was first introduced, most people did not like it as well as "regular" coffee, and it took several years to gain general acceptance (market development stage). At one point, though, instant coffee grew rapidly in popularity, and many brands were introduced (stage of rapid growth and competitive turbulence). After a while, people became attached to one brand and sales leveled off (stage of saturation and maturity). Sales went into a slight decline when freeze-dried coffees were introduced (stage of decline). At the present time, freeze-dried coffee is just reaching the beginning of the stage of maturity. Perhaps you can think through the product life cycle for products like hot cereals, frozen orange juice, digital watches, and mechanical calculators.

For a fad product like Hula Hoops and Pet Rocks, the product life cycle is very short; sometimes a matter of months. But for other products, such as microwave ovens, the introductory stage may last for many years, and the entire life cycle may take decades.

The importance of the product life cycle to marketers is this: Different stages in the product life cycle call for different strategies. Table 8.2 summarizes the entire concept rather well. The table shows how a product manager changes his or her objectives and strategies over the life of a product. It is important to recognize what stage a product is in because such an analysis leads to more intelligent marketing decisions.

Marketers must be careful not to put too much emphasis on the product life cycle, however, because it provides only guidelines, not rules for action.[17] Used as managerial input, the product life cycle is a valuable tool.

The Product-Adoption Process Donna O'Reilly is always the first to try a new fashion or to buy a new product. Donna is known in marketing as an *innovator*. Innovators are defined as the first 2.5 percent of the people to buy a new product.

Homer Brown is a rather conservative guy. He always waits until he is absolutely sure that a product is "good" and widely accepted before he buys. Homer is called a *laggard* in marketing. Laggards are the last 16 percent of the people to buy a new product.

Kim Sanborn, Bruce King, and Sharon Smith are neither the first to buy nor the last. Kim is in the *early adopter* group—that 13.5 percent of the population who buy after the innovators. Bruce is in the *early majority* group—that 34 percent of the people who buy after the early adopters. Sharon is part of the *late majority*. They are defined as the 34 percent of the people who buy just before the laggards. The adopter categories are listed in Table 8.3.[18]

[17] See Nariman K. Dhalla and Sonia Yuspeh, "Forget the Product Life Cycle," *Harvard Business Review*, January–February 1976, pp. 102–110.

[18] See *The Adoption of New Products* (Ann Arbor, Mich.: Foundation for Research on Human Behavior, 1959), pp. 1–8. See also the classic study by George M. Beal and Joe M. Bohlen, *The Diffusion Process* (Ames, Iowa: Agricultural Extension Service, Iowa State College [Special Report No. 18], 1957).

Table 8.2 COMPETITIVE STRATEGY AND THE PRODUCT LIFE CYCLE

	Stage in the product life cycle				
	Market development	Rapid growth	Competitive turbulence	Saturation (maturity)	Decline
Strategy objective	Minimize learning requirements, locate and remedy offering defects quickly, develop widespread awareness of benefits, and gain trial by early adopters.	To establish a strong brand market and distribution niche as quickly as possible.	To maintain and strengthen the market niche achieved through dealer and consumer loyalty.	To defend brand position against competing brands and product category against other potential products, through constant attention to product-improvement opportunities and fresh promotional and distribution approaches.	To milk the offering dry of all possible profit.
Outlook for competition	None is likely to be attracted in the early, unprofitable stages.	Early entrance of numerous aggressive emulators.	Price and distribution squeezes on the industry, shaking out the weaker entrants.	Competition stabilized, with few or no new entrants and market shares not subject to substantial change in the absence of a substantial perceived improvement in some brand.	Similar competition declining and dropping out because of decrease in consumer interest.
Product design objective	Limited number of models with physical product and offering designs both focused on minimizing learning requirements. Designs cost- and use-engineered to appeal to most receptive segment. Utmost attention to quality control and quick elimination of market-revealed defects in design.	Modular design to facilitate flexible addition of variants to appeal to every new segment and new use system as fast as discovered.	Intensified attention to product improvement, tightening up of line to eliminate unnecessary specialties with little market appeal.	A constant alert for market pyramiding opportunities through either bold cost and price penetration of new markets or major product changes. Introduction of flanker products. Constant attention to possibilities for product improvement and cost cutting. Reexamination of necessity of design compromises.	Constant pruning of line to eliminate any items not returning a direct profit.

Pricing objective	To impose the minimum of value-perception learning and to match the value-reference perception of the most receptive segments. High trade discounts and sampling advisable.	A price line for every taste, from low end to premium models. Customary trade discounts. Aggressive promotional pricing, with prices cut as fast as costs decline due to accumulated production experience. Intensification of sampling.	Defensive pricing to preserve product category franchise. Search for incremental pricing opportunities, including private label contracts, to boost volume and gain in experience advantage.	Maintenance of profit-level pricing with complete disregard of any effect on market share.
Promotional guidelines *Communications objectives*	(a) Create widespread awareness and understanding of offering benefits. (b) Gain trial by early adopters.	Create and strengthen brand preference among trade and final users. Stimulate general trial.	Maintain consumer franchise and strengthen dealer ties.	Maintain consumer and trade loyalty, with strong emphasis on dealers and distributors. Promotion of greater use frequency.
Most valuable media mix	In order of value: Publicity. Personal sales. Mass communications.	Mass media. Personal sales. Sales promotions, including sampling. Publicity.	Mass media. Dealer promotions. Personal selling to dealers. Sales promotions. Publicity.	Mass media. Dealer-oriented promotions.
Distribution policy	Exclusive or selective, with distributor margins high enough to justify heavy promotional spending.	Intensive and extensive, with dealer margins just high enough to keep them interested. Close attention to rapid resupply of distributor stocks and heavy inventories at all levels	Intensive and extensive, and a strong emphasis on keeping dealer well supplied, but with minimum inventory cost to him.	Intensive and extensive, with strong emphasis on keeping dealer well supplied, but at minimum inventory cost to him.
Intelligence focus	To identify actual developing use systems and to uncover any product weaknesses.	Detailed attention to brand position, to gaps in model and market coverage, and to opportunities for market segmentation.	Close attention to product-improvement needs, to market-broadening chances, and to possible fresh promotion themes.	Intensified attention to possible product improvements. Sharp alert for potential new inter-product competition and for signs of beginning product decline.

Based on Chester R. Wasson, *Dynamic Competitive Strategy and Product Life Cycles* (St. Charles, Ill.: Challenge Books, 1974). Copyright © 1974 by Chester R. Wasson.

Table 8.3 ADOPTER CATEGORIES

Order of adoption	Percent adopting	Category	Cumulative total (percent)
First	2.5	Innovators	2.5
Second	13.5	Early adopters	16.0
Third	34.0	Early majority	50.0
Fourth	34.0	Late majority	84.0
Last	16.0	Laggards	100.0

From *The Adoption of New Products* (Ann Arbor, Mich: Foundation for Research on Human Behavior, 1959).

The adopter categories can be compared to the product life cycle. In fact, as Figure 8.2 shows, the curve represented by the number of people adopting a product looks very similar to the curve for the product life cycle.

If marketers were to learn more about the characteristics of people in the various adopter categories, they might be able to speed up the adoption process. But most of the studies done thus far have been carried out by rural sociologists who were studying farmers. There is some question whether urban dwellers and purchasing agents in businesses would act similarly. Marketers can learn a great deal from concepts borrowed from the behavioral sciences, especially as regards the adoption process.[19] The more we learn about such processes, the faster we can introduce new products and important social concepts.

This discussion shows that product development should be a cooper-

[19] For an in-depth discussion, see Thomas S. Robertson, *Innovative Behavior and Communication* (New York: Holt, Rinehart and Winston, Inc., 1971).

Figure 8.2 ADOPTION CURVE FOR A NEW PRODUCT

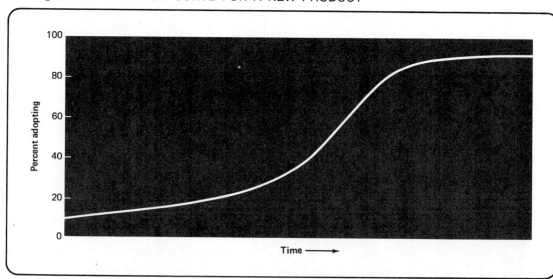

ative venture that includes buyer input. Such input helps speed the adoption process and leads to mutually satisfying exchanges. Products are made *for* buyers, and so buyers should have a major input into product design. In Chapter 21, we shall show you how to use these concepts to design your own product so that you can sell yourself to the employer that you choose.

FOR REVIEW

Key Terms

Among the more important terms and expressions discussed in this chapter are the following:

Atmospherics is a term used to describe the external factors that characterize an exchange environment.

Convenience goods and services are those products that the consumer wants to purchase frequently and with a minimum of effort.

A **physical good** is something tangible that can be weighed, measured, and evaluated according to some established criteria.

A **product** is an intangible sense of value that the consumer perceives when he or she weighs the benefits and drawbacks of making an exchange.

Product differentiation is the universal marketing function that adjusts the product offer to meet the needs of particular market segments.

Product life cycle refers to the various stages through which a product passes from its introduction to its decline or elimination.

Product management is a staff function responsible for coordinating all the marketing efforts for a particular product (product line) or brand.

A **product offer** is anything a marketer does in an attempt to satisfy another's wants and needs.

Product value to a buyer is the sum of all the perceived want-satisfying aspects of a product minus the perceived negative aspects.

Shopping goods and services are those products that the consumer buys only after comparing quality and price from a variety of sellers.

Specialty goods and services are those products that have a special attraction to consumers, who are willing to go out of their way to obtain them.

Key Concepts

Among the more important marketing concepts introduced in this chapter are the following:

> **A product is what the buyer thinks it is, not what the seller thinks it is.**

> **The way in which buyers perceive a product depends on their past experiences, cultural influences, the product offer itself, and all the other cues they receive from the market surroundings.**

> From a marketing perspective, if buyers perceive the product offer as "good" (that is, it meets their needs well), it *is* a good product, and if buyers perceive a product as "bad" (that is, it does not meet their needs), then it *is* bad regardless of how well it is made or how others feel buyers *should* react.

> The product offer and all the information related to a product offer are screened by buyers and evaluated according to their personal values.

> Perceptions of a product may or may not be based on reality.

> The value of a product to a buyer is the sum of all the perceived want-satisfying aspects minus the perceived negative aspects.

> Buyers are interested in the benefits of products rather than in features of products.

> Consumer perceptions of a product can be affected by communication (promotion), so that the product is perceived as one that best satisfies their needs.

Discussion Questions

1. "Anything that satisfies a person's wants or needs may be viewed as a product or part of a product." Do you agree? Could a person be a product? A place? An idea? A religion? Give examples to illustrate your answer.

2. "I know I have the best product on the market. I have been in this business for 30 years and know every competitive product inside and out and I *know* mine is the best product." Discuss this statement.

3. "Buyers evaluate products based on their own values and experiences." Test this concept by asking your friends what the best automobile is, what the best rock group is, and what the best business school in the country is. Do their answers reflect different values and experiences?

4. What is the "product" of the following individuals or organizations: a dry cleaner; a restaurant; a TV station; a football player?

5. One way to differentiate a product (that is, to make it more desirable to consumers) is to design it to be safer or less harmful to the environment than competitive products. Give examples of such products. Do they seem to sell well? Why or why not?

6. What is the present position of cigarettes of standard size (for example, Camels, Lucky Strike) in the product life cycle? Why? What did their manufacturers do to maintain profits? What are they doing now? Where are cigarettes in general on the product life cycle?

7. Discuss the differences between the "product offer" and the "product" of the following organizations: your school; the U.S. Army; the Republican party. How could such differences be lessened?

8. Discuss the role of product managers in today's organizations. Is it a career you would like? Why or why not?

9. Discuss how "atmospherics" affect your purchase of the following products: a haircut (style); gasoline; a place to stay (motel or hotel); movies.

10. Do nonprofit organizations have products? Give examples to prove your answer.

CASES

A New Diaper
Product Differentiation and Management

A major U.S. manufacturer recently introduced a new diaper that is designed to compete with Pampers and other disposable diapers. The major benefit of this new diaper is that it has elastic material at the legs to assure a tighter fit. Traditional disposable diapers sometimes leaked. The new diapers were almost twice as expensive, but the company felt they were much "better" than traditional disposables.

1. How could the company determine whether this new product was really "better" or not?
2. What environmental circumstances might affect the sales of this new disposable diaper?
3. The new diaper would compete directly with the best-selling disposable diaper produced by the same company. How would you assure the product manager that he would get the attention he or she deserved?
4. Why would a company make a new product that competed directly with an already established product in the same market?

A College Game Room
Improving the Product Offer

Martin Davis was manager of the game area in his college dorm. The game area had a Ping-Pong table, a pool table, several vending machines, card tables (with various games available, for example, Monopoly), and lots of comfortable chairs. Surprisingly, many dorm residents did not use the game room. In fact, Marty was concerned that the school administrators would convert the game area into something else. Marty decided to promote the game room to the dorm residents.

1. What is the product of the game room?
2. Could the product offer differ from the product as perceived by the dorm students? Explain.
3. How could Marty improve the product offer?
4. Many of the dorm residents did not participate in intramural sports either. How could recreation in general be promoted at a college?

Packaging, Branding, and Customer Service
adding value to the product offer

9

After you have read and studied this chapter, you should be able to:

1. Discuss the role of packaging in the product-differentiation function.

2. Show how service organizations can use packaging concepts.

3. Define the following terms: brand; brand name; generic product offering; customer services.

4. Explain why brand names are usually preferred by customers.

5. Using actual examples, discuss how branding concepts can be used to market politicians, services, and nonprofit organizations.

6. Compare the value of a national brand to the value of a private brand—which is better and why?

7. List at least ten customer services that may be offered by a department store.

8. Explain how a product warranty or guarantee makes a product more attractive to consumers.

9. Give several examples of how packaging and branding have added value to products and helped an organization capture a larger share of the market.

10. Discuss how you could use packaging, branding, and service concepts in presenting yourself to a potential employer.

> *The marketing view demands the active recognition of a new kind of competition that is in galloping ascendance in the world today. This is the competition of product augmentation: not competition between what companies produce in their factories, but between what they add to their factory output in the form of packaging, services, advertising, customer advice, financing, delivery arrangements, warehousing, and other things people value.*
>
> Theodore Levitt*

INTRODUCTION "You can buy the same TV set at a discount store for $35 less," the salesperson admitted, "but what are you going to do if it needs servicing? If anything goes wrong with this set, we'll see that it gets fixed, and fast. And we'll let you charge it on your store credit card. Furthermore, we can deliver the set tomorrow, and you can be sure that it will be tested in your home before the delivery person leaves. Isn't it worth $35 to be sure that you are getting a fine TV *and* good service?"

This story reflects a dialogue that goes on in stores throughout the country. It reveals that competition between sellers is more than competition between physical goods. Many stores carry the same products with the same code numbers and brand names. Would you have paid $35 more for the TV?

What causes a person to choose one store or one product over another? We have already discussed the fact that a person weighs both positive and negative benefits of a product offer, but what are some of the elements that are being evaluated? We shall answer these questions and more in this chapter. But, first, let us look at another typical consumer situation. This story emphasizes the necessity for viewing product offers broadly. It also serves as an introduction to packaging, branding, and customer service as product elements.

Chuck Peterson went out to his car one cold, wintery day and found that the battery was dead. Chuck went back to his house and began immediately to search for a good place to buy a new battery (it was a Saturday, so he had time). Chuck remembered seeing battery ads in the sports section of the newspaper, and so he dug out his old papers and went through the ads. He found that several stores were having sales and was pleased because one of his concerns was getting a good *price*.

One problem that Chuck had was that his car was not available, and so he did not feel like going too far to get a new battery (although his neighbor offered to drive him wherever he wanted to go). Another concern, therefore, was finding a *convenient* store.

Many different batteries were advertised in the paper at widely ranging prices. Chuck decided to stick to brand names with which he was familiar because he felt he would be able to get better *service* on a *brand-name* item.

* "Improving Sales Through Product Augmentation," *European Business*, April 1969, pp. 5–12.

Chuck decided to go the local Sears store and get a battery that was on sale. He asked his neighbor to help him get his car started with booster cables and drove down to the Sears store nearest him. On the way he passed several gas stations and other stores that sold batteries.

What can we learn from this example? First, notice that Chuck did not go to the most convenient place to buy batteries (the local gas station). Why not? Somehow Chuck had gotten the impression that gas stations had higher prices for their batteries. He also was not sure what brands the local stations carried. Furthermore, there were no ads in the paper announcing special deals from the gas stations. From Chuck's case, we learn that people will often pass up one store to get the same or similar items at other stores if the closer stores (1) do not advertise what brands they carry, (2) do not create an image of good value, or (3) do not seem interested in the buyer's business.

Gas stations often do not seem very interested in selling tires, batteries, and accessories (called TBA items). Even though gas stations are conveniently located and may have good prices, many people do not think of gas stations first when buying these items. Why? Because service station attendants may not promote these items, because there may be little or no advertising of these items, and because consumer perceptions of prices may be high. The same is often true of the service areas of automobile dealerships. They too are often *perceived* as being more expensive and less interested in serving customers than are stores such as Sears, Wards, and other mass merchandisers. The concept that applies here is:

› **The public's perception of prices, service, friendliness, concern, and convenience greatly affects *what* products are purchased and *where*.**

Notice that Chuck did not buy a battery sold by a nationally advertised battery manufacturer, even though he was biased in favor of brand names. Instead, he bought a Sears battery (that is, a retailer's private brand battery). Why? Chuck felt that the service, guarantee, price, and general atmosphere of Sears was superior to any other local store. For one thing, Sears had a lounge where Chuck could sit while waiting for his car. But, better yet, Sears was located in a shopping center where Chuck could shop while waiting for his car. The concepts behind Chuck's actions are:

› **People evaluate the surroundings where they make purchases as well as the goods and services they buy.**

› **Advertising affects the public's perception of which brands are best and which stores offer the best value; the information provided by advertising could thus be considered part of the total product offer.**

› **People usually evaluate the total product offer when buying a product and choose what they perceive to be the best value to them.**

Another factor affecting Chuck's decision was that he had a charge account at Sears. The availability of *credit* often is a big factor in determining what a person buys and where.

> **Product Enhancement for Nonbusiness Organizations**
>
> Whenever a nonbusiness organization adjusts its activities to meet its consumers' needs it is engaging in product improvement. Even though it shuns profits, the nonprofit organization must price its "products" to cover the costs. Moreover, the functions of distribution (e.g., delivery of health care to patients) and customer communication (e.g., making known the availability of United Fund services) can be as important to the effective functioning of nonprofit organizations as it is for firms seeking profits.

From Reed Moyer, *Macro Marketing* (New York: John Wiley & Sons, Inc., 1972), p. 9

This chapter will further explore the concepts presented in this example. We shall look at factors such as packaging, branding, credit, and customer service in determining product-selection decisions. We shall also show how marketers can use this information to improve the exchange process. We shall save the pricing element for the next chapter because of its critical importance.

PACKAGING Packaging did not affect Chuck's selection of a battery, but packaging is a critical part of the product offer for most goods. For example, while Chuck was waiting for his car he bought some items for his engine (spark plugs and an air filter). He was attracted to these items partially by the packaging. The package for the air filter, for example, gave information about the filter and the cars it would fit. It also gave directions for installation. Such packages often replace the salesperson at the point of purchase and provide the kind of information salespeople once gave.

Normally, the term packaging makes people think of boxes, wrappings, and other materials that go around a physical good. But packaging may also mean combining goods or services into a single offer (for example, packaged tours that include transportation, lodging, recreation, and meals). In this section, we shall show you how packaging changes the image and value of a product offer.[1]

Packaging Changes the Product Many years ago people had problems with table salt because it would stick together and form lumps whenever the weather was humid or damp. The Morton Salt Company solved that problem by designing a package that kept the salt dry in all kinds of weather. Thus the slogan, "When it rains, it pours." Packaging made Morton's salt more desirable than competing products, and it still is the best-known salt in the United States.

[1]For a comprehensive discussion of packaging, see William G. Nickels and Marvin A. Jolson, "Packaging—the Fifth 'P' in the Marketing Mix?" *SAM Advanced Management Journal*, Winter 1976, pp. 13–21.

The Morton Salt Company knew how to use packaging to change and improve its basic product—salt. Other companies have used similar techniques. Thus we have stackable potato chips in a can (Pringles), cigarettes in a crush-proof box, beer in flip-top aluminum cans, dinners that can be boiled in a pouch and served immediately, whipped cream in dispenser cans, and so forth. In each case, the package changed the product in the minds of consumers and opened large markets.

Could you use packaging to improve your product? College students have a tendency to wear very casual clothes and to be rather carefree about their overall appearance. Yet when companies come to interview graduates, students have learned to package themselves quite effectively. They usually wear nice clothes, comb their hair neatly, and look and act rather professional. The concept that applies in all of the above examples is:

> **Packaging changes the product by changing its visibility, usefulness, or attractiveness.**

Packaging Is Becoming More Important

Packaging has always been an important aspect of the product offer, but today it is carrying more of the promotional burden. Many goods that were once sold by salespersons are now being sold in self-service outlets, and the package has been given more sales responsibility. As such the package must do the following: (1) it must attract the buyer's attention; (2) it must explain the benefits of the good inside; (3) it must provide information relative to warranties, warnings, and other consumer matters; and (4) it must give some indication of price, value, and uses.

Corporations spent about $46 billion for packaging in 1974.[2] To give these figures some perspective, during the same period, advertising expenditures were about $26 billion. Although more money is spent for packaging than for advertising, little research has been done on packaging as a marketing tool.

Packaging has traditionally been thought of as a last step in production rather than a first step in marketing; therefore, many promotional possibilities have been missed in the past. Packaging is receiving more attention now, especially since the government and the public have been exploring nutritional labeling, Truth-in-Packaging legislation, contents labeling, and other current packaging issues.

In the following section, we shall discuss some of the marketing tasks for which packaging is being used. No doubt packaging has become a critical part of the marketing of most goods.

Different Packaging Functions

One major function of packaging is to attract the attention of the buyer. To do this a package needs *visibility*. Visibility is achieved through the creative use of color, shape, texture, design, and size. One can easily identify most popular consumer products using these cues. For example, most people can recognize a Coke bottle, a box of Tide, a package of

[2] Harry A. Lipson and John R. Darling, *Marketing Fundamentals* (New York: John Wiley & Sons, Inc., 1974), p. 374.

Marlboro cigarettes, or a package of Crest toothpaste from several yards away. The importance of package visibility cannot be overemphasized. A grocery product may get more than 15 billion potential exposures per year; to obtain as many exposures through advertising would require a budget of about $50 million.[3]

Another function of packaging is to give consumers added *convenience* for their money. You are already familiar with the convenience that packaging has given products through the use of handy spray pumps, easy-open cans, kiddie-proof bottles, clear plastic wraps, and so forth. In the future, we may expect to see packaging innovations that will enable us to keep meat and milk without refrigeration, to serve instant gourmet meals from speedy microwave ovens, and to keep fresh vegetables and other perishables for months.

But marketers must also recognize people's concern about the environment. So packaging design may have to make more items recyclable to eliminate much waste. Today one can eat a meal at a fast-food outlet and throw away a whole tray full of straws, napkins, plastic covers, and other materials. This practice in many fast-food restaurants seems wasteful. Much waste in the packaging industry could be eliminated with little effect on consumer purchasing habits. When the total cost of packaging is now over $50 billion per year, such savings can be substantial.

Another function of packaging is to *protect the goods* from environmental factors such as rain and sun. Packaging must also protect against breakage, damage, and harm from animals.

Packaging helps the middleman by grouping goods into easily managed sizes. Packaging may be designed so that the shipping carton becomes a display rack. Packaging also helps retailers to price items, store them on their shelves, and process the item through their checkout counters. The new universal product codes being developed for supermarket items and other retail goods may enable the retailer to reduce checkout time, reduce errors, and increase inventory control and the information flow from retailer to producer.

To summarize the benefits of packaging we have discussed so far, remember that packaging: (1) adds visibility, (2) adds convenience, (3) minimizes environmental damage (when done correctly), (4) protects the goods from damage, and (5) keeps the goods in manageable, controllable sizes. We also mentioned that packaging benefits middlemen as well as consumers.

Packaging and the Consumer What may be of more interest to you is the way packaging can change the perceptions of buyers toward the total product offer. We have already noted how putting on nice clothes and looking professional may change employer perceptions. Let us review some other interesting consumer reactions.

People tend to spend much more money for a product if it is packaged

[3] Dik W. Twedt, "How Much Value Can Be Added Through Packaging," *Journal of Marketing*, January 1968, p. 61.

and promoted as a *gift* rather than an item for personal use. For example, a gift box of chocolates might cost $5.00–10.00. But an equivalent amount (weight) of candy might cost less than $1.50 if bought for one's personal use. A few pieces of fruit cost very little in the store, but a gift selection of fruit packaged in a crate may cost $15.00 or more. The same is true for cheeses, jellies, shirts, ties, socks, perfumes, and other gift items. The concept is:

> **The same physical goods take on entirely new values and are bought for entirely different reasons when packaged as gifts.**

People also respond to the social-symbolic meaning created by packaging. This means that people often buy products to impress others (or themselves) and are favorably influenced by packaging that meets these needs. If a man wants to wear some kind of after-shave lotion but still maintain his masculine image, he might buy an after-shave in a leather kit that contains the lotion in a dark, heavy, manly looking bottle. Packaging may thus be used as a segmentation tool; the concept is:

> **The image created by a package should be consistent with the self-image of the target market and with the image of the total product offer.**

If the target market is concerned mainly with price and durability, the package might be sturdy and plain. If the market is more concerned with quality and social status, the package may still be sturdy, but it might be more decorative and expensive-looking.

Packaging is a marketing tool that producers can use to communicate with consumers. Packaging creates a certain image. Branding is also a marketing tool that communicates information to the buyer. Together, packaging and branding are powerful influencers. In the following section, we shall discuss further the importance of branding.

BRANDING A brand is a name, symbol, or design (or a combination of them) that identifies the goods or services of one seller or group of sellers and distinguishes them from those of competitors.[4] The term brand is sufficiently comprehensive to include practically all means of identification of a product except perhaps the package and its shape. A brand name is that part of the brand consisting of a word, letter, or group of words or letters comprising a name that differentiates the goods or services of a seller from those of competitors.[5] Brand names you may be familiar with include Chevrolet, Clorox, Del Monte, Campbell, Winston, Exxon, Borden, and Colgate. Such brand names give products a distinction that tends to make them attractive to consumers. (See the insert "Why Brand Appeal Works" to see why people are attracted to brand names.)

To measure the importance of brand names in our society, you might

---

[4] "Report of the Definitions Committee," *Journal of Marketing*, October, 1948, p. 205.
[5] Ibid.

try the following experiment. Find a group of beer drinkers who say they greatly prefer one brand of beer and dislike another brand. Pour the brand they do not like into an empty bottle of the favored brand and serve it to them. Ask them how they like it. Most will say it tastes great because the *name* on the bottle has a direct effect on the perceived taste. Many laboratory experiments[6] have proved this concept:

> **People's perceptions of a product's taste, value, and attractiveness are determined by preconceived notions that are partially maintained through branding. That is, if people expect something to be good, it usually is perceived as good. And if they expect something to be bad, it usually is perceived as bad.**

People are often impressed by certain brand names, even though they say they know there is no difference between brands in a given product category. For example, when someone who says that all aspirin is alike asks for an aspirin, put two bottles in front of him or her—one with the Excedrin label and one labeled with an unknown brand. See which one he or she chooses. Most people choose the brand name even when they say there is no difference. What does this indicate? Try the same with liquor. Vodka is an almost tasteless liquor that people often add to orange juice or tomato juice. If you offer people their choice between an expensive, well-known brand and a cheap, lesser-known brand, almost all will pick the expensive brand. Why? The taste, liquor content, and all other *physical* characteristics may be the same, but the social value is very different. The concept is:

> **People often prefer brand names for their social significance, even when they recognize that there is little or no physical difference between the products.**

Your friends may have strong preferences for certain brands of cigarettes, ginger ale, bleach, and other such homogeneous items. In blind tests, they often cannot tell one from another—yet their preferences are strong. This shows that brand names and the promotions that support them can create favorable impressions and desires for products.

You might try one more experiment just for fun. Buy an attractive, but inexpensive tie and put it in a very attractive box from an exclusive store. Then buy a similar tie from the exclusive store and put it in a box from an inexpensive discount store. Tell your friends that you can't decide which tie is better and ask them to choose. If past experience is any guide, most will choose the inexpensive tie in the more expensive box. Again, laboratory experiments support these suggestions. The concept that explains such behavior is:

> **People often cannot determine the value of products by physical inspection; they, therefore, turn to other indicators of quality such as**

[6] See, for example, "Does the Label 'Change' the Taste?" *Printers Ink*, January 12, 1962.

Why Brand Appeal Works

Why are people attracted to brand products? What is it that makes them return again and again to a certain brand, ignoring all others? Some of the appeal of brands can be broken down as follows:

Familiarity. People are generally more comfortable with something that is known than with something that is not known.

Confidence. When people like and trust a product, for whatever reasons, they will return to it again and again.

Differentiation. This emphasizes the often-forgotten fact that the great majority of products *are not* alike. The brand concept allows the consumer to differentiate one from another.

Identification. A brand stance that is different from other products allows the individual to identify with a specific product in a way that reflects his or her own taste and life style.

Prestige. This perhaps reflects a basic human frailty, but it is a fact that we often use products to gain approval of our peer group. It should be noted that reverse snobbery also falls into this category.

The application of the brand concept is certainly not new, particularly to commodity products where a real point of differentiation between products is often hard to find. What Sunkist did for the orange, Chiquita has done for the banana. And while the lowly potato may not have many distinctive elements to distinquish it from competitors, once the name "Idaho" is applied, it assumes a wholly new stance in terms of audience perception. The states of Maine and Washington are also now attempting to enhance their own potato products with linkage to their state names.

Other commodity-type products that do not have a strong point of differentiation have also benefited from the brand concept. Who today is not familiar with Morton salt, Domino sugar and Land O'Lakes butter?

There are those who say all vodkas are the same. There are also millions of people who obviously disagree in that they purchase Smirnoff, this country's leading vodka, on a regular basis.

Reprinted with permission from Walter Margulies, "Brand Marketing Power: How to Differentiate Your Product from Competitors," *Advertising Age,* September 6, 1976, p. 45. Copyright 1976 by Crain Communications, Inc.

packaging, brand names, and price. A higher priced, expensively packaged item is usually perceived as "better" regardless of its actual physical qualities.

The obvious potential for deceiving consumers makes packaging and branding a major concern of legislators, consumerists, and other consumer-minded groups and individuals. It should be noted, however, that if the consumer thinks he or she is getting value, and the product lives up to expectations, people should not criticize such choices just because the value is psychological rather than physical. After all, our egos may need as much support as our bodies if we are to be healthy and happy.

What Is the Value of a Brand Name? To calculate the value to consumers of a national brand name versus a private brand, try this experiment. Ask several individuals what they would be willing to pay for a 19-inch color TV by Zenith or RCA. Then ask them what they would be willing to pay for the same TV (including the same service and warranty) if the brand name were Discount TV or Glop TV. The difference in what people would pay may surprise you. Often people would pay $200 more for the Zenith or RCA set. The question is why.

One answer is that national brands often bring more peace of mind than do discounted brands. If a person were to buy a 19-inch color TV carrying the Discount brand, chances are he or she would worry that the set would fail or would have a lousy picture. If the set did fail, the person often would accept responsibility for the failure because "you get what you pay for." But a person who buys a Zenith or RCA usually feels satisfied that the TV is the best available, and, if something goes wrong, it is not the buyer's fault.

Furthermore, buyers of brand-name items often feel more justified in bringing the product back if something goes wrong. On the other hand, people usually feel less confident of favorable treatment when returning a private-brand, discount item. Notice that we are talking about *perceptions*, not reality. In fact, private brands often have the same guarantees, services, and return privileges as national brands. But if the customer does not *feel* secure and confident, the product is worth less. The concepts are:

> A brand-name product often is perceived as being more valuable because of the peace of mind one gets with ownership and the perceived assurance that any problems will be taken care of by the seller.

> A private-brand product often is perceived as less expensive to buy but more likely to be of inferior quality and less likely to be serviced properly.

Of course, as we showed earlier, many people buy brand names because of their social significance. That is, a brand-name TV has more snob appeal than an unknown brand.

Branding Creates and Maintains Biases All people use their past experiences to guide them in future decisions. But this practice causes almost all of us to be biased: We tend to be biased toward the things we are familiar with and have liked in the past and biased against things that are strange and untried. For example, most people would not choose fried spiders if they were offered on a restaurant menu because they are biased against what they have never tried. This is true despite the fact that fried spiders may be quite tasty.

People also tend to be biased in their attitudes toward different races,

How to Select a Brand Name

A superior product without a good name will not sell as well as an average product with a superior name. . . . [The] criteria for selecting a brand name are:

1. Projection of a meaningful image
2. Uniqueness
3. Memorability
4. Distinction and registerability
5. Non-descriptive or hard to describe verbally
6. Ability to offer long-term support to the product
7. No negative associations
8. Creative integration of all elements

Because a brand name is hard to modify and almost impossible to change completely after its introduction, marketers must take great care in selecting it.

Blair E. Gensamer, director of product management, Cat Food Group, Ralston Purina Company, as quoted in "Brand Name Most Vital Element in Developing of New Products," *Marketing News,* February 13, 1976, p. 4.

religions, political beliefs, and—more important for some marketers—goods, services, and ideas. Marketers, therefore, should learn how to create biases in favor of their products and to maintain those preferences. The guiding concept is:

> **People tend to be biased toward what they know and like and *against* what they are unfamiliar with.**

According to this concept, if marketers can make more people familiar with their products (or with the name of their products), then those people will tend to be biased toward buying those products. For example, if a seller were to offer someone the choice between a Delco battery and a battery marked Whiz Brand, the buyer would likely choose the Delco battery. Why? Because consumers are more familiar with the Delco name and tend to choose what they are familiar with. Similarly, more people choose Clorox bleach rather than cheaper, lesser-known bleaches, Del Monte peaches rather than cheaper, lesser-known peaches, and Bayer aspirin rather than cheaper, lesser-known aspirin. These are facts that are explained by this concept:

> **People will often choose products and services that are more expensive than comparable products and services because they are more familiar with the more expensive brands. This concept applies even in the case of relatively similar products such as different brands of milk.**

One reason people prefer one brand over another could be that well-known brands are actually of better quality than unknown brands. But most people do not always physically compare brands; they sometimes assume that what they have heard of is better than what they have not heard of. In fact, many name-brand goods do not differ at all from goods labeled with less well known brands; however, the products are not at all the same in the mind of the consumer.

The tool many marketers use to create and maintain brand images is television. By means of periodic repetition of their brand names on television, marketers attempt to make their products stand out from those of competitors. The goal of such ads is to create a favorable *brand image*. That is, the product seems to be a good value and of good quality as a result of the ad. The concept is:

> **Advertising may be used to create and maintain a favorable brand image that leads consumers to prefer one brand over another even though the physical goods or services are the same or very similar.**

This concept is applicable in all marketing situations. For example, industrial marketers are biased by advertising almost as much as are consumers. They are often as impressed by names like Xerox and IBM as consumers are with names like Tide and Del Monte. One study of industrial buyers showed that by altering the brand name one could significantly change the perceptions of quality among buyers.[7] But most of us have to go no further than our own homes to see our biases. Look around you and see how many decisions you make based on biases (preferences). My neighbor, for example, is biased toward a certain religion, toward a particular part of the country, toward a particular political party, toward certain products (and brand names), and he is equally biased against others. Mostly, he is biased toward what he has

[7] See Irving S. White, "The Perception of Value in Products," in *On Knowing the Consumer*, ed. J. W. Newman (New York: John Wiley & Sons, Inc., 1966), p. 102.

Historical Problems with Branding

Today the consumer is offered a multitude of products unknown to his grandparents. He must choose among a bewildering array of labels; a host of different brands of cigarettes, toothpaste, shaving cream, cosmetics, and breakfast foods are on sale in every retail store. The late George K. Burgess estimated that there are as many as 10,000 brands of wheat flour, 4,500 brands of canned corn, 1,000 brands of canned peaches, 1,000 brands of canned salmon, 1,000 brands of canned peas, 500 brands of mustard, and 300 brands of pineapple.

From Paul W. Stewart and J. Frederic Dewhurst. *Does Distribution Cost Too Much?* (New York: The Twentieth Century Fund, 1939), p. 301. The figures are from Summer H. Slichter, *Modern Economic Society* (New York: Henry Holt and Co., 1931), p. 553.

grown up with and is comfortable with and biased against strange, new ideas, goods, services, and people. Most people have similar biases, but few people like to admit it.

Private versus National Brands When Chuck bought his Sears battery, he was buying a *private-brand* product. Private brands are also known as distribution, wholesaler-retailer, house, store, middleman's, or off brands. In other words, they are not the brand name normally used by the manufacturer. For example, the Kenmore appliances sold at Sears are made by a major manufacturer that sells similar appliances under a different brand name. Manufacturers' major brands are called *national brands* (also standard or producer's brands).

There is an ongoing debate over the future competition between *national brands* and *private brands*. In fact, there are advantages to both. Private brands may enable a manufacturer to make maximum use of production facilities. That is, a manufacturer might make as many products as can be sold under its own brand name and then continue to produce additional products to be sold under a private label. Longer production enables a firm to realize *economies of scale*. That is, it costs less to make products the more that are produced.

Private brands enable middlemen, such as Sears, to have better control over the product (including quality, prices, and competition). Retailers often feel that they can make a higher profit on private brands and that store loyalty can be built by creating an image of good-quality private-brand items at low prices.

Consumers also like private brands because they are usually less expensive than national brands. A private-brand can of peaches, for example, may be several cents cheaper than the *exact same can* carrying a national brand name.[8]

As we said, there are advantages to having both national and private brands. Some consumers prefer the assured quality and established guarantees offered by national brands. Others prefer the lower prices normally charged for private brands. No doubt there will continue to be healthy competition between private and national brands in the future.[9] Such competition is felt to benefit us all. The concepts are:

> **A good with a national brand name is not the same product as the same physical good with a private brand name.**

> **There are benefits and drawbacks to buying either national brands or private brands; competition among brands enables consumers to select those benefits they most desire.**

[8] For an analysis of consumer perceptions, see Tanniru R. Rao, "Are Consumers More Prone to Purchase Private Brands?" *Journal of Marketing Research*, November 1969, p. 447.

[9] See "Trends in Share of Sales of Private Label," *Progressive Grocer*, July 1968, p. 56.

Protecting When branding its products, an organization must be careful to use
Brand Names names and descriptions that clearly differentiate that product from
others. Some names that failed that test are aspirin, cellophane, linoleum, kerosene, and yo-yo. All of these were national brand names at one
time, but they lost their rights to those names because the name was
used to describe the *generic* product class. Perhaps this example will
help clarify the problem. Scot Norman went up to a vendor at a college
football game and asked for a Coke. The vendor sold Scot a cola drink,
but it was not a Coke. Scot wondered if that was legal. It is *not* legal to
sell a person any cola drink when Coke is ordered. Coke is a registered
brand name. In fact, Coca Cola has brought more than 600 court cases
against drug stores, supermarkets, and other businesses that serve
something else when the customer orders a Coke.[10] See the ad by
Addressograph Multigraph for further discussion about generic brands.
The concept is:

> ➤ **A brand name can be registered with the government so that other
> companies cannot sell products with similar names.**

The problem with the names Aspirin and Linoleum was that people
used those names to describe the general class of good (generic name)
rather than a particular company's product (brand name). Thus Aspirin
became Bayer aspirin. Some companies that are working hard to protect
their brand names are Xerox, and Dow Chemical (Styrofoam). The
following are some of the ways in which a corporation can protect its
brand names:[11]

1. Use the generic name together with the brand name (for example,
   Vaseline petroleum jelly, Kleenex facial tissues, Styrofoam—a Dow
   plastic foam).
2. Show that the brand name is registered (for example, by using the
   letter R in a circle or "Reg. U.S. Pat. Off."—Registered in U.S. Patent
   Office).
3. Use special type to set off the brand (for example, use all capital
   letters or at least capitalize the first letter).
4. Use the name only as an adjective. Avoid using the name as a noun, in
   the plural, as a verb, or in the possessive (for example, do not say
   "Xerox this material")
5. The brand name should not be altered by additions or abbreviations.
   "Pepsi" and "Coke" had to be registered separately to protect the
   abbreviated name.

[10] See "How Coke Protects Its Good Name," *Business Week*, November 4, 1972,
p. 66.
[11] See Sidney A. Diamond, "Protect Your Trademark by Proper Usage," in
Exploring Advertising, ed. Otto Kleppner and Irving Settle (Englewood Cliffs,
N.J.: Prentice-Hall, Inc., 1970), pp. 239–247.

Companies spend a great deal of money developing a memorable brand name that they are careful to protect.

Nylon
Aspirin
Escalator
Kerosene
Zipper
Addressograph®

Sometimes a company's product becomes so well known that its name becomes generic.

It's not going to happen to Addressograph, no sir. Even though some of our competitors have lately fallen into the unfortunate habit of using variations of our trademark to describe their equipment.

For 82 years, no one's beat us in offering you the broadest, best line of addressing equipment. We make the addresser you need. We always will. And now we've added folders and inserters, too.

So the next time their salesman tells you he's got something that's "just like Addressograph", please help us protect our good name. Tell him that as far as you're

concerned "there's nothing like Addressograph."

Then call your nearby Multigraphics man. He'll show you why you're right. Or write: Dept. M., 1800 W. Central Rd., Mt. Prospect, Ill. 60056.

We make you look better on paper.

 ADDRESSOGRAPH MULTIGRAPH
MULTIGRAPHICS DIVISION

NOTE: Nylon, Aspirin, Escalator, Kerosene, and Zipper—all once registered trademarks—are now generic dictionary words. "Addressograph" remains a registered and protected trademark of Addressograph Multigraph Corp., as it has been since 1906.

Reprinted with permission of Addressograph Multigraph.

Brand Names in Politics

A man named John Adams won the Republican nomination in New Hampshire's First Congressional District. Mr. Adams was an unemployed taxi driver who did almost no campaigning. He made no speeches, issued no press releases, spent no money. He figured that with a name like his he didn't need to. This is just one more example of how people choose products, including political candidates, based on the familiarity of the name. Politicians often spend millions of dollars establishing their name. Jimmy Carter went from relative obscurity to President of the United States by making his name a household word through effective marketing. Such examples show that branding concepts are applicable in all marketing situations.

Reported in *Newsweek*, September 27, 1976, p. 36.

6. Use the brand for an entire line of products.
7. Educate people concerning proper brand-name usage.

Companies spend millions to develop a memorable brand name; they should spend a few dollars more to protect that name.

Branding of Services Because services are intangible (that is, you cannot usually evaluate them by physical comparisons), brand names are very important for symbolizing the quality and reputation of the organization. Think of all the connotations connected with names such as Midas Muffler, United Air Lines, Allstate Insurance, and McDonald's restaurants.

Brand names and trademarks are also important for nonprofit service organizations. Think of the meaning you attach to the symbol of the Red Cross and the heart of the Heart Fund. The concepts are:

› Services use brand names to represent a certain standard of excellence that has great impact on the consumer.

› In all organizations, brand names are the vehicles for establishing a certain reputation that people can recognize anywhere in the world.

✳ The reputation of an organization may be *maintained* through brand names, but it is often established through customer service. The following section discusses this important element of a total product offer.

CUSTOMER SERVICE ✳ Customer services may be defined as all offerings of value to an organization's customers or clients beyond the generic product offering.[12] The **generic product offering** is the basic good, service, or idea that is offered the customer such as food at a restaurant or clothes at a clothing store.

[12] Adapted from Alfred R. Oxenfeldt, *Executive Action in Marketing* (Belmont, Calif.: Wadsworth Publishing Company, Inc., 1966), p. 599.

Customer services add to the generic product offer and help to differentiate the offer of one seller from that of others. Included in customer services are such things as guarantees, credit, delivery, maintenance, installation, free parking, return privileges, postsale remembrances, store atmosphere, rest rooms, information booths, gift wrapping, lay away, phone-ordering systems, adjustments, and consulting services.

An example may help you visualize what is involved in customer service. Irving Siegel wanted to buy a suit to wear to job interviews. He wanted the suit to fit well and to give him an image of "modern conservatism." Irving went to several stores to shop for the suit. At one men's store, Irving found a salesman who really seemed to understand his needs. The salesman asked Irving what he would be using the suit for, how much he wanted to pay, and what style he preferred. The salesman recommended a couple of different styles and helped Irving to visualize the suit as part of his job-getting program. In fact, the salesman also recommended that Irving buy shoes, socks, a tie, a shirt, and a belt to go with the suit. Irving said he could not afford all those things at that time because he did not have a job. The salesman was very understanding and showed Irving how he could use the firm's credit system to postpone payments until Irving had the money. The suit was to be an investment in a job, and so Irving decided to buy the whole image—shirt, tie, and all.

One other time when Irving went to the store (about a year later), the salesman actively discouraged him from buying a suit. He explained that the suit did not fit well and that it probably could not be tailored to look right. The salesman mentioned that a new shipment of suits would arrive in 10 days and that he would call Irving when they came. The salesman followed up on Irving's purchases by writing a letter thanking Irving for his business and reminding him that the store guaranteed satisfaction or the merchandise could be returned. The store's policy was to make a customer, not to make a sale. Customer services at the store included delivery (at a small charge), alterations, credit, lay away, return privileges, good parking, friendly help, a warm store atmosphere, gift wrapping (free), and advice on clothing quality and value.

Irving learned later that this store was one of the fastest-growing in the city. He noted that the quality of the merchandise was similar to several other stores, but that the quality of the service was far superior. The concepts are:

> **Customer service adds value to a product offer and can give one organization a distinct advantage over other organizations that provide less service.**

> **One of the most important elements in a total customer-service package is the atmosphere created by the people the customer deals with; friendliness, helpfulness, and graciousness add immeasurable value to a product offer.**

Here are three more examples of how service can add to the product offer. We include these examples to drive home the point that a marketer

> ## Service Overtones
>
> Certain services that meet customers' intangible needs are *overtones*. . . .
> The term is used here . . . to mean *all the intangibles that can make*
> *customers like or dislike doing business with a particular company*. . . .
> Overtones can be thought of as a company's personality; a company can
> be a nice guy or not, depending on the general impressions its overtones
> create. Many customers may not patronize the nice-guy type of company
> if they can get a substantially better deal elsewhere; but if the deals
> offered are nearly equal, the company they like to do business with will
> get their orders.

From Alfred R. Oxenfeldt, *Executive Action in Marketing* (Belmont, Calif.:
Wadsworth Publishing Company, 1966), p. 599.

can use service as an important tool to satisfy customers and increase
business.

Susan Murray wanted a new lamp for her living room, but she had a
hard time deciding what kind of lamp would look best. She hesitated to
buy a lamp for fear that it would look out of place in her home. Sue
found that one of the local lamp stores allowed customers to take home
lamps on trial for several days. The store also accepted the credit card
Sue preferred to use. Sue decided to select a lamp from that store, and, if
they did not have what she wanted, she would order one from their
catalog.

Marvin and Betty Lincoln wanted to have their suede jackets cleaned,
but they were afraid to take them to a cleaner because they could be
ruined. One local cleaner guaranteed its services and had a reputation
for quality care. Marvin and Betty decided to try that cleaner.

Bob and Mary Henderson needed some work done on their furnace.
They were eager to have someone come immediately because it was
supposed to get cold that night. Bob talked to several neighbors. He
learned that one repair company had a reputation for prompt service
and they came when they said they would come. Bob decided to call that
company first.

Each of these examples further emphasizes the fact that services are a
very important aspect of a total product offer. Many stores sell lamps,
and many lamps seem very similar, but services such as credit, free
home trials, decorating tips, and delivery can make one lamp store stand
out from the others.

Marv and Betty found that warranties (guarantees) often were a
critical part of a product offer. Those dry cleaners, tree nurseries, TV
manufacturers, automobile dealers, and other producers that guarantee
their products have a tremendous advantage over those that do not.

Have you noticed how many people are upset by the delivery and
installation personnel employed by most stores? How annoying it is to
wait all day for an installer and not have him or her show up—or even
phone. The same is true of delivery persons. They often seem to have a
total disregard for the consumer's time. When Bob and Mary found a

repairman that came when he said he would, they knew they had found an exception. It is too bad that so few sellers recognize that delivery, installation, and repair services are often the most important part of their product offer.

One more example will emphasize another key point. Bert and Karen Lucetto usually shop at one supermarket because the people are so friendly there. They often mention the fact that so few service employees are friendly, even though their income depends on it. Bert is really upset by waitresses and hotel clerks who are unfriendly and seemingly uncaring. Karen's pet peeves are bus drivers, phone operators at department stores, and "anyone in credit!!" Karen and her friends find that phone inquiries about bills and other such credit problems seem to be handled by the "grump-of-the-year" award winners.

Have you had similar experiences with clerks, phone operators, salespersons, delivery people, waiters, and other customer-contact people? If you have, you know that rude and nasty treatment can ruin the best product offer. You also know that a friendly, courteous, and helpful person can make a rather mediocre restaurant, nightclub, retail store, or doctor's office seem nicer and a better place to do business. The concept is:

> **A product offer may be greatly enhanced (or ruined) by the services that accompany it.**

One of the more important aspects of a product offer in this age of consumerism is the product warranty or guarantee. When consumers perceive products as being of lower quality than in the past ("They don't make 'em like they used to."), guarantees can create much favorable reaction.

Product Warranties Traditionally companies have worded their warranties so that they were difficult to read by the buyer and protective of the rights of the seller. Recent legislation has made product warranties a major strategic marketing tool. In the future, those firms that guarantee their products may have a significant advantage over those that do not.

Warranties are especially effective in the case of those products that are purchased infrequently, have a high price, and are mechanically complex.[13] But any product offer can be enhanced by the inclusion of an effective guarantee. Note how Shaeffer pens and Zippo lighters have been using their guarantees as an important element in their promotions. The concept is:

> **Product warranties and guarantees add value to product offers; a product with a guarantee of satisfaction is much different from the same product without the guarantee.**

[13] See Jon G. Udell and Ewan E. Anderson, "The Product Warranty as an Element of Competitive Strategy," *Journal of Marketing*, October 1968, pp. 1–8.

One of the most successful promotions of the last decade was the Buyer Protection Plan of American Motors (AMC). This plan offered one of the most comprehensive guarantees ever offered by an automobile company. "If it's our fault," AMC ads read, "we'll fix it. Free." Furthermore, AMC offered to extend the guarantee for an extra year for only $149. As a result of this promotion, AMC sales increased dramatically. Here is what Cyril Freeman, general marketing manager at AMC, said: "Our research shows that one person out of four who visits an AMC dealer does so because of the Buyer Protection Plan; that 82% of the AMC shoppers know about the plan before visiting the showroom; and that 47% say it is important in promoting their visit.[14]

The Buyer Protection Plan is just one example of how a company can enhance its product offer by its guarantee program. Often such a guarantee can turn around a company's sales as it did with AMC cars.

Business Services Customer service is just as important when selling to businesses as it is in the case of consumers. Many services are the same (for example, credit, delivery, installation, maintenance, adjustments, and friendly help), but other services are also very important. A manufacturer, for example, could help retailers by giving them display assistance, promotional assistance, inventory guidance and help, in-store demonstrations, and free consulting advice on all aspects of the business including accounting, personnel, and marketing. The concepts are:

> **Customer service is important in all marketing exchanges, including industrial marketing exchanges.**

> **Purchasing agents (buyers for business organizations) often weigh customer service, especially delivery and credit, as heavily as any other element of the sale, including price and quality.**

It is the extras that make one product offer seem to be a better buy (value) than its competitors. But sometimes extras add so much to the price that the consumer turns to the less expensive product. The next chapter discusses this key element in the product offer—price.

[14] Cyril Freeman, "Buyer Protection Plan: Biggest Automobile Innovation in Years," *Advertising Age*, July 8, 1974, p. 40.

FOR REVIEW

Key Terms

Among the more important terms and expressions discussed in this chapter are the following:

A **brand** is a name, symbol, or design (or a combination of them) that identifies the goods or services of one seller or group of sellers and distinguishes them from those of competitors.

A **brand name** is that part of the brand consisting of a word, letter, group of words or letters comprising a name that differentiates the goods or services of a seller from those of competitors.

Customer services consist of all offerings of value to an organization's customers or clients beyond the generic product offering.

The **generic product offering** is the basic good, service, or idea that is offered to the customer.

Key Concepts

Among the more important marketing concepts introduced in this chapter are the following:

> **People usually evaluate the total product offer when buying a product and choose what they perceive to be the best value to them.**

> **Packaging changes the product by changing its visibility, usefulness or attractiveness.**

> **The image created by a package should be consistent with the self-image of the target market and with the image of the total product offer.**

> **Advertising may be used to create and maintain a favorable brand image that leads consumers to prefer one brand over another even though the physical goods or services are the same or very similar.**

> **A good with a national brand name is not the same product as the same physical good with a private brand name.**

> **Services use brand names to represent a certain standard of excellence that has great impact on the consumer.**

> **Customer service adds value to a product offer and can give one organization a distinct advantage over other organizations that provide less service.**

> **Product warranties and guarantees add value to product offers; a product with a guarantee of satisfaction is much different from the same product without the guarantee.**

Discussion Questions

1. Take out a few of the products you have purchased recently (for example, cereal, soap, cosmetics). What information is printed on the package? Does the package enhance the product's image? Why or why not?

2. Try some experiments in class in which people evaluate various beers (can they really tell which is which?), cigarettes (can they identify their own brand?), and beverages (for example, see if students can tell Pepsi from Coke from Diet Rite Cola). Discuss your results.

3. Go through your medicine chest and list the brand names of the products you own. (What kind of toothpaste, mouthwash, soap, after-shave, and so on, is there?). Did you buy mostly *names* or *price?*

Why? Were you consistent in emphasizing brand names or price? Why or why not?

4. Evaluate one or two of your latest major purchases (for example, a car, suit, dress, furniture). What customer services were involved (tailoring, delivery, credit, return privileges, and so on)? Did any of these have a major influence on your purchase? Why or why not?

5. How often have you had a product fixed under the warranty? Was the service prompt and friendly? Are warranties an important part of your product-selection criteria? Why or why not?

6. What image comes to mind when you read the following names: Ford Pinto, Ajax, American Airlines, B. F. Goodrich, H & R Block? Which images were good and which were not? What caused those impressions? Could your impressions be changed? How?

7. Do you buy your tires, batteries, and auto accessories at the local gas station or elsewhere? Why? What would get you to change?

8. Explain how packaging adds value for the middleman (for example, the retailer). Give examples of products that have gained prominent retail exposure because of effective display or packaging efforts.

9. Would you rather own a TV set with a *good* picture and a beautiful cabinet or one with an *excellent* picture and a drab cabinet? You have to choose one or the other. Discuss your answer as an indicator of the importance of packaging.

10. Can a person "package" services, ideas, or nonprofit organizations? Why or why not? Support your answer with examples.

CASES

A New Toothpaste
Branding Strategy

Proctor & Gamble had a best-selling toothpaste named Crest. There seemed to be a market for a toothpaste with a more minty flavor than Crest. Procter & Gamble developed such a toothpaste. It had all the cavity-fighting power of Crest plus a new, refreshing taste. Proctor & Gamble decided to name the new toothpaste "Mint-Flavored Crest."

1. What factors might Procter & Gamble have considered before deciding on the new brand name?

2. Would you have named the new brand "Mint-Flavored Crest"? Why or why not?

3. Most companies give their competitive products different brand names. Why would Procter & Gamble make an exception for Crest?

4. If Listerine mouthwash were to be formulated to taste better, would you recommend the product be named something like "Mint-Flavored Listerine"? Why or why not?

The National Kidney Foundation
Branding Strategy

Kidney disease is one of the most important diseases in terms of number of people who die from it. The National Kidney Foundation was formed to find a cure for kidney diseases and to treat people already suffering from disease. One problem is that people are not very excited about donating to a cause with "kidney" in its name. It is not nearly as glamorous as organizations that stress the heart, cancer, crippled children, muscular dystrophy, and the like. In fact, the National Kidney Foundation was sixteenth in the amount of funds raised in 1971. The American Cancer Society raised over thirty times as much money.

1. If you were in charge of the National Kidney Foundation, would you change its name? If yes, what name would you use? If no, why not?
2. Would you recommend that the National Kidney Foundation become part of United Way of America and not have its own fund-raising effort? Why or why not?
3. How could you increase awareness of the National Kidney Foundation and its national importance?

Pricing Concepts
adjusting to the market

LEARNING GOALS After you have read and studied this chapter, you should be able to:

1. Explain why price is part of the product-differentiation function.
2. Explain why price is important to the valuation function.
3. Define the following terms: break-even analysis; elasticity; marginal analysis; penetration pricing; price lining; cost-oriented pricing; demand-oriented pricing; market price; target pricing.
4. Describe how consumers react to prices.
5. Explain the concept of "value" and describe how consumers determine value.
6. Outline the relationships among price, value, and utility.
7. Contrast the price of a product with its total cost.
8. Explain the economic concepts of supply and demand and how they affect price.
9. Draw charts that explain break-even analysis and marginal analysis.
10. Describe how pricing concepts can be used to increase social welfare.

INTRODUCTION "We have a special price on gloves today," said the clerk. "Buy one at $20, and we'll give you the other one free." The humor in this story reflects the attitude of many consumers toward pricing. They often feel that pricing is just one more way to confuse and deceive them. Often they are right. This chapter will discuss pricing concepts and strategies. We hope it will give you a better idea of *how* prices are established and *by whom*. We shall also look at consumer reaction to price and at the relation of price to the valuation function. Finally, we shall discuss pricing strategies and ways to increase social welfare through pricing concepts.

PRICING CONCEPTS "How much is it?" This question is repeated many times a day in stores around the world. It shows that consumers and organizations will buy lots of things *if the price is right*. One can design the finest products in the world, but if the price is perceived as too high, the effort may be for nothing. Pricing decisions, therefore, should be completely integrated with product decisions, for price is part of the product offer, just as the package and the brand are.

Price is one way in which a seller can differentiate his offer from those of competitors. Pricing may thus be considered part of the product-differentiation function in marketing. But pricing is also part of the valuation function:

Since the price at which the consumer purchases a product involves his evaluation of the satisfaction it will yield, it can be said that the total sales of a firm represents the sum of the satisfactions, as measured in dollars and cents, which it has delivered to its customers.[1]

* *Introduction to the Marketing System* (San Francisco: Canfield Press, 1973), p. 224.

[1] Weldon J. Taylor and Roy T. Shaw, Jr., *Marketing: An Integrated Analytical Approach* (Cincinnati: South-Western Publishing Co., 1975), p. 23.

Price Closes the Deal

Product, price, and service all enter into the design of a bundle of utilities [product] to be offered to the consumer. Yet price, in a sense, is the final element which closes the deal and makes due allowances for all of the other elements.

From Wroe Alderson, *Marketing Behavior and Executive Action* (Homewood, Ill.: Richard D. Irwin, Inc., 1957), p. 257.

246

Consumer Reactions to Price   Price is often an indicator of quality to the consumer. For example, liquor is often evaluated by price rather than by taste or ingredients. Top-shelf liquor (expensive) is usually considered "better" because it is more expensive. The same is true for many other consumer products.

Leavitt reported that people often chose the higher priced of two products when the only difference between them was price. This was more likely to occur when the people perceived a difference between products (for example, floor wax) than when the products were perceived to be all alike (for example, moth balls). As the price differential increases, people tend to feel that quality differences also increase.[2]

Many more recent studies have confirmed the fact that consumers often use price as a major criterion in determining value. High-priced products are usually considered "superior" and low-priced products "inferior." These results should not be surprising; the surprising thing is that they hold true even for relatively homogeneous goods and services such as gasoline, motels, dry cleaners, and bleach.

Even more surprising is the fact that many consumers do not know the price of many, if not most, of the products they buy regularly. People tend to have a price range within which they shop and do not particularly care what the exact price is as long as the product seems to meet their needs and is in that acceptable range. Many consumers are more

[2] Harold J. Leavitt, "A Note on Some Experimental Findings About the Meaning of Price," *Journal of Business*, July 1959, pp. 205–210.

"Are any of these prices negotiable?"

Do Prices Indicate Quality?

Inability to judge quality places the customer at a disadvantage vis-à-vis the marketer. For example, consider a certain men's clothing store in a major city. It has gained a reputation as the place to go for highest quality clothing. Service is excellent; salesmen are well trained and well paid; the store exudes an atmosphere of comfort and luxury. And prices bear this out. But let us look at their pricing practices. Sport shirts are typical. A certain line of shirts cost the store $3.60 each. They are sold for $7.98, $9.98, and $12.95, depending on the pattern and minor style characteristics. Is the $12.95 shirt of better quality than the $7.98 one? Of course not. In an unguarded moment, the proprietor was asked the difference in the shirts. "The price," he said.

Robert F. Hartley, *Marketing: Management and Social Change* (New York: Intext Educational Publishers, 1972), p. 104.

concerned with *image* than with price. A low-priced product may seem the same as a high-priced product in all other ways, but, if everyone knows it is cheap, many people will not buy it. After all, who wants to be known as a "cheapie"? The concepts are:

> **Price varies in importance among different products and consumers.**

> **Price is often an indication of quality, and higher priced products *seem* better (even when they are not), especially when the products have the potential for having large differences in quality.**

> **Many people keep their purchases within a certain price range and choose only products that fit their perception of what that product "should cost."**

> **Price is often less important than image for highly visible or socially important products such as liquor, cosmetics, and automobiles; that is, the higher-priced products are often preferred for their social appeal.**

Unit Pricing Many supermarkets have introduced a policy of posting unit prices for their food items. This means that most items are listed as having a certain price per pound or per ounce. The idea was to make it easier for consumers to compare prices and values between competing products. It is difficult, otherwise, for consumers to determine whether the item selling for 38¢ for 7 ounces is a better buy than the "economy size" selling at 75¢ per pound. One problem with unit pricing is that the consumers who need it most (the poor and uneducated) often do not use it. And unit pricing might tend to put undue emphasis on *price* and give insufficient recognition to *quality*. Even with unit pricing, consumers still may not be able to tell which product is the better value because quality often varies greatly among food items. In periods of tight money, more and more emphasis is placed on price, and that often forces producers to lower quality to be competitive.

┌──┐

Price Not Always Important

Actually many purchases are made without inquiring about the price. When the consumer buys razor blades or cigarettes he is likely to assume that the price remains unchanged. . . . In specifying a need for items such as wearing apparel, the consumer may set a price limit rather than an exact price.

└──┘

Wroe Alderson, *Dynamic Marketing Behavior* (Homewood, Ill.: Richard D. Irwin, Inc., 1965), p. 31.

Price Terminology Is Sometimes Confusing

There is a potential in marketing to underplay the importance of price in service and nonbusiness organizations. Often the term price is not used and some other term is used instead. For example, you pay tuition to a school and doctors charge a fee. Social clubs often make an assessment or ask for a donation. Highway administrators establish tolls and insurance companies charge a premium.

In each of these examples, the price represents what you must give up in order to get the products you want. The price of something and the value of something are not necessarily the same. The concepts explaining the differences are discussed below.

The Concept of Value

As was discussed in Chapter 8, the "value" of an exchange relationship is determined by the sum of the satisfactions the person perceives minus the costs or dissatisfactions involved. Perhaps an example would help you to visualize this process as it applies here.

Imagine a woman trying to decide whether or not to buy a new pair of shoes. Her valuation procedure may look like this:

Costs	*Benefits*
1. Search time	**1.** Comfortable standing and walking
2. Money (about $25)	**2.** Admiration of others (new style)
3. Alternative uses of money (opportunity costs)	**3.** Fun of shopping
	4. Protection from the elements

After weighing all the factors, the woman might decide to buy a new pair of shoes, but not immediately. She might wait until she is near the shopping center and then get the shoes so she can minimize the cost of shopping time and still get all the benefits. Such a strategy would increase the overall value of the purchase.

Cost-benefit analysis helps a person weigh the "value" of a new pair of shoes versus a night on the town, a bigger donation to charity, or some other alternative. Value is thus a function of costs versus benefits, and the benefits of one exchange versus the benefits of some other exchange. The concept behind all of this is:

» **A person will enter exchange relationships when the perceived benefits of the exchange are greater than the perceived costs involved and/or are greater than the perceived benefits of alternative exchanges.**

Sometimes people will buy things that they *must* have even though the benefits are short term and they dislike the whole idea. For example, people will go to a dentist or a doctor simply because the alternative may be pain or death rather than because they perceive the dentist or doctor as a good value or a positive long-term benefit. No matter how much such people complain, the fact is that the benefits (utility) of the exchange must be perceived as greater than the costs (at the time), or else the exchange will not take place. The following summarizes the relationships among price, value, and utility:

> *Any good [product] that has the capacity to satisfy a human want is said to possess* utility. *The power of such utility or of the good [product] possessing it to command other goods [products] in normal and regular exchange is its* value. *Such value, expressed in monetary terms, is the* price *of the good.*[3]

All Exchanges Demand Price Concepts Pricing concepts have been developed partially to explain economic (money) exchanges. But marketers are also concerned with many noneconomic (nonbusiness) exchange relationships. Does this mean that pricing is not a relevant concept in noneconomic exchanges? Of course not, but often the terms are different as we detailed earlier. The concept that applies in all marketing exchanges is that of the valuation function. Pricing is merely a convenient way to adjust product offers until the perceived values of all participants are such that an exchange is made possible.

Although an exact figure may not be stated, we all know that there is a price we must pay to get an education that goes way beyond the cost of tuition and books. There is also a price we pay for big government that

[3] Theodore N. Beckman, William R. Davidson, and W. Wayne Talarzyk, *Marketing*, 9th ed. (New York: The Ronald Press Company, 1973), p. 358. The word "product" in brackets was inserted to show that services and other nongoods are included in the concept.

Value Is in the Mind of the Consumer

Popular economic discussion often assumes that things have an "intrinsic" worth . . . however, it becomes clear that what a thing is worth to us depends on how much of it we have, and that therefore the "worth" is not anything "in" a commodity. It is not a physical property of an object like weight or volume, but is simply "how we feel about it." Things are "valuable" because somebody thinks they are, and for no other reason whatever. This is true . . . even of gold, [which] like everything else is valuable only because people think it is.

From Kenneth E. Boulding, *Economic Analysis*, 3rd ed. (New York: Harper & Row, Publishers, 1955), p. 22.

exceeds the taxes we pay, and a price we pay to join a union that is more than union dues. The concepts are:

> **All exchanges involve a valuation function whereby the participants weigh the advantages (benefits) and disadvantages (costs or price) of the transaction.**

> **Pricing concepts are applicable in all exchange situations, but the terms are not always made explicit.**

✳ You should be careful to note that *prices may be set by either the buyer or the seller*. Note also that the final price is one that is agreed upon by *both* buyers and sellers. It is the result of an exchange agreement:

Without prices there can be no marketing. Products may be matched with markets, but only when buyers and sellers agree on prices *do ownership transfers actually occur. Either a buyer or a seller may propose a price, but it does not become one until accepted by the other.*[4]

It should be clear by now that nonprofit organizations are often as concerned with pricing as are profit-oriented firms. For example, the U.S. Postal Service has had very difficult pricing decisions to make in the last few years. The same is true of many universities, hospitals, and mass transit operations. Pricing strategies enable such organizations to adapt to the wants and needs of rapidly changing markets and to the organization's internal needs as well.

Price and Noneconomic Exchanges   To get some feel for the role of price in various marketing exchanges, consider the following questions:

1. Would you like to have a dog?
2. How big a home would you like to own?
3. What grades do you want in college?
4. Would you like to travel for the rest of your life?
5. Would you like to live where the air is clean and pure and the water as fresh and cold as a mountain stream?

To answer these questions realistically, you must consider what the price would be in each case. Maybe you would love to have a dog, but you have no place to keep it. If you did get a dog, you would have to pay to have it licensed, wormed, and so forth. You would also be expected to feed it, care for it, and maintain its health. The price of a dog is quite high when you consider *all* the costs.

The same is true of grades. Everyone would like to have all A's, but few are willing to pay the price. After all, the amount of time one must

---

[4] Edward W. Cundiff, Richard R. Still, and Norman A. P. Govoni, *Fundamentals of Modern Marketing*, 2nd ed. (Englewood Cliffs, N.J.: Prentice-Hall, Inc., 1976), p. 376.

spend to get a C is often considerably less. "And what is so bad about a gentleman's C, anyhow?" you may ask. No one can answer that question for you. The concepts are:

> **All exchanges have a price or cost associated with them.**

> **The value of a particular exchange varies between individuals and is based on individual wants and needs.**

> **To determine the real value of an exchange, one must measure the costs against the benefits.**

The concepts apply whether the "product" is a dog, a home, good grades, clean water and air, or anything else. One can see then that price is a key variable in the valuation function for both buyer and seller.

The Price We Pay Is Not the Total Cost One thing we can learn from the example of getting a dog is that the price of something in monetary terms is not the same as its cost. The cost of getting and keeping a dog is much greater than the money price. The same is true of all goods and services. On the other hand, the benefits we get from an exchange are not always reflected in the price either. Who can put a price on the joy a young person gets from having a dog?

One of the costs associated with many marketing exchanges is that of credit. For example, the answer to the question about how big a home a person would like to own often depends more on the cost of credit than on the price of the home. At today's rates the amount paid for credit greatly exceeds the price of a home.

Information Has a Cost Part of the price we pay for things goes for information. *Information is part of the product.* Suppose you want to buy a tennis racket, but you are not sure whether to get wood or metal, gut or nylon, new or used, or what price to pay. You could spend lots of time (and money) going from friend to friend and store to store gathering bits and pieces of information. You could go to the library and read books and magazines, go through the paper looking for sales, and spend weeks getting a "good deal on a racket." *Or,* you could go to a tennis pro's shop, discuss your questions, and buy the racket there. Which racket would cost you more? Oh sure, you may pay more for the racket at the tennis shop, *but would it cost you more?* What is your time worth? How much is tennis expertise worth? The search for information on your own may have taken 16 hours if you include all the time reading, traveling, and comparing. At $3.00 per hour, that information would have cost you $48.00. And would you be sure that the racket you buy is best for you?

Some people do not consider their own time in evaluating the cost of a product. Do you agree? Is it cheaper to make a dress or buy one? A lot depends on the value a person puts on time. Is it cheaper to take a bus or fly? Again, it depends on the value you place on time. A college student may feel the bus is cheaper, but a busy business executive cannot afford the time to take a bus. That is one reason why market segmentation becomes such an important function for sellers. It helps select those people whose values are best suited to the product to be exchanged. The concepts are:

> **Information has value that greatly affects the price of a product.**
> **One should seek information about products and prices until the cost of getting more information exceeds the value of having more information.**
> **Time spent in making or obtaining products is part of the cost, but the value of that time varies among individuals.**

HOW ARE PRICES DETERMINED? We are so accustomed to thinking of marketing as something done by the seller that it is difficult to think of pricing decisions coming from anyone other than the seller. But a moment's reflection will show you that it is often the buyer who sets the price. For example, how many times have you told a seller that you would give him or her a certain amount of money for something. In this section we shall show how prices are determined by the *interactions between* buyers and sellers.

People also feel rather intuitively that the price charged for a product must bear some relation to the cost of producing the product. In fact, we would generally agree that prices are usually set somewhere *above* cost. But as we shall see, prices and cost are not always related.

Perhaps it would be best to begin the analysis of how prices are determined by reviewing some basic economic concepts. After all, much of micro-economics[5] deals with price, and so economists have much to offer marketers in their study of pricing.

Why Cost of Production Is a Poor Basis for Price Karl Marx was perhaps the most widely known economist who tried to explain the relation between the cost of production and price. He felt that the price of a good was, and should be, based on the amount of labor needed to produce it. But it does not take much research to show this just is not so. In fact, there is often very little correlation between the price of something and its cost of production. Does a quarterback earn more than a physician because it costs more to produce a quarterback? Does a rare stamp cost a thousand times more than a regular stamp because one cost more to produce? Obviously not.

Nevertheless, producers often use cost as a primary basis for setting price. They develop elaborate cost-accounting systems to measure production costs (including materials, labor, and overhead), add in some margin of profit, and come up with a satisfactory price. The question is whether the price will be satisfactory to the market as well. In the long run, the market determines what the price will be, not the producer. This concept is explained best by economic theory.

---

[5] Micro-economics is the study of individual areas or elements of economic activity (a firm, a household, prices). Macro-economics, on the other hand, is the study of entire economic systems (for example, the United States) and aspects of those systems (unemployment, economic cycles, economic growth, and so forth).

Economic Law of Demand

Because of the difficulty most people have in trying to understand the difference between the terms "wants" and "needs," economists use the word "demand" instead. Demand as an economic concept relates the amounts of anything that people want to the sacrifices (costs) that must be made to get what they want. The idea is that people will demand less of something the more it costs. The economic principle (law) is this: *There is a negative relation between the price of anything that people want and the price (cost) they must pay for it: that is, the higher the price, the less they will buy, and the lower the price, the more they will buy.*

Although economists call this a "law," the number of exceptions to it make it wiser to call it a principle. One exception is high-status items such as automobiles, homes, and clothes. For some people, the more expensive these goods are, the more attractive they are; and people will buy the expensive ones often at great sacrifice. The same is often true of personal-care items such as perfume, lotions, and cosmetics. Lowering the cost (price) of such items does not necessarily lead to more sales. In fact, the opposite is sometimes true. One manufacturer, for example, brought out a very good face cream for a very reasonable price. But it did not sell well at all. After the company raised the price considerably, people began to perceive the product as "better" because of the high price, and they bought much *more* of it.

Price Partially Determined by Supply and Demand

Recently, an article in the *Washington Post* announced that medical schools in the Washington, D.C., area were considering raising their tuition 100 percent or more. Because tuition was already $5,000, one can see the significance of the statement. Who can afford $10,000 per year just for tuition? Well, as long as there is a very high demand for doctors

Figure 10.1 DEMAND CURVE

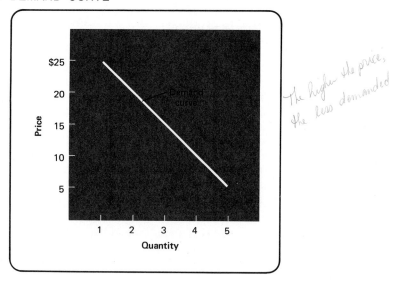

Figure 10.2 SUPPLY CURVE

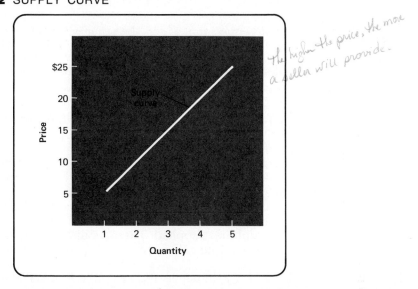

The higher the price, the more a seller will provide.

and as long as they are paid good wages, there will be a high demand to get into medical school, even with tuition costing $10,000. The concept is:

> **When the demand for a product is high, the price will tend also to be high.**

You may get confused by our use of economic terms such as demand, so let us pause here to point out that there is a difference between the *quantity* of a product *demanded* and the *demand* itself. Demand is the relationship between *quantity demanded* and *price*. The principle (law) of demand we discussed earlier stated that there is a negative relation between the price of something and the quantity demanded. If the price of beef or oil or eggs goes up, the *quantity demanded* goes down. But this statement assumes there is some *demand* for beef, oil, and eggs in the first place. That demand (not *quantity demanded*) is based on factors such as consumer income and consumer preferences.

The other side of the coin is supply. If the supply of something is high, the price will tend to be low. For example, most people pay little or nothing for water to drink. But in the middle of the desert, where supply is very low, the price can be quite high.

If we put the two factors together—supply and demand—we can fairly well predict what the price will be. The economic explanation is relatively easy to follow, so let's give it a try. It is easiest to picture with a chart. We begin with the chart shown in Figure 10.1.

What this chart says is that at $25, people would only buy one item. At $20, they would buy two, and so on until at $5, they would buy five items. Basically, this shows in chart form the principle that the lower the price, the more will be demanded. Now let's look at a supply curve (Figure 10.2).

This chart shows that at $25, the seller will sell five units. At $20, he will only sell four, whereas at $5, he will only sell one. The concept is:

> **The higher the price of a product, the more sellers will provide of that product.**

Combining the two charts, we can determine the exchange price. It is the price where the supply and demand curves cross, that is, where supply equals demand (see Figure 10.3).

Figure 10.3 shows that the best price is $15, for there supply equals demand. If the price were higher, say $20, the demand would be for only two items, but sellers would be willing to sell four. There would be a *surplus*, according to the theory, and the price would fall to get rid of the surplus. If the price were $10, the demand would be for four items, but only two would be supplied. There would be a *scarcity* of the product, and the price would rise until demand equaled price. The concept is:

> **The price of a product in the long run is determined by supply and demand; the equilibrium price (long-term exchange price) is where supply equals demand.**

Let us explain these concepts in more basic terms. If you were a stamp collector and found a stamp that no one else had, you could charge a very high price for it (assuming there was a demand). If somebody else suddenly discovered 10,000 stamps just like yours in the basement and decided to sell them, the price you could get for your stamp would go way down. Why? The stamp did not change. Yes, but the supply changed. The greater the supply, the lower the price. By the way, a stamp has been sold for over $200,000. What would happen to the buyer

Figure 10.3 SUPPLY AND DEMAND CURVES

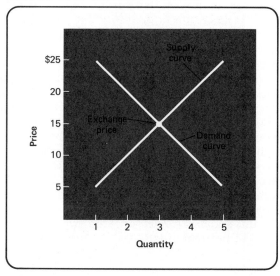

if no one wanted to buy it from him? What is the stamp really worth? Price often has little to do with quality or any other product feature.

Imagine that you own an empty lot far from the city in the middle of farm country. Let us say you paid $300 an acre for it. One day you hear that the government has decided to build a giant complex of buildings on the lot next door for defense research. How much would your lot be worth now? It has not changed at all in size, but the demand for your land might go up considerably. But if the government were to build a fence all around your land cutting off access, no one might want it, and the price you could get would go way down. Again, it is supply and demand, not inherent quality or location per se, that determines the price of a product.

Strategies Based on the Law of Demand Marketers recognize the fact that the less something costs, the greater the number of people who will *be able* to buy it, and they use this fact in strategy decisions. When bringing out a new product, for example, a firm could use one of two strategies: a skimming strategy or a penetration strategy. If they use a **skimming strategy**, they will introduce the product at a high price to cover the costs of research, development, and promotion. They hope to sell the product to those people who have money and who would like to have the "newest" products. They thus "skim" the most favorable customers from the top of the market as one would skim cream from the top of milk.

A **penetration strategy** involves pricing the product relatively low to capture the largest possible share of the market. The idea is to discourage competitors from entering the field (they couldn't make much at such a low price) and to get wide exposure for the product.

These strategies are used not only for new products, but also for old products with new features and for many other situations where a price change is called for.

What Happens When the Price Goes Up? How much flexibility one has in setting a price for his or her products is based on a number of factors, including competition, need for the product, and the nature of the product. Economists use the term **elasticity** to refer to the responsiveness of the market to a change in price. If a small change in price (downward) creates a large change in demand (upward), demand is called *highly elastic*. If a large change in price results in a small change in demand, demand is said to be *highly inelastic*. Well, so what?

If you find that the demand for your product is highly inelastic, that means that you can raise the price considerably, make much more money, and sell about the same amount. Some people feel that gasoline fits that description. Apparently some foreign suppliers thought so. After they raised the price of oil considerably throughout the world, the demand did not fall off very much, and they became quite wealthy.

In the long run, the inelasticity of demand, even for gasoline, may not be as high as supposed. As prices go higher, people begin to form car pools and take public transportation. As their old car needs replacing, they tend to buy smaller, more economical cars. If the price got too high, they might buy a bicycle or motorcycle and move closer to work. As the demand for gasoline went down, suppliers would be left with a surplus, the price would go down, and their wealth would increase much more slowly.

On the other hand, if a firm found that the demand for its product was very elastic, it could lower its price just a little and capture a much larger share of the market—if competition did not do the same. The guiding concepts for marketers are:

> **If the demand for a product is highly *elastic*, a *small* increase or decrease in price will cause a large decrease or increase in purchases respectively.**
> **If the demand for a product is highly *inelastic*, it means that consumers will buy about the same amount whether the price is raised or lowered.**
> **In the long run, the demand for most products is partially elastic; that is, people will buy less if the price is increased and more if it is decreased.**

PRICING STRATEGIES We have already discussed two pricing strategies of importance: penetration and skimming strategies. This section will briefly discuss some other basic pricing strategies and concepts. Included is a list showing some key pricing terms and what they mean in a marketing setting. One cannot hope to cover all pricing strategies in a book of this type. We hope you do get some feel for the complexity of the subject nonetheless.

Building Products to Fit Predetermined Prices Sometimes manufacturers arrive at the price for a product by determining the cost of production and adding on some profit margin, as we outlined earlier. But quite often the process is reversed. Price comes first, then profit margins are subtracted, and finally the product is designed based on the available funds. For example, a manufacturer of candy bars may see that most candy bars sell for 20¢. The manufacturer would then subtract the retail margin, distribution costs, and his own profit margin. He may find that the candy bar must be produced for 5¢ to sell it at 20¢ at the retail store. The guideline for production is thus 5¢. To meet that guideline, the candy bar may have to be made smaller (have you noticed this happening?) or the production process made more efficient.

Automobiles are often designed the same way. A competitive price comes first; say $5,500. From that price must be subtracted dealer margins, transportation costs, and so forth, and the remainder, say $3,000, is what is available for production.

One reason manufacturers often set the retail price first is that consumers are often very sensitive to slight changes in price. Retail stores may practice **price lining**, which means that the store will try to maintain a certain stable price over time. A shoe store, for example, might sell shoes at $9.95 and $19.95. Manufacturers would design shoes to match these prices. The concepts are:

> Consumers have the final say as to what price is acceptable, and so manufacturers often have to work backward from consumer prices to determine available production funds.

> Many stores have a policy of price lining, whereby prices remain relatively stable over time at a fixed rate; such practices force producers to produce to fit the price rather than set the price to fit production costs.

Pricing Objectives
A widely quoted study of corporate pricing objectives was conducted in the late 1950s.[6] It found that the most common marketing objectives among major firms were a target return on investment (for example, Alcoa, Du Pont, General Electric, and Union Carbide), maintenance of market share (for example, American Can, Kroger, and Swift), and meeting competition (for example, Goodyear). The study dealt only with larger corporations, and so it does not reflect the diverse pricing objectives of retailers and other smaller market entities.

Imp

Pricing objectives are based on the overall objectives of the firms, the market segments being served, competition, market conditions, and many other variables. The basic overall objective is to establish mutually satisfying exchange relationships with selected target markets.

Pricing objectives should be influenced by other marketing decisions regarding product design, packaging, branding, channel selection, and promotion. All of these marketing decisions are interrelated and should be approached from a systems perspective that takes into account not only the needs of the seller, but also those of the channel of distributors and consumers as well (see the insert "Pricing in the Channel").

Price Discounts
Producers must consider pricing strategies that will be effective throughout the channel of distribution, including the retail price. *Trade discounts* (functional discounts) are given various middlemen for performing specific marketing functions. For example, a manufacturer selling both through wholesalers and directly to retailers would have two different pricing strategies; the wholesaler would receive a bigger discount. It should be noted that such discounts must not be discriminatory, or else the producer would be subject to legal challenge.

Cash discounts are often given middlemen for paying their bills promptly. The terms might be 2/10, net 30, which means that a 2 percent discount is given if payment is made within 10 days, but the full amount is due in 30 days.

Promotional discounts are often given to middlemen in recognition of their efforts to help promote the product. Again, such discounts must not

[6] Robert F. Lanzellotti, "Pricing Objectives in Large Companies," *American Economic Review*, December 1955, pp. 921–940.

Pricing in the Channel

The final price of an article is not a simple thing arrived at as a result merely of the interaction of the forces in play at the point of sale and purchase. It is compounded of a whole system of interlocking price relationships reaching back through the retailer, the wholesaler, the manufacturer, and all the other marketing agents who may have had a hand in the movement of the product to the point of ultimate sale. It is the final fruit of an elaborate price structure complicated by such conditioning and obscuring factors as quantity allowances, credit terms, delivery arrangements, and services rendered at each of the several stages through which the product passes in its often devious and tortuous way to the point of final sale.

From Ralph S. Alexander, "Marketing's Contribution to Economics," in *Economics and the Public Interest*, ed. Robert A. Solo (New Brunswick, N.J.: Rutgers University Press, 1955), pp. 71–72.

be given in a discriminatory manner, or else there could be legal problems.

Quantity discounts are often given distributors or dealers that buy in volume. The idea is to recognize the savings involved in one large transaction versus several small ones. Such discounts are subject to legal action if they are not justifiable.

The whole idea of discounts and various pricing strategies throughout the channel is to generate a smooth flow of the product to consumers. Producers do not usually have a single pricing policy; they have pricing *policies* that apply to various circumstances.

Break-even Analysis   One strategic decision marketing managers must make is whether or not to produce a product at all. **Break-even analysis** is one tool that helps in such decisions. It is used in both product and price decisions. Managers usually know the approximate cost of producing a product. They are more concerned with what price to charge. Break-even analysis tells them whether the firm would be able to make money (or break-even) at a particular price, given a certain sales volume.

Break-even analysis usually involves break-even charts that show total costs and total revenues. The total revenue curve shows the revenue expected *at a given price*. A different chart is constructed for each price and a break-even point (BEP) is determined. At the break-even point, total cost equals total revenue. Beyond that point the firm will make money on each unit; below that point, the firm will lose money on each unit sold (see Figure 10.4).

Figure 10.4 shows that sales above 60 units would result in a profit given a particular price. Sales below 60 units would result in a loss. Marketers can develop a series of break-even charts to eliminate obviously unrealistic prices. But break-even analysis assumes a straight-line total revenue curve and a straight-line total cost curve, and that is not

Figure 10.4 BREAK-EVEN ANALYSIS FOR A PARTICULAR PRICE

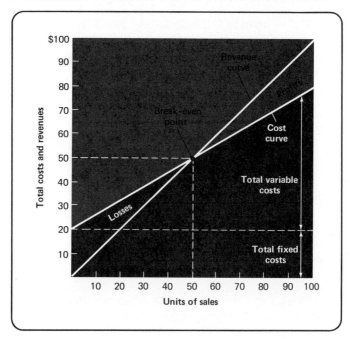

realistic. Therefore, break-even analysis should be used only to give some general feel for an appropriate price. A more realistic price can be determined using marginal analysis.

Marginal **Marginal analysis** is used for determining the price that will maximize
Analysis profits. It is more realistic than break-even analysis in that variable costs are assumed to fall as more units are produced and then rise again at some point. We have already discussed supply and demand curves, and so you have some feel for how prices are determined by demand factors. Marginal analysis is similar, but it looks at *marginal* cost and *marginal* revenue. **Marginal cost** is the change in total cost that results when one more unit is produced. **Marginal revenue** is the change in total revenue that results from the sale of one additional unit.

To maximize profits, a firm should produce and sell additional units until marginal cost is equal to marginal revenue. Any unit that adds more to revenue (marginal revenue) than it adds to cost (marginal cost) is a profitable unit to sell, no matter how small the increase may be.

A very basic marginal analysis chart is presented in Figure 10.5.

Actually, marginal analysis is much more complex than this and involves average costs and marginal profits. The basic concept, however, is:

> **To maximize profit for an organization, set the price where marginal cost is slightly less than, or equals, marginal revenue.**

261

If you want to learn about the details of marginal analysis, you should consult any modern text in micro-economics or on pricing.[7] The point to be made here is that marketers have many tools available to help in making pricing decisions and to formulate pricing strategies.

Making the Price Look Lower Many people are eager to buy various items at the store but hesitate to spend the money. Often they can be persuaded by slight changes in price. For example, marketers have long practiced the policy of *odd pricing*. This means they will price an item at 99¢ rather than $1 because psychologically 99¢ seems like much less. A person might be able to justify spending "less than a dollar" for something that they would like to have. Notice for example how much junk people will buy at an 88¢ sale.

Another way marketers make the price seem "better" is through *markdowns*. Few people can resist the appeal of a "½ off" sale. An item that is marked "was $40.00, now $19.99" uses both strategies. Notice how the higher price is $40.00, not $39.99 and the lower price is $19.99, not $20.00. Often such strategies will capture many people who would not normally pay $20.00 for the item in the first place.

Obviously, there is much room for deception in price markdowns. There is very little attempt to police such actions in retail stores, and so many people are being tricked into believing prices were dropped when they were not. But, strange as it may seem, many people would hesitate to buy without such manipulations. They want something, but they want a "bargain" even more. This does not excuse such practices; it just explains why so few people complain about them.

[7] For more detailed treatment of marginal analysis and other pricing strategies, see Kristian Palda, *Pricing Decisions and Marketing Policy* (Englewood Cliffs, N.J.: Prentice-Hall, Inc.. 1971), Donald Harper, *Price Policy and Procedure* (New York: Harcourt, Brace & World, Inc., 1966), and other texts devoted exclusively to pricing.

Figure 10.5 MARGINAL-ANALYSIS CHART

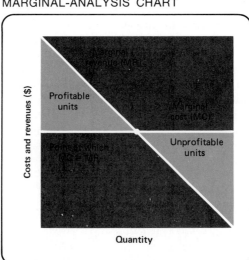

Some Pricing Terms

In a book of this type it is impossible to cover all pricing concepts in detail. However, you should at least be familiar with the following terms:

1. *Adaptive pricing* allows an organization to vary its prices based on factors such as competition, market conditions, and resource costs. Rather than rely on one set price, the firm adjusts the price to fit different situations.

2. *Competition-oriented pricing* is a strategy based on what competitors are doing. It may be the opposite of pricing leadership.

3. *Cost-oriented pricing* is the strategy of setting prices primarily on the basis of cost. For example, retailers often use cost plus a certain markup, and producers use a system of cost-plus pricing.

4. *Customary pricing* means that most sellers will adapt the product to some established, universally accepted price such as the price for gum or candy bars. Notice that when the customary price goes up, almost all producers adjust their prices upward.

5. *Demand-oriented pricing* is the strategy of setting prices on the basis of consumer demand rather than cost. Sometimes different prices are charged different consumers (discriminatory pricing), as is the case with movie theaters (less for children), drug stores (senior citizens get a discount), and airlines (first class costs more).

6. *Market price* is that price that is determined by supply and demand and is not controllable by the seller. For example, farmers have little control over the price they receive for grain or cattle. Market prices exist for many goods and services besides farm products.

7. *Pricing leadership* is the procedure by which all the competitors in an industry follow the pricing practices of one or more dominant firms. When one firm lowers or raises its prices, the others follow almost immediately. You may have noticed this tendency among oil companies and cigarette companies.

8. *Product-line pricing* is the procedure used to set prices for a group of products that are similar but are aimed at different market segments. For example, a beer producer might have a "low-priced" beer, a "popular-priced" beer, and a "premium-priced" beer.

9. *Target pricing* means that an organization will set some goal such as a certain share of the market or a certain return on investment as a basis for setting a price. Usually market conditions prevent a firm from establishing prices this way, but such goals do give some direction to pricing policies.

10. *Uniform pricing,* also known as a "single-price policy," means that all customers buying the product (given similar circumstances) will pay the same price. Although the most common policy in the United States, uniform pricing is unusual in many foreign markets, especially among private sellers.

Nonprice Competition In spite of the emphasis placed on price in micro-economic theory, marketers often compete on product attributes other than price. You may have noted that price differences between products such as gasoline, cigarettes, candy bars, and even major products such as compact cars are often small, if there is any price difference at all. Very rarely will you see price as a major promotional appeal on television. Instead marketers tend to stress product images and consumer benefits such as comfort, style, convenience, and durability.

Many organizations promote services that accompany basic products rather than price. The idea is to make a relatively homogeneous product "better." For example airlines stress friendliness, promptness, more flights, better meals, and other such services. Motels stress "no surprises," or cable TV, swimming pools, and other extras.

Quite often the reason marketers emphasize nonprice differences is because prices are so easy to match. Few competitors can match the image of a friendly, responsive, consumer-oriented company.

PRICE AND SOCIAL WELFARE All of the things we want as members of society (for example, clean air and water, freedom, opportunity, and so forth) are products—products that have costs. Many of the products have been sacrificed to get other, more attractive products. For example, people in most societies want basic food, clothing, and shelter first of all. To get those goods, they are willing to sacrifice the benefits of clean air and water. When they have the basic goods (the present situation in most of the United States), people put more emphasis on products such as the environment. Although the *price* of clean air and water was once considered too high (during the development stage), now the *price* we pay for dirty air and water (illness, discomfort) is considered too high. The concept is:

› **Social products such as clean air and water will be provided when the benefits of having them exceed the costs.**

One problem with this concept today is that those who benefit from dirtying the air and water (auto drivers, cities, farmers, and manufacturers, to name a few) do not have to pay the price. That is, they are not immediately affected if the people around them are made uncomfortable or ill by their efforts. The way to prevent such problems is to bring *social costs* more in line with *social benefits*. For example, taxes could be placed on activities whose social costs exceed private costs. Some cities charge very high sewage rates (prices) for those firms that refuse to clean up their water discharge. Eventually it becomes cheaper to clean up the water than to pay the taxes.

Another way to balance social costs with benefits is to pass laws prohibiting certain practices. For example, a utility may not be permitted to burn coal unless it puts pollution-control devices in its smokestacks. The concept is:

› **To get people to recognize the social cost of their actions, those costs may have to be charged to the initiator in the form of taxes, regulations, or similar procedures.**

Note what happens when no cost is associated with what people do. People who smoke often think nothing of throwing their cigarettes on the floor of public buildings when they would never do such a thing at home. Why? Because the cost of cleaning up is borne by someone else away from home. Some students carve up the desks at school for the same reason, and some campers leave bottles, cans, and other debris all over the place. We therefore need more often to apply this marketing concept:

➤ **Unless individuals and organizations are made responsible for their actions (assume the costs), they may not act in a socially beneficial way.**

In our zeal to obtain the social benefits of a clean environment, freedom, and opportunity, we should be careful to balance these desires with other social goals such as economic growth and survival. The goal should *not* be to get rid of *all* pollution, but to reach an acceptable balance between *some* pollution and *some* economic stability. The costs of no pollution would be too high. Similarly, in our quest for freedom, we must recognize limitations on that freedom. For example, almost everyone realizes the benefits of not being free to speed, to murder, or to steal. The concept is:

➤ **Socially desirable products such as a clean environment and freedom can be balanced with other socially desirable products such as economic survival and growth.**

As we discussed in Chapter 3, marketing is a process that enables members of society to work out mutually satisfying agreements relative to economic factors and social factors. It is the basis for a societal orientation in marketing. One of the tools we have to establish such relationships is price.

In any discussion of price and social welfare, at least brief mention must be made of the pricing strategies of the government. Of all organizations—both public and private and profit and nonprofit—federal, state, and local governments are most heavily involved in providing services designed to ensure social welfare. Obviously, a price must be put on these social services, just as one must be put on any other good or service.

Pricing of Government Services Pricing of government services is one of the more difficult marketing problems. The problems arise partially because governments try to accomplish several different objectives with price. For example, certain health services are provided free or at very low cost. The objective is to encourage use by low-income people and improve community health. On the other hand, the fee charged for illegal parking is set rather high. The objective is to discourage people from driving or parking in certain areas and to encourage the use of mass transit. Sometimes governments use pricing as a means of redistributing income. Thus, the rate of income tax charged wealthy people is greater than that charged poor people.

The government is also faced with the problem of deciding who should pay for certain services. For example, should a new waste-treatment plant be paid for by homeowners or should there be some fee based on usage rates?

The cost of government has been rising at an alarming rate. Paying for government services has become a major political and economic issue. There is no doubt that pricing is one of the critical marketing decisions in government. But it is equally important in business and other organizations. You will learn more about pricing strategies in various organizations if you take courses in marketing management and other advanced marketing courses.

FOR REVIEW

Key Terms

Among the more important terms and expressions discussed in this chapter are the following:

Break-even analysis is a marketing tool that is used to determine the price for a product at which the total cost of producing the product equals the total sales revenue.

Cost-oriented pricing is the strategy of setting prices on the basis of cost.

Demand-oriented pricing is the strategy of setting prices on the basis of consumer demand.

Elasticity is a term used by economists to describe the responsiveness of a market to a change in price.

Marginal analysis is a marketing tool that relates marginal costs and marginal revenues in order to determine a price and volume of sales that will maximize profits.

Marginal cost is the change in total cost that results when one more unit is produced.

Marginal revenue is the change in total revenue that results from the sale of one additional unit.

Market price is the price that is determined by supply and demand and is not controllable by the seller.

A **penetration pricing strategy** refers to the selling of a product at a low cost to capture the largest possible market share.

Price lining is the practice of maintaining a relatively stable price for a given product over time.

A **skimming pricing strategy** refers to the selling of a product at a high enough price to cover all costs and ensure profit, despite the fact that the product will thereby capture only a very small market share.

Target pricing means that an organization will set some goal such as a certain share of the market or a certain return on investment as a basis for setting a price.

Key Concepts

Among the more important marketing concepts introduced in this chapter are the following:

> **Price varies in importance among different products and consumers.**

> **A person will enter exchange relationships when the perceived benefits of the exchange are greater than the perceived costs involved and/or are greater than the perceived benefits of alternative exchanges.**

> **To determine the real value of an exchange, one must measure the costs against the benefits.**

> **Time spent in making or obtaining products is part of the cost, but the value of that time varies among individuals.**

> **When the demand for a product is high, the price will tend also to be high.**

> **The price of a product in the long run is determined by supply and demand; the equilibrium price (long-term exchange price) is where supply equals demand.**

> **In the long run, the demand for most products is partially elastic; that is, people will buy less if the price is increased and more if it is decreased.**

> **Consumers have the final say as to what price is acceptable, and so manufacturers often have to work backward from consumer prices to determine available production funds.**

> **To maximize profit for an organization, set the price where marginal cost is slightly less than, or equals, marginal revenue.**

Discussion Questions

1. If a firm's major goal is to maximize profits, why not set the product's price to achieve the desired profit?

2. "You paid $80 for that chair? Why I got the same chair for only $55 at the discount store." Who got the better deal? What criteria did you use?

3. Cost-plus pricing is still a very popular pricing procedure. Why? What are its limitations?

4. "Barbara Walters is paid $1 million per year. That is way too much." Discuss. By what criteria can one evaluate such a statement?

5. "A college education is well worth the price." Do you agree? What does "worth" mean?

6. Name several products whose price is usually considered to be an indication of quality. Is price an accurate indicator of quality? What is "quality"?

7. "I made this dress for only $10 and it costs $30 in the store. It only took one weekend to make it. Making your own clothes sure is a good deal." Do you agree? Why or why not?

8. How can manufacturers and consumers be made more responsible for the social costs of their exchanges; for example, the cost of pollution?

9. When would a product best be introduced using a skimming strategy? A penetration strategy?

10. Do nonprofit organizations have pricing decisions to make? Explain.

CASES

Gary's 10-Speed Bike
Determining Market Price

Gary Baird bought a 10-speed racing bike for $140. Gary rode the bike a lot the first month he had it, but he rides it very rarely now. Gary needed some money for a vacation to Florida and decided to sell his bike. The bike is now 2 years old but is in "nearly new" condition. Gary put an ad in the paper offering the bike for $110. The highest offer he has received for the bike is $90.

1. How important should his cost be to Gary when establishing a price for the bike?

2. What price do you suppose Gary will finally ask for the bike? Why? How much do you think he will get? Why?

3. What could Gary do to get a better price for his bike? That is, how could he increase the perceived value?

4. Why are people not willing to pay more than $90 for the bike? That is, what affects their perception of the bike's value?

Pollution in Surrey County
Price and Social Welfare

The citizens of Surrey County are very concerned about pollution in the Tukahawnee River, their main source of recreation and drinking water. Volunteers from the Surrey County Pollution Research Group have discovered that most of the pollution comes from three sources: (1) overflow from the city's sewage plant; (2) discharge from several nearby factories; and (3) runoff from farmland and one mine that is no longer in operation.

1. How can the Surrey County government use pricing concepts to have the major polluters pay for their share of cleanup costs?

2. Surrey County needs a larger sewage plant. What kind of tax schedule would be most equitable in paying for the plant?

3. Explain how the municipal waterworks could use the concepts of supply and demand to set a pricing schedule for different customers.

4. Is the demand for water elastic or inelastic? Explain.

Distribution Systems and Channel Concepts

getting products to the people

11

LEARNING GOALS After you have read and studied this chapter, you should be able to:

1. Explain how middlemen add value to product offers.
2. Describe different middleman organizations and their functions.
3. Define the following terms: channel of distribution; channel captain; retailer; wholesaler; administered channel systems; distribution cost accounting.
4. Give examples of how middlemen add time, place, form, possession, and information utility.
5. Describe, and give examples of, corporate, contractual, and administered systems.
6. Explain the role of a channel captain.
7. Compare physical distribution management as an integrated managerial function to distribution management as performed in most of today's organizations.
8. Show how distribution cost accounting can benefit a marketing organization.
9. Apply channel concepts to the marketing of services.
10. Justify to your friends the fact that half of what they pay for products (on the average) is marketing costs.

> *To the extent that any middleman can do so, he should think of himself primarily as a purchasing agent for his customers, and only secondarily as a selling agent for his suppliers.*
>
> Philip McVey*

INTRODUCTION Next time you go to the supermarket to buy the week's groceries, stop for a minute and look at the tremendous variety of products in the store. Think of how many marketing exchanges were involved to bring you the 8,000 or so items that you see. Some products (spices, for example) may have been imported from halfway around the world. Other products have been processed and frozen so that you could eat them out of season (for example, strawberries).

Supermarkets are an example of **retailers.** Retailers are marketing middlemen who sell to you, the ultimate consumer. There are approximately 2.3 million retail stores in the United States, selling everything from haircuts to automobiles. This does not include the thousands of consumer-serving outlets of nonprofit organizations. Does your state university have various branches to make attendance more convenient for students in various parts of the state? Do you have a post office nearby to service your community? Is there a fire station within a few minute's drive? Are there churches, schools, gas stations, supermarkets, drive-in restaurants, dry cleaners, beauty parlors, and thousands of other consumer-serving outlets relatively close to where you live? The answer is likely to be "yes" because middlemen exist to make your marketing exchanges more convenient. The concepts are:

> ➤ Consumers are often far away from those organizations that provide for their wants and needs; marketing middlemen act as representatives of the buyer and the seller to close the gaps between them.

> ➤ Retailers deal directly with the consumer and tend to be located within a relatively short distance of the people they serve.

> ➤ All organizations (including the government, nonprofit organizations, and businesses) may need marketing middlemen to make their exchange relationships more effective and more efficient.

MIDDLEMEN AND THE CHANNEL OF DISTRIBUTION This chapter is about marketing middlemen and the functions they perform. It contains the words "distribution systems" in the title because it is best to think of all marketing organizations as part of a larger system. For example, the supermarket where you shop buys its products from a variety of **wholesalers.** Wholesalers are marketing middlemen who buy products from various producers to sell to retailers, to other wholesalers, to institutions such as schools, churches, and hotels, and to any organization other than the ultimate consumer. Wholesalers are thus part of a distribution system that brings food to retailers. Manufacturers are also part of the system and so are all the raw materials suppliers that sell to manufacturers.

*"Are Channels of Distribution What the Textbooks Say?," *Journal of Marketing,* January 1960, pp. 61–65.

Figure 11.1 DISTRIBUTION SYSTEM FOR AIR-CONDITIONING EQUIPMENT

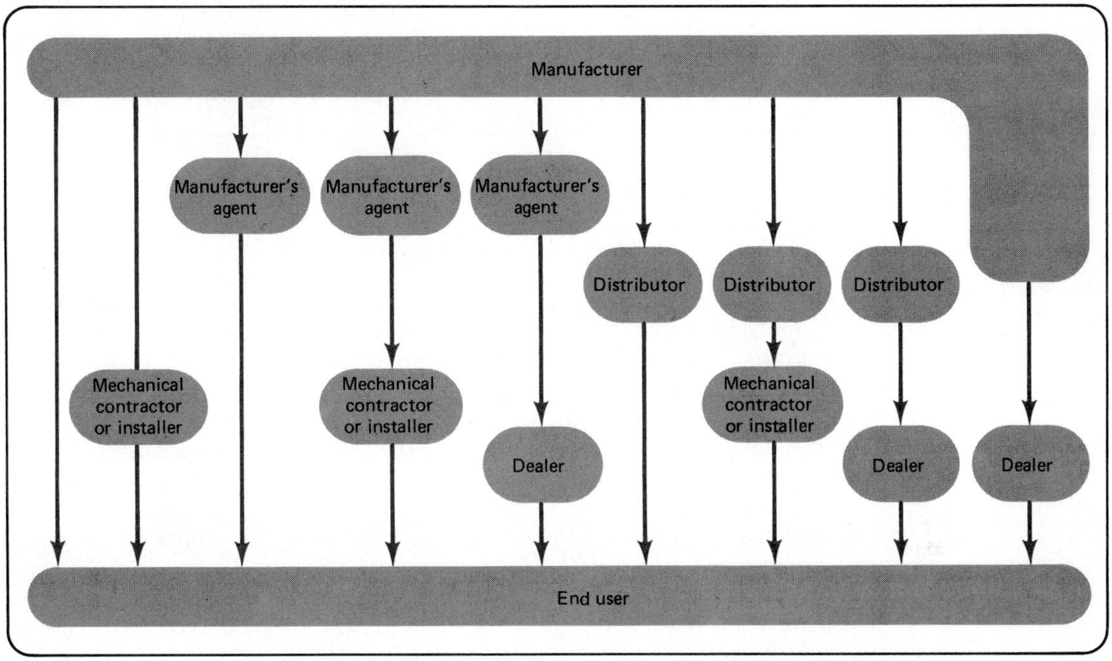

Redrawn from Louis W. Stern and Adel I. El-Ansary, *Marketing Channels* (Englewood Cliffs, N.J.: Prentice-Hall, 1977), p. 5.

A **distribution system** is, therefore, an organized network of people and organizations that performs all the marketing functions and activities required to provide consumers with whatever they want and to satisfy the needs of all the participants as well; it is sometimes called a channel of distribution. Two important concepts are:

›   **Raw materials suppliers, manufacturers, wholesalers, and retailers are all part of the distribution system for economic goods and services.**

›   **Free health clinics, libraries, schools, churches, and similar organizations are part of the distribution system for noneconomic or government services.**

In the following sections, we shall discuss the role of marketing middlemen in order to give you some feel for the importance and significance of these organizations in a society. Figure 11.1 will give you some idea of the complexity of distribution systems. Note that nine different channels may be used to distribute the product of this air-conditioner manufacturer.

Why We Need Middlemen Marketing middlemen have always been viewed with some suspicion by the public. Surveys have shown that more than half the cost of the things we buy are marketing costs that are largely due to middlemen. People reason that if we could only get rid of middlemen, we could greatly reduce the cost of everything we buy. Sounds good, but is the solution really that simple?

271

Let's take as an example a can of tomato soup. How could we, as consumers, get it for less? Well, we could all drive to Ohio where some of the soup is produced and save some shipping costs. But would that be practical? Could you imagine millions of people getting in their cars and driving to Ohio just to get some soup? No, it doesn't make sense. It is much cheaper to have some middlemen bring the soup to the major cities. That might involve a *trucking firm* and a *warehouse operator*—two middleman organizations. But they add cost, don't they? Yes, but they add value as well, the value of not having to drive to Ohio.

Well, the soup is now somewhere on the outskirts of the city. We could all drive down to the warehouse and pick up the soup. In fact, some people do just that. But is that the most economical way to buy soup? Not really. If we figure in the cost of gas and time, the soup would be pretty expensive. Instead, we prefer to have someone move the soup from the warehouse to another truck, drive it to the corner supermarket, unload it, unpack it, stamp it with a price, put it on the shelf, and wait for us to come in to buy it. To make it even more convenient, the supermarket may stay open 24 hours a day, 7 days a week—think of the *costs*. Think also of the *value*. For less than a quarter we can get tomato soup *when* we want, *where* we want, and with little effort on our part.

If we were to get rid of the retailer, we could buy a can of tomato soup for a little less, but we would have to drive miles more and spend time in some warehouse looking for the soup. If we got rid of the wholesaler, we could save a little more, but then we would have to drive to Ohio. But a few cents here and a few cents there add up—to the point where marketing may add up to 50¢ for every 50¢ in manufacturing costs. Table 11.1 shows how middlemen share your food dollar in the case of a few items (U.S. Department of Agriculture figures). Note that the retail margin varies widely. Also note that the total marketing cost ranges from 30 to 50 percent. We do not like to pay such high costs for marketing, but there is no other way to get what we want, when we want it, and at a reasonable cost.

It should be made clear that businesses are not the only organizations in which a high proportion of costs are due to marketing middlemen. It also costs a lot to have several churches in one city when people "need"

The Same Refrain 40 Years Ago

What seem to be evidences of waste abound in every direction. In the judgment of many critics, there are "too many" retail stores; "too much" advertising and high-pressure merchandising; "too many" similar products among which the consumer must make his choice; "too much" duplication of facilities and services. The markup or price spread between what the farmer or producer receives for his goods and what the consumer has to pay appears to be "too high" and to reflect unnecessary waste or excessive distribution profit, or both.

From Paul W. Stewart and J. Frederic Dewhurst, *Does Distribution Cost Too Much?* (New York: The Twentieth Century Fund, 1939), p. 333.

Table 11.1 HOW MIDDLEMEN SHARE YOUR FOOD DOLLAR

Item	Farmer	Processor	Wholesaler	Retailer
1 pound choice beef	66.3%	5.4%	7.4%	20.9%
1 dozen grade A large eggs	69.7	11.5	5.1	13.7
1 half-gallon milk	50.8	21.6	19.8	7.8

only one. It also is expensive to have post offices, libraries, health clinics, and other such nonbusiness middleman organizations. But, again, the convenience and efficiency of having such facilities usually far outweigh the cost. Some key concepts are:

> Marketing middlemen can be eliminated, but their functions cannot be eliminated; that is, you can get rid of retailers, but then consumers or someone else would have to perform the retailer's functions, including transportation, storage, finding suppliers, and establishing communication with suppliers.

> Middleman organizations survive because they perform marketing functions more effectively and efficiently than they could be performed by others.

> Middlemen add costs to products, but these costs are usually more than offset by the values they create.

How Middlemen Add Value Of the five utilities mentioned in the literature of economics—form, time, place, possession, and information—four are created by marketing middlemen. The fifth, form utility, is often performed as well. For example, supermarkets add form utility to meats by cutting, wrapping, pricing, and displaying them. Of course restaurants and other retailers also create form utility. But marketing middlemen are noted most for the creation of time, place, possession, and information utility. Below are some examples.

Time Utility Rudy Lynch was watching TV with his brother when he suddenly got the urge to have a hot dog and a Coke. The problem was that there were no hot dogs or Cokes in the house. Rudy ran down to the corner delicatessen and bought some hot dogs, buns, Cokes, and potato chips. Rudy was able to get these groceries at 10 o'clock at night because the store was open from 8 A.M. to 11 P.M. The concept is:

> Middlemen, such as retailers, add *time utility* to products by making them available *when* they are needed.

Place Utility Mary Margaret Melchak was traveling through the badlands of South Dakota and was getting hungry and thirsty. She saw a sign saying that a drugstore with fountain service was up ahead. She stopped at the store for some refreshments. She also bought sunglasses and other drug items while she was there. The concept is:

> Middlemen add *place utility* to products by having them *where* people want them.

Possession Utility William Nathan wanted to buy a nice home in the suburbs. He found just what he wanted, but he did not have near the amount of money that he needed (over $50,000). So Bill went with the real estate man to a local savings and loan and borrowed the money to buy the home. Both the real estate broker and the savings and loan were marketing middlemen. The concept is:

> Middlemen add *possession utility* by doing whatever is necessary to transfer ownership from one party to another.

Information Utility Fernando Gomez could not decide what kind of TV set to buy. He looked at various ads in the newspaper, talked to the salespersons at several stores, and read material at the library. He also got some material from the government about radiation hazards and consumer buying tips. The newspaper, salesperson, library, and government publication were all information sources made available by marketing middlemen. The concept is:

> Middlemen add *information utility* by opening two-way flows of information between marketing participants.

If you think of how convenient it is to buy gas, food, clothing, housing, and almost anything else you want or need, you will realize the value of having marketing middlemen. Think of the bother it could be to try to

---

What Organizations Are Included in a Total Channel System for Goods?

A marketing channel should include *all* firms and individuals that perform one or more of the functions required to market the goods in question. Buying and selling are only two of the activities needed to move goods from point of production to points of use; merchandise must also be transported, stored, packaged, and financed. In addition, prospective buyers must be notified that the merchandise is available and their desire to purchase it must be stimulated. Firms undertaking these "facilitating" functions are as necessary as buyers and sellers. Consequently, facilitating agencies (financial institutions, common carriers, public warehouses, advertising agencies, factors, advertising media and other providers of business services) should be included when describing the marketing channel for a specific product. . . .

. . . The channel should be defined to include influentials as well as original sellers, facilitating agencies, middlemen, and ultimate buyers.

An operational definition of a marketing channel should also provide a basis for identifying functional relationships between firms.

From Bert C. McCammon, Jr., and Robert W. Little, "Marketing Channels: Analytical Systems and Approaches," in *Science in Marketing*, ed. George Schwartz (New York: John Wiley & Sons, Inc., 1965), p. 326. Copyright 1965 by John Wiley & Sons, Inc. Reprinted with permission.

buy stocks and bonds if there were no stockbrokers. Or how hard it would be to buy or sell a home without a real estate broker. Note that these middlemen serve both the buyer *and* the seller.

Marketing middlemen are not pawns of large manufacturers whose sole purpose is to gouge money from the public. They are the creation of an advanced society that, because of a division of labor, *needs* people and organizations to bring together people with wants and needs and people who can satisfy wants and needs. Thus, social workers may be viewed as middlemen for poor people, unwanted children, and the elderly. Middlemen try to find solutions to the needs of others by acting as representatives of government organizations and private groups. Who are the middlemen that satisfy the public's desire for entertainment? Radio and TV stations are examples. Who are the middlemen that satisfy our needs for culture, art, music, and dance? Examples include the local museum, universities, symphonies, and ballet groups. These are all marketing middlemen who bring you, the public, into contact with artists, dancers, professors, musicians, and other "producers."

Facilitating Functions of Middlemen Some marketing organizations are formed to perform one or more facilitating functions to assist the traditional distribution systems. For example, a middleman often is needed to provide financial aid to the buyer. For example, when you buy a home, you might borrow the money from a savings and loan (a middleman) and get FHA (Federal Housing Administration) financing (the government as middleman). Other middlemen assist in the communication function (advertising agencies and public relations specialists); transportation activities (trucking firms, warehouse operators); service problems (independent servicemen); and in all other aspects of the marketing exchange including marketing research and buying. (See the insert "What Organizations Are Included in a Total Channel System for Goods?") The concepts are:

> Marketing middlemen may perform a variety of functions or specialize in one or two areas.

> The total marketing system is larger than the *distribution* system because it includes organizations not involved with distribution including financial institutions, marketing research firms, and advertising agencies.

The Role of Influentials in the Channel of Distribution One might get the impression that the marketing distribution system is merely a series of organizations that handle the flow of goods from producers to consumers. But such a concept of a channel is too narrow for this discussion. (See the insert "Size of the Total Marketing System.") A channel system involves many "flows" besides the flow of goods. For example, the two-way flow of information was discussed in Chapter 6. Other flows may include negotiation, payment, promotion, risk, and finance. Let's look at a channel from your perspective and see if we can discover some personal influences that add a more personal flavor to channel concepts.

Who do you turn to for information about goods, services, vacation spots, and other products? Of course, you may ask your friends and

Size of the Total Marketing System

The marketing system may be said to consist of all those entities brought together by the process of exchanging goods and/or services. The entities include all manner of business firms, political institutions, and households. Because these units may participate in the exchange process either directly through buying and selling, or indirectly, by facilitating trade through the provision of services such as transportation, warehousing, credit, or advertising, the total number of elements is extremely large. Aside from households, and political bodies, the number of procedures, service organizations, and middlemen of all types and descriptions totals more than three million for the United States alone.

From Louis P. Bucklin, "The Marketing System and Channel Management," in Frederick D. Sturdivant et al., *Managerial Analysis in Marketing* (Glenview, Ill.: Scott, Foresman and Company, 1970), pp. 551–553.

acquaintances. They are *purchasing influentials* and are part of the information flow in the channel system. So are the other sources of information you use such as *Consumer Reports,* newspapers, magazines, government reports, books, and consumerist organizations.

Organizations that might be influentials in a distribution channel include government agencies at all levels (they establish rules and regulations of trade, for example, and publish much consumer and market information); environmentalists (they might push for recycling of bottles, for example, and affect distribution back through the channel); consumerists (they publish information and demand certain things from retailers and other marketers such as unit pricing); and foreign competitors (they might force a channel to be more efficient so that it can compete more successfully). In summary, we may define a channel of distribution as a complex system of physical flows and information flows that is subject to many outside influentials; those influentials should be viewed as part of the total marketing system.

The Consumer's Impact on the Channel of Distribution

Ultimately the people who decide what channels of distribution will be most effective for what products are the buying public. If we decide to buy our TV sets at discount stores, TV manufacturers had better distribute their sets through the discount-store channel or risk losing our business. If we decide to buy our toothpaste at the supermarket, toothpaste manufacturers should sell through supermarkets or risk losing our business. We as consumers not only dictate the distribution structure but are active participants as well.

As consumers, we perform many marketing functions: We promote products we like and talk down products we do not like; we transport goods from the store to our homes; we store goods in the pantry and the basement; we do market research; we buy; we resell; we do research; and generally we are active participants in the marketing process. Marketing functions can be shifted to the consumer if that would make marketing more efficient. We could, for example, assume more of the transportation function and thus eliminate many of the marginal gas stations, grocery stores, and smaller retail stores. But we would all lose something in the way of convenience. The concepts are:

› **Consumers ultimately decide what channel systems will succeed or fail based on their purchasing decisions.**

› **Consumers are part of the channel system because they perform many marketing functions and because middleman functions can be shifted to the consumer.**

Middlemen Who Serve the Buyer Wholesalers and retailers are the functional middlemen for manufacturers, but what kind of middlemen serve buyers? There are a number of specialists who have established institutions to serve buyers. An example is the resident buying office. These offices serve department stores, apparel stores, and other stores selling general merchandise. They act as central market representatives for retail stores, so that the retailer does not have to make as many trips to central markets like New York. By representing several retailers, these buying offices can provide marketing intelligence and buying services at a reasonable price. When company buyers do come to the market, the office buyers assist them in their search.

Other kinds of buyer services are available for businesses. For example, several independent organizations known as *purchasing agents* or purchasing companies provide a buying and market-intelligence service for wholesalers of consumer goods and for industrial distributors:[1] "Typical is an organization in the wholesale hardware and mill supply trade which serves many wholesalers by locating sources of new, superior, imported, or scarce merchandise and by securing attractive price quotations for them."[2]

These kinds of services for buyers are also performed by people called *brokers*. In the consumer area, you are probably most familiar with stockbrokers and real estate brokers who provide similar services for those searching for stocks and homes. The concept is:

› **Buyers often have middlemen that represent them in various markets and provide buying services plus marketing intelligence (information); these middlemen make the buying function more effective and more efficient.**

Suppose you wanted to sell some stock that you own. You could put an ad in the paper or try to sell it to your friends, but such a strategy could be quite costly and ineffective. On the other hand, you could contact a stockbroker. He could give you an immediate "quote," or a price offer for your stock. A stockbroker is a middleman between the buyers and

---

[1] For a more detailed analysis of middlemen representing buyers and sellers, see Theodore N. Beckman, William R. Davidson, and W. Wayne Talarzyk, *Marketing*, 9th ed. (New York: The Ronald Press Company, 1973).

[2] Ibid., p. 422.

sellers of stock. He provides his service to either buyers or sellers. Think of how *efficient* they make the exchange of stocks and bonds compared with what the market would be like without them.

A real estate broker does for the buyers and sellers of homes what a stockbroker does for buyers and sellers of stocks and bonds. He or she acts as an intermediary seeking to establish a mutually satisfactory exchange. A realtor makes the housing market more *efficient*. The concepts are:

› **Middlemen perform marketing services for both buyers and sellers and greatly reduce the costs of market analysis, communication, and the other marketing functions.**

› **Stockbrokers and real estate brokers are just two examples of middlemen who serve both buyers and sellers; there are many kinds of brokers and other wholesale middlemen in industries such as food, clothing, and industrial items.**

Middlemen in Service Industries Because there is no tangible product to sell in most service organizations, the channels of distribution tend to be short. That is, producers come into direct contact with users. This is true for beauty salons, plumbers, doctors, lawyers, consultants, and other services. But some

Figure 11.2 MARKETING CHANNELS AND TOOLS FOR A DEFENSIVE DRIVING COURSE

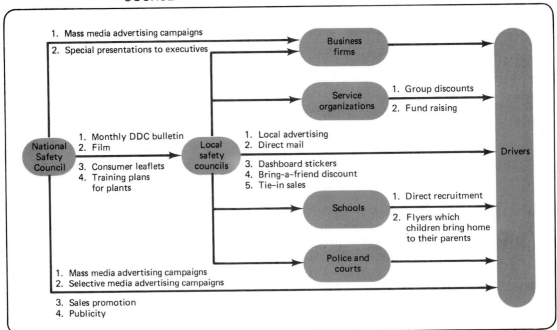

Redrawn from Philip Kotler, *Marketing for Nonprofit Organizations* (Englewood Cliffs, N.J.: Prentice-Hall, 1975), p. 299.

services have found it more efficient and effective to use middlemen to assist in the marketing function. For example, Figure 11.2 shows the channels and marketing tools used by the National Safety Council to promote defensive driving.

Airlines, bus companies, hotels, and other members of the travel industry often use travel agents as middlemen. They use tickets as a symbol of the product and exchange tickets for money. Financial institutions such as banks and savings and loan associations use retailers as middlemen. The retailer arranges credit for buyers (a loan) and uses a credit card as a symbol of the product being exchanged.

Most service organizations use advertising agencies and other information-creating middlemen. The same concepts apply in service industries as in manufacturing industries: (1) Middlemen arise in an industry when they can more efficiently or effectively perform particular marketing functions (for example, advertising); and (2) middlemen perform functions other than physical distribution (for example, credit, intelligence gathering, and buying).

Middlemen and Exchange Efficiency
The benefits of marketing middlemen can be illustrated rather easily. Suppose that 1,000 manufacturers of various food products tried to sell directly to 1,000 retailers. The number of exchange relationships that would have to be established is 1,000 times 1,000 or 1 million. Can you imagine negotiating a million exchanges just to service 1,000 stores? But picture what happens when a wholesaler enters the system. The 1,000 manufacturers would contact one wholesaler to establish 1,000 exchange relationships. The wholesaler would have to establish contact with the 1,000 retailers. That would mean another 1,000 exchange relationships. Note that the number of exchanges is reduced from 1 million to only 2,000 by the addition of a wholesaler. This process can be visualized as shown in Figure 11.3, where the number of exchanges is reduced from 25 to 10.

Figure 11.3 shows how middlemen create *exchange efficiency* by lessening the number of contacts needed to establish marketing exchanges. Not only are middlemen an *efficient* way to conduct exchanges, but they are often more *effective* as well. This means that middlemen are often better at performing their functions than a manufacturer or consumer would be.

Middleman Relationships
Marketing middlemen, like all other marketers, attempt to establish mutually satisfying exchange relationships with others. To measure whether this is being accomplished or not, the following steps should be taken:

1. Identification of marketing needs. Each member of the channel, whether manufacturer, distributor, retailer, or consumer, has marketing needs. These may include profit expectations or other more general needs.

2. Satisfaction of marketing needs. It is not enough merely to make the broad assumption that a member of the channel has needs or even to

understand what they are. Marketing programs must be developed that will assist channel members in fulfilling their requirements.

3. Assessment of need satisfaction. Again, it is not enough to recognize needs and attempt to satisfy them through marketing programs. The key is to measure whether the programs indeed did satisfy the needs of the channel member, to learn how the programs can be improved, and to reassess them from time to time.[3]

The entire process of identifying, satisfying, and assessing need satisfaction in the distribution system can be visualized as shown in Figure 11.4.

Although Figure 11.4 leaves out many potential marketing middlemen, you still can get the idea that all members of the marketing system have needs that should be recognized by the other members. No one member of the marketing channel should evaluate his satisfactions without

[3] This section is adapted from material in Reavis Cox, Thomas F. Shutte, and Kendrick S. Few, "Towards the Measurement of Trade Channel Perceptions," in *Combined Proceedings, 1971 Spring and Fall Conferences*, ed. Fred C. Allvine (Chicago: American Marketing Association, 1972).

Figure 11.3 HOW MIDDLEMEN SIMPLIFY EXCHANGES

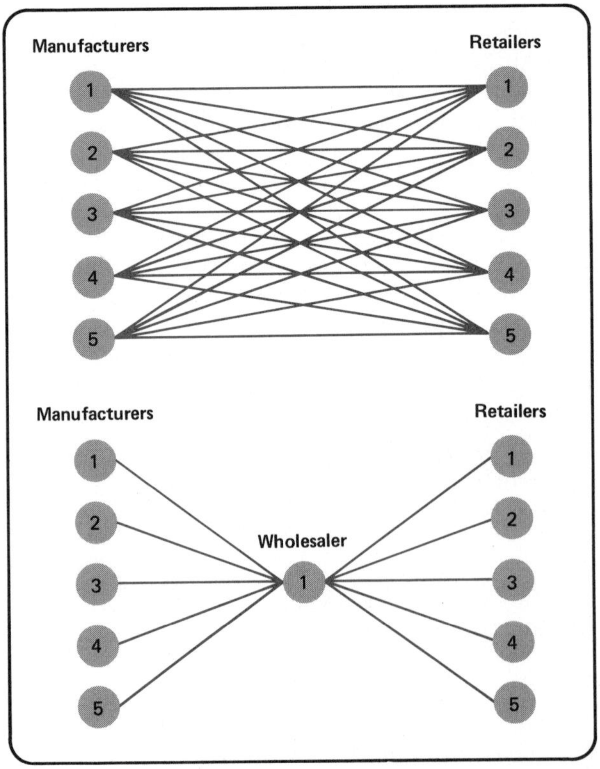

Figure 11.4 MIDDLEMAN RELATIONSHIPS

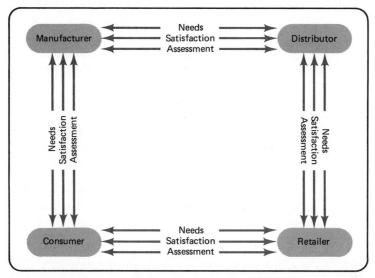

Adapted from Reavis Cox, Thomas F. Shutte, and Kendrick S. Few, "Towards the Measurement of Trade Channel Perception," in *Combined Proceedings, 1971 Spring and Fall Conferences*, ed. Fred C. Allvine (Chicago: American Marketing Association, 1972), p. 192. Reprinted with permission of the American Marketing Association.

considering whether the other members are also satisfied; if there is dissatisfaction anywhere in the system, the entire process may fail. The concepts are:

> Marketing systems consist of many participants, all of whom have needs that must be satisfied.

> Measurement of need satisfaction should not be restricted to any one organization or individual; the goal of marketing is to provide satisfaction of everyone's needs throughout the system.

> It is not enough merely to satisfy needs; there must be ongoing efforts to improve marketing programs to achieve even greater or more balanced need satisfaction.

MANAGING CHANNEL RELATIONS "Too often channel relationships do not receive due attention since they involve matters that are 'outside' the company and, hence, are more easily taken for granted than other activities such as marketing research, advertising, or personal selling."[4] Marketing managers tend to concentrate on those functions within the firm and neglect the interrelationships with other members of the channel system. Thus, marketing managers tend to concentrate on product decisions, price decisions, and promotion decisions, while channels of distribution tend to grow in an uncontrolled, uncoordinated manner. In this section, we shall look at the

[4] William R. Davidson, "Innovation in Distribution," in *Marketing for Tomorrow . . . Today,* ed. M. S. Moyer and R. E. Vosburgh (Chicago: American Marketing Association, 1967), p. 36.

channel, not as an economic system, but as a behavorial system. We have already discussed how channels create *exchange efficiency* and add value to goods and services. We shall now look at the human problems in channels and techniques for minimizing them.

Channels as Social Systems It is important to view a marketing channel as an *economic system* that facilitates exchange relationships. But it is equally important to understand a channel as a *social system*. That is, channels are not merely a structured group of *organizations* that create market exchanges. They are made up of *people* who have different attitudes, goals, and perceptions. One of the most important concepts in marketing is that the channel is really an "organized behavior system."[5] To understand channels, one must study how they are organized and how channel members behave toward one another. The concepts we shall be developing are:

> › **A channel of distribution is a social system made up of people in different organizations who must cooperate to create marketing exchanges.**

> › **The greater the degree of cooperation and coordination in a channel, the more successful the total system will be.**

Vertically Integrated Channel Systems At one time, channel relationships were more informal in that manufacturers, wholesalers, retailers, and other channel members were tied together only loosely by short-term agreements. Each organization remained rather independent of the other organizations in the channel,

[5] See Wroe Alderson, *Dynamic Marketing Behavior* (Homewood, Ill: Richard D. Irwin, Inc., 1965), pp. 43–45.

The Channel as an Organized Behavior System

Viewing the channel as an organized behavior system has several intrinsic advantages. First, this approach recognizes the fact that a channel is a purposive and rational assemblage of firms rather than a random collection of enterprises. Second, the systems concept emphasizes the existence of cooperative, as well as antagonistic, behavior within the channel. Third, the channel is perceived as a unique social organism that reflects the hopes, goals, and aspirations of its participants. Fourth, the marketing channel, from a systems point of view, is recognized as a basic "unit of competition"—a concept that broadens the study of economic rivalry. Systems theorists point out, for example, that a firm can fail not only because of its own imperfections but also because it is a member of the wrong system. Fifth, the notion that a channel is an operating system provides a basis for identifying dysfunctions that are system generated.

From Bert C. McCammon, Jr., and Robert W. Little, "Marketing Channels: Analytical Systems and Approaches," in *Science in Marketing,* ed. George Schwartz (New York: John Wiley & Sons, Inc., 1965), p. 330. Copyright 1965 by John Wiley & Sons, Inc. Reprinted with permission.

and conflict was as typical as cooperation. Many retailers were especially proud of their independence and often cooperated with manufacturers or wholesalers only when they felt it was to their advantage. Similarly, manufacturers and wholesalers often had different philosophies of business and used different language from retailers.[6] But all of this is slowly changing:

Recent changes in the structure of distribution suggests that centrally coordinated systems are gradually displacing conventional marketing channels as the dominant distribution mechanism in the American economy. Furthermore, competition, to an increasing extent, invokes rivalry between systems, as well as between the individual units that comprise them. Thus, centrally coordinated systems have emerged as a basic component of the competitive process.[7]

Today, at least three types of vertically integrated channel systems—corporate, contractual, and administered—compete in the marketplace.[8] We can learn much about where we are today and where we shall be going in the future by taking a careful look at these three systems.

Corporate Systems "Corporate systems may be regarded as roughly synonymous with integrated chain store systems, although the impetus for vertical programming may come from companies primarily regarded as retailers (e.g., Sears, Roebuck and Co.), or manufacturers (e.g., company-owned stores in the self-supply network of Firestone Tire and Rubber Co.), or wholesalers, some of whom have company-owned stores and are integrated into manufacturing."[9] Thus we may define a **corporate channel system** as a channel system in which manufacturing, wholesaling, retailing, and other channel institutions are all owned (or partially owned) by one corporation.

Sears is a particularly good example because, "A considerable volume—around 30 percent—of Sears' products are not really bought at all, but manufactured by companies in which Sears has an equity of 9 to 100 percent. Sears is, in fact, one of the largest manufacturers in the U.S."[10] Sears has gained tremendous control of the entire distribution system from production to the ultimate consumer by owning wholesaling and manufacturing organizations. Corporate systems such as Sears account for about 30 percent of all retailing and their share is growing.[11]

---

[6] See Warren J. Wittreich, "Misunderstanding the Retailer," *Harvard Business Review*, May–June 1962, pp. 147–159.

[7] Bert C. McCammon, Jr., and Albert D. Bates, "The Emergence and Growth of Contractually Integrated Channels in the American Economy," in *Economic Growth, Competition and World Markets*, ed. P. D. Bennett (Chicago: American Marketing Association, 1965), p. 496.

[8] Ibid.

[9] William R. Davidson, "Changes in Distributive Institutions," *Journal of Marketing*, January 1970, p. 7.

[10] John McDonald, "Sears Makes It Look Easy," *Fortune*, May 1964, p. 120.

[11] Davidson, "Changes in Distributive Institutions," p. 7.

Contractual Systems As its name implies, a **contractual channel system** is one in which two or more elements in the distribution system agree (contract) to perform certain marketing functions. There are three principal versions of contractual systems: wholesaler-sponsored voluntary groups, retailer-owned cooperatives, and franchise store programs.[12] Davidson reports that 35 to 40 percent of all retail trade is accounted for by some type of voluntary chain, cooperative, or franchising organization.[13] This means that 65 to 70 percent of all retailing is being done by some kind of vertically integrated system (corporate or contractual). Let's review in more detail what contractual systems are like.

Wholesaler-Sponsored Voluntary Groups Voluntary chains have most impact in areas such as food, hardware, automotive supplies, and variety goods. Perhaps names like Western Auto, IGA in food stores, and Ben Franklin Stores in the variety area are familiar to you. Thus, a **wholesaler-sponsored voluntary group** is a vertically integrated system in which a wholesaler contracts with a group of independent retailers to handle their wholesale needs; the group may then assume one name, sponsor cooperative advertisements, and generally act as a unified system.

Wholesale voluntary groups and retailer cooperatives may use sophisticated computer systems to supply dealers with marketing intelligence, profit reports, inventory reports, and other managerial information. They may also use the same accounting systems and generally behave as members of one integrated company:

The voluntary-chain concept has been successful because it gives the retailer the advantage of group identity, large-scale buying, private labels, centralized promotion, and various management aids. Control rests entirely with a wholesale operating unit, but it is a type of control which is exercised to improve the performance of the entire organization.[14]

Retailer-Owned Cooperatives A **retailer-owned cooperative** is a vertically integrated system in which a group of retailers contracts with one wholesaler to buy all or most of their supplies; the group may then assume one name, sponsor cooperative advertising, and generally act as a unified system.

Retail cooperatives are similar to wholesaler-sponsored voluntary groups. In fact, the literature usually discusses them in combination. The major difference is that retail cooperatives are initiated by a group of retailers that approach a wholesaler and contract to buy all or most of

---

[12] Bert C. McCammon, Jr., Alton F. Doody, and William R. Davidson, "Emerging Patterns of Distribution" (Paper delivered at the Annual Meeting of the National Association of Wholesalers, Las Vegas, 1969).

[13] Davidson, "Changes in Distributive Institutions," p. 8.

[14] See Edwin H. Lewis, "Channel Management by Wholesalers," in *Marketing and the New Science of Planning*, ed. Robert L. King (Chicago: American Marketing Association, 1968), pp. 137–141.

their merchandise from him. The same managerial cooperation, information exchange, and promotional cooperation take place. It is important to recognize that voluntary groups and cooperatives are a large and growing segment of retailing, especially in food, drug, hardware, and variety stores.

Franchise Systems If you were to take a walk through the main commercial district of any large city, you could not fail to be impressed by the dominant presence of franchise organizations. Many, if not most, of the gasoline stations you see are franchise organizations. So are the automobile dealerships, some appliance dealerships, and many of the motel chains. Who has not been impressed with the rapid growth of McDonald's in the United States and overseas? But Kentucky Fried Chicken, Burger Chef, Burger King, A & W Root Beer, Baskin-Robbins ice cream, International House of Pancake restaurants, Red Barn, Lums, and other such franchise organizations have also become household words to most Americans.

Franchising has even entered the service industries in dry cleaning (Martinizing), employment (Manpower), muffler repair (Midas), motels (Best Western), income-tax preparation (H & R Block), and transmission repair (AAMCO). One cannot keep up with the rapid growth of franchise organizations, and that is their strength. When someone comes up with a great idea for a new kind of fried chicken (Kentucky Fried) or different kind of restaurant (in a railroad car, for example) or a new service (steam cleaning for rugs), the best way to expand rapidly and get the financial support to do it is through franchising. Later the parent company can buy back some of the franchise outlets so that franchise systems eventually become, at least partially, corporate systems. In summary, a **franchise system** is a vertically integrated system in which a person or organization comes up with a new good, service, or idea and sells the right to sell that "product" in a given geographic area; the franchisor may also provide help in site selection, personnel hiring and training, purchasing, management training, promotion, and many other managerial aids.

Administered Systems When manufacturers want to control *their merchandise* in a retail store, but not the whole retail operation, they may try to develop an **administered system** of marketing. This means that the manufacturer (or wholesaler) will try to control everything that happens to his product including display, pricing, inventory control, and markdowns. The retailer has only to ring up the order, take his profit, and pay the principal for the product. For example, Kraft Foods (Kraftco) controls much of the cheese section of participating retailers. Kraft is so good at merchandising its products that the retailer could hardly refuse to handle them. The concept is:

➤ **A manufacturer or wholesaler can gain control over his products throughout the distribution system by developing a marketing program for all the other members of the channel (especially retailers) that is so** good that the other organizations will gladly allow the administrator to control that product; this includes display, pricing, and inventory management.

There are no figures on the overall impact of administered systems on retailing, but it is clear that this is one way for a marketer to gain control over the product throughout the distribution system.

The Channel Captain
The greatest percent of retail *volume* is being done by retailers that belong to one of the systems we have described. But by far the largest *number* of retailers are still managed as *independent organizations* that often compete directly with the larger, integrated systems. How are they doing? Well, independent retailers can offer consumers personal service and a depth of assortment that are not usually found in a larger department store. Therefore, independent retailers may actually complement the larger systems by filling in the merchandise that the systems do not provide. Thus, in a large shopping center you might find retailers that are part of corporate systems, contractual systems, administered systems, and independently managed systems.

However, it is difficult for an independent TV outlet or appliance store to compete with a member of an integrated system. Figure 11.5 helps to explain why. Note that the areas of conflict in the independent channel system are not present in the vertically integrated system. In the vertically integrated system, there is need for one purchasing department, one sales force, one transportation and storage system, one credit department, and one promotion department. In the independent system there are three of each (at the manufacturing, wholesaling, and retailing level). This is an obvious inefficiency. Furthermore, there may be con-

Go over all systems again

Figure 11.5 AN INTEGRATED CHANNEL SYSTEM VERSUS INDEPENDENTLY OWNED MEMBERS OF A CHANNEL

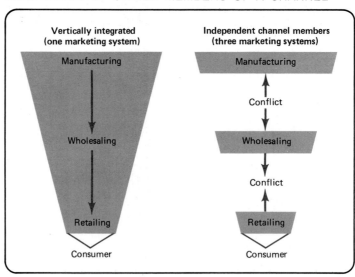

flicting goals between independent manufacturers, wholesalers, and retailers, whereas the integrated system works together toward one goal in a spirit of cooperation and coordination.

The greatest problems in traditional independent systems are *human* problems. People just do not want to give up some of their freedom to benefit the system. Thus, retailers do not like to do what wholesalers want, wholesalers do not want to do what manufacturers want, and manufacturers do not respond to their suppliers, distributors, and dealers. The channel becomes a source of conflict, antagonism, and inefficiency.

But in the wings there stands a champion of cooperation and coordination—the so-called **channel captain.** The channel captain's role is to somehow gain control over the channel members and get them to work together. The captain may be the manufacturer, the wholesaler, or the retailer. For example, in the automobile distribution system the manufacturer has much control over what the dealers do, and when and how. Retailers such as Sears have the power to control manufacturers that supply them. At times it is the wholesaler who takes charge. The concepts are:

> **Independent channel members usually cannot compete effectively against vertically integrated systems unless they resolve interorganizational conflicts and inefficiencies.**

> **One way to get control over channel conflicts and inefficiencies in an independent channel is to have one organization become the channel captain who controls the activities of the other members.**

There is a whole area of marketing that specializes in channel relationships, conflict in the channel, and power bases in the channel.[15] You should read that literature and learn more about how one organization can get other organizations to cooperate. Of course, one way is to control the information system for the whole channel, another is to control the financial support, and there are others. This is a fascinating area of study that draws heavily on the behavorial sciences.

Let us now turn away from channel systems in general and discuss one very important aspect—physical distribution. It is a major channel activity and one that deserves special attention.

PHYSICAL DISTRIBUTION Although not a universal marketing function, physical distribution is one of the most important marketing activities. The reason we should study this activity is that physical distribution of goods is often the most costly marketing function of all. Although advertising costs cause much debate among marketing critics, physical distribution costs are often five or six times the total advertising costs. Included in the cost are the physical movement of goods (raw materials) *into* a manufacturer, receiving and

[15] See, for example, Louis W. Stern, *Distribution Channels: Behavioral Dimensions* (Boston: Houghton Mifflin Company, 1969).

shipping costs, warehousing, internal movement of goods, and inventory carrying costs including interest, insurance, and obsolescence. We are all concerned about the cost of food we buy and often blame the retailer for charging us so much. Would it help you to know that the supermarket adds only 2½¢ or so per dollar of sales, whereas total distribution costs are closer to 30¢ per dollar of sales? If we could cut distribution costs, we could significantly lower the price we pay for food and other goods we buy. But how do we lower distribution costs?

Present Practices Part of the reason physical distribution costs are so high is that most firms have not adopted a "systems" perspective. That is, physical distribution activities are managed as a series of independent steps with little overall coordination and integration. For example, there is usually a person responsible for physically transporting goods *to* and/or *from* a manufacturing firm (a traffic manager). The goal of that person is to keep transportation costs to a minimum. On the other hand, the warehouse manager has a goal of keeping storage and handling costs at a minimum. But when the traffic manager tries to keep the cost of transportation low by buying in large quantities, the cost of storage may rise considerably. There should be some way to balance the costs of transportation with the costs of storage. The best way to do that is through a distribution system that is managed by one person. The present practice in most firms, however, is to have a traffic manager, a warehouse manager, a shipping manager, and a production manager who handles materials in the shop. But no one coordinates the activities of these people in order to minimize the total cost of physical distribution.

The Physical Distribution Manager The tremendous costs of physical distribution have caused special concern among marketers for over 60 years. In fact, the earliest marketing literature was about distribution. Arch Shaw, one of the earliest writers in marketing, wrote *Some Problems in Market Distribution* in

---

How Complex Is the Distribution System?

Cox and Goodman studied the distribution system of building materials to construct a two-story, masonry dwelling with six rooms and one bath. They studied forty-three different materials amounting to 186 tons of products. In traveling from place to place, these products (and their antecedents) were loaded onto carriers, moved, and unloaded 424 separate times. Some 366 business entities were involved including 148 transportation agencies. The 217 business entities that participated in the ownership flow of materials participated in 374 transactions including 330 purchase/sale transactions.

See Reavis Cox and Charles S. Goodman, "Marketing of Housebuilding Materials," *Journal of Marketing*, July 1956, pp. 36–61.

1915.[16] Many people today feel that marketing is subject to unusually close study by government, consumerists, and others, but this is nothing new. In fact, in 1939 the Twentieth Century Fund sponsored a study called *Does Distribution Cost Too Much?* The forword of this book contained the following statement:

The costs of distribution are paid by the ultimate consumer. Every time we buy a package of cigarettes, a pair of socks or a loaf of bread, we are directly and personally concerned with the expenses of getting it from its point of origin to the store counter—and of persuading us to buy it. Because these costs are as fully as large as, or larger than, the original costs of production, and because less has been done to make distribution more efficient, cutting marketing expense offers a greater opportunity to get lower prices and a higher standard of living for all of us.[17]

Yes, physical distribution costs have been a concern of marketers for many years, but there has been more talk and theory development than action. But more recently, the development of computers, marketing information systems, and integrated channel networks have led to a new position called *physical distribution manager.* This position is responsible for coordinating and integrating *all* movement of materials including transportation, internal movement (materials handling), and warehousing. Few organizations actually have such a position, but the concept has been accepted by many organizations, and the process of implementing a "total systems approach" is slowly being carried out. Only very recently have firms begun to recognize the need for physical distribution management throughout the channel system. That is, one department at one firm could coordinate and integrate as much of the movement of goods through the channel as possible. The idea is to keep distribution costs low *for the whole system* as well as for each individual organization in the channel. The concepts are:

➤ **A physical distribution manager is responsible for the coordination and integration of materials movement to, through, and from the firm; this involves control over traffic management, transportation management, materials handling, warehousing, and all other distribution activities, including inventory control and order processing.**

➤ **Physical distribution management should be broadened to include the whole channel system, so that control over distribution costs can be more effectively managed.[18]**

[16] Arch W. Shaw, *Some Problems in Market Distribution* (Cambridge, Mass.: Harvard University Press, 1915).

[17] Paul W. Stewart and J. Frederic Dewhurst, *Does Distribution Cost Too Much?* (New York: The Twentieth Century Fund, 1939), p. vii.

[18] This is sometimes called logistics management, or rhocrematics, but the concepts are the same.

There are many problems associated with implementing physical distribution management in a firm. Of course, there are even greater problems associated with implementing such a concept among several firms. But such control is possible in vertical marketing systems where various organizations are under one ownership (corporate systems) or are subject to the control of one dominant firm (contractual system).

A Classic Case of Distribution Conflict   A classic example of the conflict that can happen in a channel of distribution is provided by the furniture industry. Goods such as beds, chairs, and couches are bulky to ship, expensive to store, and subject to rapid depreciation because of style changes. Therefore, no one likes to store much furniture. The manufacturer does not want a huge inventory, wholesalers do not like to clutter their warehouses, and most retailers just do not have the room. Consequently, the consumer often has to wait 6 months or longer to get a special piece of furniture. What happens is that the manufacturer makes the piece *after it is ordered*, and that minimizes potential losses in storage and obsolescence. *But*, the consumer is forced to wait and wait and wait.

There was a big shakeup in the furniture industry a few years back when Levitz (a retailer) decided to accept the storage problem. Levitz built several huge warehouse/display outlets that enabled consumers to see furniture in the appropriate setting, select what they wanted, and *take it home the same day*. What a difference between waiting several months and having it now! As a result, Levitz experienced very rapid growth and forced other retailers to follow the same warehouse/display format.

This is a classic case of someone in the channel accepting a function no one else wanted and profiting greatly from it. There are conflicts in almost all channels of distribution that make the marketing process less effective and more expensive. That is why there has been such a trend toward integrated channel systems such as the Sears system. In this way, conflicts can be kept to a minimum.

Distribution Cost Accounting   Manufacturers have developed quite sophisticated cost-accounting systems to measure the cost of *producing* a product. But production costs are only half the total cost we pay for products. The other half are marketing costs. What we need if we want to get better control over marketing costs is an accounting system that is as diligent in measuring distribution (marketing) costs as production costs. That accounting function is known as **distribution cost accounting.** (It has also been termed distribution cost analysis, marketing cost analysis, and marketing cost accounting. We accept any of these terms so long as the basic concepts are understood.)

Distribution cost accounting is a relatively new concept in marketing. In fact, as late as 1957, the American Marketing Association was still conducting studies on *The Values and Uses of Distribution Cost Analyses.*[19] The committee felt there were "two basic steps in distribution cost

[19] AMA Committee on Distribution Costs and Efficiency, "The Values and Uses of Distribution Cost Analysis," *Journal of Marketing*, April 1957, pp. 395–399.

analysis: (1) the determination of the cost of performing each distribution activity or function of the business, and (2) the determination of the costs of those functions which are associated with products, customers, territories, or other segments of the business."[20] It should be noted that the costs being referred to as distribution costs include the costs of *all* marketing activities, including personal selling, advertising, and sales promotion as well as transportation and storage. That is why the term "marketing cost analysis" may be more accurate. The concepts are:

(Distribution)

> **Marketing costs should be analyzed with the same vigor as production costs.**

> **Whether the process of measuring marketing costs is called distribution cost accounting or marketing cost analysis, the idea is to allocate costs to particular products, customers, territories, or salespersons to determine where costs could be lowered (or where more effort is needed).**

The measurement of marketing costs is very difficult because it is hard to allocate the costs of a salesperson or an advertising campaign to a particular product or customer. Managerial accounting procedures may be used rather than financial accounting procedures. That is, the data are used for managerial decision making rather than for tax reporting or annual report preparation.

We shall not go into detail here about the procedures of distribution cost analysis or accounting.[21] There is still much uncertainty about the correct procedures. The point to be made here is that accounting and marketing personnel are working together as part of a total system to analyze distribution costs and to make the distribution process more efficient. A recent Federal Trade Commission rule *requires* line-of-business reports (that is, profits for each product line) from the nation's 300 largest firms. This may someday force businesses to do more accurate studies of distribution costs in order to comply with the law.

Although middlemen add many costs to the goods we buy, we hope you understand now that those costs also represent added value that you get when you buy products. This does not mean that distribution costs are as low as possible or as low as they should be. This chapter provides some of the concepts and tools marketers need to make the distribution process more effective and more efficient. Distribution cost accounting is one of those tools.

---

[20] Ibid., p. 396.

[21] See K. Fred Skousen, "A Format for Reporting Segment Profits," *Management Accounting*, June 1971, pp. 15–20; L. Gayle Rayburn, Analyses of Current Marketing Cost Methods," *The CPA Journal*, November 1973, pp. 985–991; Leland L. Beik and Stephen L. Buzby, "Profitability Analyses by Market Segments," *Journal of Marketing*, July 1973, pp. 48–53; and especially Committee on Cost and Profitability Analysis for Marketing, "Committee Report," *Accounting Review*, Supplement, 1972, pp. 575–615.

FOR REVIEW

Key Terms

Among the more important terms and expressions discussed in this chapter are the following:

An **administered channel system** is one in which the manufacturer or wholesaler maintains control over its product throughout the distribution system, especially at the retail level.

A **channel captain** is a manufacturer, wholesaler, or retailer who exercises marketing control over the other members of a particular channel of distribution.

A **channel of distribution** is basically a distribution system; more specifically, it is a complex system of physical flows and information flows that is subject to many outside influentials.

A **contractual channel system** is a channel system in which two or more elements in the distribution system agree, or contract, to perform certain marketing functions; examples include wholesaler-sponsored voluntary groups, retailer-owned cooperatives, and franchise systems.

A **corporate channel system** is a channel system in which manufacturing, wholesaling, retailing, and other channel institutions are owned (or partially owned) by one corporation.

Distribution cost accounting is the measurement of all marketing costs associated with the distribution of goods and services from producer to consumer, including the costs of selling, advertising, transportation, storage, and credit.

A **distribution system** is an organized network of people and organizations that performs all the marketing functions and activities required to provide consumers with whatever they want and to satisfy the needs of all the participants as well.

A **franchise system** is a vertically integrated system in which a person or organization comes up with a new good, service, or idea and sells the right to sell that "product" in a given geographic area; the franchisor may also provide help in site selection, personnel hiring and training, purchasing, management training, promotion, and many other managerial aids.

Retailers are marketing middlemen who sell to the ultimate consumer.

A **retailer-owned cooperative** is a vertically integrated system in which a group of retailers contracts with one wholesaler to buy all or most of their supplies; the group may then assume one name, sponsor cooperative advertising, and generally act as a unified system.

Wholesalers are marketing middlemen who buy products from various producers to sell to retailers, to other wholesalers, to institutions, and to any organization other than the ultimate consumer.

A **wholesaler-sponsored voluntary group** is a vertically integrated system in which a wholesaler contracts with a group of independent retailers to handle their wholesale needs; the group may then assume one name, sponsor cooperative advertising, and generally act as a unified system.

Key Concepts

Among the more important marketing concepts introduced in this chapter are the following:

> Consumers are often far away from those organizations that provide for their wants and needs; marketing middlemen act as representatives of the buyer and seller to close the gaps between them.

> Marketing middlemen can be eliminated, but their functions cannot be eliminated.

> Marketing middlemen survive because they perform marketing functions more effectively and/or efficiently than they could be performed by others.

> Middlemen add costs to products, but these costs are usually more than offset by the values they create.

> Middlemen add form, time, possession, place, and information utility to products.

> The total marketing system is larger than the *distribution* system because it includes organizations not involved with distribution including financial institutions, marketing research firms, and advertising agencies.

> Consumers are part of the channel system because they perform many marketing functions.

> Middlemen perform marketing services for both buyers and sellers and greatly reduce the costs of market analysis, communication, and the other marketing functions.

> A physical distribution manager is responsible for the coordination and integration of materials movements to, through, and from the firm.

> The concept of physical distribution management should be broadened to include the whole channel system, so that control over distribution costs can be more effectively managed.

Discussion Questions

1. My friend Dick says he buys his personal groceries wholesale. Is this possible? What do you suppose the difference in cost is between buying food at wholesale and at retail? What costs should be considered besides monetary (dollar) costs?

2. Do you feel it is stretching a point to view a church or a school as a middleman? Why or why not?

3. Give arguments for and against including the following people in the marketing channel: ad agencies; consumer organizations; credit agencies; government regulators; and consumers.

4. Real estate agencies charge about 6 percent of the sale price of a home for their service. This amounts to $2,400 on the sale of a $40,000 home. Is this an example of middlemen charging too much? Defend your answer.

5. How can an independent retailer effectively compete against an integrated retailer like Sears? What is the product offer of each?

6. The highest marketing costs for most manufacturers are distribution costs. Total marketing costs are often half of what consumers pay for goods. Are marketing costs too high? Are distribution costs too high? What criteria should one use in answering such questions?

7. A retailer spends $20 to buy a lamp and sells it to me for $25 because I am a friend. He says, "We will both benefit from this deal because I will make $5 and you will get a good price for the lamp." If the retailer had a system of distribution cost accounting, would he make the same statement? Why or why not?

8. "A channel of distribution is a social system." Explain what this means and what problems it causes for marketers.

9. Make a list of all the independent retailers in your immediate area and all those that are part of a system. Which do you prefer to deal with? Why? Which have the greatest sales volume? Why?

10. What role do consumers have in determining which marketing channels will succeed or fail? What stores have failed recently in your area? Why do you feel they failed?

CASES

Middleman Margins
Are Profits Too High?

"Marketing is nothing but a huge rip-off," Mario Borrado said. "I read where farmers are losing money on the cattle they sell because the price they get is going down. But the prices at the supermarket have gone up! The real problem today is with marketing middlemen. They gouge the public with high prices and get away with it. The farmer suffers, the consumer suffers, and the wholesalers and retailers live in fat city. Middlemen get away with it because they are in cahoots with the congressmen in Washington. What is the government doing about middlemen rip-offs? Nothing. And meanwhile we can hardly afford to eat."

"You sure are right about the rise in food prices," Mario's friend Saul Anders said. "But I'm not sure it's the middleman who is at fault. Remember when the employees at the Shop and Save supermarket went on strike last year? Well, the checkout people now make over $5 an hour, and they get double-time on Sunday. How can the store make money when the clerks make $10 an hour? I read where Shop and Save makes less than 2¢ on each dollar of sales. If someone steals an $8 steak, the store has to sell something like $400 worth of groceries to make up the loss. And you know how people have been stealing things down at the Shop and Save. I think high food prices are caused by high labor costs and increased costs of everything. Think of all the electricity the Shop and Save must use for all those freezer chests and lights. You know how much your folk's electric bill went up last year. I'm not sure about wholesalers, but I think their profit margins are even smaller than retailers. Wholesalers are also faced with increased labor costs. Didn't Joe Minardi just get a good raise? He works for a wholesaler."

1. What is your reaction to this discussion?
2. Is Mario right when he says that middlemen are gouging the public?
3. Are labor prices and energy prices going up so fast that your local supermarkets are making minimal profits? Where would you go to get answers to such questions? Would the annual reports of various supermarkets help in the analysis?
4. What role do you feel Congress should play in the battle to keep down food prices?

Rowet Furniture
Distribution Cost Accounting

Dan Rowet of Rowet Furniture was friendly with one of the appliance salesmen who calls on his store. One day the appliance salesman spotted a nice Zenith color TV that he really liked. He asked Mr. Rowet if he would sell it to him at a good price. Mr Rowet looked at his invoice from Zenith and found that the set cost him $375. So Mr. Rowet said to the salesman, "I'll tell you what. The set cost me $375. I'll sell it to you for $400. I'll make a little bit, and you will save a lot over what you'd have to pay somewhere else." "It's a deal," said the salesman, "send it out to my house."

1. What costs did Mr. Rowet include and what costs did he not include in his cost figure of $375?
2. How would Mr. Rowet benefit from adopting a distribution cost accounting system for his store?
3. How much do you think the Zenith set really cost Mr. Rowet? How did you figure that amount?
4. Do you think this case is typical of pricing in small retail stores or not? Explain your answer.

4

Communicating with the Market

One of the problems with marketing is that communication between and among buyers and sellers is often faulty. How many times have you heard complaints that organizations are not responsive to the public? For marketing to work effectively, there must be free and open two-way communication between buyers and sellers.

Chapter 12 introduces the basic concepts behind marketing communication and suggests some strategies for making marketers more responsive to market needs. One way to let people know about responsive organizations and the products they produce is through advertising. Chapter 13 discusses the role of advertising in marketing, advertising institutions (for example, advertising agencies), and advertising media (for Example, TV, radio, and newspapers).

Public relations is a marketing activity that is very closely related to advertising. Public relations is not just a talking function, however. It is one department in an organization that has explicit responsibility for listening to the public and responding to the public's needs. Chapter 14 discusses public relations and its role in creating responsive and responsible organizations. Chapter 14 also explores publicity, which is one aspect of public relations. The chapter ends with a discussion of sales promotion—the communication function that unites the others in a comprehensive communications effort.

Marketing Communications and Promotion

the marketing dialogue

12

LEARNING GOALS

After you have read and studied this chapter, you should be able to:

1. Explain the difference between marketing communications and promotion.

2. Use examples to show how listening may minimize the need for promotion.

3. Define the following terms: promotional mix; promotional synergism; selective perception; marketing communications.

4. Describe the role of a marketing communications manager.

5. Show the relationship between marketing communications and product managers.

6. Explain why traditional measures of promotional effectiveness are incomplete and what is needed to make them complete.

7. Construct an exchange model of communication and describe how it differs from traditional communication models.

8. Explain the following concepts: source effect, message effect, media effect, and receiver effect.

9. Give examples of times when you have practiced selective exposure, selective perception, and selective retention.

10. Show how nonprofit organizations can benefit by applying concepts from the marketing communications literature.

> *The first test of a communication goal should be that it serve the interest of the communicator—and also that of the intended audience. This latter requirement is often overlooked.*
>
> Marion Harper, Jr.*

INTRODUCTION Although the two are often viewed as synonymous, marketing communication is different from promotion. Marketing communication is a *two-way* exchange of information among marketing participants. This two-way exchange is sometimes known as the *marketing dialogue.* Promotion, on the other hand, is a *one-way* flow of information and/or persuasion. To promote is to further the cause of one particular organization or individual, but marketing communication increases the satisfaction of *all* participants. This chapter will discuss both marketing communication (an exchange process) and promotion (a furthering process).

"There is a real problem in much of the marketing literature today," according to Stidsen and Shutte, "in that the communication process is designed and implemented, for the most part, according to seller needs rather than those of the consumer."[1] That is, too much emphasis is placed on promotion. It is felt that "the ideal marketing process is a functioning dialogue involving a communication system which enables consumers and producers to significantly influence each other's goal attainment."[2] This chapter will discuss techniques for creating such an ideal marketing communication system.

THE MARKETING COMMUNICATION SYSTEM All participants in the marketing communication process go through a similar procedure of listening, reacting, and talking until a mutually satisfying exchange relationship is formed. Information exchanges, persuasive arguments, and negotiation are all part of the process. The elements of the marketing communication system are shown in Figure 12.1.

Marketing Communications Defined One reason for the apparent overemphasis on promotion in marketing is that most textbooks stress marketing management and thus marketing communication is presented as a tool of the *seller*. To correct such practices, we need a new definition of marketing communication. For our purposes, we shall define **marketing communications** as those communication activities performed by both the buyer and seller that aid marketing decision making and lead to more satisfying exchanges by making all participants more aware and better informed.

* "Communications Is the Core of Marketing," *Printer's Ink*, June 1, 1962, p. 52.
[1] Bent Stidsen and Thomas F. Shutte, "Marketing as a Communication System: The Marketing Concept Revisited," *Journal of Marketing*, October 1972, p. 26.
[2] Ibid.

Marketing communications help to bring buyers and sellers together in an exchange relationship; they create flows of information among buyers and sellers that make exchange activities more efficient; and they enable participants to negotiate an exchange agreement that is satisfactory to everyone. Emphasis in the definition just given is placed on decision making because both buyers and sellers use marketing communications to aid in decision making. The concept is:

➤ **Marketing communications aid both buyers and sellers by: (1) establishing exchange contacts; (2) maintaining flows of information that enable an exchange to occur; (3) creating aware and informed buyers and sellers who are more likely to negotiate a satisfactory exchange; and (4) improving decision making in marketing so that the whole exchange process is made more effective and efficient.**

One part of the total communication process is *promotion*. Promotion helps marketing participants to improve their exchange relationships with others. Another part of the communication process is *feedback*. Feedback tells marketing participants what the effect of their communication efforts has been and enables them to adjust their promotions to the market's needs.

An important element in the total communications effort is marketing research. Research enables the buyer and seller to gain more knowledge of the market and to structure the rest of the communications effort more intelligently. The insert "Market Communications Not Perfect" indicates how imperfect information causes imperfect markets.

Listening Is Half the Communication Process The communication function in marketing is *not* simply a talking function. It begins with listening and proceeds as a series of discussions that involve listening, reacting, responding, listening again, reacting, and responding again, so that the marketing exchange process becomes more and more satisfying to everyone involved. Let us look at such a system in action.

Figure 12.1 A BASIC MODEL OF THE MARKETING COMMUNICATION SYSTEM

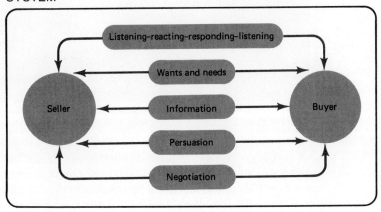

Truly human communication is essential to life. It is also essential if such organizations as the American Speech and Hearing Association are to promote their causes successfully.

Courtesy of Asha, a Journal of the American Speech and Hearing Association.

A large restaurant chain asked the residents of a local community what kind of food they preferred in a restaurant. (This was the first phase—seeking and listening to consumer wants.) There seemed to be a large demand for steak and beef dishes, and so the owners decided to open a restaurant that served nothing but beef and steak. The restaurant

Market Communication Not Perfect

The market does not perform its function in a perfect manner. In many instances the market fails to provide individuals with the maximum satisfaction available for the expenditure of their funds. Such failures may occur because communication between all possible buyers and all possible sellers at all market levels is imperfect. Therefore, the best possible choice is not always made. For example, assume that a suit of clothes pleases you and you make a purchase. At a subsequent date you might visit another store and discover several suits that would have given you more satisfaction for the same price. This failure was due in part to your failure to shop more and to seek more information, and it was due in part to the failure of the second merchant to promote his better values to the extent that you were made more aware of them before your purchase. In order for one to make the best possible choice, he would need to keep perfectly informed on all offerings. Since changes are constantly taking place in the products offered and since many institutions are involved, it is impossible to keep completely up to date on every purchase. Perfection in getting the best value offered on the market is a goal that can only be approached.

In other instances information given to buyers by sellers may convey the wrong impression. In such cases choices are sometimes made that would not have been made if complete and accurate information had been communicated. For every person to get all the information about desired products would require a great deal of shopping. To reach every possible prospect with accurate promotional information about his product would be equally difficult for the seller. The extent to which each fails to achieve perfection in this unattainable objective measures the extent to which imperfection of market dealings may occur. Nevertheless, buyers and sellers gain their objectives in proportion to the extent to which they do successfully communicate. Marketplace communication is improving, for more buyers are seeking more information in order to improve the quality of their product choices. As a result sellers must be more alert to the forces of the market in setting their prices.

From Weldon J. Taylor and Roy T. Shaw, Jr., *Marketing: An Integrated Analytical Approach* (Cincinnati, Ohio: South-Western Publishing Co., Inc., 1975), p. 27. Reproduced by special permission.

opened and was an immediate success. No reservations were accepted, and there were long lines nightly. This was one of the problems; people did not like waiting in line and said so.

The managers *listened* to the complaints and opened a large cocktail lounge where diners could have a drink while they waited for a table. This proved very popular with the customers and very profitable for the restaurant (another mutually satisfying exchange). But some other problems arose. Some customers complained about the restrooms being too small and dirty. Others complained about the long wait to be served. Management responded by remodeling the restrooms and by putting in a serve-yourself salad bar.

Eventually the restaurant offered "all the beer or wine you can drink" with meals and changed the menu to include some nonbeef dinners. (Some people were not dining at the restaurant simply because their friends or dates did not want beef.) The restaurant is now a very popular eating spot, and the owners are making more money than ever.

This case does not seem to be a very good example of marketing communications to some people. "What about the restaurant's advertising?" they say. "This case says nothing about how to inform and persuade the market to buy." Such people reveal one major problem with some marketers today. They tend to look at marketing communication as something sellers send *to* buyers. The seller is supposed to talk, and the buyers are supposed to listen. The restaurant manager in this case shows us that marketing communication is often more effective when the seller *listens* and adjusts the product to consumer needs. Consumers then learn about the product through word of mouth, publicity, and other means, and the seller has to do only a minimum of promotion.

In this case, the restaurant advertises only in the Yellow Pages and by means of a prominent sign on the main road near the restaurant. The restaurant has an excellent communications system even though it has a minimal advertising function. Word of mouth is sufficient to make the restaurant crowded almost every night. The concepts are:

› **Marketing communication is a two-way exchange of information (and sometimes persuasion) between marketing participants.**

› **For an effective communication system, listening (and then doing something about the information you hear) is often more important than talking.**

› **Consumer wants and needs are discovered through communication and are partially satisfied through communication.**

The Marketing Multilogue Throughout the marketing process, there should be a constant flow of information between and among the marketing participants. This multidirectional flow may be called a multilogue because it is a dialogue among many members of a marketing system. The marketing multilogue would look something like the diagram in Figure 12.2.

If Figure 12.2 looks confusing, it is because the marketing communi-

---

The Listening Function

An essential, and perhaps the most important, part of the communications task is to listen, carefully and attentively, to critics as well as friends. Not all criticism is justified. Illegal or improper business behavior, shoddy products, or callousness toward the consumer may be rare, but they are devastating to business credibility. Occasionally we will find we have to clean up the act before we expect applause.

From "Private Enterprise in a Changing Society," an address by L. G. Rawl, senior vice-president of Exxon Company, U.S.A., delivered at St. Mary's College of California, Moraga, Calif., February 5, 1976.

Figure 12.2 THE MARKETING MULTILOGUE

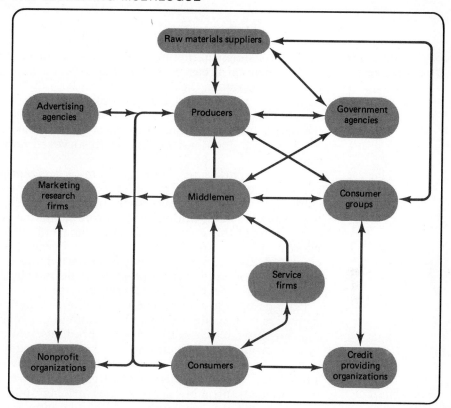

cations multilogue is a complex system of two-way flows that link together diverse institutions such as producers, wholesalers, retailers, government agencies, nonprofit organizations, consumer groups, service organizations, banks, and individuals. When one looks at how complex the communication links are among marketing participants, one can understand why Markin says that, "The complete and total activity of a firm's marketing strategy might very well be summarized as that of developing and maintaining useful communication between the firm and the market."[3] It also explains why Myers and Reynolds say that, "If communication is not the critical element in competitive consumer marketing today, it is very nearly so."[4] The concept is:

> **Marketing communication involves a series of multidirectional flows among producers, middlemen, government agencies, consumers, and other marketing entities; control over these flows is the heart of any marketing system.**

[3] Rom J. Markin, *The Psychology of Consumer Behavior* (Englewood Cliffs, N.J.: Prentice-Hall, Inc., 1969), p. 231.

[4] J. H. Myers and W. H. Reynolds, *Consumer Behavior and Marketing Management* (New York: Houghton Mifflin Company, 1967), p. 263.

Growing Interest in Marketing Communications

Traditionally, management of the communication function has been rather uncoordinated, with separate people in charge of advertising, personal selling, marketing research, sales promotion, and the other communication areas. In the last few years, there has been a trend toward integrating these functions under one person whose title is manager of marketing communications, director of marketing services, communications manager, or some similar title. A survey conducted for the Association of National Advertisers found that nearly one-fourth of 100 leading industrial firms that were surveyed now have such a position.[5]

The new marketing communications managers provide a *two-way* communication service for the other marketing functions. That is, the communications managers provide marketing intelligence (for example, marketing research findings) and promotional assistance of all kinds. Furthermore, the communications managers may assist production personnel in improving the product, package, and label. Marketing communications managers may also participate in the creation of a unified corporate identification system and may help various company spokespersons develop their presentations.[6]

Perhaps the most valuable contribution marketing communications managers make is their constant pressure to improve the overall corporate planning process. In the past, products tended to be produced before promotional decisions were made. Today, communications managers try to integrate promotional decisions with production decisions. This forces top management to make more precise analyses of market needs, promotional strategies, pricing objectives and strategies and to carry out more careful product planning and development. The marketing communications manager thus has assumed a corporate position that enables him or her to put the new marketing concept into action. The desired result is a coordinated and integrated system-wide effort to provide consumer and societal satisfaction at a profit.

Marketing Communications and Brand Management

Some firms already have a manager who coordinates and integrates marketing functions for particular products. The title of such a person is brand manager or product manager. Procter & Gamble is the organization most noted for its product managers.

Those organizations that have product managers are also experiencing what has been called a "quiet revolution" in marketing communications management.[7] This revolution involves a new corporate position called director of communications, director of communications services, or more generally, director of marketing services. The duties of this position

[5] A full report on this subject is available. See Milo E. Ziegenhagen, *Marketing Communications: What's It All About?* (Princeton, N.J.: Center for Marketing Communication, 1975).

[6] Ibid.

[7] Much of the material in this section is based on Stephen Dietz and Rodney Erickson, "Director of Marketing Services: The Quiet Revolution," *Advertising Age*, June 7, 1976, pp. 51–56.

How Marketing Communications and Advertising Differ

The basic advertising and sales promotion function:

1. Concentrates almost entirely on increasing the effectiveness of sales-men and distributors, using space advertising, sales literature, direct mail, shows and exhibits, and the like.
2. Is mainly used near the *end* of the marketing process, when the product or service is ready to be sold.
3. Is primarily a *one-way* flow of information to customers and pros-pects.

The steps to marketing communications:

1. The advertising function provides communication services not only to field sales, but also to all other functions and management levels that can help strengthen marketing. Services marketing managers, the functional managers of sales, engineering, service, etc.—and also general and top management in areas such as corporate identification and corporate-level advertising.
2. Becomes increasingly involved in setting the *strategy* for marketing and its communication programs, and with the marketing research needed to get facts on which to base the strategy.
3. Collaborates with the marketing head to do these things *early* in the marketing process, when strategies should be set.
4. Becomes—in its most advanced form—a *two-way* marketing commu-nication service for *all* company functions, provided throughout the *entire* marketing process.

Reprinted with permission from M. E. Ziegenhagen, "Marketing Communica-tions Supplants Business Ads," *Advertising Age*, June 21, 1976, p. 43. Copyright 1976 by Crain Communications, Inc.

vary in detail among different firms, but the trend is to have the director responsible for advertising agency relations, market research, sales promotion, public relations, consumer relations, home economics, package design, in-house promotion design, media, and photo and audiovisual operations.[8] This is true at organizations such as Best Foods, Vick Chemical, Clairol, and Quaker Oats.

What led to the emergence of this new position was the trend among consumer products firms to have product managers who were respon-sible for all the marketing decisions relative to one brand or several brand-name products. Many firms found that product managers had too many responsibilities and were not effectively managing the communi-cation function. The new directors of communications provide the needed assistance to product managers and enable the firms to coordi-

[8] Ibid.

nate and integrate promotional efforts. Also, some effort is made to get market feedback through market research.

In most firms, there still appears to be an overemphasis on management of communications *to* the market and an underemphasis on management of communications *from* the market. Some firms have established a position called *consumer ombudsman* to manage consumer inquires and complaints. But there is still much room for improvement in almost all organizations in the other half of marketing communications—that is, the *listening* half.

What may be needed is a position with a title such as director of communications *from* the public. A director of this department could be responsible for seeking out input from all the "publics" of an organization, including customers, suppliers, distributors, stockholders, community spokespersons, and government regulators. The director of communications from the public would work with the director of communications services to ensure that the flow of information from the organization met the needs of the various "publics."

It is not necessary to have separate individuals in charge of listening to the public and talking to the public But someone should be responsible for both. It is no longer an effective strategy to have coordination and integration of promotional communications (outgoing messages) without giving equal attention to marketing intelligence (the listening function).

Communications from the Consumer Because marketing communications involve an *exchange* of information, half the burden for establishing and maintaining communication is on the buyer. Consumers (buyers) have the obligation to state their needs clearly and to make some adjustments to the needs of the seller.

Consumers need not wait for business, education, government, or any other organizations to meet their needs. They can make their needs known and organize their efforts to find satisfaction for their needs. Most organizations will respond to consumer needs, but they often need much prompting by customers to do so. Consumers may temper their demands in recognition of the seller's economic situation, but, by communicating with organizations consumers often can improve their own satisfaction and the entire marketing process in general. The concept is:

> **Consumers need not wait for someone to recognize their needs; instead, they should make their needs known through effective marketing communication and should maintain their communication efforts until their needs are met.**

Measuring the Effectiveness of Communications When most people write about communication effectiveness, they mean how effective the seller (sender) is in influencing the buyer (receiver) to do what the seller wants. Thus communication effectiveness is usually measured by increased sales, increased share of the market, consumer awareness, or some similar measure. But such measures weigh only half the exchange process. They tend to ignore whether the communication was effective for the buyer. Let us look at an example.

> **New Look at Meaning of Communication**
>
> The word COMMUNICATE comes from the Latin—*commun-i-care.* Savor that word slowly—and allow me an added touch of meaning of my own. *Commun-i-care. Commun*—meaning community or group. *I*—the stalwart erect pronoun which stands for *yourself.* And *care*—which in modern terms means "to give a damn.". . . The dictionary goes on with many amplifying words that shade the word with—to impart—to inform—to participate—to share.

From Douglas Johnson, "Agency Employment Trends," in *Proceedings of National Conference for University Professors of Advertising,* Arizona State University, 1973, p. 65.

A carpet manufacturer went to a leading advertising agency and asked the agency to design a campaign that would expose a certain target market to their new oriental carpet line. The agency analyzed the target market, designed an attractive advertisement, and placed the ad in various media. The ad-effectiveness scores were quite high. That is, a good percentage of the target market had seen and read the ads. Nevertheless, sales were very poor, and the carpet company wondered why. Several groups of consumers were interviewed and said that the ads were interesting but did not contain enough information for them to spend thousands of dollars for an oriental carpet. (The needs of consumers were not being met.) The agency prepared another campaign that provided information about prices and ways to evaluate oriental carpets. The ads also encouraged people to inspect the large display of carpets at the showroom and ask questions of several experts who were available. The response was very good, and the store owner *and* consumers were both satisfied.

This example shows that measures of ad effectiveness should involve both sellers and buyers. The concepts are:

> **Communication effectiveness is measured by determining whether the seller *and* the buyer are better informed or are closer to reaching their goals as a result of the communication effort.**

> **Effectiveness measures that concentrate on the seller—for example, increased sales or increased consumer awareness—are incomplete in that the goal of marketing communication is mutually satisfying exchanges and the buyer's needs must be given attention.**

PROMOTION As was pointed out in the introduction to this chapter, marketing communication is a two-way exchange of information among marketing participants. **Promotion,** on the other hand, has been traditionally thought of as a one-way flow of information or persuasion designed to move a person or organization closer to the point of making a marketing exchange. Promotion is one of the more important aspects of marketing management. It has been described as a "furthering process," because it advances (furthers) the position of a marketer in some measurable way.

Table 12.1 THREE MODELS OF EXCHANGE DECISION MAKING

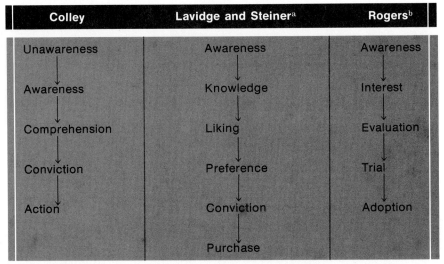

Colley	Lavidge and Steiner[a]	Rogers[b]
Unawareness	Awareness	Awareness
Awareness	Knowledge	Interest
Comprehension	Liking	Evaluation
Conviction	Preference	Trial
Action	Conviction	Adoption
	Purchase	

[a] Robert Lavidge and Gary Steiner, ''A Model for Predictive Measurements of Advertising Effectiveness,'' *Journal of Marketing*, October 1961, pp. 59–62.
[b] Everett M. Rogers, *Diffusion of Innovations* (New York: Free Press of Glencoe, Inc., 1962), pp. 76–120.

Table 12.1 presents three models of the stages through which a consumer (the object of promotion) proceeds before accepting a product or idea. Each of these models emphasizes that the object of promotion is to move the consumer from a state of unawareness to a final exchange commitment. One of these models—that of Colley—will be discussed in greater detail later in this chapter when we get into communication theory. There are other similar models, but regardless of which one is used, the following concepts apply:

> **Promotion is the process of moving a person or organization closer to the point of making a marketing exchange.**

> **Buyers, sellers, and marketing middlemen may perform promotion functions.**

The second concept may need some explanation. It is no doubt clear how sellers can use promotional tools such as advertising and personal selling to further their goals. But many people do not recognize the fact that buyers may use these same tools. For example, a buyer may place a want ad in the newspaper or use his or her selling skills to obtain needed goods or services from others. Buyers and sellers may also turn to communications middlemen such as advertising agencies and selling agents to do their promotional work. Thus, it may be said that buyers, sellers, and middlemen may all be involved in promotion. The objective in each situation is to further the goals of the organization, place, person, or idea being promoted.

The Promotion Mix In the past, advertising, personal selling, public relations, publicity, and sales promotion were viewed as the only elements in the **promotion mix** (see Figure 12.3). But today marketers are becoming more aware of the fact that everything an individual or organization does or says has promotional impact:

More and more it is becoming apparent that marketing is almost entirely communications. The product communicates; the price communicates; the package communicates; salesmen communicate to the prospect, to the trade, to management and to each other; also, prospects, dealers, management, competitors communicate.[9]

Throughout this book we have tried to emphasize the systems approach to marketing. The systems approach to promotion recognizes that all the marketing variables have promotional significance as do all the activities of an organization and its employees. From a systems perspective, everything an organization says or does (or doesn't say or do) is part of a total communications effort that creates either a favorable, unfavorable, or neutral effect on the public. The new corporate position of marketing communications manager enables a firm to create a unified corporate image and communications program.

[9] Marion Harper, Jr., "Communications is the Core of Marketing," *Printer's Ink,* June 1, 1962, p. 53.

Figure 12.3 SOME ELEMENTS OF THE PROMOTION MIX

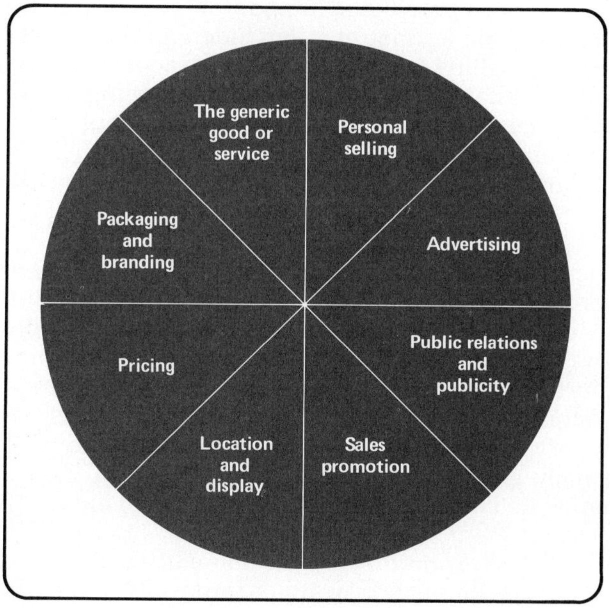

Communications and the Marketing Mix

In the past, promotion was viewed as the firm's communication link with prospective buyers. Today it is becoming increasingly clear that promotion must be viewed as only one part of the firm's overall communications effort with consumers. The roles of price, product, and place are beginning to receive greater attention as communications variables. To view promotion as the sole communications link with consumers is to run the risk of greatly reducing the effectiveness of the firm's total communications program. In some cases, the promotional effort runs counter to the message the consumer receives from product, place, or price.

. . . All marketing mix variables, indeed all company actions, must be considered as parts of the total message the company is attempting to share with consumers about its "offering." Each company action should be considered as a communicative element in the overall communications effort of the firm, and as such, each must be viewed in terms of the other variables and their interactive effects in designing marketing communications strategy.

From M. Wayne DeLozier, *The Marketing Communications Process* (New York: McGraw-Hill Book Company, 1976), p. 163.

Promotional Synergism

Promotional synergism refers to the simultaneous use of separate promotional elements (such as advertising, personal selling, publicity, and sales promotion), such that the total effect of the joint effort is greater than the sum of the effects of the individual efforts. This means that a coordinated and integrated promotional effort is much more effective than a series of independent promotional programs. Therefore, personal selling strategies should be coordinated with advertising strategies. Similarly, pricing, packaging, branding, sales promotion, publicity, public relations, and channel strategies should all be combined to create one unified image and one salable product for desired market segments. The insert "Communications and the Marketing Mix" expands upon this concept.

Nonverbal Promotional Communication

There is a tendency in marketing to think of promotional communications as verbal and written symbols (words). But much of the image generated by marketers comes from what they do, not from what they say. In many instances, actions speak louder than words. For example, courteous, friendly salespeople may mean much more to potential customers of a retail store than ads that stress "friendly service." Or a factory that keeps the grounds around its building attractive and clean usually generates more favorable reaction than one that merely promotes its community spirit. The concepts are:

> › **Nonverbal promotional communication—that is, what a person does—often is as important, or more important, than what a marketer says in a promotional message.**

> **An effective communications program calls for a combination of verbal and nonverbal message cues that convey to the receiver a consistent and clear image that leads to an exchange relationship.**

Nonverbal cues in advertising help support the message in the copy. And nonverbal cues by a salesperson (for example, appearance, gestures, facial expressions) can create a more receptive attitude in a customer. Again, marketers should be aware of both the verbal and nonverbal image they are creating and should work to make all such impressions favorable ones.

Promotion and Communication Theory   Marketing borrows many of its concepts and principles from other academic areas. One area that is particularly beneficial to marketing communicators is communication research and communication theory. Scholars in areas such as journalism, speech, psycholinguistics, psychology, sociology, English, cybernetics, and others have all contributed to our knowledge of communication. One can only briefly explore this rich literature in an introductory marketing text, but you are encouraged to explore these other disciplines if marketing communications interest you.

A classic verbal model of the communication process is that of Harold Lasswell.[10] He says that communication is best understood by answering the following questions:

1. Who?
2. Says what?
3. In which channels?
4. To whom?
5. With what effect?

This model becomes the basis for the following discussion. We shall explore the "who" question in the section on the *source* effect. "Says what?" will be discussed in the section on the *message* effect. "In which channels?" is covered in the section on the *media* effect. "To whom?" is discussed under the *receiver* effect. "With what effect?" is discussed in the section on measuring results. The basic communication model is diagramed in Figure 12.4.

It should be clear as we discuss the following concepts that we shall be viewing the communication process from the viewpoint of the seller. The concepts would be equally valid if we were to look at the process from the viewpoint of the buyer. In fact, the model that best describes the marketing communication process is an exchange model (see Figure 12.5).

This model in Figure 12.5 emphasizes the point that both buyers and

[10] Harold D. Lasswell, "The Structure and Function of Communication in Society," in *Mass Communications*, ed. Wilbur Schramm (Urbana: The University of Illinois Press, 1960), p. 117.

Figure 12.4 BASIC COMMUNICATION MODEL

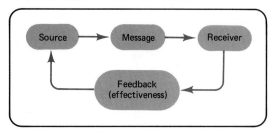

sellers may initiate marketing communications. The idea is to exchange information and to use persuasion to create mutually satisfying relationships. In their attempts to persuade others, both buyers and sellers experience communication problems that are discussed in the following sections.

**Source Effect—
"Who?"** Those who receive promotional messages are likely to have opinions and predispositions regarding the source of a message, and this image affects the ability of the sender to influence the receiver. For example, the source of a sales message may be perceived as the producer of the product, the medium in which the message is presented, or the person actually giving the message. Sources that are viewed as knowledgeable, honest, and reliable are more likely to be viewed favorably. The concept that marketers should follow is:

> **Design the marketing organization's policies, practices, and promotions in such a way that the target market perceives the source as knowledgeable, honest, and reliable; this means there must be careful selection of media and organizational representatives.**

**Message Effect—
"Says What?"** The content and structure of a promotional message also have an effect on the persuasiveness of the promotional effort. There has been much research on message content, but little of it involved field studies of actual promotional messages. For this reason, the conclusions of these studies are not to be held as gospel. Nevertheless, it seems clear that messages that are simply constructed, are clearly stated, and have something to say are more effective than complex, ambiguous statements. Sometimes it is more effective to present both sides of an issue, especially in the case of more highly educated markets. Repetition is often an effective way to reach a selected market, but it can be overdone. Humor also may be overdone (straightforward ads usually outpull

Figure 12.5 EXCHANGE COMMUNICATION MODEL

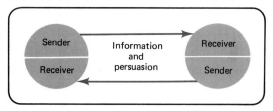

"cute" ads).[11] Further studies done on fear appeals (if you don't buy our new lock, your house will be burglarized), order of presentation (for example, should key points be made early or late?), and other elements of the message have had mixed results. The key concept for marketers is:

> **The structure and content of messages have a significant effect on the persuasiveness of promotions; therefore, design messages with the specific target audience in mind and keep the content simple, honest, and benefit-oriented.**

Media Effect— "In Which Channels?" The promotional vehicles (channels) a marketer uses to reach his target markets may have positive or negative effects on the audience. For example, word of mouth tends to be an effective vehicle for influencing people because the sender is usually perceived as being reliable and believable. Publicity is also effective because the audience usually accepts the opinions and suggestions of media representatives. Personal selling may also be an effective vehicle, but it is very expensive. Advertising is much more efficient, but believability and reliability usually are harder to convey.

Within advertising, certain media and media types can add persuasiveness to a message. For example, a magazine such as *Good Housekeeping* that gives its seal of approval to ads may increase the believability of an advertiser. The selection of a proper vehicle for reaching target audiences is based on these concepts:

> **How to reach a target market is based on the nature and characteristics of the market, the objectives of the promotion, the message itself, and the circumstances surrounding the promotional campaign.**

> **Marketers should obtain some balance between the effectiveness of communication vehicles such as personal selling and the efficiency of competing vehicles such as advertising.**

> **The most effective promotions use a combination of media and communication vehicles including word of mouth, personal selling, advertising, sales promotion, public relations, publicity, display, packaging, and labeling.**

Receiver Effect— "To Whom?" Consumers do not react the same to all promotional messages. They actively avoid some messages (*selective exposure*), they do not believe other messages (*selective perception*), and they tend to forget messages that conflict with their predispositions (*selective retention*). The following three examples illustrate receiver effects.

Allan Kaplan is a moderate smoker (about three-quarters of a pack a day). Allan has heard about the dangerous effects of smoking, but he finds it very hard to quit. Allan actively avoids stories or ads about Smokenders or other stop-smoking clinics.

[11] For other interesting advice on copy, see John Caples, "50 Things I Have Learned in 50 Years in Advertising," *Advertising Age,* September 22, 1975, pp. 47–48.

Allan's avoidance of such messages is an example of selective exposure. It basically means that people will avoid messages that conflict with their beliefs or actions and will seek out messages that support their views.

Joanne Grant is one of many Americans who feel that businesses make "excess" profits. Joanne has a masters degree and reads extensively. She says she has read many ads and articles in *The Wall Street Journal* that say that business does not make profits of 35 percent, as many people suppose, but make closer to 5 percent. Joanne simply does not believe such articles. She has read about the fabulous salaries key corporate people make (in *Business Week*) and has concluded that profits must be excessive in order to pay such salaries. Joanne refuses to discuss the issue (selective exposure) and questions any article that conflicts with her beliefs (selective perception).

Joanne typifies the average American consumer who is skeptical about advertising and obvious corporate publicity. She feels most ads are deceptive and/or misleading and does not trust them. She has much the same attitude toward salespeople.

Joe d'Amico agreed to listen to a speaker from NOW (the National Organization for Women). The speaker outlined several important areas in which NOW has made some impact and discussed several issues of importance to women today. Another speaker spoke briefly against the Equal Rights Amendment (which the NOW speaker supported) and mentioned several points about the rights of men. After the meeting, Joe's wife asked about the meeting. Joe remembered very little about the NOW speaker's points, but he repeated almost by heart the brief talk given by the second speaker. Joe was and is against what he calls "women's lib" and tends to dismiss or forget any arguments counter to his views. This is called *selective retention*.

Joe, Joanne, and Allan are all consumers. Each of them has established beliefs and behavior patterns that are difficult to change. The stories concerning them illustrate how receiver effects can frustrate a person who is trying to communicate. The following summarizes what we've learned of receiver effects:

1. **Selective exposure** means that most people tend to expose themselves to communication (promotions) in which they are interested or that support their existing attitudes or behavior and to avoid communication (promotions) that might be irritating or uninteresting or incompatible with their own attitudes or behavior.[12]
2. **Selective perception** means that under certain conditions people misinterpret or distort a promotional message so that it will be more compatible with their own attitudes, habits, or opinions.[13]
3. **Selective retention** means that people tend to forget those messages that conflict with their views or behavior and remember those that tend to support their predispositions.

[12] Adapted from Donald F. Cox, "Clues for Advertising Strategists," *Harvard Business Review*, November–December 1961, pp. 160–182.
[13] Ibid.

Even when a person has been exposed to a message, correctly perceives the meaning, and remembers the key points, he or she may still resist being influenced by the communicator. How do marketers get through to such people?

The following section explains how marketers are sometimes able to create changes in attitudes and behavior in spite of selective processes. As you will see, sometimes it is best *not* to attempt such changes.

Overcoming Receiver Effects A marketer can sometimes penetrate the barriers of selective exposure, perception, and retention. Some people will never change their attitudes and behavior toward particular subjects, whereas others are quite open to change. Often the idea is to find people who are most likely to change or to appeal to attitudes and behavior that already exist.

How is it that some promotions are very effective in changing people's attitudes and behavior and others are not? For example, why is it so easy to get people to try different restaurants and so difficult to get people to stop smoking? Why do promotions for rock concerts often result in sold-out performances with little effort, whereas promotions for chamber music are so widely ignored?

The concept that seems to explain much of people's acceptance or rejection of change is called degree of commitment.[14] The more strongly people are committed to their attitudes and behavior, the less apt they are to respond to messages that attempt to change them. For example, people who are strongly religious are not likely to pay any attention to the arguments of an atheist.

The question becomes, "How can a marketer change people who are committed to a particular attitude or behavior?" The answer is, "Usually he or she can't!" In fact, a wise marketer does not try to change committed people but instead tries to appeal to already existing attitudes and behavior. But sometimes a marketer wants to change people. For example, some marketers want people to change their attitudes and behavior with regard to smoking, planned parenthood, littering, voting, driving large cars, and so forth. What chance do these people have of successfully changing people and how can they do it? One generalization is that attitudes about an idea, person, organization, or product are more likely to be changed by promotions when the existing information about the subject is relatively scanty.[15] For example, most people know very little about their state senators, and so they are usually quite open to information about a new candidate.

Attitudes and behavior toward relatively unimportant subjects are more likely to change than are attitudes toward important subjects.[16] For example, people are more likely to change their brand of gum or detergent than they are to change their political party or perfume.

Subjects that affect people quite personally are also less susceptible to

[14] See C. W. Sherif and R. E. Nebergall, *Attitude and Attitude Change* (New Haven, Conn.: Yale University Press, 1961).

[15] See T. N. Newcomb, R. H. Turner, and P. E. Converse, *Social Psychology* (New York: Holt, Rinehart and Winston, Inc., 1965), p. 91.

[16] Ibid, p. 92.

change. For example, people are not likely to readily accept radical restructuring of their neighborhood, but they might be in favor of urban renewal in general. Similarly, poor people might be quite receptive to appeals to "tax the rich" until the day when they personally become more wealthy. The concepts are:

> A marketer is most likely to receive a favorable response to his or her promotional efforts if the message supports already exisiting attitudes and behavior.

> People are more likely to change their attitudes and behavior if present behavior is based on scanty knowledge, if the topic is relatively unimportant, or if the change does not affect them personally.

> Generally speaking, it is more effective to "find a need and fill it" than to find a cause and try to get previously disinterested people to support it.

Measuring Results—"With What Effect?" Traditionally, companies have measured promotional results (that is, advertising effectiveness) in terms of sales. The goals of a promotional campaign, for example, might have been "to increase sales by 10 percent in the Los Angeles area." But some people felt that advertising and other promotional efforts (for example, personal selling) only *contributed to* increased sales and were not a direct cause that could be measured.

Russell Colley, prepared a report for the Association of National Advertisers that emphasized the fact that sales were the result of a total *marketing* effort, not just a promotional or advertising effort.[17] Colley suggested that marketers concentrate on the measurement of *communications* goals for advertising. He felt that marketers should measure how effective a given promotional effort was in moving consumers from unawareness to action. His model of exchange decision making, presented earlier in Table 12.1, looks like this:

Unawareness $\longrightarrow$ Awareness $\longrightarrow$ Comprehension $\longrightarrow$ Conviction $\longrightarrow$ Action

According to Colley, each promotional element should have specific communication objectives designed to further people along the decision-making path. One advertising goal, for example, might be to "increase the awareness of Boston men and women between the ages of 25 and 40 that a new instant camera is available from Kodak." That objective is readily measured and would indicate the success or failure of the advertising campaign. Note, however, that the campaign *would not necessarily increase sales*. But it would move people closer to a sale and make it easier for personal selling and display to move people through the decision-making process to "action."

Every promotional tool—personal selling, packaging, public relations, and so on—should have similar, clear-cut objectives. Such objectives could be rather accurately measured, and marketers could gain more control over the promotional process. They could also understand better

[17] R. H. Colley, *Defining Advertising Goals for Measured Advertising Results* (New York: Association of National Advertisers, 1961).

the relationships between promotional elements and the contributions of each. This could lead to more effective and efficient promotional efforts.

The best way to get the coordination and integration of promotion called for in Colley's paper is to have a marketing communications manager such as described earlier. Such a manager could develop a comprehensive promotional program. Colley called his system DAGMAR, which means "Defining Advertising Goals for Measured Advertising Results." His concepts could be expanded to form several key concepts:

> **Every promotional element should have specific communication objectives; those objectives should be measured in light of their contribution to, rather than their direct effect on, sales.**

> **Because marketing communications, including promotional communications, are designed to create mutually satisfying exchanges, promotional effectiveness must measure consumer satisfaction as well as contribution to sales.**

In the following chapters, we shall look at some promotional elements in more detail. Special attention will be given advertising, personal selling, public relations, publicity, and sales promotion because these elements are the heart of most promotional strategies. As you read those chapters, keep in mind that the goal of all marketing promotional efforts is the establishment of mutually satisfying exchanges.

FOR REVIEW

Key Terms

Among the more important terms and expressions discussed in this chapter are the following:

Marketing communications are those communication activities performed by both the buyer and seller that aid marketing decision making and lead to more satisfying exchanges by making all participants more aware and better informed.

Promotion is basically a one-way flow of information or persuasion designed to move a person or organization closer to the point of making a marketing exchange.

Promotional mix refers to the particular combination of elements (advertising, personal selling, public relations, and so forth) used by an organization as part of its promotional strategy.

Promotional synergism refers to the simultaneous use of separate promotional elements such that the total effect of the joint effort is greater than the sum of the effects of the individual efforts.

Selective exposure means that most people tend to expose themselves to communication (promotions) in which they are interested or that support their existing attitudes or behavior and to avoid communication (promotions) that might be irritating or uninteresting or incompatible with their own attitudes or behavior.

Selective perception means that under certain conditions people misinterpret or distort a promotional message so that it will be more compatible with their own attitudes, habits, or opinions.

Selective retention means that people tend to forget those messages that conflict with their views or behavior and remember those that tend to support their predispositions.

Key Concepts

Among the more important marketing concepts introduced in this chapter are the following:

› Marketing communications aid both buyers and sellers by: (1) establishing exchange contacts; (2) maintaining flows of information that enable an exchange to occur; (3) creating aware and informed buyers and sellers who are more likely to negotiate a satisfactory exchange; and (4) improving decision making in marketing so that the whole exchange process is made more effective and efficient.

› Marketing communication is a two-way exchange of information (and sometimes persuasion) between marketing participants.

› For an effective communication system, listening (and then doing something about the information you hear) is often more important than talking.

› Buyers need not wait for someone to recognize their needs; instead, they should make their needs known through effective marketing communication and should maintain their communication efforts until their needs are met.

› Communication effectiveness is measured by determining whether the seller *and* the buyer are better informed or are closer to reaching their goals as a result of the communication effort.

› The most effective promotions use a combination of media and communication vehicles including word of mouth, personal selling, advertising, sales promotion, public relations, publicity, display, packaging, and labeling.

› A marketer is most likely to receive a favorable response to his or her promotional efforts if the message supports already existing attitudes and behavior.

› An effective communication program calls for a combination of verbal and nonverbal message cues that convey to the receiver a consistent and clear image that leads to an exchange relationship.

Discussion Questions

1. Explain the difference between marketing communication and promotion, using a college as your example.
2. Discuss how your local movie theatre might benefit by having someone in charge of listening as well as promotion.
3. Show in a diagram where people like Ralph Nader and other con-

sumer spokespersons fit into the marketing multilogue (see Figure 12.2).

4. Prepare a statement explaining why marketing communications is or is not the most important marketing function.

5. Explain the function of a marketing communications manager in a firm that has product managers.

6. How would a manager of marketing communications benefit a nonprofit organization such as your local church or temple?

7. Give at least two examples of how you, as a buyer, used your communication skills to get what you wanted from a seller.

8. How would you measure the effectiveness of a promotion for a new play in town?

9. Give examples of situations in which your friends have practiced selective exposure, selective perception, and selective retention.

10. List as many promotional tools as you can think of that could be used by your local dog pound to find homes for stray animals.

CASES

An Income Tax Service
Communicating with the Market

Betty Lassuten has her own income-tax preparation service that is located on the outskirts of a major southeastern city. The location is convenient to both city and suburban residents. Betty has a good reputation among her clients and is doing a relatively good volume of business each year. But Betty wants to increase her business, and she wants to spread it out more evenly between January and April. Most of her clients seem to come in late March and early April.

1. How could Betty communicate her need for a more balanced demand and create more business for herself as well?

2. Betty now advertises in the city newspapers and has a store sign on a main commuter street. What other promotional tools would you recommend she use? Would you recommend continued use of the newspaper?

3. Most of Betty's clients have relatively simple income-tax needs. Betty wants to service wealthy people who have more complex needs. How could Betty communicate with that market? Would you recommend that she pursue such clients? Why or why not?

4. Could Betty benefit by listening more to the public's wants and needs? Why or why not?

A College AMA Chapter
Promoting Professional Meetings

Paul Thompson is president of his college's chapter of the American Marketing Association. The college chapter is designed to create an interface between marketing majors and the business community. Various business leaders are invited to visit the college to discuss topics such as careers in retailing, the marketing research function, media-selection strategies, and other key subjects.

The meetings are held in the late afternoon at 4:00 P.M. because most students are finished with classes by then. Paul is responsible for getting speakers, arranging for a meeting room, providing refreshments, and publicizing the meetings to students. Most meetings are promoted through announcements in marketing classes and signs in the business building.

The problem for Paul is that the college is attended mostly by commuters from nearby cities, and many students go home before 4:00 P.M. Paul often has fewer than twenty students at the meetings.

1. Discuss how Paul could use marketing communication concepts to get more people to come to the meetings and to participate actively in the college chapter.

2. What promotional tools could Paul use besides announcements and signs. He has no promotional funds.

3. Using the concept of "find a need and fill it" for a base, list what needs Paul is and is not filling for students. How could Paul better meet student needs?

Advertising
reaching mass markets

LEARNING GOALS

After you have read and studied this chapter, you should be able to:

1. Give examples of ads that (1) inform, (2) persuade, (3) create an image, and (4) satisfy the needs of buyers and sellers.

2. Define the following terms: advertising; information utility; product analysis.

3. Report how much is spent on advertising in the United States in total and list the most important media in order.

4. Describe the role of an ad agency.

5. Explain how ad agencies are compensated by a firm that has an agency prepare its ads.

6. List the advantages and disadvantages of the leading media.

7. Explain how to effectively use signs, window displays, and internal displays.

8. Show how a nonprofit organization can further its goals by using advertising concepts.

9. Explain how advertising benefits both sellers and buyers by making the communication function more efficient.

> *Never write an advertisement you wouldn't want your own family to read. You wouldn't tell lies to your own wife. Don't tell them to mine.*
>
> David Ogilvy*

INTRODUCTION There are several ways to view the role of advertising in a society. One view is that advertising is a relatively inexpensive way to transmit *information*. Advertising thus adds information utility (value) to product offers. Another view is that advertising is a means of *persuasion*. The costly efforts by many advertisers to persuade the public to buy or try a product is evidence of advertising's persuasive function. A third view is that advertising is a means for *creating an image*. "Advertising always has the short-range task of creating some immediate action," says Pierre Martineau. "But it always has a far more important long-range goal—to create a rich, positive product image or institutional image. . . ."[1] A fourth view, and the one emphasized in this book, is that advertising is *a means for satisfying the needs of both buyers and sellers*. From this perspective, advertising informs, persuades, and creates images in order to create exchanges that will satisfy people's needs.

Before taking a detailed look at these functions of advertising, we should say something about what it is and is not. **Advertising** has been defined as "paid, nonpersonal communication through various media by business firms, nonprofit organizations and individuals who are in some way identified in the advertising message and who hope to [communicate with] members of a particular audience."[2] Note that advertising is paid for; advertising that is published free because of its newsworthy content is called **publicity**. Note also that advertising may be used by anyone, including nonprofit organizations. In addition, it is a tool of the *buyer* and the *seller*. Furthermore, advertising is different from propaganda in that the promoter is identified. The goal of advertising should be to *communicate with* people rather than to persuade them to do something without taking their wants, needs, and opinions into consideration.

FUNCTIONS OF ADVERTISING

Advertising Provides Information

Economists have placed great emphasis on time, place, form, and possession utility—and for good reasons. A product is worth more to a person when he can get it any time, at a convenient place, and charge it on a credit card. It is also obvious that form utility (for example, changing rubber into tires) adds value to a product. But what is less obvious and given little attention in the literature is the value of information to the consumer.

* *Confessions of an Advertising Man* (New York: Atheneum, 1963), p. 99.
[1] Pierre Martineau, *Motivation in Advertising* (New York: McGraw-Hill Book Company, 1957), p. 199.
[2] Adapted from S. Watson Dunn and Arnold M. Barban, *Advertising: Its Role in Modern Marketing*, 3rd ed. (Hinsdale, Ill.: The Dryden Press, 1974), p. 7.

This ad creates a favorable impression for the firm and provides information as well

With each new life begins an insatiable urge to communicate.

To live. To breathe. To love. To understand. To be understood.

These compelling human needs greet every newborn child, grow more intense with every passing year and, though constantly fulfilled, never become less demanding.

Yet of all the fundamental needs, it can be said that the abilities to understand, to reason, to communicate are the things that separate humankind from all other forms of life.

We at United Telecom are in the business of communications. In fact, every day we help millions of people in nearly 3,000 communities talk to each other through United Telephone, the nation's 3rd largest telephone system.

And in this year of the Bicentennial we think it particularly fitting to remember one other inherent drive. One that is called an inalienable right. One that is too often repressed.

To be free.

United Telecom
United Telecommunications, Inc.

We operate the United Telephone System, America's 3rd largest.

United Telecommunications, Inc., P.O. Box 11315, Plaza Station, Kansas City, Missouri 64112.

Reprinted with permission of United Telecom.

Let's review an example we have used before. Suppose that a new play called *Bizarre* was coming to town. How much would you be willing to spend to see that play? Until you received more information, you might not be willing to pay anything. But if you were told in an advertisement that the play was a very successful comedy that had played for 3 years

325

on Broadway to rave reviews, you might pay quite a bit to go. You might pay even more if you learned from the ad that a famous person was starring and would give autographs afterward. The concept is:

> Advertising adds value to products by providing information to consumers.

Of course, some ads provide much more information than others, but the mere mention of a product, its price, and availability provides information of value to consumers. The value created by advertising may be called **information utility**. Advertising adds value to products by telling people what the product is, what it can be used for, where it is available, who else has it, and other such information. Without such information, people would not be willing to spend as much (that is, they would not recognize all the value in products).

One indication that advertising's primary role is that of providing information is the fact that advertisers as a whole spend more dollars in newspapers than in any other medium. If you analyze newspaper advertising, you will find that most of the ads are used to inform consumers of the availability of certain products at certain prices at certain locations. The purpose is usually not to persuade, but only to inform. In the classified section, you will find that buyers have placed ads looking for products they need and sellers have placed ads trying to sell products. Newspapers thus provide a forum in which buyers and sellers can make their wants and needs known to others. If you were to eliminate this forum, local markets would become very inefficient unless radio or some other advertising medium could assume the informational role that newspapers have taken. The concept is:

> Advertising provides a means for sellers and buyers to *inform* one another about their wants and needs so that those needs can be met through mutually satisfying market exchanges.

Advertising Persuades   Some advertising not only *informs* audiences of the availability of products (as in newspapers), but also tries to *persuade* potential buyers that one product will satisfy their needs better than a similar product. The role of persuasion is more likely to involve the medium of television or magazines.

A thorough analysis of advertising in the United States would reveal that more effort and money is spent on informing people of the supply of, and the demand for, goods, ideas, and services than is spent on persuasion. People usually do not need to be persuaded to buy products that clearly satisfy their wants and needs. But when two products seem to meet a need equally, the sellers are likely to spend much time and effort persuading people that their product is better. Often some of that money would be better spent in *making* the product better rather than in merely saying that it *is* better.

Persuasive advertising has caused considerable criticism from certain individuals and groups. They feel that advertising is being used to

Advertising Provides Consumer Information

Man's earliest attempts to satisfy his needs consisted of hunting or searching for game or for natural objects which were suitable for his purpose. That type of initiative from the ultimate user of a product is still very much in evidence, but today it is exerted mainly through the available channels of trade. Usually, this means searching by the consumer through the displays or stocks of accessible retail stores. . . . The search activity of the shopper is facilitated by retail advertising.

From Wroe Alderson, *Marketing Behavior and Executive Action* (Homewood, Ill.: Richard D. Irwin, Inc., 1957), p. 15.

manipulate, deceive, and exploit innocent consumers. There was an especially vocal group opposed to such advertising directed at children. In fact, there were several actions taken by the Federal Trade Commission and the advertising industry to minimize such advertising to children.

But many people also feel that it was advertising that persuaded the public to buy big cars, to be generally materialistic, and to be morally and mentally corrupt. Such people give advertising more credit and power than it deserves. It is very difficult to change people through the media.

If you have ever tried to *persuade* someone to change political parties, religious attitudes, or brands of cigarettes, you know how resistant people are to persuasion of even the most logical sort. The concepts are:

> • People resist attempts to change their attitudes, activities, and beliefs; therefore, self-centered persuasive messages usually fail to change people or to create exchanges.

> • Buyers do not buy simply because they are manipulated by the seller; they buy because they perceive the exchange as creating more value than they would have without an exchange: Advertising does not force people to do anything.

It is often socially beneficial to *try* to change people's attitudes and behavior, although most such attempts are not very successful. For example, advertising has been used to remind parents to have their children immunized against childhood diseases; to encourage people to stop smoking, to love their neighbor, and go to church; to guide teenagers to more nutritional eating habits; and to urge people to plan the size of their families. In such cases, persuasive messages would be welcomed by many people in society. Still, it is very difficult to *persuade* people to do anything with advertising—even when it is for their own good and the good of society. This is what one leading marketing scholar has to say about persuasive ads:

A primary application for advertising is in helping the individual to overcome his confusion and uncertainty as to relative values. Advertis-

Mobil Oil went to the people with this ad to explain the natural gas shortage and the need to decontrol the price of gas.

328

> **Various Advertising Theories**
>
> There are a number of theories about advertising and the way it works. Some of these theories hold that advertising makes its impact by conveying information, but most recognize that persuasion is an essential part of its function. There are many variations in the persuasive theory of advertising with respect to the relative importance of rational and irrational appeals and the interaction of information and persuasion. The present view suggests that the consumer should be approached primarily as a problem solver who must first be convinced that he has a problem and then that the product offered will facilitate a solution.

From Wroe Alderson, *Marketing Behavior and Executive Action* (Homewood, Ill.: Richard D. Irwin, Inc., 1957), p. 260.

ing messages can help to persuade him that a given activity is really the best one for him and that he has chosen this activity in its most agreeable form relative to others. . . . It can help him relate this activity to other aspects of his style of living and to his more fundamental life objectives.[3]

Imp.   Advertising Defined.

Advertising thus performs two basic functions: (1) providing information and (2) attempting to persuade people to act on that information. But advertising is also a means for creating images and for establishing mutually satisfying exchanges.

Advertising Creates Images Advertising today is much more than the presentation of a few facts and figures to make a point. It does not rely on words and logical arguments alone to "win the customer over." Instead, advertising uses a variety of techniques and images to create a *favorable impression* with viewers. Besides appealing to a person's basic sense of values through price appeals and quality claims, advertising also stresses beauty of design, pride of ownership, increase in status, and other noneconomic appeals.

The creators of advertising messages have at their disposal many techniques and tools to create product images. They can use color and sound, artwork and photographs, illustration and layout, and well-known people to dramatize and glamourize product offers. In attempting to capture the market, sellers often rely more on such gimmicks than they do on good products designed to satisfy recognized needs. And often they succeed, but they succeed only once! People will often buy a new this or that for a couple of dollars to "give it a try." They do this mostly because they saw it on TV or heard about it from a friend (who saw it on TV). But will they buy it again? Not unless the product offers them good value and partially satisfies their needs.

Much criticism is today directed at marketers for emphasizing nonrational, noneconomic appeals in their ads. But whether we think it is

[3] Wroe Alderson, *Marketing Behavior and Executive Action* (Homewood, Ill.: Richard D. Irwin, Inc., 1957), p. 287.

right to do so or not, people buy many, if not most, products because having the product makes them feel good rather than because they need it or because of its durability and reliability. For example, many best-selling liquors are the more expensive brands, not necessarily because they taste better but because *they say something about the buyer.* Many people also choose cigarettes, cars, homes, clothes, and other visible signs of "making it" not on the basis of economic value per se, but on social values as well.

Other sellers can offer the buyer a product offer with similar ingredients or at a better price, but they can rarely match the nonrational, noneconomic appeal of an established brand. The marketing concepts behind this discussion are:

> People buy products and accept ideas for a variety of reasons (rational and nonrational, economic and noneconomic); advertising reflects their preferences by creating images for products that satisfy these different needs.

> Product differentiation for a product is created by advertising as much as by physical changes in the factory, and much of the differentiation is created by imagery.

> Marketing success depends on good products that meet people's needs; advertising images add to the value of products by showing people how particular products will enhance their economic or social well-being.

Remember that the product is what the consumer thinks it is. An important function of the advertiser is to show consumers that a particular product is the answer to their needs. It is shocking today to see what junk people buy to satisfy their needs, but the fault is not with advertising—it is with people's tastes, values, and judgment. Part of the responsibility of social marketing is to raise people's standards through consumer information and education. We shall discuss this point in greater detail in Chapter 19.

Advertising Satisfies Needs People can get so involved with arguments about the style and techniques used in advertising that they forget its basic purpose: To create the flows of information that enable buyers and sellers to satisfy their wants and needs efficiently through market exchanges. Sometimes people need to be *informed* before they can intelligently select products. For example, they need to know more about nutrition, additives, and prices before they can choose the best foods for their families.

Sometimes people need to be *persuaded* to do things that are good for them or for society. They must often be persuaded to brush their teeth; to help the poor, the sick, and the aged; and to get a good education.

Usually the most persuasive ads are those that use imagery to convey to people a mood or a feeling that prompts them to act. For example, the image of an innocent little girl struggling to learn how to walk with crutches may encourage people to donate funds to an appropriate charity.

But information, persuasion, and imagery are all *means* used to

> **Advertising Agencies and Product Images**
>
> When a product which is not completely new changes its advertising agency, what actually is the agency's real assignment? The ingredients of the product will rarely be changed. Pricing, packaging, and distribution won't be changed. It is the product image which the advertising is expected to change—its collar of purely psychological meanings. Same product, same appropriation, same physical everything—but presumably it can be invested with new desirabilities. The perfectly obvious course . . . will be to fill in the image with many other meanings beside the mere rational claims about what the product can do.

From Pierre Martineau, *Motivation in Advertising* (New York: McGraw-Hill Book Company, 1957), pp. 150–151.

accomplish an *end,* and that end is a mutually satisfying marketing exchange. Advertising is one of the most efficient communication tools marketers have. They should use it to best serve other individuals, society, and themselves. There should be no toleration of deception or fraud in advertising or any other phase of marketing. Many laws, self-regulating agencies, and consumer groups attempt to minimize such practices. The guiding concepts are:

> **Advertising is a marketing tool that facilitates communication among marketing participants.**

> **Information, persuasion, and imagery are all important aspects of effective advertising messages.**

> **The goal of advertising is the efficient creation of marketing exchanges through communication.**

> **Deception and fraud in advertising hinder the creation of mutually satisfying exchanges and are thus antimarketing; therefore, one objective of advertisers should be to minimize such practices.**

Advertising as a Communication Tool Advertising is a tool for opening two-way communication between sellers and buyers, so that the needs of both are clearly presented and satisfied in the most efficient and effective way possible; such communication will lead the way to mutually satisfying marketing exchanges.

There is no question that advertising in the past has been used by marketers to attempt to change or persuade the public to act in accordance with the will of the seller. But more and more we see consumers and consumer advocates using advertising as a tool to improve the market position of *buyers*. For example, Ralph Nader uses advertising to raise money for his consumer causes. Consumers also use advertising to find jobs, locate lost items, complain about faulty merchandise and poor marketing practices, and persuade politicians to pass more consumer-oriented legislation.

The problem is that consumerism today is mostly negative—*against* dangerous products, *against* unfair marketing practices, *against* mo-

Advertising to Find a Mate

Bob Kemper, Jr., found that advertising can be an effective way to find a potential wife. He placed an ad in the Miami Herald that said in part:

> Wife Wanted. I want a wife. A wife who will be my friend too. It's a bit unusual to advertise for a wife—but there's no time for the conventional methods, you know, social clubs, pubs, singles trips, cruises and the "computer." What's a fella to do when time is running out and he hasn't found his life's companion? ADVERTISE!!! (His picture was at the bottom).

Mr. Kemper got 1,000 or so letters from all over the world. He will be busy for some time sorting out the letters and calling the most likely prospects. Hopefully he will be able to make a mutually satisfying marriage with one of the respondents.

From "Wife Ad Replies Pour In," *Advertising Age*, October 27, 1975, p. 78.

nopoly power. For this reason, consumers are often put in the position of being against business, government, and other institutions. Advertising is used by them to attempt to persuade others of their "rights" and their causes.

If we are to end the conflicts between and among consumers, businesses, government, and other organizations, we must learn to *work with* one another, and advertising is one very efficient and effective tool for opening such dialogues.

This discussion is not meant to show that advertising should not be used to inform and persuade. It is meant to show that advertising begins with listening—listening to the wants, needs, and objections of the other party. The persuasive messages are then designed to show others that what they want is now available because someone was listening to them. Furthermore, advertising should be thought of as a tool available to everyone who wants to get his ideas known:

True, [advertising's] communication function has been confined largely to informing and persuading people in respect to products and services. On the other hand, it can be made equally available to those who wish to inform and persuade people in respect to a city bond issue, cleaning up community crime, the "logic" of atheism, the needs for better education facilities, the abusive tactics of given law and enforcement officers, or any other sentiment held by any individual who wishes to present such sentiment to the public.[4]

[4] C. H. Sandage, "Using Advertising to Implement the Concept of Freedom of Speech," in C. H. Sandage and V. Fryburger (eds), *The Role of Advertising* (Homewood, Ill.: Richard D. Irwin, Inc., 1960), pp. 222–223.

The advertising council participates in many education efforts. This ad was prepared in cooperation with the U.S. Department of Health, Education, and Welfare.

ONE-SEVENTH OF YOUR EMPLOYEES MAY BE DYING. HELP SAVE THEIR LIVES.

High Blood Pressure is the country's leading contributor to stroke, heart disease and kidney failure. Any of which can kill.

And, one out of every seven of your workers has it. Half have no idea they're walking around with this time bomb inside them: there are usually no symptoms.

But you can help. By sending for a special kit, "Guidelines for High Blood Pressure Control Programs in Business and Industry." Write to: National High Blood Pressure Education Program, 120/80, National Institutes of Health, Room 1012—Landow Bldg., Bethesda, Md. 20014.

HIGH BLOOD PRESSURE.
Treat it...and live.

**The National High Blood Pressure Education Program,
U.S. Department of Health, Education, and Welfare.**

A Public Service of this Magazine & The Advertising Council

Courtesy of the Advertising Council, Inc.

THE SCOPE AND COST OF ADVERTISING Now that you have some idea of the functions of advertising, you should know something about advertising institutions and the media they use. The balance of this chapter will deal primarily with these topics. However, before we begin our discussion of advertising institutions, we should make you aware of just how big the advertising business is.

Advertising Volume in the United States Advertisers in the United States now spend over $35 billion per year. As you probably have noticed, those companies that spend the most on national advertising are in industries where product innovation is frequent and product differentiation often is small. For example, in 1975, Procter & Gamble, which produces many food and soap products, spent over $360 million on advertising. Other big spenders are in industries such as drugs, automobiles, cosmetics, and tobacco. For example, in 1975, Sterling Drug, Inc., spent over $69 million on advertising, Philip

Morris, Inc., spent almost $100 million, and Ford Motor Co. spent over $91 million (see Table 13.1).

In 1975, the top hundred national advertisers spent a total of over $6 billion. This means that about $22 billion was spent by millions of other businesses, nonprofit groups, and individuals in all the different media. Table 13.2 will give you a better feel for where advertising monies are being spent.

Reach and Cost of National Advertising Advertisers often spend what seems like an unbelievable amount of money on TV ads, but the figures show that such advertising may be a real bargain. For example, a 1-minute ad during the telecast of Super-bowl IX (the 1974–1975 pro football championship game) cost $107,000. This seems like a tremendous amount of money for a 1-minute commercial. But Nielsen estimated that over 71 million people watched the game.[5] That means that the advertisers were able to talk with 1,000 sports-minded people for only $1.50. In what other way could a sponsor reach such a vast audience for so little money?

Advertisements are often costly to make as well as run: One ad for H. J. Heinz Co.'s "Great American" soups is estimated to have cost $200,000 to produce. One reason ads are so expensive is the cost of talent. Football star Joe Namath is reported to have signed a $5-million contract to do ads for Fabergé.[6] Margaux Hemingway also was reported to have signed a 5-year contract for $1 million to promote Fabergé. One can easily see how costly it may be to produce and run a 1-minute commercial on TV.

In spite of the seemingly large amount of money spent by firms on advertising, this amount as a percent of sales tends to float slightly over *1 percent!* For example, in 1967–1968, it was 1.17 percent, in 1968–1969, 1.16 percent, in 1969–1970, 1.13 percent, in 1971–1972, 1.08 percent and in 1972–1973, 1.06 percent. As might be expected, some industries spend much more. For example, in 1972–1973, the drug industry spent 7.78 percent, soaps, cleaners, and toilet goods, 8.79 percent, and the tobacco industry, 4.37 percent. Other industries spend considerably less. Meat products spent 0.36 percent of sales on advertising, life insurance, 0.25 percent, and repair services (not auto), 0.55 percent.[7] The basic concept is:

> ➤ National TV advertising is very expensive in terms of total dollars, but when measured by the cost of reaching 1,000 people or as a percent of sales, it is a very efficient and effective way to get a message to the people.

[5] These figures come from James P. Forkan, "NFL, College Pack in Sponsors Despite Price Tag, Competition," *Advertising Age,* August 18, 1975, p. 3.

[6] *Advertising Age,* October 13, 1975, p. 3.

[7] See "Percentage of Sales Invested in Advertising in 1972–1973," *Advertising Age,* October 20, 1975, p. 74.

Table 13.1 100 LEADING NATIONAL ADVERTISERS (AD DOLLARS IN MILLIONS, 1975)

#	Advertiser	$	#	Advertiser	$	#	Advertiser	$
1	Procter & Gamble Co.	$360.0	35	Goodyear Tire & Rubber Co.	67.8	69	H. J. Heinz Co.	34.0
2	General Motors Corp.	225.0	36	Pillsbury Co.	65.4	70	Seven-Up Co.	33.4
2	Sears, Roebuck & Co.	225.0	37	Beatrice Foods Co.	64.0	71	American Motors Corp.	32.9
4	General Foods Corp.	203.0	38	Seagram Co. Ltd.	63.0	72	Pfizer, Inc.	32.0
5	Bristol-Myers Co.	170.0	39	Kellogg Co.	60.8	73	Toyota Motor Sales U.S.A.	31.5
6	Warner-Lambert Co.	169.0	40	Loews Corp.	60.5	74	North American Philips Corp.	31.0
7	American Home Products Corp.	138.0	41	Ralston Purina Co.	60.0	75	Nissan Motor Corp. U.S.A.	30.8
8	Mobil Corp.	135.9	42	CBS, Inc.	57.2	76	Polaroid Corp.	30.5
9	R. J. Reynolds Industries	113.6	43	Brown & Williamson Tobacco Co.	57.0	77	Carnation Co.	30.3
10	U.S. Government	113.4	44	Schering-Plough Corp.	56.0	78	Exxon Corp.	30.2
11	Colgate Palmolive Co.	108.0	45	Johnson & Johnson	55.5	79	Thomas J. Lipton, Inc.	30.0
12	Heublein, Inc.	103.7	46	Eastman Kodak Co.	55.2	80	American Express Co.	29.5
13	American Tel. & Tel. Co.	101.7	47	Gulf & Western Industries, Inc.	55.0	81	Trans World Airlines	28.1
14	Philip Morris, Inc.	99.5	48	Liggett Group, Inc.	53.0	82	Block Drug Co.	28.0
15	Chrysler Corp.	98.2	48	Greyhound Corp.	53.0	83	Clorox Co.	26.7
16	Richardson-Merrell, Inc.	94.5	50	Chesebrough-Pond's, Inc.	50.0	84	Kimberly-Clark Corp.	26.6
17	General Mills	94.0	51	Campbell Soup Co.	49.0	85	Time, Inc.	26.2
18	Ford Motor Co.	91.0	52	SmithKline Corp.	47.8	86	Royal Crown Cola Co.	25.7
19	RCA Corp.	89.0	53	CPC International	46.5	87	Hiram Walker-Gooderham & Worts Ltd.	24.8
20	Norton Simon, Inc.	86.4	54	Rapid-American Corp.	46.1	88	UAL, Inc.	24.6
21	Lever Bros.	85.0	55	Miles Laboratories	46.0	89	National Distillers & Chemical Corp.	24.0
22	Gillette Co.	84.0	56	Revlon, Inc.	45.9	90	American Airlines	23.9
23	Nabisco, Inc.	80.7	57	Borden, Inc.	43.6	91	Wm. Wrigley Jr. Co.	23.4
24	Kraftco Corp.	76.6	58	Anheuser-Busch, Inc.	43.0	92	Mars, Inc.	22.3
25	Coca-Cola Co.	75.3	59	Hanes Corp.	42.5	93	Mattell, Inc.	21.0
26	McDonald's Corp.	75.0	59	Jos. Schlitz Brewing Co.	42.5	94	Pan American World Airways	20.5
27	American Cyanamid Co.	74.0	61	Morton-Norwich Products	38.6	95	Squibb Corp.	20.1
27	American Brands	74.0	62	Esmark	38.0	96	Delta Air Lines	19.3
29	Int'l. Tel. & Tel. Corp.	73.1	63	Volkswagen of America	37.8	97	Scott Paper Co.	19.1
30	Standard Brands, Inc.	72.0	64	Carter-Wallace	37.3	98	Noxell Corp.	19.0
31	PepsiCo, Inc.	70.0	65	S. C. Johnson & Son	36.0	99	Shell Oil Co.	18.5
31	General Electric Co.	70.0	65	Nestle Co.	36.0	100	Mazda Motors of America, Inc.	18.1
33	Sterling Drug, Inc.	69.0	67	Quaker Oats Co.	35.6		**All advertising totals are for U.S. only.**	
34	J. C. Penney Co.	68.0	68	Union Carbide Corp.	35.5			

Reprinted with permission from the August 23, 1976, issue of *Advertising Age*. Copyright 1976 by Crain Communications, Inc.

Table 13.2 ADVERTISING VOLUME IN THE UNITED STATES, 1975 AND 1976

Medium	1975 (Revised) Millions	1975 (Revised) Percent of total	1976 (Preliminary) Millions	1976 (Preliminary) Percent of total	Percent change
Newspapers					
Total	$ 8,442	29.9	$10,022	30.0	+18.7
National	1,221	4.3	1,480	4.4	+21.2
Local	7,221	25.6	8,542	25.6	+18.3
Magazines					
Total	1,465	5.2	1,775	5.3	+21.2
Weeklies	612	2.2	750	2.2	+22.5
Women's	368	1.3	455	1.4	+23.6
Monthlies	485	1.7	570	1.7	+17.5
Farm publications	74	0.3	85	0.3	+15.0
Television					
Total	5,263	18.6	6,575	19.7	+24.9
Network	2,306	8.2	2,785	8.3	+20.8
Spot	1,623	5.7	2,125	6.4	+30.9
Local	1,334	4.7	1,665	5.0	+24.8
Radio					
Total	1,980	7.0	2,228	6.7	+12.5
Network	83	0.3	104	0.3	+25.0
Spot	436	1.5	488	1.5	+12.0
Local	1,461	5.2	1,636	4.9	+12.0
Direct mail	4,181	14.8	4,725	14.1	+13.0
Business publications	919	3.3	1,020	3.0	+11.0
Outdoor					
Total	335	1.2	388	1.2	+16.0
National	220	0.8	255	0.8	+16.0
Local	115	0.4	133	0.4	+16.0
Miscellaneous					
Total	5,571	19.7	6,602	19.8	+18.5
National	2,882	10.2	3,418	10.2	+18.6
Local	2,689	9.5	3,184	9.6	+18.4
Total					
National	15,410	54.6	18,260	54.6	+ 18.5
Local	12,820	45.4	15,160	45.4	+ 18.3
GRAND TOTAL	$28,230	100.0	$33,420	100.0	+ 18.4

Reprinted with permission from the December 27, 1976, issue of *Advertising Age*, p. 46. Copyright 1976 by Crain Communications, Inc.

ADVERTISING INSTITUTIONS Advertising is such an important marketing function that many middlemen have emerged to specialize in various advertising activities. For example, there are specialists in writing creative copy (advertising boutiques), in media buying, in advertising research, and in art, photography, and other related activities. Of key importance are full-function advertising agencies (that is, agencies that perform all these activities) and advertising departments at various organizations. The following material discusses these advertising institutions.

Advertising Agencies Most of the ads that you are most familiar with were not prepared by the companies whose products are advertised. Instead, the ads were prepared by an advertising agency. The question that immediately comes to mind is, "Why don't companies prepare their own ads rather than have them done by an outside agency?" The answer in a greatly simplified form is that (1) agency people are usually more skilled in advertising management and (2) ad agencies do much of their work for free.

The second point needs some explanation, because many people are confused by the way agencies earn their income. Ad agencies were originally sales agents for the various media. That is, they bought space or time at one price and sold it to advertisers at a higher price. The difference between what agents paid for advertising space and time and what they sold it for was called a commission. But what does this have to do with free services?

At first, ad agencies did nothing for advertisers but sell them space or time in the media. But over time different agencies began to offer additional services to "differentiate their product." One agency would offer to write the ad for the advertiser. Another would counter by writing the ad and preparing pictures. Another agency would do these things plus do market research, prepare media studies, and perform several other services.

Note that the source of income for ad agencies remained the same through all of this! They still earned their pay by buying advertising space and time at a given price and then charging the advertiser a higher price. The price paid by an agency is generally 15 percent less than the price they charge advertisers. In essence then, ad agencies work for advertisers, but they get their income from the media! A strange relationship, indeed.

Another question that arises is, "Why don't advertisers get similar discounts from the media?" The answer is that advertisers cannot get the 15 percent discount from media because they are not "agents" of the media. So if advertisers were to buy space or time directly from the media, they would *pay the same as they would if they went through an agency.* But the agency provides many services to advertisers that buy through them. That is why the services of an ad agency are considered "free" for the advertiser and why most manufacturers use ad agencies.

The mathematics of the agency relationships look like this, assuming the advertiser wanted a $100,000 ad on television:

$$
\begin{array}{rl}
\text{Cost of ad to advertiser} = & \$100,000 \\
\text{Cost of ad to agency } (-15\%) = & \underline{85,000} \\
\text{Agency commission} = & \$15,000
\end{array}
$$

The agency makes its 15 percent commission every time the ad is run! So if a $100,000 ad for a particular product were to run three times during a TV program, the agency would make $15,000 each time the ad is run, or $45,000. Of course, not all of that is profit because the agency must pay copywriters, artists, and others on their staff plus rent, other overhead, and so forth.

Without advertising, you'd pay a lot more for a lot less.

Yesterday's black & white 6" TV: around $300.   **Today's black & white 12" TV: under $90.**

A lot of people think advertising adds to the cost of things. If that were true, you'd pay over $300 for a 6" TV instead of under $90 for a 12" TV. How advertising and our free enterprise system help reduce the cost is what this ad is about.

Advertising expands the market.

The first televisions were costly. An expensive gimmick, most people thought. But advertising explained how television worked. What it would bring into people's homes. And fired the imagination. Advertising created interest and demand. Demand increased production. Increased production and larger sales dropped the cost per unit.

Today, the cost of the average black and white portable is less than one-third of what it was. While the picture is larger. With superior quality and reliability.

Free enterprise creates competition.

When a successful product appears, it's not long before there's competition. The original product must be improved to keep its competitive edge. Good products get better. Inferior products disappear. And the consumer wins.

We share the profit.

Too many people think only business profits from profit. Sure, some of it pays dividends. But it also pays for expansion, more jobs, and better products at lower prices. And both business and consumers share the result: the highest standard of living in the world.

Advertising works.

We're Combined Communications Corporation. And our business is delivering advertising information to consumers through our television and radio stations, our big-city newspaper, our supermarket merchandising system, and our network of outdoor advertising companies.

Advertisers use these media to increase their sales. As a result, we've increased our sales. CCC has been profitable every year we've been in business. In 1976 our gross revenues were in excess of $200,000,000 compared to $151,000,000 in 1975.

Our advertisers know advertising works. We know advertising works. If it didn't, we wouldn't be spending our hard-earned money advertising in this publication.

There's more.

If you want to know more about us, or more about advertising's role in our free enterprise system, write to Ray Cox, Vice President/Corporate Relations, P.O. Box 25518, Phoenix, Arizona 85002. Our symbol on the NYSE is CCA.

Combined Communications Corporation
Free Enterprise Keeps America Working

Television: WXIA-TV (ABC) Atlanta. KBTV-TV (ABC) Denver. WPTA-TV (ABC) Fort Wayne. KARK-TV (NBC) Little Rock. WLKY-TV (ABC) Louisville. KOCO-TV (ABC) Oklahoma City. KTAR-TV (NBC) Phoenix.

Radio: WWDJ-AM Hackensack. KIIS-AM & FM Los Angeles. KBBC-FM Phoenix. KTAR-AM Phoenix. KEZL-FM San Diego. KSDO-AM San Diego. MUZAK Arizona.

Outdoor: Eller in San Francisco, Denver, St. Louis, Detroit, Flint, Grand Rapids, Oakland, San Jose, Tucson, Sacramento, Kansas City, Phoenix, Houston. Pacific in San Diego, Los Angeles. Claude Neon in Montreal, Quebec, Winnipeg, Ottawa, Hamilton, Toronto.

Sign Manufacturing: Claude Neon Industries, Limited, Canada. Tennessee Continental Corporation (TENCON), Centerville, Tennessee.

Newspaper: The Cincinnati Enquirer.

Supermarket Merchandising: PIA Merchandising Company, throughout California, Arizona and Nevada.

Ad developed for Combined Communications Corporation by Jennings & Thompson Advertising Agency, Phoenix, Arizona

Some ad agencies charge a fee for special client services in addition to the normal 15 percent commission, and other special arrangements can be made. At this point it is enough to understand that ad agencies are popular because they provide numerous services for advertisers for free or for very low cost.

Advertising Agency Functions

Some of the services that advertising agencies provide to their clients are:

1. Marketing research
2. Copywriting, art, and layout
3. Media buying
4. Production of ads
5. Market intelligence

Marketing research may consist of three major elements: market analysis, product analysis, and advertising pretesting and posttesting. We have already discussed market analysis as researching the demand for, and supply of, a given product or product line. Often both the advertiser and the agency will do this kind of analysis.

Product analysis is the agency's way of determining what benefits to feature in the ads. For example, an ad agency with a beer account might emphasize "fire-brewed flavor" or "made from mountain stream water" or "beechwood aged." The agency often gets such inspiration by touring the manufacturer's facility, conducting consumer interviews, and generally getting to know the product as viewed by both the seller and the buyer.

Sample ads are then prepared by the agency and pretested by using consumer panels or some other research technique. The ads are usually prepared by people who write the words (copywriters), others who prepare the visuals (artists and photographers), and still others who blend the words and visuals into an attractive whole (layout specialists). All of these people might work together with a "creative director" and other agency personnel to prepare an ad that will attract consumers and hold their interest long enough to inform or persuade them.

After ads are run in the media, the agency might do more research of the ad's effectiveness. Furthermore, the agency might conduct market interviews and otherwise gather data that would be of interest to the advertiser.

Given the fact that agencies may provide all of these services for free or for a minimum fee, is it any wonder that most national advertisers use agencies to prepare their ads? Not only do the agencies prepare the ads and research them, but they also evaluate the various media and try to get optimum exposure for each advertising dollar. For many companies, ad agencies have thus become a marketing auxiliary that provides many valuable services. Some agencies even provide public relations and publicity materials, sales promotion programs, and personal selling aids. Thus, ad agencies often serve as the communications arm for their clients.

The Company Advertising Department Because most producers use an ad agency to do advertising research, production, and placement, what does the ad department in the firm or organization do? First, ad department personnel must prepare a budget and integrate advertising decisions with sales and the other promotional areas. Second, the ad department must help in the selection of an agency. After that, the ad department becomes a liaison area that provides two-way communication between the agency and the advertiser.

Some ad departments go beyond this essentially managerial role and get involved with ad production and other internal services. For example, the ad department might prepare all direct-mail materials, might help prepare the company newsletter and annual report, and might generally assist in the creation of signs, sales aids, and other creative materials.

But the typical ad department is rather small (less than five employees) and concentrates on budgeting and control over the ad agency. This includes reviewing the agency-prepared ads, managing cooperative advertising programs, handling billing, and coordinating the advertising plan with the total marketing effort.

Retail Advertising Departments Most retailers do not use an ad agency to prepare their ads (except for the larger retailers that promote on TV or in magazines). The retail ad department serves as an in-house agency and prepares the ads for all the various departments. Ad departments are usually preferred because agencies usually cannot or will not prepare ads in the limited time available (retailers often advertise every day). Furthermore, most retail ads stress availability and price, and so there is little perceived need for agency creativity or research.

Often the retail ad department is coordinated and integrated with display, special events, signs, and press releases (public relations). The display department prepares window displays, interior displays, and special exhibits. The special-events department is responsible for periodic promotions such as fashion shows, parades, demonstrations, consumer-education classes, contests, merchandise fairs, and shopping-

BROOM HILDA *By Russell Myers*

center promotions such as sidewalk sales. At times, the promotion personnel get assistance from comparison shoppers, fashion coordinators, home economists, consumer-affairs specialists, and a marketing research staff.

Many small retailers entrust all of their advertising preparation to the media representatives and the media staff. Those retailers large enough to have a full-time advertising department might have only one person performing all the functions or it might divide the work among several people (for example, copy, art, layout, and production).

Ad agencies might be used on a consultative basis and might also be retained for ads other than those to appear in newspapers. But of the over 1.8 million retailers in this country, only a very small fraction can afford either an ad agency or an ad department. Too often small retailers have no coordinated, integrated advertising plan but instead rely on periodic cooperative ads with manufacturers and occasional newspaper or radio ads to generate business. These stores would benefit greatly from hiring a marketing consultant to help in the planning and execution of a totally integrated promotional effort.

ADVERTISING MEDIA Marketers may choose from many different media for communicating with the market. The five leading media are newspapers, television, direct mail, radio, and magazines. But marketers should not neglect the supplementary media of advertising specialties, window and internal displays, outdoor signs and billboards, transit advertising, and directories such as the Yellow Pages. In the following sections, we shall briefly discuss the advantages and disadvantages of each medium and give some general hints on effective media usage. We devote much space to the media because advertisers spend most of their money in the media and need to know which media are best for various goals.

Newspaper Advertising The newspaper medium is basically a local communication device that enables retailers and nonprofit organizations such as churches and schools to maintain contact with the public. One advantage of newspapers is their ability to reach almost all people in a given community for a relatively low total cost. Another advantage is that the preparation of newspaper ads is relatively easy; in fact, newspapers will often prepare ads free for their clients. Newspapers also allow an advertiser some flexibility in the timing of ads. An ad usually can be placed a few hours before publication time.

But the most significant advantage of newspapers is that local marketers (both buyers and sellers) can reach a given geographic region daily with an up-to-date listing of available products, prices, and special deals.

Newspapers are an especially effective medium for individuals who wish to buy, sell, or trade *used* merchandise. Advertising of cars, furniture, antiques, and garage sales often takes up several pages of the classified section. Such ads cost only a few dollars and are often very effective in creating a market for hard-to-sell merchandise.

Department stores, discount chains, and other larger retailers have found newspapers to be an excellent distribution vehicle for periodic minicatalogs that list special sale items. Perhaps you have noticed the inserts in your local paper (many are in color and are several pages long).

It is important to remember that advertisers spend more money in newspapers than in any other medium. This is a good indication that newspapers have proved to be an effective and efficient medium, especially for local advertisers.

Disadvantages of Newspaper Advertising Perhaps the greatest disadvantage of newspapers is the number of competing ads by other local marketers. Newspaper ads also lack the clarity that enhances product images (the image is often too grainy). Newspaper ads also have a short life span; that is, few people keep the newspaper around for more than a day. Two easily corrected disadvantages are: (1) Newspaper ads are often too similar for competing retailers (for example, all grocery ads might look the same); and (2) newspaper ads sometimes offer misleading bargains and thus tend to annoy consumers and make them less responsive to true bargains. Concepts a marketer might use in evaluating newspaper advertising include:

> Newspapers are often the most effective and most efficient medium for reaching local markets for both buyers and sellers.

> Newspapers serve as a daily catalog of goods, services, and other offers; they provide information on prices, product benefits, and other helpful shopper's information.

> Newspaper ads should create some differentiation for advertisers to make them more desirable to the market.

> Everybody may use newspapers to buy or sell anything because a classified ad may cost only a few dollars.

Television Advertising We have already discussed the very real advantage of using television to establish brand names and to create favorable images for those brands. Television has the advantage of using sight, sound, and demonstration to show product benefits. Compared with print media (newspapers and magazines), in the television medium, fewer competing commercials and editorial materials vie for the viewer's attention.

Television viewers must literally refuse to view a commercial that is run during a program they are watching, and so chances are that they will be exposed to the message. This is a special advantage for those advertisers introducing new products that would not normally attract the attention of the public.

Another advantage of television is that the full commercial time can be devoted to product benefits. Unlike magazines or newspapers, TV does not have to devote much of its space to get the viewer's attention. Most ads are in color, and because over 70 percent of the homes with TV have color, the product may be shown in vivid surroundings.

Television is also a very flexible medium. Ads can be shown locally or nationally, and, once the ad is made, it can be placed on a program whenever there is available time.

The primary reason for using television, though, is that the cost of the ad per thousand viewers may be quite low given the benefits of sight, sound, color, and demonstration. Viewers may be exposed to a new product for less than 1¢, but a direct-mail piece designed to convey the same message might cost 15¢ or more.

Television is the number-one medium for nationwide advertisers. Its rapid growth is a testimony to the benefits marketers have received from using this outstanding medium.

Disadvantages of Television Advertising The greatest drawback to television advertising is the total cost. A commercial may cost $25,000 or more to make and a 1-minute commercial often costs $45,000 or more to run during prime time. Naturally such costs preclude the use of television by most small producers, retailers, and nonprofit groups.

Television is not a very selective medium; that is, many people might be exposed to commercials, but few might be in the market for the product. For example, notice the TV commercials for computers, steel companies, and office copiers. The average person is not in the market for these products. Furthermore, even though the total TV audience for TV programs is large, the number of people watching a particular show is significantly smaller. And the most popular shows may not be available to an advertiser because others may have already bought the time. So, although TV is a very effective, potentially efficient medium, it is too expensive for most advertisers and must be used cautiously by even the largest organizations.

Concepts one might use in evaluating television advertising are:

> **Television is an effective and efficient mass medium that creates brand awareness and brand images.**

> **The benefits of sight, sound, and demonstration give TV an advantage over all other mass media.**

> **Because TV commercials reach people when they are already watching a program, the full commercial time may be devoted to brand development and product benefits.**

> **Television may be used as a national or local medium.**

Direct-Mail Advertising The cost of mail is rising so rapidly in the United States that a marketer would be wise to think of alternative ways of distributing promotional pieces other than through the U.S. Postal Service. Nevertheless, direct mail is still the third largest medium in terms of dollars spent and deserves special attention.

One advantage of direct mail is that it may be directed to specific individuals or groups, unlike mass media that may reach many *people* but not so many *prospects*. Direct mail is also relatively simple to do; a few postcards to the right people may be enough.

If direct mail is sent only to good prospects, the cost of a direct-mail campaign may be quite low. Direct mail should not be viewed as a mass medium in direct competition with TV or magazines; it is too expensive for that. Used correctly, though, direct mail is an effective *and* efficient medium.

One advantage of direct mail is that the cost of a large, multipage mailer is not significantly greater than the cost of a single sheet. Unlike the other media, direct mail may be used to send out much information at little increase in cost.

Direct mail is the most flexible of media. It can be sent out anytime to anyone with any message. Furthermore, there is little competition from competitive ads compared with most media (that is, few people get more than two or three pieces of advertising in the mail each day). Direct mail is also a very effective way to expose people to a product—a sample or a coupon to buy a sample at a low price can be included in the mailing piece.

The best prospects for direct-mail pieces are people who have responded in the past—past customers, clients, or patrons. Other good prospects may be found in the local community. Direct-mail lists of particular kinds of people (for example, college graduates, nurses, engineers, theater lovers, and so forth) may be bought from specialists.

Disadvantages of Direct-Mail Advertising Probably the greatest disadvantage of direct mail is the high cost per thousand people reached compared to the other media. As mentioned the cost of mailing the material is increasing drastically. This cost may be lessened greatly by using alternative techniques. For example, local retailers may have their flyers distributed door to door by local boys and girls for a fraction of the cost of mailing. Or pieces may be handed out at shopping centers, sports arenas, or other public places. The point is that the disadvantage of cost may be lessened greatly by some careful thought and imagination.

Another severe problem with direct mail is its image as "junk mail." Mailed pieces that have "free offer" or other inducements on the envelope do appear "junky" and lessen the impact of this potentially powerful medium. This disadvantage may be minimized by hand addressing the envelope. Such a practice would also encourage marketers to send direct mail only to good prospects and leave mass advertising to the other media.

Other disadvantages include the cost of getting mailing lists, the cost of postal permits, and the high rate of returned mail due to people moving or out-of-date mailing lists.

In the future, marketers may be looking away from direct *mail* advertising and toward direct advertising of a different sort. Perhaps more delivery firms will emerge to handle direct mail, plus magazines, and samples. There are already many such services. Some advertisers are joining with several others and having their promotional pieces delivered in one package by a delivery firm. Regardless of the delivery system used, direct advertising will continue to be a primary advertising medium. Concepts that help guide the use of direct mail are:

> **Direct mail is most effective when used to reach *selected* individuals and groups rather than mass audiences.**

> Direct advertising may be delivered by mail or through several other distribution channels.

> Direct advertising's most responsive markets are past customers and people in the surrounding community.

> Because the cost of a direct advertising piece does not rise significantly with greater size, marketers should include in their promotional pieces all the information that prospects would want and need.

> Direct advertising literature may be delivered at a reasonable cost by inserting it in local newspapers.

Magazine Advertising The medium of magazines is at present going through a transition period. Advertisers are turning away from general-interest magazines (due to TV's superior ability to reach mass markets) and toward special-interest magazines read by particular market segments. General-interest magazines are far from dead, however, because they can offer a large audience at a relatively low cost per thousand readers.

One of the best features of magazine advertising is that specific target markets (for example, tennis enthusiasts, golfers, dog owners, and art lovers) can be reached at a minimum cost. These same markets could be reached with direct mail, but the lists are expensive and may be incomplete and out of date. Special-interest groups are most effectively and efficiently reached through magazines.

A magazine's image may also rub off on advertisers and their products. For example, a full-page ad in *Playboy* or *Cosmopolitan* may give a product an image of sophistication. Magazines have the benefits of high-quality printing and vivid colors to enhance the visual effect of products.

Magazine ads also have a longer life span than similar ads in the broadcast media. That is, people often save magazines for a week or more. Also, magazine ads may contain much product information that can be clipped and stored until the reader goes shopping.

Marketers are finding that magazines are the best medium for reaching special-interest groups and business people. Hundreds of magazines are designed to reach any group that has a special hobby or outside interest. The ads in these magazines offer readers the kind of products that have special interest to them. The ads do not have to be large or fancy because readers of special-interest magazines often actively search through the ads for interesting or new products.

Many magazines are specifically directed toward business people in all occupations. Over 175 different occupations have one or more of their own magazines. Marketers selling equipment, supplies, and services to businesses find such magazines an effective communication tool.

Disadvantages of Magazine Advertising Ads in magazines often suffer because there is so much competition from other ads and editorial material in the same issue. Magazines also have much "waste coverage," which means that general-interest magazines reach many people, but all of them may not be prospects for a

This magazine ad is effective in attracting attention to an important organization and its benefits to society.

A kid could get in trouble with this.

A knife in the hands of some kids could be a problem. But in the hands of a Scout? That's a different story. You see, in Scouting, a boy is taught to use a knife as a tool. Not as a weapon. He learns to start a campfire with a knife. To use it for craft-making. To prepare food. And to administer first aid which could save a life.

But beyond that, a Scout learns to respect a knife. Just like he learns to respect many other things in life. Like other people. The ecology. And himself. And developing that kind of respect is not easy. It's tough. But once he does, he discovers what life is all about. He discovers that helping others, meeting challenges, and doing his best is rewarding and a lot of fun. And that's what Scouting is all about.

Scouting. It's not kid stuff.

One of a series in Campaign '76.
For information call 897-1965

Created and produced by Young & Rubicam, Detroit

given product. That is why there is such a growth in special-interest magazines.

The lead time for magazines is also relatively long—an advertiser might have to place an ad several weeks before it will be run. Magazines also lack the action and sound that are part of television's major appeal. Some concepts that might guide the use of magazines are:

> Magazines are an excellent supplement to television in that they may reach audiences not reached by television and they enable readers to clip and store information until they are ready to buy.

> Special-interest magazines can reach particular clearly defined market segments such as golfers or boaters more effectively and efficiently than any other medium.

> Magazines may be used as a national or local medium. Even national magazines have regional editions, and magazines such as *Time* or *Newsweek* add a special image to their advertisers.

> The high-quality printing and sharp colors in magazines can enhance the visual presentation of products better than almost any other medium.

Radio Advertising Radio has become the local medium best suited to reach particular market segments in a community. Whereas newspapers appeal to *all* segments of a given area, radio stations appeal to particular people such as teenagers, housewives, lovers of classical music, specific ethnic groups, and so forth.

An advantage of radio is that it may reach people with messages that might be ignored in a newspaper ad. Because people are already listening to the station, they may listen to the ad also, even though they may have had no initial interest in the product. For example, most people do not change banks very often and tend to ignore bank advertising. Radio often enables bankers and other such marketers to tell people about new services better than do print ads that people might avoid.

Radio also has the advantage of reaching selected audiences for a minimum cost. For example, local FM stations might reach an older, more affluent market for a very low cost. Ethnic radio shows such as church services and special programs of foreign music reach special markets in their own language and again at relatively low cost.

Radio commercials are rather easy to prepare—the station will usually provide them free if you ask. Radio is also an effective way to reinforce the image and themes created in the other media. For example, a television commercial for Coca Cola might show attractive visuals supporting the theme "Coke adds life." Radio commercials would pick up the same theme song and reinforce the brand name and imagery. Radio is a good complement to TV because it reaches people when TV is not as effective (for example, during hours of heavy commuting, during vacations, and during the summer when people are outdoors).

Radio is especially effective when the announcer gives his personal support and recommendation to the product. Many such commercials are unrehearsed and have the effect of word-of-mouth publicity.

Many retailers could benefit by using radio to supplement their newspaper advertising. Radio has the flexibility to give an extra boost to a special promotion. The ability of the announcer to use his voice to create excitement and interest cannot be matched by any other local medium except television—and TV ads are often too expensive for local advertisers.

Disadvantages of Radio Advertising Radio listeners often switch channels during commercials, and so the impact of careful program selection might be lost. Radio is often used as a background for other activities, and people may not pay any attention to the ads. It is also difficult to get accurate audience figures for radio because people are usually in their cars during the best radio times, and market research is very difficult.

Because radio is limited to one dimension—sound—it is more difficult to show product benefits. Also, people cannot clip and keep radio commercials as they can newspaper ads, and so radio does not have the same long-term benefits provided by print media.

Specialty Advertising Advertising specialties are those pieces of merchandise, like pens, calendars, rulers, and matches, given to customers and potential customers so they will remember the giver. The objective of giving away specialty items is to create goodwill and to keep the advertiser's name before the public. Such items reach specific audiences with a short, but important message. The greatest advantage of such items is that people may carry them with them wherever they go and thus have a constant reminder of the giver. Of course, the number of repeat exposures to the message is high, and the flexibility of specialty items enables the giver to send any message desired. Children are especially fond of specialty gifts such as a balloon, a yo-yo, or a T-shirt.

One disadvantage of specialty items is their high cost and the potential careless use to which they may be put. Like direct mail, specialty items should be given or sent only to *selected* prospects. Another disadvantage is that the message must be short.

The use of specialty items may be an important supplement to other advertising. But because of the cost and potential abuse, marketers would be wise to seek expert counsel in the design and distribution of any specialty items.

Outdoor Signs and Billboards If a person has never been inside a store, the only things he or she may know about a store are what they learn from billboards or the store sign. If the signs are torn and tattered, the image of the store is one of decay and obsolescence. If the sign contains little information, the potential customer will know little about the product, and the less customers know, the less likely they are to buy. Think of the billboards and signs you have seen while driving on vacation. Which places attracted you and why? What information was most pertinent to you? Notice how often your total evaluation was based solely on the sign and the information it gave. Some concepts to be followed in sign design are:

> **For people unfamiliar with a store or a product, the sign *is* the product, and the image created by the sign will either attract people or not.**

> **Signs should convey the total image of the product offer including price, quality, reputation, and special services.**

> **The wording on billboards and other traffic signs must be kept to a minimum; therefore, much information must be conveyed by visuals such as pictures or symbols (for example, AAA approved).**

Store signs normally should include the name, the kind of merchandise carried, and other pertinent data. It is usually not enough to put up a name without also indicating what is available. Exterior signs might also include the address (clearly shown), hours of operation, and phone number. Additional signs might indicate special sale items or special differentiating features (for example, "free tailoring," "repairs while you wait," or "satisfaction guaranteed or your money back").

For most small retailers, the store sign and window display are the primary advertising media. As much care should go into their design and evaluation as in the case of any other media. It is not enough to quickly slap up a sign and stick something in the window and forget about them. There should be some measure of customer response, the image created, and suggested improvements.

Window and Internal Displays A whole book could be written about how to design and maintain displays. Because we have limited space in this book, let us emphasize some key concepts about displays:

> **Window displays should attract attention and draw people into the store. They should be changed periodically and cleaned weekly so that they always appear fresh and attractive.**

> **Window displays serve as a calling card for the store and as such should convey the total personality of the store, including the kind and variety of products, the price level, and the features that make the store different from others.**

> **Internal displays should continue the theme of the window displays and should lead people to the items they most want or need.**

> **Internal displays should also be coordinated with advertising.**

> **Often internal displays take the place of sales assistance and consequently must give product benefits, differentiating features, price, use and care information, and other pertinent data. The trend toward self-service will increase the need for more complete point-of-purchase displays.**

Transit Advertising There is a nationwide growth in interest and development of mass transportation in the larger cities. Such trends open new possibilities for placing ads in buses, rapid transit cars, and at the various stations and stops. Advertising may also be placed on the outside of vehicles.

The advantages of this advertising are: (1) It reaches people on the way to work; (2) the impressions are repeated daily and may last 30 minutes or more; and (3) the signs serve as excellent reminders of product benefits and images.

The disadvantages are: (1) The message must be relatively short; (2) there may be too much "waste coverage"; and (3) the money may be better spent in other media.

Transit advertising is a growing medium with many possibilities. For reminder advertising, it is one of the best media for reaching people on the go.

Directory Advertising The most effective and widely used directory of advertisers is the Yellow Page section of the phone book. Marketers dealing in services should be especially concerned about placing an effective ad in the phone book. The advantages of Yellow Page advertising are: (1) People use the Yellow Pages as a buying guide; (2) such ads expose the marketer to a wide range of buyers the seller may not know exist; and (3) the ads are a relatively inexpensive way to have continuous exposure to potential customers.

Other directories are available for a marketer's use and should be given some consideration. Which directories to use depends much on the kind of product and the kind of customer.

ADVERTISING AS A MARKETING SPECIALTY Many schools have an entire course on advertising, and so it is obvious that we cannot give you a thorough treatment here. You may want to learn more about advertising management, including how to budget, how to measure ad effectiveness, how to select media, and so forth. You may want to take a course in advertising if you have the time, but you could also learn much from reading advertising textbooks and "how to" books by practitioners.[8]

The last chapter in this book discusses careers in advertising and how to begin early to prepare for such a career. We hope this chapter has given you some incentive to learn more about advertising because it is a fascinating subject to study and an interesting career opportunity as well.

[8] An interesting starter is Pierre Martineau, *Motivation in Advertising* (New York: McGraw-Hill Book Company, 1957).

FOR REVIEW

Key Terms

Among the more important terms and expressions discussed in this chapter are the following:

Advertising consists of paid, nonpersonal communication through various media by business firms, nonprofit organizations, and individuals who are in some way identified in the advertising message and who hope to communicate with members of a particular audience.

Information utility is a term used to describe the value added to a product by means of advertising and other promotional communications.

Product analysis in advertising refers to the study of a product in order to determine what product benefits to feature in advertising.

Key Concepts

Among the more important marketing concepts introduced in this chapter are the following:

› **Advertising adds value to products by providing information to consumers.**

› **Advertising provides a means for sellers and buyers to *inform* one another about their wants and needs, so that those needs can be met through mutually satisfying market exchanges.**

› **Marketing success depends on good products that meet people's needs; advertising images add to the value of products by showing people how particular products will enhance their economic or social well-being.**

› **Information, persuasion, and imagery are all important aspects of effective advertising messages.**

› **The goal of advertising is the efficient creation of marketing exchanges through communication.**

› **Newspapers serve as a daily catalog of goods, services, and other offers; they provide information on prices, product benefits, and other helpful shopper's information.**

› **Television is an effective and efficient mass medium that creates brand awareness and brand images.**

› **Direct mail is most effective when used to reach *selected* individuals and groups rather than mass audiences.**

› **Special-interest magazines can reach particular clearly defined market segments such as golfers or boaters more effectively and efficiently than can any other medium.**

› **For people unfamiliar with a store or a product, the sign *is* the product, and the image created by the sign will either attract people or not.**

› **Window displays serve as a calling card for the store and as such should convey the total personality of the store, including the kind and variety of products, the price level, and the features that make the store different from others.**

› **Internal displays should continue the theme of the window displays and should lead people to the items they most want or need.**

Discussion Questions

1. Do you feel that advertising is used *primarily* to inform, persuade, create an image, or satisfy the needs of buyers and sellers? Support your answer with examples from a variety of media (for example, TV, radio, newspapers, magazines).

2. Think of the last time you went to a movie or a play. How did you get information about the movie or play? How much value did that information add? Would you have been willing to go without such information?

3. When was the last time you were persuaded to buy something because of advertising? What was the appeal?

4. List all the products, if any, you were persuaded to buy that you did not *want*. Can advertising get people to buy products they do not want? If so, give some examples.

5. Do people feel that the U.S. public buys most of what it buys because of the influence of TV? Discuss if the introduction of TV has changed people's purchases of the following products: homes; cars; furniture; carpeting; food and appliances.

6. Direct mail is often referred to as "junk mail." Is that an accurate description? Why or why not? How could direct mail advertisers improve the image and effectiveness of direct mail?

7. How often do you use the Yellow Pages of the phone book to find what you want? Do you notice the ads? Why or why not? How would you improve ads in the Yellow Pages?

8. Over $35 billion is spent on advertising in the United States each year. Is that a waste of resources? Why or why not? What benefits do consumers receive from advertising? What costs do they incur because of advertising?

9. Look over the point-of-purchase displays at several different retail stores (for example, an appliance store, a carpet store, a department store, and a discount store). Do they contain the kind of information you need to make intelligent product choices? How could they be improved?

10. Evaluate the effectiveness of advertising for various nonprofit organizations. How does it affect you and your friends? Could such advertising be more effective in reaching you and your peers?

CASES

College Fashions
The Power of Advertising

"It's unbelievable how much power advertisers have over the American public," Carol Masterson said. "Take fashions, for example. Marketers keep changing styles every year, and advertising makes everyone run out and buy the latest fashions. Why, we even were talked into buying those platform shoes that were so dangerous to wear. And think of how skirt lengths keep going up and down. And men are talked into buying button-down shirts one year, colored shirts another, and something else the next year. There is no doubt that advertising is the most important influence on what we wear. At least I think so."

"I don't agree," her friend Sheryl Sanchez said. "Look at what college students have been wearing. I had never seen an ad pushing wire-rim glasses, wide watch bands, or wide belts until long after the students were already wearing them. And students do not wear the latest in shirts—button down and all that you said. Guys are more likely to wear T-shirts and actively avoid ads for suits, ties, and other fashion items. I think that people do what they want, and ads help them choose what is available. For example, my dad still wears the same white shirts and conservative ties he wore 20 years ago. And my mom doesn't buy the latest fashions. Advertisers have no control over them. And my little sister refuses to wear anything but Levis. Advertisers haven't reached her either. And I never bought platform shoes, although I must admit many of my friends did. I think that advertising is very successful in selling what people want, but not very good at selling what people don't want. For example, nobody bought those maxi skirts that were so heavily promoted a few years ago. And many people were buying Earth Shoes long before there was much advertising. Do you think advertisers have the power to get college women to wear dresses and college men to wear sport coasts and ties? I don't think so."

1. How much influence do you feel advertising has on college fashions and other such decisions?
2. Has advertising ever persuaded your friends to buy particular clothes? What other influences were at work to create such exchanges?
3. Can you think of examples where advertising failed to motivate the public?
4. Why is advertising sometimes very effective in getting people to buy new fashions and other times very ineffective?

Texas Instruments
Advertising a New Product

Texas Instruments has developed a new plastic-cased digital watch that is expected to sell for as low as $10. It also is producing a new metal-case line that starts at $20. Many other producers either are gearing up to produce a similar watch or already have competitive watches on the production lines.

Only 3.5 million digital watches were sold in 1975, but overall sales for 1976 were in the 15 to 20 million range. Prices for digital watches dropped dramatically over the last few years from $100-plus to this new, low competitive price.

Digital watches may be *the* watch of the future, and Texas Instruments wants to capture a large share of the market early.

1. Would you use an ad campaign for the new watch that was informative, persuasive, image creating, need solving, or some combination? Why? How?
2. What media would you use in your campaign? Why?
3. Would you use an ad agency to prepare your ads? Why or why not?
4. Would you direct your advertising at ultimate consumers, retailers, or both? Why?
5. In your ads, how would you meet the competition of other firms making similar watches?

Public Relations, Publicity, and Sales Promotion

earning public support

LEARNING GOALS

After you have read and studied this chapter, you should be able to:

1. Explain why public relations and publicity are two key marketing functions.
2. Define the following terms: public relations; publicity; sales promotion; and institutional publicity.
3. Show how public relations is the key to making an organization more socially responsive and responsible.
4. List at least eight activities of a PR department.
5. Explain the relationship between the PR function and a firm's marketing information system.
6. Give examples to show the difference between product publicity and institutional publicity.
7. List the advantages of publicity over advertising.
8. Discuss the following sales promotion tools and give examples of each: samples, coupons, premiums, trading stamps, contests, rebates, and display.
9. Explain the importance of sales promotion for generating the support of employees and middlemen.
10. Illustrate how public relations, publicity, and sales promotion can be used in a nonprofit organization.

INTRODUCTION What do the following people have in common: Henry Kissinger, Marilyn Monroe, Muhammad Ali, Jacqueline Kennedy Onassis, Joe Namath, Evel Knievel? The answer: All of the people are well known largely because of *publicity.* When a person gets his or her name in the various media *for any reason,* that exposure to the public may be called publicity. Sometimes the publicity is unfavorable, as it was for former President Nixon at the end of his term. Sometimes the publicity is so overwhelming that it interferes with a person's life, as it does with Jacqueline Kennedy Onassis.

If a person wants to be famous (or infamous) the surest and best way to do it is to generate publicity about oneself. The same is true of organizations. This chapter is about publicity and its use as a marketing communications tool. Publicity is part of a broader area called *public relations,* which we shall also discuss. At the end of the chapter, we shall discuss sales promotion as a marketing tool that ties publicity, public relations, advertising, and personal selling into a total promotional program.

PUBLIC Public relations (PR) is defined by the *Public Relations News* as the
RELATIONS management function that evaluates public attitudes, identifies the policies and procedures of an individual or an organization with the public interest, and executes a program of action to earn public understanding and acceptance. Notice that public relations starts with good marketing research ("evaluates public attitudes").

Public relations is one department in an organization that has explicit responsibility for listening to the public. The second step in a good PR program is the development of policies and procedures that are in the public interest. Public relations should *not* be just a promotional tool or a communications device; it should be an action-oriented department with responsibility to adapt the organization to the public's wants and needs. The final step in a PR program is to take action to *earn* public understanding and acceptance. One does not earn understanding by bombarding the public with propaganda; one earns understanding by having programs and practices in the public interest and letting people know that you have them. It is not enough to act in the public interest; you must also inform people of that fact. The concepts are:

> ‣ **Public relations is the marketing activity that recognizes the organization's obligation to be socially responsive, helps the organization to**

* *Advertising, Sales Promotion, and Public Relations—Organizational Alternatives* (New York: The Conference Board, 1968), p. 1.

356

develop programs, and establishes two-way communications with the public to be sure everyone is satisfied with the organization's policies, personnel practices, and procedures.

› Public relations is an action-oriented program of meeting the public's demands; it is not just a communication function.

Responsibilities of the PR Department You may get a better idea of what public relations involves if we list some of the activities of PR departments:[1]

1. Establishing contact with civic groups, consumer organizations, and other concerned citizens to learn their views of the organization, to answer their questions, and to provide information (or education).

2. Opening lines of communication with customers, suppliers, distributors, retailers, stockholders, government agencies, educators, and community leaders.

3. Conducting studies to find the economic, environmental, and social consequences of organizational practices and to learn how to make a more positive contribution to customers, stockholders, and society.

4. Providing any assistance needed to adjust the goals, policies, practices, personnel policies, products, and programs of the organization to meet the needs of changing markets.

5. Assisting all members of the firm in developing effective programs of consumer information and consumer education.

6. Sending speakers to schools, clubs, and other such groups to maintain an open dialogue with students and other socially active members of society.

7. Creating incentives for employees to participate in public-affairs activities such as raising funds for charitable groups, advising young people in the Boy Scouts, Girl Scouts, or Junior Achievement, and being active in community associations.

8. Answering consumer and other complaints promptly and correcting whatever it was that caused the complaint.

9. Training employees or volunteers to provide prompt, friendly, courteous, and helpful service to anyone who contacts the organization in person, by phone, or by written correspondence.

10. Demonstrating to society that the organization is listening, reacting, adjusting, and progressing in its attempt to provide satisfaction to its diverse publics.

11. Opening two-way communications with employees to generate favorable employee opinion and to motivate employees to speak well of the organization to others.

This list is not a complete description of all the activities and responsibilities of the PR staff, but it should give you some feel for what they do. It also helps to sharpen our definition of public relations.

---

[1] These ideas are developed further in William G. Nickels, *Marketing Communications and Promotion* (Columbus, Ohio: Grid, Inc., 1976), p. 241.

The word "public" in public relations means every individual, organization, government agency, or group that has the potential for affecting or being affected by a person or organization. This includes employees, stockholders, suppliers, customers, and community leaders.

The word "relations" means the establishment of open two-way communications with the goal of creating mutually beneficial relationships including marketing exchange relationships. The concept is:

> **Public relations is responsible for establishing and maintaining open two-way communications with all publics of an organization and for creating favorable public opinion about the organization (or individual or place or cause).**

Public Relations in Nonbusiness Organizations

The PR function in many nonbusiness organizations is almost synonymous with marketing. Most nonbusiness organizations do not have a marketing department. Instead they have a PR department that is responsible for (marketing) research, (product) program design, advertising, personal selling (soliciting), sales promotion (display), and all the other "marketing" activities. Nonbusiness organizations often hesitate to use the word "marketing" because the public associates marketing with deception, manipulation, and "hard-sell" tactics. The words "public relations" are also beginning to have negative connotations ("It's just institutional propaganda"), and some organizations are using different terms such as community relations, press relations, or customer relations.

You might be surprised to see how sophisticated the PR area is in some nonbusiness organizations. For example universities, schools, hospitals, financial institutions, government agencies, charities, social causes, unions, foundations, political organizations, and museums all may have large and active PR departments or staff.

International Scope of Public Relations

Pause for a moment and think of nations such as Spain, Mexico, China, Japan, and India. What are your initial impressions? Why? A few moments reflection will tell you that almost everything you know or feel about a country is based on what you heard on radio or TV and read in the newspapers or magazines. If you have a favorable impression, that country has done a relatively good PR job. If you have a negative impression, it may be that the media have tried to create that impression or that the country may have ignored its PR role.

One of the key industries for many countries is tourism. The best way to increase tourism is to get favorable publicity in the media of other countries and through travel agents, tour clubs, and other major influentials.

We do not want to belabor the point that public relations is important for countries as well as businesses, nonprofit organizations, and social causes. But we want you to expand your horizons a bit to see public relations and its main concern (public opinion) as a critical function for all organizations and individuals that hope to establish mutually satisfying relations with others.

**Public
Relations and
the Marketing
Information
System**

"Two-way communications is the keystone of public relations," says one writer. "Often there is a tendency to slight the inbound communication and to focus too much attention on what goes out, but this is wrong."[2] Most people think of public relations as an outward flow of information and persuasion. The reason for this is explained as follows:

> Outbound communication is the most conspicuous element of public relations. A good many people do not realize that there is anything else involved. Inbound communication, planning, and evaluation are not visible activities. But outbound communication is designed to attract attention, and, as a consequence, it is seen and heard in varying degrees by everyone. In addition, much more time and money are spent on outbound communication than on all other public relations activities, so it naturally becomes the center of attention.[3]

To make public relations an effective two-way flow of communications, there should be careful coordination and integration between PR

[2] Lawrence W. Nolte, *Fundamentals of Public Relations* (New York: Pergamon Press Inc., 1974), p. 283.
[3] Ibid., p. 321.

Public Relations, Publicity, and Advertising

Of the three major promotional/communications functions, the one most often handled centrally at corporate headquarters—and least often decentralized to the company's operating divisions—is public relations. Nine out of ten companies report having a central public relations function, while only one in three maintains such a function within any of its divisions. . . .

When public relations work is carried on at the division level, it is most frequently confined to one phase of public relations which does bear directly on the marketing function—product publicity. . . .

Half the time, the same unit responsible for corporate advertising also looks after all or a substantial part of a company's corporate level public relations work. In three out of four cases where some facet of public relations is left to the operating divisions, this is carried out in combination with the divisional advertising effort. . . .

A method sometimes used to assure that different kinds of public relations requirements of the company will properly be met is to break the function into specialized parts—with perhaps one unit working in support of marketing programs and another dealing with such publics as the financial community, stockholders, and the like.

From David L. Hurwood and Earl L. Bailey, *Advertising, Sales Promotion, and Public Relations—Organizational Alternatives* (New York: The Conference Board, 1968), pp. 12–13.

activities and the marketing information system. Marketing research data and all other marketing intelligence should provide some base for determining problems in the area of public relations.

Internal processing and distribution of marketing intelligence helps PR personnel to show management the need to adjust corporate policies and practices when such changes are necessary.

Publicity and all other outward communications by public relations may be considered as part of the promotional-communications function of marketing. Most organizations now coordinate and integrate public relations with the other promotional elements. The concepts are:

> **Public relations begins with good marketing research to determine public opinion and to define the PR task.**

> **Marketing information systems provide the structure for opening two-way communications with all the publics of an organization (or individual, or cause).**

> **Public relations and publicity should be coordinated and integrated with the other promotional elements.**

Internal Public Relations Although most people think of public relations as something organizations do with outsiders, internal public relations (to employees) is a critical aspect of a total PR program. Internal public relations should involve two-way flows of communication just as external public relations does. But too often organizations have the PR department send all kinds of materials *to* employees (for example, films, newsletters, and magazines) but do little to get information and suggestions *from* employees. It is not enough to put in a suggestion box or to ask "how are things going" every once in a while. Employee relations must be given serious attention so that everyone in the organization is working together in a common cause.

Everyone Responsible for Public Relations "Employees are the most important tool of public relations," says one consultant. "Properly motivated and properly utilized, this can accomplish more than all other tools combined. On the other hand, if they are not motivated or used in the right way, they can undo all the other constructive elements in the program."[4]

Although authority and responsibility for public relations are usually assigned to a particular department, everyone in the firm should be made to feel that he or she is part of the PR effort. Firms like General Motors, General Electric, IBM, and AT&T and organizations like the U.S. Postal Service, the Red Cross, and the Heart Fund employ or involve millions of employees and volunteers. Each of those people should be trained to be spokespersons who inform and educate the public about their organization and its policies, practices, and procedures. This should not be a quick, one-time training session; rather, it should involve a continuous effort to get people interested and involved in the organization, so they will feel motivated to tell others about it.

[4] Ibid., p. 355.

> **Budgeting for Public Relations**
>
> As a general rule, but certainly not true in every case, the advertising budgets of large corporations selling directly to the public average approximately 12% of gross sales. Of this budget, allotments to specific public relations activity extend from half of 1% to a maximum of 2%. These allotments are usually assigned to one of three potential practicing units: public relations departments within the advertising and promotion section of the corporation; the public relations department of the corporation's advertising agency; or individual public relations agencies. Surveys show that the three categories share about equally the total number of assignments.

From L. Roy Blumenthal, *The Practice of Public Relations* (New York: The Macmillan Company, 1972), p. 45.

The PR System It should be clear by now that public relations begins with an analysis of the public and public opinion. Often the best way to analyze what the public is thinking is to read what the media are writing, because public opinion influences, and is influenced by, the media. A second step is to integrate the organization with its environment. That means getting the organization to adapt its policies and practices to fit the demands of relevant publics. The new policies and practices should be implemented, and the public should be informed of those actions. Finally, the effects of such activities should be evaluated and any necessary adjustments made. The total PR system is shown graphically in Figure 14.1.

Figure 14.1 ELEMENTS OF THE PR SYSTEM

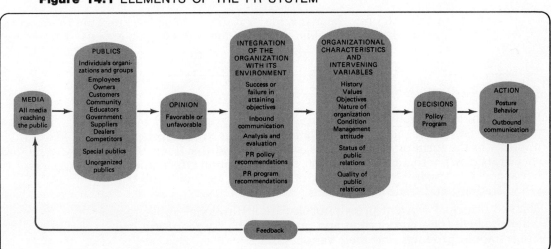

Redrawn from Lawrence Nolte, *Fundamentals of Public Relations* (Elmsford, N.Y.: Pergamon Press, Inc., 1974), p. 16.

Notice that public relations is involved in two major activities: (1) establishing policy and (2) carrying out programs for generating favorable public opinion. In many organizations, the first activity is often neglected. Although the people in public relations have monitored public opinion and recommended changes, often those changes are not made. Public relations is a *staff function*. That means that there is no direct authority for making policy or procedural changes. Without the authority to make or significantly influence policy, public relations becomes more of a propaganda function and is relatively ineffectual.

One major activity of the public relations department is to generate publicity. The concepts and principles behind the dissemination of publicity are explained in the following sections.

PUBLICITY   A woman had quintuplets a couple of years ago, and newspapers and magazines throughout the country ran stories about the family. These stories resulted in hundreds of free gifts from individuals and companies, and dozens of local people volunteered to help with the children.

An airplane crashed in the Washington, D.C., area during a storm, and many people were killed. All the media reported the incident for months because mistakes were allegedly made by the air controllers and/or the pilot.

A lumber company spent over $11 million on pollution control in 1 year and received much favorable publicity for its efforts. Another company located one of its production facilities in a disadvantaged neighborhood, hired and trained local people for the plant, and received much favorable comment in the various media.

All of these stories are examples of publicity in action. **Publicity** is any information about an individual, a product, or an organization that is distributed to the public through the media and that is not paid for, or controlled by, the sponsor. You should understand several important concepts about publicity:

> **Publicity may be favorable or unfavorable. (The story about the quintuplets was favorable, the story about the airline crash was unfavorable.)**

Public Opinion and Publicity

Public opinion is largely formed from information transmitted by the press, television, and radio. Public relations departments supply press publicity in the form of news releases, scripts for radio and television, special articles, photographs, clip sheets, and background information to newspapers, magazines, wire services, news syndicates, radio and television stations, and trade publications.

The two principal types of press publicity are institutional publicity to build goodwill for a corporation and product publicity to inform consumers about products and their various uses.

From Bertrand R. Canfield, *Public Relations—Principles, Cases, and Problems* (Homewood, Ill.: Richard D. Irwin, Inc., 1964), p. 172.

> Publicity may be released voluntarily or involuntarily; an individual or organization normally has little control over the media. (The lumber company made great efforts to get its story published, but the airline preferred not to have the story of the crash extensively reported.)

> Publicity is not paid for. (Often the only difference between advertising and publicity is that advertising is paid for.)

> Publicity cannot be controlled by an individual or an organization; it is subject to changes by the media. (Advertising messages may be published *as is*, and some publicity releases are also, but there is no guarantee that publicity releases will be published as submitted)

Publicity and Marketing Imagine that you have just invented a new product that enables people to dry-clean their clothes at home in their own washing machines. The problem is that you have very little money to promote the product, and you want to get some initial sales to generate funds. One effective way to

---

Springsteen: The Merchandising of a Superstar

"You don't go right to the public to sell a new performer," says CBS Records' Bruce Lundvall. "You sell him to your own company first, then to the trade, and then to the record buyers." That was the plan behind the marketing of Bruce Springsteen, a 26-year-old singer from New Jersey who has been acclaimed as the 1975 counterpart of Elvis Presley or The Beatles. And who, not inconsequentially, has sold $2 million worth of records in the few weeks that his latest album, *Born to Run*, has been out.

Springsteen's first album two years ago sold only 20,000 copies, when the record company publicity was calling him "a new Dylan." Bob Dylan, whose *Blowin' in the Wind* had made him the voice of rebellious youth in the '60's, had virtually retired, and the Columbia label needed a successor. Trying again, the company issued a second Springsteen album, this time playing down the "new Dylan" image. Sales were only slightly better, but CBS saw the beginnings of a Springsteen cult of fans.

Its investment by now was around $150,000, and marketing man Lundvall, CBS Records Group head Walter R. Yetnikoff, and Irwin Segelstein, head of the domestic division, laid plans for an all-out effort to recoup with *Born to Run*. Springsteen's songs are too long and complex for airing on "top 40" radio stations, which play the same 40 hits over and over and only occasionally promote a new number. CBS decided to concentrate instead on FM "underground" radio stations that specialize in playing entire albums for serious music fans.

Months before *Born to Run* was ready for the public, the CBS promotion staff was called to a meeting to listen to it. Cassettes were made so the field men could play it in their cars as they drove from town to town to tell radio program managers and record distributors that "something big is coming." Audio-visual casettes showing TV and print ads for the album were made, with "teasers" or brief snatches of the actual music used to build expectations.

The big "hype." Last February CBS bought a radio and print campaign promoting the first two Springsteen albums and telling the public a new one would be ready soon. Trade papers then got stories of the pressures and delays the performer was experiencing while trying to make his new album something special. Sales of the first two records climbed toward the 150,000-copy mark. Then, in August, Springsteen was set for a handful of personal appearances—not in a large concert hall, but in a 400-seat New York club. CBS took one-fourth of the tickets for the press, radio people, and friends, causing fans to scramble for the remainder and wait in block-long lines. The *Village Voice* and *New York Times* covered the resulting stampede with major stories and favorable reviews. *Time* and *Newsweek* covers followed just as *Born to Run* reached the stores. And sales zoomed.

"Is it all publicity?" asks Lundvall. "Some of it, sure. But Springsteen has to be good enough to sell records over the long haul. We know that too much "hype" can be dangerous, that it makes critics look at an act more closely, trying to find flaws. When they do, if publicity is all the act has, it goes down fast. Our intent is to have artists who will last, and Springsteen is one."

Reprinted from the December 1, 1975, issue of *Business Week* by special permission. © 1975 by McGraw-Hill, Inc.

reach the public is through publicity. You might prepare a news release describing the new product and how it works and send it to the various media. (We shall not go into vast detail of how this is done, but there is much skill involved in writing the story so that the media will want to publish it.) Release of the news about the new product will reach many potential buyers (and/or investors, distributors, and dealers), and you will be on your way to becoming a wealthy marketer.

Publicity is an effective complement to other tools of marketing promotion such as advertising, personal selling, and sales promotion. The best thing about it is that the various media will publish publicity stories free *if the material is felt to be interesting or newsworthy.* The idea, then, is to write publicity that meets these criteria.

Publicity about products (goods, services, people, and places) is called **product publicity.** Most publicity seems to fall in that category. But there is also publicity about organizations in general. This is sometimes called **institutional publicity.** Publicity in this sense involves the reporting of an organization's day-to-day activities that are deemed newsworthy. This includes notable promotions, ground-breaking celebrations, special attempts to recruit the disadvantaged, new pollution-control efforts, and unusual events such as a strike.

Publicity often has several advantages over other marketing promotions, such as advertising. For example, publicity may reach people who would not read an advertising message. Publicity may be placed on the front page of a newspaper or in some other very prominent position. Perhaps the greatest advantage of publicity is its believability. When a newspaper or magazine publishes a story as news, the reader treats that story as news, and news is more believable than advertising. Of course, publicity is much cheaper than advertising, because it is published free.

But publicity is not a substitute for advertising or any other promotional tool. It *supplements* other promotional methods and should be considered as one element in a total marketing-communications program.

Effectiveness of Publicity One should never underestimate the power of the media to influence public opinion and preferences. A story in the national media about a person or organization can either make or break their efforts to attain a favorable image with the public.

Many movie stars, singers, politicians, athletes, and other personalities have become famous and popular because of the media. Think of people like Evel Knievel, Muhammad Ali, Elton John, and Bruce Springsteen. These people have received tremendous exposure through the media, and, as a result, they have become famous and rich. People would not pay much to see Mr. Muddles sing at a nightclub. Why? Because they have never heard of Mr. Muddles. But if Muddles got the publicity of a Tiny Tim or an Alice Cooper, he might become the next superstar of the music industry.

But remember that negative publicity can hurt people as much as positive publicity can benefit them. Many politicians have failed because the media concentrated on some statement or position that the public did not like. For example, many people feel George McGovern's presidential race was hurt by media emphasis on his "$1,000-per-person welfare plan." Former President Ford was often portrayed as being "clumsy" or "dumb" in the media and had to overcome such negative publicity throughout his term. President Carter had to overcome his "ethnic purity" remarks. You can probably think of many examples on your own of how specific politicians have benefited or suffered because of publicity.

Organizations also may rise or fall in popularity because of good or bad publicity. Think of how negative the public was during the oil crisis, when oil companies were being accused daily of making "excess profits," of "withholding oil from the market," and of other such abuses. The oil companies tried to counter such publicity with publicity of their own, but much of it was not published. (Remember the media control what is published and what is not.) The oil companies then turned to advertising to explain their position, but advertising is not nearly as believable as publicity, and the effects were less than spectacular.

Companies are always subject to negative publicity because of hiring practices, strikes, product failures, pollution problems, and other such issues. It is critical, therefore, for companies to foster a constant flow of positive publicity in order to keep the public informed (and educated) about their side of such issues. As Abraham Lincoln once said: "Public sentiment is everything. . . . With public sentiment nothing can fail. Without it, nothing can succeed. He who moulds public sentiment goes deeper than he who executes statutes or pronounces decisions."

Coordinating Public Relations with Marketing All of the major elements of promotion—advertising, personal selling, public relations, publicity, and sales promotion—should be coordinated and integrated to create a uniform impression with the public. This is often very difficult to do because advertising and public relations are often delegated to outside organizations. To coordinate the activities of several different organizations so that the programs of all of them are united is a key marketing task.

Often the sales-promotion area provides the link that ties together all the other promotional elements. The next section discusses sales promotions and its role as an integrative marketing activity.

SALES PROMOTION Sales promotion consists of those marketing activities, other than personal selling, advertising, and publicity, that stimulate consumer purchasing and dealer effectiveness by means of such things as displays, shows and exhibitions, demonstrations, temporary offers of material rewards, and various other nonrecurrent selling efforts.[5]

Those free samples of products that people get in the mail, the cents-off coupons that they clip out of the newspapers, the contests that various retail stores sponsor, and those rebates that have been so popular in recent years are all examples of sales promotion activities. Sales promotion programs supplement personal selling, advertising, and PR efforts by coordinating such efforts throughout the channel and creating enthusiasm for the overall promotional program. Consumer promotions are just one aspect of a total program. Sales promotion activities are also directed at company employees (especially salespersons), wholesalers, retailers, and institutions such as schools and hospitals. This section will explore this important marketing tool and its importance to both sellers and buyers.

[5] *Marketing Definitions: A Glossary of Marketing Terms*, Definitions Committee of the American Marketing Association (Chicago: American Marketing Association, 1960).

What Is Sales Promotion?

Sales promotion is concerned with the creation, application, and dissemination of materials and techniques that supplement advertising and personal selling. Sales promotion makes use of direct mail, catalogues, house organs, trade shows, sales contests and other dealer aids. Its purpose is to increase the desire of salesmen, distributors, and dealers to sell a certain brand and to make customers more eager to buy that brand. Personal selling and advertising can go only so far in these decisions: sales promotion provides an extra stimulus.

Albert W. Frey, "Promotion," a supplement to *Business Horizons*, February 1961.

Objectives of Sales Promotion Before we go into details about specific promotional techniques, let us take a minute to review just what businesses are trying to accomplish with sales promotion.

Internal Sales Promotion Objectives One sales promotion objective is to get company employees more interested in the company's products and promotions. For example, the Great Atlantic & Pacific Tea Co. (A & P) has used video cassettes to reach all employees from senior executives to checkers.[6] Such cassettes can be used for sales training or to explain advertising strategies, special promotions, company policies, new procedures, or any other promotion-related information.

About a score of companies are showing their employees TV shows—for example, "The Du Pont TV News," and "The Smithkline TV News"—that keep employees informed of developments that affect the company (for example, new legislation) and other topical information.[7] Such news can help keep employees up to date on products, policies, and promotions of the firms.

The most important internal sales promotion efforts are directed at salespeople and other customer-contact persons such as complaint handlers and clerks. Sales promotion tries to keep the salespeople enthused about the company through sales training, the development of sales aids such as flip charts, portable audiovisual displays, and movies, and participation in *trade shows* where salespeople can get leads. Other employees who deal with the public may also be given special training to make them more aware of company programs and a more integral part of the total promotional effort. The concepts are:

> **Sales promotion efforts begin at home with the company's employees—especially the sales staff, clerks, and other customer-contact people.**

> **The objectives of internal employee promotions are to raise or maintain employee morale, to train employees how to best serve customers, and to gain employee support, cooperation, and enthusiasm for various promotional efforts.**

> **Sales promotion supplements the activities of the PR department by providing some of the equipment and materials needed to conduct an internal PR program (for example, slides, films, displays, bulletin boards, and pamphlets).**

Middleman Sales Promotion Objectives Sales promotion efforts with middlemen (wholesalers, retailers, credit agencies, and service organizations) may be used to smooth out seasonal fluctuations in orders, to encourage larger-quantity purchases, to get more channelwide support for a particular promotion, to get more or better shelf space, or to capture a new account.

[6] See *Advertising Age*, December 29, 1975, p. 29.
[7] Eric Morgenthaler, "Some Firms Like It If Their Employes Watch TV at Work," *The Wall Street Journal*, November 17, 1975, p. 1.

To smooth out seasonal fluctuations in orders, for example, a middle-man might be offered a special deal, such as "two free items when you buy ten" or "an off-season discount of 20 percent." Larger-quantity purchases may also be gained through such promotional techniques.

Channelwide support for a promotional program may be gained in a variety of ways. For example, the company could offer special discounts during the period of the promotion or special cooperative advertising allowances. It could sponsor sales contests for wholesale or retail sales-persons or place demonstrators in stores to help with sales. Furthermore, the company could offer "push money" (special bonuses) to retail or wholesale salespersons and, in general, keep distributors and dealers informed about upcoming promotions.

Better shelf space may be earned by offering retailers an attractive display package, by giving unusual discounts or retail margins or by involving retailers in a popular contest or other consumer promotion.

New dealers may be won through any of the techniques just mentioned. The idea is to use some short-term incentive to win the support and cooperation of everyone involved, including the consumer, to make an overall promotion work. The concepts are:

> **Sales promotion efforts with middlemen are designed to gain support, cooperation, and enthusiasm for various promotional efforts, to move merchandise through the channel on a regular basis, and to reach the consumer through coordinated display, advertising, and personal selling efforts.**

> **Sales promotions with middlemen give added support to a promotional effort by getting everyone in the channel to work together to give the consumer a good deal; such coordination and cooperation creates mutually satisfying exchanges throughout the distribution system.**

> **Sales promotion supplements channelwide PR efforts by designing timely promotional programs that keep the general public and channel members interested in, and involved with, the firm.**

Consumer Sales Promotion Objectives

Sales promotions for consumers may be used to get people to try new products, to broaden sales by, for example, getting them to try a particular brand, to increase the volume per sale (20 percent off when you buy a dozen), to encourage new uses for products (for example, putting baking soda in the refrigerator as an air freshener), or to counter a competitor's promotion and maintain sales. We shall discuss such consumer sales promotion techniques as contests, trading stamps, cents-off deals, coupons, sampling, and rebates. Often publicity releases are used to generate interest in such promotions. Thus, again you can see the relationship between public relations, publicity, and sales promotion.

Consumer Sales Promotion Methods

You can learn about the details of, and managerial problems connected with, consumer promotions if you take a course in marketing communications or promotion. Here, we shall briefly discuss some of the promotions with which you may be familiar to give you some idea of how both buyer and seller benefit from sales promotions.

You should recognize the fact that specific sales promotion techniques tend to have cycles of popularity. For example, trading stamps were once a big thing because everyone wanted to get in on the action. When stamps became less popular, almost everyone seemed to drop them. No doubt stamps will return as a popular promotional tool. The same was true of rebates. In the mid-1970s, the auto companies started a rebate fad that lasted for a couple of years and then dropped off somewhat. A promoter should be careful to plan sales promotions based on the needs of the company and market characteristics, not on the latest fad or gimmick. Figure 14.2 shows the trend in sales promotion techniques from 1968 to 1975. We shall discuss each of these techniques later, but first let's look at product sampling because it is a very effective sales promotion tool.

Product Sampling Product sampling means that the promoter gives the consumers a free item to try. It is one of the most expensive sales promotions of all, but one of the most effective as well. Sampling is especially effective for introducing a new or improved product. No doubt you have received samples of a new toothpaste, soap, or other cosmetic product recently. If a producer feels that his or her product is superior, sampling is often the best and fastest way to prove it to consumers. Even highly skeptical consumers might try a sample, although such consumers might be almost impossible to reach with advertising. Samples may be delivered by mail (although high mail rates are making this less desirable), distributed door to door or in stores, or attached to another product sold in a store. Students, newlyweds, mothers, and other such groups have also learned that many companies send samples in gift packs that contain several different products.

Figure 14.2 MAJOR ADVERTISED PROMOTIONS BY TYPE (MAGAZINES AND SUPPLEMENTS ONLY)

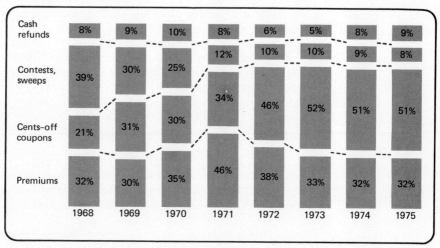

Redrawn with permission from the September 22, 1975, issue of *Advertising Age*, p. 23. Copyright 1975 by Crain Communications, Inc.

Sample Distributors, Inc., uses milkmen to distribute hard-to-handle products like frozen foods. They will distribute groups of products under the name "Pantry-Pak" or individual product samples. Kimberly-Clark Corporation sampled its new Kotex Lightdays in magazines such as *Family Circle* and *Women's Day* and in newsstand editions of *Seventeen*. A firm called Selective Sampling distributes Treasure Chest gift packs with fifteen to twenty samples each to financial institutions. Its affiliate, Associated Marketing Systems, distributes gift packs to new mothers in the hospital. The company also *sells* cosmetic packs to retailers for resale to consumers. These are only a few of the many different ways companies distribute sample products to selected market segments. Notice how many new middleman companies have formed to help manufacturers with their sampling problems. These middlemen "found a need and filled it" and are quite successful as a result.

Dan Ailloni-Charas, president of Stratmar Systems, notes the following objectives for massive sampling programs:

1. To best reach potential users of the product
2. To deliver a large enough sample to enable a potential user to make a judgment about the product or take a user out of the market for a period of time
3. To demonstrate the effectiveness of the product
4. To get accelerated trial or establish a repeat purchase pattern as quickly as possible
5. To gain lowest possible cost and best possible target audience
6. To coordinate with an advertising campaign or market rollout[8]

Students should recognize that the sampling of services is often as important as or more important than the sampling of goods. The benefits of a new health spa, miniature golf course, automobile diagnostic center, or any other such service are often best demonstrated through free samples. Coupons may be sent to selected people offering them a free trial. Satisfied people will tell their friends, and word of mouth will spread the message about the new service.

Nonprofit organizations might offer sample services as well. When people move to a new area, they need to find churches, libraries, recreation areas, and other such services. If a volunteer from a local church would invite the people to visit, a long-term mutually satisfying relationship could develop. Local museums, libraries, and recreation areas could offer special tours to new people through coupons delivered by Welcome Wagon or some other service organization. The concepts are:

> **A promoter can often establish a mutually satisfying relationship with a target market faster and more effectively by exposing that market to the product through a sample; this is true of both goods and services, including the services of nonprofit organizations.**

[8] Cited in Louis J. Hough, "Postage Increase Raises Ante for Product Sampling," *Advertising Age*, December 8, 1975, p. 6.

> Product sampling is one of the most expensive sales promotion tools, and so target markets must be carefully selected.

> Sampling benefits consumers by giving them an opportunity to try new products without having to spend their own money.

Coupons as a Sales Promotion Tool Every Thursday Marilyn Washington goes through the food section of her local paper and cuts out coupons for her next shopping trip. She was pleasantly surprised when she began receiving packages full of coupons for nonfood items in the mail. Marilyn figures she saves several hundred dollars a year by carefully clipping and using available coupons.

Because people like Marilyn shop for food so often, they are more aware of prices and price changes in the supermarkets than they are in the case of most other stores. People also love to find a bargain. That is why cents-off coupons are so popular among consumers and promoters. Manufacturers distributed 35.7 *billion* coupons in 1975, more than double the amount sent 5 years earlier and more than triple the amount sent 10 years earlier (see Figure 14.3).[9] Sixty-five percent of those households responding to a Nielsen survey in 1975 used such coupons, up from 58 percent in 1971.[10] Not all coupons are for food, of course, but food is a key promotional item.

As Figure 14.2 shows, cents-off coupons made up over half of the major advertised promotions in the mid-1970s. "The number of companies using coupons is already more than 1,000; every home in the United States will be the target of close to 500 coupons . . . and, for all their

[9] See *Marketing News*, July 18, 1975, p. 3, and *Advertising Age*, January, 5, 1976, p. 32.
[10] *Marketing News*, July 18, 1975, p. 3.

Figure 14.3 TREND IN COUPON DISTRIBUTIONS, EXCLUDING IN-AD COUPONS (BILLIONS OF COUPONS)

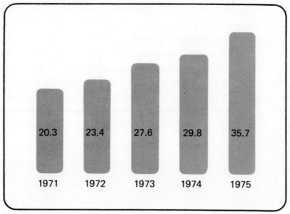

From "A New Look at Coupons," *The Nielsen Researcher*, no. 1 (1976), p. 3.

popularity, only 3% to 4% of all coupons distributed are ever redeemed."[11]

Nielsen reports that about 20 percent of the merchandise sold in food stores has a cents-off price. "The revenue loss due to the cents-off promotion is not charged generally to advertising, but is charged as a reduction to the manufacturer's gross margin. The aggregate reductions in gross margin because of cents-off promotions are in the multi-billion dollar range. . . ."[12]

We, as consumers, can benefit from using cents-off coupons because they do represent a true savings in price. The problem for manufacturers is that many people rely too heavily on cents-off deals and do not develop any loyalty to a certain brand. The Reuben H. Donnelley Corp. introduced the Carol Wright direct-mail "heavy-user" coupon program to minimize the costs of coupon promotions and to optimize results. The program is designed to reach heavy users of coupons, such as larger families. Other sales promotion middlemen have developed programs to assist marketers in delivering coupons in the cheapest and most effective way. The key concepts behind coupon promotions are:

> **Coupons are an effective way to motivate consumers to try a new product or to continue using an established product; the advantage over sampling is that couponing is much less expensive.**

> **Coupons should be used selectively; otherwise, consumers may drift from brand to brand seeking the best coupon deal rather than establishing a mutually satisfying relationship with one firm.**

> **Coupons benefit consumers by giving them an opportunity to try new products at a discount or to buy established products for less.**

> **Coupons are especially effective for service organizations because they can increase traffic in the off-season and introduce new services quickly and efficiently.**

Premiums Brian Lastovika is a college freshman who enjoys the college life. He has been exposed to many products in what he considers rather clever ways. For example, he has noticed many students wearing T-shirts with slogans from leading manufacturers or with their brand name (for example, Budweiser). He has also seen towels, glasses, umbrellas, and other products with promotional messages or brand names in a prominent position. Brian asked his advertising professor about this and found that these products were called *self-liquidating premiums.* That is a fancy way of saying that a manufacturer or other marketer sells a product like a T-shirt for the price he pays for it. The idea is to get publicity for a

---

[11] William A. Robinson, "How Marketers Responded to the Money Crunch in '75," *Advertising Age*, January 5, 1976, p. 32.

[12] H. D. Wolfe and D. W. Twedt, *Essentials of the Promotional Mix* (New York: Appleton-Century-Crofts, 1970), p. 152.

product by having people wear the shirt or use the glasses where others will see them. The name "self-liquidating" means that the consumer pays for the full cost of the item and, in effect, promotes the product at little or no cost to the seller. A retailer might use a self-liquidating premium such as low-priced pop (soda) to generate store traffic. Again, the idea is to give the consumer a good deal and get some recognition in return.

Self-liquidating premiums are just one example of various premiums offered the public. In-pack or on-pack premiums are often very effective. The idea is to attach or enclose some product that consumers would like. Examples include the "gifts" in Cracker Jack boxes, toothbrushes attached to toothpaste tubes, and towels in a soap box. Consumers like such premiums because there is no special effort needed (like mailing a coupon) to get the bonus product.

Another rather interesting premium in this age of recycling is the reusable container. Examples include jelly in a reusable drinking glass and coffee in a carafe. The consumer is often willing to pay more for a product that is packaged in such an attractive, useful container.

Other premiums are offered through the mail. This involves saving labels or box tops and mailing them in for some kind of merchandise. This is not as popular a promotional tool and is much less easily managed by the organization.

The whole idea of premiums is to attract a consumer to a product because of the "extra" premium, so that he or she will buy the product, learn of its benefits, and become a regular customer. As a sales promotion tool for sellers, premiums are second only to cents-off promotions in popularity.

Trading Stamps Trading stamps may be considered a kind of premium because they are given to consumers as a reward for buying in a particular retail store. The stamps are saved by consumers and later redeemed for merchandise or cash (usually merchandise).

Stamps were very popular during the 1960s. They were used in a variety of stores including gasoline stations, supermarkets, department stores, drugstores, and dry cleaners. The cost of giving stamps tended to be quite high, however, and many stores felt that price cutting would be more effective.

One of the factors that hurt stamp programs was the energy crisis in the early 1970s. Gasoline stations no longer needed to promote gas (there was a shortage) and trading stamps and other such premiums were eliminated. Supermarkets also became quite price conscious in the early 1970s because of unit pricing, beef shortages, and other such factors, and they too stopped giving stamps. When gasoline stations and supermarkets stopped giving stamps, many other stores followed suit because stamps are most effective when several stores offer them at the same time.

Trading stamps are still an interesting and effective promotional tool that will no doubt become popular again. Consumers now seem to be more interested in coupons, contests, and other sales promotion tools.

Contests and Sweepstakes Contests and sweepstakes are popular sales promotion tools for both promoters and consumers. But such promotions are difficult to manage and often have many legal implications. Contests and sweepstakes are too complex to discuss in detail here. However, the key concepts are:

> **Contests and sweepstakes may be used to generate enthusiasm for a product among salespersons, middlemen, and consumers.**

> **Contests and sweepstakes can develop store traffic by bringing people in to deposit entry blanks or check winning numbers.**

> **Contests and sweepstakes are the hardest sales promotion tools to manage and evaluate—for marketers *and* for consumers; they should be used with great care, and expert advice should be sought.**

Rebates (Cash Refunds) As you can see in Figure 14.2, cash refunds have always been a factor in sales promotion strategy. But they were never so popular as they were in the mid-1970s when the automobile companies used cash rebates to promote the sales of an excess inventory of cars that built up during the "energy crisis." The success of automobile promotions prompted other companies to try rebates as well, and rebates became the fad of the mid-1970s. But like all fads, this one did not last, and cash refunds have returned to being an occasional promotional tool.

The primary use of cash refunds is for the introduction of new products. They are also used to encourage repeat purchases. For example, often the consumer must send several box tops or other proof of purchase to get a refund. Sometimes cash refunds are used to encourage purchase of high-margin (profitable) items. For example, an offer might be to give 50¢ off on frozen strawberries if you buy ice cream.

Because of all the fuss involved (clipping, form filling, and mailing), there is a low redemption rate for most refund offers. The company thus generates some interest for a product without incurring much cost.

Display One sales promotion tool that links manufacturers with retailers is display. Salespeople who call on retailers often have primary responsibility for getting good shelf space and for setting up attractive displays. There is much competition for shelf space in most retail stores, and so the manufacturer that provides attractive, compact, easy-to-use display materials often can get a priority position.

Window displays are effective in drawing the consumer into the store. Point-of-purchase or internal displays serve as reminder advertising and attract the consumer to a particular brand.

You could learn much about retail display and other promotion tools in advanced marketing courses or by reading books on the subject.[13] The

[13] For example, see John F. Luick and William L. Ziegler, *Sales Promotion and Modern Merchandising* (New York: McGraw-Hill, Inc., 1968).

point to remember is that sales promotion tools such as display help link manufacturers with retailers and make promotion a total channel effort.[14]

Ad Agencies, Sales Promotion, and Public Relations   Advertising agencies often manage all or almost all the mass promotion activities for firms, including advertising, public relations, publicity, and sales promotion. In fact, among the larger advertising agencies, 72 percent of those in the $40–$90 million category and 92 percent in the over $90 million category have separate units for the sales promotion function.[15] This means that a manufacturer or wholesaler can turn to his or her communication specialist for assistance in the complex sales promotion area. This includes help in promotion research, display design, display purchasing, layout and printing, and audio/visual aids (these are usually extra costs).[16] Assistance in promotion planning, promotion strategy, premium selection, and arrangment for contest judging, coupon planning, and cash refund handling are likely to be free.

One benefit of using one ad agency for advertising, public relations, publicity, and sales promotion is that there is likely to be more coordination and integration among the various promotional elements. The other major promotional tool, personal selling, is easily coordinated by having the advertising department of the firm act as a liaison between the sales area and the ad agency.

[14] For a systems perspective on promotion, see William G. Nickels, *Marketing Communications and Promotion* (Columbus, Ohio: Grid, Inc., 1976).

[15] "A Study of the Advertising Agency Sales Promotion Function," Sales Promotion Committee of the American Association of Advertising Agencies, 1974, p. 11.

[16] Ibid., p. 43.

FOR REVIEW

Key Terms

Among the more important terms and expressions discussed in this chapter are the following:

Institutional publicity is publicity that concerns organizations in general.

Product publicity is publicity that concerns goods, services, people, and places.

Publicity is any information about an individual, a product, or an organization that is distributed to the public through the media and that is not paid for, or controlled by, the sponsor.

Public relations is the management function that evaluates public attitudes, identifies the policies and procedures of an individual or an organization with the public interest, and executes a program of action to earn public understanding and acceptance.

Sales promotion consists of those marketing activities, other than personal selling, advertising, and publicity, that stimulate consumer purchasing and dealer effectiveness by means of such things as displays, shows and exhibitions, demonstrations, temporary offers of material rewards, and various other nonrecurrent selling efforts.

Key Concepts

Among the more important marketing concepts introduced in this chapter are the following:

› **Public relations is the marketing activity that recognizes the organization's obligation to be socially responsive, helps the organization to develop programs, and establishes two-way communications with the public to be sure everyone is satisfied with the organization's policies, personnel practices, and procedures.**

› **Public relations is an action-oriented program of meeting the public's demands; it is not just a communication function.**

› **Public relations begins with good marketing research to determine public opinion and to define the PR task.**

› **Public relations and publicity should be coordinated and integrated with the other promotional elements.**

› **Publicity may be favorable or unfavorable.**

› **Publicity may be released voluntarily or involuntarily; an individual or organization normally has little control over the media.**

› **Sales promotion efforts begin at home with the company's employees—especially the sales staff, clerks, and other customer-contact people.**

› **Sales promotion supplements the activities of the PR department by providing some of the equipment and materials needed to conduct an internal PR program (for example, slides, films, displays, bulletin boards, and pamphlets).**

› **Sales promotions with middlemen give added support to a promotional effort by getting everyone in the channel to work together to give the consumer a good deal; such coordination and cooperation creates mutually satisfying exchanges throughout the distribution system.**

Discussion Questions

1. Public relations has been defined as "the management function that evaluates public attitudes, identifies the policies and procedures of an . . . organization with the public interest, and executes a program of *action* to *earn* public understanding and acceptance." Do most organizations seem to follow that definition? Give examples to prove your point.

2. Name several persons and/or organizations that have suffered recently from negative publicity. Could such publicity have been

avoided? Can such publicity be countered by an effective PR program? Why or why not?

3. Is public opinion important to your college or university? Do present attitudes seem mostly favorable or unfavorable? How could public opinion be improved?

4. Think of any organization you have had contact with as an employee or member. Was internal public relations very effective? Were employees and/or members enthused about the organization? Why or why not? What would you do to increase internal support?

5. Are you affected much by such sales promotion schemes as contests, coupons, rebates, premiums, or cents-off sales? Which are most attractive to you and your classmates? Why? Would most people feel the same?

6. Notice which movie stars and entertainers are getting the most publicity lately. Did their popularity come before or after the publicity? If before, how did they become popular?

7. Evaluate the effectiveness of publicity versus advertising. Should an organization spend more, less, or about the same on publicity as they do advertising? Why?

8. What could your school do to generate more favorable publicity through its students. Does a good basketball team help or hinder a school's public image? Why?

9. Which is more important to an effective PR program: an effective program of listening to customers and other "publics" or a great group of writers? Explain your answer by giving real-life examples.

10. Discuss the effect of the media on the political ambitions of presidential candidates and congresspersons. Which candidates made effective use of publicity and how did they do it?

CASES

A Local Band
Generating Publicity

Ron Gerhard, Bud Fransdale, and several of their friends got together in high school and started a band. They could play all kinds of music, but they preferred to play rock 'n' roll and Top 40 songs. After high school, several members of the band drifted off, but they were replaced, and Ron and Bud became serious about launching their band. The band played several high school dances and was fairly well known in the area, but the future was too uncertain for some of the band members. Ron and Bud decided they needed some marketing help. They wanted to advertise in the local papers and make up some posters for schools and local stores. But Ron felt that such advertising would not be effective and would not get them the exposure that they needed. The band had five members now and had to make it soon or risk losing some of the members.

1. How could Ron and Bud generate favorable publicity for their band?
2. Would you recommend that the band go ahead with its plans to advertise in local papers?
3. What "publics" should the band consider in launching a PR effort?

The Lion's Club
Publicity and Sales Promotion

The Lion's Club of Montgomery County, Maryland, is sponsoring a carnival to raise funds for eye research. The carnival will be held on the grounds of a local church and will feature rides, games, and an old-fashioned weiner roast. The Lion's Club has contacted a group that will set up all the rides, games, and food. All the Lions have to do is publicize the event to get people to come.

1. How would you publicize the carnival? To what groups would you direct your efforts?
2. Would you spend much money on advertising in the local media? How much?
3. The Lion's Club is thinking of making the carnival an annual event. How could this year's carnival be used to publicize next year's event?
4. What kind of sales promotion devices or strategies could be used to generate interest in the carnival?

5

Face-to-Face Communications

Often the most effective way to establish long-term marketing relationships is through personal contact and negotiation. This is usually accomplished by means of salespeople. Chapter 15 explores personal selling and sales management. Salespeople may be viewed as communications middlemen who provide a means for buyers and sellers to have free and open discussions. In Chapter 15, we shall look at consultative selling, the most sophisticated version of selling, and we shall show how selling techniques help people achieve more satisfying exchange relationships.

Selling is only half of face-to-face marketing exchanges. The other half is buying. Chapter 16 explores the buying function among consumers, retailers, and other marketing institutions. Buying is a critical marketing function and is increasing in importance as shortages become more widespread.

Selling and Sales Management

the personal touch

15

LEARNING GOALS After you have read and studied this chapter, you should be able to:

1. Explain why selling is such an important and interesting career possibility.
2. Define the following terms: personal selling; sales development; sales maintenance; consultative selling.
3. Describe the various functions salespeople perform.
4. Describe the selling process.
5. Show how selling skills can be used by anyone in their daily interactions with others.
6. Contrast consumer selling with industrial selling.
7. Give examples of how consultative selling may be used to improve the selling process.
8. Discuss the advantages and disadvantages of being a sales manager.
9. List the functions of a sales manager and briefly explain each.
10. Explain how nonprofit organizations could benefit from the application of selling skills.

> *The most fruitful way to view selling is to see it as a buying process which the [salesperson] brings about in the prospect and customer. Thus the process begins with the discovery of the needs to be met by the product or service being sold.*
>
> Harold C. Cash and W. J. E. Crissy*

INTRODUCTION Give selling a chance. Studies show that many college students are turned off by the whole idea of personal selling as a career. Such students may be making a mistake in that they might not understand how interesting and challenging a sales career can be. This chapter is about personal selling, sales management, and selling's role in marketing.

To give you some idea of the importance of personal selling in our economy and career opportunities it provides, let's look at a few figures. First, U.S. Census data show that nearly 10 percent of the total labor force is in personal selling. Considering the fact that many people who work for nonprofit organizations in a selling role are not included, this means that over 7 million people are employed in sales.

Consider also the fact that about 20 years ago the cost of an industrial sales call was estimated to be just over $17. By 1969, the cost had run to over $49. And more recent figures show costs are over $60 *per call* and climbing! The cost of calling on ultimate consumers is much lower, but

* *Guiding Buying Behavior* (Flushing, N.Y.: Personal Development, Inc., 1965), p. 6.

The Joy of Selling

[Salespeople] are lucky people. At a time when many discussions of work focus on such dismal topics as alienation, dehumanization, and boredom, [salespeople] do work that brings them into contact with other people, lets them establish productive human relationships, and is seldom repetitious or dull. At a time when many people feel estranged from, or indifferent about, their jobs, [salespeople] do work that can be engaging and engrossing. And, at a time when many people feel that their jobs lack challenge and exhilaration, [salespeople] do work that can be deeply satisfying and fulfilling.

. . . We can say the same of sales managers. They enjoy most of the satisfactions their [salespeople] enjoy; in addition, they experience the special gratification that comes from helping men [and women] develop and grow. More than many jobs, sales management is deeply fulfilling because, like selling, it is inseparable from relationships with people.

From V. R. Buzzotta, R. E. Lefton, and Manuel Sherberg, *Effective Selling through Psychology: Dimensional Sales and Sales Management Strategies* (New York: Wiley-Interscience, 1972), pp. 1–2. Copyright © 1972 by John Wiley & Sons, Inc. Reprinted by permission of the publisher.

Everyone lives by selling something

Robert Louis Stevenson

From the beginning to the end of everything, whether
it be one lifetime, or the span of a civilization, the art
of persuasion is employed to convince someone of the
value of an idea. Those of us in business have the
responsibility to make our way within the framework of
recognized human values, and in this regard selling is
an important means of communicating. The innovations
of a man or an organization are necessary to meaningful
existence and selling is as much a part of the idea cycle
as are technical formulae.

 **ADDRESSOGRAPH MULTIGRAPH**
20600 CHAGRIN BOULEVARD • CLEVELAND, OHIO 44122

Courtesy of Addressograph Multigraph Corporation.

there is no doubt that personal selling is an extremely expensive form of
persuasive communication. Given the fact that a marketer can reach
mass markets through advertising media for less than a penny per
exposure, it takes much analysis and statistics to show that a salesperson
is often well worth the money.

Over all, one can conclude that personal selling is a very expensive,
very important part of marketing and deserves our attention. Personal
selling is also a very interesting career (see the insert "The Joy of
Selling"). In addition, the financial rewards of a selling career are high
and getting higher (see Table 15.1).

You are no doubt familiar with many salespeople through your personal contacts. There are salespersons at retail stores and service sta-

Table 15.1 AVERAGE EARNINGS OF SALESPEOPLE

Annual salary	Percent of salespeople at salary level	
	1972	1975
Less than $10,000	6	2
$10,000–$12,500	26	3
$12,500–$15,000	32	19
$15,000–$20,000	30	48
$20,000–$30,000	5	25
$30,000 and over	1	3

Reprinted by permission from *Sales & Marketing Management* magazine, March 8, 1976. Copyright 1976.

tions; there are salespeople who call on prospects to sell insurance, real estate, brushes, encyclopedias, vacuum cleaners, cosmetics, and magazines; and there are auto salespersons, and a host of other such salespersons. Every sales job is slightly different but all of them call for certain basic skills, techniques, and human understanding. The following section contains the story of a student who has had a long and successful sales career. Marge Burns is much like many marketing majors, and so her story reveals many interesting insights into personal selling.

BASIC CONCEPTS OF SELLING— THE STORY OF MARGE

Marge Burns was a hard-working person from the time she was very young. She helped her mother and father around the house when she was 4 years old, and, as she got older, she helped mow lawns, shovel snow, paint, clean the house, and do other necessary chores. When Marge was 13, she was exposed to her first outside job in personal selling. Marge got a paper route with the daily paper and built her territory from thirty-five customers to fifty-five customers. Marge was very pleased with her results. Through her paper route, Marge earned $12.65 per week—enough to buy many of her "extras."

At 16 Marge went to work at a local drive-in restaurant as a waitress. She was paid $1.10 per hour, but, with her tips, her weekly earnings often exceeded $120. Marge became more adept at working for and with people on this job and found that most people responded favorably (in this case with a tip) to a conscientious, friendly, dedicated salesperson (waitress).

After high school, Marge got a job at one of the leading department stores. She worked in various departments, but her tasks always included selling. Marge was given several salary increases and more job responsibility as management recognized her dedication and ability to work with people. Marge was surprised by her continual success in her various jobs because she felt she was basically a rather shy person. She always believed that successful salespersons had to be outgoing, fast-talking individuals with lots of personality. Marge hardly fit that description. She was relatively quiet; she talked easily to people, but was not particularly "quick with words," and she had a rather reserved personality. Nevertheless, Marge felt she had been successful at selling and was eager to try other selling jobs.

A year and a half after graduation from high school, Marge enrolled in State College. She was unsure about what would be a good major, and so she sampled courses in psychology, sociology, journalism, and other areas. One of her courses was on the principles of marketing, and it was in this course that Marge learned the basics of personal selling, advertising, and other marketing functions. Marge was still working part-time in a local retail store and found much of what she learned in marketing to be interesting and directly applicable in her work. She was especially interested in the potential marketing careers for women. But Marge was very hesitant about selling, because she did not feel she had the right kind of personality.

Marge eventually majored in marketing and took courses in sales management, marketing research, promotion, marketing management, and consumer behavior. Marge was surprised to find that much of the material she had discussed in psychology and sociology was being applied in marketing. Her consumer behavior and marketing research

"The commercial said, 'No salesmen will call.' I'm a saleswoman."

courses were particularly fascinating. One of Marge's teachers encouraged her to pursue a sales career when she graduated because selling was an entry into all aspects of marketing management.

It was with great hesitancy and doubt that Marge began applying for sales jobs with companies like Procter & Gamble, General Foods, and other consumer-goods firms. Because of her past experience, she was much more comfortable in discussing careers in retailing with Sears and the other major stores. But when Procter & Gamble offered Marge a starting annual salary that was $2,000 over what most retailers offered, plus a company car and good benefits, Marge said yes.

Marge was surprised to see that the Procter & Gamble interviewers were as interested in her outside activities and work experience as they were in her grades. They were especially pleased by her obvious dedication to her jobs and her drive to succeed. Procter & Gamble trained Marge in selling techniques, including the use of prepared (canned) sales talks that were used for practice and for gaining confidence. Marge enjoyed her contacts with retailers and the challenge of winning shelf space, setting up attractive displays, and introducing new products. Marge was surprised, though, at how little "selling" she had to do. That is, she did not have to practice the get-your-foot-in-the-door, overcome-objections, close-the-sale aggressive sales techniques she felt were part of all selling. Instead, Marge used her friendliness, sincerity, and professionalism to *work with* her customers to generate more sales for them and for her company. Marge did quite well in this job, and her salary was satisfactory.

Then one day Marge met a man who was in sales at IBM. He had heard about Marge through a friend and was impressed with her ability. He told her about sales opportunities at IBM and the special opportunities for women. Marge had heard from some of her college friends that many companies were going out of their way to hire women and minorities. The man at IBM confirmed this notion. He talked Marge into meeting his boss at IBM and discussing career opportunities. Marge was hesitant because her technical skills were not one of her strengths.

After much discussion and interviewing, Marge decided to switch to IBM. She went through a very comprehensive training program and eventually became a very successful member of the sales force. Marge felt like a professional marketer at IBM because she was given so much responsibility. She was trained to be a consultant to her clients and to work with them in solving many different problems, not merely marketing problems.

Marge never did acquire the sales personality she had felt was necessary on such a job. She continued the same professional, yet friendly style she had found successful throughout her career. Her income varied at IBM, but it usually ranged between $19,000 and $30,000 per year.

Marge left IBM after several years of successful selling. She is now pursuing a career as a mother and part-time salesperson for a local newspaper. Marge is now back in class studying for her MBA degree. She hopes some day to be a product manager, so that she can become involved with all phases of marketing on a managerial level.

Let's review some of the things you can learn from Marge and other salespersons. Personal selling is an art that may be applied in all aspects of a person's life. People can apply the same techniques to sell their ideas and their political philosophy as they use to sell soap and computers. Marge showed us that a person can begin very early to practice selling strategies (at first, to get jobs mowing lawns and shoveling snow and later to get contracts for large firms). One misconception people have is that salespersons have a recognizable personality and sales approach. But Marge taught us that successful salespersons do *not* differ from the general population on most measures. There is no correlation between sales success and intelligence, personality, age, level of education, or most other such measures.[1]

In other words, one cannot group salespersons into a common bundle and analyze them. All of them are different, all use slightly different approaches, and all have different personalities, skills, and educational backgrounds. We have seen, though, that Marge was able to succeed at many different kinds of sales jobs, and so there must be some similarities between salespersons.[2] The basic concepts are:

> **There is no such person as a "born" salesperson or sales manager. People become good in these fields by applying effectively certain well-established principles of the behavioral sciences (and, of course, by mastering the many technical aspects of their jobs).**

> **Selling strategies may be learned by anyone. But above all a salesperson must be flexible enough to adjust to the wants, needs, and demands of individual customers. Being a good listener and developing a warm, responsive manner is often more important than being a good talker or clever manipulator.**

> **Part of sales training is personal development. It is important for all salespeople to study their personal strengths and weaknesses. Such self-knowledge enables a person to develop the interpersonal skills needed for successful selling.**

THE ROLE OF PERSONAL SELLING Personal selling may be defined as interpersonal, face-to-face interaction for the purpose of creating, modifying, exploiting, or maintaining a mutually beneficial exchange relationship with others.[3] "Based on limited surveys, it has been estimated that approximately 55 percent of total sales expenses of U.S. industry have involved personal selling, with the

---

[1] A survey of the literature by Samuel N. Stevens supports these conclusions. See J. Allison Barnhill, *Sales Management* (Glenview, Ill.: Scott, Foresman and Company, 1970), pp. 13–23.

[2] For an interesting review of different sales personalities and buyer types, see V. R. Buzzotta, R. E. Lefton, and Manuel Sherberg, *Effective Selling Through Psychology: Dimensional Sales and Sales Management Strategies* (New York: Wiley Interscience, 1972). This book shows that many different styles are possible in sales, but there is a professional approach that is best.

[3] Adapted from Patrick J. Robinson and Bent Stidsen, *Personal Selling in a Modern Perspective* (Boston: Allyn & Bacon, Inc., 1967), p. 14.

remainder allocated to nonpersonal means (36 percent for advertising and 9 percent for point of purchase and all other)."[4]

Most people are somewhat familiar with the role of salespeople who call on *consumers* because they have observed their behavior in many different situations. Therefore, the following material will concentrate on the responsibilities and selling activities of industrial salespeople. As you will see, many of the concepts and principles are the same for *all* sales jobs.

We shall show how salespeople establish "mutually beneficial exchanges" by performing a variety of activities. We shall then discuss how these activities may be applied in any situation that calls for "interpersonal, face-to-face interaction for the purpose of creating, modifying, exploiting, or maintaining" exchange relationships. Such situations occur for politicians (while campaigning), for government agencies (in dealing with other organizations), for nonprofit organizations (when soliciting funds), and for all other individuals and organizations that must rely on others for what they want and need.

The Salesperson's Functions

One of the unexpected, yet rewarding aspects of a sales career such as Marge's is the variety of tasks an industrial salesperson is expected to perform. Face-to-face selling is just one of many important functions. Other functions include:

1. Market analyzing
2. Prospecting
3. Communicating
4. Gathering intelligence
5. Servicing
6. Developing customers
7. Maintaining customers
8. Defining problems
9. Solving problems
10. Managing time
11. Allocating resources
12. Self-improvement

Market analysis includes forecasting future sales, monitoring competitors, and keeping up with the current economic and social environment. Selling jobs are almost always interesting because everything that affects the economy affects the salesperson's role. A good salesperson is aware of what is happening in many areas besides business.

Prospecting involves the searching out of potential new accounts, building new orders from present accounts, and generally finding market needs.

Communicating is the heart and soul of a salesperson's function. The emphasis is *not necessarily* on persuasion, but on opening and maintaining a friendly dialogue with prospects. Persuasive communication is just one element of a total communication function.

Gathering intelligence is one of the more important, yet widely overlooked, functions. Salespersons do not like to make out reports or spend time in the office reporting what is going on in their areas. They prefer to be out "selling," usually because they are paid a commission to "sell,"

[4] Ibid.

not to report. Nevertheless, salespersons provide key data on customer complaints, competitors' behavior, and other marketing intelligence. Included are reports on the salesperson's daily activities and results.

Servicing includes consulting with customers about their needs and problems, providing technical assistance (or arranging for such help), finding financial (credit) assistance, arranging for delivery, monitoring installation, supervising training of the buyer's personnel in product use, and maintaining a liaison between the service department of the selling firm and customers.

Developing customers means that the salesperson is responsible for helping customers to increase their business (profits). This may involve giving personal advice or finding professional help in areas such as inventory control, promotion, product development, and pricing. The idea here is that by developing the customer's sales, salespeople increase their own sales. Often information is the most valuable product a salesperson can give customers.

Sales maintenance is a crucial function that basically involves establishing goodwill and maintaining good relationships with customers.

Defining problems goes far beyond responding to customer demands. It means carefully analyzing the customer's business to determine where problems exist. It also involves finding and reporting *potential* problems with the products, services, prices, and delivery system of his own firm.

Solving problems is an overall function that basically calls for flexibility, innovativeness, and responsiveness. If a problem demands the resources of several firms, the salesperson may help find those resources. A salesperson thus could become a general consultant, rather than a one-firm representative, and could earn the respect and trust of clients.

Managing time is one of a salesperson's biggest problems. Much time is often wasted in travel, unproductive calls, and waiting. Time management is one area where salespersons need periodic training.

Allocating resources is often necessary during times of scarcity or when certain customers prove unprofitable to serve. The salesperson provides key input into managerial decisions about opening new accounts, closing unprofitable accounts, and allocating efforts to various accounts.

Self-improvement involves training, retraining, and personal efforts to keep physically and mentally fit. A salesperson needs to be self-motivated, and one cannot maintain the right frame of mind and physical pace that selling demands without keeping healthy. Other training involves learning more about customers and their needs, competitors and their activities, and the products, policies, and programs of one's own firm.

It is apparent from this discussion that personal selling may involve a variety of tasks that call for a person with outstanding ability. It is important that you recognize the diverse tasks of salespeople because so much of the public feels selling is synonymous with persuading or manipulating. Some salespeople apparently feel that way also from the way they act.

The Selling Keeping in mind the fact that face-to-face selling is just one role of an
Process industrial salesperson, let us examine in more detail the selling process
itself. It usually includes the following steps: (1) preapproach, (2) approach, (3) presentation, (4) the sales dialogue, (5) the close, (6) follow-up.

The *preapproach* is one of the most important steps in the entire sales
process because it establishes the background and strategy to be followed. The preapproach follows prospecting and includes gathering
information about prospects to see whether they have a need and the
resources to buy. The preapproach also involves finding *who* to talk with
and *when* and *where*, and *how* to tailor the discussion. Discussions with
salespeople who have called on the firm previously might help, as might
postsales records, journal articles, and other such information. The more
information a salesperson can gather about a firm and its employees, the
better (within obvious limits). Often such research will reveal the personality characteristics of various influentials within the firm, their
interests, and their attitudes toward the seller and competitors. A final
step in the preapproach is to arrange a convenient time and place to
meet the person or persons who are able to get the salesperson into a
position where his or her products will be most favorably reviewed.

The *approach* establishes the tone for the entire selling relationship,
and so it must be carefully planned. Often *where* the approach takes
place is as important as what is said. If a client can be approached
outside his or her office, away from phone calls and other distractions,
the sales call might be more effective. Because first impressions are
important, a salesperson's appearance and actions should be appropriate to the occasion.

Often the approach is used simply to establish a potential sales relationship—no further immediate attempt is made to make a sales presentation. Instead, the salesperson might ask to be allowed to study the
wants, needs, and specifications of the buyer. That process might take
days or months, depending on the product. The salesperson would be
searching for areas where a need exists and determining who would be
involved in a purchase decision.

Often the salesperson will go back to his company with a detailed
analysis of the customer's needs. A product offer will be designed, a
price will be determined, and a sales presentation will be designed.
Charts may be made, financing arrangements may be determined, and
all aspects of the sale might be prepared *before* the sales presentation.

The actual *sales presentation* may have to be made to more than one
person. Often the salesperson will bring several assistants (for example,
an engineer, a finance person, and so on) to aid in the presentation. The
presentation is designed to establish a dialogue with the customer
whereby all of his or her needs, objections, and opinions are free to be
aired. If the customer seems receptive, a close might be attempted
immediately, but, if not, there is usually plenty of time to get answers to
questions and to return. After all, the goal is to establish a long-term
relationship, and so one should not rush the process. On the other hand,
unnecessary delays should be avoided as well.

After the order is closed, the salesperson must follow-up with the
customer development, customer maintenance, and service functions

"OK, you've got five minutes"

CORPORATE PRESIDENT

Would this situation intimidate you or motivate you?

The people we are looking for would be motivated by the opportunity to convey their ideas to the President of a Fortune 500 Company. They would not view him as a fire breathing dragon, but rather as a policy maker and a man who makes decisions. Therefore, when you are marketing a service such as ours, he's the right man to see.

We're not suggesting that it would be easy. On the contrary it's a difficult assignment and not everyone is qualified to handle it. That's why we become very selective when we decide to add to our marketing team.

You must have a proven record of achievement in business, education or the military service and a confidence that goes beyond your years. You must be subtle yet bold, aggressive yet tactful. You must want to help top executives define problems . . . and present solutions—much like a consultant.

Our successful Time-sharing Marketing Representatives have come to us from a diverse range of educational and business backgrounds; from

Finance to Science and from Sales to Education.

We are The Service Bureau Company, pioneers in the management time-sharing industry. An industry that has literally boomed in the last decade. Our growth has been both dynamic and sure. All forecasts for the future see an increased demand for the services we provide to the international business community.

We are an equal opportunity employer with positions currently available throughout the U.S.

We would like to know more about you, and we're sure you'd like to know more about us. Drop us a resume or a brief letter. Today.

The Service Bureau Company

SBC® Director of Marketing
Management Time-sharing
500 West Putnam Avenue
Greenwich, Conn. 06830

A Division of Control Data Corporation

The Salesperson as Market Manager

The old-time [salesperson]—the story-telling, hard-living, back-slapping salesman of playwright Arthur Miller—is dead. He has been replaced by a company representative who is a market manager of his territory, who sells within a keenly competitive business structure, who functions as an educator, and who is intelligent and mature. He is also a problem solver always aware of the business needs of the buyer or firm and always sensitive to the emotional needs of those with whom he is conducting business. This changing character of the salesman's role came to light in the early fifties, gathered momentum in the late fifties, and by the sixties was well accepted by the business community.

As a market manager, the salesman has become increasingly responsible for planning and managing his sales effort, functioning as a market analyst in his territory, acting as the eyes and ears of his company in his territory, and representing his company on the highest ethical plane.

As a problem solver, he must understand his customer's business needs. He must know how his product can best service the needs of his customers or prospects. He must differentiate his product and service in competition with other products and the services of other salesmen. The salesman, however, is increasingly acting as a consultant to his customers, especially the smaller firm. Depending on the salesman, the product, and the customer's situation, salesmen may be required to give assistance in one or more areas such as cost control, sales promotion and advertising, stock control, training of a sales force, training of employees to use equipment, production methods, quality control, design and layout of equipment, etc. This type of *systems selling* is especially important today in the electronics and computer fields. More and more salesmen are required to sell to a group of men representing various interests within the purchasing company. He also is called upon to function as one member of a group of experts from his company who survey the needs of a potential user company and present a solutions program to a group of men representing the surveyed firm.

This is the new world of selling.

From Joseph W. Thompson, *Selling: A Behavioral Science Approach* (New York: McGraw-Hill Book Company, 1966), p. 21.

described earlier. As you can see, the modern salesperson is really a market manager in his territory (see the insert "The Salesperson as Market Manager").

PERSONAL SELLING SKILLS Everyone could benefit from learning more about personal selling techniques and strategies. Personal selling teaches one to (1) analyze the wants and needs of others, (2) view situations from the perspective of both buyer and seller to make necessary adjustments, (3) persuade others that one product would meet their needs better than another, (4) satisfy the needs of others through every means at one's disposal, and

(5) establish open two-way communication that enables established relationships to continue and grow. These skills are useful not only for business representatives, but also for teachers, lawyers, politicians, and anyone else who wishes to communicate openly and persuasively with others.

Personal selling is a useful tool for all organizations as well. All organizations must have members to survive, and membership is usually best increased through personal selling efforts. Personal selling may also be used to raise funds, to persuade others to support the organization in any way that is desired, and to establish and maintain friendly relations with the community, government, other organizations, and the general public.

Finding Needs As we mentioned earlier, the first task of marketing and of selling is to analyze the wants and needs of a particular person or group. The guiding concept is still "find a need and fill it." An important skill in selling, therefore, is the ability to listen and ask questions to find out what wants and needs a prospective buyer has. What does he or she want from the product, service, or organization the salesperson represents?

For example, a marketer of washing machines should begin early in his contact with a customer to determine things like the following: (1) How many people are in the family? (2) How many children and what ages? (3) What kinds of fabrics will be washed? (4) What happened to the old machine? (5) What price do they expect to pay? (6) When do they need the machine? Given such information, the salesperson can guide the buyer toward the machine best suited to his or her needs and ability to pay. If necessary, financing may be arranged to make sure that the customer is not forced to buy a machine that will fail to satisfy all of his or her needs.

The same search for customer needs is necessary whether the product is a car, a church, a class in school, or a computer system. The concept is:

> **Selling begins with an analysis of the buyer's wants and needs.**

Satisfying Wants and Needs The second half of personal selling is finding solutions to customer problems. Again the guiding concept is "find a need and fill it." But what if the salesperson does not have what the customer wants? Either the salesperson should explain to the customer that he or she would be better off going elsewhere (and helping him or her find other solutions) or the salesperson should search elsewhere until the right solution is found.

Many sales relationships today involve many contacts over time and many different transactions. Personal selling establishes and maintains communicative relationships that enable such exchanges to continue. This increases the satisfaction of both buyer and seller. The concept guiding sales efforts is:

> **Selling is a continuous process that finds solutions to problems and increases the satisfaction of both buyers and sellers.**

> **Selling Establishes Mutually Satisfying Relationships**
>
> The increasing complexity and sophistication of many buying systems tends to emphasize the advisory or consultative capacity of the salesman. In the broader context, then, selling is communication oriented toward the development of dynamic, mutually beneficial relationships, or toward the achievement of some mutually compatible goals between producers and users.

From Patrick J. Robinson and Bent Stidsen, *Personal Selling in a Modern Perspective* (Boston: Allyn & Bacon, Inc., 1967), p. 207.

Selling does not end with an exchange. Salespeople should continue to service their customers after the exchange to assure that everything was satisfactory. The other half of this task is to be sure that the seller is satisfied with the exchange relationship. The sales concept is:

> **Selling establishes and maintains mutually satisfactory exchanges between buyers and sellers by continually monitoring all participants and adjusting the product offer as needed.**

The Salesperson's Image as a Selling Skill Research has shown that successful salespeople are those that most closely resemble their customers on a number of dimensions such as age, income, and religious preference.[5] A truly effective and skillful salesperson is one who can adapt his or her style to fit the needs of diverse customer groups. Thus, salespersons must be exposed to all kinds of subjects, so that they can talk intelligently and openly about any topic of interest to the customer, including sports, business, economic conditions, government restrictions, and various hobbies.

Salespersons also should dress as their customers would expect them to dress. Research has shown that the clothes a salesperson wears create a conditioned positive or negative response in prospects before the presentation is even begun. Books have been written on the subject of proper business dress.[6] Some even come with comprehensive questionnaires that, when processed, will tell a person what kind of wardrobe he or she should have for particular kinds of customers.

Marge found that there often was some initial reaction to the fact that she was a woman when she called on new accounts or new people within established companies. But she was usually able quickly to establish her professional role and to develop an open relationship with her clients. Marge learned that salespersons who are members of minority groups also may experience an initial reaction from some cus-

[5] For example, see F. B. Evans, "Selling as a Dyadic Relationship—A New Approach," *The American Behavioral Scientist*, April, 1963, pp. 78–79.

[6] One interesting one is John T. Molloy, *Dress for Success* (New York: Peter H. Wyden, Inc., 1975).

Minorities in Sales—More Blacks, More Women

In the last four years, the number of women and blacks in selling has doubled, reports a survey by Research Institute of America.

In the Jan. 21st [1976] issue of *Alert*, its weekly newsletter, RIA reports that its queries of a large group of top marketing executives show that 25% now employ blacks in the sales force, compared with only 13% in 1972. Thirty-eight percent of the executives said they now have women as salespeople, up sharply from 15% in 1972.

Reprinted by permission from *Sales & Marketing Management* magazine, March 8, 1976. Copyright 1976.

tomers, but usually they have no problem establishing their role as problem-solving professionals. The concepts for sales are:

> **Salespersons are generally most effective when dealing with customers whose interests, backgrounds, age, sex, and nationality are similar to their own.**

> **Appearance is an important element in creating a favorable impression with customers, but different customers respond favorably to widely different hair and clothing styles. The principle is that dress should be appropriate for the market.**

> **Salespersons can overcome any initially unfavorable first impressions by being professional, by establishing their problem-solving ability, and by shifting attention away from themselves to customer needs and the product.**

One reason that some buyers are surprised to find a woman calling on them is the fact that, in the past, most companies did not employ women in sales. The Research Institute of America found that 81 percent of the companies they surveyed did not employ women.[7] Those that did found them to be good salespersons. Today this situation is changing, and the opportunities for women have never been greater as companies scramble to make up for their past neglect. Women are moving into consumer sales and industrial sales. Women are also moving into consumer-affairs departments and, in general, have many more marketing opportunities today than ever before. The same is true for minorities in marketing. Opportunities are greater than ever and the success rate is quite favorable (see the insert "Minorities in Sales—More Blacks, More Women").

CONSUMER VERSUS INDUSTRIAL SELLING Much of the selling function at the consumer level is performed by advertising, publicity, display, and other promotional elements, in addition to personal selling. Salespersons often do little more than close the order. This varies greatly by product, however. For example, life insur-

[7] *Marketing News*, July 15, 1974, p. 1.

ance and encyclopedia salespersons perform the full gamut of selling activities from market analysis through follow-up.

At the industrial level (that is, sales from one firm to another), most of the promotional task is given to sales. Advertising merely opens the door for salespersons; publicity and sales promotion are support functions that increase the salesperson's effectiveness. But most of the basic negotiating is done face to face between a salesperson and a buyer or buying committee.

Marge had been employed in both consumer sales and industrial sales and found advantages and disadvantages in each. Consumer sales seemed to be more structured, and the salesperson was often given less responsibility. But the opportunity to meet new people all the time and to help them solve their problems was quite rewarding.

Industrial sales seemed to be more professional, more demanding, and more rewarding financially, although this varied considerably among firms. The firms that adopted the consultative selling or systems selling approach, which will be described shortly, were quite professional, and their training programs were extensive.

Marge enjoyed all the training sessions she had at both the consumer and industrial levels. She learned that sales was *the* revenue-producing function for the firm and that sales careers were much more rewarding, both personally and financially, than she expected. Salespersons were problem solvers for customers and their employers, and that is an important role.

Sales Development versus Sales Maintenance Industrial selling strategies have taken on new importance now that markets are tighter and competition is more intense. Some firms have found it best to divide the selling task into two entirely different functions—sales development and sales maintenance.[8] **Sales development** involves seeking out *new* customers, showing the buyers the selling organization's problem-solving capabilities, motivating the customers to buy, and converting the customer into a long-term account. **Sales maintenance** involves *keeping* the customer and making him or her a better account.

Extech International, for example, divided its sales force by specific markets covered (for example, the university research field, the medical hospital field, and the chemical processing field).[9] Previously, each salesperson covered a particular geographic area; now salespeople go wherever their category of customer is located. Furthermore, Extech trained a specialized sales force to go after new business. A sales-development specialist should be trained to be a "creative strategist, a tactician capable of designing and implementing original, effective sales approaches . . . custom tailored for each prospect and for each person influencing the purchase."[10]

[8] George N. Kahn and Abraham Schuhman, "Specialize Your Salesmen," *Harvard Business Review*, January–February, 1961, p. 90.

[9] Howard M. Anderson, "Selling by Marketargeting," *Sales & Marketing Management*, December 9, 1975, pp. 65–66.

[10] Kahn and Schuhman, "Specialize Your Salesmen," p. 93.

Extech found that by dividing its market twice—into customer categories and into new clients versus established clients—it was able to increase sales by 31 percent with no increase in sales personnel.[11] They called the whole sales-development and sales-maintenance process *"marketargeting."* This is what they say about it:

You know from the outset that you will be less efficient because of duplication of selling effort, but that effort will be well worth it. Markets today aren't an inch deep and a mile wide; they are a mile deep and an inch wide.

Such specialization in selling is making obsolete the whole process of assigning territories, measuring territory potential, and establishing quotas based on those potentials. Instead of concentrating on territories, effective industrial salespersons may concentrate on particular customer groups. Specialized selling (that is, sales maintenance and development) also calls for new methods of compensation, new ways of establishing sales goals, and new ways of allocating funds.[12] For example, sales-maintenance people would be paid a salary rather than a commission, and sales goals would be based on maintaining and building accounts rather than soliciting new ones. Furthermore, sales budgeting would take into account the differing needs of new-account salespersons versus maintenance salespersons. Some concepts to guide sales managers in the future are:

> Industrial salespersons are often most effective when they deal with specific kinds of customers such as banks, universities, and government agencies.

> Industrial selling is often more effective when the selling task is divided between sales development (getting new accounts) and sales maintenance (keeping old accounts).

> Specialized selling means that salespersons should *not* be limited to territories and that traditional compensation techniques should be changed.

Consultative Selling When Marge was a trainee at IBM, she learned for the first time about a concept called **consultative selling.** Marge was told that, as a consultative salesperson, she was the manager of a personal-service business; she managed her territory, her time, and her customer contacts. She was also taught that a consultative salesperson sells not just a product, but a *system of products* and the inherent benefits of a total system (that is, equipment maintenance, customer service, and so forth). Rather than concentrate on sales, Marge was to concentrate on profit (that is, the best net return on investment possible within her territory). She was also trained to help manage the business of her customers. Marge often felt

[11] Anderson, "Selling by Marketargeting," p. 66.

[12] For a more detailed discussion of these points, see Alton F. Doody and William G. Nickels, "Structuring Organizations for Strategic Selling," *MSU Business Topics*, Autumn 1972.

she knew much more about the day-to-day problems and operations of her customers than she did about IBM. She felt that by increasing her customers' business, she would increase her own sales as well. Finally, Marge learned to be flexible and to not let short-run sales possibilities ruin the long-run profit outlook.

Marge learned to sell profitable products to profitable customers effectively and efficiently. That was the essence of consultative selling. She wished that she had learned these concepts earlier in her career, for they are applicable in all sales situations. In brief, the consultative salesperson:[13]

1. Performs a long-term business planning function for customer-clients.
2. Helps customer-clients define their businesses, their markets, and their product-service systems.
3. Maintains wide, multifunctional access inside client companies and their key customers.
4. Sells systems of services and products, with primary emphasis on services.
5. Draws on the full complement of company functions and services for support.

What consultative selling tells most salespersons is this:[14]

1. Segment your markets and concentrate on heavy buyers.
2. Seek out their needs.
3. Sell solutions to their problems by offering a whole bundle of products and services designed especially for them.
4. Provide educational, consultative, and other personal services for clients.
5. Act as a representative of the buyer as well as the seller and try to know as much about buyers' needs as they themselves do.

What impressed Marge most about consultative selling is that it put the buyer's needs first. Selling was not viewed as a process of persuading or manipulating but of assisting and solving problems. Wouldn't it be wonderful if salesclerks, car salespersons, and all other salespeople would treat their customers that way? Some already do, and the best ones will in the future. The idea is to establish long-term friendly relations with clients, not to make sales at any cost. When a salesperson adopts the style of consultative selling, he or she has become a true professional.

[13] Mack Hanan, J. Cribbin, and H. Heiser, *Consultative Selling* (American Management Association, 1970), p. 14.
[14] Based on Mack Hanan, "Join the Systems Sell and You Can't Be Beat," *Sales Management*, August 21, 1972.

Industrial Salespersons—An Endangered Species?

Mistraining and misuse of industrial salespeople, skyrocketing costs, and social changes are making them an endangered species, according to Henry Lavin, chairman, Lavin Associates, Inc., Cheshire, Conn., industrial marketing consultants. Interpolating McGraw-Hill research statistics, he predicts the average industrial sales call will cost $230 by 1980, compared with $84 in 1974. For traditional sales channels (ads, reps, direct mail, etc.), he says, astute marketing managers already are substituting key account selling techniques, team selling, mobile marketing, TV and phone conferences, conference selling, in-plant and out-plant customer seminars, creative sales promotions, catalogue microfilming, and computerized salesperson reporting. "Today's industrial sales engineer must either be the guiding light in these sales promotions or his place will be taken by specialists, machines, or even by management itself," Lavin said.

From *Marketing News*, January 17, 1975, p. 2. Reprinted with permission of the American Marketing Association.

Consultative Selling in Nonbusiness Organizations

Many people feel that personal selling is a function confined to business organizations. But can you imagine a successful church, school, union, government agency, or any other organization (individual) that could exist without applying personal selling skills? Salespersons in nonbusiness organizations often have different titles (for example, fund raiser, membership chairperson, negotiator), but the goals are still the same—to create, modify, exploit or maintain a mutually beneficial exchange relationship with others. Such relationships include union/management relationships, educator/student relationships, charity/donor relationships, and so forth.

Can you see how nonbusiness organizations could apply the concepts of consultative selling? Can you imagine a pastor consulting with his congregation or a school administrator consulting with students? Sometimes it *is* hard to imagine because so few nonbusiness organizations are adept at selling (communicating). But *all* individuals and organizations could improve their relationships with others by applying established strategies and concepts of personal selling.

SALES MANAGEMENT

It seems from our discussion with students that many are eager to become sales managers, but they are not nearly so eager to become salespersons. Entire courses are devoted to sales management; the following sections are designed to give you only a brief introduction to this topic. The functions of a sales manager include:

1. Participating in sales to key accounts
2. Hiring good salespersons
3. Sales training

4. Motivating the sales force
5. Sales forecasting and planning
6. Providing sales support
7. Sales control

A sales manager's job may not seem as glamourous and desirable when one considers all of his or her responsibilities and duties. Often sales managers make less money than the people they supervise. The sales force might work on a commission basis that can lead to very high incomes, whereas the sales manager may be limited by a salary-plus-bonus arrangement. Salesmen are relatively free to manage their own time and to be outside calling on customers. Sales managers usually spend more time behind the desk handling paperwork and preparing reports relative to budgeting, forecasting, or evaluating salespersons and sales results. Managers must also become so involved with the day-to-day planning, organization, and control of the selling process that they often lose much of the excitement that comes from winning a new

"Now get out there, Herman, and put your foot in the door, tell them a joke, get their attention, show them the product, demonstrate its features, nail the sale, and make a killing. Momma needs a new pair of shoes!"

Reprinted by permission from *Sales & Marketing Management* magazine. Copyright 1974.

account or finding new sales challenges. This is not meant to discourage people from sales management, but to *encourage* people to see the benefits of personal selling. Sales management is a very rewarding occupation for those people who have had the thrill of being in the field and doing a good job and are now ready to settle down more and earn a more steady, yet very acceptable income. Let's look in more detail at what sales management involves.

Participating in Sales Sales managers often call on key accounts and participate in the sales efforts of their sales force. Part of the sales-training function might include getting out in the field and working with trainees. More recently, sales managers and higher-level corporate executives have become involved in selling because of poor market conditions.[15] Such sales efforts can hinder the planning, organization, and control activities that managers normally pursue.

Field selling enables sales managers to better keep abreast of current developments in the market and gives them different perspectives on market problems and competitive conditions. Nevertheless, sales managers should normally keep their personal selling activities to a minimum. They usually have enough to do without getting deeply involved in selling.

Hiring Good People Good salespeople are not born that way. Yes, it is true that certain individuals do have the kind of personality and drive needed for many sales jobs, but many others could be trained to do as well. In the past, too much emphasis may have been placed on recruiting and too little on training. Even the best people cannot do well without some training.

The selection process in many, if not most, companies is still a rather difficult, unscientific process, often involving some questionable standardized tests and a casual, unstructured interviewing process. Friends recommend friends, and somehow some people get hired and others do not. Students often are surprised to find that appearance, personality, and attitude are usually given greater weight than grades. But it should be apparent that sales jobs, more than most careers, demand people with unusual drive, friendliness, and empathy. Standardized tests together with other selection procedures seem to do a relatively good job of screening out the least acceptable candidates. But the final selection process is often left to the sales manager because he or she is responsible for the performance of the person who is hired.

Sales Training The sales manager may also be responsible for all or part of sales training. There often is a person responsible for sales training to assist in this effort. Sales training involves educating salespersons in the following key areas:

Internal Organizational Data

1. The organization's policies, practices, and procedures
2. Industry facts and figures

[15] See "Executive Suite Salesmanship," *Business Week*, October 20, 1975.

3. The relationship of marketing to other functions
4. The sales structure and relationships with other marketing functions
5. Sales-support activities and procedures

Product Information

1. Product features and benefits
2. New applications of current products
3. Delivery, installation, and servicing policies, practices, and procedures
4. Price guidelines and policies

Competitor Information

1. Competitive features, benefits, and prices
2. Competitor's selling strategies (including systems selling)
3. New products from competitors
4. Comparative analysis of competitor products versus the company's products

Customer Information

1. Persons who influence the sale
2. Personal information about buying influences
3. Past experiences with each customer
4. Present status of customer needs
5. Key accounts and prospects
6. Territory boundaries and limitations

Personal Development Information

1. Compensation system and fringe benefits
2. Promotion criteria and procedures
3. Expected performance levels
4. Available training programs within and outside the firm
5. Time management
6. Territory (customer) management
7. Continuing education programs

Selling Skills

1. Listening skills
2. Finding customer needs
3. Practicing sales situations (simulation techniques, role playing, on-the-job observation)
4. Strategies for finding buying influentials
5. Communication strategies and skill development

It is readily apparent that sales training is a major responsibility. Sales training never ends because salespersons should be periodically exposed to new information and should be allowed to provide input into future sales courses. Often salespersons will go outside the company to learn specific selling skills, strategies, and procedures. But selling is more a matter of being responsive and flexible than applying known techniques or strategies. Therefore, many sales courses now stress listening, finding customer needs, solving customer problems, and learning how to utilize all the resources of the firm to accomplish these objectives. The sales manager then counsels the salesperson on how to implement these new ideas.

Motivating the Sales Force   The sales manager is responsible for maintaining the morale and productivity of the sales force. This responsibility is usually considered under the heading of "motivating the sales force." But people cannot be made more productive or happier by any magic formula. When you light a fire under some people, they just get burned. So the sales manager must learn how to *work with* his people. He becomes part counselor, part teacher, part father or mother figure, and part slave driver.

The task of motivating salespeople varies greatly from organization to organization. In organizations where the sales force must be able to face rejection day after day and still go forth with enthusiasm and confidence, the motivation task is often most important. This is true in most firms that sell real estate, insurance, encyclopedias, automobiles, and all products sold door to door such as cosmetics, vacuum cleaners, brushes, magazines, and pots and pans.

In industrial sales situations, the task of the sales manager is more sales support rather than motivation. The sales force does not normally face the same rejection rate, and it works with clients over a long period of time.

When a sales manager does wish to motivate his people, there are many tools at his disposal. They include direct monetary incentives, indirect financial incentives, and nonfinancial incentives.[16] Financial incentives are controlled by setting up compensation systems based on a fixed salary, salary plus commission, straight commission, or bonuses. Normally a company that wishes to motivate its sales force will use some sort of commission system so that more effective and more efficient efforts lead to more financial rewards for the salespersons.

Indirect financial incentives include contests, fringe benefits, expense accounts, and other reward techniques such as a better company car, a better territory, or a nicer office.

Nonfinancial incentives are often the real key to a manager's success at motivation. The sales manager should be perceived as a silent partner who is fighting for financial rewards for the sales staff and who also is there to provide training, counseling, and other personal assistance. The sales manager must strike an effective balance between being supportive of the salesperson and being task-oriented. That is, he must help the salesperson to be productive *and* to be reasonably satisfied doing his or her work.

[16] See H. Robert Dodge, *Field Sales Management* (Dallas: Business Publications, Inc., 1973), pp. 256–306.

Sales Forecasting and Planning One of the sales manager's major duties is to allocate the organization's selling effort among alternative uses. He must decide how to allocate resources to various products, salespersons, and customers. He does this by developing a *sales budget*, which should be coordinated with an overall promotional budget, and by preparing a *sales forecast* that becomes the basis for the budget.

First, the sales manager analyzes *market potential*, or the total demand for a product or group of products of an industry during a particular period of time. Then the manager looks at *sales potential*, which is the potential demand for his particular firm:

$$\text{Sales potential} = \text{market share} \times \text{market potential}$$

The sales forecast (that is, dollar revenue expected for a given period) is often used to determine production levels, size of the work force, and other crucial managerial decisions. The sales forecast may also be the basis for *sales quotas* or goals for the various functions of the organization, especially sales. It is beyond the scope of this book to discuss techniques of sales forecasting, budgeting, and quota setting. It is important, though, to recognize these important functions.

Providing Sales Support One of the important jobs in selling is to identify the actual and potential key customers for the organization. In almost all markets (for profit or nonprofit organizations) the "80–20" rule will generally hold. That is, 80 percent of the transactions or donations will come from 20 percent of the target markets. Heavy buyers or donors, therefore, are the key targets. Not only do they buy more, but they may also buy more often.[17]

The sales manager should work closely with the salesperson to provide any sales support needed to establish and maintain close relationships with key accounts. The salesperson might need the assistance of a financial expert, an engineer, or other such experts. Often the sales manager calls on the key accounts personally.

The result of a comprehensive sales support effort is "system selling." This means that the sales organization makes available to the buyer a whole bundle of services to back up the product; the basic product plus service package is called a "system." Services may include expert advice relative to the needs of the buyer; financial advice and aid; delivery, installation, and repair; warranty provisions; training aids; and any other desired services. The idea is *not* to sell the "system" itself, however; it is to sell the *benefits* of the "system." Thus the salesperson will stress cost reduction, profit increase, and peace of mind. Such assurances are based on sales support from the sales manager and, often, a full-scale sales-support staff.

Often the most important service a salesperson can provide his customer is information—information about products, market conditions, government actions, and economic changes. The sales manager, through

---

[17] Mack Hanan, "Join the Systems Sell and You Can't Be Beat," p. 42.

his or her marketing information system, is able to keep the sales force up to date on these issues and thus provide a valuable service to customers.

Sales Control Sales managers must, first and foremost, be managers. As such, they must plan, direct, and control the activities of the sales force. For example, they must establish objectives, plans, programs, and schedules. They also supervise, counsel, and coordinate. Finally, they measure, evaluate, and correct performance.

Of course, a sales manager may ultimately move up to become marketing manager, marketing vice-president, and president. Traditionally, marketing has been an excellent career path to top management. But one does not start as a marketing manager normally. One usually starts as a salesperson and moves up; each step on the hierarchy is interesting and challenging.

FOR REVIEW

Key Terms

Among the more important terms and expressions discussed in this chapter are the following:

Consultative selling is the effective management of sales relationships by determining and satisfying the total needs of customers, by providing them with broad systems of product and service benefits, by using the total resources of the selling firm, and by concentrating on profitable sales.

Personal selling consists of interpersonal, face-to-face interaction for the purpose of creating, modifying, exploiting, or maintaining a mutually beneficial exchange relationship with others.

Sales development is a specialized selling strategy designed to seek out new customers.

Sales maintenance is a specialized selling strategy designed to foster and preserve a good exchange relationship with present customers.

Key Concepts

Among the more important marketing concepts introduced in this chapter are the following:

› There is no such person as a "born" salesperson or sales manager. People become good in these fields by applying effectively certain well-established principles of the behavioral sciences (and, of course, by mastering the many technical aspects of their jobs).

› Selling strategies may be learned by anyone. But above all a salesperson must be flexible enough to adjust to the wants, needs, and demands of individual customers. Being a good listener and developing a warm, responsive manner is often more important than being a good talker or clever manipulator.

> Selling begins with an analysis of the buyer's wants and needs.

> Selling is a continuous process that finds solutions to problems and increases the satisfaction of both buyers and sellers.

> Industrial salespersons are often most effective when they deal with specific kinds of customers such as banks, universities, and government agencies.

Discussion Questions

1. Discuss with your classmates their attitudes toward selling as a career. What image do they have of a salesperson? Is it a good or bad image? Why?

2. Do you feel that Marge (the woman we discussed in the chapter) had an unusual sales career or a typical sales career? Explain your views. Explain why you would or would not enjoy such a career.

3. "There is no such thing as a 'born' salesperson or sales manager." Do you agree? What characteristics, if any, should a salesperson have that others lack?

4. How much of a salesperson's time do you feel is involved in actual face-to-face selling? Review the many responsibilities a salesperson has before answering this question. Does selling seem more complex or less complex than you thought it was?

5. What are the main differences between an industrial sales representative and a salesperson in a retail appliance department? Which would you rather be? Why?

6. How do the salaries for salespeople listed in Table 14.1 compare to the salary levels of other occupations? Do salespeople seem to work harder or less hard than other professionals? Why?

7. Describe how sales development would differ from sales maintenance in the case of a firm that sells office machines.

8. Compare consultative selling with what you know about traditional sales practices. Which seems more effective? What are the major differences?

9. Would you prefer a career as a salesperson or sales manager? Why? How do their responsibilities differ? Which one works harder? Longer? Earns more money?

10. What would be the responsibilities of a sales representative in a nonbusiness organization such as the Heart Fund or your local college? What would his or her title be? How would he or she be paid? Would such a career be rewarding? Why or why not?

CASES

Wyland's Men's Store
Selling Techniques

Wyland Thompson opened an exclusive men's store in Atlanta, Georgia. Wyland wanted to reach those men who wanted the finest clothes but were not interested in the conservative, older-looking styles that were offered by the other, more established men's stores. Wyland decided to create his own image rather than rely on established names like Gant or Hathaway in shirts or Hickey Freeman in suits. Wyland developed his own exclusive label and put it in his shirts, ties, and suits. Wyland's advertising stressed quality, service, and youthful stylishness. All merchandise was guaranteed by the store and unusual care was taken with alterations and the proper "look."

As a final touch, Wyland decided to train all his own salespeople and managers. All managers would be promoted from within (Wyland had successful stores elsewhere and shifted personnel to management when they were ready). Wyland heard about IBM's consultative selling system and wondered if it would be applicable in his sales-training program. He also heard about systems selling and felt that his store could use such concepts because they were selling a "total look" that included shirts, ties, shoes, socks, suits, sport jackets, slacks, and accessories.

1. How could Wyland's salespeople implement a consultative selling strategy in a clothing store?
2. Would such salespeople be paid a salary or a commission? What are the benefits of each?
3. Would some people be offended if the salespeople tried to sell a total package (system selling) that included shirts, ties, shoes, and so forth? How could such conflicts be minimized?
4. What is the product in Wyland's store? Is it a good product? How could it be made better?
5. Would Wyland's salespeople follow the stereotype of a fast-talking, back-slapping, hard-sell, traditional sales type?

Community Church
Fund Raising Strategies

Sonny Youngblood and his wife Bonita accepted responsibility for soliciting annual pledges for their church. Each year all the members of the church pledge a certain amount, and that becomes the basis for the church budget. Most people put their pledge cards in a basket that is passed around during the service. But about one-third of the congregation usually has not pledged by the end of the pledge period. Sonny and Bonita then ask a group of volunteers to call these people personally and ask for their pledges. This is not a pleasant task, because many people use this occasion to air their complaints against the church and the pastor.

1. How should Sonny and Bonita prepare their assistants to call on church members; that is, should the assistants be given any sales training and if so what kind?
2. Is it ethical to train church members in selling strategies for fund-raising purposes? Why or why not?
3. Should Sonny and Bonita accept help from every volunteer who wants to solicit pledges? Why or why not?
4. What kind of knowledge besides selling would be helpful to the volunteer solicitors?

Buying and Market Exchanges

the other half of marketing

LEARNING GOALS

After you have read and studied this chapter, you should be able to:

1. Explain the importance of buying in the marketing process.
2. Define the following terms: consumer buying; industrial buying; retail buying; broker; and consumer cooperative.
3. Draw a basic illustration of the buying process.
4. Describe how buyers can use the six universal marketing functions.
5. Discuss the role of retail buyers.
6. Show how centralized buying and computerized buying affects the selling process.
7. Describe the industrial buying process.
8. Give examples to show the role of influentials in industrial buying.
9. Explain why the purchasing (buying) function is becoming more important in industrial organizations and what this means for future careers.
10. Show how nonprofit organizations could benefit from more effective and efficient buying efforts.

> *It was the contribution of the marketing concept to recognize that, in a free enterprise economy, the buyer has more power than the seller in most market relationships.*
>
> Frederick E. Webster, Jr., and Yoram Wind*

INTRODUCTION Every market exchange involves a buyer. To understand market exchanges, therefore, you should know something about buyers and how they think and act. Because you are a buyer (consumer), you already have some insight into how consumers approach buying activities. But ultimate consumers are just one group of buyers in the total marketing process. Manufacturers buy all kinds of goods, services, ideas, and people as inputs to the manufacturing process. Middlemen such as wholesalers and retailers buy for resale. Institutions such as hospitals and schools buy materials for their own use and for their "customers." A product that someone buys from a retail store may have been bought and sold several times previously. What this means for a student of marketing is that there are many career opportunities in buying (purchasing) and that buyer behavior is one of the more important subjects in marketing. In fact, buying may be called "the other half of marketing," because without buying there can be no selling.

BUYING CONCEPTS

The Buying Process

Joel Tingelhoff was an economics major when he took his first marketing course. Joel said he would never want to be a buyer for an organization because "buyers don't do anything but sit around and get manipulated by a bunch of fast-talking salespersons." Many people are like Joel; they feel that buying is a relatively unimportant, routine activity that consists basically of placing orders. But buying is not a passive response to selling efforts. Buying is a very active process that involves several steps:[1]

1. Anticipation or recognition of a problem (need) and a general solution
2. Determination of characteristics and quantity of needed item
3. Description of characteristics and quantity of needed item
4. Search for, and qualification of, potential services
5. Acquisition and analysis of proposals
6. Evaluation of proposals and selection of supplier(s)
7. Selection of an order routine
8. Performance feedback and evaluation

* *Organizational Buyer Behavior* (Englewood Cliffs, N.J.: Prentice-Hall, Inc., 1972), p. 108.
[1] Patrick J. Robinson, Charles W. Faris, and Yoram Wind, *Industrial Buying and Creative Marketing* (Boston: Allyn & Bacon, Inc., 1967), p. 14.

The buying process varies considerably depending on whether the needed merchandise has been purchased before or is being purchased for the first time.[2] Furthermore, the buying process is influenced by the personality of the purchasing agent, the organizational setting, the state of the economy, and other factors. The concepts are:

> **The buying process in marketing is an active attempt to optimize exchange benefits for the buyer, not merely a passive response to selling efforts.**

> **The buying process varies among different organizations and is affected by the personality of the buyer, the organizational setting, and environmental factors.**

> **The buying process, like the selling process, may be described as "find a need and fill it," but this time it is buyers who analyze their own needs and actively search for others to satisfy them.**

The basic buying process is shown graphically in Figure 16.1. Note that the buying process does not end with the actual purchase. There is a follow-up procedure that provides input into future purchase decisions.

Functional Approach to Buying
The *market analysis* function is as important to buyers as it is to sellers. If they are to be effective, buyers should have a thorough knowledge of market conditions, sources of supply, and economic trends. Data provided by the government may be combined with private research to analyze such factors. But buyers also need more detailed information about particular firms, products, quantities and qualities, and prices. Factors such as certainty of supply, dependability in meeting schedules, and available technical assistance must also be evaluated. Such information often can be gained only through experience or through careful marketing research.

The market-analysis function is performed by buyers at all levels in the channel of distribution. Consumers analyze the market by shopping,

[2] Ibid.

Figure 16.1 THE BASIC BUYING PROCESS

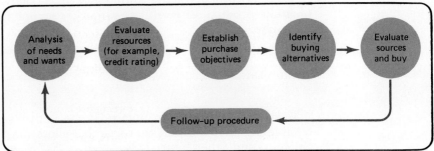

by seeking information from published sources and from friends, neighbors, and relatives, and by testing products in the home. Retail buyers also shop in key trade centers and seek inputs from published data and personal sources. The same is true for buyers at industrial, institutional, and nonprofit organizations.

The *communication* function enables buyers to transmit their needs to sellers and to negotiate the best terms. Open two-way communication among buyers and sellers is the key to establishing mutually satisfying exchanges. Consumers are becoming more aware of the power of communication in letting their views be known among governmental, business, and private organizations. Perhaps the greatest potential for improving the total marketing system comes from better communications among buyers, sellers, and society as a whole.

Buyers use the *market-segmentation* function to find those suppliers most likely to satisfy their wants and needs. Much of the narrowing-down process would result from market analysis. But decisions still have to be made about particular suppliers. For example, should price be a dominant factor, or quality, or some combination of price and quality? Which suppliers have the best reputation, prestige, technical know-how, and ability to provide needed services? The market-segmentation function enables the buyer to concentrate his or her buying power among those firms that can best satisfy the organization's needs.

Product differentiation is also a key buying function. During periods of scarcity, the buyer must design an offer that is attractive to sellers. This may mean providing the seller with market information, offering a higher price, assuming the transportation function, paying cash, or otherwise becoming a particularly attractive customer.

Through the *valuation* function, buyers can weigh all the variables that emerge from careful marketing research. For example, the valuation function would help establish criteria for evaluating products and suppliers. Some suppliers will have a good price. Others will offer special services. The valuation function puts values on each of these factors so that the best total offer can be determined.

Finally, buyers can use the *exchange* function to complete the sale. This may involve finding sources of credit. It may also involve negotiating final terms with the seller including delivery schedules, quality control procedures, and payment schedules. The concepts are:

> Buyers perform all the marketing functions—market analysis, communication, product differentiation, market segmentation, valuation, and exchange.

> By applying the six universal marketing functions, buyers can gain more control over the marketing process and can optimize exchange relationships.

Today sellers are more aware of the active search by buyers for reliable suppliers. To aid that search, sellers may provide directories, catalogs, and other buyer aids.

Directories and Catalogs Buyers in most organizations often use directories and catalogs to find needed merchandise and suppliers. Therefore, it is wise for a seller to be listed in various directories that will be used by potential customers. It is also helpful to publish a catalog that customers can use to find and order merchandise.

Ultimate consumers often use the Yellow Pages of the phone book as a handy directory of retailers. Consumers also consult the daily paper and look through the minicatalogs that are often inserted in newspapers. Sears, Wards, and Penny's have found that catalog sales are growing yearly. Catalog showrooms are one of the newer, more popular means of shopping for consumer goods.

Retail buyers also use the Yellow Pages. They may also consult directories such as *Sheldon's Buyers' Reference Book*, which lists items available to various retail buyers. Retail buyers also use catalogs, trade magazines and papers, and other sources to find needed merchandise.

Industrial buyers may use *Thomas' Register* and specialized industry registers. Retail and industrial buyers also attend trade shows, read trade magazines (industrial magazines), and use many catalogs. The concepts are these:

› **Directories, catalogs, trade shows, trade magazines, the Yellow Pages, and other sources are helpful resources to consumer, retail, and industrial buyers.**

› **Sellers who hope to reach various buyers should place information in various directories and catalogs to facilitate the market analysis and communication function for their buyers.**

Different Types of Buying Most people tend to think of selling as being the dominant marketing activity. Buying is usually viewed as the result of selling activity. But today buying has become so advanced that, more often than not, buying is the dominant activity and selling is the result of buying.

The following sections will look at buying activities as performed by consumers, retailers, institutions such as churches, schools, and hospitals, and industrial firms. As you approach this material, try to visualize marketing exchanges as an interaction between buyers and sellers and remember that buyers can and do initiate sales relationships as often as sellers.

Think of what you have bought lately and how active you were in buying and how passive the seller sometimes was in comparison. For example, think of your last trip to the supermarket or drugstore, your purchase of car insurance, your signing up for college, or your most recent trip to a restaurant. It is likely that you, as the buyer, initiated the contact, conducted a thorough market search (shopping), and *bought* what you needed. We shall see that this is true at all levels in the channel of distribution: Buying is a major determinant of exchange relationships.

CONSUMER BUYING The importance of buying is apparent when one studies the behavior of ultimate consumers. When consumers recognize a want or a need, they usually begin an active search to find satisfaction. Sellers recognize this active search by consumers and do everything possible to facilitate and stimulate such behavior. Sellers advertise heavily in newspapers and design catalogs so that consumers can easily shop at home for items such as food, appliances, automobiles, and other such goods and services. The personal search by the ultimate consumer for a product that will satisfy one of his or her wants or needs is called **consumer buying.**

Retail stores have further adapted to the active nature of consumer buying by making more and more of their outlets self-service. It was not until the 1930s that supermarkets became self-service, but the idea spread quickly. Today, most consumer goods, even insurance and automobiles, can be purchased without dealing with salespeople. The consumer's tasks are becoming more complex:

The more the retail selling and service functions are curtailed, the greater become the tasks and responsibilities of the consumer as buyer. The constant increase in the variety of products offered to him, the growing tendency to procure more goods and services in the market rather than to produce them in the home, the multiplicity of brands, the frequency of relatively small quality differentials, and the widely differing services offered by stores, all combine to add to the difficulty of the consumer's choice and to stress the importance of his being able to buy with intelligence.[3]

Consumers are forced to do more and more research in order to become effective buyers. Magazines such as *Consumer Reports* and *Moneysworth* are experiencing continued growth as consumers search for more objective information to aid their buying. Consumers also discuss products, prices, and retailers with their friends, neighbors, and family to learn where the best deals are. In short, consumer buying is becoming more and more important and is demanding more time, effort, and skill than ever before. The concepts are:

› Consumer buying is an active process that involves a careful analysis of available goods, services, and other products; a thorough search for alternative sources; and much research and discussion.

› Sellers can better serve consumers by providing more of the kind of information and education that would enable buyers to make more knowledgeable purchase decisions.

Consumer Cooperatives The rapid rise in food prices and other commodities over the last decade or so has increased the interest in consumer cooperatives. A **consumer cooperative** is a group of ultimate consumers who organize in order to buy goods and services for their personal use or for resale to the cooperative's members. A cooperative can be quite simple in concept. For example, five or six neighbors might pool their funds and take turns

[3] Theodore N. Beckman, William R. Davidson, and W. Wayne Talarzyk, *Marketing*, 9th ed. (New York: The Ronald Press Company, 1973), p. 408.

buying grocery products from wholesale outlets where prices might be lower and quality higher. But cooperatives may also become quite large and complex.

One of the largest consumer cooperatives in the country is Greenbelt Consumer Services, Inc. This cooperative has run its own supermarkets, pharmacies, gas stations, and furniture stores. Competition from large, efficient, profit-making companies has forced the closing of many of the food, gas, and pharmacy operations, however. It is easier to maintain control over a cooperative when it is small and has the active involvement of the membership. Large cooperatives tend to become more like profit-making operations and may not compete successfully with large, commercial competitors.

The idea of consumer cooperatives is a good one. Several people get together to increase their buying power or their volume in purchases. Food cooperatives often provide savings in transportation costs as well as food costs in that one person does the shopping for several others. The concepts are:

> **Consumers sometimes can pool their resources to buy better merchandise at lower prices through an effective and efficient consumer cooperative.**

> **A consumer cooperative is a group of ultimate consumers who organize in order to buy goods and services for their personal use or for resale to its members (and sometimes outsiders as well).**

Brokers: Middlemen for Buyers or Sellers A broker is an independent agent who negotiates the sale or purchase of goods or services for someone else. Usually, in the marketing of goods, the broker represents the seller and receives a commission or brokerage fee for the sale. But in periods when supplies are generally short, as we are experiencing in many areas today, brokers may be hired by buyers to search out and obtain scarce supplies. The broker is paid a fee for this function. Brokers may serve anyone who needs their services, but trade ethics and legal constraints prevent them from representing both buyer and seller in the same exchange.

Brokers are a big help to buyers and sellers because they can provide information about products, prices, and market conditions. A broker can help sellers make their products more attractive and can help with pricing and promotional decisions. A broker can help buyers in much the same way. The buyer can learn about prices in general, sources of supply, and the best way to obtain a consistent supply of materials.

Most people are familiar with real estate brokers and stockbrokers. Notice how these brokers represent both buyers and sellers. Both brokers may buy and sell for the same person. For example, a real estate broker will find people a new home when they move into a new city. If the people wish to move again, the broker may sell the home for them and arrange with a broker elsewhere to find another home. Furthermore, the real estate broker may help the seller prepare the home for sale, set a realistic price, and promote the sale in the papers. Brokers perform similar services for their corporate clients who wish to sell canned foods, raw materials, sugar, and other such products. The concepts are:

> Buyers and sellers can use brokers to learn about market conditions and to negotiate the best purchase or sale agreement.

> Brokers are a valuable marketing aid because they supply information about products, prices, sources of supply, available buyers, and other market conditions.

RETAIL BUYING There is an old saying in retailing that goods well bought are half sold. This means that if the retail buyer buys the kind of goods that consumers want and need, the selling process is made easier. Some people like to think of the retail buyer as a purchasing agent for his or her customers. A retail store is viewed as a place to store goods until consumers are ready to buy. In general, **retail buying** consists of the purchase of goods for eventual resale to the ultimate consumer.

Retail buyers have varying degrees of power. A huge retail chain such as Sears has tremendous buying power and can demand much from suppliers. Sears can even design its own products and have suppliers make them to their specifications. A small, local variety store, on the other hand, may have very little purchasing power. Often the buyers for such stores rely heavily on salespeople from the manufacturer or wholesaler to help them with ordering, inventory control, and promotions.

Who Initiates the Contact? Retail buyers may divide their time between hours spent in the store and hours spent traveling to various markets. Many salespeople contact retail buyers at the store and demonstrate their merchandise on the spot. Retail buyers look for reliability, honesty, and quality from their suppliers as well as good prices. Most retail stores rely very heavily on the salespeople from wholesalers and manufacturers for obtaining needed merchandise. Salespeople also provide needed market information, pricing data, and promotional assistance (including funds for cooperative advertising). Retailers expect certain salespeople to initiate the sales contact and to keep the retailers informed.

But retailers also spend much time out in the field searching for new sources of supply. Such buying trips will take buyers to New York, Chicago, San Francisco, Paris, Brussels, London, and other major market centers. Such trips often make retail buying an exciting and broadening career. Retailers are constantly searching for new ideas and new merchandise that will excite their customers or better serve their needs. Thus, retail buyers are not passive people who simply wait in their office for salespeople to call. They are active market researchers who get out into the field and look for new merchandise. The concepts are:

> Retail buying calls for a person who can deal with many salespeople from all kinds of firms and who can go into the field and negotiate deals with new suppliers.

> Retail buyers also must supervise several employees (for example, clerks), keep inventory, and generally manage one area of the store; buying is usually only one aspect of the job.

Resident Buying Offices Retailers such as department stores and clothing stores often use **resident buying offices** to help in their purchasing function. These resident buying offices have a staff of well-qualified persons who supply retailers with the latest market information and best sources of supply. This lessens the need for retail buyers to make frequent trips to key market centers. One buying office may serve many different retailers; thus, small retailers can have the benefit of up-to-date market information and share the cost with others. When resident buyers spot particularly good deals, they may be authorized to purchase the goods for their clients. Resident buyers may also generate group buying exchanges to get the benefits of volume purchases.[4] The concepts are:

> Resident buying offices serve as a permanent buying office for one or more buyers and provide market information, buying services, and other marketing assistance.

> Resident buying offices offer their clients expertise in purchasing; lower costs through shared purchasing with others and volume buying; constant contact with the market to take advantage of new fashions (fads) or special deals; and a constant flow of market information relative to prices, new suppliers, and other relevant data.

Centralized Buying In Chapter 11 we discussed retailers that belong to corporate and contractual systems. Such systems included giant retailers such as Sears (corporate system), retailers such as McDonald's, Holiday Inns, and Kentucky Fried Chicken (franchise systems), and retailers who belong to cooperatives or voluntary chains such as Western Auto and Ben Franklin Stores. These large integrated systems have a tendency to centralize their buying function to make optimum use of volume discounts and purchasing expertise. Salespersons who call on such huge-volume retailers must use special techniques because the buying process is so complex and subject to so many influences.[5]

Sometimes centralized buying involves committee buying. That is, several experts in a firm (for example, a finance person, an accountant, a purchasing agent, an engineer, and a marketing expert) will form a committee to evaluate a purchase from different perspectives, including financing and return on investment. Making a sales presentation before such a committee is quite different from facing a purchasing agent in his

---

[4] For a listing of resident buyers and the people they serve, see *Phelon's Resident Buyers and Merchandise Brokers of Department Store Merchandise, Ready to Wear, Millinery* (New York: J. S. Phelon and Company, published annually).

[5] For a detailed analysis of how sales forces can adapt to powerful buying centers, see Alton F. Doody and William G. Nickels, "Structuring Organizations for Strategic Selling," *MSU Business Topics*, Autumn 1972, pp. 27–34.

or her office. Often the seller will send a sales team to offer the same expertise in selling as the buyer has on the committee. The concepts are:

> The buying function in many organizations has been centralized to gain more market power, to share market information, and to negotiate the best deal for the total system.

> The expertise of centralized buying, including buying committees, calls for a new selling approach that recognizes the needs, procedures, and importance of these new buying centers.

Centralized buying creates greater effectiveness and efficiency for retailers and other organizations. It lessens the number of people involved in buying, concentrates buying power to negotiate the most favorable market exchanges, and generally improves the market position of the total system.

Computerized Buying   You may have noticed that many retail stores have new, electronic cash registers that are able to read coded prices on merchandise. Such machines are just one part of a total system of inventory control and ordering that goes all the way back to the manufacturer. Some stores are able to keep daily checks on inventory and have systems for automatically ordering merchandise when supplies get low. The retail store's computer will feed an order into the computer of a wholesaler, and the merchandise will be on its way with the next shipment. The wholesaler may have a similar computer link with several manufacturers.

Computer inventory keeping and ordering makes the buying process much more efficient by minimizing the need for repetitive buying. This allows purchasing agents to concentrate on finding new suppliers, when needed, and to negotiate new marketing agreements. Computerized buying strengthens the ties between retailers and their suppliers and often makes it difficult for new suppliers to break into the system. This is just one more example of how the increasing complexity of the buying process demands new sales strategies. Too often, firms use traditional sales approaches with buyers who no longer want or need such sales approaches. The concepts are:

> Computerized buying links retailers with suppliers in an efficient system of distribution.

> Computerized buying puts new demands on sales people and calls for new sales procedures.

INDUSTRIAL BUYING   Industrial buying consists of the purchase of goods and services necessary for the operation of the firm or for the production of the firms basic products. The purchasing function in industrial organizations has always been important. But today's business environment is placing more and more responsibility on this key area. Read what *Business Week* says about these new developments:

> . . . *the purchasing agent suddenly is moving into management's top ranks. First it was shortages that propelled him [or her] into the spotlight. Now it may be excessive inventories. Either way, the purchasing [agent] today is likely to be juggling a lot of new duties under the catch-all title of "materials manager" and to be poking into practically every aspect of business operations, from new products to capital spending.*[6]

To give the purchasing function more buying power, the department is being centralized in many firms, and more time is being spent on planning. Purchasing agents are anticipating shortages in all kinds of materials and are searching for alternative sources of supply as well as alternative materials. For example, electric utilities must make very careful choices among various power sources such as coal, oil, and

[6] "The Purchasing Agent Gains More Clout," *Business Week*, January 13, 1975, p. 62.

Complexity of Industrial Buying

Buying is a complex process, not an instantaneous act. Buying involves the determination of the need to purchase products or services, communications among those members of the organization who are involved in the purchase or will use the product or service, information-seeking activities, the evaluation of alternative purchasing actions, and the working out of necessary arrangements with supplying organizations. Organizational buying is therefore a complex process of decision making and communication, which takes place over time, involving several organizational members and relationships with other firms and institutions. It is much more than the simple act of placing an order with a supplier.

Responsibility for organizational buying is often delegated to specialists within the organization. Buyers (or "purchasing agents") are usually assigned responsibility for only a limited part of the total organizational buying process—namely, the actual purchasing activity consisting of the identification and evaluation of alternative sources of supply and the administrative details in establishing working relationships with vendors of goods and services. Other aspects . . . such as the determination of the kind of materials or items to be purchased and the standards to be used in evaluating potential suppliers, are often the responsibility of other members of the organization. . . .

From Frederick E. Webster, Jr., and Yoram Wind, *Organizational Buyer Behavior* (Englewood Cliffs, N.J.: Prentice-Hall, Inc., 1972), pp. 1–2. Copyright 1972. Reprinted with permission.

Figure 16.2 A MODEL OF THE BUYING ORGANIZATION

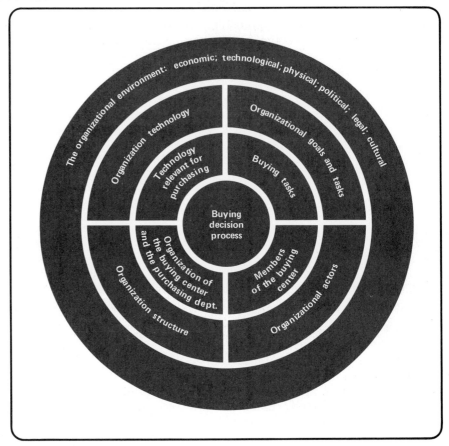

Redrawn from Frederick E. Webster, Jr., and Yoram Wind, *Organizational Buyer Behavior* (Englewood Cliffs, N.J.: Prentice-Hall, Inc., 1972), p. 54.

atomic energy. The cost of such energy may make up one-third or more of the cost of running a utility, and so one can see the importance of cost control in fuel purchasing. "At Gillette Co., where 90% of the cost of a typical product is in the materials, the materials management group . . . oversees inventories, warehousing, and shipping of products, and even works with research personnel on the development of substitute materials."[7]

Most people have a tendency to think of market research as the study of the buying market by sellers. But in an economy of shortages and increasing materials costs, market research often means careful research by the buyer for potential sellers. Figure 16.2 illustrates the complexity of the buying organization today.

When materials costs make up half or more of the cost of a manufactured product, purchasing management may be *the* key to profits. Therefore, purchasing has been moved up to the vice-presidential level

[7] Ibid., p. 63.

in many firms. Many firms are hiring MBAs (Masters of Business Administration) for their purchasing departments. "To make career opportunities in purchasing . . . more attractive, some companies are considering incentives for buyers similar to the compensation granted salesmen. . . . [Many] companies. . . would [need] a 20% increase in sales to achieve the same bottom-line change in profit that only a 1% reduction in the cost of materials would bring."[8] One can see that purchasing is likely to be a key marketing function for many years to come. The concepts are:

> **In an era of materials shortages and increasing costs, purchasing often becomes the key to increased profits.**

> **Market research may involve the search for needed supplies by buyers as well as the search for potential markets by sellers.**

> **As purchasing assumes more responsibility for corporate profits, the function will tend to become more centralized, to demand more highly trained personnel, and to pay some bonus for substantial cost savings.**

Supplier Development In addition to their functions as market researchers and purchasing agents of the firm, buyers may also be quite active in developing close interpersonal relationships with suppliers:

The basic concept of supplier development . . . is relatively simple. Supplier development is the creation of a new source of supply by the purchaser. A company can through its marketing efforts develop new customers. Exactly the same parallel exists on the procurement side. A company can through its procurement efforts develop new suppliers . . . thus the initiative in developing new sources of supply lies, not with the supplier, but with the purchaser.[9]

Robinson and Faris explain the concept further:

The buying companies' interest in being a good customer is based upon more than a spirit of altruism. As a purchasing agent expressed it, "In the long run, my job is a lot easier if my suppliers think of me as a good customer. I want them to want my business, because when they do they will hustle to get it and to keep it." The establishment, cultivation, and maintenance of good supplier relationships are considered to be intrinsically more important than the outcome of individual transactions.[10]

---

[8] Ibid.

[9] Michiel R. Leenders, *Improving Purchasing Effectiveness through Supplier Development* (Boston: Harvard Business School, 1965), p. 7.

[10] Patrick J. Robinson and Charles W. Faris, "Industrial Buying and Creative Marketing," (unpublished manuscript, Marketing Science Institute, 1966), p. 159.

Purchasing agents, therefore, must learn to work closely with salespeople in the interest of creating mutually satisfying long-term exchange relationships. The seller and buyer are both actively trying to develop the business of the other, so that both might survive and grow in a competitive economy. The concepts are:

> **Supplier development is a process whereby the buyer develops new sources of supply and assists present suppliers in making the exchange relationship long lasting as well as mutually beneficial.**

> **Purchasing agents and salespeople are both agents of their firms who are trying to establish, develop, and maintain satisfactory exchange relationships with other organizations.**

Reciprocity in Industrial Buying and Selling Although they may feel ethically and legally bound to buy from sellers who offer the best overall deal, some buyers also feel compelled to buy from those they sell to. This is called **reciprocity.** For example, the purchasing agent for a large tire-producing firm might feel obligated to lease cars that use their tires.

The federal government is very concerned about reciprocal trading relationships because they may restrict competition.[11] Naturally, purchasing agents develop interpersonal ties with certain suppliers, but ethical considerations should dominate such relationships so that the best interests of the public are served.

Understanding the Industrial Buying Process There were few studies of the industrial buying process until the 1960s. Since then, several studies have tried to develop models to explain the process. One basic model is based on the buyer's decision process and looks like this:[12]

1. Problem recognition
2. Identification of alternatives
3. Evaluation of alternatives
4. Selecting a course of action
5. Implementation

A similar model has four phases:[13]

1. Problem recognition
2. Assignment of buying authority and responsibility
3. Search process
4. Choice process

---

[11] See Reed Moyer, "Reciprocity: Retrospect and Prospect," *Journal of Marketing*, October 1970, pp. 47–54.

[12] Frederick E. Webster, Jr. and Yoram Wind, *Organizational Buying Behavior* (Englewood Cliffs, New Jersey: Prentice-Hall, Inc., 1972), p. 21.

[13] Frederick E. Webster, Jr., "Modeling the Industrial Buying Process," *Journal of Marketing Research*, November, 1965, pp. 370–376.

Neither of these models gives full recognition to the many internal and external forces that may influence the buying decision in a firm. The COMPACT model, developed by Robinson and Stidsen, recognizes the decision-making process (from awareness through commitment), the roles of various organizational members in the buying process (including the purchasing agent, operating management, and top management, and various levels of individual buying competence).[14] This model is very helpful in understanding the interactions and relationships involved in buying. But it too is incomplete.

A study by the Marketing Science Institute found that the buying process differed significantly depending upon whether the purchase was of a product that had never been bought before (new task), one that called for a slight modification of a past exchange (modified rebuy), or one that was bought regularly before (straight rebuy).[15] The resulting model of buying behavior was called BUYGRID. There has been some effort to simulate the buying process (that is, create a buying situation that could be placed on a computer and analyzed) using the BUYGRID model.[16] Such simulations can better reveal the relationships among buyer variables and the effect of various marketing strategies on buyer behavior.

We are now at a point where the buying task can be broadened to include internal and external variables. Webster and Wind have developed a model that recognizes individual factors, interpersonal factors, organizational factors, and environmental factors (see Figure 16.3). It also recognizes task and nontask variables. The point is that the buying process is now being studied rather intensively by marketers to learn more about what influences the buying decision and about techniques for making the buying function more efficient.

Buying Influentials The Robinson and Stidsen study that led to the COMPACT model of buyer behavior also reported on the number of people (called "influentials") involved in purchase decisions. The number of influentials varied from as many as forty people in "new" product purchases to as few as two or three in "straight rebuy" situations.[17] Perhaps you will be able to understand this process better if we give an example.

Linda Vincenzo is a secretary at a large college in the Southwest. Linda was not satisfied with the copying machines that were available in her office. She noticed that her friend Sharon had a Xerox machine that did a great job for her office. Linda asked her supervisor to push for a Xerox machine. Linda's supervisor asked several faculty members and other staff people what kind of copier they preferred, and most said Xerox. So the supervisor went to the college dean and requested a new

[14] Patrick J. Robinson and Bent Stidsen, *Personal Selling in a Modern Perspective* (Boston: Allyn and Bacon, Inc., 1967), p. 146.

[15] Robinson et al., *Industrial Buying and Creative Marketing*, p. 14.

[16] Yoram Wind and Patrick J. Robinson, "Simulating the Industrial Buying Process," in *Marketing and the New Science of Planning*, ed. Robert L. King (Chicago: American Marketing Association, 1968), pp. 441–448.

[17] Robinson and Stidsen, *Personal Selling in a Modern Perspective*, p. 139.

Figure 16.3 A MODEL OF ORGANIZATIONAL BUYING BEHAVIOR

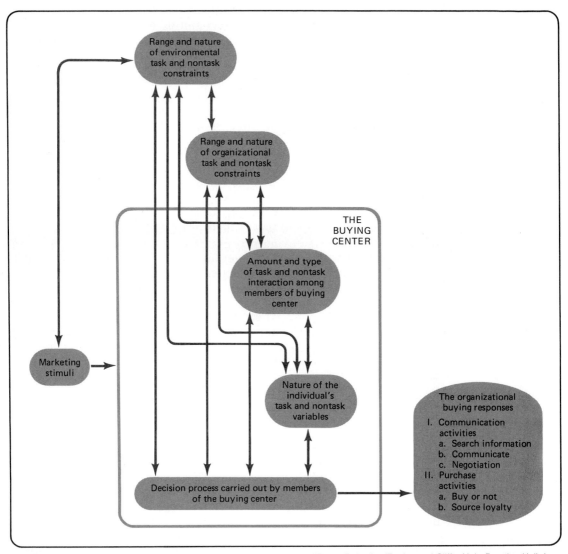

Redrawn from Frederick E. Webster, Jr., and Yoram Wind, *Organizational Buyer Behavior* (Englewood Cliffs, N.J.: Prentice-Hall, Inc., 1972), p. 30.

Xerox copier. The dean put in a request to the provost, who in turn put in a request to the top administrators who ordered the machine bought through the purchasing department. Notice how many people influenced the purchase: Linda, her friends in other areas, the supervisor, faculty and staff, the dean, the provost, various administrators, and the purchasing department staff. Sellers must recognize that the buying process depends on many influentials and should try to reach as many of these persons as possible to win the order. Often the seller (such as Xerox) will advertise on television, because TV reaches everyone who might influence a purchase—including secretaries, administrators, and faculty. It is easy to see why Xerox and the other large copying machine producers tend to dominate the market—they dominate the input that is received by influentials. The concepts are:

> **Buying decisions are usually the result of a series of interactions between people (called influentials) who have tremendous impact on the final purchase decision.**

> **Sellers who wish to influence a purchase decision must reach multiple influentials, not just the purchasing agents who negotiate the final sale.**

Leasing (Renting) Versus Buying
There is a growing trend among buyers in all organizations to lease rather than buy needed merchandise. Industrial buyers may lease everything from the building they are in, to machinery, airplanes, trucks, tools, cleaning supplies (rags), and part-time secretaries.

Consumers are also learning the benefits of renting versus ownership. Thus, consumers are renting everything from homes to cars, lawn mowers, tools, furniture, and garden equipment.

The growing trend toward leasing will have a significant effect on marketing in the future. Negotiations with individuals and organizations that want to rent are quite different from sales transactions. Some of the advantages of leasing are: (1) It frees capital for other uses; (2) it minimizes service problems (they are the responsibility of the lessor); (3) it enables the user to have the most modern equipment; and (4) it enables users to lease equipment only when needed, and so the equipment does not take up space when not needed. Buyers should learn as much as possible about leasing to optimize the use of capital and to explore all market alternatives.

BUYING BY INSTITUTIONS AND NONPROFIT ORGANIZATIONS
The purchasing function in many institutions (for example, hospitals, schools, prisons) and nonprofit organizations (for example, charities, social clubs, causes) is often less professional and scientific than it is in profit-making organizations. The process may be similar, and the purchasing agents as well educated, but the resources available to conduct market research and market analysis often are scanty. As a consequence, many institutions and nonprofit groups pay more for capital goods, equipment, and services than do similar profit-making corporations.

There is a greater recognition today of the importance of the buying function in all organizations. Nonprofit groups are now starting cooperative-buying schemes and other procedures to lower their costs of resources.

There are many opportunities for marketing majors to assist institutions and nonprofit organizations in their buying function. In fact, the entire purchasing area is one of great promise for the future. Remember, for every sale there is a buyer as well as a seller. Careers in buying, therefore, are available at all levels in the channel—industrial, wholesale, and retail. Purchasing careers can also be followed in nonprofit organizations and institutions. We hope this chapter has increased your interest in this area and has encouraged you to read more.

FOR REVIEW

Key Terms

Among the more important terms and expressions discussed in this chapter are the following:

A **broker** is an independent agent who negotiates the sale or purchase of goods or services for someone else.

Consumer buying is the personal search by the ultimate consumer for goods or services that will satisfy his or her wants or needs.

A **consumer cooperative** is a group of ultimate consumers who organize in order to buy goods and services for their personal use or for resale to the cooperative's members.

Industrial buying consists of the purchase of goods and services necessary for the operation of a firm or for the production of the firm's basic product.

Resident buying offices serve as a permanent buying office with a well-trained staff that provides one or more buyers with market information, buying services, and other marketing assistance.

Reciprocity means that firms will tend to buy from the same firms that buy from them.

Retail buying consists of the purchase of goods for eventual resale to the ultimate consumer.

Key Concepts

Among the more important marketing concepts introduced in this chapter are the following:

> The buying process in marketing is an active attempt to optimize exchange benefits for the buyer, not merely a passive response to selling efforts.

> The buying process varies among different organizations and is affected by the personality of the buyer, the organizational setting, and environmental factors.

> Buyers perform all the marketing functions—market analysis, communication, product differentiation, market segmentation, valuation, and exchange.

> Directories, catalogs, trade shows, trade magazines, the Yellow Pages, and other sources are helpful resources to consumer, retail, and industrial buyers.

> Buyers and sellers can use brokers to learn about market conditions and to negotiate the best purchase or sale agreement.

> Retail buying calls for a person who can deal with many salespeople from all kinds of firms and who can go into the field and negotiate deals with new suppliers.

> The buying function in many organizations has been centralized to gain more market power, to share market information, and to negotiate the best deal for the total system.

> Supplier development is a process whereby the buyer develops new sources of supply and assists present suppliers in making the exchange relationship long lasting as well as mutually beneficial.

> Buying decisions are usually the result of a series of interactions between people (called influentials) who have tremendous impact on the final purchase decision.

Discussion Questions

1. Give at least four examples of things you own that you *bought* with little or no effort on the part of the seller.

2. Discuss how consumers could use the market-analysis function to get the best deal on a new car (that is, what sources would they use, what procedures, and so forth).

3. How has the growth in self-service retailing increased the importance of the consumer-buying function?

4. Describe how a consumer cooperative could save money for members on food, drug items, and clothing.

5. Explain the role of a real estate broker as an agent of both buyer and seller.

6. Explain why a retail buyer might be called a "purchasing agent for consumers."

7. Discuss how centralized and computerized buying would change the sales approach for suppliers.

8. List some of the factors that have given more status and responsibility to industrial purchasing agents.

9. Explain what "supplier development" is and describe how a consumer could use it to improve relations with the local gas station.

10. Discuss how nonprofit organizations could benefit from cooperative buying agreements.

CASES

McNamara's Sporting Goods
Retail Buying

Shawn McNamara went to work in his father's sporting goods store after he graduated from college. Shawn had worked at the store for several years during high school and college and was eager to help his dad increase profits. The store was located in a suburban shopping center near Columbus, Ohio. The store did an especially good business in tennis and golf equipment, sports clothing, and backpacking supplies. In fact, the store did more business than most of the other sports stores in the area. Shawn felt that the store had more problems with buying than with selling. His dad did not like to travel, and he bought most of his supplies from salespeople who had called on him for years. Shawn talked with some other store owners and learned that his dad was paying more than they were for similar products. This prompted Shawn to begin a search for better suppliers.

1. Show how Shawn could use the six universal marketing functions to improve his purchasing system.
2. What could Shawn do to draw important sellers to *his* store rather than those of his competitors?
3. Which is more important to McNamara's store—buying or promotion? Discuss both sides of the issue.

Moving to a New Town
Learning Effective Buying Strategies

Guillermo Quinnones has just moved his family to the Washington, D.C., area. The family moved into an area that has many Spanish-speaking families as well as other ethnic groups. Guillermo is very concerned about the high cost of living in the area (one of the highest in the nation). He is especially concerned about food prices, the cost of homes, and the cost of transportation (almost everyone drives automobiles). The Quinnones family has rented an apartment for the time being; meanwhile they are searching for a home that they can afford.

1. How can Guillermo and the other people in his apartment building lower their food bills?
2. What sources might Guillermo use to find a home he could afford?
3. There is no mass transportation that services the area where the Quinnones family lives. How could Guillermo and his family minimize transportation costs?
4. What procedure would you recommend for finding the best bank, church, clothing store, doctor, dentist, and supermarket for the family?

6

Special Situations in Marketing

Although consumers spend only slightly less than half their money on services, the marketing of services is given comparatively little attention in the marketing literature. We have tried to integrate service marketing throughout the text, but there is need for one chapter to focus entirely on the special problems of service organizations. Therefore, Chapter 17 summarizes the concepts of this book as they relate to service organizations.

There has been some debate about the nature and scope of marketing in the last few years. One consequence of that debate is that few articles are being written about the very real problems that nonbusiness organizations have in carrying out marketing tasks. The position here is that marketing is a *tool* that all organizations can use to further their exchange relationships with others. Nonbusiness managers have learned to "find a need and fill it," but often they are less effective or efficient at the task than are business managers. Chapter 18 explores nonbusiness marketing and the application of the six universal marketing functions to the nonprofit sector.

Marketing of Services
the marketing revolution

17

LEARNING GOALS After you have read and studied this chapter, you should be able to:

1. Draw a chart illustrating where consumers spend their money for services.

2. Explain why the marketing of services is so important today by citing employment figures and other facts and figures.

3. Define the following terms: service; convenience, shopping, and specialty services; demarketing strategies; exchange services.

4. List where service careers are most prevalent.

5. Describe the differences in the marketing of convenience, shopping, and specialty services.

6. Explain why rental services are growing in importance and how this growth will affect marketing.

7. Show how an airline could use the six universal marketing functions to better serve its customers.

8. Explain why productivity is a problem in the service industry and what this means to the economy.

9. Discuss industrial services and how they differ from consumer services.

10. Explain why women may have greater opportunities for successful careers in service industries.

America was the first nation to become a service economy. Today close to 60% of its labor force is engaged in providing services, not in producing products, and the service industries continue to grow.*

INTRODUCTION Sally Anderson was a junior at a large Eastern college. While taking an introductory course in marketing, she heard that almost half of what consumers spend is for services. Sally found this figure hard to believe because she did not spend much of her money on services, or so she thought. After all, how much does one spend on haircuts, laundry, and other such services?

Sally's professor thought it would be a good experience if Sally were to make note of her expenditures for services throughout the semester to see for herself where the money went. Sally agreed, and this is what she found.

Sally discovered that one of the major service expenditures she made was for rent. In fact, housing is one of the largest service expenditures for all consumers (about 34 percent). Another major outlay was for tuition at the university. (Educational expenses are about 4 percent of all service expenditures.) In the middle of the semester, Sally went skiing with the ski club on a chartered bus. After some investigation, Sally learned that transportation services were an important factor in total service costs (about 7 percent) and recreation was another (over 4 percent). One of Sally's friends sprained her ankle while skiing and had to go to the hospital. Sally was surprised at the cost of medical care and how much it took of the consumer's service dollar (over 15 percent). (The advertisement titled "You might die if he doesn't operate" explains one reason why medical and insurance costs are rising.)

During the semester Sally had her hair cut and styled, took her clothes to the dry cleaner, went to a music festival, attended services at her church, sent letters to her friends, called her parents on the phone, saw a couple of movies, joined some friends at a couple of football games, and helped her sorority gather funds for a charity. Each of these activities involved a service organization, and Sally saw more clearly where consumers spend their money on services. Of course, a good share of a person's income goes for government services in the form of taxes; some is given away for church activities, charities, and social causes (about 3 percent), and the rest goes for service expenditures such as rent, insurance, health care, entertainment, utilities (water, electricity, phone, gas) repairs, transportation, credit charges, education, communications (radio, TV, telegraph), and legal aid. Table 17.1 summarizes consumer spending for services.

Sally reported what she found to the class. The professor reminded Sally that she had not mentioned the services that are provided for *businesses,* for *institutions* such as hotels, motels, schools, and hospitals, and for the *government.* The class then discussed the phenomenal growth of computer services, leasing services (for example, of cars,

* "The Outlook," *The Wall Street Journal,* October 2, 1972, p. 1.

An interesting ad for a service organization explaining the rising cost of insurance coverage.

Reprinted with permission of Crum & Forster Insurance Companies.

trucks, copiers, buildings, and so forth), and consulting services. The professor also brought up the tremendous outlay Americans make for credit. For example, the total cost of a house may be $50,000, but the cost of financing the house may be over $70,000. It costs more for financing (a service) than it does for the house itself!

We hope you can learn something from Sally's experiences. This chapter will discuss the marketing of services because they are such a major part of the economy and because the marketing problems are quite different—even though the concepts are much the same. We shall begin by looking more closely at the growth of the service sector and what this will mean for you.

THE SERVICE ECONOMY

One thing that Sally learned in her class discussions was that it was no longer accurate to think of the United States as an industrial society. If one defines an industrial society as one where the production of *goods* is the main occupation of the labor force, the United States is already a

Table 17.1 CONSUMER SPENDING FOR SERVICES

Service category	Percent of total spending
Housing	35
Medical care	16
Household operation	14
Personal business	13
Transportation	7
Recreation	4
Private education	3
Personal care	4
Religion and charities	3
Foreign travel	1
	100

Adapted from figures published by the U.S. Department of Commerce, "Survey of Current Business: National Income Issue." Figures were rounded to nearest percent, 1974 figures. These figures were the basis for much of Sally's class report and represent after-tax expenditures.

postindustrial society. It is more accurately called a *service economy*. Let us pause for a moment to look at the insert "Rushing Toward a Service Economy." Think of what these figures will mean to you and your future in marketing.

The figures in the insert show that the economy of the future will be very different from that of the past. The impact on marketing will be especially strong. Marketing has traditionally stressed goods-producing industries. Even today the vast majority of marketing texts draw almost all their examples from *goods-producing* firms and channels of distribution of *goods*. By 1980, seven out of ten workers will be employed in the

---

Rushing toward a Service Economy

During the last 100 years or so the United States has changed from an agricultural economy to an industrial economy and now to a service economy. For the first time in the history of the world, a nation now employs more than 50% of its labor force in services. During the next 10 to 30 years, the changes that have occurred in the United States economy will likely be replicated in many of the industrial nations of Western Europe.

The percentage of the U.S. work force employed in agriculture has declined from 90% in 1790 to 4% today. The percentage of the work force employed in manufacturing . . . has declined in recent years from 30% of the work force in 1947 to 24.9% in 1968. . . . Looking into the future, a RAND Corporation mathematician forecasts that by the year 2000 only 2% of the labor force will be required to turn out all the necessary manufactured goods.

From Dennis Little, "Post Industrial Society and What It Means," *The Futurist*, December 1973, p. 259. Reprinted with permission of the World Future Society, Washington, D.C.

434

service sector.[1] What will this mean for the economy and for you as a future marketer and consumer?

Moving into a service economy may put tremendous inflationary pressures on the country. During the last half of the 1960s, prices of cars rose 15 percent and durable goods rose 18 percent (TV sets, appliances, and so forth), but medical care, insurance, schooling, and recreation (the services) went up over 42 percent. One problem with service industries is productivity. Labor costs in service industries are close to 70 percent, whereas they are closer to 30 percent in manufacturing industries. The problem is that productivity of service workers is hard to increase: A doctor can see only so many patients, an orchestra can play just so fast, a teacher can handle a given number of students, and those figures are difficult to change. So if labor costs rise at 7 percent per year and productivity rises at less than 2 percent, there is inflationary pressure and prices rise.

Of course, when one talks about services in the United States, it is important to discuss the government. People often complain about price increases in food and energy, but the government is often the biggest drain on our income. In 1974, for example, a family of four with an income of $14,466 had an increase in social security taxes of 21.6 percent *in one year.*

The net result of all of this is: Marketing in the future will be primarily the marketing of services; at least that will be where the major problems will be. This includes the marketing of government and nonprofit organizations. But it also involves the marketing of medical care, education, insurance, recreation, real estate, travel, communication systems, and financial institutions. The breakdown of employment in the service sector is shown in Table 17.2.

Marketers must seek ways to apply the six marketing functions to the service sector more effectively. Educators could help by increasing the amount of time spent on the service and government sectors in marketing courses. And all marketers should work on techniques for increasing the productivity of service workers.

What Is a Service? At this point in the book, you are likely to be tired of definitions, but try to be patient because this is one area where some clarification is necessary. There is really no widely accepted definition of services that marketers use. In fact, there is no clear boundary between those organizations that are part of the channel for goods and those that provide services. Restaurants, for example, are considered by some writers as part of the channel of distribution for foods because they are an alternative to supermarkets. But it is clear that the primary activities of a restaurant are service activities. Furthermore, some services are subject to free market exchanges and others, such as government services, are paid for through mandatory taxes. Later we shall discuss the special problems of marketing for nonprofit organizations such as the govern-

[1] "How Growth of Services is Changing America," *U.S. News and World Report,* November 9, 1970, pp. 34–35.

Table 17.2 EMPLOYMENT IN THE SERVICE SECTOR

Service category	Percent of total service employment
Retail and wholesale trade	31.5
Government	26
Personal and business services	26.5
Transportation, communication, utilities	8
Finance, insurance, real estate	8
	100

From Bureau of Labor Statistics, 1976 figures.

ment, charities, churches, and social causes. But here we shall concentrate on those services that are bought and sold in the market. We will call these services exchange services, intangible products that are bought and sold in the marketplace in a mutually satisfying transaction.[2]

One key to this definition is the idea that services are *intangible* products. If you have nothing you can hold in your hands as the result of an exchange, you have purchased a service—an intangible product. You may be given something tangible to "represent" the service, such as an insurance policy, a credit card, or a student identification card, but what you have bought is not the policy, but insurance "protection," not a credit card but "credit," and so forth.

Whereas goods are *produced,* services are *performed;* thus, the quality of an intangible product (a service) derives from its performance, not from its physical characteristics.[3] Furthermore, the place of marketing in the exchange process is different. "Goods are produced, sold, and consumed. Services are sold and then [performed] and consumed simultaneously. . . . In place of the one interface between buyer and seller of goods—marketing—there are *two* interactions between the buyer and seller of services—marketing and production."[4] Think, for example, of the interaction between buyer and seller in a doctor's office, a classroom, a beauty parlor, or an airplane. In fact, the value of a service and the benefits derived from it are often dependent upon the skills, knowledge, and participation of the buyer as much as the seller.[5] Think, for example, of the contribution a student makes to education or a knowledgeable viewer makes to a play or a football game. The concepts are:

> ▸ A service is an intangible product that is performed rather than produced.

> ▸ The value and benefits of a service may vary from user to user because part of the input into service performance may be provided by the buyer.

[2] Based on a definition in John M. Rathmell, *Marketing in the Service Sector* (Cambridge, Mass.: Winthrop Publishers, Inc., 1974), p. 25.

[3] Ibid., p. 58.

[4] Ibid., p. 6.

[5] Ibid., p. 17.

MARKETING CONSUMER SERVICES Services may be divided into two broad classifications. The first broad general class is industrial services. These services are provided for a broad range of organizations, including manufacturing, mining, agriculture, nonprofit, and the government. A selected list of such services may be found in Table 17.3.

The second broad general class is consumer services. You are likely to be more familiar with these services. Like goods, consumer services can be divided into three types—convenience, shopping, and specialty. This *IMP* section will explore how the emphasis in marketing changes for these three types of consumer services. Table 17.4 lists a few selected consumer services to give you an idea of what we are talking about.

It is important for you to recognize that it is the consumer who determines to which category a service belongs. For example, some people might consider dry cleaning a convenience service and go to the closest store. Someone else might feel that dry cleaning is a very special service and may drive way across town to have his or her clothes cleaned. To this person, dry cleaning is a specialty service. The concept is:

> **A service is classified as convenience, shopping, or specialty based on the shopping behavior of individual consumers.**

Table 17.3 SELECTED INDUSTRIAL SERVICES

Accounting, auditing, and bookkeeping
Architectural services
Building maintenance
Cleaning (building, linen, uniforms)
Communication
Computer services
Consulting
Credit
Detective agencies and other protective services
Educational services
Employment
Engineering services
Financial services (for example, factoring)
Insurance
Leasing services (auto, building, computers, and so forth)
Legal services
Marketing intelligence and research services
Medical
Promotional services including all the media
Repair
Stenographic services
Testing laboratories
Transportation
Utilities (gas, water, electricity)
Window cleaning

Table 17.4 SELECTED CONSUMER SERVICES

Amusement (movie theaters, bowling alleys, and so forth)
Automobile (insurance, parking, repair, rental, and storage)
Barber shop, beauty parlor, and shoe shine services
Brokerage services for stocks and bonds
Child-care, baby-sitting, and animal-sitting services
Cleaning, painting, repair, and maintenance (of homes, for example)
Clothes cleaning, alterations, and repair
Delivery services
Financial services (banking and credit)
Funeral services
Home utility services (gas and electricity)
Income-tax preparation services
Legal services
Life insurance services
Lodging (hotels, motels, and camper parks)
Medical care and sickness prevention
Photography sales and processing
Private education
Radio and television broadcasting and repair
Real estate services
Rental services (boats, cars, homes, and so forth)

Marketing Convenience Services

Convenience services are those consumer services that the public purchases rather frequently and with a minimum of effort. Examples of such services may include repair services (auto, shoe, watch), haircutting services, and dry cleaning services. The definition is based on the method of purchase employed by the typical consumer. The convenience involved may be in terms of nearness to the buyer's home, easy accessibility to some means of transportation, or nearness to places where the buyer shops or works.[6]

It has been said that the three most effective appeals for convenience services are location, location, and location. Most consumers want to obtain convenience services with a minium of time and effort. Consumers are often willing to pay extra for that convenience. For example, the neighborhood dry cleaner may not be as inexpensive as another dry cleaner farther away, but most people would prefer to pay extra rather than drive across town. In fact, dry cleaners that pick up and deliver clothes are usually the most expensive *and* the most convenient. This does not necessarily hurt sales. The convenience of home delivery was once a very important marketing plus for sellers of milk, bread, and coffee, but the price became too high.

Although location is usually the most important marketing variable for convenience services, other factors may be critical. In the case of bread and milk, price became so important to consumers that most of them now look upon these products as shopping goods and no longer buy

[6] This discussion is based on the definition of convenience goods in "Report of the Definitions Committee," *Journal of Marketing*, October 1948, p. 206.

them from door-to-door delivery persons. However, price is usually not an important factor in the purchase of convenience services—not when compared to the importance of location.

The image of a convenience service *is* an important marketing variable. If a service outlet can establish a reputation for fast, friendly, and reliable service, the marketing task is much easier. Word of mouth is very important in establishing an image, and so is advertising. An example of a convenience service is a motel. Consumers want to stop *when* they get tired and *where* they do not have to go out of their way. But consumers will go slightly out of their way for a particular motel if the *image* is one they prefer. Names like Best Western motels, Holiday Inn, and Howard Johnson's mean a certain standard of quality at a certain price. Motels recommended by the American Automobile Association also may have a favorable consumer image. It is important for all convenience services to have a clear, attractive image *and* to be located close to where people will be when the service is needed.

Marketing Shopping Services

Shopping services are those consumer services that the public selects after comparing quality, price, and reputation. Examples of such services may include auto repair shops, insurance companies (auto and life), and various rental services (auto and home, for example). Consumers need *information* to compare shopping services, and so marketing communication rather than location may be the key marketing variable.

Let us look at the life insurance industry, for example. Most consumers do not fully understand basic concepts like whole-life policies, term policies, and mutual life insurance companies. To get a person's business, a life insurance company must communicate effectively *with* the buyer. Normally this means hiring and training good salespersons who can relate to the people they serve. For shopping services such as life insurance, information provided by sales representatives often is the key difference between sellers.

How do you select which bank or savings and loan to use? Do you go to the least expensive barber or beauty parlor and how did you decide? Was word of mouth important? Often consumers do not feel comfortable choosing among shopping services because they do not feel that they have sufficient information. The company that provides that information can often win their business. Think of how uncertain most consumers are when choosing an auto repair shop. They ask questions (often of themselves): Will I be cheated? How much will this cost? What guarantee do I have that this will not happen again? How much work do I really *need?* The auto repair shop that gives *free estimates*, *explains* what needs to be done and why, and *guarantees* its service will get more business than it can handle *if* it communicates with the public through advertising, word of mouth, and publicity. *Imp.*

Because consumers compare price, quality, and reputation of shopping services, the marketing task is clear. Give consumers that information and show them how your service compares with the competition. For some reason, service organizations often do not promote with the same competitiveness and consumer appeal as organizations selling goods. But for shopping services, promotion (communication) is the key to success *if* the product is what consumers want.

Marketing Specialty Services **Specialty services** are those consumer services for which buyers are willing to make a special purchasing effort by traveling out of their way or by paying a premium. Examples may include medical specialists, lawyers, and financial advisors. Marketing emphasis for these people and organizations should be placed on product development and consumer satisfaction. Word of mouth and publicity will serve as their promotional tools.

Product development for such services means giving the client the time and attention he or she wants and deserves. It also means providing the consumer with pleasant surroundings and keeping waiting time to a minimum. But most of all, it means performing the service better than competitors. A financial analyst who can help people make money and minimize taxes will soon be in demand. A criminal lawyer who wins important cases will always be in demand. Again, emphasis is on success and performance.

Price and location are relatively minor factors in specialty service marketing. By definition, people will go out of their way to get such a service and will pay a premium price. But they demand satisfaction and set high standards of performance.

Demarketing and Synchromarketing Strategies Many service organizations are unlike manufacturing organizations in that increased volume does not necessarily lead to economies of scale. Most manufacturing firms use marketing to *increase* sales, but often in service organizations the major goal of marketing is to manage (get control of) sales or demand. For example, once they are established, doctors usually have as many or more patients than they can handle. Doctors may then limit the number of patients by refusing to accept new clients, by raising their prices, or through other marketing procedures. These strategies have been termed **demarketing strategies** because their goal is to lessen rather than increase the market.[7]

Utility companies practiced a demarketing strategy in the 1970s. Utilities encouraged people to use energy wisely and gave tips on how to cut consumption of gas and electricity, especially that used for home heating. The state of Oregon used a demarketing strategy to keep people from moving to Oregon. In this case, a governmental unit used marketing to *regulate* a demand rather than to increase it.

One problem with service organizations is that they cannot store their product to meet consumer demand when it occurs. For example, a resort cannot store extra rooms for the busy season. Service organizations, therefore, often try to smooth out irregular demand.

Many examples of irregular demand can be cited. In mass transit, much of the equipment is idle during the off-hours and in short supply

[7] See Philip Kotler, "The Major Tasks of Marketing Management," *Journal of Marketing,* October 1973, p. 47.

during the peak hours. Hotels in Miami Beach are insufficiently booked during the off-season and overbooked during the peak season. Museums are undervisited during the week days and terribly overcrowded during the weekends.[8]

No doubt you can think of examples from your personal experiences (for example, beauty parlors, gas stations, furnace repair, golf courses, airlines, and so forth). Kotler recommends services use a *synchromarketing* strategy to (1) alter the supply pattern to fit the demand pattern, (2) alter the demand pattern to fit the natural supply pattern, or (3) alter both to some degree.[9] One technique is to charge a higher price when demand is high. You may have noticed this practice among resort hotels, tennis clubs, the phone company, movie theaters, and other service organizations. Another technique is to promote more heavily when demand is normally low. You may have noticed such promotions for the airlines, universities (summer school, for example), and sports facilities. The concepts are:

➤ Service organizations, more than manufacturing organizations, are concerned with *managing* demand; this means that marketing strategies may not be designed to *increase* demand but to maintain or even lessen demand.

➤ Overdemand for a service calls for a strategy of *demarketing*, whereby an organization actively discourages more customers on either a temporary or permanent basis.

➤ Irregular demand for a service calls for a strategy of *synchomarketing*, whereby an organization attempts to bring supply and demand into balance throughout the year; this is critical for service organizations because they cannot store products.

In general, the marketing problems of service organizations are more difficult because demand varies greatly and there are no simple manufacturing or storage changes that can adapt the supply of a service to demand. The burden falls on marketing to regulate demand through pricing, promotion, and product changes.) *Imp.*

The Trend toward Rental Services   The United States has recently changed from an industrial economy to a service economy. In addition, it is slowly changing from an economy of abundance to one of scarcity. One notable example was the shortage of gasoline in the early 1970s. But other examples abound, including shortages of various metals, food, housing, and public transportation. Along with selected scarcities come various changes in buyer behavior. For example, many people are moving away from ownership of goods toward renting of goods; that is, they are shifting purchases from the goods sector to the service sector.

Housing is a good example of what is happening in the service sector. More and more people are choosing not to live in detached single-family

[8] Ibid., p. 46.
[9] Ibid.

homes. Often this choice is involuntary, caused by the high cost of homes. The net result is a tremendous growth in rental housing. About 40 percent of the housing in the United States today is rental property, but the percentage should increase dramatically over the next 10 years. There are many more families being formed than houses being built, and so young married couples may be forced to live in rental housing. Most young people prefer such an arrangement anyhow because young couples tend to be highly mobile, and ownership often restricts one's ability to move.

There are other factors that are leading consumers toward the *use* of goods rather than *ownership*. These include:

1. *Ecological awareness*. As consumers become more aware of the wastefulness connected with ownership, and this will be reflected in higher prices as it already has in the case of cars, there will be a growing trend toward renting and sharing of products. Apartment living and town-house living will accelerate this trend, because people will find it convenient to share tools, lawn mowers, hedge clippers, ladders, and other household materials. Not only can people afford less in a period of scarcity, but there is no place to store such things in most apartments and town houses. Car pools are one indication of this trend.

2. *Living for today*. Young people today want everything their parents had when they were middle-aged. Dishwashers, garbage disposals, stereos, TV sets, washers, and dryers are now considered standard equipment in new homes. Many young people cannot afford to buy such equipment, but they can rent them with their apartment or home. This is especially true of seasonal items such as air conditioners.

3. *Consumerism*. Today's consumer is greatly concerned about quality and service. Rental merchandise tends to be of higher quality, durability, and reliability—and servicing is no problem to the renter.

4. *Sports participation*. More people than ever are participating in sports such as skiing, tennis, bicycling, and golf. Few people can afford the equipment associated with all these sports (much less find room to store it), and so there is a real growth in the rental of ski equipment and other sports-related goods.[10]

These are only a few of the reasons why consumers are moving toward the renting of goods rather than ownership. Look around you and make note of the things people are renting these days—automobiles, furniture, sports equipment, recreational equipment (campers, tents, sleeping bags, and so on), apartments, cleaning tools, lawn-care equipment, vacation homes, paintings, TV sets, extra beds, movies, and even social

[10] These ideas were developed in a paper by Michael R. Padbury, "Consumption Without Ownership—A Contemporary Analysis" (unpublished, The University of Maryland, 1974).

companions. Marketers must be aware of such trends and adjust their strategies accordingly.

Industrial buyers are moving toward leasing and renting at a similar pace. Automobiles and trucks are notable examples. But everything related to transportation, including shipping containers and airplanes, are experiencing growth. The industrial market rents everything from major items such as the building they are in to computers, copiers, typewriters, and everyday items such as uniforms, towels, and maintenance equipment. In the future, marketing of rental property, equipment, and supplies will be an exciting and challenging career. You should keep abreast of this rapidly growing service area.

SERVICES AND THE MARKETING FUNCTIONS The six universal marketing functions outlined in Chapter 2 apply to service organizations as well as to industrial firms, but the implementation is often different. In this section, we shall discuss each of the functions and some basic concepts to use when planning marketing programs for services.

The Market-Analysis Function Market analysis is a universal marketing function that enables marketing participants to learn about the future demand for, and supply of, products, including intangible products. The existence of a potential for the exchange of services is called the *services market* and it is a large and growing part of the economy (see Figures 17.1 and 17.2).

Just about everyone can make some money in the service sector, and it usually does not take much of a capital investment—just a little know-how.

Tommy Leete was a 14-year-old student when he started his own window-cleaning service in his neighborhood. Eventually Tommy expanded the service, hired people to help, and still operates the service

---

Future of the Service Sector

Probably in the not-too-distant future not only the manpower but also the output of tangibles will be curbed to slow down the depletion of resources and to abate the degradation of the environment. Much greater emphasis will then be placed upon consumption of services. . . .

Only services have a potential for unlimited growth in this environment of scarcity. If the disasters inherent in continuing exponential growth are to be averted, services will have much higher priority than is now the case. Above all, what is now one of the minor life-cycle services, the family planning agency, will assume prime importance. . . . Secondly, in the values of investment and consumer choice, services in general . . . will probably be given overall preference because by and large these services are not wasteful of scarce material resources nor do they appreciably raise pollution levels.

From Carl Gersuny and William R. Rosengren, *The Service Society* (Cambridge, Mass.: Schenkman Publishing Company, 1973), p. 145.

Figure 17.1 TOTAL CONSUMER SPENDING AND OUTLAYS ON SERVICES, 1970–1980

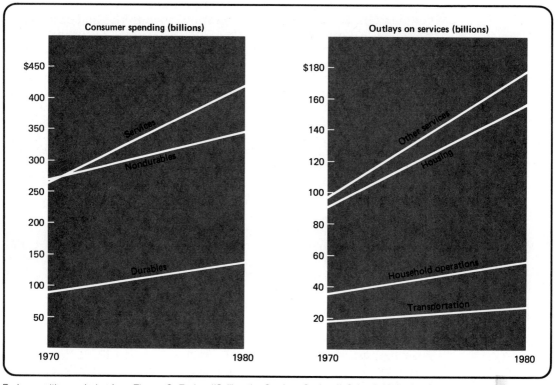

Redrawn with permission from Thayer C. Taylor, "Selling the Services Society," *Sales & Marketing Management*, March 6, 1972. Copyright 1972.

part-time. Tom is now a college graduate with a full-time job in marketing.

Remember Marge Burns from the chapter on personal selling? She started her own service businesses when she was very young, including lawn care, snow removal, window cleaning, baby-sitting, animal-sitting, plant care, and house cleaning.

The idea is to find something you enjoy (for example, swimming) and find someplace where you can make money doing it (for example, giving swimming lessons at the local pool). People who enjoy music can learn to teach or perform. The same is true of those who like art, drama, or dance.

If you were to carefully analyze consumer and industrial markets, you would see that there is a definite limit to the amount of *goods* individuals and organizations need. But the need for *services* keeps growing, and the opportunities for continued growth seem endless. Take education, for example. You can study subjects all of your life and still be interested in more knowledge. Higher education grew from 1960 to 1973 at a rate of almost 6 percent per year. Higher education (continuing education) for adults is just beginning to grow. Education and related knowledge fields (for example, consulting, accounting, publishing, research and development, and communication) are all growth areas of the future.

Another obvious growth area is medical services. The government may become more involved in programs such as national health insurance, but, regardless of who manages the system, health care (including dental care) will keep expanding—at least for the immediate future.

Another prospect for the future is more leisure time. This opens up exciting prospects for marketers in areas such as spectator sports, travel, and photography.

More and more women are finding rewarding careers outside the home. This greatly increases the demand for services such as child care, housekeeping, restaurants, and shopping services.

Market analysis helps a person like yourself find opportunities to serve others and be rewarded in return. Remember the basic concept:

> **Find a need and fill it, and your needs will be met as well.**

Market analysis also enables individuals and organizations to find expert help in solving their problems. For just about every problem you can name, there is someone out there with a service to help solve it. That

Figure 17.2 NONAGRICULTURAL AND SERVICES EMPLOYMENT, 1970–1980

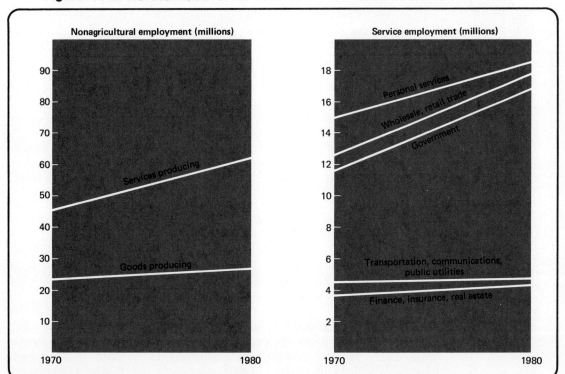

Redrawn with permission from Thayer C. Taylor, "Selling the Services Society," *Sales & Marketing Management*, March 6, 1972. Copyright 1972.

Opportunities for Women in the Service Sector

Some of the most startling comparisons between the industry and service sectors concern the characteristics of their respective labor forces. One simple, but profound, difference is that many occupations in the service sector do not make special demands for physical strength. This means that women can compete on more nearly equal terms with men, perhaps for the first time in history. In the service sector, we find women holding down almost one-half of all jobs, compared with only one-fifth in industry.

From Victor R. Fuchs, *The Service Economy* (New York: National Bureau of Edocomic Research, 1968), p. 10.

someone may work for himself or herself, for a business, a church, a charity, a social cause, or the government. The concept is:

> **Market analysis enables the providers and users of services to find each other and begin the process of establishing mutually satisfying exchange agreements.**

The Product-Differentiation Function   Earlier we discussed the idea that a product is what the customer thinks it is. This is especially true for services. The "product" cannot be examined, compared, and evaluated *before* it is purchased like most goods, and so much of the consumer's selection process is based on past experience, word of mouth, brand names, and promotional communications. One could say that the product that causes a customer to buy from a service organization is information, but the product the customer receives is the benefits gained from the service. For example, a person might go to a movie because of the advertising or the publicity, but the product the person gets is his or her pleasure from viewing the movie. Remember that part of the product's value (benefits) is determined by the consumer The more he or she knows about good acting, and so forth, the more the movie might mean. The concepts are:

> **The product of a service organization is determined by the *interaction* between buyer and seller; the buyer is part of the input.**

> **Information is a more important element of intangible products (services) than tangible products (goods); because services cannot be evaluated before purchase, information serves as a product substitute until a sale is made.**

Some service organizations offer a standard product that is the same for all customers. Utilities, parking lots, and savings account rates at banks are examples. Other organizations vary the product for each customer. Consulting firms, beauty parlors, doctors, and lawyers are some examples. Other service organizations try to tailor a relatively standard product to fit each customer. Insurance companies, for example, may stress, "There's nobody else exactly like you," and so they have different policies for everyone. Travel agents might develop a product package for each client.

Usually service organizations are not restricted to a particular product. Rather, they have a *potential for satisfying needs*. Consultants, for example, develop a product after the customer has spelled out his or her needs. This flexibility in product offer is a big plus for service organizations in that they can give each individual what he or she wants. The problem is, how does a service communicate that fact? How does a service organization convince people that they will solve a wide range of problems? This is a task for the communications function, which will be discussed shortly. First, let's discuss a few ways in which services differentiate their products.

Packaging and the Service Product One does not usually think of packaging in relation to services, but the concepts of packaging are very important. For example, a producer of cosmetics might put rouge, lipstick, mascara, and other face preparations in a beauty package that is more attractive to the buyer than are the separate items. Similarly, a travel agency might combine transportation services with housing, recreation, and meals in a package that is more attractive to the buyer than are the separate items. It is often called a "tour package." Even several charities can package their services in one organization (for example, United Way), so that the consumer minimizes the inconvenience of multiple contacts.

Branding and the Service Product Brand names in service industries are often more important than brand names of goods because the customer cannot physically compare competing brands before buying. Thus, brand names like Howard Johnson's, Holiday Inn, Midas, AAMCO, and TWA are very important for establishing a differential advantage for intangible products. The customer learns to expect a certain level of quality and a certain consistency of service that is unavailable from little known service organizations.

Pricing and the Service Product The service sector usually uses terms other than "price" to describe the cost of exchange. Common terms include fee, rate, toll, tuition, rent, interest, retainer, admission, and charge. There seem to be few principles that would apply to service pricing because, as indicated by the variance in terms, pricing strategies differ greatly among service organizations.

Several service industries have their prices regulated by the government—including transportation firms (railroads, truck lines, and airlines) and utilities (oil, gas, electric, and phone). Some services charge according to the season (resorts, hotels, motels, airlines). Some charge more for adults than for children (movie theaters, sports events, circuses). Other services may set their rates to match a particular consumer's ability to pay (doctors, lawyers, dentists).

Even those service organizations that seem to have a fixed price often manage to adapt to different market segments. Universities, for example, may charge the same tuition for all undergraduates—*but* poor students might get a scholarship or a job, athletes may get a scholarship plus free room and board, and out-of-state students may pay a premium.

Because the product is often decided between the seller and buyer, service pricing tends to be very flexible. "You get what you pay for" is often true in this industry. Quality is very difficult to measure in service organizations, but very important for pricing strategies. A doctor who charges very low fees, for example, may appear to be not very good. On the other hand, a doctor who charges outrageous fees often has a reputation for quality.

Generally, service organizations establish prices on much the same basis as producers of goods. One input into the decision is cost of providing the service. Most services are highly labor intensive (that is, labor makes up much of the cost), and so the price is set to cover labor costs plus capital costs plus some profit level. Supply and demand also have a big influence on price. If a radio station has unsold time, it might lower its price to a potential buyer. A resort hotel may take whatever price a wandering customer might offer in the off-season, but during the prime season prices will skyrocket.

People tend to believe that the price of services rises faster than the price of goods. In many cases this is true, but not in all cases. Those industries that are labor intensive (medicine and education, for example) have had tremendous increases in prices over the last decade. You should look closely at each service industry before you make any generalizations about price levels or price increases. You might be surprised at the diversity.

One issue in the pricing of services is the question of payment. Services that are not paid for cannot be repossessed like a TV set, and so some service organizations demand payment before delivery. Hospitals are particularly noted for this practice. Advertising agencies are beginning to put more emphasis on this because of an increase in late payments. Some motels make you pay in advance as do most theaters, sports events, and schools. Those people who do not require payment in advance often are left with huge income losses. Doctors and dentists seem particularly vulnerable. Perhaps that is the public's way of protesting the price?

The Marketing-Communication Function   Marketing communication is a universal marketing function that narrows the perceptual gaps between marketing participants, and this is particularly important in the marketing of services. Consumers do not always understand the benefits of services such as life insurance, continuing education, opera, and preventative medicine. The sellers of such services must develop more effective communication strategies to *talk with* consumers about these services. One-way promotional tools such as advertising are not very effective in convincing people of the merits of products such as life insurance or symphony music.

Remember that listening is half the communication function. If school teachers would listen more to students, if managers of concert halls would listen more to the public, and if doctors would listen more to patients, they would all discover better ways to serve the public (find a need) and better ways to increase their returns (and your needs will be met as well).

Service organizations usually find it more effective to use indirect promotional strategies. Word of mouth, for example, is very effective for doctors, lawyers, dentists, and other professionals. Publicity is also very effective for professionals and for marketing organizations such as theaters, sports arenas, race tracks, and convention halls.

Service outlets are wise to make optimum use of the Yellow Pages and other directories. Signs and the physical appearance of service centers are also very important promotional tools. Who wants to sit in a messy, dirty waiting room while his or her car is being serviced? Who wants to have a dozen sick people breathing on them in a doctor's office? Who really enjoys waiting for a bus in the rain and snow? Service organizations must recognize that *comfort in use* is part of their product offer, and they should do everything possible to make the consumer happy. Marketing communication helps service organizations find out what consumers want and then enables the organization to tell people it is available.

One car dealership in the Washington, D.C., area, for example, has a free car wash, a laundry, and a barber shop available to customers using the service center. Much of this dealer's advertising stresses the benefits of their service department, and the results are impressive.

The Market-Segmentation Function
Market segmentation resolves market separations by helping the seller of services concentrate marketing efforts on those people who are in the right place at the right time and who have the kinds of perceptions and price orientation that are compatible with the service in question. Of course, market segmentation also helps buyers to narrow the market to a few sellers that could satisfy their needs.

The Valuation Function
The service sector provides a unique problem in the case of the valuation function because, unlike products, one cannot evaluate a service *before use*. One can only *estimate* the value of an advertising agency, a consultant, or a lawyer. Similarly, it is difficult for a service organization to communicate its value to the public. Nevertheless, the valuation function takes place, but the input is less reliable. Buyers rely on cues such as past experience, brand names, price, location, word of mouth, publicity, and advertising to evaluate a service organization. The organization evaluates its potential relationship with consumers by similar indirect measures.

How does a college decide whom to serve? How does a utility (for example, a gas company) select which customers to serve? In other words, what criteria should a service organization use to evaluate the market? Notice that hospitals often require that you prove you can pay before treating even an *emergency!* Apparently their prime evaluation criterion is *ability to pay*. Universities may use *admission standards* to screen their customers. The concepts are:

➤ **Valuation is a universal marketing function whereby each of the participants tries to determine whether the benefits of a transaction would exceed the costs.**

> **The valuation function applied to service exchanges often must occur before the benefits of an exchange are known; therefore, the valuation function becomes an ongoing process in which services that provide satisfaction may create great customer loyalty.**

The Exchange Function   Exchange is a universal marketing function that represents a transfer of benefits (need satisfaction) between or among the participants. One of the primary facilitating functions to the exchange of services is credit. In most service situations, the buyer and the seller must cooperate to make the exchange mutually beneficial. For example, a woman must help the hairstylist give her the kind of hairstyle she prefers. The actual cutting and styling is done by the professional, but the customer helps determine the benefits of the exchange. The same process takes place at a university. Students work *with* the faculty to facilitate the *exchange* of ideas. Similarly, the customer helps an insurance agent to draw up a policy that is most satisfying to both.

Often the production function and the exchange function are one in the same. That is, the performance of a service *is* the exchange function. Therefore, a service can be adjusted continually *during the exchange process* so that the needs of buyer and seller can be met most fully.

SERVICE ORGANIZATIONS   It may seem strange to you to talk about channels of distribution for services. After all, services are intangible, and so one cannot transport them and store them like goods. But services *can* be made easily accessible through retail outlets, and many of the same middleman organizations are as necessary in the case of services as they are in the case of goods. Financial services (credit arrangements), for example, are often necessary to support the marketing of services such as transportation, hotels and motels, education, and health care. Service organizations may also need communications middlemen such as advertising agencies, PR firms, and sales agents (brokers).

Service Organization Channels   We have already discussed how middlemen add form, time, place, possession, and information utility. The need for time and place utility are especially apparent for service organizations. People want to be able to use the phone at all times of the day and night. The same is often true of hospitals, motels, and other service organizations. Most services must also be located where they can be reached by users. Movie threaters, gas stations, banks, and other service organizations provide multiple outlets in a city to make customer contact easier. Notice also how some services are grouped in "service centers" to make their use convenient. Examples include medical centers, visual arts centers, and sports complexes. Note also how colleges, libraries, health clinics, legal-aid services, symphony orchestras, and other such services are going "to the public" with branch outlets, mobile units, temporary facilities, and other such techniques.

The most visible middlemen in service channels are agents and brokers. You are no doubt familiar with insurance agents, and agents for performers of all kinds (sports, stage and screen, speakers, writers, and so on). You are also likely to have met people who are stockbrokers or real estate brokers. Remember that agents and brokers can represent both buyers and sellers.

Imp ✳ Perhaps the most important middlemen in service channels are those who create information utility (the communications middlemen). Take the travel industry, for example. The average person takes a vacation away from home once a year. Think of all the service organizations that must be contacted by such a vacationer—hotels, motels, airlines, car-rental firms, tour buses, and recreational sites. The average traveler would be overwhelmed by the problem. That is where service middlemen come into being. They provide two-way information flows between the public and various service organizations and serve as marketing information centers. Travel agents, for example, help the public with transportation, housing, recreation, and tour arrangements throughout the vacation period. Some service organizations are forming integrated systems to better serve the public. Like integrated systems in the manufacturing industries, these huge organizations are beginning to dominate the field.

In the hotel/motel industry, for example, corporate systems and contractual systems (franchises) dominate the field with names like Holiday Inns, Howard Johnson's, Motel 6, Ramada Inns, and Best Western. Some of the systems link two major service industries; for example TWA (airline) and Hilton International (hotels) and American Airlines/Americana Hotels. Such vertically integrated systems can be expanded to include car-rental services, tour accomodations, credit arrangements, and restaurant services.

You are probably familiar with other integrated service systems in the service field: AAMCO (transmissions), Midas (mufflers), Rayco (seat covers), H & R Block (preparation of income-tax returns), KOA (camp grounds), and Century 21 (real estate). Not only are these service organizations large, but they are very effective in providing good, reliable, reasonably priced services.

Regulation of Service Industries Through some rather unexplainable events, the marketing of services has come under more government regulation than the marketing of goods. The insurance industry, for example, is regulated by various state agencies. Interstate marketing (commerce) is regulated by the Interstate Commerce Commission. Broadcasting is regulated by the Federal Communications Commission, banking by the Federal Research Board, airlines by the Civil Aeronautics Board, and utilities by the Federal Power Commission. Many services are also subject to Section 5 of the Federal Trade Commission Act regarding unfair methods of competition and unfair or deceptive acts. Various other federal and state regulations affect service industries. The important thing to understand is the large government involvement in the service sector. ✳

Certainly you can understand the need for the government to regulate the practices of monopoly industries such as the telephone company and electric utilities. But you may share the concern of many businesspersons and congresspersons about overregulation of services. There was some discussion in the 1970s of deregulating the airlines, trucking, and

---

Public Policy and Services

Public policy in the service sector takes on a variety of forms which are quite similar to those found in the goods sector, but there are several exceptions. (1) Some services are restricted to public ownership. . . . (2) Others may be performed by private enterprises subject to varying degrees of restriction on marketing efforts, particularly pricing: consider public utility and telephone services. (3) Increasingly, public agencies are participating as partners with private enterprises in the performance of certain services: property insurance. (4) Some services are subsidized by government: ocean shipping. (5) . . . Some privately determined professional standards have the support of public policy: certified public accounting and dentistry.

From John M. Rathmell, *Marketing in the Service Sector* (Cambridge, Mass.: Winthrop Publishers, Inc., 1974), p. 44.

other service industries. It is interesting to follow this debate and listen to both sides of the issue. We encourage you to keep up with this debate because it is very important to marketing and the free enterprise system in general.

Some services are subject to rules and regulations of their own making. Physicians, for example, must meet certain standards before entering a practice. Lawyers are also subject to strict standards. Other professions such as accounting, architecture, and barbering may also be subject to certain restrictions (for example, certified public accountants).

It will be interesting to follow future interaction between the government and the service sector. A recent debate centered on the restrictions that prohibit some professional services from advertising. Government intervention in the 1970s has opened up various professions to advertising. The idea is to provide the public with more information about the availability of various services and the prices charged for them so that consumer choice in the service sector is more informed. How far this will go is not clear at this time, but you might watch the medical, legal, accounting, and dental professions to see what happens if advertising is permitted.

Increasing Service Productivity One of the major challenges of marketers and of society in the next decade or two is to raise the productivity of service workers. As mentioned, service industries tend to be labor intensive (that is, they use people power rather than machines for production). As a consequence, the cost of services rises as fast or faster than wages. Note, for example, how rapidly labor-intensive services such as education, medicine, and mail delivery have risen in price. Marketers must strive to make the distribution system for services as effective and efficient as the distribution system for goods.

One problem with measuring productivity in service sectors is that quality varies so greatly. One can vastly increase the number of students

The Consumer's Role in Service Productivity

In services . . . the consumer frequently plays an important role in production. Sometimes, as in the barber's chair, the role is essentially passive. . . . But in the supermarket and laundromat the consumer actually works, and in the doctor's office the quality of the medical history the patient gives may influence significantly the productivity of the doctor. Productivity in banking is affected by whether the clerk or the customer makes out the deposit slip—and whether it is made out correctly or not. This, in turn, is likely to be a function of the education of the consumer. . . . Productivity in education . . . is determined largely by what the student contributes, and . . . the performance of a string quartet can be affected by the audience's response. Thus we see that productivity in many service industries is dependent in part on the knowledge, experience, and motivation of the consumer.

From Victor R. Fuchs, *The Service Economy* (New York: National Bureau of Economic Research, 1968), pp. 194–195.

taught by one faculty member, but the quality of education might drop as well. Similarly, doctors could see more patients and barbers could cut more hair—but at what cost in quality? It should be apparent that one cannot measure service productivity using the same standards one uses in measuring the production of goods. Productivity is the ratio of output to input—usually expressed in terms of quantity. That is, so much resources become so many products. Quality is assumed to be constant. Obviously, in the service sector this is not possible.

Major issues in the service sector are productivity, government regulation, and self-regulation. The successful marketer of the future will be one who can increase service productivity through application of systems concepts such as marketing information systems and integrated systems concepts. Marketers must also cooperate with the government to make the United States the first (and only) *productive* service economy.

FOR REVIEW

Key Terms

Among the more important terms and expressions discussed in this chapter are the following:

Convenience services are those consumer services that the public purchases rather frequently and with a minimum of effort.

Demarketing strategies are designed to lessen rather than increase market demand.

Exchange services are intangible products that are bought and sold in the marketplace in a mutually satisfying transaction.

A **service** is an intangible product that is perfomed rather than produced.

Shopping services are those consumer services that the public selects after comparing quality, price, and reputation.

Specialty services are those consumer services for which buyers are willing to make a special purchasing effort by traveling out of their way or by paying a premium.

Key Concepts

Among the more important marketing concepts introduced in this chapter are the following:

› The value and benefits of a service may vary from user to user because part of the input into service performance may be provided by the buyer.

› A service is classified as convenience, shopping, or specialty based on the shopping behavior of individual consumers.

› Service organizations are concerned with *managing* demand; that is, marketing strategies may be designed, not to *increase* demand, but to maintain or even lessen demand.

› Excessive demand for a service calls for a strategy of *demarketing,* whereby an organization actively discourages more customers either on a temporary or permanent basis.

› Irregular demand for a service calls for a strategy of *synchromarketing,* whereby an organization attempts to bring supply and demand into balance throughout the year.

› An economy of scarcity leads to more renting of goods rather than ownership and moves resources from the goods sector to the service sector.

› The six universal marketing functions may be applied to service organizations; they are market analysis, communication, product differentiation, market segmentation, valuation, and exchange.

Discussion Questions

1. What consumer services do you feel will experience the most growth in the next 10 years? What marketing jobs will be available in those areas?

2. Give examples of convenience, shopping, and specialty services you have used recently. Evaluate the marketing programs of the organizations you dealt with. How do they compare to the marketing programs of manufacturers?

3. "Young people today want everything their parents had when they were middle-aged." Do you agree? How do young people today differ in their marketing attitudes from young people 20 years ago?

4. Why is productivity a problem in the service sector? How does this

problem affect the national economy? What can be done to improve productivity in the service sector?

5. Discuss why service organizations such as schools and hospitals may be more interested in *managing* demand than in *increasing* demand for their services? Does this make marketing harder or easier? Why?

6. "A RAND Corporation mathematician forecasts that by the year 2000 only 2 percent of the labor force will be required to turn out all the necessary manufactured goods." What could this mean for blue-collar workers? What could this mean for marketing majors?

7. How important is student input to the value of a college education? Give other examples of situations in which the buyer is as important as the seller to the satisfactory performance of a service. How does this affect the marketing of such services?

8. Over 40 percent of the dollars spent for services are in the industrial sector rather than the consumer market. Do you feel this split of the service dollar will continue. Why or why not? What are the largest industrial service areas?

9. Do the marketing functions discussed in Chapter 2 apply to service organizations as well as to manufacturing organizations? Where are the major differences, if any?

10. Discuss opportunities for women in the service sector. Does this mean that women will have more or less job opportunities in the future? How will this affect job opportunities for men?

CASES

Real Estate Sales
Promoting a Service

Jim and Bonnie Lindstrom are a husband and wife real estate team. They both work for the same agency. They deal primarily in residential housing in the suburban areas of Washington, D.C. They do very well selling real estate but would like some assistance in the area of marketing. Jim and Bonnie use newspaper advertising much like all the other real estate people, but they feel that there is more to the marketing of a service than advertising. They feel they have a unique product to sell because a customer of either gets the assistance of the other for no added cost. For example, if Bonnie is not home to answer the phone or to show someone around, chances are Jim will take over and see that everything is done for the customer.

1. Is real estate sales a convenience, shopping, or specialty service?
2. Show how Bonnie and Jim could use each of the six universal marketing functions to improve their service.
3. What kind of promotion other than newspaper advertising would you recommend for this sales team?
4. Show how Bonnie and Jim could benefit by having their own personal marketing information system.

Insurance Sales
What Is the Product?

John Williams was a star quarterback for the state university football team. He is well known throughout the state by college-age people and older people as well. John hurt his knee in his senior year and couldn't go on to professional football. One of John's friends found a good job for him selling life insurance for one of the leading companies.

1. What is John's total product offer?
2. What market segments should John concentrate on if he wishes long-run success in his career?
3. Is John selling a convenience, shopping, or specialty service?
4. What would be an effective way for John to generate leads for his insurance business?

Marketing and Nonbusiness Organizations 18

broadening the concept of marketing

> *For years, certain successful marketing techniques that were once con-*
> *sidered to belong almost exclusively to profit-motivated business enter-*
> *prises have been used advantageously by alert managers in private*
> *nonprofit organizations. However, many other managers of nonprofit*
> *organizations have failed to recognize that marketing is as intrinsic to*
> *the nonprofit sector as it is to the business community.*
>
> Benson P. Shapiro*

INTRODUCTION Tony Bianchi was a marketing student at a major university who hoped to find a managerial position in some large business firm. One day Tony's professor brought up a subject Tony had never heard about in his undergraduate classes. The professor called it "social marketing" or **nonbusiness marketing**. Tony was rather disturbed to be "wasting time" discussing this subject because he did not feel it was helpful to a "business" career. You may tend at first to agree with Tony's views on this subject. However, you should be patient and read on. What you learn about this subject may be more relevant to your future career than you imagine. In this chapter we shall discuss marketing for nonbusiness organizations such as the government, charities, social causes, and politicians—what is generally called "nonbusiness marketing." Most people feel that social marketing (the marketing of causes) is just one aspect of nonbusiness marketing. The terms "nonbusiness" and "non-profit" organizations are often used synonymously, and we shall use them interchangeably. Perhaps you will be surprised to learn about the importance of marketing in nonprofit organizations and the many career opportunities it provides.

Broadening In 1970, two professors at Northwestern University, Philip Kotler and
the Concept Sidney J. Levy, won an award for writing the best article of the previous
of Marketing year in the *Journal of Marketing*. It called for **broadening the concept of marketing**, and it was to cause quite a stir among marketing scholars. Here are some of the things the authors said in that article:

Political contests remind us that candidates are marketed as well as soap; student recruitment reminds us that higher education is mar-keted; and fund raising reminds us that "causes" are marketed. Yet these areas of marketing are typically ignored by the student of mar-keting. . . .

. . . the authors see a great opportunity for marketing people to ex-pand their thinking and to apply their skills to an increasingly interest-ing range of social activity. . . . Marketing will either take on a

* "Marketing for Nonprofit Organizations," *Harvard Business Review*, September–October 1973, p. 123.

458

broader social meaning or remain a narrowly defined business activity . . .

. . . Many . . . organizations . . . require the same rarefied management skills as traditional business organizations. Managing the United Auto Workers, Defense Department, Ford Foundation, World Bank, Catholic Church, and University of California has become every bit as challenging as managing Procter & Gamble, General Motors, and General Electric. . . .

. . . All organizations must develop appropriate products to serve their sundry consuming publics. The business heritage of marketing provides a useful set of concepts for guiding all organizations.

The choice facing those who manage nonbusiness organizations is not whether to market or not to market, for no organization can avoid marketing. The choice is whether to do it well or poorly. . . .[1]

You should read this entire article carefully and think about its implications for students of marketing. What it means is that a marketing student can seek employment in *all* organizations, not just businesses, and that the greatest challenges in the future might be in nonbusiness organizations. The article discusses the marketing problems of police departments, museums, public schools, developing nations, anti-smoking groups, political organizations, the American Medical Association, the YMCA, the Republican party, and other such groups.

Broadening Too Far? The favorable reaction to the article by Kotler and Levy was not unanimous, however. David Luck felt that they broadened the concept of marketing too far. As Luck put it: "A manageable, intelligible, and logical definition of marketing can be fashioned when its scope is bounded within those processes or activities whose ultimate result is a *market transaction.*"[2]

Kotler and Levy answered Luck in this way: "The crux of marketing lies in a *general idea of exchange* rather than the narrower idea of market transactions. Exchange involves two (or more) parties who voluntarily agree to enter into a "trading agreement."[3]

In reality, there is no "right" or "wrong" solution to this debate. Marketing *is* concerned with *market* transactions, but it is *also* concerned with nonmarket exchanges. There is no reason why marketers should not study *both*, because both are important in an advanced economy. Figure 18.1 summarizes all business and nonbusiness marketing exchanges, both voluntary and nonvoluntary.

[1] Philip Kotler and Sidney J. Levy, "Broadening the Concept of Marketing," *Journal of Marketing*, January 1969, pp. 10–15.

[2] David J. Luck, "Broadening the Concept of Marketing—Too Far," *Journal of Marketing*, July 1969, p. 54.

[3] Philip Kotler and Sidney J. Levy, "A New Form of Marketing Myopia: Rejoinder to Professor Luck," *Journal of Marketing*, July 1969, p. 57.

Figure 18.1 SATISFACTION OF CONSUMPTION THROUGH VOLUNTARY AND NONVOLUNTARY EXCHANGE

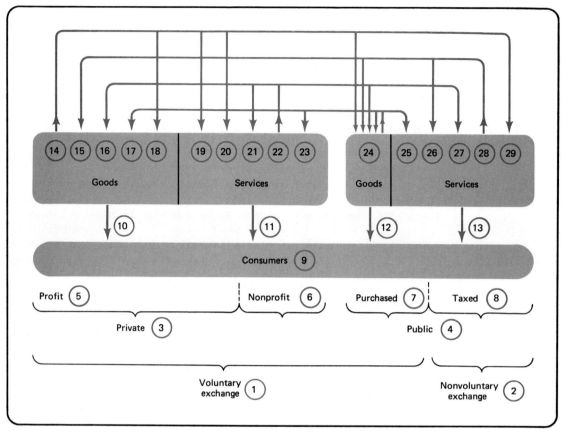

Key to Chart: (1) All market transactions. (2) All purchases through taxation. (3) Transactions between consumers and private sellers. (4) Transactions between consumers and public bodies. (5) Transactions between consumers and, for example, retailers or lawyers. (6) Transactions between consumers and, for example, private universities. (7) Transactions between consumers and public bodies (postage, for example). (8) Services rendered by public bodies: financed by taxes (fire protection, for example). (9) Ultimate consumers. (10) Food; automobiles. (11) Telephone service; Red Cross. (12) Government publications. (13) Highway tolls; sewage treatment. (14) Goods sold to other than ultimate consumers (computer hardware, for example). (15) Commercial purchases of government services (voluntary or nonvoluntary) by goods-handling firms. (16) Commercial purchases of private services (goods handling). (17) Voluntary or nonvoluntary purchases of government goods. (18) Purchases of goods for resale or industrial use. (19) Commercial purchases of goods by private services. (20) Purchases of government services (voluntary or nonvoluntary) by private service firms or institutions. (21) Purchases of private services by private services and institutions. (22) Services sold to other than ultimate consumers. (23) Voluntary or nonvoluntary purchases of government goods by private service firms or institutions. (24a) Purchases of private goods and services and government services by government goods producers. (24b) Sale of government goods to private goods and services and government services producers. (25) Purchases of government goods by government services. (26) Purchases of government services by government services. (27) Purchases of private services by government services. (28) All sales of government services to other than ultimate consumers. (29) Purchases of private goods by public services. *Note:* Many services are offered by both private and public bodies: utilities, insurance, and outdoor recreation, for example. Mixed ventures (partly public and partly private) are not reflected on chart.

Redrawn from John M. Rathmell, *Marketing in the Service Sector* (Cambridge, Mass.: Winthrop Publishers, Inc., 1974), pp. 31–32.

MARKETING IN NONPROFIT ORGANIZATIONS You may be still uncertain whether marketing concepts, principles, and strategies can be effectively applied in nonprofit organizations. Almost the entire July 1971 issue of the *Journal of Marketing* was devoted to that subject. Here are some of the titles from that issue: "Marketing's Application to Fund Raising," "Health Service Marketing: A Suggested Model," "Marketing and Population Problems," "Recycling Solid Wastes: A Channel of Distribution Problem," and "Incorporating Ecology into Marketing Strategy: The Case of Air Pollution." If you read these articles, you will discover that the functions of marketing and the management activities are much the same for all organizations.

There has also been an increase in the amount of attention paid to marketing in nonprofit organizations in marketing courses. An article by Nickels in the *Journal of Economics and Business* reported the results of a poll of marketing professors taken in 1974.[4] It showed that the large majority (95 percent) of college marketing educators felt that the scope of marketing should be broadened to include nonbusiness organizations. Over 75 percent of the respondents felt that marketing textbooks did not devote enough space to the special problems of nonprofit organizations. Much progress has been made in the few years since that poll was taken.

In 1975, an important book on this topic was published. In it, Kotler discusses in detail the ways in which the basic principles of marketing

[4] William G. Nickels, "Conceptual Conflicts in Marketing," *Journal of Economics and Business*, Winter 1974, pp. 140–143.

Nonbusiness Marketing

In recent years, marketing has become a subject of growing interest to managers of public and private nonprofit organizations. The concepts, tools, and models that have worked so effectively to manage products and services in the profit sector are becoming increasingly relevant to the management of products and services in the nonprofit sector. Nonprofit organizations face a host of problems that would be analyzed as straightforward marketing problems if found in the profit sector. Museums and symphonies have a difficult time attracting sufficient funds to carry on their cultural activities. Blood banks find it hard to enlist enough donors. Churches are having difficulties attracting and maintaining active members. Many colleges face serious problems in attracting a sufficient number of qualified students. Police departments are hampered by a poor image in many communities. Family planners face formidable problems in selling the idea of "zero population growth." Safety councils seek more effective ways to persuade motorists to wear their safety belts. National parks such as Yellowstone are plagued with overdemand and are seeking ways to discourage or "demarket" the parks. There is hardly a public or private nonprofit organization in existence that is not faced with some problems stemming from its relations to its markets.

From Philip Kotler, *Marketing for Nonprofit Organizations* (Englewood Cliffs, N.J.: Prentice-Hall, Inc., 1975), p. ix.

can be applied to nonbusiness organizations.[5] That book, plus other articles on this topic, provide the basis for this chapter. (The insert "Nonbusiness Marketing" contains a portion of the preface of Kotler's landmark text.)

Social Marketing

Business organizations use marketing concepts and tools to create mutually satisfactory product exchanges, and their return is called "profit." Nonprofit organizations also try to create mutually satisfying exchanges, but the return is sometimes called "social improvement," a "better standard of living," or a "higher quality of life." Though there are differences between marketing in profit-making and nonprofit organizations, there is also much that is similar. This is clear when one reviews the definition of social marketing (management). **Social marketing (management) is the design, implementation, and control of programs that seek to foster the acceptance of a social idea, cause, or practice by a target group or groups.**[6] It utilizes market segmentation, communication, and the other marketing functions (see Chapter 2).

The idea is still to "find a need and fill it," but the needs are often those of society rather than of individuals and the whole society benefits (gains) from such exchanges. Population control, crime prevention, environmental protection, energy conservation, drug control, economic stability, and world peace are all goals of social marketing. The concept is:

> **Marketing is an attempt to establish mutually satisfying exchange relationships to satisfy *all* of society's wants and needs—some of those needs can be met only through nonbusiness organizations; therefore, the marketing of nonbusiness organizations is a major concern.**

Social Marketing in the Future

The future of marketing in the business (profit-making) sector will no doubt follow the same evolutionary changes that have occurred over the last 75 years. But there may be revolutionary changes in the area of *social* marketing. We have already noted that there are few marketing positions, as such, in the government, nonprofit organizations, and social causes. As a consequence, some people feel that the U.S. public is receiving an unbalanced marketing effort—an effort that stresses expenditures on personal satisfactions and gives little support to public expenditures.

Marketing's role in society is to provide for all our needs both social and economic. Therefore, the marketing of social causes could be given more attention in the future to balance the satisfaction of individual's needs with the satisfaction of society's broader needs. Included among these latter needs are pollution control, health care, workable transpor-

[5] Philip Kotler, *Marketing for Nonprofit Organizations* (Englewood Cliffs, N.J.: Prentice-Hall, Inc., 1975).

[6] Philip Kotler, *Marketing Management: Analysis, Planning, and Control*, 3rd ed. (Englewood Cliffs, N.J.: Prentice-Hall, Inc., 1976), p. 495.

This ad shows how Blue Cross/Blue Shield, a nonprofit organization, uses marketing to explain some of its services.

A broken arm shouldn't cost an arm and a leg.

Protecting the subscriber's pocketbook is part of the theory behind UCR — a better way to prepay doctor bills. UCR stands for "Usual, Customary or Reasonable" fees, and basically, it means this: When a Blue Shield subscriber is treated by a participating doctor, we pay the doctor's bill in full for the services we cover. There's no problem finding a participating doctor — 4,500 physicians in the area are participating. And UCR applies to a range of physicians' services from x-rays to lab work. From setting that broken arm to major surgery or a visit in the hospital. See the person who handles employee benefits where you work and inquire about UCR. If you're in a group of five or more employees, send for our booklet. Nearly two thirds of our subscribers already have this kind of full-payment coverage.

Blue Cross®
Blue Shield®'

Group Hospitalization, Inc. and Medical Service of D. C.
The Blue Cross and Blue Shield Plans of the National Capital Area.
®Registered Marks Blue Cross Association ®'Registered Service Marks of the National Association of Blue Shield Plans

Courtesy of Blue Cross and Blue Shield Plans of the National Capital Area.

Marketing Challenge of the Future

At present, society possesses the capacity and even the will to meet most material needs. But our experience has shown us . . . that man has many needs that are not specifically material. Can business methods, which have made the U.S. the most productive society in history, contribute to the fulfillment of these other needs—like personal freedom, sense of community, pride in work, aesthetic pleasure, reunion with nature? If they cannot, business is in danger of becoming irrelevant to the primary challenges of our time.

From an editorial in *Fortune,* July 1968.

tation systems, international peace and world trade, and world population control. The concept is:

› **Marketing in the future could do more to balance social needs with economic needs and the needs of individuals with the needs of society; therefore, the future of marketing may involve more efforts to satisfy the social problems of poverty, overpopulation, pollution, international conflict, disease, and ignorance.**

The Ethics of Marketing in the Nonprofit Sector You might have the feeling that there is something distasteful about the marketing of organizations such as churches. It might be difficult for you to imagine churches applying the same kind of tactics that are used by some discount stores. As a matter of fact, top people in many nonprofit organizations seem to feel that there is something inherently deceptive and manipulative about marketing. For this reason, very few nonprofit organizations have a "marketing department." They prefer to call this area public relations or some other, less controversial term. Levy suggests we use the term "furthering" rather than "marketing" in nonprofit organizations:

Nonbusiness groups, institutions, and organizations resist application of the term "marketing" to their activities, feeling that it stigmatizes them by implying that they value and seek money or sucess instead of less meretricious social and professional goals. This is a semantic and conceptual problem. . . . Perhaps the overall concept encompassing the determination of audience needs and the generation of audience interest and supportive response to one's aims might use the term further-ing instead of marketing.[7]

But whether we call it marketing, public relations, furthering, or anything else, there is no getting around the fact that nonprofit organi-

---

[7] Sidney J. Levy, "Promotion Behavior," in Frederick D. Sturdivant et al., *Managerial Analysis in Marketing* (Glenview, Ill.: Scott, Foresman and Company, 1970), p. 431.

zations are involved in different markets and must learn how to best deal with the markets.

It is not unethical to attempt to establish mutually satisfying exchange relationships with people. It *is* unethical to use deception or misrepresentation in such attempts. But this is true of law, medicine, and all other professions—not just marketing. Marketing is a tool that can be used or abused. We hope this text will help all organizations to use marketing more effectively and to eliminate the abuses.

Structure and Cost of a Marketing Department

Many people feel that it costs a lot to hire marketing experts and that a nonprofit organization would have to establish some kind of marketing department that would add to the bureaucracy.

It is true that a marketing department may add some costs to a nonprofit organization; however, the benefits could greatly exceed such costs. It is not necessary to add a large staff or to spend a lot on promotion, because marketing may be more of a philosophy of management (an attitude) than a position in the organizational hierarchy. The marketing concept calls for the coordination and integration of multiorganizational systems to provide mutually satisfying exchanges for individuals and for society.

A marketing approach means that the nonprofit organization should listen to its publics. It should design its products, policies, and practices to meet their needs and should establish open two-way communications with employees or volunteers and with outside groups and individuals. These functions could be performed by the organization's present staff, and consultants could be used to help in conducting marketing research, setting up a marketing information system, or establishing effective product, promotion, and distribution strategies.

Of course, it would be best if one person were given the responsibility and the authority to coordinate and integrate marketing functions in a nonprofit organization. The added cost of such a position would be more than offset by efficiencies in fund raising and client services.

THE FUNCTIONAL APPROACH TO NONBUSINESS MARKETING

One benefit of studying marketing from a functional approach is that the concepts are applicable in all marketing situations, including nonbusiness marketing. Marketing in the nonprofit sector is much the same as marketing in the service sector, because the product is intangible, productivity is a real problem, and communication is a key function. But there are differences that make nonprofit marketing more complex. For one thing, nonprofit organizations often get their revenue from two sources—clients and donors. For example, a nonprofit hospital may charge whatever patients can afford and make up the difference through public donations or from government funding. Nonprofit organizations thus may have primary exchange relationships with several different markets: the donor market, the client market, and the government market. Each of these markets should be approached with a separate marketing program designed to meet the needs of that market segment. In the following sections, we shall discuss the special problems that nonprofit organizations have in applying the six marketing functions: market analysis, communication, product differentiation, market segmentation, valuation, and exchange.

The Market-Analysis Function   Nonbusiness organizations have a special problem in defining which people to serve. For example, should a nonprofit, public university serve *all* high school graduates or just those with good grades? Should special programs be designed for adults? How much of the cost should be borne by students and how much by the public? How should students from other states be treated? These are difficult questions to answer, but they are typical of the kinds of questions faced by nonprofit organizations.

Take hospitals as another example. Should a nonprofit hospital serve *all* people, regardless of ability to pay? Who should get first priority? Who should absorb the costs of nonpaying patients?

The public may also find it difficult to carry out the market-analysis function. What charities and causes should be supported and how? Where can a person learn about the effectiveness and efficiency of various nonprofit organizations? Should we vote to increase local taxes for the schools or not? Which politicians should we elect in order to have the kind of government we would like?

As you can see, there is a tremendous need for careful marketing research in the nonprofit sector. Government organizations, charities, social causes, foundations, and other nonprofit groups must choose what social needs they will attempt to satisfy and must clearly spell out the specific segments they will serve within the total population. Without careful market analysis and segmentation, nonprofit organizations may find themselves in serious financial difficulty. The government is one example of how rather loose marketing management of various programs may hurt everyone in society. At the city level, New York suffered financial problems so severe that the consequences were felt throughout the nation. New York, and all other cities, must analyze the social market and carefully manage the programs so as to maintain financial stability. This takes serious and detailed marketing research. The same market analysis must be conducted at the county, state, and federal level.

At the micro (organizational) level, market analysis means that nonprofit organizations such as schools, hospitals, charities, and causes must recognize limitations to their programs. World problems with hunger, poverty, disease, and war cry out for attention, but all problems cannot be solved at once. Each organization must carefully select some aspect of a broad social need and satisfy that need effectively and efficiently.

There is evidence to show that many nonbusiness organizations are far behind profit-making organizations in their market-analysis efforts. Some nonprofit organizations seem to be where business was 100 years ago. For example, Eckles studied an agency of the government that prepares maps from aerial photographs. The agency appeared to have a production orientation much like businesses had in the early 1900s:

Further investigation of the agency uncovered a number of shortcomings that the use of marketing concepts could be helpful [*in solving*].

After two months of investigation, it became obvious that the agency did not understand the value of studying . . . user needs. The agency did not attempt to define its market, identify its market target, or understand its consumer's profile. By not sufficiently defining its direction, the agency did not achieve the most realistic allocation of its resources so as to optimize its output of timely and relevant . . . products.[8]

Investigations of other nonprofit organizations by Eckles revealed the organizations' tendency "to overlook the more critical and sophisticated marketing concepts of marketing research, demand analysis and forecasting, isolation of the market target, and product identification."[9]

If all nonprofit organizations and all individuals would apply marketing concepts to their activities, we could make better progress toward solving the many problems of the world. The concepts are:

> **Market analysis for nonprofit organizations is the process whereby organizations learn about unmet needs in society and analyze which of those needs can be satisfied by a marketing program.**

[8] Robert W. Eckles, "Using Marketing Concepts in the Not-For-Profit Organizations" (Paper delivered at the 1973 annual meeting of the Southwestern Social Science Association—Marketing Section, Dallas, Texas), p. 5.

[9] Ibid., p. i.

Why Government Agencies Need Marketing

Government agencies, like other organizations, are surrounded by several publics with whom they must maintain good relations. Many agencies are established specifically to provide a public service, such as transportation, protection, relief, commercial information, health service, education, and so on. Although they often provide the service as a monopolist, there are usually substitutes that consumers can resort to if the quality of the public service offering is poor. Public agencies that do a poor job of meeting the needs of their clients are subject to criticism from public interest groups and media, as well as withdrawal of client patronage. One of the agency's most important publics is the legislature, which presumably scrutinizes the quality of service the agency offers in deciding on its funding. Thus there are many publics that an agency must satisfy if it is to function effectively.

The government agency that wishes to operate smoothly, receive adequate funding and powers from the legislature, and avoid bad press relations must pay attention to its level of service to each of its publics. The role of marketing in the agency is to establish the needs of its various publics, develop the appropriate products and services, arrange for their efficient distribution and communication, and audit the degree of satisfaction. In this way, it achieves and fulfills its goals as an agency.

From Philip Kotler, *Marketing for Nonprofit Organizations* (Englewood Cliffs, N.J.: Prentice-Hall, Inc., 1975), p. 329.

> Market analysis for the public in the nonbusiness area includes the search for nonprofit organizations that can satisfy those needs that are not being met by the business sector.

The Communication Function If there is one area of marketing where nonprofit organizations have developed expertise, it is in the area of promotion. Many nonprofit groups have developed quite sophisticated promotional programs that include advertising, public relations, publicity, personal selling, and sales promotion. We shall briefly discuss each of these promotional tools to show you what the present situation is in the nonprofit sector.

These two ads show how marketing may be used to promote social causes—here, energy conservation and pollution control.

Courtesy of The Advertising Council, Inc.

Advertising Many nonprofit organizations do not budget money for advertising but rely on the media to publish their advertisements free. The media are required to do a certain amount of such public service advertising, and the various nonprofit groups compete for that free space and time. Some organizations use direct mail very effectively and have quite sophisticated, computerized mailing procedures.

Businesses have offered their advertising expertise to nonprofit organizations through the Advertising Council. The Advertising Council arranges to have someone from business coordinate the advertising program for the causes they support. The Council also invites an ad agency to write the ads, and the various media are solicited to get free space and time. You have probably seen many of the ads that the Council has sponsored. Notable ones include "Smokey the Bear" for fire prevention and ads to encourage young people to stay in school and stay away from drugs. The Council supports governmental, religious, charitable, educational, and other social agencies.[10]

The problem with many nonprofit organizations is that they rely almost exclusively on promotion as a marketing tool. This means they give too little attention to marketing research, product design, channel selection, distribution, market segmentation, and other marketing activities.

Public Relations Often nonprofit groups are far ahead of businesses when it comes to public relations and publicity. Organizations such as the Red Cross receive much favorable coverage in the media. The problem recently has been a rash of unfavorable publicity about nonprofit groups, especially charities and government agencies. Some charities have been accused of being very inefficient and even fraudulent. Not surprisingly, much of the inefficiency being cited is marketing inefficiency. The successful causes of the future will be those that develop efficient and effective marketing systems, including a good PR department.

Personal Selling Although most nonprofit organizations do not have people with titles such as"sales representative," they do have salespeople (fund raisers) on the staff. These people are especially important for soliciting funds from businesses, foundations, and government agencies. All of the personal selling skills we have discussed previously are used by these solicitors. One problem with some nonprofit organizations is that they fail to train their volunteer salespeople (for example, door-to-door solicitors) in even the fundamental principles of selling or product knowledge. Untrained, unskilled personal representatives can cause many problems for an organization by creating a bad image and by misrepresenting the organization.

[10] For more details about the work of the Council, see Thomas V. Greer and William G. Nickels, "The Advertising Council: A Model for Social Marketing?" *Marquette Business Review*, Spring 1975, pp. 17–22.

Sales Promotion Many nonprofit groups have quite sophisticated sales promotion programs that give support to the other promotional tools. You have probably seen window displays in stores promoting various charitable functions. But sales promotion also coordinates social affairs at which volunteers are solicited and sets up displays in various public facilities.

We need not dwell too long on the promotion function, because nonprofit organizations usually are quite good at it. But some mention should be made of the fact that nonbusinesses are often as unresponsive as business organizations to public inquiries and suggestions. No one seems to be in charge of listening! Nonprofit organizations must learn to be as progressive in the listening end of communication management as they are in the talking end.

Wiebe feels that nonprofit organizations must give their potential supporters some *mechanism* (agency or group) by which the public can translate motivation into action. He also says that such organizations must give supporters *direction.*[11] That is, supporters must know where, when, and how they should act in response to an appeal. And nonbusiness organizations should show the public that their programs are *compatible* with what the public wants and *adequate* to do what they promise. All of these goals require two-way communication. Listening is required to find out what potential supporters are looking for in an organization. Promotion is required to tell the public about programs and progress. The concepts are:

> Communication flows in the nonprofit sector should open a dialogue between and among all social organizations and the public; communication is the marketing tool that enables nonprofit organizations to learn about and resolve social problems in cooperation with other organizations.

> Nonprofit organizations have a special responsibility to listen to the public, because such organizations are often the last resort for people with unmet needs.

> To get support for their programs, nonprofit organizations should provide a *mechanism* (an organization) to mobilize support; they should give *direction* to supporters by telling them *what* to do, when, and how; and they should show supporters that they are succeeding in their mission by informing people of their progress in meeting a recognized need.

The Product-
Differentiation
Function Have you ever analyzed why you give money to some charities and not to others? What is the product you are buying when you give? What differentiates one charity or social cause from another? If you stop to answer these questions, you will realize that nonprofit organizations, like all other organizations, have a "product" to sell. That product is really an image or a series of impressions rather than something tangible.

[11] These concepts are from G. W. Wiebe, "Merchandising Commodities and Citizenship on Television," *Public Opinion Quarterly*, Winter 1951–1952, pp. 681–682.

For example, what is the product of a small private university? Why would a student choose to spend four or five times as much to go to a small private school rather than to a major state university? Do images of small classes, "personalized" instruction, and friendly student relations come to mind? What about status, "quality" education, and "sound" academics? Do big schools make you think of large classes, "impersonal" TV instruction, and mass education? No doubt, you have your own impressions, but those impressions are very real to you, even though you may never have visited a university different from your own. "The product is what the consumer thinks it is!"

A university does not turn out a standard product. It is a resource that is as good or bad as each student makes it. But a university's product is much more than education; it is a social environment, a home away from home, a place to show one's athletic prowess, a place to find a mate, and an escape from work. Therefore, each school can differentiate its product to appeal to a different market segment. Thus we have schools for radicals, schools for engineering "stars," schools for athletic "stars," schools for marginal students, schools for the elite, and so on. Each school needs a different product that enables it to compete in today's market of declining enrollments.

Churches go through much the same process. For example, there are very liberal Christian churches, very conservative churches, and many in between. The same concept is true in Judaism. There is a church, temple, or religious group to appeal to almost any belief or persuasion. Churches often adapt their "products" by changing the service, revising the songs, and emphasizing different issues. Those churches or church leaders that fail to adapt to their market usually lose attendance and income. Most churches attempt to establish a mutually satisfactory relationship between their members and some meaningful God. To do this, they must behave as all middlemen and "fill the needs" of their members. They do this by developing their product.

All organizations market products, and their success at doing so depends partially on their ability to differentiate their product from competitors and meet the needs of some target group. This is as true for nonprofit organizations as it is for IBM or any other firm. The concepts are:

- Nonprofit organizations must develop product offers that appeal to a particular market segment.
- The product of nonprofit organizations is intangible, and so much of product development (image creation) relies on marketing communication (promotion).
- The public gives its support to those nonprofit organizations that best meet the public's needs by developing products that satisfy some social need.

A couple of examples may help you to visualize these concepts. Try to imagine what the product of the Lung Association would be. The association feels that its core product is the control and prevention of lung disease.[12] But there are many other products to sell including antipollution programs, antismoking legislation, professional education programs (for various kinds of doctors), and direct services to lung disease patients. Some people feel that Christmas seals are the main product of the Lung Association, but Christmas seals are merely the visible, tangible representation of the basic product—the prevention of lung disease.

The Lung Association even has a registered trade mark (the red, double-barred cross) and a registered slogan ("It's a Matter of Life and Breath"). The Lung Association tries to use its trade mark and slogan on all of its literature and promotional materials.

The Lung Association also experienced a product life cycle with one of its major products. The core product at one time was the eradication of tuberculosis. This appeal was new at the time (1907) and received limited public attention (introductory stage). The tuberculosis movement experienced *rapid growth* from 1921 until 1954. In 1954, a treatment was found for TB that ended the need for a vast national fund-raising effort. Rather than suffer the *decline* stage of the product life cycle, the organization changed its *product* from the eradication of tuberculosis to the control and prevention of lung disease (note that the products are rather closely related). Later the Tuberculosis Association changed its name to the Lung Association to reflect its new product emphasis. (This is the same kind of thinking that led the Radio Corporation of America to become RCA and the Minnesota Mining and Manufacturing Company to become 3-M).

Are you getting the feeling that nonprofit organizations not only have products, but brand names, slogans, and life cycle problems as well? Perhaps another example would help.

The National Foundation–March of Dimes once had as its product the treatment and care of polio victims. When a polio vaccination was discovered, the name was changed from the Polio Foundation to the National Foundation, but the same March of Dimes campaign continues. Today, the Foundation's product is the treatment and prevention of birth defects. Notice that this cause (product) also went through a classic life cycle.[13]

The products of various nonprofit organizations can be combined into a "package of services" that would have more appeal than separate products. The United Fund, for example, provides support for hundreds of services. Similarly, the Commerce and Industry Combined Health Appeal (CICHA) supports thirteen health agencies, including the Eye Bank, the American Lung Association, the Planned Parenthood Associ-

---

[12] Information about the Lung Association comes from Greg Walling, "Marketing for a Nonprofit Organization: The Lung Association" (unpublished paper, University of Maryland, 1975).

[13] For more about the stages in the life cycle of various causes, see Philip Kotler, "The Five C's: Cause, Change Agency, Change Target, Channel, and Change Strategy," in *Creating Social Change*, ed. Gerald Zaltman, Philip Kotler, and Ira Kaufman (New York: Holt, Rinehart and Winston, Inc., 1972).

Marketing efforts are used to market causes—here, preventive medicine.

Perform a death-defying act.

Have regular medical check-ups.

Give Heart Fund
American Heart Association

Courtesy of the American Heart Association.

ation, and the American Cancer Society. This is what Kotler and Zaltman have to say about product design in nonprofit organizations:

Product design is typically more challenging in the social area than it is in the business area. Consider the problem of marketing "safer driving." The social objective is to create safer driving habits and attitudes in the population. There is no one product that can accomplish this. Various products have to be designed that will make partial contributions to the social objective. A public-education media campaign providing tips on safe driving is one such product; the offering of "defensive" driving courses is another. . . .[14]

One could go on listing ways in which nonprofit organizations manage product concepts, but you should by now have an idea of how they do so. The concepts are:

- Nonprofit organizations have products, brands, and slogans much like those of a manufacturing firm, but their products more closely resemble service industry products.
- The products of nonprofit organizations may go through a product life cycle; if so, the organization must then develop new products or face possible extinction.
- Nonprofit organizations must learn to differentiate their products from other, similar organizations if they are to realize market success.

Many people in the United States are not familiar with the thousands of causes that appeal to them for money. The nonprofit organization that develops a product that satisfies a real need, establishes a good image for the organization, and uses marketing tools such as trademarks, slogans,

[14] Philip Kotler and Gerald Zaltman, "Social Marketing: An Approach to Planned Social Change," *Journal of Marketing,* July 1971, p. 7.

advertising, packaging, and pricing, can generate much public support for its cause. Of course, this is true for *all* organizations, but it is not recognized as being true in many nonprofit organizations.

The Market-Segmentation Function   You may have been surprised to find that nonprofit organizations are so involved with product concepts such as product development, branding, pricing, and the product life cycle. Another area of importance to nonprofit organizations is market segmentation. Pause for a moment and think of how you would segment the market for the March of Dimes.

Mindak and Bybee analyzed the fund-raising efforts of the March of Dimes and here is what they found: "The first handicap the authors encountered in conducting the marketing analysis was the lack of primary research data about the "heavy giver," his demographic characteristics, the location and size of this particular market, and his basic motivation for giving or not giving."[15] It is difficult to conduct an effective and efficient fund-raising campaign without ample market-segmentation data.

Mindak and Bybee felt that the March of Dimes was in the late stages (decline) of the "charity" life cycle. Their research showed that many people still associated the March of Dimes with polio (although a cure was found almost 20 years previously). You should read about the details of their research in their article in the *Journal of Marketing*. It is interesting to note that much of their emphasis was placed on defining and segmenting the market.

Many nonprofit organizations use market-segmentation strategies for both fund raising and for allocating their services to the public. The Lung Association segments donors on the basis of (1) past donations, (2) residential classification, (3) select job categories, and (4) organizational and business classification.

Client markets are segmented in a similar way. For example, smokers are segmented for certain types of health service programs *and* by age, sex, and occupation. The antipollution program segments markets by industries that are polluting, potential carpoolers, and activists who would help in the legislative area. Even doctors are segmented by specialties and are invited to attend special seminars.

At times, market-segmentation efforts can be quite difficult for nonprofit organizations. People do not support a cause simply because they are young, old, rich, or poor. Often they support a cause because they *want to;* but how do you find people who are already interested? Read what Kassarjian found in his study of air pollution:

Demographic variables such as age, sex, socioeconomic status, and political party membership do not seem to be relevant. . . . The important variable of concern to the marketer is not related to the usual segmentation criteria, but rather the level *of concern about the issue at hand, whether it be nonreturnable bottles, high-phosphate detergents,*

---

[15] William A. Mindak and H. Malcolm Bybee, "Marketing's Application to Fund Raising," *Journal of Marketing*, July 1971, pp. 13–14.

aluminum cans, or excessive use of paper bags dispensed at supermarkets.[16]

With competition among various social causes becoming more intense, the need for market-segmentation research and practice is critical for nonprofit organizations. All of the segmentation variables we discussed earlier (for example, demographics and psychographics) are applicable. So are the positioning strategies outlined in Chapter 4. The concepts are:

> **Nonprofit organizations need market-segmentation strategies for two purposes: resource gathering (fund raising) and resource allocation (serving clients).**

> **All the segmentation variables used by profit-making organizations are applicable to nonprofit organizations, but often concern about the issue at hand is the most important variable.**

The Valuation Function and Pricing We have said that valuation is a universal function in marketing whereby each of the participants tries to determine whether the benefits of an exchange would exceed the costs. Such an analysis is as important to a nonprofit organization as it is to a business firm. Here is what was said about the valuation function in an organization concerned with family planning: "Although the program is part of a nonprofit foundation, attention is being paid to the cost of providing the services. Cost-benefit analysis is performed and vigilant cost analysis and control reports are being instituted."[17]

Pricing is often an important element in the valuation function. The cost to the consumer in time may be considered as well: "Although the services provided to the customers were free, clinic personnel were taught that the customer had an *opportunity cost* involved. In essence, the customer had an alternative use for her time, and the cost of spending several hours to receive this service might be prohibitive."[18]

Many nonprofit organizations do charge a price for their services, but the price tends to be flexible. If you are attending a university, you know that the price can be quite high even if you attend a subsidized state institution. The price of hospital care might also be quite high, partially because those who cannot afford to pay are often subsidized by those who do pay. Museums, symphonies, public gardens, and other nonprofit organizations may also charge a fee to partially offset the costs. But the price of something does not have to be expressed in monetary terms. The client must "pay" a lot to receive the full services of a *free* stop smoking clinic or a drug rehabilitation center.

Flexibility in pricing is evident when one looks more closely at what

[16] Harold H. Kassarjian, "Incorporating Ecology into Marketing Strategy: The Case of Air Pollution," *Journal of Marketing*, July 1971, p. 65, emphasis added.

[17] Adel I. El-Ansary and Oscar E. Kramer, Jr., "Social Marketing: The Family Planning Experience," *Journal of Marketing*, July 1973, p. 4.

[18] Ibid., p. 3.

The Need for Product Differentiation and Market Segmentation

The experiences in the cases [analyzed] indicate that problems of marketing such as selling and promoting may not be the critical areas of need for not-for-profit organizations. The critical needs that are not being met . . . appear to be in the areas of marketing research, demand analysis, isolation of market potential, identification of market target, and above all, product identification. The not-for-profit organizations investigated seemed to lack an understanding that being responsive to the needs of society and/or presenting an effective program could be assisted by other marketing concepts such as:

1. Defining the existing need.
2. Properly identifying the market target or those who have the greatest need.
3. Realistically allocating resources to meet these needs.

Therefore, knowing how to sell and promote is very necessary, but knowing *what* is being sold to *whom*, and *why*, appears to be even more important.

From Robert W. Eckles, "Using Marketing Concepts in the Not-For-Profit Organizations" (Paper delivered at the 1973 annual meeting of the Southwestern Social Science Association—Marketing Section, Dallas, Texas), pp. 11–12. Reprinted with permission of the American Marketing Association.

people pay various nonprofit groups. Some students are given scholarships to lower the price of their education. Students may receive discounts at museums and art shows. Some people give nothing to their church, while others give 10 percent of their gross income. What the organization fails to raise through its pricing programs, it must raise through fund-raising programs. The concepts are:

> Nonprofit organizations and their clients use the valuation function to determine whether the costs of an exchange (in time, money, or effort) are less than the benefits received; if they are, exchange relationships likely will end.

> Pricing is an important issue for all nonprofit organizations; the price may not be expressed in terms of money, but price concepts are equally valid.

The Exchange Function At one time marketing educators were concerned mostly with defining marketing terms and describing marketing institutions. But today marketing is viewed as "a conceptual system about exchanges and transactions that helps analyze, explain, and control them."[19]

Exchange, then, is the core of marketing and a key marketing function

[19] Kotler, *Marketing for Nonprofit Organizations*, p. 34.

Efficiency in the Nonprofit Sector

The growing importance of the nonprofit sector will probably pose some disturbing questions about how to promote efficiency and equity in such organizations (for example, the problems associated with increasing costs in voluntary hospitals). When nonprofit operations represent only a minor exception to an essentially private-enterprise economy, the problem is not very serious. But if we ever reach the stage where nonprofit operations tend to dominate the economy, we probably will be faced with the need for radically new instruments of regulation and control.

From Victor R. Fuchs, *The Service Economy* (New York: National Bureau of Economic Research, 1968), p. 192.

in all organizations. All the other functions are designed to facilitate exchange relationships. In nonprofit organizations, the two central exchange relationships are (1) those established between donors and the organization (resource gathering) and (2) those between the people served and the organization (resource allocation).

One of the more important ways to facilitate exchanges is to make it easy for others to enter such relationships. In seeking donors, nonprofit groups may come to your home (for example, the Girl Scouts), place people in heavily trafficked areas (for example, the Salvation Army), establish easy-to-use donation forms (for example, self-addressed envelopes), and generally minimize the effort involved in volunteering one's time or money.

Similarly, nonprofit groups try to establish locations where they can serve their clients best. We shall discuss these programs in more detail in the following section.

Distribution Channels   Nonprofit organizations can better serve the public by applying many of the business concepts relating to channels and distribution management. For example, a state university might want to reach students throughout the state. Rather than force the students to come to some central campus, the university might set up branches in several major cities. This often saves the students the housing and eating costs associated with living away from home. Each of the branches may be thought of as retail outlets for the producer—that is, the university.

The idea is to serve the public as efficiently and effectively as possible. Thus the Lung Association has mobile X-ray units that travel from community to community, libraries have bookmobiles that do the same thing, and welfare organizations have counselors that go directly to people's homes to provide aid. "Meals on Wheels" programs deliver food to the sick and the aged, and churches have "drop-in" services. In each case, the goal is to distribute the services of the nonprofit organization to those who need them.

Nonprofit organizations must determine some cost-benefit trade-off in establishing distribution systems. The idea is to balance public service with some reasonable cost-control program.

Systems concepts are sometimes useful in controlling the delivery cost of nonprofit service. Public hospitals, for example, are most effective and efficient when they coordinate and integrate their efforts. This minimizes duplication of effort. Hospitals, schools, and other nonprofit institutions can form buying pools to lower resource costs and can share marketing intelligence data. The idea is to run the health-care system, the educational system, the charity system, and the government agency system like a large corporate system.

The American Lung Association, for example, is the equivalent of corporate headquarters. There are regional headquarters and local "retail" outlets as well. Together, these agencies form a system that has as its goal the prevention of lung disease. Other organizations are just now beginning to recognize the benefits of distribution middlemen.

For example, a few years ago the Whitney Museum of American Art opened a branch near Wall Street in New York City and was successful in attracting a good many people to its displays. Similar projects were started in Indianapolis and Baltimore.[20] The Louisiana Family Planning Program also was made more successful by carefully selecting clinic sites and by improving service levels.[21] These are just two examples of how nonprofit organizations can use marketing distribution concepts to establish mutually satisfying exchanges with the public. This is the thinking behind the new museum branches: "Curators are discovering an untapped "market" in business districts, often far removed from traditional museums. They reason that if art were nearer where people work, it might become a routine part of their lives."[22]

Here is what the marketers said about the family planning distribution system:

To reduce travel time, strategic locations were selected for the program's clinic satellites. Also, clinic layout was planned to reduce the time consumed in information and physical flows. The areas assigned for waiting rooms were limited to force faster customer flows. Bottlenecks in the system were identified and eliminated. It was realized that improving the service level would result not only in a higher percentage of kept appointments and active customers, but also in better utilization of physical facilities and human resources.[23]

[20] See Roger Ricklefs, "Will an Art Break Help Lunch Break? A Museum Hopes So," *The Wall Street Journal*, March 29, 1976, p. 1.

[21] El-Ansary and Kramer, "Social Marketing: The Family Planning Experience," pp. 1–7.

[22] Roger Ricklefs, "Will an Art Break Help Lunch Break? A Museum Hopes So," p. 1.

[23] El-Ansary and Kramer, "Social Marketing: The Family Planning Experience," p. 3.

New Educational Opportunities

Several years ago the Ohio State University changed the name of the business school from the College of Business Administration to the College of Administrative Science. This change was made to reflect the new emphasis in the business school on the marketing of nonprofit organizations, especially private hospitals. This is just one example of how universities are adapting to meet the needs of future managers in nonprofit organizations.

More recently, UCLA initiated a Management in the Arts program. Similar programs are offered at Wisconsin and York (in Toronto). Other schools offer short seminars for managers of various nonprofit groups. Recently, for example, I had the pleasure of discussing marketing concepts at a seminar sponsored by the University of Delaware for managers of arboretums and public gardens.

All across the country managers of nonprofit organizations are seeking advanced degrees in marketing to help their organizations become more effective and efficient. Perhaps you will find a rewarding career in hospital administration, government service, educational administration, or some similar field. You will find that courses in marketing will be a tremendous benefit in such a job.

You can see that the directors of nonprofit organizations can benefit greatly from studying channel and distribution concepts. The insert "New Educational Opportunities" discusses where people can learn more about marketing and management in nonprofit organizations.

MARKETING IN THE GOVERNMENT The largest nonbusiness organization that is vitally concerned with marketing is the U.S. government. We have already discussed the government as buyer; in this section we shall briefly explore the government as seller. The government is particularly interested in marketing the benefits of employment in the armed services. Creation of an all-volunteer army has placed tremendous pressures on the military to design an attractive product, to segment its market, and to promote its programs to potential recruits. Millions of dollars are spent on advertising alone to attract men and women to the various military services.[24]

The government also has rather comprehensive marketing programs for Amtrak (railroad), the U.S. Postal Service, the U.S. Travel Service, and other such agencies. The Postal Service, for example, employs nearly 700,000 clerks, inspectors, and letter carriers. It operates a fleet of 220,000 cars and trucks and operates 40,000 post offices, branches, and stations.[25] The Postal Service also has a separate marketing department

---

[24] See *Advertising Age*, August 27, 1973, pp. 159–160.

[25] Figures are from "A Gathering Mail Storm," *Newsweek*, March 22, 1976, p. 61.

Product Research and the Postal Service

"In the last 14 months . . . we've had to do the kind of market research that P & G and others did 50 years ago. For the first time in the history of the Post Office, we know which services make money and which lose the most. We have two dozen "products" available, and now we know who uses each one and why. It might seem elementary to even a semi-sophisticated marketing operation, but we could not go anywhere without the information."

. . . Postal Service ads for several "new products" will begin in a handful of test markets about Nov. 1.

. . . The test-market program . . . involves the preparation of sales training brochures and manuals, a slide presentation, and a telephone program to ferret out prospects and give quick replies to inquires.

. . . the new Postal service "has no 'civil service' mentality. It views itself like any other corporation, looking for areas it should get into, then developing a plan to get there, and knowing it must reach a certain profit level in a specific time."

"The Postal Service Tries the Hard Sell," *Business Week*, October 21, 1972, pp. 38–39.

as would be expected of any large organization. The insert "Product Research and the Postal Service" describes some of the activities of the Postal Service's marketing department.

The Government as Retailer   Did you know that the government is the third largest retail organization (after Sears and Penney's)?[26] The government operates retail stores (called post exchanges or more simply the PX) all over the world. Each of these stores is run in a manner similar to competing establishments off military bases, but the prices are usually lower and the income is tax free. These stores need managers who must evaluate the needs of consumers, order products, maintain inventory, price the items, and generally market the store and its products to military customers.

Government retail operations extend into services as well. The government operates barber shops, auto repair shops, restaurants, social clubs, hospitals, and other service facilities.

A person can find many interesting and challenging careers in government retailing, including procurement specialists, supply officers, and store managers. The total market for all new retail sales by the government is over $4 billion per year—an impressive figure by any standards.

The government also markets used merchandise to the public. Items include automobiles, trucks, office equipment, clothing, and just about anything else that government agencies may use. These items are sold

[26] This section is based on material in Robert M. Fulmer, *The New Marketing* (New York: Macmillan Publishing Co., Inc., 1976), p. 255.

Figure 18.2 THE GOVERNMENT AS MIDDLEMAN IN EXCHANGE RELATIONSHIPS

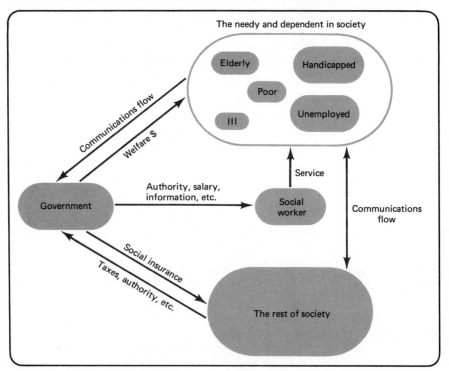

Redrawn from Richard P. Bagozzi, "Marketing as Exchange," *Journal of Marketing*, October 1975, p. 38. Reprinted with permission of the American Marketing Association.

through surplus outlets that prepare catalogs and place announcements in the various media. Most of the items are sold by auction or to the highest bidder (via sealed bids).

Sometimes the government gets involved in real estate sales to dispose of surplus property or buildings. Local governments also sell property at sheriffs auctions to pay back taxes. Again, these properties are normally sold through sealed bids or at public auctions.

One can see that the government is deeply involved in the marketing of goods and services—often in direct competition with private business. Of course, the government also tries to sell its needs for more funds to Congress and the people. No organization has a larger staff of PR people, salespersons (recruiters), and marketing research specialists than the government (most research is contracted for from private researchers). Table 18.1 will give you some feel for the importance of government employment in a typical Midwest city. Notice that five of the ten employers are nonprofit organizations. Also, the first four employers are all government organizations. It is rather apparent that the key employment opportunities in this and many other cities are in the nonprofit sector. Figure 18.2 illustrates how government acts as a middleman in exchange relationships between society and needy people within society. This is a growing function in the U.S. economy.

Table 18.1 TOP TEN EMPLOYERS IN COLUMBUS, OHIO

1. The Ohio State University
2. State of Ohio
3. Federal Government (excluding military)
4. Columbus Public Schools
5. Western Electric
6. F & R Lazarus
7. City of Columbus
8. Nationwide Insurance
9. Ohio Bell Telephone
10. Borden

From Columbus Area Chamber of Commerce, 1974.

SPECIAL TYPES OF NONBUSINESS MARKETING We cannot possibly give you all the details about the special marketing problems of nonbusinesses such as churches, schools, charities, foundations, social causes, unions, fraternities, politicians, youth groups, libraries, and nonprofit health care agencies. A book like Kotler's *Marketing for Nonprofit Organizations* gives such details if you are interested. We should take a brief look at some of these organizations, however, to give you some feel for the problems involved.

Marketing of Causes Often the goals of marketing are to mobilize the public behind some cause that seems beneficial to everyone. Many of these causes develop a slogan or some basic statement that everyone can recognize and support. You are probably familiar with slogans such as the following:

Give blood.
Love your neighbor.
Drive defensively.
Fasten your seat belt.
See America first.
Stop smoking.
Buy bonds.
America, love it or leave it.
Help fight pollution.

Give to the college of your choice.
Help prevent forest fires.
Stay in school.
Legalize abortion.
Children have a right to life.
Support your local police.
Drive slower.
Help prevent crime.
Hire the handicapped.

The promotion of such causes is part of the area we have called social marketing. Other important causes that students are concerned with today include pollution control, world freedom, women's and men's liberation, integration, and world hunger. All of these causes must generate support among the public if they are to be successful. This calls for effective and efficient marketing programs.

Marketing of Educational Institutions The U.S. education industry employs 3 million people in over 120,000 educational institutions. It serves over 60 million customers at an annual cost of $74 billion, or 7 percent of the gross national product.[27] Yet schools have had serious problems getting funds. Bond issues for school

[27] Kotler, *Marketing for Nonprofit Organizations*, p. 344.

districts have been voted down in cities throughout the country. Many private colleges are in serious financial condition.

The education industry must recognize that its image is slipping among the public and must establish a comprehensive marketing and PR effort to change its programs and regain public confidence and support. Individual institutions also must establish better and more sophisticated marketing departments to analyze market needs, must set up programs to meet those needs, and must promote those programs to the appropriate market segments.

Political Marketing Politics is a very important part of American life, and marketing is becoming an increasingly important part of the political scene. Market analysis, market segmentation, marketing communication and the other marketing functions are as important to politicians as they are to any other marketer. Some concepts of note are:

> **Mass advertising for a political candidate has the same function as national advertising for products—to establish the name and a favorable image.**

> **Political candidates must rely heavily on organization—getting their supporters to recruit other supporters and to keep the momentum going throughout the campaign, including getting voters to the polls.**

> **Political candidates need very careful market-segmentation strategies to ensure that pertinent issues will be discussed with different market segments as needed.**

Politicians need marketing middlemen for the same reasons that manufacturers do. It is impossible for a candidate to contact every one of his or her constituents, and so middlemen must be organized to contact various market segments. If a candidate has a hundred close political supporters and each of those supporters contact five people each and ask those five to contact five more through five layers, then 312,500 people would have been personally contacted and encouraged to vote for the candidate. In the case of presidential elections, such pyramiding often takes place within each state and within each city. Well-organized campaigns carry such support to each precinct and each neighborhood. The candidate can thus reach various market segments with persons who can answer questions and generate enthusiasm.

Marketing for Charities There are more than half a million charitable organizations in the United States today.[28] Each of them is competing for the public's support. The National Center for Voluntary Action estimates that 50 to 60 million people belong to volunteer groups of some sort. John Dixon from the Center for a Voluntary Society estimates volunteerism's "gross national product" at about $50 billion a year.[29]

[28] See Ann C. Scott, "Charity: Where Does the Money Go?" *Ms*, October 1974, pp. 130–132.

[29] Figures are from "50,000,000 Helping Hands," *Reader's Digest*, December 1974, p. 147.

Politicians must use effective marketing strategies too.

"First, the good news . . . we got you a tv spot. Now the bad news . . . it's between Sesame Street and Batman."

In spite of the willingness of Americans to volunteer their time and money for charitable causes, there is much discontent and hesitancy about charitable giving. As we mentioned earlier, many negative articles and books have been written about charities. One of the most damaging criticisms of charities has been their inefficiencies in one area—you guessed it, marketing! Some charities spend as much as 70 to 90 percent of their income on fund raising. There is little doubt that charitable organizations are desperately in need of marketing assistance.[30]

MARKETING CAREERS IN NONBUSINESS ORGANIZATIONS We strongly encourage you not to limit your career selection to business organizations. The biggest employer in the United States is the government (one out of six people now works for the government), and many challenging marketing careers are available. Somebody has to help market the benefits of mass transit systems, make the Postal Service more efficient, and generate more cooperation between businesses and organizations like the Product Safety Commission and the Food and Drug Administration. These are marketing tasks that call for marketing personnel.

Often, the path to a managerial position is much faster in nonprofit

[30] For a more comprehensive look at marketing in charities, see William G. Nickels, *Marketing Communications and Promotion* (Columbus, Ohio: Grid, Inc., 1976), Chapter 19.

organizations because the whole idea of marketing is rather new to them, and a good person can pretty much create his or her own department. Jobs are available in advertising, marketing research, consumer analysis, publicity, public relations, fund solicitation, and other marketing areas. We hope this chapter has given you some insight about this new, interesting area of social marketing.

FOR REVIEW

Key Terms

Among the more important terms and expressions discussed in this chapter are the following:

Social marketing is the design, implementation, and control of programs that seek to foster the acceptance of a social idea, cause, or practice by a target group or groups.

Nonbusiness marketing is the use of marketing concepts and tools to establish exchange relationships between individuals or groups and organizations, other than business, that can partially satisfy their wants and needs.

Broadening the concept of marketing means expanding the nature and scope of marketing to include all exchange relationships, including those initiated by nonprofit organizations.

Key Concepts

Among the more important marketing concepts introduced in this chapter are the following:

› **Marketing is an attempt to establish mutually satisfying exchange relationships to satisfy *all* of society's wants and needs**—some of those needs can be met only through nonbusiness organizations; therefore, the marketing of nonbusiness organizations is a major concern.

› **Marketing in the future could do more to balance social needs with economic needs and the needs of individuals with the needs of society**; therefore, the future of marketing may involve more efforts to satisfy the social problems of poverty, overpopulation, pollution, international conflict, disease, and ignorance.

› **Market analysis for nonprofit organizations is the process whereby organizations learn about unmet needs in society** and analyze which of those needs can be satisfied by a marketing program.

› **Communication flows in the nonprofit sector should open a dialogue between and among all social organizations and the public**; communication is the marketing tool that enables nonprofit organizations to learn about and resolve social problems in cooperation with other organizations.

> To get support for their programs, nonprofit organizations should provide a *mechanism* (an organization) to mobilize support; they should give *direction* to supporters by telling them *what* to do, when, and how; and they should show supporters that they are succeeding in their mission by informing people of their progress in meeting a recognized need.

> Nonprofit organizations have products, brands, and slogans much like those of a manufacturing firm, but their products more closely resemble service industry products.

> Nonprofit organizations need market-segmentation strategies for two purposes: resource gathering (fund raising) and resource allocation (serving clients).

Discussion Questions

1. Many top-level people in nonbusiness organizations dislike marketing and everything that it represents. Why do you suppose they have that attitude? Do you think it can be changed? How?

2. Should college courses in marketing devote some time to the marketing of nonbusiness organizations? Why or why not?

3. Is it proper to use sophisticated marketing strategies in political campaigns? Could there be abuses? How could such abuses be minimized?

4. Is marketing for nonbusiness organizations easier or more difficult than marketing for business? Explain your answer and give examples.

5. How effective and efficient do you feel the marketing efforts of nonbusiness organizations such as charities and social causes have been? How could these efforts be improved?

6. What is "social marketing"? How does it differ from the marketing of business organizations?

7. Explain how a private college could use the six universal marketing functions to recruit more students.

8. Will there be fewer or more opportunities for marketers in nonprofit organizations in the future? Why? Does such a career sound interesting? Why or why not?

9. How can marketing contribute to efforts designed to solve the problems of racism, sexism, hunger, disease, environmental decay, and international conflict? Or are such problems beyond the scope of marketing? What organizations, if any, have no need for marketing concepts and techniques?

10. What do you dislike about the marketing of charities? What do you like? How would you improve the marketing efforts of the Girl Scouts, the United Fund, and the Red Cross?

CASES

St. Mark's Church
Can Marketing Help?

St. Mark's Church is located in the heart of a declining neighborhood in a large Midwestern city. The population in the area at one time consisted of relatively wealthy white-collar workers. The neighborhood now consists of many low-income minority groups and blue-collar workers. St. Mark's is a beautiful old church, but it is expensive to maintain. Many of the older, wealthy parishioners still attend services there, but there seem to be fewer every year. The church now services many different ethnic groups and has many excellent programs to serve the needy in the area including "Meals on Wheels" (to feed the old and the sick), a clothes closet (to give clothes to those in need), a day-care center (for working parents), courses in English as a second language, and a counseling service for families with personal problems. The problem is that St. Mark's is spending more than it earns. There has been talk of closing the church. There do not seem to be any new funds available from the national church body, and the parishioners do not seem to have the funds to support the church and its many programs. The pastor of St. Mark's notes that his church is only one of many that are facing similar problems.

1. Can St. Mark's be helped by taking a marketing approach to its problems? How?
2. Where is St. Mark's in the product life cycle?
3. How could St. Mark's raise additional funds?
4. What arguments would you give for keeping the church open or closing it down?
5. Show how St. Mark's could apply each of the six universal marketing functions to solve its problems. Would you recommend that it begin such a marketing program?

The Marketing Curriculum
What About Nonprofit Organizations?

Professor Herbert Heffron is teaching a college course called Marketing for Nonprofit Organizations. The professor had some trouble getting such a course into the curriculum and he has been asked to discuss the course before a campus-wide curriculum committee. Members of the committee have expressed their concerns in public already. One member feels that marketing is an inherently deceptive area and shudders to think of it being used in churches and schools. Another member feels that marketing is being taught in the *business* school and that, therefore, nonprofit organizations should not be discussed. A third member feels that there are too many marketing courses already and that this new one is particularly useless because "nonprofit organizations don't have a marketing department anyhow."

1. Prepare a statement for Professor Heffron that would answer his critics.
2. Would a marketing course for nonprofit organizations differ significantly from a normal marketing course? Why or why not?
3. What kinds of organizational leaders might benefit from Professor Heffron's course?
4. Would you expect this to be a growing course in the future or not? Why?

7

Contemporary and Future Issues

There is some question whether marketers should give consumers what they want if such exchanges result in damages to the environment, morals, or the ability to satisfy others (for example, depletion of resources). Chapter 19 explores such issues and the role of government in regulating marketing exchanges. This chapter can only introduce some of the issues in marketing. We hope you will add to this material through your discussions with friends and in class.

Most discussions about marketing seem to get involved with the future. Will there be enough food to feed populations throughout the world? Will there be sufficient natural resources to meet our energy needs 30 years from now? Will we suffer from cultural shock as a result of technological innovations? Chapter 20 briefly explores such questions and serves as a foundation for more research into the future.

We saved what most students have considered the most important chapter until last. We wanted you to have some idea of what marketing was before we exposed you to marketing careers. But Chapter 21 gives some important facts and figures to help you make a more informed career choice. It also gives you strategies for landing the job *you* want in the organization *you* choose. We hope you find this chapter helpful in choosing a career in any field, but we also hope that this book has convinced you that marketing offers careers that cannot be beat.

Social Issues in Marketing

responsive and responsible marketing systems

LEARNING GOALS After you have read and studied this chapter, you should be able to:

1. Differentiate between the terms consumer information and consumer education.

2. Describe what is meant by the marketing correspondence function and what it means for tomorrow's consumers.

3. Illustrate the need to balance the social need for economic growth with the need for environmental protection.

4. Briefly describe the major provisions of the Sherman Act, the Clayton Act, the Federal Trade Commission Act, and the Robinson-Patman Act.

5. Describe how legislation affects all areas of marketing management, including product, place, promotion, and price.

6. Discuss the benefits of a corporate social audit to the corporation and to society.

7. Give examples of social indicators that might be used to measure the quality of life in the United States.

8. List what you consider to be the five major social issues in marketing today and give some indication of what could be done to resolve them.

9. Discuss the role of consumerism in today's society and indicate what you think the future issues may be.

10. Write your own code of conduct relative to marketing behavior and use it in your everyday exchange activities.

> *During the 1970's a [new] thrust seems to be emerging [in marketing]. It is evidenced by a concern for such areas as the impact of marketing on the quality of life; marketing and community affairs; marketing and social problems; the reduction of poverty; the opportunity to develop human capital to its fullest potential; the provision of good health care, education, and training; the development of better communities; the reduction of pollution and the protection of the environment; the provision of ample jobs and opportunities; and greater consideration for one's fellow man. The result is a movement from the consideration of profits or sales only, to a consideration of the societal implications and dimensions of marketing decisions and actions.*
>
> William Lazer and Eugene J. Kelley*

INTRODUCTION A basic proposition that has been presented throughout this book is that marketing is a process of satisfying wants and needs. But should marketers satisfy *all* wants and needs? And should they encourage people to get what they want even though it may not be good for them? What is marketing's responsibility for protecting the health, safety, and well-being of society? These are hard questions that must be resolved if marketing is to meet the needs of society as well as of individuals within society. This chapter discusses these questions and other social issues in marketing.

The U.S. economy was originally based on a system of free markets, but over time more and more rules, regulations, and legislation have been imposed on market participants. The United States now has a "mixed" economy that has some elements of free enterprise, some elements of socialism, and a large measure of government regulation. One social question that will dominate marketing for the near future is, "How much freedom will consumers and sellers have in the marketplace?" That is, how much exchange activity will be subject to government regulation? Another dominant question will be, "How should organizations implement more socially responsible and socially responsive programs in the future?" Let's begin the analysis of these problems by looking at what is happening in the food industry.

What Shall We Eat for Breakfast? Many, if not most, Americans seem to prefer cereal that contains lots of sugar. There is some question whether sugar is good for people or even whether it is harmful to eat. Most people feel that sugar is bad for teeth and that it has little nutritional value. Should marketers offer consumers cereal that is very high (up to 50 percent) in sugar content? Should marketers promote such cereals heavily? What obligation do marketers have to educate consumers to eat more nutritious food? What if con-

Social Marketing: Perspectives and Viewpoints (Homewood, Ill.: Richard D. Irwin, Inc., 1973), pp. 3–4.

sumers do not like nutritious food? Is a breakfast of coffee and donuts any better than sugared cereal?

There is much controversy over the cholesterol content of eggs and the use of sodium nitrate in bacon. White bread is said to be less nutritious than it once was. Is a breakfast of bacon, eggs, coffee, and toast "better" for people than orange juice, cereal, milk, and toast? Should Americans be taught to eat an entirely different kind of breakfast? And, if so, by whom? At whose expense? There are no easy answers to these questions. Most people have decided that the best way to resolve such issues is to let each person decide for himself or herself. But every effort should be made to help people make intelligent decisions. For example, nutritionists should have access to mass media to teach people about health and foods.

But given a certain state of knowledge, most marketers in the United States feel that people should be free to choose for themselves. Freedom is also a product people want, and marketers should recognize that obligation as well. The concept is:

> **Marketers in the future may increase their efforts to educate the public in matters of health, safety, and social welfare and then leave the selection of particular products to individual consumers.**

If a person feels that consumers should eat different foods, use different forms of transportation, or refrain from smoking, drinking, or taking drugs, that person is free to use every marketing tool at his or her command to let his or her views be known and try to persuade others. But most marketers feel that no person or organization should have the power to *force* people to change such behavior. If a person wants to eat sugared cereal once in a while and if bacon, eggs, white bread, and other foods and nonfoods seem particularly attractive to a person, marketers feel that he or she should have the freedom to choose.

What consumers want today is more and better information and education so that unwise marketing exchanges can be kept to a minimum. Such information and education could benefit all organizations, individuals, and society in general. The concept is:

> **From a marketing perspective, the best judge of products of all kinds (including people, places, ideas, goods, services, and causes) is an informed consumer who has been taught to use that information; for this reason, a major obligation of marketing is to provide consumer information and education.**

CONSUMER INFORMATION AND EDUCATION A major social issue in marketing today is the demand by consumers for more information about products (including product safety, durability, and contents) and more readable product warranties. But how much information can marketers provide before "information overload" occurs? There is much evidence that consumers do not effectively use the information that is already provided. The problem may be one of consumer *education* rather than consumer *information*. Consumer

information involves the *presentation of facts and figures* about goods, services, and other products through advertising, labeling, consumer bulletins, and other information channels. **Consumer education,** on the other hand, is the process of teaching the public *how to use relevant facts and figures* to make more intelligent exchange decisions; it involves special pamphlets, personal counseling, and similar educational efforts.

There is no question that marketers could provide more information to consumers about product use, care, safety, and so forth. Marketers could also do more to tell consumers about *significant* product differences and ways to improve product selection. But *information* will not solve today's consumer problems. What is needed is consumer education. Read what Dean Canoyer, the first chairperson of the Consumer Advisory Council, says about consumer education:

It is my conclusion from a good many years' experience in the fields of economics and home economics, that the basic problem underlying all so-called "consumer problems" is the lack of education. It is not enough, in fact it is impossible, to represent consumers in a meaningful way if they are ill-informed and irresponsible. It is not enough to offer them isolated pieces of information about specific problems, if they do not have a broad framework of understanding about their role in our economy as responsible consumers. . . .[1]

A survey by *Grey Matter* in 1972 found that marketing people feel that consumer education is the most effective way to protect the consumer. Respondents felt that, "An informed consumer is his own and the economy's best protection."[2] Ninety percent of the respondents also felt that consumers can be taught to get more value and satisfaction from products through more informative advertising. Of course, consumers would make much more intelligent market choices if they were taught how to use marketing information.

Consumer Education Programs Consumer education could start in the grade schools where children could learn to use marketing information to improve their purchasing behavior throughout their life. Students would learn how to use unit pricing and nutritional labeling, how to read care-and-use labels and warranties, and how to obtain useful market information from *Consumer Reports* and similar publications. There has been some progress in implementing such courses already.

Consumer education could also be a major concern of the government. Special attention might be given the needs of the poor, the uneducated, the young, and non-English-speaking minorities. Many government programs are designed to educate consumers, but there is little coordination and integration and the people who seem to need it most are not being served adequately.

[1] Helen G. Canoyer, "The Consumer Advisory Council: Its Origin, Purpose, and Problems" (Speech before the American Home Economics Association, Kansas City, Missouri, June 1963).
[2] *Grey Matter,* April 1, 1972.

An example of an ad emphasizing consumer information.

This is what little girls are made of.

Every minute, three billion cells in a little girls' body are being replaced by new ones.

The material for each new cell comes from the nutrients in the food she eats. What these nutrients do once they reach her body, and what they do with each other will make her different from every other little girl.

Her life depends on nutrition. She'll grow to live life well or ill because of it. We study nutrition. And we've learned that although poverty is the chief cause of malnutrition, it isn't the only cause.

Almost half of us are under-nourished. And through nothing more than a lack of knowledge about the food we eat.

Every day we're learning more. You should learn more too.

To give you some basic information and valuable guides to preparing meals and diets, we've put together a book entitled "Food Is More Than Just Something to Eat."

Write for it. Nutrition, Pueblo, Colorado 81009. And we'll send it to you.

Free.

Ad Council A Public Service of This Magazine & The Advertising Council

U.S. Departments of Agriculture and Health, Education, & Welfare. Grocery Manufacturers of America.

Courtesy of The Advertising Council.

Businesses are especially involved with consumer education because information and information use are part of the total product offer. Many firms have established consumer affairs departments that have taken preliminary action toward establishing consumer education programs. But the impact is still minimal, even though the need for such programs is growing more intense.

> ## The Challenge of Consumerism
>
> Consumerism is nothing more and nothing less than a challenge to business to live up to its full potential—to give consumers what is promised, to be honest, to give people a product that will work and that is reasonably safe, to respond effectively to legitimate complaints, . . . and to return to the basic principle upon which so much of our nation's business was structured—satisfaction guaranteed or your money back.

From Virginia Knauer, former Special Assistant to the President for Consumer Affairs, as cited in E. T. Garman and S. W. Eckert, "Consumer Education in Junior High Schools," *Business Education Forum,* March 1973, p. 23.

One benefit of such consumer education programs is that they put the control over the exchange process back in the hands of the consumer. No one can legislate consumer protection. Consumers must learn to protect themselves by seeking information and education. One cannot blame the institutions of society for *all* of the consumer ignorance that exists. Half the problem is due to the apathy and laziness of consumers. Organizations cannot force people to become better consumers; it takes cooperation and participation. With such cooperation, consumers will receive many benefits and will benefit society as well. The U.S. Office of Consumer Affairs said this:

Consumer education should help each person understand his own value system; develop a sound decision-making procedure in the marketplace based upon his values; evaluate alternatives in the marketplace and get the best buy for his money; understand his rights and responsibilities as a consumer and as a member of society; and fulfill his role in directing a free-enterprise system.[3]

Evidence that the consumer is becoming more involved in the marketing process is found in the consumerism movement of the 1960s and 1970s.

CONSUMERISM Consumerism has been defined as a social movement that seeks to increase and strengthen the rights and powers of buyers in relation to sellers.[4] Former President Kennedy proposed four basic rights of consumers: (1) the right to safety, (2) the right to be informed, (3) the right to choose, and (4) the right to be heard. These rights will not be gained if consumers passively wait for organizations to recognize them; they will come partially from consumer action in the marketplace. Consumerism

[3] *An Approach to Consumer Education for Adults,* Office of Consumer Affairs, Executive Office of the President (Washington, D.C.: Government Printing Office, 1973), p. 3.
[4] See Philip Kotler, "What Consumerism Means for Marketers," *Harvard Business Review,* May–June 1972, pp. 48–57.

is the people's way of getting their fair share in marketing exchanges. It is not a new movement, but it is a movement that has taken on new vigor and direction in the 1970s.

Consumer involvement in the marketplace is a benefit to those organizations that respond positively to such involvement. Consumers are becoming more aware of those organizations that are trying to give them safer, better, more long-lasting products. Consumers also are better informed about those organizations that listen to their wants and needs and provide prompt answers to their inquiries and complaints.

Consumerism is becoming institutionalized into organizations such as those sponsored by Ralph Nader. It is also finding support in government organizations and legislation. The issues are many and complex. The following are a few of them:

1. Bait-and-switch tactics[5]
2. False and/or misleading advertising
3. Price deception
4. Product safety issues
5. Planned obsolescence
6. Poor nutrition from processed foods
7. High prices for almost all goods and services
8. Inefficiencies in distribution
9. Unresponsive businesses and nonbusinesses

Surely you can think of other areas in which you as a consumer wish businesses, government, and other organizations would improve. Consumerism is here to stay, but there is some question about what form it will take. There is serious question whether consumer discontent can ever be satisfied by large government bureaucracies or consumerist groups. In the future, consumers are likely to seek legal solutions to their grievances more frequently (for example, in small-claims courts) and will seek more education and information so that they are aware of questionable establishments and practices. The best way to make organizations responsive is by using market forces. Consumers should buy where they are satisfied and not buy where they are not satisfied and they should tell others to do the same. In that way, consumerism would become a *personal* matter of *personal* concern and would take on renewed strength.

No doubt consumerism in the future will shift its emphasis from relatively minor problems such as bait-and-switch selling to more general issues such as discrimination in selling or buying, ecology, unemployment, and population control. Marketers are responsible for monitoring such changes and acting as middlemen between the public and major social institutions. Surely the future holds much promise for those

[5] This means a retailer will advertise a low-priced product in the newspaper (the bait) and try to sell people a higher-priced product when they come in (the switch).

An example of advertising used to correct false advertising.

FALSE ADVERTISING IS STEALING

- It steals your money when you are tricked into buying inferior goods or services.
- It steals your opportunities to make intelligent choices about how you spend your money.
- It steals business from honest competitors.
- Check out the truthfullness of claims like these, before you buy:

- *Repossessed — Full balance due — Credit department.*
- *Unclaimed layaway.*
- *Freight damage, Salvage, etc.*
- *Going out of business, Lost our lease, etc.*
- *Fire Sale, Smoke damage, etc.*
- *30% off regular price, etc.*
- *Regular price $49.95 — Sale price $39.95*
- *List price $259 — Our price $189.*

- Penalties for false, deceptive or misleading advertising, under the Seattle false advertising ordinance are fines of up to $300 and/or jail of up to 90 days for each violation.
- Report violations to the City of Seattle, Consumer Affairs Division, 102 Municipal Building. Telephone 625-2712.

This ad was prepared by the City of Seattle Department of Licenses and Consumer Affairs and was paid for by a person who served ten days in jail following his conviction of four misdemeanor counts in Seattle Municipal Court and King County Superior Court for falsely advertising stereo equipment and as a condition for suspension of 350 additional days in jail sentence.

Courtesy of City of Seattle, Consumer Affairs Division.

students who want to become involved in consumerism, marketing, and public policy issues in general. Some problem areas and possible solutions are listed in Table 19.1.

Corporate response to consumerism is evidenced by more activity in the consumer affairs area and more attention being given to two-way marketing communications.

The Marketing Correspondence Function One major consumer issue of the 1970s has been the lack of responsiveness of major institutions to the wants and needs of the public. The public has been especially concerned about its lack of power to influence institutional decision making without resorting to violence, demonstrations, and other disruptive behavior. Businesses should be much more open to consumer criticism and suggestions; and there should be some area responsible for creating such an open atmosphere. That area has been called "the marketing correspondence function":

It is time for manufacturers, retailers, and others who deal with the public to establish . . . strategies for anticipating and satisfying consumer inquiries and complaints. Each firm should have personnel in charge of marketing correspondence. . . .

An effective marketing correspondence function has many advantages; most important, it must generate long-term customer relations. Advertising, sales, sales promotion, and publicity may result in a sale, but the sale is only a start toward establishing the client as a customer. Long-term relationships demand two-way flows of information, listening as well as talking, and responding as well as persuading. The function that encompasses all these activities is marketing correspondence.[6]

[6] William G. Nickels and Noel B. Zabriskie, "Corporate Responsiveness and the Marketing Correspondence Function," *MSU Business Topics,* Summer 1973, pp. 53–58.

Table 19.1 CHANGING MARKETING'S IMAGE AMONG CONSUMERS

Ten negative consumer perceptions of present marketing practices	Ten future marketing practices to counteract these negative perceptions
Marketing encourages consumption of scarce resources.	More attention given to the environment and social responsiveness.
Advertising encourages consumption of unhealthy and/or dangerous products, especially by children.	Better regulation of advertising practices by the industry and the creation of clearer guidelines.
Marketing is a tool of business that promotes excess profits by exploiting consumers.	Training future marketers to use marketing in all organizations to improve the quality of life for all people.
Businesses are forever messing up on billing, overcharging, and failing to answer inquiries and complaints.	Developing a consumer correspondence department with authority and responsibility for answering complaints and taking corrective action.
Marketers use packaging to excess and encourage the use of throwaway materials rather than recyclable ones.	Becoming more responsive to society's ecological needs and more conservation-oriented.
Marketers overcharge the poor for food, credit, and other goods and services.	Increasing citizen involvement in marketing programs and making special efforts to train the poor and disadvantaged in marketing skills.
Marketers take advantage of consumers through deception, fraud, and unethical behavior in general.	Developing consumer-education programs for various social groups to prepare consumers to police the market themselves.
Marketers monopolize markets and discourage competition to optimize profits and manipulate profits.	Support all efforts to prevent illegal restraints of trade, but educate people on the benefits of large corporations that are consumer-oriented.
Marketers encourage the use of huge cars, huge homes, and generally make people wasteful and materialistic.	Stress the many marketing efforts designed to save energy, to encourage the use of economical cars, and to create responsible consumers through education.
Marketers introduce new products and new designs to make old products and designs obsolete before their time (planned obsolescence).	Show people the benefits of development of new products and minimize change for the sake of change.

Government Needs to Improve Its Marketing Correspondence

A private study of complaint-handling systems at various federal agencies has found unsatisfactory performance in many areas. The report was compiled by Technical Assistance Research Programs, Inc., for Virginia Knauer's Office of Consumer Affairs. The report said replies from the Federal Communications Commission often aren't clear or are inappropriate to the question raised because the agency uses too much legalese and relies too much on forms. The Federal Energy Administration averaged 49 days to make final response to specific complaints. The 15-agency average was 18 days, with Knauer's office itself taking the shortest time, 9 days.

From *Marketing News*, July 18, 1975, p. 11.

Usually, the marketing correspondence function has been delegated to the consumer affairs section of the public relations department. It has been estimated that more than three hundred U.S. firms have a consumer affairs area.[7] But most directors have been in office less than 10 years because the function is so new.

Many consumer affairs departments concentrate on complaint handling and do little to educate consumers. Furthermore, few of these departments have real input into managerial decision making relative to major consumer issues. But all of this is changing, and some consumer affairs directors have had tremendous impact on corporate policy and practices.

In the future, more and more institutions will have active departments specializing in marketing correspondence (two-way communication with the market) and consumer affairs. People in these areas will be responsible for such things as (1) listening to the public, (2) working with marketing and public relations to distribute educational materials, (3) establishing consumer workshops, (4) acting as consumer spokespersons with top management about product design and other areas of concern such as pollution control, hiring practices, and sexism, and (5) establishing friendly relations with all the organization's "publics." These departments will also be responsible for monitoring the public's attitudes toward broader issues such as pollution control and product safety.

Environmental Concerns Pollution control is a major social issue in marketing. To give you some idea of the attitudes of marketers toward this important subject, let's review the results of a survey taken of American Marketing Association members in 1972. Of those responding, 56 percent agreed and only 38 percent disagreed that pollution control should be given *greater* consid-

[7] E. Patrick McGuire, *The Consumer Affairs Director: A Statistical Profile* (A Special Report from the Conference Board, 1973).

eration than profitability when developing marketing plans.[8] These results reflect the attitudes of the time, but they also show a growing concern among marketers for environmental matters.

Some idea of the complexity of this subject can be learned from the controversy over returnable containers. In 1972, Oregon became the first state to ban the sale of beer and soft drinks in nonreturnable bottles and cans. The goal of the law was to minimize litter. This law did have some impact on litter according to a report by the Environmental Protection Agency, but National Can Corporation closed one plant in Washington and Emerald Canning Corporation went out of business, with the loss of 142 jobs.[9] The question then becomes, "Even assuming that Oregon-type laws reduce litter, are the benefits worth the cost?" Will consumers pay more for beverages? Will such laws help alleviate the more pressing solid-waste problem?[10] The burden on retailers and on the entire distribution channel is great because bottles must be recycled back up through the channel at great cost. Furthermore, consumers are greatly inconvenienced by the necessity of returning bottles—not too much of a burden for some, but a very great burden for others. People at canneries lose jobs, and, in general, the entire beverage industry is affected. But beverage containers account for only 7 percent of municipal solid

[8] Robert J. Lavidge, "AMA Members Favor Government Actions to Protect Consumers, But Oppose Limits on Aid Expenditures," *Marketing News,* October 1, 1972, p. 1.
[9] "Oregon: A Test Case for Returnable Containers," *Business Week,* July 28, 1973, p. 76.
[10] Ibid., p. 77.

Marketing and Society

Participants in the marketing system constitute a closed group having expectations and responsibilities among them, but they also are but a subset in the larger social order. Recognition of this increased as society identified its collective values as superior to mere economic values. Consequently, marketing has increasingly been held responsible for not only supplying consumption goods, but for doing so in ways which preserve and augment the well-being of people in all ways. It is expected that marketers minimize the pollution of the environment, desist from exploiting children markets, assist in the employment of minority members, [and] protect consumers from dangerous products. . . . Past marketing practices often passed to society costs which marketers themselves avoided, and often which society did not reckon with at the time. An accumulation of social problems related to marketing drew marketing into closer relation to society, and added another dimension to the concept of marketing as a social—and socially responsible—process.

From Robert Bartels, *The History of Marketing Thought,* 2nd ed. (Columbus, Ohio: Grid, Inc., 1976), p. 169.

waste.[11] Are the benefits worth the cost? This question is still to be resolved in many people's minds. However one thing is for sure, the answers are not obvious or simple. These trade-offs between the economy and the environment are never easy to make. It is important to see that marketers are facing these decisions and are giving serious consideration to environmental concerns in their programs (see the insert "Marketing and Society").

The controversies are such that even more consideration must be given this problem. We need oil, but the Alaskan pipeline threatened the environment and demanded further study. Resulting delays cost all of us millions and millions of dollars. In the future, businesses might work more closely *with* environmentalists (versus *against* them), so that such costs could be lessened. America has become a throwaway society. Witness the tremendous clutter left after a family meal at a fast-food restaurant. In contrast, at a soft drink vending machine in Russia there was *one glass for everyone.* Quite a contrast. Certainly somewhere between these extremes is a rational balancing point. The concept is:

> › **Marketers attempt to satisfy the needs of individuals and of society, including the need for environmental protection; this calls for coordination and cooperation among all social organizations to work out sensible trade-offs between economic concerns and environmental concerns.**

Direct costs to private industry in meeting standards for clean air and water and for solid-waste disposal easily total more than $10 billion annually.[12] "According to the McGraw-Hill Economics department, the paper industry is putting 43 percent of new investment into pollution control, non-ferrous metals the figure is 22 percent, for petroleum 10 percent."[13] This gives you some feel for the effort being put behind pollution control *and* the costs involved.

Consumer Safety   Before we get too deeply into consumer and environmental issues, we should say something about the area of consumer safety. A National Advertising Review Board (NARB) report emphasized the seriousness of the problems in this area:

Each year at least one of every ten Americans suffers a painful or disabling injury from an accident associated with a consumer product. The magnitude of the problem has prompted the federal government to allocate more than $100,000,000 annually to a drive to improve the quality and safety characteristics of consumer products.[14]

[11]Ibid.

[12]"Environmentalists at Bay," *The Wall Street Journal,* January 3, 1974, p. 10.

[13]Ibid.

[14]"Product Advertising and Consumer Safety," *Advertising Age,* July 1, 1974, p. 47.

The NARB panel concluded that warning statements are more appropriately and effectively displayed on packaging and labeling than in mass media advertising. Advertising was considered only part of the product-related communication process regarding safety. Other elements of the communication process are packaging, labeling, and care-and-use instructions to fully inform the buyer.

Marketers have not always placed sufficient emphasis on the education of consumers in the safe and prudent use of products that are potentially hazardous when misused. According to the NARB, "Safety in advertising requires a degree of focus comparable to the attention [given] to matters of legality, truth and accuracy and minority group representation." [15] Of course, this is especially true of products promoted to children, and the National Safety Council issues bulletins concerning potentially dangerous toys. Here is what one writer has to say about consumer protection and safety:

Modern society is saying that the business community definitely and specifically has not only a moral, but a legal, liability to protect the user against her own carelessness! That liability may not be total. But neither will business again be totally free from liability because of user carelessness!

Customers today expect products to perform satisfactorily, to provide dependable functional performance, and to be safe. [16]

LEGAL ISSUES One social issue that has tremendous implications for marketers is that of government regulation and legislation. How much should there be? Should the government take a more active role in attempting to create safer, more nutritious, and more durable products? How much regulation should there be of the marketing of services and nonprofit organizations? We shall review some of the major legislation in this section to give you some feel for how things are now. Then we shall discuss future prospects. We begin with the Sherman Antitrust Act of 1890 because it was one of the first significant pieces of legislation to affect marketers.

The Sherman Antitrust Act, 1890 The Sherman Act was designed to prevent large organizations from stifling the competition of smaller or newer firms. The Act forbids the following: (1) contracts, combinations, or conspiracies in restraint of trade and (2) actual monopolies or attempts to monopolize any part of trade or commerce.

[15] Ibid.
[16] E. B. Weiss, "In Near Future Marketing May Be Quasi Utility," *Advertising Age,* November 15, 1971, p. 48.

The Sherman Act and the laws that followed it are most effective, not because the government has been so diligent in enforcing them, but because businesses are forced to make marketing decisions knowing the threat of legal action is there. Government thus becomes an all pervasive force in marketing decision making.

Periodically the government gives businessmen a stiff reminder that the law is not to be ignored. One such reminder was the "electrical equipment" cases of the 1960s. Several producers of electrical equipment were charged with violating one section of the Sherman Act by conspiring (1) to fix and maintain prices, terms, and conditions for the sale of specified products, (2) to allocate among themselves the business in heavy electrical equipment, (3) to submit noncompetitive bids for supplying specified equipment to various organizations, and (4) to refrain from selling certain types of equipment to other manufacturers of electrical equipment.

As a consequence of this case, some top managers of several electrical-equipment companies were given prison sentences. Several people actually served time in prison, and others were given suspended sentences. Furthermore, some companies were charged with triple damage claims for alleged overcharges on various pieces of equipment, with penalties reaching as much as $16 million. Such actions by the government force businesses to be very concerned about any marketing actions that might be construed as violating the Sherman Act or any of the other laws affecting marketing.

The Clayton Act, 1914 The Clayton act was an attempt to clarify some of the legal concepts in the Sherman Act. It is really a supplement to the Sherman Act. Various practices are prohibited "where the effect will be to substantially lessen competition or to create a monopoly."

One of the practices prohibited is discrimination in setting prices charged purchasers of like grade, quality, or quantity of a commodity sold. Note that products not considered "commodities" (for example, TV or radio time) are *not* covered by the Act.

The Act also prohibits organizations from selling or leasing goods with the condition or agreement that the "buyer" will not deal in goods supplied by a competitor. This is called "exclusive dealing." The law also prohibits "interlocking directorates" (where a member of the board of directors is on a competitor's board) in competing corporations (except banks and common carriers) where one of the corporations has a capital and surplus of more than $1 million and where the elmination of competition between them would constitute a violation of any of the provisions of the antitrust laws. The law also prohibits any corporation engaged in commerce from acquiring the shares of a competing corporation or from purchasing the stocks of two or more competitors. Notice that the Clayton Act is more concerned with the *prevention* of practices that would lessen competition, whereas the Sherman Act emphasizes *punishment*.

The government continued its actions to minimize restraint of trade with the Celler-Kefauver Act of 1950. It was an amendment to the

Clayton Act and prohibited the acquisition of stocks or assets where in any line of commerce, in any section of the country, the effect of such an acquisition may be substantially to lessen competition, or to tend to create a monopoly. Note that the government has kept a watchful eye on businesses throughout the last 100 years or so and has progressively cleared up the language of legislation.

Federal Trade Commission Act, 1914 Like the Clayton Act, the Federal Trade Commission Act supplements the Sherman Act with additional prohibitions and makes the provisions clearer. The Federal Trade Commission (FTC) is an independent regulatory agency with enforcement responsibility. The Federal Trade Commission Act prohibits *unfair methods of competition in commerce.*[17] Note the words "in commerce." It was not until 1938 that the Wheeler-Lea Act gave the FTC power to prevent practices that injure the public.

The FTC is the agency that enforces the Federal Trade Commission Act, part of the Clayton Act, and the Wheeler-Lea Act. It also enforces various labeling acts covering products such as wool, furs, and flammable fabrics.

Of most interest to the public in the last decade or so have been the FTC's actions against deceptive advertising. The FTC has a group of lawyers who screen national ads and process complaints from the public. The FTC may force an advertiser to cease and desist deceptive advertising and may even force an advertiser to place "corrective ads" that explain past deceptive actions. In only a few cases has this occurred thus far, but the threat is there. Most advertisers have learned to avoid creating any commercials that would come under FTC investigation. Obviously this does *not* cause informative or interesting ads—it only eliminates blatantly deceptive ads.

[17] Unfair competition includes individual practices against a competitor involving misrepresentation, deception, and fraud, and methods of competition having a dangerous tendency to unduly hinder competition or to create a monopoly.

The Cost of Regulation

The FTC has a statutory obligation to look out for the interest of the consuming public. . . .

I suggest, however, that we bear in mind that protecting the public from the cost of consumer abuse is not itself a costless process; and that there are occasions where the latter cost greatly exceeds the former cost.

There is such a thing as over-regulation, and for it we all must pay a price. The issue of whether or not to regulate is not one which pits the consumer against someone else. It is an issue which pits the consumer's left pocket against his right.

From Lewis A. Engman, "Horseshoes, Eyeglasses, and Milk—the Costs of Over-Regulation" (Address before the National Association of Attorneys General, Hot Springs, Arkansas, December 1974).

Robinson-Patman Act, 1936 The Robinson-Patman Act expanded federal regulation of marketing even further than the previous laws mentioned here. The Act had four basic purposes: (1) To make it unlawful for any person engaged in interstate commerce to discriminate in price between purchasers of commodities of like grade and quality; (2) to prohibit the granting of brokerage fees to large buyers who purchase directly from producers or through "dummy" brokerage houses manned by regular employees of the purchasing organization; (3) to prohibit any payment to a customer unless such payment is made on proportionally equal terms to all other competing customers (for example, special advertising allowances); and (4) to protect independent merchants, the public, and manufacturers from unfair competition.

One interesting aspect of the Robinson-Patman Act is that it applies to both sellers *and buyers* who "knowingly" induce or receive an unlawful discrimination in price. It also stipulates that certain types of price cutting shall be criminal offenses punishable by fine and imprisonment. As you can see, the laws have grown more precise and the punishment more definite as the years have passed. More recent legislation goes beyond describing what marketers *cannot do* and lists what they *must do* to engage in commerce. For example, they *must* put the ingredients on certain food products. A brief look at some of the laws passed in the 1970s will give you some idea of the trend in legislation toward more exacting legal demands.

Legislation in the 1970s Every year, many new bills that would establish more regulations and laws affecting marketing are introduced. In 1970, the Public Health Smoking Act banned cigarette advertising on radio and television. Legislation has also been considered to ban *all* commercials for cigarettes and to ban cigarette smoking in certain public areas. You might be interested in following this legislation because it could set the stage for more legislation against other forms of advertising, such as that for liquor.

The Poison Prevention Labeling Act of 1970 requires special safety packages for products that may be harmful to children. Similarly, the Consumer Product Safety Act of 1972 was designed to protect the public from unreasonable risks of injury from products, to assist the consumer in evaluating product safety, to develop safety standards for consumer products, and to promote studies of the ways to prevent product-related injuries and deaths. Other significant legislation of the 1970s includes the Federal Environmental Pesticide Control Act (1972), the Noise Control Act (1972), the Agriculture and Consumers Protection Act (1973), the Emergency Petroleum Allocation Act (1973), and the Water Resources Development Act (1974).

You will find that there are literally dozens of consumer-related bills before federal and state legislators every year. Concerned marketers should try to learn as much as possible about forthcoming legislation because the effect of legal decisions on marketing practices is always important.

Legislation and Marketing Management As you can see from the previous discussion, legal constraints affect all areas of marketing management, including product, place, promotion, and price decisions. To give you a quick overview, let's review each area and briefly outline some additional regulations.

Product Legislation Product-related legislation includes the various patent laws that give producers protection for their new ideas. For example, the Lanham Act of 1946 specifies the procedure for registering brand names and trademarks. Product legislation also takes the form of various labeling acts, such as the Wool Products Labeling Act of 1939, the Fur Products Labeling Act of 1959, the Textile Fiber Products Identification Act of 1958, and the Fair Packaging and Labeling Act of 1966. Also included in this category is product-quality legislation such as the Food, Drug, and Cosmetic Act of 1938, which authorizes the Food and Drug Administration (FDA) to establish quality standards for foods. Other regulation concerns product safety, warranties (implied and actual), and pollution standards. In short, there is regulation affecting each stage of product development.

Place Legislation Place-related legislation (that is, what channels to use and how) includes the Clayton Act's prohibition against tying contracts (that is, making a buyer buy one product to get another); constraints against exclusive dealings (for example, requiring the buyer to purchase all his materials from one supplier); prohibitions against paying allowances to buyers in lieu of middleman costs (brokerage part of Robinson-Patman Act); and prohibitions against various unfair policies as spelled out in the Robinson-Patman Act.

Promotion Legislation Promotion-related legislation includes the Wheeler-Lea Act, which outlaws false advertisements of foods, drugs, devices, or cosmetics, the Federal Trade Commission Act, which set up the FTC to regulate deceptive ads, and the Robinson-Patman Act, which prohibits offering one distributor promotional allowances (for example, advertising funds or store demonstrators) without making them available to others. Also included is much legislation regarding advertising to children, the use of premiums, bait advertising, and price advertising. Legislation has also been passed to give consumers a "cooling off" period after buying an expensive item from a door-to-door salesperson. Perhaps no area of marketing is given more detailed analysis and subsequent legislation than promotion.

Price Legislation Price-related legislation includes the Clayton Act and Robinson-Patman Act, which prohibit price discrimination among purchasers, minimum-price legislation (for example, prohibiting firms from driving others out of business with below-cost pricing), and the Sherman Act, which prohibits conspiracy to control prices (remember the electrical-equipment cases).

"By Jove, Hopper, you've got yourself a shady deal!"

Reprinted by permission of Chicago Tribune-New York News Syndicate, Inc.

Future Legislation

Thus far, the various government agencies have given little attention to the marketing activities of nonprofit organizations and social causes. But recent investigations of charitable organizations and other nonprofit organizations indicates that this may soon change.

In this chapter, we obviously could not discuss all the legislation affecting marketing. Besides, as mentioned earlier, it is not the laws per se that are important as much as the *interpretation* of those laws by the courts, the FDA, the FTC, and other regulatory bodies. You can keep up with the latest decisions by reading the "Legal Developments in Marketing" section of the *Journal of Marketing.* You might also ask for a free copy of the FTC newsletter and watch the daily newspaper for news of marketing legislation. *Advertising Age* is also a good source for learning about new legal challenges and decisions.

CORPORATE SOCIAL AUDITING

The consumerist movement of the 1970s, together with increased pressure from legislation, has made businesses much more concerned about their social responsibility. Firms are looking beyond profits to explore their social contribution (see the insert "New Social Goals of Business").

The most visible evidence of this trend is the development of social-auditing concepts and procedures. This section will review some of the

New Social Goals of Business

In recognition of the network of social consequences of business activity, we can no longer measure the influences of business solely in terms of economic well-being and national wealth. The ultimate purpose of business, as of any institution in society, is to be "socially profitable." The firm must be appraised, then, in terms of its total contribution to society, not merely its economic contribution.

From Alvar O. Elbing, Jr., "The Value Issue of Business: The Responsibility of the Businessman," *Academy of Management Journal*, March 1970, pp. 79–89.

major concepts from the social-auditing area. Let's begin by defining what we are talking about: **A corporate social audit** is a systematic evaluation of a firm's activities as they affect society.

One of the most difficult problems with social auditing is defining what is meant by "socially responsible behavior." Another major problem is establishing procedures for measuring a firm's activities and their effects on society. What should be measured? One writer feels that the following social activities offer the greatest promise for early quantification and measurement:

1. Aid to arts and cultural activities.
2. Aid to higher education and health-related activities.
3. Employee-related activities: improved benefits, equal opportunities in promotion, participation in job enrichment programs, self-development programs, job safety, the right to dissent, and encouraging participation in political activities of the employees' own choice.
4. Community-related activities: local fund-raising campaigns, executive time devoted to improving the efficiency of various local governing and planning bodies, urban development, and inner-city programs.
5. Minority groups: hiring, job training, development, and promotion; and encouragement of minority-owned enterprises through loans, technical assistance, subcontracting, and purchasing.
6. Consumerism: product safety, product warranties; adequate consumer information, fair pricing policies, nondeceptive advertising, and complaint handling.
7. Political activities (external and internal): taking a position on war, apartheid, and so forth; supporting public-interest legislation on such issues as gun control, stringent antipollution laws, better standards for consumer protection, and mass transit.
8. Restructuring of corporate organization: inclusion of minority groups and other public-interest representatives on the board of directors, federal chartering of large corporations, and so forth.[18]

[18] S. Prakash Sethi, "Getting a Handle on the Social Audit," *Business and Society Review/Innovation*, Winter 1972–1973, p. 38.

Linowes feels that companies should apply the "system" of economic and fiscal measurement to social areas.[19] He calls this "socioeconomic measurement" and the result would be a socioeconomic operating statement (SEOS) that would resemble a firm's balance sheet:

It will be a tabulation of those expenditures made voluntarily to improve the welfare of employees and the public, product safety, or environmental conditions. . . . Set off against these . . . expenditures would be "detriments"—the cost of such above-mentioned items which have been brought to the attention of management, and which a reasonably prudent, socially aware management would be expected to undertake, but which it chooses to ignore.[20]

There is some question whether a social audit should be reported as the sum of all the socially beneficial activities minus the socially detrimental activities. Most people seem to feel that the emphasis should be on the positive action, with some recognition given the areas where more action is needed:

. . . It seems we should steer clear of the traditional accounting approach of matching bad things (costs) with good things (revenues) in order to develop a net dollar amount as a basis for objectively evaluating the periodic performance of corporate management. Dollar-matching just does not seem appropriate when benefits are primarily external to the firm. . . . In fact, that which is not done should not be subtracted from what is done, since it does not reduce the benefit of what has been achieved.[21]

There is rather general agreement, however, that a social audit would be beneficial for most organizations. We shall not be able to explain all the details of such an audit here because the procedures are quite complex. Bauer and Fenn conducted extensive research on the topic and reported the results in their book *The Corporate Social Audit.*[22] Consulting firms such as Abt Associates, Inc., and Arthur D. Little help other firms conduct social audits. The American Institute for Certified Public Accountants has created a Committee on Social Measurement to give some guidance to interested organizations. In general, much progress has been made toward defining what is meant by "socially responsible corporate behavior" and some progress toward measuring such behavior through social auditing.

[19] See David F. Linowes, "Let's Get On With the Social Audit: A Specific Proposal," *Business and Society Review/Innovation,* Winter 1972–1973, pp. 39–43.

[20] Ibid., p. 40.

[21] John C. Burton, "Commentary on Let's Get On With the Social Audit," *Business and Society Review/Innovation,* Winter 1972–1973, p. 43.

[22] Raymond A. Bauer and Dan H. Fenn, Jr., *The Corporate Social Audit* (New York: The Russell Sage Foundation, 1972).

One social goal is conservation of energy resources.

National Advertising Program, National Rural Electric Cooperative Association, Washington, D.C.

The Future of Social Auditing All marketing organizations should investigate the benefits of implementing a periodic social auditing system. The results of such an audit do not have to be reported to the public. In fact, the companies that pioneered this research have used the information primarily as a managerial aid. The information should be part of a total marketing information system designed to achieve the marketing goal of benefiting both individuals *and* society.

Many individuals and organizations have pledged not to invest in companies that are socially irresponsible. A corporate social audit, therefore, not only aids in managerial decision making but may lead to more investor interest, better public relations, and less government regulation. We encourage you to read the latest articles and books on the subject because it is one road to establishing mutually satisfying exchanges in society.[23] In fact, social auditing may become a norm for all organizations—not just businesses.

Profit as a Socially Responsible Goal   In Chapter 3, we outlined a philosophy of marketing that stressed socially responsible behavior, but we made it clear that a profit orientation was one way the corporations could benefit society. Perhaps an example would help clarify the concept:

> When the businessman wastes resources on a bad risk, it is the consumer who principally pays. . . . When he reduces his costs or innovates successfully, it is the consumer who benefits.
>
> And so, precisely because the businessman's drive for profitability is identical with his drive for lower costs, his profit is a pretty good measure of social welfare. Suppose two companies make similar products and sell them at about the same price. Company A nets $10 million, but Company B nets twice as much. . . . To an individual consumer, the two companies might seem to offer little choice. But so far as society at large is concerned, Company B has done a much better job, because it has used $10 million less of our resources, i.e., raw material and manpower, in doing the same job.[24]

As consumers, we should recognize the ways in which everyone benefits from profitable businesses. Furthermore, business managers should be careful not to overemphasize social goals to the detriment of their primary responsibility to customers and stockholders. The idea is to strike an acceptable balance between the needs of individuals (for example, customers) and the needs of society. A social audit makes such a commitment more precise and sets up procedures for measuring progress.

Social Indicators   While individual firms are trying to establish some measure of their social effectiveness through social auditing, society as a whole is trying to measure its own progress through **social indicators**. A social indicator is "a statistic of direct normative interest which facilitates concise, comprehensive, and balanced judgments about the condition of major

[23] See, for example, Raymond A. Bauer and Dan H. Fenn, Jr., "What *Is* a Corporate Social Audit?" *Harvard Business Review*, January–February 1973, pp. 37–48, and Nabil Elias and Marc Epstein, "Dimensions of Corporate Social Reporting," *Management Accounting*, March 1975, pp. 36–40.

[24] Gilbert Burck, "The Hazards of Corporate Responsibility," *Harvard Business Review* (June 1973), pp. 114–117, 214, 216, 218.

aspects of a society. It is in all cases a direct measure of welfare and is subject to the interpretation that, if it changes in the 'right' direction, while other things remain equal, things have gotten better, or people are 'better off.'"[25]

A government study of this subjects says that "the National Income statistics are, in fact, one kind of social indicator; they indicate the amount of goods and services at our disposal. But they tell us little about the learning of our children, the quality of our culture, the pollution of the environment, or the toll of illness. Thus other social indicators are needed to supplement the National Income figures."[26]

For example, the *Economist* magazine (London) compiled an index for fourteen countries using fifteen social indicators including car ownership, divorce, economic growth, and the ratio of TV sets and telephones to people. The National Wildlife Federation has an index that emphasizes things like soil, air, water, and living space. Other indexes emphasize noneconomic and economic factors such as love, status, information, money, goods and services.[27] The anthropologist Margaret Mead suggests we look at the quality of life in terms of patterns: "One might look at a pattern of life—what is available with a given level of technology, a given level of education, a given set of resources—and examine whether that pattern supplies people with a degree of dignity as human beings that is comparable to the degree of dignity of other people."[28]

The whole idea of measuring economic and noneconomic social indicators is to determine whether marketing and other social institutions are bettering the "quality of life" of people or not. There have been several "social indicator" conferences, and some progress is being made. Marketers are directly involved in such issues and are beginning to have some impact on social studies of this nature. As you can see, marketing is becoming involved with *all* aspects of human wants and needs. We hope you will become more interested in marketing's potential for creating a better quality of life and will do your part in whatever organization you join.

[25] Robert S. Raymond, "Social Indicators and Marketing Decisions," in *Combined Proceedings 1971 Spring and Fall Conferences*, ed. Fred C. Allvine (Chicago: American Marketing Association, 1972), p. 609.

[26] U.S. Department of Health, Education and Welfare, *Toward a Social Report* (Washington, D.C.: Government Printing Office, 1969), p. 97.

[27] Richard D. James, "Measuring the Quality of Life," *The Wall Street Journal*, May 18, 1972, p. 18.

[28] Cited in James, "Measuring the Quality of Life."

FOR REVIEW

Key Terms

Among the more important terms and expressions discussed in this chapter are the following:

Consumer education is the process of teaching the public how to use relevant facts and figures to make more intelligent exchange decisions.

Consumer information involves the presentation of facts and figures about goods, services, and other products through advertising, labeling, consumer bulletins, and other information channels.

Consumerism is a social movement that seeks to increase and strengthen the rights and powers of buyers in relation to sellers.

A **corporate social audit** is a systematic evaluation of a firm's activities as they affect society.

A **social indicator** is a statistic of direct normative interest that facilitates concise, comprehensive, and balanced judgments about the condition of major aspects of a society.

Key Concepts

Among the more important marketing concepts introduced in this chapter are the following:

> **Marketers in the future may increase their efforts to educate the public in matters of health, safety, and social welfare and then leave the selection of particular products to individual consumers.**

> **From a marketing perspective, the best judge of products of all kinds (including people, places, ideas, goods, services, and causes) is an informed consumer who has been taught to use that information; for this reason, a major obligation of marketing is to provide consumer information and education.**

> **Marketers attempt to satisfy the needs of individuals and of society, including the need for environmental protection; this calls for coordination and cooperation among all social organizations to work out sensible trade-offs between economic concerns and environmental concerns.**

Discussion Questions

1. Write a list of ten issues you feel are most important in marketing. Compare your list with those prepared by others in your class and discuss in depth the five issues that appear most often. Why are those issues so dominant today? What issues may be dominant 10 years from now?

2. Should marketers give people what they want or should they try to change people's wants to create a better society? Give examples to explain your position.

3. What effect do you feel legislation has had on marketers over the last 85 years or so? Has there been a significant improvement in exchange relationships? Why or why not?

4. Discuss the role of individual consumers in forcing marketers (and people in general) to be more honest, reliable, and open. Is the consumer the boss? Why or why not?

5. Discuss consumerism today and the issues that are receiving the

most attention. Are these issues easily resolved by better marketing? Would more consumer information and consumer education help?

6. Should social auditing be made mandatory in business organizations? In government organizations? What should be included in such an audit? Are such audits better as an internal management device or a means for regulating marketing?

7. Discuss the merits and drawbacks of banning throwaway bottles. What are the benefits and costs of having throwaway bottles and cans?

8. Some of the most dangerous toys for children are bicycles and roller skates. Should such products be taken off the market? Why or why not? Who should decide such issues?

9. Cigarette advertising was banned from television, and yet sales rose both in England and in the United States. Warnings have been placed on cigarette packs. Should further legislation be enacted regarding cigarette smoking or cigarette marketing? What are the guidelines you used in your answer?

10. Do marketers have an *obligation* to be socially responsible? Is social responsiveness good managerial practice? By what criteria do you evaluate "good" marketing management?

CASES

Red's Snackmobile
A Marketer's Social Obligation

Red Becker got an inspiration for "finding a need and filling it" while vacationing at a large ocean resort. Red noticed that there were long stretches of beach with no stores of any kind, and people were hot and thirsty. Red decided to go into the vending business. He got the necessary permits and began selling ice cream, cold drinks, and other snacks on the beach. Red made a very substantial income from his business and had to work only 4 months a year. But Red ran into trouble with local citizen groups. His customers were leaving paper cups, straws, wrappers, and other junk all over the beach. Furthermore, Red charged 50¢ for a cola drink and similarly high prices for his other products. Few customers complained to him, but many were unhappy with the price. Many complaints were filed against Red, and he was in danger of losing his license.

1. Does Red have any social obligations to the local residents of the beach community. If so, what are they?

2. Is there anything unethical about charging 50¢ for a cola drink? Would there be any reason to charge less?

3. What "publics" must Red be concerned about besides his customers? Why?

4. Was Red violating any laws that you are familiar with? Are laws an effective way to protect the consumer interest in such cases?

Wholesale Food Sales
What Is Ethical Behavior?

Sandy Kaplan is a salesman for a food wholesaler. One of Sandy's customers is a particularly big account. The manager of this chain of stores, Mr. Brennan, has a reputation for demanding special "gifts" for himself when he places orders. Sandy learned that many of his competitors do give substantial "gifts" to buyers like Mr. Brennan, but that the large, national organizations give large discounts on merchandise instead. For example, one national supplier gives thirteen cases of merchandise for every ten bought during special promotions. Sandy cannot match the discounts given by the larger firms and questions the use of "gifts" to win accounts, but word is out that most buyers will not deal on any other terms.

1. What would you do if you were in Sandy's position and your sales manager was pushing you to get more sales or be fired?
2. Is it unethical, in your view, to give substantial discounts to some buyers? How does this differ from giving those accounts "gifts" such as money or free trips?
3. Who is more unethical in your view—the manager who demands "extras" or the seller who gives them?
4. Many U.S. firms have admitted to giving foreign governments "bribes" to purchase U.S. products. Such bribes are said to be the norm in such deals. Should U.S. firms refuse to deal with any country or companies that demand such payments? What consequences might this have for foreign trade?

The Future of Marketing

more of the same or new challenges?

LEARNING GOALS

After you have read and studied this chapter, you should be able to:

1. Discuss the role of marketers in preventing "future shock."
2. Describe which areas of marketing will change slowly in the future and which will experience radical change.
3. Give examples to show how marketing will change as the economy changes.
4. Explain the role marketing plays in resolving environmental problems.
5. Show how marketing can be used to better control population growth.
6. Give examples of marketing programs that could begin to solve many of the world's food problems.
7. Discuss which service industries will have the greatest growth in the future.
8. Show how future changes in marketing communications will affect salespeople and other marketers, including consumers.
9. Explain the productivity problem in marketing and indicate what can be done to solve it.
10. Define a marketing audit and explain how it improves marketing productivity.

> *We should all be concerned about the future because we will have to spend the rest of our lives there.*
>
> Charles F. Kettering*

INTRODUCTION "Too often colleges of business are accused of teaching how it has been, not even how it is, and it is said that [students] should be taught how it may be in the future," says Donald Mulvihill. "Plans by forward-looking companies, at least as discussed in business and trade publications, indicate that they are attempting to add to their staff young men and women who will be capable of dealing with problems which will occur twenty to thirty years from now."[1]

Every indication is that Mulvihill is correct. A cursory review of marketing texts shows that very little space is devoted to the future of marketing. On the other hand, there is much evidence that marketers everywhere (especially in business and government) are beginning to plan long-range marketing programs and are starting now to adapt to future demands. The energy crisis, which came to prominence in the 1970s, has shaken many people and has prompted them to look ahead for future problems in other areas, including technology, space, health, and ecology. Other concerns have centered on population problems, unemployment, worldwide inflation, and worldwide hunger. This chapter will explore a few of the major issues that will affect marketing in the future.

Introduction of New Technology and Social Values Your parents and grandparents have witnessed an almost unbelievable growth in new, advanced products. Such people have seen the introduction of automobiles, airplanes, television, tape recorders, computers, motion pictures with sound, dishwashers, automatic washers and dryers, refrigerators, air conditioning, aluminum siding, and much more. In your lifetime there will be similar advances in appliances, transportation, communications, and household aids.

It has been predicted that the rapid growth of new products and ways of living in the future will cause "future shock."[2] It is up to marketers to make sure that new products and services are introduced in such a way that people accept them as readily as the innovations of the past. In the last 40 years, there have been radical changes in people's attitudes toward religion, sex, family size, the role of men and women, and entertainment. Future changes may be just as radical, but not necessarily more so.

Marketers are responsible for monitoring society's attitudes, values,

* *Seed for Thought* (1949).

[1] Donald F. Mulvihill, "A Look Into the Future," in *Combined Proceedings: 1971 Spring and Fall Conferences*, ed. Fred C. Allvine (Chicago: American Marketing Association, 1972), p. 16.

[2] Alvin Toffler, *Future Shock* (New York: Random House, 1970).

and life-styles and for keeping organizations in line with what is acceptable. There will be no "future shock" if marketers continue to introduce change at an acceptable rate. Technological growth, like any other aspect of a business, must be managed. Social change must also be anticipated, evaluated, and used as input for marketing planning. The future will be an exciting, challenging period of tremendous change, but future marketers will be ready. The concept is:

> **Marketing will not just adapt to environmental changes in the future; it will also influence those changes and adjust markets to new situations so that disruptions are minimized.**

Marketing Evolution and Revolution History indicates that the marketing of goods and services in the next century will experience many evolutionary changes.[3] Distribution systems will become more mechanized, computerized, and systematized. Marketing information systems will improve the two-way flow of information up and down the channel and among marketing systems. The marketing process in general will be more effective and more efficient. These changes will be evolutionary rather than revolutionary, however, and traditional marketing organizations should be able to adapt to the new technological and behavioral changes. *As an economic and a managerial process*, marketing in the future will still be concerned with providing consumer satisfaction at a profit. Marketing management decision making may involve multifirm channel systems, but the concepts will remain much the same.

As a *social process*, however, marketing may experience *revolutionary* changes that will challenge even the most progressive marketing organizations. As society's physical needs are satisfied through more advanced production and marketing processes, there will be a tremendous demand for business, government, and private organizations to satisfy society's other needs. As society's physical needs are met, there tends to be an increased demand for better educational programs, improved health-care services, more efficient and effective pollution-control systems, and higher standards of social welfare. Marketing will have to be involved in many governmental and other nonbusiness programs if these future demands are to be satisfied. Such involvement will demand new perspectives on marketing's goals.

The future of marketing will thus consist of two major thrusts. One development will be the slow, evolutionary adoption of a systems perspective and the emergence of fast, efficient distribution systems. The second development will involve changes in the area of social welfare. Marketing experts will be asked to apply their knowledge and skill to international efforts to build a better world society.

Marketing offers no cure-all for solving society's problems, but it has

---

[3] This section is based on William G. Nickels, "Metamarketing and Cultural Dynamics," in *Combined Conference Proceedings, Spring and Fall, 1972*, ed. Boris W. Becker and Helmut Becker (Chicago: American Marketing Association, 1973), pp. 533–534.

the expertise for analyzing people's wants and needs, developing programs to satisfy those needs, and designing information and distribution systems to implement the desired solutions. The real challenge for marketing in the future will be to structure an effective macro-marketing system that is responsive to the dynamic social environment of a global society. In the following sections, we shall discuss some of the issues that might dominate marketing decision making. Emphasis is placed on macro-marketing issues because they will likely be the most pressing in the future.

ECONOMY, ECOLOGY, AND ENERGY

Some people feel that the three E's will shape future thought for some time; these are economy, ecology, and energy.[4] Many changes are expected in the *economy* in the future. One change that particularly affects marketers is shortages. Marketers in the United States are used to operating in a society characterized by an abundance (even an over-abundance) of manpower, raw materials, and capital. But today there are manpower shortages in some areas (for example, doctors), raw materials shortages in other areas (for example, silver and cobalt), and capital shortages almost everywhere.[5]

Under pressure from ecologists, environmentalists, conservationists, and the public in general, marketing organizations are searching for products and processes that are less damaging to the environment. This is evidenced by the growth in recycling and recycling laws, the installation of all kinds of pollution-control devices on factories and cars, and the growing concern over cigarette smoking in public places.

Concerns over energy are reflected in the growing popularity of smaller cars, the installation of storm-windows and doors on homes, and the search for new sources of energy (for example, the Alaskan pipeline). The following sections will give more details about the 3 E's.

Economy and Shortages

Economics is a discipline that studies in part how to allocate scarce resources. There are not enough resources in the world today to assure that everyone can have the life-style of an average U.S. citizen. In less developed countries, individuals consume about 400 pounds of grain per year, whereas a U.S. citizen consumes 2,000 pounds (mostly indirectly through the eating of meat). Despite having only 6 percent of the world population, the United States consumes two-thirds of the world's raw materials such as copper, coal, and oil. One can see that the United States is a consumption society that is using much more than its share of world resources. Of course, the United States also produces much more than its share of food and other critical resources.

The question for marketers and economists is how to best allocate scarce resources among individuals, societies, and the world. Can we afford to be as wasteful as we have been in the past? Every year the

[4] For example, see Gerald Garvey, *Energy, Ecology, Economy* (New York: W. W. Norton & Company, Inc., 1972).

[5] See "The Capital Crisis," *Business Week*, September 22, 1975, pp. 42–48.

industrial nations of the world throw away 60 billion bottles, 100 billion cans, 11 million cars and trucks, 44 million tons of paper and other wood products. Can marketers develop a better way to use these materials so that natural resources are used at a slower pace and environmental decay can be slowed? This is the kind of question organizations must ask as they design the products, packages, and distribution systems of the future.

Although there is much talk about future shortages of food and housing, perhaps the greatest scarcity the United States faces in the near future is money (capital):

Between 1955 and 1964, the U.S. economy consumed $760 billion in capital in turning out all the cars and TV sets, in building all the houses and factories and shopping centers that a growing population wanted. Between 1965 and 1974, the nation's consumption of capital doubled to $1.6 trillion. By the best estimates available, the U.S. will need the incredible sum of $4.5 trillion in new capital funds in the next 10 years. . . .[6]

Without needed capital, the United States cannot begin satisfying future needs for food, housing, and other goods and services. Unemployment could also be a real threat. This is what *Business Week* says in summation of this problem:

Some factors . . . must change or the U.S. economy of the late 1970s and 1980s will be unlike anything the American people have seen in nearly four decades: an economy marked by slower growth, higher unemployment, and fewer fulfilled promises for nearly everyone.[7]

The potential capital shortage of the future demands greater cooperation between government and business and more attention to national priorities. There does not seem to be enough money available to solve all domestic and world problems at once. Therefore, marketers must learn to do careful *market analyses* of our national needs, to *segment* those needs that are most pressing, and to develop coordinated programs to provide economic *and* social stability.

The problems of unemployment and inflation in the U.S. and world economies can be solved only through the kind of long-range planning that marketers have used for years in industry. A strong economy is the basis for solving other social needs, including environmental improvement, full employment, and welfare. The concept is:

➤ **One role of marketing is to use resources (including capital) wisely, and that calls for long-range planning and economic analysis.**

[6] Ibid., p. 42.
[7] Ibid., p. 48.

Economy and The cost of detached single-family homes in the suburbs is already out of
Living Styles the reach of most American families. In the future, it is likely that the
costs will be even higher, and people will have to adopt new (and
perhaps better) life-styles. Many household items such as furniture and
appliances could be made more durable and could serve different
functions. For example, a dining room may be designed to be used as a
storage area and a game area as well as an eating place.

More rooms could be used for multiple purposes. For example, bed-
rooms could be converted into play areas for children by installing easily
movable beds and furniture. Several families could join together to
purchase a home, and the "extended family" concept may see a rebirth.
That is, grandparents, parents, and children may all share one dwelling.
Regardless of how living patterns change, it will be the function of
marketers to recognize such changes and to adjust both producers and
consumers to the new realities. The concept is:

> **Living styles in the future will reflect the social, technological, and
> political environment; marketing practitioners should monitor such
> changes to adapt people and organizations to the new life-styles.**

Ecology We may be slowly ending the period when marketers will be eager to
satisfy the consumer's desire for convenience by producing throwaway
products. There is a gradual trend toward nonobsolescence rather than
planned obsolescence. We may be approaching an era when recycled
products will be the norm rather than the exception. No longer would
people be able to afford disposable products such as diapers, packaging

---

Managing Future Demands

The need for new, clear goals is transcendentally important, because 20
years of increasing affluence in the U.S. have given us an unreasoning,
and, ironically, unsatisfying appetite for more material gains, with many
deeper human longings unsatisfied. We have moved from *wistfully
longing* for a better living in the 1930s to hoping for a better quality of
life in the late 1940s, to *expecting* greater material and human gains in the
1950s, and now to *demanding* them since the mid-1960s. The deteriora-
tion of the environment as a result of our accelerating quest for more
goods, better services, more education, and greater freedom has been
extensively documented and poses some of the major paradoxes and
problems of the 1970s. The better things get, the worse they seem to be!
We now need to reassess our levels of social, material, and educational
aspirations, futures research tells us as we determine what the biosphere
can provide; and we now need to identify new, equitable, human, yet
realistic levels of aspiration toward which we can afford to move.

From Harold G. Shane, "Education for Tomorrow's World," *The Futurist*, June
1973, p. 104. Reprinted with permission of the World Future Society, Washington, D.C.

"It's a special issue on the paper shortage."

Reprinted with permission from the January 28, 1974, issue of *Advertising Age*. Copyright 1974 by Crain Communications, Inc.

materials, and newspapers. Marketing terminology might be changed so that "consumers" would be called "users," for materials would be recycled rather than consumed or thrown away.

Recycling means more than collecting old beer cans and pop bottles; it means that almost all materials can be reused:

In such a society the present materials situation is literally reversed; all waste and scrap . . . become our major resources, and our natural untapped resources become our backup supplies. This must eventually be the industrial philosophy of a stabilized society and the one toward which we must work.[8]

In order to implement a less wasteful consumption pattern, products would have to be made more durable and easily repairable with standard, replaceable parts. One function of marketing is to monitor such trends and adjust the policies, products, and procedures of various organizations to meet future needs of society.

Energy "Energy use tends to outstrip other main indicators of expansion, such as population growth and increases in gross national product. Between 1960 and 1968, for example, population increased by 11% while total energy consumption jumped 39%."[9] We witnessed an energy crisis in the

[8] Glenn T. Seaborg, "The Recycle Society of Tomorrow," *The Futurist*, June 1974, pp. 108–115.

[9] Garvey, *Energy, Ecology, Economy*, p. 23.

early 1970s, which caused some rather minor inconveniences for many people, and spot shortages ever since. We have seen schools and businesses closed down because of a shortage of natural gas. However, every indication today is that there is ample energy available in the United States and the world. But the cost of getting it may be high. Coal reserves alone could provide all the energy the United States would need for several generations. The problem, and it is partially a marketing problem, is to balance the world's need for energy with its needs for environmental protection.

If we could solve international tensions through adopting the societal marketing concept worldwide, there might be much less of a problem. Oil-rich nations would trade freely with other nations having greater technological skills (for example, Japan and the United States), and energy problems could be minimized.

In the future, there may be so many sources of energy to tap that energy might not be a major problem. There are many potential sources of energy including fuel cells, liquefied natural gas (LNG), oil, wood, coal, wind, solar, tidal, geothermal, shale oil, nuclear, and so on. Marketers must act as middlemen to bring together governmental, business, and environmental leaders to work out the energy problems of the future. The concept is:

> **Marketers can help solve the energy problems of the future by establishing trade-offs between energy acquisition and environmental deterioration so that the world's energy needs can be met at a minimum of ecological harm.**

POPULATION MANAGEMENT, FOOD PROBLEMS, AND WORLD TRADE

Population Management

While most countries of the world may be trying to minimize or stop population growth (for example, India), others may be trying to promote growth to keep the economy growing (for example, the USSR). In either case, government officials can apply marketing principles and concepts to the task. People will not adapt their family size to some government standard without some incentive and some sense of participation in a nationwide program of some importance *to them personally*. It is the job of marketers to show people the importance of family planning and to design incentives that would encourage participation.

The United States will experience a relatively mild rate of growth over the next 30 years or so. The Census Bureau projects a population of somewhere between 250 and 300 million by the year 2000. Some of our problems may stem from having such a slow growth rate (see the insert "Birthrates"). Already we see schools being closed and people losing jobs. With fewer children to feed, house, and have children of their own, the United States may shift from an emphasis on quantity to quality. But do not be misled into thinking the population problem is solved just because the United States is in *relatively* good shape. The greatest problems in the future will probably be due to overpopulation rather than underpopulation.

The United States is just a small entity in terms of the world population. There are about 4 billion people in the world now, and, if we keep growing at present rates, we will reach 7 billion people by 2005.

Birthrates

A few months ago the polymath Herman Kahn appeared at a meeting to debate the limits to national growth. He asked how many in his audience thought the American birthrate should be lower. Nearly all of the hands went up. Mr. Kahn then asked how they felt about life in a country where the average age was over 40 (compared with the present age of 28) and the population was declining. His audience, most of them young and many of them academics, wavered. Mr. Kahn chided them sharply for their failure to realize that even the present American birthrate has fallen well below the replacement level and, if it holds constant, will result over the next half-century in precisely that pattern of an aging and diminishing population. People who talk about the country's future, he correctly declared, have no business not knowing where the numbers are leading.

It seems unlikely that the birthrate will in fact hold constant, since it has always been among the most volatile and unpredictable of social statistics. But regardless of its future movement, it has already dropped low enough for long enough to ensure substantial changes in the tenor of American life for decades to come.

The country changed its mind about big families about 20 years ago. The sharpest measure of it is the fertility rate, which means the number of babies born for every thousand women of child-bearing age. It reached its postwar peak of 123 in 1957. Last year it was 67, and it is still dropping rapidly. To put it another way, in 1960 4.26 million babies were born, more than any year before—or since. This year, the number will be somewhere around 3.15 million.

Of all the predictions that you might make about this country and its people in the year 2000, there is hardly any that you could calculate with more assurance than the number of 25-year-olds. They have already been born. You can assume with equal confidence that there will be fully one-fourth fewer 25-year-olds than 40-year-olds. It will be the first time in our history that an inversion of this magnitude will have occurred in our population.

This reversal of the usual pattern promises to have interesting effects on things as disparate as politics, music and marketing. Population change in the other direction, after all, was one of the most influential ingredients of the transformation of this country and its culture in the 1960s. It was not only that Americans were better educated, richer and more mobile than ever before, but also that a vast number of them were very young. It was the period in which the children of the postwar baby boom reached their late teens and early 20s. Suddenly the interests and concerns of that age group carried more weight than they had ever seemed to before. It will be highly instructive to see whether, as time passes, the national mood continues to telegraph the particular preoccupations of this generation as it moves into middle age: homes and mortgages, jobs and promotions, orderliness and security.

Perhaps the falling birthrates constitute a referendum on the principles of population control. Perhaps they are only a demand for more personal freedom than small children allow their parents. It is true that an American in his mid-50s has seen the population of this country double in his lifetime; an American of 80 has seen it triple. For most people, the old sense of unlimited and uncrowded space has disappeared. But it is hard to believe that people make decisions about having children merely on the basis of abstract principles and statistical truths. Whatever the reason, these decisions are about as binding as any that mortals can make. It is already clear that the United States will approach the millennium more lopsidedly middle aged, in demographic profile and perhaps in spirit as well, than at any time in its long history.

From an editorial in *The Washington Post*, April 26, 1976, p. A22. Copyright 1976 *The Washington Post*.

Let us look at a nation with huge population problems. India has one-third as much land as the United States and three times as many people. In 1900, India had a population of 236 million, with 26 million (11 percent) living in cities. Today, the population of India is over 600 million, with 120 million (20 percent) living in cities.[10] The conditions caused by such rapid growth are deplorable. "Bombay . . . has a population of 6.5 million, of whom 2.6 million live in slums, and 100,000 are pavement dwellers with no shelter of any kind."[11] Of course, widespread hunger, disease, and death accompany runaway population growth. Furthermore, per capita income in India is about $100 annually, less than the average U.S. worker earns per week.

Marketers have the tremendous challenge of helping the nations of the world solve their population problems. Partially, it is an educational task, but it is also a religious, political, social, and technological problem. Marketing's knowledge of consumer behavior, consumer research, and communication techniques can all be used to benefit humankind in its quest to satisfy its basic needs for food, clothing, and shelter. One approach is to help gain some control over population growth.

Feeding the World There is little doubt that in many areas of the world (including parts of the United States) there will not be enough nutritious food for everyone. But much of that deficiency may be solved by the use of such products as "meats" made from soybeans, "foods" made from wood, oil, and other materials, and other protein sources (for example, algae) that are largely untapped today. One of the more important marketing challenges of the future may be to market such products.

But the resistance to such foods may be expected to be high. People will not accept such foods simply because they are needed for good health. The food must be produced, packaged, and tested to meet the taste and consistency standards of the various markets to be served.

[10] Rashmi Mayor, "The Coming Third World Crisis: Runaway Growth of Large Cities," *The Futurist*, August 1975, p. 168.
[11] Ibid.

Today such foods are being introduced through nutritious beverages and by other such "hidden" means. But tomorrow's food products must meet people's need for bulk as well. Marketers will provide invaluable assistance to those companies and government agencies that wish to study consumer attitudes and values in order to design new foods that will be acceptable.

Marketers in the future will also be responsible for developing exchange agreements and distribution networks for a worldwide food system. Food production and marketing will be a major marketing problem for many years, and farm marketing will become a major area of interest.

International Trade All of the nations of the world are dependent upon other nations for many or most of their basic resources. But in the future there will be even greater interdependence between and among nations. The European Common Market is just one example of how several countries can join together to work out complex marketing (exchange) agreements. Underdeveloped countries of the world will form similar trading blocks to pool their resources so that they can become active traders in world markets.

All of these developments will be dependent upon, and will be led by, people who understand international markets and marketing. These people will have important positions in government and industry and will have tremendous impact on national trade policy.

World Trade and the Marketing Concept Much of the promise for the future depends on how quickly people adopt the new societal marketing concept as outlined in Chapter 3. Many recent articles have pointed out the need to balance self-interest with mutual interest (a societal orientation in marketing), to improve cooperation among different peoples and nations (through multinational and international marketing systems—both governmental and private), and

---

Population, Food and Life Expectancy

The food problem is intensified by world-wide population growth. . . . some 25% of all the persons who ever lived on this planet are alive today. With each passing minute some 120 new lives come into being. . . .

World population grows some 2.1% yearly. This seemingly small figure means that the population is doubling each 33 years. If this increase continues, a whole new world of people will be added to this world in the next generation. . . .

. . . Since people are living longer, they require more food per lifetime. . . . Average life expectancy in U.S. for both sexes has increased by 20 years just since 1910.

From Graham T. T. Molitor, "The Coming World Struggle for Food," *The Futurist*, August 1974, p. 169.

to establish more balanced priorities (for example, economic growth together with pollution control and conservation of resources).

It is important to recognize the need to apply the societal marketing concept worldwide, because pollution problems, economic problems, and international conflict are best resolved through international cooperation. When nations try to solve their economic problems internally and ignore the plight of other nations, tensions may build as they did in Germany in the 1930s, and that could lead to another major war. One nation can pollute the water of another (especially in the large rivers of the world), and it is often best to resolve such issues at an international level.

There have been many criticisms of the United Nations, but many promising programs have emerged to solve international marketing problems. For example, the International Monetary Fund (IMF) helps bring order to the international monetary system, an important first step

An ad used to encourage the British public to conserve water during the summer drought in 1976.

"If we want to save jobs, we have to save water."

Are you using less water at work as well as at home? If not, you could be putting your own job in danger–and those of others too.

Aim at cutting your own use of water by half from today–and help your firm to do the same.

After all, it's not just water you're saving.

It's jobs.

Len Murray, General Secretary, Trades Union Congress.

SAVE WATER

National Water Council

Courtesy of McCann-Erickson, London.

toward world trade. The General Agreement on Tariffs and Trade (GATT) also helps reduce trade barriers. The World Bank (The International Bank for Reconstruction and Development) provides capital to help poor countries set up better communications, roads, and power systems. Finally, there are agencies such as UNESCO, the World Health Organization (WHO), and others that deal with problems of illiteracy, hunger, and disease. These programs have not solved world marketing problems, but they do show that nations can work together to increase trade (GATT), establish monetary exchange systems (IMF), and generally act together to establish *mutually satisfying exchange relationships worldwide.*

GROWTH OF THE SERVCE SECTOR AND DISTRIBUTION SYSTEMS We have already discussed the ways in which the United States has become a service economy. In the future, services will become an even greater factor in consumer budgets. This is true in many different areas, including housing (rentals will grow faster than ownership in the near future at least), transportation (for example, more reliance on mass transportation), recreation (because of more leisure time), education (especially continuing education for adults), health care (perhaps nationalized), communications (cable TV, citizen's band radio, computer conferences), and child care (for example, day-care centers and camps). Let's look in greater detail at a few specific areas to get some idea of the growth of services in the future.

Health Care Increases in the cost of health care have been the cause of much concern; in the United States, the amount of money spent annually on health care more than doubled between 1960 and 1969—from $26 billion to $60 billion. The costs of health care continue to rise, and marketers must begin to try to counter the trend. Inefficiencies in hospitals must be dealt with, more outpatient services must be provided, and the entire health-care system, including government and private insurance, should be given a high priority.

Marketing concepts are relatively new in the health-care industry, but there has been encouraging progress. Marketers were especially interested in studying Health Maintenance Organizations and in winning acceptance of them by the public. Thus far the impact has been disappointing, but the research goes on, and everyone involved is beginning to see the need for a marketing approach to health-care delivery.

The whole idea of *preventive* medicine must be sold to the medical profession and to the public. Some doctors and dentists are leading this trend, but the public tends to resist. Most people, even in advanced countries, do not brush their teeth as recommended by dentists in spite of millions of dollars in promotion for toothpaste. Most hospitals and doctor's offices are geared to handle patients *after* they become ill, and comparatively little effort is made to inform the public of the value of balanced nutrition, preventive checkups, and other such measures. Health Maintenance Organizations are one promising step in that direction. But often people ignore the free chest X rays, blood-pressure checks, and other services offered today. Many children are not being immunized against polio and other such diseases, even though prevention is now possible with modern drugs. These are marketing problems! They involve consumer information, consumer education, and the careful cooperation of the medical world with the world of marketers.

Future of Marketing Communications One of the tremendous growth areas in the future will be in the general area known as communications. Radio, TV, computers, communication satellites, laser-beam technology, transistors, microfilm, and microfiche are all elements that will be combined to create a communications revolution in marketing. Marketing has the general function of bringing products and people together. In general, it is cheaper to move products than people, but it is even cheaper to move information.[12] It is also cheaper to communicate through the mass media rather than through salespersons. The concepts that apply are:

› **Marketing is more efficient when it concentrates on moving products rather than people, and most efficient when it moves information rather than products; instead of having people personally inspect products, for example, they could see the product demonstrated on television and could purchase it through the mail.**

› **Personal selling may decline in relative importance in the communications mix as mass communication (advertising) assumes more of the function of marketing communications and promotion.**

Some of the more interesting developments in the future will involve cable TV and two-way cable TV. Present technology would enable a consumer to contact a store, government agency, doctor, or any other marketer and conduct a complete transaction over a two-way cable TV system (or a video-phone system). A sick person would be able to show a doctor what is wrong, get a diagnosis, order a prescription, have it delivered, and never leave his or her bed. Think of the advantages of such a system in rural areas where no doctor is available. Remember, it is cheaper to move information than people!

Students would be able to take courses at home and still have the ability to ask questions and participate actively in the class. Again, think of the advantages to students in rural areas and to handicapped students. Again, it is cheaper to move information than people!

Can you think of other examples of how two-way cable TV or video-phone systems could revolutionize marketing of particular products? What might be the effect on the movie industry? How could social workers benefit? How could salespersons minimize travel time with such a system? How could it improve shopping for people too busy to drive to the shopping center? Try to think of applications for the marketing of

---

[12] This concept is developed in Wroe Alderson, *Dynamic Marketing Behavior* (Homewood, Ill.: Richard D. Irwin, Inc., 1965), p. 368.

everything from homes, insurance, cars, boats, and clothes to the marketing of social causes, politicians (remember that two-way conversations are possible), lawyers, and tax consultants.

Transportation Changes We have emphasized the fact that it is cheaper to move goods than people and cheaper to move information than goods. Increased costs of transportation in the future will force people into moving more information than ever before. Note this release in *Newsweek* magazine:

> The world's hard-pressed airlines face a new competitor—closed-circuit TV. Dow Chemical Co., for example, has been spending more than $700,000 annually on air tickets and the same amount in man-hours to fly company executives back and forth between its headquarters in Michigan and its manufacturing center in Texas. Nowadays, closed-circuit color-TV conferences that cost $2,000 an hour are replacing these meetings—at an initial cost of only $260,000 a year. In England, the British Post Office is touting its telephone-line TV service called Confravision as a way to save on long-distance conferring: a 90-minute TV "meeting" transmitted between special studios in London and Glasgow costs $125 less, the BPO says, than flying three men from one city to the other.[13]

What this means for marketers is that the communications revolution will be a tremendous challenge to the transportation industry. Closed-circuit TV, two-way cable TV, computer conferences, video-phone systems and other new developments may make the traveling salesperson a thing of the past. Why travel when you can contact customers by video-phone, give elaborate demonstrations over two-way cable TV systems, and transfer photocopied information over phone lines?

[13] *Newsweek*, August 26, 1974, p. 15.

Computer Conferences

Using ordinary telephone lines, people can now join an invisible network and attend a conference that runs continuously, 24 hours a day, for as long as the participants want. . . .

Our studies to date indicate that computer conferencing has unique potential for enhancing the exchange of ideas among people. In current field tests, we are exploring its usefulness in bargaining and negotiation, conflict resolution, crisis management, and some educational applications. . . . We believe that the potential of computer-based communication remains largely unexplored.

From Jacques Vallee, Robert Johansen, and Kathleen Sprangler, "The Computer Conference: An Altered State of Communication?" *The Futurist*, June 1975, pp. 116–121. See also the *The Futurist*, August 1975, pp. 182–195.

Mass transportation (including buses and various rail systems) will continue an evolutionary growth in the future, nonetheless. Travel by private automobile will continue to be a primary source of movement, but the costs might keep such travel to a minimum. You may want to keep an eye on revolutionary new concepts in transportation in the future such as coal pipelines, monorail systems, personalized air-travel systems, underground pipelines for distribution of goods, and superior rail transport. All of these developments will affect physical-distribution management and marketing in general. But note also the partial *replacement* of travel with *communications,* for that will be the most revolutionary change in marketing.

Channel Systems of the Future It is the year 2000, and Diane Winton wants to go grocery shopping. What kind of store do you think she will go to? Or will she go to a store? There is some evidence to indicate that much of our grocery shopping in the future will be from home. There will be a handy catalog of everyday grocery items in the kitchen. When we want something, we will just pick up the phone, call the local food distribution center, order what we want, and have it delivered in an hour or two. The principle is: Move goods, not people. Those items we like to shop for, such as meats, bakery goods, and produce, we could buy at a local "farmer's market" where such goods are on display in a wide variety of shops.

If in the future people do go shopping for food as they do today, it is quite likely that they will shop at huge supermarkets where many nonfood items will be sold. The idea is to minimize the number of places a person must visit to shop and to increase the margin on items sold at supermarkets (the markup on nonfood items tends to be much higher than that on foods).

More significant than the changes in the retail system, which will go through a slow, evolutionary change, will be the increased movement toward vertically integrated channel systems (that is, the merging of manufacturing, wholesaling, and retailing firms). The most significant development in channel systems could be the growth of interfirm marketing information systems that will involve computerized inventory systems, system-wide promotional programs, and a generally more efficient physical distribution flow. This may mean lower prices for consumers, but it would lead to more centralization of market power among a few giant corporations that would be diversified into many areas, such as food, clothing, appliances, books, and furniture.

MARKETING PRODUCTIVITY One of the major concerns of marketers in the future will be to increase marketing productivity. Marketers will be better able to solve the serious problems outlined earlier when they improve the effectiveness and efficiency of marketing programs. There had been few studies of marketing productivity until the mid-1970s, but at that time the American Marketing Association began a major study of the problem, a study that will no doubt continue for many years. One of the problems has been to define just what is meant by "productivity." At the 1973 AMA Spring

Conference, **productivity** was defined as "useful, nonpolluting output per unit of useful, nonpolluting input," with "useful" being defined as "having value in the marketplace." [14]

There is some indication that marketers will be much more concerned with concepts of mutually satisfying exchange than they have been in the past. Productivity measures, for example, may include measures of seller efficiency (inputs versus outputs), measures of consumer satisfaction, and measures of social satisfaction. This is how Robert Eggert, former president of the AMA, views the problem:

Productivity means "useful" output per unit of input. The term "useful" helps to define the difference between productivity in its purely technical sense from productivity in a practical marketing sense. Also, I would hope that the word "useful" would include not only what values consumers would be willing to pay for in the marketplace, but in addition would help improve the quality of human life. However, this area requires considerable skill on the part of the marketer for it often is very difficult for even successful companies to take social values (quality of life) into their productivity equation. The reason for this is that frequently the average consumer will not pay more for a product of a marketer who recognizes social values vs. a marketer who ignores such values.

Because of this, in many instances social values entering into productivity considerations will have to be of a regulatory nature so that all competitors are "encouraged" to toe the mark. There are, of course, instances of "quality of human life" values that consumers would be willing to give recognition in the "price paid" equation, but I believe the majority of instances are in the other direction. This suggests that the marketer of the future must not only concern himself with providing outputs of goods and services that satisfy consumers directly, he also must plan to work closely with the regulatory agencies so that the quality of life aspects of the problem are equitably initiated and administered. [15]

Because productivity is a measure of "output" given various "inputs," one of the primary tasks of marketers in the future will be to define just what the "inputs" of marketing are (for example, labor, capital, machinery, risk) and what the "outputs" are (for example, goods, services, consumer satisfaction, pollution—a negative output—and social well-being). An AMA Advisory Committee on Measuring Marketing Productivity gave this rather pessimistic report:

There is no body of data that has been, or is being, systematically gathered and organized to provide a basis for measuring marketing productivity. . . .

[14] Reported in "Plenary Session Speakers Tell How to Measure, Increase Productivity," *Marketing News,* May 15, 1973, p. 1.

[15] Robert J. Eggert, "Productivity or Death," *Marketing News,* April 1, 1973, p. 3. Reprinted with permission of the American Marketing Association.

Private industry and some trade associations undoubtedly have made some efforts—possibly some progress—toward understanding and measuring marketing productivity. Much or most of this is safely guarded behind the wall of fear of competitive disclosure.

Educators have made sporadic and partial advances in this or closely related fields. Few of these efforts have been coordinated in a systematic or conclusive way, and only some of these have ever been published.[16]

As you can see, marketers are just on the threshold of productivity analysis. All areas of marketing could be made more effective and efficient through such careful research. For example, the need to increase the productivity of salespeople is dramatized by the statement that "only 25 percent of the sales force produces 75 percent of the total sales volume":[17]

According to Joseph P. Saner, national sales manager, Dun & Bradstreet, Inc., New York, to help the remaining 75 percent generate their share of higher commissions and improved reserves, D & B has developed "quick start," a service geared to key marketing facts on nearly three million U.S. companies. . . . The package includes a computer-generated statistical profile to define good prospects by size and type, information cards to identify up to 1,000 best prospects, mailing labels to get promotional materials to prospects quickly, a territory management program, and enrollment in D & B's salesmanship correspondence course.[18]

Victor Buell of the University of Massachusetts says this about advertising productivity: "In my opinion, there is no objective means of measuring productivity in advertising. But ad productivity—effectiveness—is at present decreasing and will probably get worse before it gets better. I'm a short-term pessimist but a long-term optimist."[19] David Harden of Market Facts, Inc., feels that marketing research productivity is suffering because it is "surprisingly subjective (individual views are more important than scientific support of various techniques), too fadish, too time pressured, too labor intensive, and too swamped in unnecessary data."[20] Similar problems are present in areas such as

[16] Reported in "Absence of Data to Measure Marketing Productivity Causes Lack of Trust in Marketing as a Productive Business Effort," *Marketing News*, December 1, 1974, p. 4. Reprinted with permission of the American Marketing Association.

[17] This concept is discussed in *Marketing News*, March 15, 1973, p. 2.

[18] Ibid.

[19] "Plenary Session Speakers Tell How to Measure, Increase Productivity," *Marketing News*, May 15, 1973, p. 4.

[20] Ibid.

physical distribution and product development. The American Marketing Association and various researchers will be studying the overall problem of marketing productivity.

More Use of Computers in Marketing Marketing has lagged behind many of the other functional areas of organizations in making optimum use of computers. One area where computers are especially important is that of marketing information systems. Salespersons and other employees should be able to feed information to a data bank that could easily manage all the intelligence flows so critical to the future. Included would be data about the government, suppliers, competitors, distributors, dealers, world conditions, and internally generated facts and figures. The computer is also useful in analyzing and sorting data into meaningful form.

The growth of time-sharing systems by which several firms can use one large computer will enable even relatively small organizations to benefit from computer technology. Computers will help in *marketing research* by making cost-benefit projections of research projects more precise. Of course, computers also help in data analysis. Computers will also help *promotion* managers in their media-selection process, in budgeting decisions, and in preparing distribution-cost accounting reports. *Pricing* decisions are also aided by computerized cost estimates, market-demand analyses, and by simulating competitive reactions.

There is no need to elaborate further on how the computer can benefit *all* areas of marketing and marketing management in government, business, and nonprofit organizations. We are just beginning to realize the potential of computers to help make marketers more productive. One should be careful not to put too much reliance on computers and computer technology in the future, however. Marketing will still be an exchange relationship that will demand personal, friendly two-way exchanges of information, and computers can provide only background support for such dialogues.

THE MARKETING AUDIT One way to measure the effectiveness and efficiency of the marketing process in the future is to conduct careful marketing audits. A **marketing audit** has been defined as, "a systematic, critical, and unbiased review and appraisal of the basic objectives and policies of the marketing function of the organization, and methods, procedures, and personnel employed to implement the policies and achieve the objectives."[21] It should be made clear that a marketing audit covers the entire marketing system, not just one function or department. It might be conducted by the organization's auditing department, or, to avoid bias, it could be done by an outside consulting firm.

A marketing audit would be conducted only occasionally and would be very thorough. Such audits are helpful in revealing inefficiencies of operation and in generally improving the effectiveness of the overall

[21] Alfred R. Oxenfeldt, *Executive Action in Marketing* (Belmont, Calif.: Wadsworth Publishing Company, Inc., 1966), p. 746.

marketing program. But each functional area of marketing (for example, sales and advertising) should also do periodic performance reviews to concentrate on the productivity of individual departments. In the future, there is likely to be much more emphasis on marketing audits and performance evaluations in all organizations, not just businesses.

As each organization begins to analyze its own internal productivity, marketing will become more and more efficient and will do a better job of meeting the wants and needs of individuals and society as a whole.

"One of the strongest arguments in favor of environmental scanning and 'futures' programs is the power it gives business to affect the course of coming events, rather than to react to them on a crisis management basis. It's a way to receive—and act on—early warning signals in the environment before they become forces too powerful to deal with."[22] A marketing audit gives early warning signals that indicate whether the organization is effectively responding to environmental changes.

Will the future of marketing be more of the same or will there be new challenges? The answer is both! Marketing will continue to provide satisfaction of individual wants and needs. But it will also become more involved in social problems and world trade. The future promises to be an exciting period for tomorrow's marketers.

[22] *Grey Matter*, a publication of Grey Advertising, Inc., vol. 47, no. 1 (1976), p. 4.

FOR REVIEW

Key Terms

Among the more important terms and expressions discussed in this chapter are the following:

A marketing audit may be defined as "a systematic, critical, and unbiased review and appraisal of the basic objectives and policies of the marketing function of the organization, and methods, procedures, and personnel employed to implement the policies and achieve the objectives" (from Alfred R. Oxenfeldt, *Executive Action in Marketing*).

Productivity, in terms of marketing, may be defined as useful, nonpolluting output per unit of useful, nonpolluting input, with "useful" being defined as "having value in the marketplace."

Key Concepts

Among the more important marketing concepts introduced in this chapter are the following:

- Marketing will not just adapt to environmental changes in the future; it will also influence those changes and adjust markets to new situations so that disruptions are minimized.

- The future of marketing will consist of two major thrusts. One development will be the evolutionary adoption of a systems perspective and the emergence of fast, efficient distribution systems. The second development will involve changes in the area of social welfare. Marketing experts will be asked to apply their knowledge and skill to international efforts to build a better world society.

> Three major concerns of American marketers in the future will be economy, ecology, and energy.

> Three concerns of marketers worldwide will be population management, food marketing, and international exchange agreements.

> Marketing of services in the United States will experience greater growth than will the marketing of goods.

> Much effort in the future will be placed on increasing marketing productivity through marketing audits and other management efforts.

Discussion Questions

1. What evidence is there today that people do suffer "future shock" from too rapid introduction of technological and social change?

2. Will Americans necessarily be forced to lower their standard of living as a result of a slow-growth economy?

3. Discuss the role of marketing in solving the problem of population management throughout the world.

4. What would happen to the economy of the United States and the rest of the world if a major disaster were to destroy the U.S. food crop? How could the results of such a disaster be minimized?

5. What are some of the changes in social values that will have a major effect on marketing in the future?

6. How could a state increase the productivity of its elementary schools? Is this partially a marketing problem? How?

7. "It is cheaper to move products than people, but it is even cheaper to move information." Discuss how this concept could be applied to the health-care field.

8. How could an organization apply a marketing audit to its purchasing function?

9. Will marketing in the future be subject to more or less government influence?

10. How could one increase the productivity of the money-gathering function of charities in the future?

CASES

The Future of Marketing
What Are the Issues?

Margaret Hargrove has just entered the MBA program at her state university. She was assigned a term paper on "The Future of Marketing." Margaret read this chapter as part of her preparation. She also explored several books and magazines that discussed issues of the future. Margaret found many areas of marketing that would be affected in the future that were not discussed in this chapter.

1. What are some issues that you feel will dominate marketing in the future?
2. Will future challenges make marketing more or less of a social influence? Discuss.
3. Dave Hilton feels that marketers should not waste time trying to predict the future. He feels we could learn more from the past and need to improve present practices first. Discuss.
4. Margaret's paper concluded that the economy in the United States would be greatly affected by shortages in raw materials, manpower, and capital. Give arguments to show that Margaret may be wrong in those conclusions.

Food Marketing
Problems of the Future

The consulting firm of Nash, Carroll, and Lamone specializes in the marketing of agricultural products. Special attention is given to the establishment of farm cooperatives to help grow, distribute, and sell food products. There is some worry among the independent farmers in the Midwest that a severe drought will hit their region. That would mean that much of the wheat and corn production of the United States would be destroyed. The consulting firm is called in to make a recommendation.

1. What can farmers do to minimize the losses from a major disaster like a drought?
2. How would the marketing task change if the United States had a deficit rather than a surplus of food? How would this affect world exchanges?
3. How could marketing consultants help developing nations to increase their food production and improve distribution systems?
4. Discuss the role of government in farm marketing and international trade.

Careers in Marketing
but can I find a job?

21

LEARNING GOALS After you have read and studied this chapter, you should be able to:

1. List at least ten marketing careers and briefly describe what they involve.

2. Explain the difference between a product manager and a venture manager.

3. Describe how marketing prepares people to be better economists.

4. Discuss what marketing careers are available for a person with your background and interests.

5. Prepare an effective cover letter and resume.

6. Conduct an effective job interview.

7. Improve your product offer so that you can get the job *you* want where *you* want it.

8. Evaluate alternative career choices and pick the one best for you.

9. Gather additional career information to better prepare you for the future.

10. Relax, because this is the last chapter in the book.

> *. . . With the exception of technical school graduates, only one out of four high school graduates and but two of four college grads have any idea of what they want to do. Further, less than 2 percent of those who said they knew what they wanted could give sound reasons for their choice.*

Sidney Edlund and Mary Edlund*

INTRODUCTION When all is said and done, probably the questions students ask most about marketing are: What's in it for me? Are there jobs available? Would I enjoy them? Do marketing jobs pay well? Are there opportunities for women and minorities? Can I "move up" in my career through marketing? What kinds of organizations could I work for?

If a student is satisfied that marketing is an interesting and rewarding career choice, the questions often become: How do I go about getting a job in marketing? Where do I apply? How important are my grades, extracurricular activities, and course selection? How do you write a good resume that sells? What should I say in the cover letter? How can I prepare for my interviews?

These questions come from marketing majors and from all other students. They are often of utmost importance in a student's mind. So we shall try to answer many of these questions in this chapter. We are sure that you will find some area of marketing that you would enjoy. We hope to show you how to get a job in that area and how to plan a long and successful career in marketing. If you are a marketing minor, we hope to show you how marketing courses will open up new career horizons for you. Finally, we hope to show you that marketing concepts and principles can be applied toward any task, including getting a job.

WHAT CAREERS ARE AVAILABLE No business discipline and few other professions have as many different career possibilities as marketing. There are marketing jobs available for majors in almost any discipline, but marketing majors enjoy a much wider range of career possibilities. Many students today are majoring in subjects such as sociology, psychology, anthropology, and social psychology. With some marketing training, such students would have a good background to go into careers in marketing research, consumer behavior analysis, and personal selling. Opportunities are available for social science/marketing majors in advertising agencies, marketing research firms, advertising departments, and retailing and wholesaling firms, to mention but a few.

Journalism majors with some marketing training are especially qualified for careers in advertising and sales promotion. Marketing/finance majors have good success working in banks, life insurance companies, and brokerage houses (selling stocks and bonds). Marketing/accounting

---

* *Pick Your Job and Land It,* rev. ed. (Englewood Cliffs, N.J.: Prentice-Hall, Inc., 1954), pp. 16–17.

majors have tremendous opportunities in consulting firms and in managing their own businesses. Marketing/economics majors may find work with the government, consulting firms, and most large manufacturing firms.

Those who do well in math and statistics would enjoy working for an ad agency in media selection. They might also make good marketing researchers and consumer behavior analysts. Engineers with a BA or MBA in marketing continue to be in demand for well-paying industrial sales careers. Home economics majors have done very well in retail buying, consumer education, consumer affairs, and a host of other marketing areas.

No matter what your major may be, marketing courses are certain to benefit your career and your personal life. After all, we are all consumers and need to know about the economics of consumer buying and other marketing subjects.

In the following sections, we take a closer look at the more popular marketing careers. Perhaps you will find some job category that sounds particularly appealing to you. Before moving on, however, take a look at the comprehensive list of marketing management careers that are available in some government agencies, nonprofit organizations, and business firms (Table 21.1). This list will serve as a broad introduction to the scope of marketing careers.

Personal Selling   We have already mentioned the fact that over 7 million people are employed in sales, and so it obviously is one of the more widely available careers. You might want to review the discussion in Chapter 15 on personal selling and sales management. The important thing to keep in mind is that salespeople are made, not born, and there is no such thing as a "good" sales personality. There are literally hundreds of different sales positions that call for widely different skills and techniques. You surely would fit one of those positions.

There are salespeople in retailing, wholesaling, manufacturing, insur-

---

A Career in Sales?

In 1974, the number of salespersons employed in various marketing institutions was as follows: retailing, 2,758,000; wholesaling, 768,000; manufacturing, 357,000. The total number of salespersons employed by all industries, including insurance and real estate, was 5,417,000 in 1974. This does *not* include sales/marketing/promotion positions in nonprofit organizations (total positions = 7,000,000).

There obviously is a lot of potential for a person interested in a sales career. One of the fastest growing areas is the service sector. Here are some job categories and the number of workers in each: advertising agents and salespeople, 34,762; insurance agents, brokers, underwriters, 369,230; real estate agents and brokers (rental), 195,742; stock and bond salespersons, 29,018; other service industries, 185,591.

Table 21.1 SURVEY OF MARKETING POSITIONS

Position	Other names for position	Duties
Marketing manager	Vice-president of marketing, marketing director, chief marketing officer, marketing administrator	The marketing manager is a member of the top administration. His or her tasks include providing a marketing point of view to the top administration; staffing, directing, and coordinating marketing activities; and proposing new products and services to meet evolving market needs.
Product manager	Program manager, brand manager	A product manager is responsible for managing a particular product or program of the organization. His or her job is to propose product objectives and goals, create product strategies and plans, see that they are implemented, monitor the results, and take corrective actions.
Marketing research manager	Marketing research director	The marketing research manager has responsibility for developing and supervising research on the organization's markets and publics, and on the effectiveness of various marketing tools.
Communications manager	Advertising manager, advertising and sales promotion director	The communications manager provides expertise in the area of mass and selective communication and promotion. He or she is knowledgeable about the design of commercial messages, media, and publicity.
Personal representatives manager	Sales manager	The personal representatives manager has responsibility for recruiting, training, assigning, directing, motivating, compensating, and evaluating personal representatives and agents of the organization. He or she is responsible for coordinating the work of the personal representatives with the other marketing activities designed to accomplish the organization's objectives.
Innovation manager	New-product manager, new-product director	The innovation manager has responsibility for conceiving new products and services, screening and evaluating new product ideas, developing prototypes and testing them, and advising and helping to carry out the innovation's introduction in the marketplace.

Table 21.1 *Continued*

Position	Other names for position	Duties
Logistics manager	Channel manager, physical distribution manager	The logistics manager has responsibility for planning and managing the systems that make the organization's products and services accessible to the potential users.
Client relations manager	Customer service manager, account executive	The client relations manager has responsibility for managing client services and handling client complaints.
Government relations manager	Legislative representative, lobbyist	The government relations manager provides the organization with intelligence on relevant developments in government and manages the organization's program of representation and presentation to government.
Public relations manager	Public affairs officer	The public relations manager has responsibility for communicating and dealing with various publics in matters involving the organization's image and activities.
Territory manager	Regional manager, district manager	The territory manager has responsibility for managing the organization's products, services, and programs in a specific territory.

From Philip Kotler, *Marketing for Nonprofit Organizations* (Englewood Cliffs, N.J.: Prentice-Hall, Inc., 1975), pp. 233–234.

ance, banking, transportation firms, newspapers (and the other media), brokerage houses, real estate firms, and other service organizations. The level of sophistication varies from salesclerks in retail stores to multi-million-dollar sales consultants who sell computers, high-rise buildings, and other sophisticated products.

Selling is a career in which you can begin low and work your way up through the firm or into other firms. The pay is high compared to most other occupations, you work away from the desk much of the time, and the chances of getting into management, even top management, are good. Talk to a few sales representatives in your area and learn about opportunities, salaries, and duties. You may be pleasantly surprised that there are truly interesting sales jobs you have never even thought of before.

Advertising and Promotion There are many interesting careers in promotion, including everything from designing and installing window and floor displays in retail stores to writing ads for General Motors. Ad agencies employ copywriters (people who write the words for ads), artists, photographers, graphic artists, media selection people, consumer behavior analysts, computer specialists, accountants, budget specialists, production and printing experts, sales representatives, PR experts, and others. There is a job in advertising and promotion for many specialties, but the job market is tight (there are not many new opportunities).

This is one field where experience is as important as, or more important than, education. Often you must prove your worth *before* you are hired. This means that you should have some evidence of your ability, such as an art portfolio or sample ads you have written or essays that are especially good. This also means that you might have to work *free* for a few summers to get the experience and the needed portfolio, but that is often *the* way for many students to get into the field.

If you want to get into radio and TV, you should offer your services free long before you complete college. This is an unusually exciting, dynamic area to work in, and so you will have much competition. The idea is to be the "firstest with the mostest." That means taking whatever jobs you can get during your college career, working days *and* nights, and being totally involved. Broadcasting is like acting; you must be dedicated and persistent to get ahead.

Marketing Research Marketing research as a specialized marketing field is relatively new. Even as late as 1940, it was the exception rather than the rule for an organization to have a marketing research department.

In the last 40 years or so, the number of companies with research departments has grown tremendously. One study found that 50 percent of those organizations with memberships in the American Marketing Association had formal research departments, but more than half of them were formed after 1957.[1] In the last few years, marketing research budgets have increased, compensation levels have risen, and there is increased recognition of equal pay and opportunity for women.[2] All of this means that marketing research is a new, growing, well-paying career opportunity for men and women.

You should have a good, basic grasp of math, statistics, computer uses, and consumer behavior to be a marketing researcher. Although the opportunities are there, they are not always easy to find. While still in college, you should begin contacting people in major firms throughout the country. Learn what skills they are looking for early and then plan your course work accordingly.

Wholesaling and Retailing There are over 1.7 million retail stores in this country, and they all need good managers. Could you be one? Most college graduates aim for a career with one of the leaders in retailing, such as Sears, Montgomery Ward, Saks, or Garfinkels. That leaves about 1,699,000 stores for those students who want to work in a smaller store where they can "run the

---

[1] See Dik W. Twedt, *Survey of Marketing Research—1968* (Chicago: American Marketing Association, 1969).

[2] Dik W. Twedt, "Six Trends in Corporate Marketing Research: Show Budget, Productivity, Pay, and Opportunity Increases," *Marketing News*, March 14, 1975, p. 3.

Summary of Findings of the American Marketing Association 1973 Survey of Marketing Research

1. More than half of 1,121 respondent companies reported having a marketing research department. Marketing research departments are most common among consumer companies (70 percent), publishers and broadcasters (66 percent), and in industrial companies (59 percent).

2. Since 1922, there has been a steady growth in marketing research departments.

3. About half the research departments of industrial and consumer goods companies represented in this study have been formed within the past 11 years.

4. Marketing research directors are reporting more to top corporate management and less to sales and marketing management than they did in 1968.

5. For the total sample, there was a relatively modest 10 percent increase (compared with 1968) in the average marketing research budget.

6. Consumer goods companies outspend industrial companies in marketing research in every size classification.

7. Since the 1968 study, there has been a slight decrease in the percentage of total marketing research budget spent for outside services.

8. Compensation of senior research staff members is most directly related to experience of individual, and much less to type of company. For the four top job levels, the rate of increase has not kept up with inflationary pressures.

9. Although compensation for women engaged in marketing research is less than that of men at comparable job levels, the differences are lessening.

10. In the subject matter of research, there are many more parallels between consumer and industrial research than there are differences.

Other results were that one-fourth of the responding firms reported doing research on corporate responsibility, studies of consumer's right to know, ecological impact, social values, and legal constraints on ads and promotion. Other research studies included ad research, product research, sales and market research, test markets, store audits, packaging, ad effectiveness, and a host of other topics. Truly, marketing research is important in all areas of marketing and a promising career. Average income for research directors in ad agencies is $40,800; $30,300 in consumer product companies; and $25,400 in industrial products companies (1973 figures).

From Bernice Finkelman, citing a survey by Dik W. Twedt, in "AMA Study Finds Research $, Status Gains," *Marketing News*, March 1, 1974, pp. 1, 3. Reprinted with permission of the American Marketing Association.

whole show." Often students will work for a larger firm to get the needed training and experience before moving into a smaller store.

Small store or large, retailing is an especially wide-open career opportunity. Every major city has dozens of stores that could use a highly motivated, knowledgeable marketing person. Large stores have the advantage of sophisticated training programs and a variety of career ladders, but the competition is tough and career growth may be slow.

Product Manager, Project Manager, or Venture Manager?

There appears to be much confusion between the job titles and corresponding activities performed by product managers, project managers, and venture managers. How one firm defines a product manager may be what another firm defines as a project manager or what still another firm defines as a venture manager. This confusion is partially due to: 1. Top management and the personnel departments desire to attach more fashionable titles to existing activities and 2. Different kinds of product management tasks being performed in small, medium, or large firms. There are some basic organizational factors which provide clearer insights into what kind of manager one is actually speaking of.

It is necessary to first establish operational definitions for three of the more common systems of managing products.

1. The *product manager* is a staff role with product-profit responsibility over both existing products and new extensions to his product line. In large firms he usually reports to a group product manager or a divisional officer and in smaller firms he may report to a functional officer or to top management.

2. The *project manager* is a line role with a small and somewhat temporary team of specialists from functional areas. He operates within a matrix organizational structure and is responsible for bringing new products through the firm and well into the marketplace. A product manager as described above may be assigned to the same product at a later point in time, or the new product may result in the formation of a new division. The project manager may report to a new products department director or a divisional manager.

3. A *venture manager* is a line manager employed by complex-large organizations to manage totally new products from conception to full commercialization with the assistance of a team of specialists. His activities are seen as organizationally separate from the other areas of the firm and he usually reports to top level management or a corporate committee. Large firms with many ventures will place them under a corporate development department or a new enterprise division. The venture manager role exists in large firms as a device to overcome the more numerous bureaucratic obstacles to new product management. It also provides a means for more entrepreneurial freedom to exist.

From James D. Hlavacek, "Product Management," *Marketing News*, April 1, 1972, p. 8. Reprinted with permission of the American Marketing Association.

Small stores may fail altogether (80 percent do in the first 2 years of operation), but the opportunity to get into management, make money, and use all your skills is often much greater.

The service area of retailing offers many career opportunities. For example, there are over 87,000 hotels, motels, tourist courts, and camps; 498,000 personal care service organizations such as beauty shops, shoe repair shops, and laundries; 139,000 auto repair services; 138,000 other repair services (for example, watch, electrical); 16,000 motion picture theaters; and 96,000 recreation services such as bowling alleys and dance halls.

Visit some retail stores and talk to the people there about salaries, training, opportunities, and responsibilities. Do not ignore the small boutiques. Spend a few weeks doing this, and you will be much better prepared to make a decision on whether a retail career is for you.

So many students are interested in retailing that they tend to forget about wholesaling. There are over 300,000 wholesale organizations in the United States. These firms need buyers, traffic managers, salespeople, promotion specialists, advertising experts, and other marketing types. Because there is less competition for these jobs, the chances are good that you might get one. Look up some wholesalers in the phone book, visit them, ask questions, and learn about salaries, and so forth. Believe it or not, wholesalers in the United States do more volume of business than do retailers. Do not ignore such potential in your career quest.

Buyer/ Purchasing Agent Those people who go into the market and buy merchandise for retail stores have titles such as assistant buyer and buyer. Sometimes these people work exclusively for one store, and sometimes they represent several stores. Resident buyers have offices in places like New York and act as on-the-spot representatives for several firms. There are many rewarding careers in retailing, but few seem as exciting and rewarding as buyer. They are usually able to travel to the trading centers of the world and can work with the kind of merchandise that interests them.

The equivalent of a retail buyer in industrial firms is called a purchasing agent. Purchasing agents too have a very active role to play in analyzing markets, negotiating transactions, and acting as information source for the firm. They play a very important role in the firm and find marketing a very helpful background. They also should know something about credit, transportation, and finance, but marketing is the foundation.

Transportation There are many rewarding careers for marketers in the airlines, railroads, shipping, and trucking firms of the United States. But, beyond that, there are many challenging careers in traffic management, physical distribution management, and warehousing in industrial firms. Somebody has to move materials from the mines to the manufacturer, through the firm (inventory control specialists), and from the manufacturer to wholesalers, retailers, other firms, and consumers. The key position is physical distribution manager. Such a person handles *all* the physical flows to, through, and from the organization.

Visit a manufacturing plant and talk to purchasing agents, inventory control specialists, traffic managers, and warehouse operators. Also see what jobs are available with the airlines and other carriers. This is a very competitive field, but the careers are often worth the effort. If some of these terms do not mean much to you (for example, traffic manager), that is good. It means that there are lots of careers out there that you have never even heard of in your marketing classes. If you begin now to search for a job that you will find interesting, you will be years ahead of most students.

Product Management One job in marketing where a person can apply all his or her skills is product management. The names differ, but many firms have such a position. The Association of National Advertisers, in a recent study, found that the following percentages of participating companies had product managers: packaged goods, 85 percent (but 93 percent of those firms with annual advertising expenditures exceeding $10 million); other consumer goods, 34 percent; industrial goods, 55 percent.[3]

Some people find product management *the* most challenging job other than top marketing management. The insert "Product Manager, Project Manager, or Venture Manager?" will give you a feel for the challenge of this career. It is one of the most competitive careers available, but it is also one of the more interesting. It has been an especially attractive position for people with a marketing MBA.

Economist/ Consumer The word "economist" is made up of two parts: eco- comes from *oikos*, which is Greek for "house"; -nomist comes from *nemein*, which is Greek for "to manage." An economist, therefore, is one who manages a house. Almost all of us share in this task: We must manage our household budget, purchase what we need, and try to become effective and efficient household managers. Marketing concepts and principles help us to understand how to deal in the "market" and how to optimize our purchases. Such concepts also teach us how to get involved in the affairs of business and government, so that we can use our influence to create an atmosphere of free and open exchange. We can also influence legislation and act with others to get rid of fraudulent and deceptive business practices. Marketing is therefore a key subject for everyone to study: It helps make us good "economists."

Marketing also shows us how to be good consumers. In addition to our full-time careers, all of us spend time and money shopping, buying, and analyzing markets (for example, house markets, stock markets, food markets, and so forth). Many people make a full-time career out of home

[3] *Current Advertising Practices: Opinions as to Future Trends* (New York: Association of National Advertisers, 1974). Cited in Victor B. Buell, "The Changing Role of the Product Manager in Consumer Goods Companies," *Journal of Marketing*, July 1975, p. 4.

management and consumerism. There are rewarding careers for people who counsel home managers and help in their consumption behavior. Marketing, therefore, is a key subject for home economists, homemakers, and all of us who are active consumers.

Product Testing and Consumer Protection There are several rewarding careers in business and government in product testing and consumer protection. Product testing involves analysis of fabrics and other materials for safety, fire hazards, durability, and other characteristics. People following such careers need to understand something about consumer behavior and market behavior so that they can help design safe, durable products. The government is deeply involved with product testing and consumer protection, and the area is expanding all the time.

Consumer-affairs departments, consumer-protection agencies, extension services, and other such organizations need people trained in marketing and home economics. These people help strengthen the consumer side of the marketing relationship and help assure fair and equal exchanges. Many organizations have consumer-affairs advisors who act as spokespeople for the consumer in marketing decision making. This is truly a rewarding and fascinating career for those people concerned with consumer protection.

Other Careers No one chapter can even begin to list *all* of the careers and opportunities available in marketing. Little mention has been made, for example, of the many marketing careers available in the government and nonprofit organizations. If you want to serve your country or your favorite cause

Table 21.2 BUSINESS BACKGROUNDS OF KEY INDIVIDUALS AND GROUPS—640 COMPANIES

Key Positions	Business Background						
	Engineering	Finance	Legal	Manufacturing	Marketing	Research and development	General
Board chairman	15%	25%	5%	16%	26%	4%	9%
Vice board chairman	12	22	4	22	23	1	16
Internal board of directors	8	16	3	16	24	1	32
Outside board of directors	5	37	19	7	4	1	27
President	15	16	5	22	31	2	9
Chairman of the executive committee	14	23	5	19	30	3	6
Executive committee	6	19	3	15	23	1	33
Group executive	13	3	1	30	34	2	17
Operating executive	14	5	0	37	30	1	13
Product or brand manager	14	1	0	7	71	2	5

From Carlton P. McNamara, "The Present Status of the Marketing Concept." *Journal of Marketing*, January 1972, p. 54.

and make money doing so, marketing is certainly one of the best fields to do it in.

Marketers have key positions in schools, foundations, museums, unions, hospitals, charities, causes, political parties, show business, sports, and almost all other organizations. Where would you most like to work? Have you gone there to talk with their employees about career opportunities yet? Well, what are you waiting for? We are talking about your future for the next 40 years or more. This is not something to be taken lightly or without long, detailed, and serious research. It may take a lifetime to find what you really want and enjoy, but the sooner you start the better.

Whether you choose to follow a marketing career in the profit, non-profit, or government sector, you can be sure of one thing—marketing is the best route to top management in any organization. As Table 21.2 shows, 31 percent of the presidents and 26 percent of the board chairmen of 640 large organizations have a business background in marketing. This is perhaps the best proof of the rewards of a career in marketing.

GETTING A MARKETING JOB

One can apply the concepts and principles of marketing to any exchange situation, including getting a job. Because your first and perhaps most important marketing task is likely to be finding a job and determining a career, this section will discuss how to use the ideas you have learned to find a job. We shall use the universal marketing functions discussed in Chapter 2 as a base: There will be sections on product differentiation, market analysis and segmentation, valuation, and communication. Hopefully, this analysis will lead to a mutually satisfying exchange between you and a good employer. First, let's look at the product.

Product Differentiation— What Is Your Product Offer?

The procedure for identifying your product offer is much the same as that used by any organization. You must be particularly careful, however, not to be too biased, either positively or negatively, when analyzing your product. Remember also that your product has many different aspects, and a comprehensive product analysis involves looking at all of the benefits you have to offer and at all of the drawbacks.

You can begin the analysis of your product offer by listing your strengths and weaknesses. Be sure to be complete in this analysis. Go back to when you were young. Did you have a paper route? Did you help around the house? Did you mow lawns, rake leaves, or do other such chores in the neighborhood? If so, these experiences show the employer, and yourself, that you have a long history of being self-motivated, self-reliant, and an active worker. Do not keep these things a secret; they are part of your product.

Use this same technique to analyze your high school and college years. What did you do that was different from the average student? Did you edit the school paper, march in the band, sing in the choir, act in the school play, play any sports, win any awards, accept any part-time jobs, or do anything else other than go to school? Do not be modest at this point. Be sure to *list* all of your strengths.

Now make a separate list of your weaknesses. What are the things you could improve upon? Are you overly shy or aggressive? Do you tend to avoid work? Are you often late for appointments? Do you find it difficult to start a task or complete it? Be as honest with yourself as you can, so that you can get a true picture of your value to an employer. Such an analysis may also reveal the kind of jobs in which you would *not* be happy. For example, a person who recognizes that he or she is not a self-starter would probably not be happy in selling.

Product Development After you have made an honest effort to analyze yourself and have made a list of your strengths and weaknesses, you should begin to redesign your product to fit your chosen occupation. You may need more education, more training, or more experience. But do not stop with skill training—work on your personality as well.

You are what you think you are. If you think you are shy or backward socially, you will act that way, and other people will think you are shy or backward. But there is no such thing as a shy person: Only people who *think* they are shy. If your self-image is not what it should be, work on it as hard as you would work on your education or on learning to play the piano or to ride a bike. Personality development takes practice, just as any self-improvement program takes practice.

Be sure that as you develop your product you keep the employer in mind, for it is the employer who will ultimately decide whether your product is acceptable or not. Learn about the requirements of the job *before* you sign up for courses or training. Learn what skills are needed, how much personal contact is involved, and what kind of person the organization is looking for.

When it comes time for a job interview, and the interviewer says, "Tell me about yourself," you will now be prepared to give an interesting and thorough answer. You can discuss your strengths and give examples, you can mention any weaknesses and your program for improving on them, and, most of all, you will be confident, friendly, and warm. In short, you will be a good potential employee (product).

Packaging Yourself "You can tell about a person from the way he or she dresses," or so the saying goes. Whether you think it *should be* this way or not, organizations base much of their initial impression of persons on the way they look and carry themselves. Therefore, a potential employee should "package" his or her product in clothes, shoes, and hairstyles that fit the desired image of the buyer (employer).

No one wants a TV set that looks funny or is all scratched and banged up. Similarly, no one wants to hire an employee who looks out of place or is messy or sloppy. The outside appearance of a TV set is important to a sale, and so is the outside appearance of a potential employee—for the same reasons. Buyers want to be proud of what they own and want to be eager to let anyone see it. Remember that when you are designing your product.

Try Not to Pinch Pennies

College students and other potential employees often have very little money to spend at the time they are applying for a job. Nevertheless, this is not the time to be cheap. Everything you say or do will make an impression on potential employers, and so you must begin early to look and act sharp.

First of all, make sure that any correspondence with a potential employer is typed on good bond paper with a good, clear typewriter. If you do not have access to such materials, pay to have your letters typed—the results are worth the small investment.

Everything you do at this point is an investment in a career that may span 40 years or more, and so a few extra dollars spent now is a good investment.

Any time you want to reproduce multiple copies of a resume or any other materials to send to an employer, *do not* use a normal office copier. Instead, take the letter or whatever to a printer and have it reproduced properly (that is, so it looks like the original).

Also spend some money on good clothes and grooming. Not only will the employer be favorably impressed by an appropriately dressed person, but you will feel more confident and more self-assured knowing that you look right. Again, look upon these "recruiting clothes" as an investment.

Remember the concept we are working under: The product is what the customer thinks it is. Therefore, every effort should be made to create a favorable impression. It is not enough to *be* capable, confident, and skilled: You must *look* that way. Spend some money on your product—you are worth it!

Market Analysis and Segmentation

Before you begin trying to market your product, you should have a clear idea of what the market wants. You cannot possibly be all things to all people, and so you must segment the market to a few target organizations.

Many potential employees use a shotgun approach to getting a job. That is, they send letters and resumes to over a hundred prospective employers. They are often disappointed when only a few reply. Selling without first segmenting the market is seldom very effective.

A better strategy is to do comprehensive marketing research about a *few* potential employers. Read their annual reports; look them up in the publications of a stock-information service; and read about them in *Forbes, Fortune, Business Week, Dun's Review,* or some other business periodical. Talk to employees at the organization (especially those holding the position you desire). Ask them about training, salaries, opportunities, strategies for applying, and so forth.

Do some research and *you* will be able to select where to work; otherwise, someone else will decide for you. By learning what is wanted of you early, you can begin to adapt your product to the market. It is much, much easier to sell a custom-made product than one made for an unknown, general audience.

Do not approach the job market with the attitude that you need a job and hope someone will offer you one. Instead, adopt the attitude that organizations always need good employees and that you will be a good employee; therefore, they need you as much as you need them. Do not accept an offer from just anyone; get an offer from the organization you want to work for. You can do that only by marketing yourself, not by merely offering yourself for sale. And marketing means doing careful market analysis, market segmentation, product design, packaging, promotion, and establishing "mutually satisfying exchanges."

The Valuation Function and Careers   When evaluating a potential employer, be sure to evaluate the total product offer and not just the most visible dimensions. For example, many employees picked their job because the pay was better than most or because the job was available when they were. But many of those employees are now dissatisfied with their jobs and are trying to get another.

It is important to analyze every aspect of a job offer. One consideration is the organization's training program: Is it complete? Does it prepare you for the job? Is it continuous? Another consideration is location: Is the organization in a desirable location? Does the company shift employees around the country? Salary, fringe benefits, the retirement system, and other considerations are also important. Do not neglect to look into the organization's policy toward continuing education (many organizations will pay for advanced degrees, for example). It is also important to analyze the future of the industry and of the organization, the kind of co-workers you will have, and the working conditions (for example, size, location of office, access to mass transportation, noise levels, and so forth).

Finally, pick a job that will lead to the career *you* want. Do not be overly influenced by parents, friends, professors, or any other "experts" when choosing your career. Use their counsel, evaluate it, and decide for yourself what *you* want and what *you* will enjoy. After all, *you* have to do the work, not your parents or friends. If you pick a job you enjoy doing, you are more apt to do it well and be a success. If you pick a job because *others* think it pays well or because it is respectable, you are apt to be indifferent to the work and unsuccessful—even if you make lots of money. You will find that success in life means more than money.

Be Career-Oriented Rather Than Job-Oriented   Many people get rather nervous about their first job and get unnecessarily upset about choosing the "right" organization. Few people have kept the same job for a lifetime. The first job is an especially uncertain one, and most people are not happy at it. Therefore, you should be more concerned about whether your first job is a step toward the career you want rather than a place to spend the rest of your life.

Keeping this in mind, you might look for different things in your first job than you would look for in a subsequent job. For example, you might be more concerned with an excellent training program, opportunities to further your education, and good experience. Factors such as retirement benefits, sick leave, and vacations may be of little or no importance.

Choose your first job with the idea that you have not developed your product offer fully yet, and think of your first job as an opportunity to do so. Be careful in choosing this job, though, for it often sets the tone for the rest of your career. So choose the job with your career goals in mind and pick an organization that furthers your career rather than one that offers you a good paying job per se.

Books and Pamphlets on Marketing Careers

General Marketing

Angel, J. L., *Modern Vocational Trends: Reference Handbook*, 7th ed. (New York: Simon and Schuster, 1970).

Holbert, Neil, *Careers in Marketing*, American Marketing Association, 222 S. Riverside Plaza, Chicago, Ill. 60606 ($1.50).

Hopke, W. E., ed., *The Encyclopedia of Careers and Vocational Guidance* (Chicago: J. G. Fergusen Publishing Co., 1972).

U.S. Department of Labor, *Employment Outlook for Advertising Workers, Marketing Research Workers, Public Relations Workers*, U.S. Government Printing Office, Washington, D.C. 20402 (no charge).

Advertising

American Advertising Federation, 1225 Connecticut Ave. N.W., Washington, D.C. 20036. *Jobs in Advertising* (no charge).

American Association of Advertising Agencies, 200 Park Ave., New York, N.Y. 10017 *Advertising—A Guide to Careers* (no charge).

International Newspaper Advertising Executives, P.O. Box 147, Danville, Ill. 61832. *Careers in Newspaper Advertising.*

Advertising Management

Association of National Advertisers, Inc., 155 East 44th St., New York, N.Y. 10017. *Educational Preparation for Positions in Advertising Management* (no charge).

Distribution

National Association of Wholesalers, 1725 K St. N.W., Washington, D.C. 20036. *Your Career in Wholesale Distribution.*

National Food Brokers Association, 1916 M St. N.W., Washington, D.C. 20036. *Job Preview—Food Broker.*

Public Relations

Public Relations Society of America, 845 3rd Ave., New York, N.Y. 10022. *Careers in Public Relations, Public Relations—Profession and Growth Industry* (no charge).

Rosenberg, T. J., "Health Industry: New Opportunities for PR Professionals," *Public Relations Journal*, August 1972, pp. 6–8.

Purchasing

National Association of Purchasing Management, 11 Park Place, New York, N.Y. 10007. *Purchasing as a Career.*

Radio and Television

National Association of Broadcasters, 1771 N St. N.W., Washington, D.C. 20036. *Careers in Radio, Careers in Television* (no charge).

Retailing

Duncan, D., C. Phillips, and S. Hollander, *Modern Retailing Management: Basic Concepts and Practices*, 8th ed. (Homewood, Ill.: Richard D. Irwin, Inc., 1972), pp. 49–74.

U.S. Department of Labor, SBA # 150: *Business Plan for Retailers*, SBA # 18: *Starting and Managing a Business*, U.S. Government Printing Office, Washington, D.C. 20402.

Selling

Council on Opportunities in Selling, Inc., 630 3rd Ave., New York, N.Y. 10017. *Opportunities in Selling* (25¢).

Institute of Life Insurance, 277 Park Ave., New York, N.Y. 10017. *A Life Career.*

Life Insurance Marketing and Research Association, Hartford, Conn. *The Life Insurance Career* (no charge).

Statistics

Blankenship, A. B., "What Marketing Research Managers Want in Trainees," *Journal of Advertising Research*, February 1975, pp. 7–14.

Committee of Presidents of Statistical Societies, c/o American Statistical Association, 806 15th St. N.W., Washington, D.C. 20005. *Careers in Statistics.*

Establishing a Price One of the more important considerations for job candidates has always been salary. But what should that salary be? Keep in mind that you are still unproved merchandise to the employer and usually cannot demand a salary out of line with the normal range, even if you feel you are superior. It is better to get the job you want, *prove* you are superior with superior performance, and *then* request appropriate compensation. The prime consideration is getting the right job; if compensation does not come naturally, you can always move up if the first job prepared you by giving you needed training, experience, and exposure to people in your chosen field.

This principle is especially true in some hard-to-get marketing jobs such as copywriter in a New York ad agency or buyer for a leading woman's store. One effective strategy for job candidates without experience is to offer to work *free* in order to get the right job with the right

WE'D LIKE TO PUT AN END TO THE GREAT CAREER COUNSELOR MYTH.

It seems there's a common feeling around that career counselors who spend all their time inside the college, can't possibly know what's going on outside the school.

Maybe if you knew a little more about career counselors, you'd change your mind.

For instance, we at Mobil, like many other large corporations, go to career counselors when we're looking to hire graduates.

They know what qualifications are needed for what jobs, so they don't even bother to send us someone who isn't qualified.

And they know how to put together a good resume (the kind that helps you get jobs).

They also teach you interview techniques. (It's not hard to make a fool of yourself at an interview.)

There's more to getting a good job than just getting good grades in school.

So don't underestimate career counselors.

The 30 minutes you spend with them now might determine what you'll do the next 30 years of your life.

Mobil
An equal opportunity employer. M/F

© 1976 Mobil Oil Corporation.

organization. Most people laugh at the suggestion and immediately dismiss such an idea. But, again, the principle is to *get the job first*, prove your ability, and then negotiate compensation.

A walk-on football player, for example, would find it difficult to demand $100,000, to play for the Washington Redskins. But if he were to prove his worth by getting the job at $15,000 the first year, he might be able to demand $50,000 the second year. The same is true of a talented copywriter, a good marketing researcher, a clever PR person, a persuasive salesperson, or an insightful buyer.

Some college students get experience by offering to work free during the summers or on days when there are no classes. They sometimes work for the campus radio station or newspaper to get experience. But often they select one of the best firms in town and offer their services free. They look upon such service as an *opportunity to get a free education*, not as a sacrifice of their time for no compensation. Employers are usually impressed with a person so dedicated to a chosen career, and, of course, the student can either prove his or her worth or learn early in the game that this is not the career for them.

Often, experience is more important to an employer than education. But how does one get experience when no one will hire an inexperienced person? There often is little choice but to work for free to get the needed experience. If you look upon such experience gathering as *free* on-the-job training, you will approach the job with the enthusiasm you will need to prove yourself. You can smile at those poor souls who have to *pay* to go to a trade school while you are being trained for *free*.

Marketing Communication and Careers

Sources of Career Information

There are dozens of catalogs and other materials available for people interested in marketing careers. Consult your local library and the career library at your school for these sources. But this information can give you only general, background data. To get a real feel for a job, you must get into different organizations and see for yourself. Spend some time with an industrial salesperson, a buyer, a copywriter, a marketing researcher, a retailer, or any other person you might learn from. Ask them pointed questions about salaries, training, opportunities, good points and bad, and job openings. Such research is worth more than several days in the library. Do not be shy about asking people to help; they will be flattered at your attention and will give you more time than you would expect.

To learn about careers and career opportunities, you should also join the local chapter of the American Marketing Association and the student chapter on campus, if there is one. You might subscribe to the *Journal of Marketing, Business Week*, and *The Wall Street Journal* to get current facts and figures about the business world in general and about the marketing world in particular.

Talk to your friends who have already graduated about their experiences. Talk also with professors, neighbors, and friends of your parents. Be open to new ideas, suggestions, and opportunities. A good marketer is an alert marketer, an aware marketer, and an informed marketer. "Be prepared" as they say in scouting.

What to Do While in School   In addition to the suggested talks you have with people in various occupations, there are other things you can do to enhance your career while in school. First, you can join marketing clubs such as the American Marketing Association, Alpha Delta Sigma (an advertising club), and related organizations. Second, you can work summers, evenings, and vacations at various jobs to see if you really enjoy them. Remember, do this free if you must. Third, you can become active in extracurricular activities such as sports, drama, fraternity or sorority affairs, clubs, and so forth. Many employers are as interested in these activities as they are in your grades. Fourth, grades are important, so you should keep them up. Finally, the kinds of courses you take often help. Almost any course could be helpful to a marketing career; therefore, you should try to choose a career as early as possible so that you can select appropriate courses. You cannot go wrong with courses in marketing management, promotion, consumer behavior, statistics, marketing research, economics, and computer sciences. Other helpful courses include English, journalism, speech, social psychology, psychology, sociology, math, and management.

One purpose of belonging to clubs, working, and generally being active in college is to show potential employers (and yourself) that you are a self-starter, a go-getter, and a contributor. In tight markets, these kind of people get the jobs first. It is also best to major in a field related to marketing and to have a good background in marketing principles and concepts. This course should give you a good start. One final note about school: Try to get to know one or two professors who will write recommendations for you and counsel you on career decisions. Do not be "just another face," but speak up in class and show the professor that you are the kind of person he or she can recommend when job openings arise.

Job Interviews   If you are to be effective at a job interview, you must be prepared, relaxed, and professional. Being prepared means to have done your homework about the organization. What do they do? Where do they operate? You can learn much from the organization's annual report (if it has one), from stock-information services, and from other such sources. But the best source is an employee. Try to talk to a couple of people at the organization *before* the interview. Learn about training, and other matters, so that you can ask *informed* questions and present yourself as a *prepared* candidate.

Being prepared also means being ready to answer any questions the interviewer might ask. Often to be good at this you must practice. You can do this with a fellow student or with anyone else who is willing to help. Usually the college career center will give you helpful hints. Your product analysis will be invaluable to this stage.

Being prepared enables you to be relaxed. If you are nervous, you will tend to make the interviewer nervous or, at least, less impressed. When you are relaxed, you can think more clearly and will be more friendly and more alert. If you practice your interviews, you will eventually be relaxed, because the situation will become familiar to you.

Finally, you should be professional. As we have made clear, you should look, act, and feel professional. That means you should be confident, poised, relaxed, alert, and prepared. You are looking for a job that pays thousands of dollars a year, and you should act the part. You are no longer a student; you are a job candidate. You will get a better feel for how a professional in your field looks and acts by talking with some of them and watching them on the job. When you feel comfortable talking with them, you are ready to begin interviewing.

Writing a Resume A resume is a document that lists all the information an employer would need to evaluate you and your background. It includes information such as your name, address, phone number, age, marital status, and health. It also explains your immediate goals and career objectives. This information is followed by an explanation of your educational background, experience, interests, and other relevant data.

Remember that your product is what the buyer (employer) thinks it is, and so what you put on your resume *is* your product. If you have exceptional abilities and do not communicate that fact to the employer on the resume, those abilities are not part of the product he or she will evaluate. You must be comprehensive and clear in your resume if you are to communicate all of your attributes.

Most resume counselors suggest that you keep your resume short and precise. They feel that employers will not "waste their time" reading a long resume. But such advice is bad for a person who wants to market himself or herself. If an employer is going to pay a person $8,000–15,000 per year, he or she will be willing to read a two- or three-page resume before making such a commitment—and do not let anyone convince you otherwise.

Your resume is an advertisement for yourself. If your ad is better than the other person's ad, your product is more likely to sell. In this case, "better" means that your ad highlights your attributes in an attractive way.

In discussing your education, for example, be sure to highlight your extracurricular activities such as part-time jobs, sports, clubs, and other such activities. If you did well in school, put down your grades. The idea is to make your product as good on paper as it is in reality.

The same is true for your job experience. Be sure to describe what you did, any special projects you participated in, and any responsibilities you had.

For the "other interests" section, do not just *list* your interests, but describe how deeply you are involved. If you organized the club, volunteered your time, or participated more often than usual in an organization, make sure to say so in the resume. Figure 21.1 shows an edited version of an actual resume. It shows Tom Thomlynson's strengths clearly, and yet it is suitably brief. Your own resume might be somewhat different from this one, but Tom's is a pretty good model.

The Cover Letter A cover letter is the letter one uses to announce his or her availability and to introduce the resume. The cover letter is probably one of the most important advertisements a person will write in his or her lifetime—so you should do it right.

Figure 21.1 SAMPLE RESUME

RESUME

Thomas J. Thomlynson
4956 Key Lock Road
Tempe, Arizona 86394
Phone: (907) 063-3497

Age: 22
Sex: Male
Health: Excellent
Marital status: Single

Date available for employment: June 10, 1981

Career Objective: To have a successful career in industrial
    sales that would eventually lead to sales management.

Education: B.S., Arizona State University; marketing major; 3.02 grade
    average on a 4.0 scale; earned 100% of college expenses;
    activities included vice-president of American Marketing
    Association chapter, fraternity treasurer, captain of intramural
    football team, and member of the ski club. Worked 20 hours per
    week during school and full time each summer at local shoe store
    as salesman.

Experience: (1977-1981) Korvalis Shoes, Tempe. Began as clerk and
    worked up to assistant manager. Now supervise three salespersons,
    keep inventory, make buying trips to key supply centers, and
    generally manage the business when the owner is away. Have
    introduced several innovations in display and advertising and
    have had good response to quarterly promotions that I handled
    entirely.

Early Experience: (1971-1977) My selling career began when I was 12
    and delivered papers for the Tempe Daily where I increased
    deliveries from 30 to 74. This was followed by several jobs
    throughout high school and during the summers: lifeguard for
    two summers; magazine sales; window-cleaning business (my own);
    also helped my neighbor campaign for state representative by
    distributing literature, making calls, etc.

Other Interests: Active in ski club and have arranged two trips to
    Colorado; as vice-president of AMA chapter, I arrange for
    speakers and set up tours of local businesses and social
    activities; defensive back on intramural football team (8-1-1
    last season); also enjoy spectator sports, bicycling, swimming,
    and politics.

References: Available on request.

First, the cover letter should indicate that you have researched the organization in question and are interested in a job with them. Let the organization know what sources you used and what you know about them *in the first paragraph* to get their attention and show your true interest.

You may have heard that, "It is not what you know, but whom you know that counts." This is only partially true, but it is important nonetheless. If you do not now know someone, you can get to know someone. You do this by calling the organization (or better yet, visiting their offices) and talking to people who already have the kind of job you are hoping to get. Ask about training, salary, and other relevant issues. Then, in your cover letter, tell the firm that you have talked with some of the firm's employees and that this discussion increased your interest. You thereby show the letter reader that you "know someone," if only casually, and that you are interested enough actively to pursue the organization.

Second, in the description of yourself, be sure to say what benefits your attributes will be to the organization. For example, do not just say, "I will be graduating with a degree in marketing." Say, "You will find that my college training in marketing and marketing research has prepared me to learn your marketing system quickly and begin making a contribution right away." The sample cover letters in Figures 21.2 and 21.3 will give you a better feel for what we mean.

Third, be sure to "ask for the order." That is, say in your final paragraph that you are available for an interview at a time and place convenient for the interviewer. Again, see the sample cover letter in Figure 21.3 for guidance. Notice in this letter how Tom subtly showed that he read business publications and drew attention to his resume. Can you think of any ways in which to improve this letter?

Some principles to follow in writing a cover letter and preparing your resume are:

1. Be self-confident and list all your benefits and attributes.
2. Do not be apologetic or negative about anything. Write as one professional to another—not as a humble student begging for a job.
3. Research every prospective employer thoroughly before writing anything. Use a rifle approach rather than a shotgun approach. That is, write effective marketing-oriented letters to a few select companies rather than to a general list.

Figure 21.2 A WEAK COVER LETTER

```
Dear Sir:

    I will be graduating from the state university in June with a
degree in marketing.

    I am very interested in working with Ajax Corporation and will
be available in June.  Enclosed is a copy of my resume.  I hope that
you will read it and will find that my qualifications are appropriate.

    Please let me know if you are interested.

                                        Sincerely,


                                        Thomas J. Thomlynson
```

Figure 21.3 A MODEL COVER LETTER

Dear Sir:

    A recent article in <u>Business Week</u> mentioned that Ajax Corporation
is expanding its operations into the southwest. I have always had
an interest in your firm, and so I read more about you in <u>Forbes</u> and
<u>Standard & Poor's</u>. It seems as though you will be needing good
salespeople to handle your expanding business. Harold Jones, your
Detroit sales representative, is a neighbor of mine. He told me about
your training program, compensation system, and career opportunities.
He convinced me that Ajax is the place for an ambitious college
graduate.

    I will be graduating from state college in June with a degree in
marketing. My courses in marketing management, sales management,
consumer behavior, and marketing research have given me some insight
into marketing for a growing organization like yours. My 3 years'
experience as a salesman for Korvalis Shoes has given me valuable
skills that I could apply at Ajax. You will notice when you read the
attached resume that I have always been active in the organizations
I have joined. Could I do as well at Ajax?

    I will be in the New York area the week of November 17-25. Please
let me know which time and date would be convenient for you to discuss
a future at Ajax. I am looking forward to hearing from you.

                  Sincerely,

                  Thomas J. Thomlynson

4. Have your materials typed on a good typewriter by an experienced typist.

5. Have someone edit your materials for spelling, grammar, and style.

6. Do not send the names of references until asked. Put "References furnished upon request" at the bottom of the last page of your resume. You may send *letters* of reference to those firms requesting reference materials.

7. For those firms interested in interviewing you, you may send a few letters of recommendation from former employers or teachers. This is an unusual practice and thus one that differentiates your product from those of others.

A FINAL COMMENT

Marketing is an interesting subject to take in school, but, more importantly, it is an interesting and rewarding career choice. The wide variety of available jobs means that there is one to fit just about everyone's personality and desires. We hope this chapter puts you on the right track toward finding a successful career.

In your job search, be sure to apply the concepts you have learned in this book. Use *market analysis* to find the organizations that you would most enjoy working for. Then *segment* the market to a choice few. Differentiate your *product* so that you can choose where you want to work. Be sure to *evaluate* all the job characteristics, including environment, future opportunities, training, and compensation. Finally, we wish you well in your lifetime goal of establishing mutually satisfying exchange relationships with your family, friends, employers, acquaintances, and the marketing world in general.

FOR REVIEW

Discussion Questions

1. Discuss the wide variety of career opportunities in marketing. Which areas seem to have the most promise for college graduates in the future?

2. Discuss in general what the product of a college graduate is. What are the best features of that product and what are the weakest? How can the overall product be improved?

3. Pick some career in marketing and interview at least two people in that profession. Learn about salaries, opportunities, advantages, and disadvantages of the job. Then have an open discussion of marketing careers with your classmates and exchange findings.

4. Write a cover letter to some firm that you would like to interview. Have an English major and a marketing faculty member review the letter. Then exchange letters with your classmates and read a few before the class (anonymously, if you prefer) for overall comment.

5. External appearance and personality often are important to an interviewer. Do you feel this is a misplaced emphasis? Explain your position.

6. One of the suggestions in this chapter is to consider your job search as an investment and not to cut corners on clothes, correspondence, and so on. Do you agree? Discuss your views with others, especially the job-counseling service.

7. Have one of your classmates assume the role of an interviewer and others assume the role of interviewee. Prepare difficult questions beforehand and evaluate the answers given by various candidates. Practice job interviews yourself in class or with friends. What questions are particularly difficult to answer? How can you prepare yourself for such questions?

8. Go to the library and read career literature. Also visit the placement center at your school, if there is one. What is the present job situation for college graduates? What can students do before graduation to increase their job opportunities?

9. One way to get experience is to work for free in the chosen area. Do you feel this is a good strategy? Explain your answer.

10. Analyze your product from the perspective of an employer. Be sure to look at extracurricular activities, personality, drive, responsibility, academic excellence, promptness, and appearance. What could you do before graduation to better that product?

CASES

A College Sophomore
Making Career Decisions

Paul Formane is a sophomore at a large California college. He has absolutely no idea what he wants to do when he graduates, and he has not chosen a major yet. Paul's father is an engineer and wanted Paul to study engineering. But Paul was not good at math and could not see becoming an engineer. Paul's grades have not been good enough to get him into law school or medical school, but his parents would like him to be a professional. Accounting is one alternative, but Paul refuses to even think about accounting because he thinks of it as being "numbers, numbers, numbers," and he hates working with numbers.

Paul does not seem to have any particular strengths in the academic area, although he has earned good grades in English, sociology, history, and in some other courses in school. Paul is more interested in sports. He was not good enough (he thinks) to make the football team or any other school team, but he has had good success on intramural teams in football, basketball, and baseball. Paul is a friendly person; he gets along with others well and is generally outgoing. But Paul is not very confident in himself because he has not lived up to his parents' expectations or his own.

1. What steps could Paul take to find an interesting and challenging career *before* he graduates from college?
2. What is Paul's product offer now and how could he make it better?
3. How would you recommend that Paul segment the market when looking at career possibilities?
4. What factors should Paul consider when evaluating his first job?

A College Graduate
What Do I Do Now?

Michelle Riemenschneider is graduating from Bouregard Community College in June. She has a job offer from one of the local retailers to enter the management-training program. Michelle also has an opportunity to travel through Europe with her family for several months. If Michelle goes to Europe, she will miss the start of the training program and perhaps lose the job entirely—at least for a full year. Michelle also has a chance to get a job with one of several manufacturers as a sales representative. One is with a lingerie firm and the other is with a cosmetics firm.

1. What criteria should Michelle use when deciding what to do now?
2. Should Michelle go to Europe with her family and risk losing her job offer? Why or why not?
3. How could Michelle use a trip to Europe to improve her product offer?
4. Do you feel that Michelle would have a more rewarding career in retailing or in selling to retailers? What criteria did you use in your answer?

Name Index

Subject Index